# TOP BACKPACKER
# DESTINATIONS
# AUSTRALIA

EXPLORE
AUSTRALIA

## LEGEND
$ $15 and under
$$ $16–$30
$$$ TOP TREAT!! Over $30

♡ City favourite
◈ Hidden gem

★★★ Top pad
★★ Good place to stay
★ Mediocre accommodation

# CONTENTS

**Before you go**
Planning your trip                                  2
Travelling by car                                   4
Travelling by air, train, bus and boat              6
Health and safety                                   7
Money and opening hours                             8
Accommodation, food and drink                       9
Top 10s                                            10

**NEW SOUTH WALES**                                12
**Sydney**                                         14
TOP REGIONS:
Blue Mountains                                     24
North Coast                                        29
Snowy Mountains                                    35
Hunter Valley                                      39

**QUEENSLAND**                                     42
**Brisbane**                                       44
TOP REGIONS:
Gold Coast and the hinterland                      54
Cairns, the Tropics and the
    Great Barrier Reef                             58
Sunshine Coast                                     63
Fraser Island and the coast                        66

**VICTORIA**                                       70
**Melbourne**                                      72
TOP REGIONS:
Great Ocean Road and the Grampians                 84
Dandenongs and the Yarra Valley                    89
Phillip Island and Gippsland                       92
Goldfields and Spa Country                         96

**NORTHERN TERRITORY**                            100
**Darwin**                                        102
TOP REGIONS:
Kakadu and Arnhem Land                            111
Red Centre                                        115

**WESTERN AUSTRALIA**                             120
**Perth**                                         122
TOP REGIONS:
Rottnest Island                                   131
The South-west                                    133
Outback Coast and the Mid-west                    138
The Kimberley                                      143
Esperance and the Nullarbor                       148

**SOUTH AUSTRALIA**                               150
**Adelaide**                                      152
TOP REGIONS:
Barossa Valley and the Adelaide Hills             161
Kangaroo Island                                   165
Flinders Ranges                                   170
Limestone Coast                                   174

**TASMANIA**                                      178
**Hobart**                                        180
TOP REGIONS:
The South-east                                    188
East Coast and the Mid-north                      193
The North-west                                    198

**Road atlas**
Australia-wide distance chart                     200
Road atlas introduction                           202
Road atlas maps                                   204

**Index**                                         242

Sydney Opera House and Sydney Harbour Bridge, New South Wales

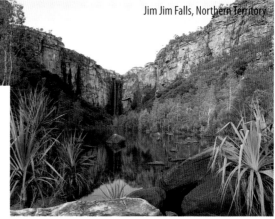
Jim Jim Falls, Northern Territory

The Great Barrier Reef, Queensland

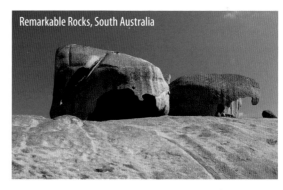
Remarkable Rocks, South Australia

Port Arthur, Tasmania

Federation Square at night, Victoria

Lake Argyle, Western Australia

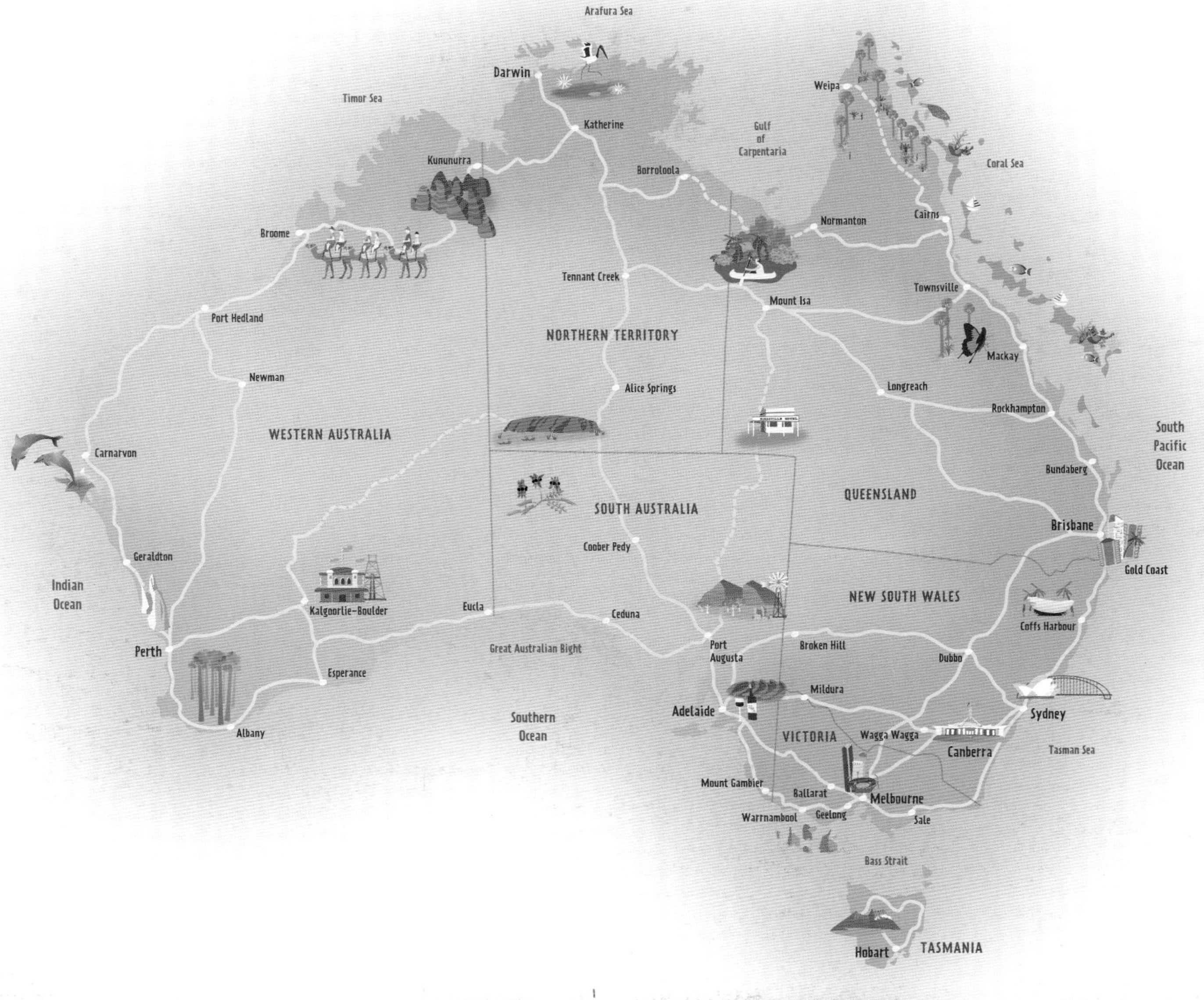
Arafura Sea
Timor Sea
Darwin
Katherine
Kununurra
Gulf of Carpentaria
Weipa
Coral Sea
Borroloola
Broome
Normanton
Cairns
Tennant Creek
Mount Isa
Townsville
Port Hedland
NORTHERN TERRITORY
Mackay
Newman
Alice Springs
Longreach
Rockhampton
WESTERN AUSTRALIA
South Pacific Ocean
Carnarvon
Bundaberg
QUEENSLAND
SOUTH AUSTRALIA
Brisbane
Coober Pedy
Geraldton
Gold Coast
Indian Ocean
NEW SOUTH WALES
Kalgoorlie-Boulder
Eucla
Ceduna
Coffs Harbour
Perth
Great Australian Bight
Port Augusta
Broken Hill
Dubbo
Esperance
Mildura
Adelaide
Sydney
Southern Ocean
Albany
VICTORIA
Wagga Wagga
Canberra
Tasman Sea
Mount Gambier
Ballarat
Melbourne
Warrnambool
Geelong
Sale
Bass Strait
Hobart
TASMANIA

# Planning your trip

## Passports and visas

Travellers to Australia must have a passport that is valid for longer than the intended period of stay. All visitors must also have a visa. There are three forms of Australian visitor visas:

➡ **ETAs (Electronic Travel Authority)** are for short-term visits up to three months, and are not extendable. ETAs are issued online and incur a $20 service charge, payable by credit card only.

➡ **Tourist visas** are valid for three to six months, cost $75, and are extendable (for a fee). In certain circumstances, long-stay tourist visas of 12 months are granted. Once in Australia, ETA visa holders can apply for a tourist visa to extend their stay. All visa applications can be made online through the Department of Immigration and Citizenship website, or obtained through your travel agent or airline. Tourist visa applications can also be lodged through Australian missions overseas.

➡ **Sponsored Family Visitor visas** are for longer-term stays up to 12 months. Applicants must have an eligible relative in Australia willing to guarantee that their visitor will leave Australia before the visa expires. Applications cost $75 and can only be made in Australia by the sponsor.

Australia has diplomatic missions in countries around the world offering information on entry requirements, customs and general issues of concern to travellers. A list of missions is available from the Department of Foreign Affairs website. Embassies and high commissions are located in Australia's capital of Canberra.

### Working Holiday visas

If you are aged 18–30 with no children, you may be eligible for a 12-month Working Holiday visa. Residents of the following countries can apply: Belgium, Canada, Cyprus, Denmark, Estonia, Finland, France, Germany, Hong Kong, Ireland, Italy, Japan, Korea, Malta, the Netherlands, Norway, Sweden, Taiwan and the UK. Visas must be arranged prior to travel to Australia and can be applied for online through the Department of Immigration and Citizenship website or in paper form. Conditions include a return airfare and sufficient funds ($5000). The visa costs $185 and must be activated within 12 months of the date the visa was granted. You can work in any field, but only for the same employer for up to six months.

If you complete three months seasonal work in regional Australia (e.g. fruit picking) you may be eligible for a second Working Holiday visa. Seasonal fruit picking work is available all year round in Australia. See the Harvest Trail website for information about vacancies and fruit picking seasons. Agencies such as Grunt Labour Services and T4 Group can also set you up with harvest jobs. Hostel notice boards are useful sources of job information. WWOOF (Willing Workers on Organic Farms) is a volunteer organisation that arranges work on organic farms in return for food and board. This can be counted for your three months.

**Department of Immigration and Citizenship** 13 1881; www.immi.gov.au/immigration.htm
**ETA** www.eta.immi.gov.au
**Embassies and consulates** www.dfat.gov.au/embassies2.html
**National Harvest Labour Information Service** 1800 062 332; www.jobsearch.gov.au/harvesttrail
**Grunt Labor Services** www.gruntlabour.com
**T4 Group** www.t4group.net
**WWOOF** www.wwoof.com.au

## When to travel

With a few exceptions, you can travel to most areas of Australia all year round. Most travellers avoid the tropical north during the wet season (Nov–April), which brings dense humidity, torrential downpours and tropical storms. The desert and outback areas have melting-hot temperatures (regularly in the 40s) during summer. At this time of year, many Australians head for the coast to cool off. Australia's busiest holiday periods are the school summer break (late December to the end of January), the Easter break (late March or April), and school holiday periods (Jun–Jul and Sept–Oct). The high season in Queensland runs from April to Sept.

In winter, Tasmania, southern Victoria and Canberra can be chilly with daytime temperatures around 12 degrees. In the Australian Alps and parts of Tasmania, the temperature dips below freezing, often accompanied by snow. Alpine resorts are heavily booked during the ski season (Jun–Sept).

Major festivals and sporting events put pressure on cities and towns, so travellers should keep up-to-date with what's on.

## Student and youth travellers

For students under 26, an International Student Identity Card (ISIC) is a must, providing cardholders with a wide variety of student discounts. Apply at youth travel agencies such as STA. There are several organisations in Australia providing travel services and backpacker accommodation for youth travellers such as the Australian YHA and VIP Backpackers. Youth travel agencies also provide discount travel for students, such as Peterpans Adventure Travel, Backpackers World Travel, Student Flights and Trailfinders.

**YHA** www.yha.com.au
**VIP** (07) 3395 6111; www.vipbackpackers.com
**STA Travel** 13 47 82; www.statravel.com.au
**Peterpans Adventure Travel** 1800 252 459; www.peterpans.com
**Backpackers World Travel** 1800 676 763; www.backpackersworld.com.au
**Student Flights** 1800 046 462; www.studentflights.com.au
**Trailfinders** 1300 780 212; www.trailfinders.com.au

## Staying in touch

Mobile phone use is widespread in Australia, although phone networks do not cover many rural and remote areas. Buying a prepaid SIM card is a good way for jobseekers to get an Australian number and useful for keeping in touch. Telstra, Optus and Vodafone are the main mobile phone companies with a host of others also around. Internet cafes abound in major cities and can be found in smaller towns, but may be more expensive. Reasonably priced international phone cards are sold at newsagents, internet cafes, post offices and most hostels. You can use an Australian post office as a mailing address – simply mark the envelope 'Post Restante' with your name, and the location and postcode of the relevant post office.

**Telstra** 12 58880; www.telstra.com.au
**Optus** 1300 301 937; www.optus.com.au
**Vodafone** 1300 650 410; www.vodafone.com.au

### Electrical appliances

You may need to purchase an adaptor to use your electrical appliances in Australia. The electrical current is 240–250 volts AC and plugs have either two or three pins. Some hostels may provide hairdryers as well as 110-volt sockets for shavers. Adapters can be purchased at chemists, electrical or hardware stores. If required, make sure you also purchase a converter to change the voltage, as an adapter alone will not be sufficient.

## Gay and lesbian travel

Most Australians are pretty open-minded when it comes to homosexuality. Melbourne and Sydney have vibrant gay and lesbian scenes, and most other capital cities have gay and lesbian venues and events. Sydney is well known for its Mardi Gras, and Melbourne for its Midsumma Festival. The rainbow sticker is a ubiquitous symbol of gay pride in Australia, and appears on many gay-friendly premises.

There are several Australian gay and lesbian websites with good information on nightlife, events, accommodation and travel advice. Organisations such as Q Beds also provide listings of gay and lesbian-only accommodation. State-based publications feature news and entertainment information, such as the Melbourne-based *BNews* and *MCV* street newspapers. Gay and Lesbian Counselling and Community Services of Australia provide support and telephone counselling.

**Sydney Gay and Lesbian Mardi Gras** www.mardigras.org.au
**Midsumma: Melbourne's Gay and Lesbian Festival** www.midsumma.org.au
**GALTA (Gay and Lesbian Tourism Australia)** (08) 8267 4634; www.galta.com.au
**Rainbow Tourism International** 1800 822 668 ; www.rainbowtourism.com
**Q Beds** www.qbeds.com.au
**Gay and Lesbian Counselling and Community Services of Australia** 1800 184 527; www.glccs.org.au
**BNews** www.bnews.net.au
**MCV** www.evolutionpublishing.com.au/mcv

# Travelling by car

## Licences

To drive in Australia, you must hold a current drivers licence from your home country. If your licence is in another language, you will need an International Drivers Permit (some car rental companies require it too – even if your licence is in English).

## Car and campervan rental

Rental cars are widely available throughout Australia. Prominent rental companies have outlets at airports, in city centres and other high-volume tourist areas. Always check the conditions of hire carefully, particularly with regards to insurance. Major rental companies impose a high insurance excess (around $2750) to be paid by the driver in the event of an accident. A daily payment of around $20 will reduce this to around $300. Many rental companies will not cover standard vehicles for travel on unsealed roads.

Camper hire is a moderately cheap, hassle-free alternative to buying a campervan, with pick-up and drop-off in the city of your choice. Most companies offer 24-hour roadside assistance and will supply you with a new campervan to get you back on the road.

## Car rental

**vroomvroomvroom** Compares prices of major hire car companies www.vroomvroomvroom.com.au
**Avis** 13 6333; www.avis.com
**Budget** 1300 362 848; www.budget.com.au
**Europcar** 1300 131 390; www.deltaeuropcar.com.au
**Hertz** 13 3039; www.hertz.com.au
**Thrifty** 1300 367 227; www.thrifty.com.au

## Campervan rental

**Wicked Campers** 1800 246 869; www.wickedcampers.com.au
**Britz Campervan Hire and Car Rentals** 1800 331 454; www.britz.com
**Maui – Motorhome and Car Hire** 1300 363 800; www.maui.com.au
**Backpacker Campervan Rentals** 1800 670 232; www.backpackercampervans.com
**Hippie Camper** 1800 777 779; www.hippiecamper.com
**Travellers Autobarn** 1800 674 374; www.travellers-autobarn.com.au
**Apollo Campervan and Car Rentals** 1800 777 779; www.apollocamper.com

## Buying and selling cars and campervans

For listings of vehicles for sale, consult the Trading Post (www.tradingpost.com.au), classified ads in *The Age* (Saturday), *The Sydney Morning Herald* (www.drive.com.au) and *Herald Sun* (Friday). Hostel notice boards advertise cars and campers for sale – often complete with camping gear. The Australian Gum Tree also has listings.

When buying a car privately, get a mechanic's check through a state-based motoring organisation or by going to a local mechanic. Also be sure to check the rego (registration) paperwork, as conditions vary from state to state. (Western Australia's is the cheapest and does not require a compulsory roadworthy certificate.) Most states require a roadworthy certificate to transfer ownership of a second-hand car, so check with the relevant state department of transport before buying a vehicle.

Backpacker rental companies such as Travellers Autobarn, Travellers Mate (Sydney-based), Backpackers Auto Sales (Melbourne-based) and Wicked Campers sell vehicles on buy-back schemes, giving you up to 50 per cent of the purchase price back depending on how long you keep the vehicle. Buying through a company will save you the hassle of having to sort out your roadworthy status and paperwork.

**The Australian Gum Tree** www.gumtree.com.au
**Travellers Mate** (02) 9556 2113; www.travellersmate.com.au
**Kings Cross Car Market** 1800 808 188; www.carmarket.com.au
**Backpackers Auto Sales** (03) 9372 5077; www.backpackersautosales.com.au
**Boomerang cars (Adelaide)** 0414 882 559; www.boomerangcars.com.au

# Roadside assist

For a small annual fee, state-based motoring organisations provide roadside service throughout Australia. Reciprocal arrangements between organisations ensure complete coverage. Various levels of cover are available: enquire about the different features to find out what will work best for you.

**New South Wales and Australian Capital Territory (NRMA)** 13 1122; www.mynrma.com.au
**Victoria (RACV)** 13 7228; www.racv.com.au
**South Australia (RAA)** (08) 8202 4600; www.raa.net
**Western Australia (RAC)** 13 1703; www.rac.com.au
**Northern Territory (AANT)** (08) 8981 3837; www.aant.com.au
**Queensland (RACQ)** 13 1905; www.racq.com.au
**Tasmania (RACT)** 13 2722; www.ract.com.au

# Road rules

Uniform road rules apply in Australia, but some rules vary to suit local conditions. Some outback roads in the Northern Territory have no speed limit. In Melbourne there are additional tram-related rules: do not overtake a tram on the right; stop behind stationary trams to allow passengers on and off; and where signed in the CBD, you turn right from the left-hand lane – these 'hook turns' leave the right lane free for through-traffic and the tram tracks clear for trams. A blood alcohol level of 0.05 is the maximum throughout Australia.

**National Transport Commission (NTC)** (03) 9236 5000; www.ntc.gov.au

# Safe driving tips

➡ Always leave a 2-second gap between your car and the vehicle ahead
➡ Keep left unless overtaking
➡ Indicate 30 m before turning or changing lanes
➡ Drive defensively: bad drivers are everywhere
➡ Avoid fatigue: don't drive when you would usually sleep, take a break every 2 hours, limit driving to 10 hours per day and watch for fatigue symptoms such as daydreaming and sore eyes
➡ Avoid distractions: don't use your mobile phone, light cigarettes or fiddle with the radio as you drive
➡ When driving on outback roads, be extra careful of native animals, especially kangaroos, at dawn and dusk – they can jump out of the middle of nowhere and are mesmerised by the headlights

In all states and territories of Australia, any accident in which someone is injured must be reported to police within 24 hours. It is advisable to report any accident that involves substantial property damage in order to avoid and/or simplify legal and insurance problems. Exchange names, addresses and insurance details with other parties involved in the accident, but do not discuss details or admit liability. Wait until you are thinking clearly again before making a statement to police.

# Car sharing and relocations

Hostel notice boards are a good place to start when looking for rides or people to share fuel costs. There are also some websites that can hook up drivers and passengers. If you drive, relocations are another cheap option for transport between major cities. For a nominal amount you can relocate a vehicle for a hire car company from one city to another. Many rental companies including Britz provide this option.

## Car sharing

**Share your Ride** www.shareyourride.net
**The Gum Tree** www.gumtree.com.au
**Need a Ride** www.needaride.com.au

## Relocations

**Wayward** www.waywardbus.com.au
**Standby Cars** www.standbycars.com.au

## Hitching

Hitching – by its very nature – is risky. Horror stories of the Ivan Milat hitchhiker murders and films like *Wolf Creek* have given it a bad name in Australia. In remote areas, most locals are friendly and are more likely to pick up hitchhikers than people in cities. If you choose to hitch, take care and ensure you are well equipped with water and supplies. Travel in pairs for safety, and let someone know where you are going.

# Travelling by air, train, bus and boat

## International air travel

Australia has several international airports, the busiest being Sydney and Melbourne. Most flights from Europe stop over in Asia (usually Bangkok or Singapore). Prior to landing in Australia, passengers are asked to fill in customs documents. It is important to answer the questions as honestly as possible; Australia has strict customs regulations and failure to make a full declaration can result in heavy fines.

## Domestic air travel

Australia's three major domestic airlines, Qantas, Jetstar and Virgin Blue offer a range of discount fares and regularly advertise sale fares in newspapers and online. South East Asian budget airline Tiger Airways will operate domestic routes in Australia from late 2007. The best way to get a cheap flight is to book early (more than three weeks in advance) via the internet and avoid peak travel periods (Fri–Sun and weekdays before 9am). Transfers from airports range from $5–$20.

**Qantas** 1300 HOLIDAY (4654329); www.qantas.com.au
**Virgin Blue** 13 67 89; www.virginblue.com.au
**Jetstar** 13 15 38; www.jetstar.com
**Tiger Airways** www.tigerairways.com

## Train travel

Rail is a fun way to traverse the great expanse of Australia in comfort. There are several classic overland routes: the *Indian Pacific* (Sydney–Perth), the *Ghan* (Adelaide–Darwin) and the *Queenslander* (Brisbane–Cairns). NSW, Queensland and Victoria have a good range of country rail services. Their respective rail companies offer discounted travel passes. Countrylink has a Backtracker Pass, which offers unlimited journeys between Melbourne and Brisbane from $232 for two weeks. The East Coast Discovery Pass allows travel in one direction along the east coast with stopovers (Sydney to Melbourne $110). Great Southern Railway have a backpacker pass for the *Ghan* for six months unlimited travel for $590.

**Great Southern Railway** 13 2147; www.gsr.com.au
**Transwa (Western Australia)** 1800 662 05; www.transwa.wa.gov.au
**V/Line (Victoria)** 13 6196; www.vline.com.au

**Countrylink** 13 2232; www.countrylink.info
**Queensland Rail** 13 1617; www.qr.com.au

## Bus travel

Bus is a cheap and flexible mode of travel in Australia. Major companies such as Greyhound Australia and Premier Motor Service offer a range of travel passes that allow passengers flexible stops as well as direct services. For those who want to party around Australia, companies such as Oz Experience offer hop-on hop-off bus tours, stopping at sights along the way and dropping you at selected hostels.

**Greyhound Australia** 1300 4739 46863; www.greyhound.com.au
**Premier Motor Service** 13 34 10; www.premierms.com.au
**Firefly** 1300 730 740; www.fireflyexpress.com.au
**V/Line** 13 61 96; www.vline.com.au
**Oz Experience** 1300 300 028; www.ozexperience.com.au
**Easyrider Backpacker Tours** 1300 308 477; www.easyridertours.com.au

## Boat travel

Ferries service a number of islands off the mainland including Tasmania. The *Spirit of Tasmania I* and *II* cross the Bass Strait between Melbourne and Devonport daily with additional voyages in peak periods.

Boat cruises are a great way to see remote areas in a relaxed setting. The Whitsunday Islands off Queensland's north coast are a popular destination for sailing adventures leaving from Airlie Beach.

**Spirit of Tasmania** 1800 634 906; www.spiritoftasmania.com.au
**Prosail** (07) 4946 7533; www.prosail.com.au
**Sailing Whitsundays** 1800 550 751; www.sailing-whitsundays.com

# Health and safety

## Sun and surf

Soaking up the sun is an essential part of an Australian holiday, but it can be a risky practice. Even if your skin never burns in your home country, think again. The sun is much stronger in Australia than in Europe and other parts of the world, so it is quite easy to burn after a short period outside. To avoid heatstroke and sun damage, stay in the shade between 11am and 3pm, and when in the sun wear protective clothing (including a hat) and apply broad-spectrum sunblock regularly. Sunblock should be applied 20 minutes before going outdoors to ensure the best protection.

Many Australian beaches have dangerous riptides or currents that can drag swimmers away from the shore. You should never swim alone or at unpatrolled beaches. Red and yellow flags mark the patrolled areas at swimming beaches. Surflifesavers may be around to provide further information.

## Floods and bushfires

In possible flood situations, keep well informed of prevailing conditions, particularly in remote areas. Flash floods can occur without warning. Only camp in riverbeds or close to the edges of creeks or streams if you know it's safe.

### EPIRBs

EPIRBs (Emergency Position Indicator Radio Beacons) are very useful emergency tracking beacons for bushwalkers, sailors and drivers in remote locations. If you activate an EPIRB (and this should only be done in extreme emergencies) you send a signal that allows rescue authorities to pinpoint your exact location. EPIRBs are cheap (around $200) and very portable. EPIRB suppliers can be found online.

Avoid bushfire-prone regions on days of critical fire danger (Total Fire Ban days). If you must travel, carry woollen blankets as a shield against fire and plenty of water to keep hydrated. Never light fires on days of total fire ban.

## First aid

If you are planning to travel through remote areas, consider signing up for first aid training ahead of your trip, and take an appropriate first aid kit with you. Administering first aid in the event of an accident or other medical emergency can often help save lives. St John Ambulance conducts courses in branches all around Australia and also sells a range of first aid kits (for more information go to www.stjohn.org.au).

## Dangerous creatures

Australia has more than its fair share of dangerous wildlife, but this shouldn't restrict your adventures. Risks to personal safety can be minimised by following safety precautions, avoiding contact with wildlife, obeying warning signs and using common sense. A German tourist killed by a crocodile in the Northern Territory in 2002 was swimming in a billabong that was signposted as a crocodile area – clearly not such a good idea. Examples of Australian wildlife to avoid are given below:

➡ **Box jellyfish** – found in tropical waters from Oct–May
➡ **Blue-ringed octopus** – common in rockpools around Australia
➡ **Sharks** – prevalent throughout Australian waters
➡ **Saltwater crocodiles** – found in estuaries and rivers in northern Australia
➡ **Spiders and snakes** – found across Australia; check bedding, clothes and shoes in high-risk areas

### Health and safety contacts

**Sexual Assault Crisis Support** www.aifs.gov.au/acssa/crisis for support centres and phone numbers for each state

**National Helpline for Violence Against Women** 1800 200 526

**National Lifeline: 24-hr telephone counselling** 13 1114

# Money and opening hours

## Australian currency

The local currency is the Australian dollar, which is divided into 100 cents. There is no limit to the amount of foreign or Australian currency that can be brought into or taken out of the country, but amounts of AUD$10 000 or more must be declared to customs. Exchange rates are updated daily by the Reserve Bank of Australia (www.rba.gov.au). Foreign currency can be exchanged at most banks and at foreign exchange branches.

## Banking

Many small towns do not have a single bank, let alone branches of different banks. You will need to plan ahead for over-the-counter transactions. Apart from depositing cheques, most bank services can now be accessed by ATM machine, phone or internet (unlike banks, internet cafes can now be found everywhere). Through its giroPost service, Australia Post acts as an agent for a number of banks and credit unions.

## Cash, card or cheque

For security and convenience, cards are the preferred method of payment for larger transactions these days. A credit card linked to other accounts will allow you to replenish cash, pay for purchases using a credit or debit account (EFTPOS) and pay bills as you travel. But cash still has its uses. Many small businesses (markets, cafes, roadside stalls) are strictly cash only. Other businesses impose a minimum card transaction amount of between $10 and $20. Some businesses charge an additional fee for credit card transactions. Retailers rarely accept personal cheques. It's also a good idea to carry an extra card not linked to your main account so that you can still access your cash in the event you need to cancel your primary card. Travellers cheques are still commonly accepted.

Most banks operate a 24-hour lost card service, so notify your bank immediately if your card is lost or stolen. Write down the contact numbers on the back of your cards before travelling.

## Tax and superannuation

Travellers who work in Australia have income tax and superannuation deducted from their wage. Ensure you apply for a Tax File Number (TFN) when you arrive to avoid a high tax rate. Don't forget to apply for a refund when you leave the country.

Superannuation contributions of 9 per cent of your wage are compulsory for employers in Australia. Remember to keep a record of the name of your superannuation fund and your membership number because you can apply for a refund once you've left the country. Tax returns can be completed online at the end of the financial year. You'll need a group certificate (PAYG) from your employer in order to complete your tax. If tax and super bores you to tears, there are many companies who'll do the work for you. Temporary residents departing Australia should consult the tax office website for further information.

**Australian Tax Office** www.ato.gov.au
**Taxback** www.taxback.com
**Tax Back Australia** (02) 9386 5333; www.taxbackaustralia.com.au
**Departing Australia superannuation payment essentials – online applications** www.ato.gov.au/super
**Super Return** www.superreturn.com.au

## Opening hours

Australia's working week is traditionally from Monday to Friday, 9am to 5pm. Banks are open Monday to Friday, 9am to 4pm, with some also offering services on Saturday mornings until noon. ATM machines for cash withdrawals operate 24 hours. Retail shops often have extended opening hours, covering weekends, and major department stores commonly offer late-night shopping towards the end of the working week. Some convenience stores and petrol stations remain open 24 hours. Be aware of public holidays, when many businesses are forced to close for the whole day.

# Accommodation, food and drink

## Backpacker accommodation

Backpacker hostels are a popular form of budget accommodation. Rooms are usually dormitory-style, although many hostels also offer twin or double rooms (some with private ensuites). Kitchens, bathrooms and living areas are shared. While bed linen is usually provided, travellers often use their own sleeping bags. Some backpacker hostels have curfews, but a key or PIN code is usually provided for after-hours access. There are a number of organisations in Australia that run hostels in various locations (see Planning your trip, p. 2–3). Some backpacker hostels offer discounts to members of organisations such as YHA (www.yha.com.au) and VIP (www.vipbackpackers.com).

Staying at hostels can provide invaluable opportunities for meeting other backpackers and staying in touch with travellers' news. Most hostels have notice boards for travellers to post items wanted or for sale, work wanted or available, and travel opportunities.

To search for backpacker hostels and to find out more information, check out www.bugaustralia.com, www.hostelaustralia.com, www.hostelz.com or www.hostelbeds.com

## Couch surfing

Couch surfing networks provide free accommodation for travellers worldwide, with hosts offering their couches, spare beds or floor space for travellers to crash on. Registering online as a member of the couch surfing network allows you to search and browse extensive profiles of other registered hosts and travellers, and to make accommodation arrangements. For purposes of security and trust, personal vouching and verification systems are used. For more information and to sign up go to www2.couchsurfing.com or www.HospitalityClub.org

### Accommodation deals

If you want luxury without the price tag, you may be able to score a good deal by booking hotels online in the week of intended travel. Packages and deals can be found at www.lastminute.com.au, www.wotif.com.au and www.zuji.com.au

## Camping

Most national parks have campsites, though facilities and regulations vary. In some parks, campsites are allocated on a first-come, first-served basis; in others, bookings need to be made weeks or even months in advance. Some parks charge a fee for camping and some require campers to obtain camping permits. Permits may be purchased from the Park Visitor Centre or at the relevant campground; in other cases permits may need to be organised in advance. Remember that campfires and gas barbecues, gas lights and portable stoves are prohibited on Total Fire Ban days.

## Food

Australian cuisine is extremely diverse and reflects the multicultural population. The greatest variety is found in urban centres, and vegetarian, gluten-free and organic options are also generally available. Medium-sized towns usually offer a variety of options such as Italian or Chinese food. Traditional Aussie pub meals can be found just about anywhere, and include dishes such as roasts, steaks, schnitzels and pastas. Native animals (such as kangaroo and crocodile) are not generally on the menu, but can be found in some pubs and restaurants. To eat like a local, try ordering a 'chicken parma' – a crumbed chicken fillet topped with tomato sauce (and sometimes ham), finished with cheese and grilled so that the cheese melts. For a traditional (but not necessarily healthy) meal on the go, grab a meat pie from a milk bar or service station – and don't forget the tomato sauce.

### Tipping

Tipping is not compulsory in Australia, but it is commonly practised when the service is good – and particularly when dining with large groups. In these cases, tips of 5 to 10 per cent of the total bill are appreciated.

## Pubs and bars

Going to the pub for a beer is an enduring Australian pastime. While all but the smallest towns will have at least one pub, there are plenty of options for going out for a drink in urban centres, with establishments ranging from traditional pubs to bars and clubs. Beer is the drink of choice, and the most popular Australian beer is Victoria Bitter (better known as VB). Wine and spirits are also regularly consumed in pubs and bars.

### Smoking laws

Smoking laws vary from state to state, but smoking is generally not allowed indoors – including inside pubs, bars and clubs. If you're desperate for a cigarette, you may be forced to spend some time outside the establishment.

# Top 10s

## Top tracks

1. **Australian Alps Walking Track, ACT, NSW & VIC** A 680 km track, usually completed in sections, taking in rivers, peaks and valleys.
2. **Bibbulmun Track, WA** A walk that traverses Western Australia's spectacular south-west. It can be done in total (963 km from Kalamunda to Albany) or in part.
3. **Blue Mountains, NSW** Anything from an hour's stroll to a week-long trek through some of Australia's most accessible bush. See p. 24
4. **Flinders Ranges, SA** A range of walks weaves across the ridges, gorges and river valleys of this ancient landscape. See p. 170
5. **Fraser Island, QLD** Short walks to extended treks across this massive sand island, taking in lakes, forests and dunes. See p. 66
6. **Lamington National Park, QLD** Around 160 km of walking tracks through primordial subtropical forests. See p. 55
7. **Larapinta Trail, NT** A 220 km walking track along the gorges, chasms, pools and arid habitats of the West MacDonnell Ranges. See p. 117
8. **Overland Track, TAS** Australia's best-known long-distance walk – seven days from Cradle Mountain to Lake St Clair. See p. 198
9. **Wilsons Promontory, VIC** Pristine beaches and bush accessed along 150 km of tracks in one of Australia's most beautiful coastal parks. See p. 95
10. **South Coast Track, TAS** A challenging six-to-nine-day hike that explores Tasmania's uninhabited south coast.

## Top beaches

1. **Bells Beach, Torquay, VIC** Australia's top surfing destination and the site of the legendary Rip Curl Pro each Easter. See p. 84
2. **Booderee National Park beaches, Jervis Bay, NSW** A series of near-deserted beaches, surrounded by native bush and boasting what is claimed to be the whitest sand in the world.
3. **Cable Beach, Broome, WA** A luxurious sweep of white sand fronting turquoise waters, forming the scenic centrepiece of Australia's most remote and exotic resort town. See p. 143
4. **Cactus Beach, Penong, SA** The three famous surfing breaks of this remote destination are strictly for surfers with a frontier spirit and the skill to match.
5. **Four Mile Beach, Port Douglas, QLD** A beach so beautiful that it helped turn a sleepy seaside village into an international resort. See p. 61
6. **Noosa National Park beaches, QLD** A subtropical wonderland of peaceful, pandanus-fringed coves providing a retreat from the bustling Sunshine Coast. See p. 65
7. **Watego Beach, Byron Bay, NSW** Tune out and drop in at this popular surf beach in one of Australia's most free-spirited towns. See p. 33
8. **Whitehaven, Whitsunday Island, QLD** A paradise, 7 km long, on a pristine, uninhabited island.
9. **Wineglass Bay, Freycinet Peninsula, TAS** Bushland opens up to this magnificently sculpted, crescent-shaped beach. See p. 194
10. **The Basin beaches, Rottnest Island, WA** On the island's north side, reef-protected beaches offer a great place to relax or go snorkelling. See p. 131

## Top natural wonders

1. **Uluṟu–Kata Tjuṯa National Park, NT** Massive rock formations in the desert, with numerous Aboriginal sites. See p. 119
2. **Great Barrier Reef, QLD** The world's largest reef, with the most diverse reef fauna. See p. 61
3. **Kakadu National Park, NT** Myriad natural environments and the world's oldest, most extensive Aboriginal rock art. See p. 111
4. **Fraser Island, QLD** The world's largest sand island, with a complex dune system, freshwater dune lakes and rainforest. See p. 66
5. **Purnululu National Park, WA** Home of the Bungle Bungles, beehive-shaped rock formations that speak of 20 million years of geological history. See p. 147
6. **Shark Bay, WA** A large population of sea mammals, and 3.5 billion-year-old stromatolites representing the oldest life on earth. See p. 139
7. **Australian Fossil Mammal Sites (Naracoorte & Riversleigh), SA** These two sites have yielded 20 million-year-old fossils of extinct Australian species. See p. 177
8. **Tasmanian wilderness** Forest, rivers, caves, glacial lakes and 40 Aboriginal sites pointing to at least 30 000 years occupation, and home to Australia's oldest living trees – the Huon Pine.
9. **Heard and McDonald islands, WA** An active volcano (on Heard), glacial landscapes and rare sub-Antarctic flora and fauna.
10. **Greater Blue Mountains area, NSW** A deeply incised plateau with dramatic cliffs, valleys and eucalypt forests. See p. 24

## Top skiing slopes

1. **Thredbo, NSW** Among Australia's skiing destinations, this alpine village stands out with Australia's highest run, as well as some of its longest, with an inspiring mix of terrain. See p. 36
2. **Falls Creek, VIC** Snowbound with some of Australia's best snow cover, as well as one of the nations best adventure areas for advanced skiers.
3. **Perisher Blue, NSW** This collection of four resorts has the skiable area and lift capacity to rival many North American resorts, and is know for its good snow cover and cruising terrain. See p. 36
4. **Mount Buller, VIC** This large resort has 25 lifts spanning all capabilities and is a favourite with weekenders from Melbourne.

5. **Mount Hotham, VIC** Long considered one of Australia's major resorts with a good range of runs and some challenging terrain for advanced skiers and boarders.

6. **Ben Lomond, TAS** Tasmania's premier skiing destination is set on the plateau in Ben Lomond National Park and has easy to difficult runs, as well as cross-country loops and unmarked tracks.

7. **Lake Mountain, VIC** The closest cross-country skiing area to Melbourne, Lake Mountain is renowned for its exclusive cross-country trails and is a great place for snow play and tobogganing.

8. **Mount Stirling, NSW** This is a mountain for real adventurers – there are no lifts and it is over an hour's trek to the summit from the parking area. At the top there are plenty of steep, challenging trails for intermediate to advanced skiers.

9. **Mount Baw Baw, VIC** An affordable slope situated conveniently close to Melbourne, Baw Baw is a beginner's paradise with its gentle, uncrowded slopes along with some interesting cross-country trails.

10. **Mount Mawson, TAS** This small slope in Mount Field National Park has struggled a little in recent years, but is an ideal place for intermediate to advanced skiers wanting to get away from the crowds and try out some hairy terrain, including what is considered Australia's steepest lift track.

# Top festivals

1. **Sydney Gay and Lesbian Mardi Gras, NSW** Every year hundreds of thousands of people line the streets of Sydney to witness the elaborate and exotic floats participating in this parade for gay and lesbian pride.

2. **Adelaide Fringe Festival, SA** Rivalled only by the Edinburgh Fringe Festival, this event features some of the world's best independent artists.

3. **Sydney Festival, NSW** This three-week festival of theatre, dance, music and visual art is one of the nation's biggest cultural events.

4. **Melbourne International Comedy Festival, VIC** Showcasing comic talent from Australia and around the globe, this is considered one of the three major comedy festivals in the world.

5. **WOMADelaide, Adelaide, SA** A three-day festival of arts, music and dance, held in Adelaide's Botanic Park.

6. **Perth International Arts Festival, WA** This internationally acclaimed event is Australia's longest-running arts festival.

7. **Ten Days on the Island, Hobart, TAS** Tasmania's leading, biennial cultural event, comprising of arts, theatre, dance, music and literature.

8. **Tamworth Country Music Festival, NSW** Music fans and travellers from around the globe flock to Tamworth to see performances by country music greats.

9. **East Coast Blues and Roots Festival, Byron Bay, NSW** Australia's largest international festival of blues and roots is held in Australia's most laidback coastal town.

10. **The Dreaming, Woodford, QLD** This festival on the Sunshine Coast showcases the best of Australia's Indigenous art, ranging from visual works to physical theatre.

# Top sporting events

1. **AFL Grand Final, Melbourne, VIC** The yearly final of Aussie Rules football sees Melbourne come to a standstill, with all eyes on the MCG for one day in September.

2. **NRL Grand final, Sydney, NSW** The National Rugby League grand final is one of Sydney's major sporting events, held at the Telstra Stadium in October.

3. **Boxing Day Test Match, Melbourne, VIC** More than 160 000 cricket fans come to the MCG to cheer on Australia in the world's biggest test match.

4. **Melbourne Cup, VIC** A day of fashion, champagne and barbecues, not to mention horseracing that all of Melbourne stops to watch.

5. **Australian Open, Melbourne, VIC** This Grand Slam tennis tournament draws top players to Rod Laver Arena in January.

6. **Sydney to Hobart Yacht Race, Hobart, TAS** This world-famous sailing event kicks off on Boxing Day from Sydney, with yacht crews braving the waters of the Bass Strait to reach Hobart.

7. **Formula One Grand Prix, Melbourne, VIC** Australia's most important motorsport event attracts people from around the world to watch the cars whiz around the circuit at Albert Park.

8. **Bathurst 1000, NSW** This 1000 km touring-car race sees V8 Supercars competing for the Peter Brock Trophy, named in honour of the late racing car legend.

9. **Rip Curl Pro World Surfing Championships, Torquay, VIC** The surfing championship at Bells Beach is one of the most prestigious world surfing events.

# NEW SOUTH WALES

# CONTENTS

Sydney 14
TOP REGIONS:
Blue Mountains 24
North Coast 29
Snowy Mountains 35
Hunter Valley 39

## Visitor information

New South Wales Visitor Information Line
13 2077; www.visitnsw.com.au

## FAST FACTS

**Highest mountain** Mount Kosciuszko (2228 m)
**Most remote town** Tibooburra
**Strangest place name** Come-by-Chance
**Most famous person** Nicole Kidman
**Quirkiest festival** Stroud International
Brick and Rolling Pin Throwing Competition
**Favourite food** Sydney rock oysters
**Local beer** Tooheys
**Interesting fact** The Stockton Sand Dunes (up to
30 m high) form the largest-moving coastal sand
mass in the Southern Hemisphere

New South Wales fulfils every backpacker's wish list and then some. Lush rainforests, spectacular beaches, majestic snowfields and the rugged beauty of the outback all compete for your attention. New South Wales is also guardian to some of this country's earliest history, both European and Aboriginal. Time-conscious travellers will be delighted with the fantastic weekend getaways within easy reach of Sydney, like the Blue Mountains or the Hunter Valley, while those with time to linger can wander every inch and won't be disappointed. Add to this the almost indecent amount on offer in Sydney, from its dazzling harbour to its wild nightlife.

# Top region highlights

## Three Sisters

Set in the Blue Mountains, just 2 hours by train or a 90-minute drive from Sydney, these three rock formations are the impressive, eroded remains of a giant plateau cliff-face that emerged from a river delta a mere 80 million years ago. p. 25

## Kosciuszko National Park

Kosciuszko National Park is a year-round wonderland of bushwalking, skiing, whitewater rafting, kayaking, horseriding, caving … and the country's highest mountain, Mount Kosciuszko, is just waiting to be conquered. p. 38

## Byron Bay

A laidback and environmentally 'tuned in' culture, together with exquisite beaches, make Byron Bay a magnet for visitors. It's the closest you'll get to the free-loving 70s in Australia. p. 33

## Hunter Valley wineries

Over 160 cellar doors are open and waiting for your tastebuds. Be prepared for wine and local cuisine that will knock your socks off. p. 40

## Big Banana

It's a little tacky, but we couldn't resist mentioning one of Australia's many 'big things' in Coffs Harbour. p. 31

# Other regions worth a look

## Canberra

The country's political heartbeat and so much more – honest. With attractions such as the National Gallery, you are doing your inner culture vulture a huge favour by visiting Australia's capital.

## Outback

Visit Mungo National Park to see the Walls of China, incredible weather-eroded sand formations that have revealed skeletons of megafauna.

## New England

This region incorporates Tamworth, Australia's centre of country music that's home to a massive golden guitar. But don't forget the breathtaking Wollomombi Falls and fossicking for rare black opals at Lightning Ridge.

## Central Coast and Hawkesbury

The beautiful mix of exquisite coastline and spectacular Ku-ring-gai Chase National Park ensures a rewarding weekend break, within 1 hour of Sydney.

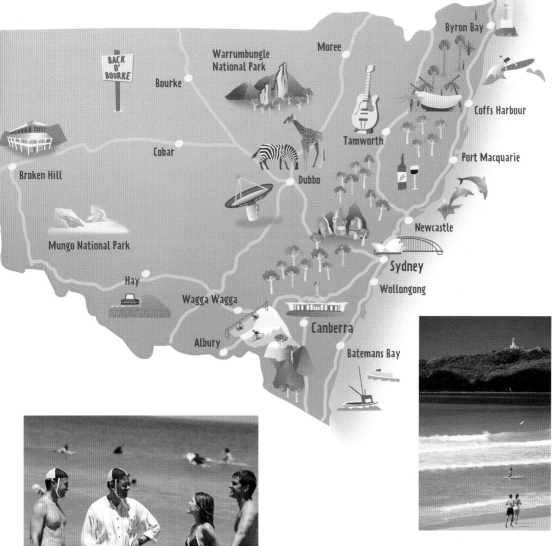

BACK O' BOURKE

Bourke

Warrumbungle
National Park

Moree

Byron Bay

Coffs Harbour

Broken Hill

Cobar

Dubbo

Tamworth

Port Macquarie

Mungo National Park

Newcastle

Hay

Wagga Wagga

Sydney

Wollongong

Albury

Canberra

Batemans Bay

# Sydney

Radiating from the sparkling waters of Sydney Harbour, Australia's biggest city is knitted together from the shores of the Pacific to the feet of the Blue Mountains. This one-time prison settlement has grown up to become the most recognised city in Australia. Proud parent to the iconic Sydney Harbour Bridge and Sydney Opera House, the city effortlessly attracts more than two million visitors per year. Along with outstanding natural assets – stunning beaches, extensive parklands and the beautiful harbour – Sydney boasts a fantastic 'to do' list of inner city standouts, including dazzling shopping and a galaxy of incredible restaurants and night spots.

## Top attractions

### Circular Quay harbour area

From the moment that Sydney was declared a settlement, Circular Quay has been where it all happens. It's a major junction for bus, rail and ferry transport (see Getting around), and a natural meeting place. There are always buskers and street performers, while the many excellent cafes and bars offer stunning views of the harbour.

Sydney Opera House stands at the far end of East Circular Quay. One of the great buildings of the 20th century, it was the natural fall of a segmented orange that inspired Jørn Utzon's design. A guided tour is well worth the effort. Bookings are essential (02) 9250 7111.

Towards the western side of Circular Quay is the Museum of Contemporary Art, occupying a brooding Art Deco structure. Once inside, the large, open, white rooms hit you with Australia's best cutting-edge contemporary artworks.

Sydney Harbour Bridge is at the western tip, dominating with its soaring arch. The second-longest single-span bridge in the world (New York's Bayonne Bridge beats it by a few centimetres), one of the best views can be had from the Pylon Lookout, which also contains an excellent exhibition detailing the bridge's history. BridgeClimb offers

unique tours to the very top of the span (see Tours and activities). Museum of Contemporary Art, (02) 9245 2396, daily 10am–5pm, general admission free; Pylon Lookout, 5 Cumberland St, (02) 9240 1100, daily 10am–5pm, admission fee applies.

### The Rocks

The heart and soul of The Rocks is Playfair Street, filled at the weekends with wandering street performers, corn-on-the-cob and live entertainment. Find a seat in Rocks Square and soak it all up. Not far from Rocks Square is Argyle Stores, a converted warehouse that now houses a collection of open-plan shops specialising in beautiful and unusual clothes. The area is also home to Cadmans Cottage, Sydney's oldest surviving residence, now the Sydney Harbour National Park Information Centre. Cadmans Cottage, 110 George St; (02) 9247 5033; Mon–Fri 9.30am–4.30pm, Sat–Sun 10am–4.30pm.

### Royal Botanic Gardens and the Domain

An oasis on the edge of the harbour, the Royal Botanic Gardens are a great place to stroll or relax with a picnic. Visit the Tropical Centre, go to Moonlight Cinema (see Cinemas), or even adopt a tree. Across the Cahill Expressway, the Domain comes into its own in January when it hosts popular jazz, opera and symphony concerts. On regular Sundays, soapbox orators and a crowd of hecklers debate the issues of the day. Mrs Macquaries Rd; (02) 9231 8111; general admission free.

### Art Gallery of New South Wales

Opposite South Domain, this gallery stands in an imposing Classical Revival-style building with ultra-modern additions. There is an impressive collection of both Australian and international artworks, including a large permanent collection of Aboriginal art and a superb Asian collection. Art Gallery Rd, The Domain; (02) 9225 1744; daily 10am–5pm, Wed 10am–9pm; general admission free.

Sydney Opera House and Sydney Harbour Bridge

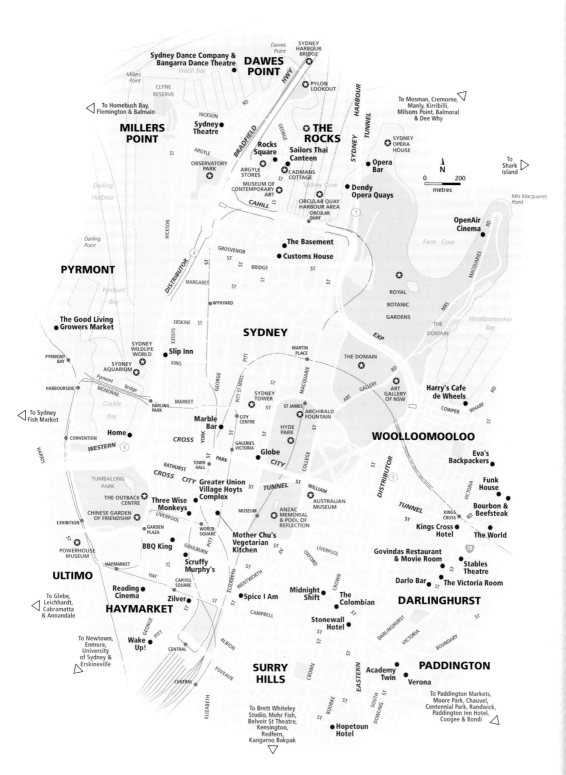

Sydney Dance Company &
Bangarra Dance Theatre

DAWES
POINT

Dawes
Point

SYDNEY
HARBOUR
BRIDGE

Walsh Bay

Millers
Point

CLYNE
RESERVE

PYLON
LOOKOUT

To Homebush Bay,
Flemington & Balmain

MILLERS
POINT

HICKSON

Sydney
Theatre

ARGYLE

OBSERVATORY
PARK

ARGYLE
STORES

MUSEUM OF
CONTEMPORARY
ART

Rocks
Square

CADMANS
COTTAGE

Sailors Thai
Canteen

THE
ROCKS

Sydney Cove

CIRCULAR QUAY
HARBOUR AREA

CIRCULAR
QUAY

Opera
Bar

SYDNEY
OPERA
HOUSE

To Mosman, Cremorne,
Manly, Kirribilli,
Milsons Point, Balmoral
& Dee Why

Dendy
Opera Quays

N

0        200
metres

To
Shark
Island

OpenAir
Cinema

Farm Cove

Mrs Macquaries
Point

CAHILL

Darling
Harbour

Darling
Point

PYRMONT

Pyrmont
Bay

GROSVENOR

BRIDGE

MARGARET

WYNYARD

ERSKINE

SYDNEY

THE
DOMAIN

ROYAL
BOTANIC
GARDENS

MRS
MACQUARIES

Woolloomooloo
Bay

The Good Living
Growers Market

SYDNEY
WILDLIFE
WORLD

Slip Inn

KING

The Basement

Customs House

The DOMAIN

ART  GALLERY

ART
GALLERY
OF NSW

Harry's Cafe
de Wheels

COWPER        WHARF

PYRMONT
BAY

SYDNEY
AQUARIUM

Pyrmont
Bridge

MONORAIL

HARBOURSIDE

DARLING
PARK

MARKET

MARTIN
PLACE

PITT ST MALL

SYDNEY
TOWER

ST JAMES

ARCHIBALD
FOUNTAIN

HYDE
PARK

MACQUARIE

WOOLLOOMOOLOO

Eva's
Backpackers

To Sydney
Fish Market

Cockle
Bay

CONVENTION

Home

WESTERN

Marble
Bar

CITY
CENTRE

GALERIES
VICTORIA

Globe

CITY

AUSTRALIAN
MUSEUM

Funk
House

Bourbon &
Beefsteak

HARRIS

CROSS

BATHURST

TOWN
HALL

PARK

CROSS   CITY

TUMBALONG
PARK

THE OUTBACK
CENTRE

CHINESE GARDEN
OF FRIENDSHIP

EXHIBITION

POWERHOUSE
MUSEUM

ULTIMO

To Glebe,
Leichhardt,
Cabramatta
& Annandale

HAYMARKET

Greater Union
Village Hoyts
Complex

Three Wise
Monkeys

LIVERPOOL

GARDEN
PLAZA

WORLD
SQUARE

BBQ King

GOULBURN

Scruffy
Murphy's

CAPITOL
SQUARE

Reading
Cinema

Zilver

HAY

MUSEUM

Mother Chu's
Vegetarian
Kitchen

PITT

ANZAC
MEMORIAL
& POOL OF
REFLECTION

WILLIAM

TUNNEL

KINGS
CROSS

DISTRIBUTOR

Kings Cross
Hotel

Govindas Restaurant
& Movie Room

Darlo Bar

LIVERPOOL

OXFORD

The World

Stables
Theatre

The Victoria Room

DARLINGHURST

Wake
Up!

CENTRAL

ALBION

FOVEAUX

SURRY
HILLS

Spice I Am

CAMPBELL

Stonewall
Hotel

Midnight
Shift

The
Colombian

CROWN

DARLINGHURST

VICTORIA

BOUNDARY

Academy
Twin

Verona

PADDINGTON

To Newtown,
Enmore,
University
of Sydney &
Erskineville

To Brett Whiteley
Studio, Mohr Fish,
Belvoir St Theatre,
Kensington,
Redfern,
Kangaroo Bakpak

BOURKE

EASTERN

SOUTH

DOWLING

Hopetoun
Hotel

To Paddington Markets,
Moore Park, Chauvel,
Centennial Park, Randwick,
Paddington Inn Hotel,
Coogee & Bondi

## Australian Museum

On the corner of William and College streets, this museum houses several unique natural history collections as well as a superb display of Indigenous Australian culture, with lots of hands-on activities and weekly sessions of Aboriginal music and dance. 6 College St; (02) 9320 6000; daily 9.30am–5pm; admission fee applies.

## Hyde Park

Originally laid out as the city's first racecourse, Hyde Park is now a place of sunny lawns and wide avenues shaded by spreading trees. Near Liverpool Street, you'll find the Art Deco ANZAC Memorial and the Pool of Reflection. Below the memorial there's an excellent ongoing photographic exhibition 'Australians at War'. At the busy end of the park stands the gorgeously kitsch Archibald Fountain, which commemorates the association of France and Australia during WW I. Find yourself a place in the sun and take in a game of giant chess, or simply watch the world go by.

## Sydney Tower

Accessed by way of the Centrepoint shopping complex in Pitt Street Mall, your ticket grants you access to the 250 m observation tower, which commands superb views of Sydney, from the Blue Mountains to the Pacific Ocean. Included in your ticket price is OzTrek, a virtual tour of Australia and the outback. For those who like to live dangerously, there's an outdoor walk over the roof of the Sydney Tower. 100 Market St; (02) 9333 9200; daily 9am–10pm; admission fee applies.

# Getting around

Sydney has an extensive network of rail, bus and ferry services. When negotiating the inner city, buses are probably best, with regular services on George and Elizabeth streets, between Park Street and Circular Quay. The Red Explorer bus covers city attractions, and the Blue Explorer bus focuses on the eastern beach and harbourside suburbs.

Trains are another option, with services every two or three minutes on the City Circle line, which runs in a loop between Central Station and Circular Quay. The Monorail, an elevated ride through the streets of Sydney, is an experience in itself. It runs in a circle that includes the north, west and south sides of Darling Harbour, and Liverpool, Pitt and Market streets. The Light Rail service runs from Central Station to the inner-west suburb of Lilyfield. As Sydney's only tram service, it is particularly useful for accessing places such as Star City and the Sydney Fish Market.

Ferries are also a great way to travel, with services to many locations on the inner and outer harbour. Enquire about Travel 10, Daytripper and weekly tickets, as these can considerably reduce the cost of your trip.

If you're driving, an up-to-the-minute road map is essential. There are six tollways in Sydney, including the Harbour Bridge and the Cross-City Tunnel. Tolls can sometimes be paid on the spot, but the Cross-City Tunnel and the M7 will only accept payment by E-tag, an electronic device which can be obtained through the Roads and Traffic Authority (RTA).

Public transport **Train, bus and ferry information line** 13 1500

Specialty trips **Monorail and Metro Light Rail** (02) 9285 5600

**Tollway Roads** and **Traffic Authority (RTA)** 13 1865

Motoring organisation **NRMA** 13 1122

Car rental **Avis** 13 6333; **Bayswater Car Rental** (02) 9360 3622; **Budget** 13 2727; **Hertz** 1300 132 607; **Thrifty** 1300 367 227

Taxis **ABC Taxis** 13 2522; **Legion Cabs** 13 1451; **Manly Warringah Cabs** 13 1668; **Premier Cabs** 13 1017

Water Taxis **Yellow Water Taxis** 9299 0199; **Water Taxis Combined** 1300 666 484

Tourist bus **Red Explorer, Blue Explorer** 13 1500

Harbour cruises **Sydney Harbour Ferries** 13 1500; **Captain Cook Cruises** (02) 9206 1111

Bike hire **Centennial Park Cycles** (02) 9398 5027; **Bonza Bike Tours** (02) 9331 1127

## Sydney Aquarium

The Sydney Aquarium rates high among aquariums of the world for sheer spectacle-value. Highlights include the fabulous underwater tunnels that enable you to walk with the stingrays and stroll with the sharks, a Great Barrier Reef exhibition that's pure magic, and the Seal Sanctuary, where you can watch the seals flirt and frolic all around you. Aquarium Pier; (02) 8251 7800; daily 9am–10pm; admission fee applies.

Sydney Opera House

### Sydney Wildlife World

Situated right next door to the Aquarium, Sydney Wildlife World takes you deep into the heart of the Australian bush, from the rainforests of the tropical north to the deserts of the Red Centre. This is your chance for a close encounter with some of Australia's most beautiful and unusual plants and animals, including reptiles, koalas, wallabies, butterflies and creepy spiders. Aquarium Pier; (02) 9333 9288; daily 9am–10pm; admission fee applies.

## Taronga Zoo

Taronga Zoo is a 12-minute ferry ride from Circular Quay (see Getting around). A world-class institution, it houses over 2000 animals, most of which enjoy stunning views of the harbour and city. There are plenty of places for picnics and barbecues, a Skyline Safari offering a unique way of seeing the animals, and the ever-popular 'Twilight at Taronga' open-air concerts, which take place in February and March. Bradleys Head Rd, Mosman; (02) 9969 2777; daily 9am–5pm; admission fee applies.

## Powerhouse Museum

One of Sydney's most fascinating museums, it is best reached by monorail. Housing an extraordinary collection of oddments and treasures, highlights include the Hall of Transport with its fleet of aeroplanes suspended from the ceiling, and the tiny 1930s-style cinema. Free guided tours. 500 Harris St, Ultimo; (02) 9217 0111; daily 10am–5pm; admission fee applies.

# Other attractions worth a look

**Shark Island** Sandy beaches, shaded grassy areas and superb views of the harbour make this the perfect place for a picnic. Matilda Catamarans runs a daily ferry service from Darling Harbour and Circular Quay. Bookings (02) 9264 7377.

**Chinese Garden of Friendship** Tucked away near Darling Harbour, this is a beautiful garden of airy pavilions and tiny, arched bridges reflected in tranquil lakes, surrounded by weeping willows and graceful bamboo. Southern end of Darling Harbour; (02) 9240 8888; daily 9.30am–5pm; admission fee applies.

**The Outback Centre** Part gallery, part shop, part performance space, the Outback Centre offers a heady mix of art, music and quality merchandise. 'Sounds of the Outback', a 30-minute live show, is performed at 1pm, 3pm and 5pm daily. Darling Walk; daily 10am–6pm; admission free.

**Observatory Park** High above The Rocks stands what is perhaps the loveliest park in Sydney. It has an old-world ambience and stunning views of the western harbour.

**Brett Whiteley Studio** Paintings and sculptures in the former studio and home of this great Australian artist. 2 Raper St, Surry Hills; 1800 679 278; Sat–Sun 10am–4pm; admission fee applies.

**Sydney Olympic Park** The site of the 2000 Olympic Games, the park now hosts Sydney's yearly Royal Easter Show and is home to the fabulous Aquatic Centre. Visitor centre, cnr Showground Rd & Murray Rose Ave, Homebush Bay; (02) 9714 7888.

## Top events

**Festival of Sydney** A celebration of the city, it includes sporting and cultural events at Sydney's most stunning indoor and outdoor venues. Jan.

**Big Day Out** The biggest and best collection of live bands, both international and local, gather at Sydney Olympic Park in Homebush to rock your socks off. Jan.

**Gay and Lesbian Mardi Gras** The glitz and glamour of this street parade tops off the Gay and Lesbian Festival. Feb.

**Tropfest** The biggest short film festival continues to grow its cult following every year at The Domain. Keep your eyes peeled for mega movie stars who attend to judge and partake in the viewing. Feb.

**Big Laugh Comedy Festival** A week of local and international comedy acts at various venues around Sydney. Mar.

**Royal Easter Show** The country comes to the city in the Great Australian Muster. Easter.

**Sydney Film Festival** A showcase for the newest offerings in cinema. Jun.

**City to Surf** Road race for all walks of life, from Hyde Park to Bondi. Aug.

**Rugby League Grand Final** The leaders of this football competition compete for the title in the final match of the season. Sept.

**Manly International Jazz Festival** Many a jazz fan has been born while visiting this live jazz extravaganza on the waterfront. Oct.

**Sydney to Hobart Yacht Race** Classic blue-water sailing event. Dec.

**Oceanworld Manly** An exciting bottom-of-the-sea experience, situated to the west of the Manly ferry terminal. There are daily shark feedings and opportunities to get up close and personal with the sharks through the Shark Dive Xtreme. West Espl, Manly; (02) 8251 7878; daily 10am–5.30pm; admission fee applies.

# Where to eat

**City centre** The variety of venues is extreme, from groovy eateries exuding uber-cool fabulousness to unpretentious local darlings. Our favourites: **Mother Chu's Vegetarian Kitchen** 🟢 Also serving meat, this kitchen still belongs to Mother Chu, now in her seventies, serving up delectable Chinese, Taiwanese and Japanese nosh for a steal. 367 Pitt St; (02) 9282 2828; lunch Mon–Fri noon–3pm, dinner Mon–Sat 5–10pm.

**Sailors Thai Canteen** 🟢/🟢🟢 Gorgeous, affordable version of the fancy Thai favourite downstairs. 106 George St, The Rocks; (02) 9251 2466; Mon–Sat noon–10pm.

**Chinatown** Bursting with cheap souvenirs and heavenly food. Our favourites: **BBQ King** 🟢🟢 ♡ Chinatown's best barbecue is perfect for groups and late-night feasts. 18–20 Goulburn St; (02) 9267 2586; daily 11.30am–2am.

**Zilver** 🟢🟢🟢 **TOP TREAT!!** ♡ Elegance and Zen are effortlessly mixed into divine nourishment here. Level 1, 477 Pitt St; (02) 9211 2232; Mon–Fri 10am–3.30pm & 5.30–11pm; www.zilver.com.au

**East** Locals will have you believing there is nowhere worth visiting outside the borough of inner East Sydney. Our favourites: **Spice I Am** 🟢 Everyone happily lines up for the incredible Thai food on offer here. The frequent rave reviews makes this Sydney's worst-kept secret. 90 Wentworth Ave, Surry Hills; (02) 9280 0928; Tue–Sun 11.30am–3.30pm & 6–10pm; www.spiceiam.com

**Govindas** 🟢🟢 Two great worlds combined – a vegetarian, Indian buffet and a boutique cinema (see Cinemas for more information). It's cheap, delicious and chilled out. 112 Darlinghurst Rd, Darlinghurst; (02) 9380 5155; daily from 5.45pm; www.govindas.com.au

**The Victoria Room** 🟢🟢 Sumptuous antique decor and great food make this place a fantastically funky night spot on weekends and an elegant late-night retreat on week nights. Level 1, 235 Victoria St, Darlinghurst; (02) 9357 4488; Tue–Thur 6pm–midnight, Fri 6pm–2am, Sat 2pm–2am, Sun 1pm–midnight; www.thevictoriaroom.com

**Harry's Cafe de Wheels** ⓢ ♡ Over half a century old, check out the photos of visiting celebs happily scoffing pies as you order. A Sydney institution. There's one in Haymarket too. Cowper Wharf Rd, Woolloomooloo; (02) 9211 2517; www.harryscafedewheels.com

**Mohr Fish** ⓢⓢ ✎ Do your best Oliver Twist impression at this crowded counter to get your share of great fish and chips. 202 Devonshire St, Surry Hills; (02) 9318 1326; daily 11am–10pm.

**Arthur's Pizza** ⓢ/ⓢⓢ ◈ Ask why the sign is upside down while you sup on the best pizza in town. 260 Oxford St, Paddington; (02) 9331 1779; Mon–Fri 5pm–midnight, Sat–Sun noon–midnight.

**Inner west** The thriving heart and soul of Italian, Greek and all good home cooking, mixed with a hippy vibe.

Our favourites: **Bar Italia** ⓢⓢ ♡ This is the place for the best Italian comfort food. 169–171 Norton St, Leichhardt; (02) 9560 9981; Sun–Mon 10am–midnight, Tue–Thur 9am–midnight, Fri 9am–1am, Sat 10am–1am.

**Thai Pothong** ⓢⓢ ✎ Lavished with awards, this beautifully decked-out haven lives up to its reputation with bargain basement prices. 294 King St, Newtown; (02) 9550 6277; lunch Tue–Sun noon–3pm, dinner Sun–Thur 6–10.30pm, Fri–Sat 6–11pm; www.thaipothong.com.au

**Steki Taverna** ⓢⓢ ✎ Fantastic and fun Greek tavern tucked away from the main road and adored by everyone. 20 O'Connell St, Newtown; (02) 9516 2191; Wed–Sun from 6.30pm.

**Badde Manors Cafe** ⓢ ◈ You'll need to get in quick to snag a table. Scrumptious grub and coffee with a hip vibe. 37 Glebe Point Rd, Glebe; (02) 9660 3797; Mon–Fri 8am–midnight, Sat 8am–1am, Sun 9am–midnight; www.baddemanorscafe.com

Harry's Cafe de Wheels

## Other areas to eat out

**Liverpool Street** Sangria and tapas are the go in Sydney's Spanish quarter.

**John Street, Cabramatta** Packed with inexpensive, authentic Vietnamese eateries.

**Darling Street, Balmain** A famous eat street with an endless selection of restaurant, cafe and pub food.

**Circular Quay** Superb cuisine with stunning views of the Opera House and the Harbour Bridge.

**Cockle Bay Wharf, Darling Harbour** Exclusive waterfront dining, with some surprisingly cheaper options tucked away.

# Out and about
## Cinemas

**Greater Union Village Hoyts Complex** 505–525 George St; (02) 9273 7431.

**Entertainment Quarter – Hoyts Cinema Complex** Driver Ave, off Lang Rd, Moore Park; (02) 9332 1300.

**Cinema Paris** (art house selection) Driver Ave, off Lang Rd, Moore Park; (02) 9332 1300

**Dendy Opera Quays** (independent world films) Shop 9, 2 Circular Quay East; (02) 9247 3800.

**Govindas Movie Room** (new and classic films) Movie and dinner deals here are a must; 112 Darlinghurst Rd, Darlinghurst; (02) 9380 5162.

**Chauvel** Paddington Town Hall, cnr Oately Rd & Oxford St; (02) 9361 5298.

**Hayden Orpheum Picture Palace** (mainstream and art house selection) 380 Military Rd, Cremorne; (02) 9908 4344.

**Academy Twin** (art house selection) 3a Oxford St, Paddington; (02) 9331 3457.

**Verona** (art house selection) 17 Oxford St; (02) 9360 6099.

**IMAX Cinema** Southern Promenade, Darling Harbour; (02) 9281 3300.

**Moonlight Cinema** (summer only, new and classic films) Woollahra Gate, Centennial Park; (02) 9266 4800.

**OpenAir Cinema** (summer only, new and highly acclaimed films) Fleet Steps, Mrs Macquaries Point; bookings essential 1300 366 649.

**Reading Cinema** Level 3, Market City Shopping Centre, Haymarket; (02) 9280 1202.

**Randwick Ritz** 45 St Paul St, Randwick; (02) 9611 4811.

## Live music

**Enmore Theatre** Everyone hopes to be rocked by their favourite band at this intimate venue. 118–132 Enmore Rd, Enmore; (02) 9550 3666; box office Mon–Fri 9am–5pm, Sat 10am–2pm, open 2 hrs prior to performance; www.enmoretheatre.com.au

**The Basement** This Sydney institution is

### Where to shop

**Pitt Street Mall, City** Sydney's major shopping area, in the heart of the CBD.

**Queen Victoria Building, City** Considered by some to be the most beautiful shopping centre in the world, with three levels of stylish shops and cafes.

**Castlereagh Street, City** Sheer indulgence with some of the world's leading designer labels.

**Galleries Victoria, City** A dazzling array of top-quality fashion and lifestyle brands.

**The Rocks** The place to go for top-quality Australian art, jewellery and clothing.

**Oxford Street, Darlinghurst** Up-to-the-minute street fashion and funky alternative clothing.

**Oxford Street, Paddington** Home to the most cutting-edge designers and a mecca for antique hunters.

**Double Bay** Sydney's most exclusive shopping suburb.

**Birkenhead Point, Drummoyne** Designer shopping at bargain prices in a historic waterfront venue.

**Military Road, Mosman** Classy shopping in a village atmosphere.

**King Street, Newtown** Strut your funky self along this incredibly mixed shopping strip, from alternative, in-your-face gear to sleek, chic boutiques.

Queen Victoria Building

## Markets

**Paddington Markets** Fashion, artworks, jewellery and collectibles in one of Sydney's trendiest suburbs. 395 Oxford St, Paddington; Sat 10am–4pm.

**Paddy's Markets** Located near Chinatown with bargains in clothing, souvenirs, toys and gifts. Haymarket; Thur–Sun 9am–5pm.

**The Rocks Market** Classic street market with some superb Indigenous art, stylish homewares and exquisite jewellery for sale. Northern end George St; Sat–Sun 10am–5pm.

**Sydney Opera House Markets** Australian souvenirs, arts and crafts in a harbour setting. Sydney Opera House Forecourt; Sun 9am (unless weather or outdoor events interfere).

**Glebe Markets** Decorative homewares, arts and crafts, new and second-hand clothing, with a background of live jazz. Glebe Public School, Glebe Point Road; Sat 9.30am–4.30pm.

**Sydney Fish Market** Fast-paced and vibrant, with a good bakery, an excellent deli and some of the freshest seafood in the world. Guided tours enable you to watch a Dutch auction (where the price actually drops every minute), but only for the early risers. Phone the Fish Line for details, (02) 9004 1122. Bank St, Pyrmont; daily 7am–4pm.

**Sydney Flower Market** Freshly cut flowers at wholesale prices, and breakfast at the market cafes. Flemington; Mon–Sat 5–11am.

**Entertainment Quarter Market** Plants, giftware, arts and crafts and movie memorabilia in a village-like atmosphere. Lang Rd, Moore Park; Wed & Sat 10am–3.30pm, Sun 10am–5pm.

**Balmain Markets** Jewellery and leather goods, arts and crafts in the grounds of an old sandstone church. St Andrews Church, cnr Darling St & Curtis Rd; Sat 8.30am–4pm.

**The Good Living Growers Market** The gourmet's choice, with superb breads, cheeses, fruit and vegetables, close to Darling Harbour. Pyrmont Bay Park; 1st Sat each month 7am–11am.

**Sydney Swap and Sell Market** Sydney's biggest garage sale, where second-hand goods are bought and sold and occasionally even swapped. Off Parramatta Rd, Flemington; Sat 6am–2pm.

the place to experience jazz, blues, acoustic and world music. 29 Reiby Place, Circular Quay; (02) 9251 2797; lunch noon–3pm, dinner from 7.30pm, happy hour from 4.30pm, performances from 9.30pm; www.thebasement.com.au

**Annandale Hotel** With a cult following, indie fans flock here for the fantastic variety of bands, both adored and up-and-coming. Cnr Nelson St & Parramatta Rd, Annandale; (02) 9550 1078; Mon–Sat 11am–midnight, Sun noon–10pm; www.annandalehotel.com

**The Forum** A great venue to see the hottest new bands on the local and international circuit. Entertainment Quarter, Moore Park; (02) 8117 6700; Sun–Thur 10am–1am, Fri–Sat 10am–2am; www.forumsydney.com.au

**State Theatre** This venue's lavish interior both clashes with and complements the various acts playing here. 49 Market St; (02) 9373 6655; Ticketmaster box office Mon–Fri 9am–5pm, performance nights from 8pm; www.statetheatre.com.au

**Hopetoun Hotel** Affectionately called the 'Hoey', this is one of Sydney's best venues for up-and-coming indie bands. 416 Bourke St, Surry Hills; (02) 9361 5257; Mon–Sat noon–midnight, Sun noon–10pm.

## Pubs and bars

**London Hotel**
Great old pub, featuring an outside counter where everyone hangs out in the sunshine. 234 Darling St, Balmain; (02) 9555 1377; Mon–Sat 10am–midnight, Sun noon–10pm.

**Paddington Inn Hotel** Huge, plush, popular hangout with room for everything and everyone. 338 Oxford St, Paddington; (02) 9380 5913; Mon–Fri 11.30am–midnight, Sat 10am–1am, Sun 11.30am–1am.

**Darlo Bar** Funky, mismatched furniture and friendly service make this place a much-loved watering hole. Cnr Darlinghurst Rd & Liverpool St, Darlinghurst; (02) 9331 3672; Mon–Sat 10am–midnight, Sun noon–10pm; www.darlobar.com

**Customs House** Suits spill out and continue to schmooze on the street square at this very popular pub, a stone's throw form the Quay. Macquarie Place, Bridge St, Circular Quay; (02) 9259 7000; Mon–Fri 11am–10pm.

**Hero of Waterloo** One of Sydney's oldest pubs, this relic rocks when bands play on Friday and Saturday nights, and is especially cosy in winter around the fireplace. 81 Lower Fort St, Millers Point; (02) 9250 7111; Mon–Sat 10am–11pm, Sun 10am–1pm.

**Lord Nelson Brewery Hotel** Sample the beer brewed on-site, plus the scrummy bar menu, at this much-loved pub behind The Rocks. Cnr Argyle & Kent sts, Millers Point; (02) 9251 4044; Mon–Sat 11am–11pm, Sun noon–3.30pm & 5–8.30pm.

**Bourbon & Beefsteak** Tacky and notorious, everyone ends up at this Sydney haunt at some point, which plays live music most nights. 24 Darlinghurst Rd, Kings Cross; (02) 9358 1144; open daily 24 hrs.

**Marble Bar** Feast your eyes on the sumptuous decor of marble, dark cedar and stained glass while you treat yourself to a top-shelf drink. Hilton Hotel, Lvl B1, 488 George St; (02) 9265 6026; Mon–Fri 3pm–1am, Sat 5pm–2am; www.marblebarsydney.com.au

**Three Wise Monkeys** Centrally located and loved by backpackers, this pub promises a good time over its three levels. 555 George St, near Haymarket; (02) 9283 5855; Mon–Thur 10am–3am, Fri 10am–4am, Sat & public holidays 11am–4am, Sun 11am–3am; www.3wisemonkeys.com.au

**Scruffy Murphy's** Swap travel stories at this boisterous Celtic pub. 43–49 Goulburn St, Central; (02) 9211 2002; daily 11am–4.30am.

**Opera Bar** Seductively positioned, pop in for a quick drink and stay for the sublime sunset. With live music and a laidback feel, the extra dollar or two for drinks is worth it. Lower Concourse Level, Sydney Opera House; (02) 9247 1666; Mon–Sat 10am–1am, Sun 11am–midnight; www.operabar.com.au

**Establishment** A huge space with a huge reputation. Often crowded 252 George St; (02) 9240 3000; Mon–Fri 11am–late, Sat 6pm–late; www.merivale.com/establishment

## Nightclubs

**The World** A refreshingly chilled door code attracts enthusiastic prancers to boogie to

the great mix of house and dub tracks. 24 Bayswater Rd, Kings Cross; (02) 9357 7700; Sun–Thur noon–4am, Fri–Sat noon–6am.
**Globe** Dress in your best to get past the door dogs at this up-market venue for energetic house mixes and big beats. Cnr Park & Elizabeth sts; (02) 9282 8082; Thur 11pm–4am, Fri–Sat 11pm–7am.
**Kings Cross Hotel** Audacious and adored by travellers, who flock here to shake a leg. Cnr Williams St & Darlinghurst Rd, Kings Cross; (02) 9358 3377; daily 10pm–5am.
**Slip Inn** Made famous by being the place where Australia's Princess Mary met Denmark's Prince Frederik. This maze of a club boasts three, differently themed rooms. A must if you're a fan of turntables, funky house and hip hop. 111 Sussex St; (02) 9299 4777; Mon–Thur noon–midnight, Fri noon–4am, Sat 5.30pm–4am; www.merivale.com.au

## Gay and lesbian culture

Gay Sydney is everything you've heard it is – a fabulous, loved-up oasis where everyone is welcome, decked and checked out to the max.

Head straight to Oxford Street for the rainbow-flagged 'pink strip' of gay coffee shops, restaurants, bookshops, nightclubs and bars. King Street in Newtown and neighbouring Erskinville are other hubs of gay culture, while lesbians have established themselves in Leichhardt, affectionately known as 'Dykehart'.

Sydney's Gay & Lesbian Mardi Gras is a carnival of flesh and glamour, with straight locals and visitors lining the parade route. It's one of the best nights out on the Sydney calendar.

Some nightspots to check out:

**The Colombian** 117–123 Oxford St, Darlinghurst; (02) 9360 2151; daily 10am–5am.

**Stonewall Hotel** 175 Oxford St, Darlinghurst; (02) 9360 1963; daily 11am–6am; www.stonewallhotel.com

**Imperial Hotel** 35 Erskinville Rd, Erskinville; (02) 9519 9899; Mon 3pm–midnight, Tue 3pm–1am, Wed 3pm–2am, Thur 3pm–3am, Fri–Sat 3pm–late, Sun 1pm–midnight; www.theimperial.com.au

**Midnight Shift** 85 Oxford St, Darlinghurst; (02) 9360 4319; downstairs daily noon–late, upstairs Thur–Sun 11pm–6am; www.themidnightshift.com

**Home** Sydney's first major club swallows 2000 boppers into its labyrinth of areas staging big-name DJs. 101/1 Wheat Rd, Cockle Bay Wharf, Darling Harbour; (02) 9266 0600; Fri 10pm–7am, Sat 10pm–6am; www.homesydney.com

## Performing arts
**Belvoir Street Theatre** 25 Belvoir St, Surry Hills; (02) 9667 3444.
**Sydney Opera House** Bennelong Point; (02) 9250 7777.
**Stables Theatre** 10 Nimrod St, Darlinghurst; (02) 9250 7799.
**Wharf Theatre** Pier 4, Hickson Rd, Millers Point, The Rocks; (02) 9250 1777.
**Sydney Theatre** Hickson Rd, Millers Point, The Rocks (02) 9250 1777.
**Theatre Royal** MLC Centre, 108 King St, Martin Place; (02) 9320 9191.
**New Theatre** 542 King St, Newtown; (02) 9873 3575.
**NIDA Theatre** 215 Anzac Pde, Kensington; (02) 9697 7613.
**The Performance Space** 199 Cleveland St, Redfern; (02) 9319 5091.
**Capitol Theatre** 13 Campbell St, Haymarket; (02) 9266 4800.
**Footbridge Theatre** University of Sydney, Parramatta Rd; (02) 9692 9955.
**Star City** 20–80 Pyrmont St, Pyrmont; (02) 9266 4800.
**Bangarra Dance Theatre** (Indigenous modern dance company) Pier 4, Hickson Rd, Millers Rd, The Rocks; (02) 9251 5333.
**Sydney Dance Company** Pier 4, Hickson Rd, Millers Rd, The Rocks; (02) 9251 5333.
**Aboriginal & Islander Dance Theatre** (02) 9252 0199.
**Ensemble Theatre** 78 McDougall St, Milsons Point; (02) 9929 0644.
**Comedy Store** Fox Studios, Driver Ave, Moore Park; (02) 9357 1419.

## Where to stay
For further information and reviews on these hostels, please visit www.bugaustralia.com, www.hostelaustralia.com or www.hostelz.com

## Sport
Having hosted the 2000 Olympic Games, Sydney is now home to some of the best sporting facilities in the world.

Although Sydney does have an AFL team – the Sydney Swans – Rugby League and Rugby Union hold more sway here, with the season for both codes beginning in March. Key games in the League season are played at Aussie Stadium at Moore Park, with the Grand Final taking place in September at Telstra Stadium, in Olympic Park. A highlight is the State of Origin competition, which showcases the cream of Rugby League talent.

The Waratahs are the NSW side in the Super 14 Rugby Union competition in which local and overseas teams go head to head. These are played at Aussie Stadium, while the Bledisloe Cup games (against the New Zealand All Blacks) are at Telstra Stadium.

In summer, cricket takes centre stage. The highlight is the New Year's Day Test, followed by the One-Day Internationals, all of which are played at the Sydney Cricket Ground (SCG).

Basketball is another summertime sport with two Sydney teams in the National Basketball League, the Sydney Kings and the West Sydney Razorbacks.

Other sporting highlights include the Spring and Autumn Racing Carnivals, with the world's richest horserace for two-year-olds, the Golden Slipper, being held just before Easter.

**Wattle House** ★★★ Dorm $27, twin or double $85 44 Hereford St, Glebe; (02) 9552 4997; www.wattlehouse.com.au
**Eva's Backpackers** ★★★ Dorm $24, twin $60 6–8 Orwell St, Kings Cross; (02) 9358 2185; www.evasbackpackers.com.au
**Wake Up!** ★★★ Dorm $28, twin or double $90–$100 509 Pitt St; (02) 9288 7888; www.wakeup.com.au
**Funk House** ★★★ Dorm, double or twin $21 23 Darlinghurst Rd, Kings Cross; (02) 9358 6455; www.funkhouse.com.au
**Coogee Beach Wizard of Oz** ★★★ Dorm $25, twin or double $55 172 Coogee Bay Rd, Coogee; (02) 9315 7876; www.wizardofoz.com.au
**Kangaroo Bakpak** ★★ Dorm $23–$25, twin or double $30 665 South Dowling St, Surry Hills; (02) 9319 5915;

www.kangaroobakpak.com.au

**Dive ★★★ TOP TREAT!!** Gorgeous Art Deco boutique hotel opposite the beach. Worth every cent. Standard room $150–$180, twin $180 234 Arden St, Coogee Beach; (02) 9665 5538; www.divehotel.com.au

## Tours and activities

**BridgeClimb** The ultimate tour of the Harbour Bridge: climb to the top of the span secured with a harness. Bookings (02) 8274 7777. www.bridgeclimb.com

**The Rocks Pub Tours** Tales of scandal and intrigue unfold on this pub crawl with a difference as you knock back a schooner or two at The Rocks' most famous hotels. Bookings (02) 9240 8788. www.therockspubtour.com.au

**Oz Jetboating Tours** Tour the harbour in a high-performance V8 Jet Boat. Bookings (02) 9808 3700.

**Destiny Tours** Sex, scandal and the supernatural – explore Sydney's darker side in a classic Cadillac hearse. Bookings (02) 9943 0167. www.destinytours.com.au

**Easyrider Motorbike Tours** See Sydney on a Harley Davidson. Bookings 1300 882 065. www.easyrider.com.au

**City Sightseeing Sydney and Bondi Tours** Cover the city and the eastern suburbs in a double-decker, open-topped bus, hopping on and off as often as you like. Enquires (02) 9567 8400.

**Chocolate Espresso Tours** Tour the city's

Circular Quay with Harbour Bridge

CBD and shopping districts, with a focus on either coffee or chocolate. Bookings 0417 167 766. www.chocolateespresso.com.au

**Aboriginal Heritage Tours** Experience the Dreamtime of The Rocks with an Aboriginal guide. Bookings (02) 9240 8788.

**Sydney Ferry Walkabout Tours** Discover Sydney's more out-of-the-way places on foot. Pick up a brochure at the Sydney Ferries Information Centre at Circular Quay, take a ferry and start walking.

# Outside the city: Bondi

Ok, so Bondi is probably why you're in Sydney in the first place. We understand. Local residents are smug in this knowledge too. You can't blame them really – they know they're at one of the most coveted, drooled-over destinations in the world. Bondi is a palace of sexy, fabulously pretentious glitterati parading past leathered, old beach geezers with hippies gliding about; this fantastic cross-section of humanity starts to hint at the fact that there is a lot more to Bondi than meets the eye. Cutting-edge clothing boutiques, an excellent weekend market and some very chic sidewalk cafes clutter the streets. Oh yes, did we mention it has a beach …?

## Top attractions

### Bondi Beach

We won't need to encourage you to visit Bondi's perfect waters, or check out the cute lifeguards at its surf lifesaving clubs. You'll also have a fantastic fill of people-watching, and if you love a bit of attention yourself, feel free to mix with the uber-cool sun worshippers. Make sure to visit the Aboriginal rock art near the cliffs at the golf club; after all, Bondi comes from the Aboriginal word for 'sound of the surf'.

### Bondi Pavilion

This place has everything: showers, change rooms, exhibitions, live performances and an open-air cinema. Queen Elizabeth Dr; (02) 8362 3400; www.waverley.nsw.gov.au

**Getting to Bondi**

Hop on a bus departing Circular Quay and head to the beach via Oxford Street, # 380, #L82 or #389.

Alternatively, catch a train from the city direct to Bondi Junction on the Eastern suburbs line (if you're going to the beach, connect with buses at the train station, #361 or #381).

## Bondi to Coogee Walk

The best way to view Bondi's surrounding suburbs is by a walking track at the southern end of Bondi Beach. From Bondi, it winds along the cliffs through the tiny boutique beach of Tamarama. In November, this section is crowded with people viewing the Sculpture by the Sea exhibition (see Events in Bondi). Bronte, a lovely beach with a natural-rock swimming pool known as the Bogey Hole, completes the track. To explore further, the walk extends through Waverley Cemetery (where you can find the grave of author Henry Lawson), past Clovelly (a popular swimming place), to Coogee. Visit the Coogee Bay Hotel, a lively pub with a sunny, waterfront beer garden directly opposite the beach.

## Bondi Icebergs Club

An Aussie country club experience. With a prime position overlooking Bondi Beach and a fantastic, 50 m lap pool, it's well worth checking out. 1 Notts Ave; (02) 9130 3120; www.icebergs.com.au

# Where to eat

**Bondi Beach** The beach strip distracts tourists from the jewels in her side streets. You'll be amazed at the funky, feasting delights to be discovered.
Our favourites: **Mongers** 🟢/🟢🟢 ♡ Rumour has it that this place is home to the best fish and chips in Bondi. All the awards can't be wrong. 42 Hall St; (02) 9365 2205; daily noon–9pm.
**Green's Cafe** 🟢 ♡ A cosy, relaxed place

Bondi Beach

with healthy feasts. 140 Glenayr Ave; (02) 9130 6181; Wed–Sun 8am–4pm.
**Gertrude & Alice Cafe Bookstore** 🟢 Fantastic atmosphere and generous portions. You'll love every book-soaked moment in this popular hangout. 46 Hall St, cnr Consett Ave; (02) 9130 5155; Mon–Fri 7.30am–midnight, Sat–Sun 8.30am–midnight.
**Gusto** 🟢 ♡ The first-class coffee, deli and delicious fare attracts a crowd. 16 Hall St; (02) 9130 4565; daily 6.15am–7.30pm.
**The One that Got Away** 🟢🟢 ♡ Divine fish including sushi. Make sure you try their yam chips. 163 Bondi Rd; (02) 9389 4227; daily 10am–9pm.
**Red Kite** 🟢 The clever menu doesn't disappoint, especially when you discover there's nothing over $12. 95 Roscoe St; (02) 9365 0432; daily 8am–6pm.
**Gelbison** 🟢 ♡ Foodies, surfies and movie stars have worn a path to this Italian darling. 10 Lamrock Ave; (02) 9130 4042; daily 5–11pm.
**Bondi Icebergs** 🟢🟢🟢🟢 ♡ When you dine here you'll know you're in the heart of exclusive Sydney. Save up and wear your most fabulous outfit while savouring incredible views, food and celebrity watching. 1 Notts Ave; (02) 9365 9000; Tue–Sat noon–midnight, Sun noon–10pm; www.idrb.com

**North Bondi** Catering more for the locals, there are a host of divine noshing experiences on offer.
Our favourite: **Speedos** 🟢 ♡ As relaxed as its name suggests, with nothing between you and the view. 126 Ramsgate Ave, North Bondi; (02) 9365 3622; daily 6am–6pm.

# Out and about
## Cinemas

**Greater Union Cinema** Level 6, Bondi Westfield; (02) 9300 1555 or Gold Class (02) 9300 1500.
**Bondi Open Air Cinema** Bondi Pavilion; (02) 9209 4614.

## Pubs and bars

**Bungabar** This funky, Balinese-style beach-

hut bar is so cool, it'll have your jaw dropping to the floor. It has tapas and a cocktail menu most can only dream about. 77 Hall St; 0410 314 725; daily noon–11pm.
**Ravesi's** Most of eastern Sydney beats a trail to this Sunday hot spot after a heavy weekend of partying . . . to start again here. Cnr Campbell Pde & Hall St; (02) 9365 4422; Mon–Sat 10am–midnight, Sun 10am–10pm.
**Hotel Bondi** You can let your hair down at this adored landmark affectionately called the 'Pink Palace'. 178 Campbell Pde; (02) 9130 3271; daily 10am–4am; www.hotelbondi.com.au
**North Bondi RSL** Make sure you bring ID to this no-nonsense venue with fantastic views. A welcome cheaper option in this tourist-laden beach town. 118–120 Ramsgate Rd; (02) 9130 8770; Mon noon–10pm, Tue–Fri noon–11pm, Sat 10am–midnight, Sun 10am–11pm; www.northbondirsl.com.au
**Bondi Icebergs Winter Swimming Club** Keep your ID about to access to this members-only prize underneath Bondi Icebergs, but with cheaper drinks and the same million-dollar views. 1 Notts Ave; (02) 9130 3120; daily 10am–late; www.icebergs.com.au

## Events in Bondi

**Flickerfest International Short Film Festival** The cream of international short films. Jan.

**Sydney Fringe Festival** Home to fringe and alternative arts performances in association with the Festival of Sydney. Jan–Feb.

**Vibes on a Summer's Day** What began as a humble party for music loving locals has graduated into an event not to be missed – it's sometimes held at Maroubra Beach so check listings. Jan.

**Sun Herald City to Surf** Join the crowds for 14 km of fun running (or walking) – and check out the crazy costumes – as everyone makes their way from the city to Bondi Beach. Aug.

**Festival of the Winds** … kites, people … kites! It's the biggest kite festival in Australia, loads of fun. Sep.

**Sculpture by the Sea** Incredible, sculptured works defying the imagination are arranged along the coastal meander for everyone to stop and gaze, from Bondi to Tamarama. Oct–Nov.

**Sunburn Christmas Beach Party** Mingle and party with all the other travellers celebrating a sunny Christmas at the beach. Dec.

## Nightclubs

**BJ's** Vivacious venue for lovers of South American beats and salsa in the two different club rooms. 195 Oxford St Mall, Bondi Junction; (02) 9388 9100; Sat 9.30pm–3am.

## Where to stay

**Bondi Beachouse YHA** ★★★ Dorm $31.50, double $73.50 63 Fletcher St; (02) 9365 2088; www.bondibeachouse.com.au

**Bondi Beach Homestay** ★★★ Twin or double $80–$135 10 Forest Knoll Ave; (02) 9300 0800; www.bondibeachhomestay.com.au

**Bondi Sands** ★★ Dorm $25, double $65–$75 252 Campbell Pde; 1800 026 634; www.bondisands.com

**Bondi Beach House** ★★★ **TOP TREAT!!** This beautiful beach house is the Australian version of summer in the Hamptons. Single $85, double $125 28 Sir Thomas Mitchell Rd; 0417 336 444; www.bondibeachhouse.com.au

# Other suburbs worth visiting

**Milsons Point** See the harbour bridge from Luna Park, then take a swim at the great, Olympic-sized saltwater pool next door.

**Paddington** Oxford Street is home to dozens of boutiques, galleries and cafes. It is at its most vibrant on weekends, when the Paddington Markets are in full swing.

**Glebe** Excellent bookshops, lively cafes and some great weekend markets here.

**Manly** Catch a jet cat from Circular Quay and see what all the fuss is about at this seaside town with the fantastic Oceanworld Manly.

**Newtown** A suburb with a funky, alternative feel: visit in the afternoon and early evening, when King Street comes alive.

**Balmain** Visit the Saturday markets, the pubs, cafes and shops along Darling Street, and you'll understand why so many of the up-and-coming are moving this way.

**Balmoral** Extremely popular in summer, Balmoral has a lovely beach with a fenced-in pool and some excellent restaurants.

**Dee Why** We agree, it's a bit of a trek, but you'll stop whinging when you catch your first glimpse of its incredible beach. Keep going around the peninsula to take in the superb coastline called the 'Northern Beaches'.

Lifesavers at Bondi Beach

# Visitor information

## Sydney Airport

Kingsford Smith Airport is located 10 km south of the CBD by car. For more information, call (02) 9667 9111 or visit www.sydneyairport.com.au

**Bus** Kingsford Smith Transport/Airporter has shuttles between the airport and Sydney hotels. Bookings (02) 9666 9988. There's also **Manly Airport Bus** with door-to-door service to and from Manly. Bookings 0500 505 800.

**Train Airport Link** runs regular shuttles to all city train stations. For more information, call 13 15 00 or visit www.airportlink.com.au

**Taxi** A taxi to Circular Quay costs approximately $25–$35 and to Central Station $20–$25.

## Internet cafes

**Internet World** (24 hrs) 369 Pitt St; (02) 9262 9700.

**Travellers Contact Point** Level 7, 428 George St; (02) 9221 8744.

**Global Gossip** 111 Darlinghurst Rd, Kings Cross; (02) 9326 9777.

**Phone.Net.Cafe** 73 Hall St, Bondi; (02) 9635 0681.

## Hospitals

For all emergencies, including police, fire, or hospital, dial '000'.

**Kings Cross Travellers Clinic** 13 Springfield Ave, Kings Cross; (02) 9358 3066.

**Travellers Medical & Vaccination Centre** Level 7, 428 George St; (02) 9221 7133.

**Royal North Shore Hospital** Pacific Hwy, St Leonards; (02) 9926 7111.

**Royal Prince Alfred Hospital** Missenden Rd, Camperdown; (02) 9515 6111.

**St Vincent's Hospital** Cnr Victoria & Burton sts, Darlinghurst; (02) 8382 7111.

**Sydney Children's Hospital** High St, Randwick; (02) 9382 1111.

**Sydney Hospital & Sydney Eye Hospital** 8 Macquarie St; (02) 9382 7111.

NEW SOUTH WALES

For more detail
see maps
204 & 207

Sydney

# Blue Mountains
# Happy to be blue

A lot of places promise beauty, but the World Heritage-listed Blue Mountains really deliver. In case you're wondering, the blue mist comes from the vast expanse of eucalyptus trees, which disperse eucalyptus oil over the bush-clad cliffs

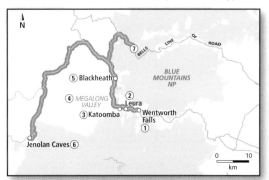

and valleys, and leave everyone feeling relaxed and rejuvenated. With all this 'magic in the air', it's no surprise that the Blue Mountains are Sydney's favourite weekend retreat. Your best bet is to base yourself in Katoomba, from where you can explore villages and bushland, and go bushwalking, canyoning, abseiling, horseriding or caving. The ideal times of year to visit are autumn, winter and spring; try to skip the summertime humidity.

**Number of days to spend in this region: 2–6 days**

## Getting here

Trains run from Central Station in Sydney to Lithgow, stopping at all the major mountain villages along the way.

There's also a daily GX255 coach service operated by Greyhound from Eddy Avenue near Central Station in Sydney, which sets you down in Katoomba at the E&W bus stop on the Great Western Highway.

Once you're in the area, Mountainlink, a local bus company, has five routes taking you to the main spots in the mountains.

**City Rail** 13 1500; www.cityrail.com.au

**Mountainlink** 68 Megalong St, Katoomba; (02) 4782 3333.

## Blue Mountains tours

**Tread Lightly Eco Tours** 100 Great Western Hwy, Medlow Bath; (02) 4788 1229; www.treadlightly.com.au

**Fantastic Aussie Tours Blue Mountains** 283 Main St, Katoomba; (02) 4782 1866; www.fantastic-aussie-tours.com.au

**Oztrek Adventure Tours** (02) 9666 4262; www.oztrek.com.au

**Wonderbus Tours** 1300 556 357; www.wonderbus.com.au

**Trolley Tours** 285 Main St, Katoomba; (02) 4782 7999; www.trolleytours.com.au

**Wildframe Eco Tours** 12 Leverton Close, St Ives; (02) 9440 9915; www.wildframe.com

**Blue Mountains Walkabout: Ancient Aboriginal Quest!** Springwood; 0408 443 822; www.bluemountainswalkabout.com

## ❶ Wentworth Falls (half- to full-day)

The town of Wentworth Falls is named after its top attraction and offers phenomenal views, bushwalks and torrents of pristine mountain water. A corridor of trees will guide you to Wentworth Falls Lake, where

crowds of ducks are wise to the promise of food from relaxed picnickers. Once you reach the actual Wentworth Falls, the delicate-looking trails of water gushing down three levels of sheer cliffs will take your breath away. Make sure you also visit the Valley of the Waters with its web of bushwalks, waterfalls and rainforests, such as Nature Track, Empress Falls Lookout and Princess Rock Lookout.

## Further information

❶ **NPWS Information Board** The Conservation Hut, Fletcher St; (02) 4757 3827; www.conservationhut.com.au

## Where to eat

**Il Postino** ❺/❺❺ Excellent cafe in the old post office. Mixed menu and fantastic value. 13 Station St; (02) 4757 1615; daily 8.30am–6pm.

**The Conservation Hut** ❺/❺❺ Great place overlooking Jamison Valley. Fletcher St; (02) 4757 3827; Mon–Fri 9am–4pm, Sat–Sun 9am–5pm; www.conservationhut.com.au/index.htm

**Grand View Hotel** ❺/❺❺ A beautiful country pub with a fantastic bistro and a grand view. 174 Great Western Hwy; (02) 4757 1001; Mon–Sat 10am–late, Sun 10am–11pm.

## ❷ Leura (half- to full-day)

Leura is a slice of heaven, considered the most sophisticated village in the mountains. Leura Mall is the major, tree-lined strip with a banquet of tea houses, shops, galleries and restaurants. Stop and stare at Everglades Gardens, a celebrated 1930s garden incorporating European and native Australian flora. For something totally different, visit Leuralla, an Art Deco mansion that's home to a major collection of trains, railway memorabilia and toys, including good ol' Barbie and Ken dolls from 1959 onwards.

Once you've seen the town, take the winding track to the spectacular Leura Cascades, which are best viewed from a rock cave. This track also leads to the radiant favourite Bridal Veil Falls. Other bushwalks in the area include the 2-hour circuit passing the Pool of Siam and Lyrebird Dell, or you can follow the easy Prince Henry Cliff Walk to Katoomba Falls (9 km, 1.5 hrs one way).

If you like your vistas from a bird's-eye vantage point, make your way to Sublime Point and Cliff Drive. Gordons Fall Reserve nearby provides another superb spot to stop for lunch.

### Further information

ℹ️ **Leura Visitors Gateway** 121 The Mall; 1800 455 582.
**Everglades Gardens** 37 Everglades Ave; (02) 4784 1938; spring & summer daily 10am–5pm, autumn & winter daily 10am–4pm; www.evergladesgardens.info
**Leuralla** 36 Olympian Pde; (02) 4784 1169; daily 10am–5pm; www.toyandrailwaymuseum.com.au

### Where to eat

**Solitary – the Kiosk** $/$$ This award-winning restaurant has thoughtfully opened a kiosk. Treat yourself to a slice of cake at the above-ordinary cafe. 90 Cliff Dr, Leura Falls; (02) 4782 1164; lunch Sat–Sun, dinner Tue–Sat; www.solitary.com.au
**Landseers** $ Cosy little cafe with large sandwiches and portions of lasagne. Make sure you leave room for their superb puddings. Shop 1, 178 The Mall; (02) 4784 1992; daily 7.30am–5pm.
**The Mountain Deli** $ Follow the locals to this friendly spot and you'll discover a huge variety of feasting options that won't break the bank. 134 The Mall; (02) 4784 1328; Mon–Fri & Sun 9am–6pm, Sat 8am–6pm.

### Where to stay

**Alexandra Hotel** ★★★ Single $56, double or twin $70  62 Great Western Hwy; (02) 4782 4422.

### Events

**Leura Gardens Festival** Come and see what all the well-earned fuss is about. Even if gardening ain't your thing, you'll be blown away by these gorgeous gardens. Oct.

## ❸ Katoomba (1–2 days)

Originally named Crushers but thankfully renamed a year later, Katoomba rests at an altitude of 1017 m. The name is an Indigenous word for 'shining tumbling water' and the area is still home to the Gundungurra people in the north, Dharug people in the south and Wiradjuri people in the west. This majestic place is rich with Dreamtime stories and over 700 heritage sites that descendants continue to watch over.

Katoomba is also a thriving tourist hot spot. Blue Mountains National Park lies to the north and south, holding all the nature your heart and eyes can handle. Here you'll discover the iconic mountain formations of the Three Sisters, which are best viewed from Echo Point during the day or night, when they are stunningly floodlit (a must-see). The name of these weathered outcrops recognises a Dreamtime story about a witchdoctor who turned three sisters into stone to protect them from a battle.

For more wonderful scenery, stroll to the lush Katoomba Falls and Cascades (also floodlit at night). Heading along Cliff Drive, you can then take a ride on the Scenic Railway, the world's steepest train ride, rising up out of the valley at a nail-biting 45-degree incline (your screams will echo all around the valley below). If that's not enough, wind your way down into Jamison Valley on the Sceniscender, an enclosed cable car.

To really see this area, make sure you do a bit of bushwalking. A great walk for beginners is the Prince Henry Cliff Walk (4 km, 1.5 hrs return), which starts at Echo Point and takes you past Katoomba Cascades and Jamison Valley. One of the most popular treks is the 6-hour hike to the Ruined Castle rock formations, beginning at the bottom of Jamison Valley. Once you've climbed the Giant Stairway (counted at 841 steps), reward yourself with a large slice of cake and a rest for your jellied legs at one of the cafes at the top. If you choose to explore without a guide, make sure you contact the visitor centre. Seriously. The weather can change suddenly and the region's vast and rugged terrain can be cruel to unprepared visitors.

Other activities in the area include abseiling, rock climbing and canyoning, which involves donning a wetsuit and finding your way through caves, waterfalls and rainforest.

### Further information

ℹ️ **Blue Mountains Visitor Information Centre** Echo Point; 1300 653 408; www.visitbluemountains.com.au

Katoomba Cascades

**Scenic World** (02) 4782 2699; www.scenicworld.com.au

**The Edge Cinema** Daily screenings of The Edge (images of Blue Mountains) on a six-storey screen. 225-237 Great Western Hwy; (02) 4782 8900; www.edgecinema.com.au

## Tours

**Katoomba Adventure Centre** 1 Katoomba St; 1800 624 226; www.kacadventures.com.au

**Blue Mountains Adventure Company** 84a Bathurst Rd; (02) 4782 1271; www.bmac.com.au

**High n Wild Mountain Adventures** 3/5 Katoomba St; (02) 4782 6224; www.high-n-wild.com.au

**The Australian School of Mountaineering** C/o Paddy Pallin, 166b Katoomba St; (02) 4782 2014; www.asmguides.com

**Blue Mountains Canyon Tours** 166 Katoomba St; (02) 4782 5787; www.canyontours.com.au

**Bicycle hire: Clyde Tech** 182 Katoomba St; (02) 4782 2800.

## Where to eat

**Cafe Zuppa** $/$$ All-day breakfast, mix of Australian/Italian food. Great value, lovely atmosphere. 36 Katoomba St; (02) 4782 9247; daily 7am–1pm.

**Parakeet Cafe** $/$$ You'll feel right at home here and have the bonus of checking out local artists' work adorning the walls as you munch on cheap and luscious meals. 195b Katoomba St; (02) 4782 6623; daily 8am–9pm (later on Sat especially if there's live music, often blues).

**Avalon Restaurant** $$/$$$ TOP TREAT!! You'll find this treat in the dress circle of the old Savoy Theatre covered with Art Deco relics. It's not often that splurging at a restaurant like this is rewarded with generous portions and divine desserts. 18 Katoomba St; (02) 4782 5532; lunch & dinner Wed–Sun.

**Paragon Cafe** $ You can't miss this Blue Mountains institution. Beautifully trapped in the 1930s, the atmosphere is almost as delicious as the food. 65 Katoomba St; (02) 4782 2928; breakfast, lunch & dinner daily.

**Blues Cafe** $ Vegetarians will be tickled pink, and meat eaters will even consider switching allegiance, in this fantastic and popular bakery that's been around for years. 57 Katoomba St; (02) 4782 2347; daily 9am–5pm.

Scenic Railway

Blue Mountains escarpment

## Pubs

**The Carrington Hotel** This sprawling, elegant building is home to a range of bars, outrageous cabaret and a nightclub called The Attic. 15–47 Katoomba St; (02) 4782 1111; daily 10.30am–midnight, until 4am Fri–Sat; www.thecarrington.com.au

**The Clarendon** Pop in for a drink and stay to watch the amazing live music and dinner theatre on offer. Cnr Lurline & Waratah sts; (02) 4782 1322; daily from 6pm, dinner daily from 7pm; www.clarendonguesthouse.com.au

**Glearins Hotel** Good pub... they have 'chocolate draught'! 273 Great Western Hwy; (02) 4782 4395; Mon–Sat 8am–late, Sun 10am–midnight.

## Where to stay

**Central Blue Mountains Backpackers** ★★★ Dorm $22–$25, single $50, double or twin $70 144 Bathurst St; (02) 4782 9630; www.centralblue.com.au

**Blue Mountains YHA** ★★ Dorm $29.50, double or twin $76.50 207 Katoomba St; (02) 4782 1416; www.yha.com.au

**No 14** ★★ Dorm $22, double or twin $59 14 Lovell St; (02) 4782 7104; www.bluemts.com.au/No14/

**The Clarendon** ★★★ Budget room $45, guesthouse ensuite $65 Cnr Lurline & Waratah sts; (02) 4782 1322; www.clarendonguesthouse.com.au

**The Carrington Hotel** ★★★★ TOP TREAT!! Budget room $119–$139 (weekend), colonial room $190–$235 (weekend) 15–47 Katoomba St; (02) 4782 1111; www.thecarrington.com.au

## Events

**Blue Mountains Music Festival** Popular three-day extravaganza of blues, folk and roots music with local and international artists. Mar.

**Yulefest** Exactly what it sounds like: Christmas in the Blue Mountains. Escape the fact that you're only halfway through the year and go along with it. Completely mad and loads of fun. Jun–Aug.

**Winter Magic Festival** Locals swear it's the biggest street party in Australia. Winter Solstice (Jun).

## Six Foot Track (2–3 days)

The Six Foot Track was originally intended as a short cut to Jenolan back in the 1800s. Today it's 42 km of enthralling bushwalking from Katoomba to Jenolan Caves. To get the most out of this ramble, hitch yourself to a local tour guide. The trek begins at Explorers Tree and traverses Nellies Glen through the mighty Megalong Valley, follows Coxs River over Mini Mini Range and onwards until you reach Jenolan. The wildlife is pretty spectacular: everything from wallaroos to wombats and echidnas, and don't forget the possums that come alive at night. Campsites are peppered along the way. The track is also the site of the annual Six Foot Track Marathon, drawing over 500 runners.

## Tours

**Fantastic Aussie Tours** (02) 4782 1866; www.fantastic-aussie-tours.com.au
**Camping: Jenolan Caves Trust** (02) 6359 3311; www.jenolancaves.org.au

## Events

**Six Foot Track Marathon** Australia's largest, 100 per cent off-road marathon. Mar.

## ❹ Megalong Valley (1–2 days)

The best way to experience the majestic Megalong Valley is on horseback. Trails follow the mighty Coxs River as it weaves its way through the valley. Amble to Mermaids Glen (*Mad Max* fans will recognise this spot from *Return to Thunderdome*) as well as Coachwood Glen. Old Ford Reserve is the perfect excuse to dismount for a picnic.

To get the most from your experience, head straight for the Megalong Australian Heritage Centre. The staff have perfected the art of the Australian bush experience. By the time they've finished with you, you'll know the meaning of 'crack a whip', 'muster' and 'make a damper with billy tea'. They'll also show you how to shear a sheep. There's a huge variety of expeditions on offer such as the Jackaroo Adventure, the Coxs River Cattle Drive and the Overnight Stockman's Ride.

Whether you're acquainting yourself with a simple horseback ride or learning how to drive cattle, you'll feel dwarfed by the incredible beauty arching overhead.

## Further information

**Megalong Australian Heritage Centre** Megalong Rd; (02) 4787 8188; daily 8am–5.30pm; www.megalong.cc
**Horseriding: Blue Mountains Horse Riding Adventures** Megalong Heritage Centre, Megalong Rd; (02) 4787 8688; www.megalong.cc
**Werriberri Trail Rides** Megalong Rd; (02) 4787 9171; www.bluemts.com.au/werriberri/

Horseriding through Megalong Valley

## Where to stay

**Megalong Ranch Guest House** ★★ Budget stay $35 (bring own linen and breakfast, or you can hire linen), bed and breakfast $85, Stockman's Lodge $20 (no linen)  Megalong Road; (02) 4787 8188; www.megalong.cc/centre/default.htm

## ❺ Blackheath (half- to full-day)

Renowned for its guesthouses, gardens and bushwalks, Blackheath is perched at the edge of Blue Mountains National Park. The area was devastated by bushfires in November 2006, forcing the closure of some walking tracks to give the charred bushland a chance to recover. Contact the Blue Mountains Heritage Centre to find out which walks are open before you set off. The centre also features an interactive display on the geology, wildlife, and Aboriginal and European history of the area, and offers historical tours and guided walks. Tip your hat in reverence at Govett Statue, named after the bushranger Govett, who is said to have ridden his horse off a cliff rather than be captured by police. Naturally he won everyone's total admiration.

The area's absolute must-see is Govetts Leap Lookout, offering incredible vistas across several waterfalls, including Bridal Veil Falls, and the Grose Valley. The lookout is accessed via the Fairfax Heritage Walk (3 km, 1 hour return). From the lookout, you can either head down into the valley to reach the base of the falls, head right to Evans Lookout and the Grand Canyon, or head left along the ridge to Pulpit Rock, a shard of sandstone jutting out from a cliff. From Perrys Lookdown, another walking trail descends into the Blue Gum Forest, a pocket of blue gums towering over the surrounding trees (5 km, 5 hrs return). If you don't mind a slight detour and some high-altitude adventure, go canyoning in the Grand Canyon, south-east of Blackheath.

Pulpit Rock, Perrys Lookdown and Anvil Rock can all be reached from town by heading down Hat Hill Road.

Hay fever sufferers beware: Blackheath is known as 'Rhododendron Town' for the myriad varieties that blossom every November and are celebrated in their own annual festival.

## Further information

ⓘ **Blue Mountains Heritage Centre** Govetts Leap Rd; (02) 4787 8877; daily 9am–4.30pm; www.nationalparks.nsw.gov.au

## Where to eat

**Victory Cafe** ⓢ If you like your food with a bit of culture, you'll love this place. Surrounded by antiques, this cafe even has a bookstall, and the delicious gourmet food is a steal. 17 Govetts Leap Rd; (02) 4787 6777; daily 8.30am–5pm.
**Vulcans** ⓢⓢ/ⓢⓢⓢ TOP TREAT!! This is the site of many a foodie's pilgrimage. Everything is delectable, including the dessert it is famous for: chequerboard liquorice and pineapple ice-cream. 33 Govetts Leap Rd; (02) 4787 6899; lunch & dinner Fri–Sun.

View from Evans Lookout

## Where to stay

**Gardners Inn** ★★★ Single $45, double or twin $80
255 Great Western Hwy; (02) 4787 8347; www.gardnersinn.com.au
**Blackheath Caravan Park** ★ Caravan site $10–$14 pp, on-site
caravan $45 per two pax BYO linen. Prince Edward St (off Govetts Leap
Rd); (02) 4787 8101; www.bmcc.nsw.gov.au/contactus/caravanparks/
blackheathcaravanpark/

## Events

**Rhododendron Festival** A riot of flowers has admirers flocking here
every year. Nov.

## ❻ Jenolan Caves (detour, 1 day)

Formed 400 million years ago, Jenolan Caves are one of the most
extensive and complex underground limestone cave systems in the
world. Of the 300 or so 'rooms', nine are open to the public and a self-
guided tour has just been added as another way to experience this
labyrinth of flowstone deposits, helictites, columns and lakes.

For those with limited time, choose between Lucas or The Temple
of Baal. Lucas is home to breathtaking Cathedral Chamber, which hosts
many concerts. The Temple of Baal, on the other hand, is hauntingly
spectacular and is widely recognised as one of the world's most
beautiful caves with the graceful 9 m-long Angel's Wing, one of the
world's longest cave shawls. To get you around the agony of choosing, a
two-cave ticket is cheaper.

If you are new to this magical world, there are easy caves like
Imperial Cave to start you off. But once you get into it, you might like
to take the self-guided tour around Nettle Cave. Adventure caving is
another fantastic option, best experienced in Aladdin's Cave. There are
also Ghost Tours operating on weekends. Above ground, check out the
amazing formations of Carlotta's Arch and Blue Lake.

## Further information

**Jenolan Caves** 1300 77 33 11; www.jenolancaves.org.au

## Tours

**Adventure Caving at Jenolan Caves** (02) 6359 3911.
**Jenolan 4WD Adventures** (02) 6335 6239 or 0428 619 709;
www.bluemts.com.au/jenolan4WD/

## Where to stay

**Jenolan Caves House: The Gatehouse** ★★ $30 each for first 2
people, then $26 for each additional person. Tip: This is a huge beautiful
retreat, so mention you'd like a room at The Gatehouse, which is the
budget arm of their luxe establishment. Plus, if you stay here you get
20 per cent discount on any show cave ticket purchase. Jenolan Caves
Wilderness Reserve; (02) 6359 3322; www.jenolancaveshouse.com.au
**Jenolan Cabins** ★★★ **TOP TREAT!!** Double from $98. These
cabins are three-and-a-half star luxury and require minimum stays on
weekends. But if you're looking for a plush overnight treat during the
week, these cabins are worth every cent. 42 Edith Rd, Porcupine Hill;
(02) 6355 6239; www.bluemts.com.au/jenolancabins

## ❼ Bells Line of Road (1 day)

Slicing across the northern section of the Blue Mountains between
Richmond and Lithgow, Bells Line of Road is one of the most scenic
routes in the mountains, surrounded by chalky sandstone cliffs and
tangled bushlands. Just turn off the Great Western Highway at Mount
Victoria and onto Darling Causeway, then hang a right onto Bells. The
road is surprisingly secluded and tranquil, and there is loads to see and
do on your journey.

Look out to your right for the start of Pierces Pass and stop to soak
up the magnificent views of Grose Gorge. If you're up for a hike, Pierces
Pass leads to the Grose River and Blue Gum Forest (8 km, 7 hrs return).
Further along is the start of the hike to the summit of Mount Banks (1.5
km, 1.5 hrs). Next in line is Zig Zag Railway, the name alluding to the
'Z'-shaped tracks (trips are 1 hr and 40 mins return). But if you really
love your flora, Mount Tomah Cold Climate Botanic Garden is a must,
with trees harking back to the dinosaur days.

Further along, Kurrajong Village is a cute little town with lots of
walkways for strolling and generally admiring the beauty enveloping
you. Look out for the orchards around Bilpin as well as the collection of
galleries, craft and antique shops along the way.

## Further information

ⓘ **Lithgow Visitor Information Centre** 1 Cooerwull Rd;
(02) 6353 1859; www.tourism.lithgow.com
**Zig Zag Railway** (02) 6355 2955; www.zigzagrailway.com.au
**Mount Tomah Botanic Garden** Bells Line of Rd via Bilpin;
(02) 4567 2154; www.bluemts.com.au/mounttomah/info.htm

## Where to eat

**Garden Restaurant – Mount Tomah Botanical Gardens** ⓢ
Don't be freaked out by the pricey menu here, there's a cheaper light
meals menu and a kiosk, encouraging you to munch away while
feasting on their incredible views. Bells Line of Road via Bilpin;
(02) 4567 2154; Mar–Sep daily 10am–4pm, Oct–Feb daily
10am–5pm; www.bluemts.com.au/mounttomah/info.htm

For more detail see maps 209 & 221

Sydney

# North Coast
# Coast with the most

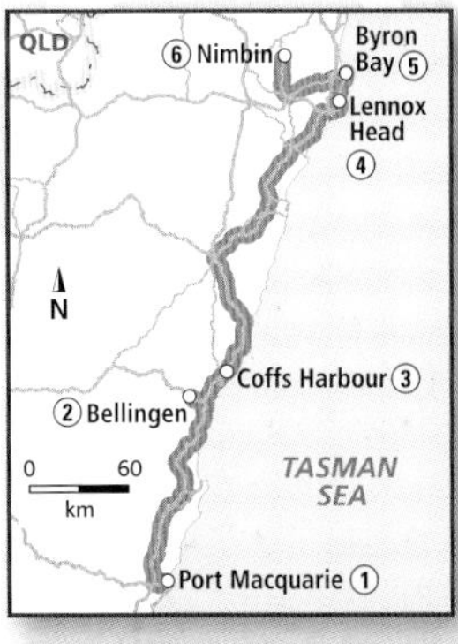
QLD
⑥ Nimbin
Byron Bay ⑤
Lennox Head ④
N
Coffs Harbour ③
② Bellingen
0 60
km
TASMAN SEA
Port Macquarie ①

Whether you like your surf with a rowdy mix of sun worshippers or prefer to paddle in tranquil solitude, it doesn't matter, everyone is catered for on New South Wales' north coast. With so much pristine beauty, it's amazing that the locals are so welcoming. But the truth is that everyone's here for a good time. This coastline proves that paradise is alive and kicking, with nature and wildlife attractions around Port Macquarie and Bellingen, and a chilled, alternative vibe when you get to the renowned hippy towns of Byron Bay and Nimbin.

**Number of days to spend in this region: 10–20 days**

## Getting here

There are flights daily into Port Macquarie, Coffs Harbour and Ballina (Byron Bay).

XPT Train has services daily from Sydney to Coffs; disembark at Wauchope for Port Macquarie and Urunga for Bellingen. Book through Countrylink.

McCaffertys coach you all the way from Sydney to Brisbane via Port Macquarie, Coffs Harbour and Byron main stops, plus the nearby towns of Wauchope and Urunga for Port Macquarie and Bellingen respectively. There are services twice daily.

**XPT** 13 2232; www.countrylink.nsw.gov.au

**McCaffertys** 13 1419; www.mccaffertys.com.au

## ❶ Port Macquarie (1–2 days)

Historically, this town at the mouth of the Hastings River was used as a place of punishment for convicts. But today Port Macquarie is a major holiday destination, considered to have the best climate in Australia, as well as loads to do and ravishing surrounds.

If you like your bushwalk with some eco-friendly messages, head off to the Sea Acres Rainforest Centre, with three different types of rainforests and a boardwalk for you to soak up the view. Nearby Kooloonbung Creek Nature Reserve is a fantastic, large nature reserve where you can do a spot of bushwalking. The incredible vegetation will have you firmly believing you are in the middle of nowhere, and yet the reserve is extraordinarily close to the centre of town.

The Koala Hospital is a must-see, and has free entry thanks to the host of volunteers that care for over 200 crook ('ill') koalas that arrive after car accidents, dog attacks or due to disease. The hospital also runs a 'Feed, Walk and Talk' tour every afternoon at 3pm. Other cuddly animals in perfect health are at the Billabong Koala and Wildlife Park, where you can handfeed the kangaroos and hug the koalas. There's also Kingfisher Park, a sanctuary for rare and threatened native animals.

Paradise is located at Lighthouse Beach: 16 km of white sand, camel rides and dolphin watching. The surf is excellent too. You can take in the stunning views up and down the coast from Tacking Point Lighthouse. Go one higher and take it all in from the air, strapped into a hang-glider. You're spoilt rotten with watersports such as surfing, diving, parasailing, sea-kayaking, jetski tours, fishing and cruises. If you're at the river foreshore at sunset, take an extra minute or two and watch the pelicans pestering the local anglers for a meal.

For a little detour, head about 13 km west to Cassegrain Winery, especially in October when they host their Discovery Concert.

### Further information

ⓘ **Port Macquarie Tourist Information Centre** Clarence St; 1300 303 155; www.portmacquarieinfo.com.au

Surfers at Port Macquarie

**Sea Acres Rainforest Centre** Pacific Dr; (02) 6582 3355.
**Koala Hospital** Feedings daily at 8am and 3pm. Roto House, Macquarie Nature Reserve, Lord St; (02) 6584 1522; daily 8am–4.30pm (can walk around grounds at other times); www.koalahospital.org.au
**Billabong Koala and Wildlife Park** Billabong Dr; (02) 6585 1060.
**Kingfisher Park** Kingfisher Rd; (02) 6581 0783.
**Cassegrain Winery** 764 Fernbank Creek Rd; (02) 6582 8377; cellar door daily 9am–5pm; www.cassegrainwines.com.au

## Tours
**Port Macquarie Sea Kayak** Sea Rescue Shed; (02) 6584 1039.
**Rick's Dive School** 0422 063 528.
**High Adventure** 1800 063 648; www.highadventure.com.au
**Port Macquarie Camel Safaris** Lighthouse Beach, Matthew Flinders Dr; (02) 6583 7650 or 0412 566 333.

## Where to eat
**Beach House 🄢** Hugely popular place with everything from burgers to oysters, right on the water. Horton St; (02) 6584 5692; lunch & dinner.
**Fisherman's Co-op Market 🄢** Explore the local fish markets and buy your own fish to fry. Town Wharf, Clarence St; (02) 6583 1604; daily 8am–4pm.
**Vista Cafe Restaurant 🄢🄢** Treat yourself to a sumptuous meal overlooking the Hastings River. Level 1, 74 Clarence Street; (02) 6584 1422; dinner daily.
**Cafe 66 🄢/🄢🄢** Make sure you try the brilliant breakfasts that'll keep you going all day. 66 Clarence St; (02) 6583 2483; breakfast, lunch & dinner daily.

## Pubs
**Port Macquarie Hotel** Starting block of many pub crawls. Cnr Clarence & Horton sts; (02) 6580 7888; Sun–Thur 10am–midnight, Fri 10am–1.30am, Sat 9am–1.30am.
**Finnian's Irish Tavern** Home to Guinness and gaudy leprechaun murals. 97 Gordon St; (02) 6583 4646; Mon–Thurs 11am–late, Fri–Sat 11am–1am, Sun noon–10pm.

## Nightclubs
**Roxys Niteclub** Boogie along to the latest tunes getting radio play, plus play a few games of pool. William St; (02) 6583 4566; Wed–Sat from 6pm.
**Downunder** You'll hear a bit of everything: brand new pop to stonewashed-jeans-big-haired rock. Downstairs, Short St; (02) 6583 4018; Wed–Sat from 6pm.

## Where to stay
**Port Macquarie YHA ★★** Dorm $26.50, double or twin $58.50 40 Church St; (02) 6583 5512; www.yha.com.au

**Limeburners Lodge ★★** Accommodation at lodge $26. 353 Shoreline Dr; (02) 6583 3381; www.limeburnerslodge.com.au

## Events
**Golden Lure Tournament** This annual deep-sea game fishing extravaganza blows the notion of sitting idly around with a fishing rod right out of the water. Jan.
**Food & Wine Festival** Local markets and wineries serve up their famous 'Taste Tempters'. Oct.

# ❷ Bellingen (2 days)
Like Byron Bay, Bellingen is overflowing with creative types who ensure a laidback, New Age vibe. Your number one priority should be a scenic drive around the aptly named Promised Land (seriously), the most beautiful section of the Bellinger Valley, with a stop to paddle in Never Never Creek. For the adventurous, the Bellinger River and forest areas are perfect for walking, cycling, horseriding and canoeing. If you're up for a walk, organise a guided tour around Dorrigo National Park and cool off with a swim at Danger Falls. It's also worth visiting Dorrigo Rainforest Centre, which houses a simulated rainforest creek.

But no one is fussed if you want to just laze about in Bellingen. For the best breakfast in town, go straight to the Old Butter Factory, which also houses galleries and shops with fantastic one-off souvenirs. The Bellingen Markets are a real treat if you're in town on the 3rd Saturday of the month. At dusk, look up and you'll see the sky filled with up to 40 000 grey-headed flying foxes (bats) in search of a meal. Wearing a hat is advised to protect you from getting . . . er . . . *rained* on.

## Further information
ℹ️ **Bellingen Visitor Centre** 1 Doepel St; (02) 6655 1522; www.bellingermagic.com
**Dorrigo Rainforest Centre** (02) 6657 2309; daily 9am–5pm; www.dorrigo.com/attractions/rainforest/index.html
**Old Butter Factory** 1 Doepel St; (02) 6655 2260; daily 9am–5pm; www.bellingen.com/butterfactory
**Bellingen Markets** Bellingen Sports Oval, Church St, 200 m from Hyde St; www.bellingen.com/markets/
**Heartland Didgeridoos** Australia's largest manufacturer of handmade didgeridoos. Ask for Tynan, the owner. He'll sort you out. Shop 2/25 Hyde St; (02) 6655 9881.

Shopping in Bellingen

## Tours

**Hinterland Tours** 10 Connell Pl; (02) 6655 2957;
www.hinterlandstour.com.au
**Valery Trails & Horseriding Centre** 758 Valery Rd, Valery;
(02) 6653 4301; www.valerytrails.com.au
**Bellingen Canoe Adventures** 4 Tyson St, Fernmount;
(02) 6655 9955; www.canoeadventures.com.au

## Where to eat

**Boiling Billy Cafe** 🟢 The place to go for breakfast. 7f Church St;
(02) 6655 1947; Mon–Fri 8am–4pm, Sat 8am–2pm.
**Lodge 241 Gallery Cafe** 🟢/🟢🟢 An institution in these parts; it'll
dazzle you with art, food and friendly atmosphere. 150 m from YHA, on
the Waterfall Way, western fringe of town; (02) 6655 2470;
daily from 8am.
**Old Butter Factory Cafe** 🟢/🟢🟢 Well worth the little journey to
get here; there's so much to wander around and browse after breakfast
or brunch or a late lunch. 1 Doepel St, east of Bellingen Golf Course;
(02) 6655 2150; daily 9am–5pm; www.bellingen.com/butterfactory

## Pubs

**Diggers Tavern** 30 Hyde St; (02) 6655 0007; Mon–Sat from 10am,
Sun from 12pm; www.diggerstavern.com.au

## Where to stay

**Bellingen Backpackers YHA** ★★ Dorm $28.50, double or twin
$63.50 2 Short St; (02) 6655 1116; www.bellingenyha.com.au
**Gracemere Grange** ★★ Single $50, twin $70  325 Dome Rd,
Dorrigo; (02) 6657 2630; www.babs.com.au/gracemere/

## Events

**Bellingen Jazz & Blues Festival** Three days of great jazz and blues
music. Aug.
**Bellingen Global Carnival** Various performances and arts and crafts
on show to celebrate cross-cultural exchange. Oct.

## ❸ Coffs Harbour (3–4 days)

There aren't many places that can play host to a giant banana and get
away with it.

The adored, kitsch and iconic Big Banana, which looks like it
might be visible from outer space, is the Coffs landmark, housing an
education display on the banana industry, as well as a skywalk over the
plantations and various other attractions. For something equally bizarre,
there's also the Clog Barn that's straight out of the Netherlands, with a
miniature Dutch village complete with windmills, and many shoes for
sale. And if there's a closet circus performer somewhere inside you, Zip
Circus will help you to let it out through their flying trapeze and circus
arts school.

Once you've dragged yourself beyond the clutches of town, prepare
to be gobsmacked. The Great Dividing Range topples into the South
Pacific and the land around you is saturated with sandy white beaches
stretching gloriously into the distance. There are many gorgeous strands
such as Jetty Beach onwards to Diggers Beach and further to Emerald
Beach.  Diving and snorkelling is on offer at the Solitude Islands Marine
Park, where the blend of tropical and temperate currents makes life
beneath the surface particularly spectacular. Further adventure awaits
aboard a raft, whitewater or surf, on the Nymboida River. All of this aqua
splendour is also the perfect training ground to learn how to surf.

Above ground, make sure you explore Muttonbird Island Natural
Reserve and say hello to these incredibly hardy creatures who fly
thousands of kilometres from South East Asia every August to breed.
This reserve is excellent for its walking trails and vantage points for
whale watching (July–August). Gaining access is fun too: 500 m walk
along the sea wall from the harbour.

The North Coast Regional Botanical Gardens Complex puts you
in the zone of rainforests, mangrove boardwalks and diverse birdlife.
For a bit of bushwalking, throw in the 9 km Coffs Creek Habitat Walk,
which snakes along the boundary of the botanical gardens and beyond,
exploring Coffs Creek via a network of bush tracks, boardwalks and
bridges. Bindarri National Park has more rough and tough hikes through
its pristine forest and amazing views (there are no facilities in the park).

If Australian wildlife is still your favourite attraction, get yourself
down to Pet Porpoise Pool. Performing dolphins and seals are one
thing, but you'll be blown away by their research and nursery facilities,
and giddy with excitement when you arrange to swim with these
free-spirited mammals.

## Further information

🔵 **Coffs Coast Visitors Centre** Cnr Pacific Hwy & McLean St;
(02) 6652 1522; www.coffscoast.com.au
**Big Banana** 351 Pacific Hwy; (02) 6652 4355; www.bigbanana.com
**Clog Barn** 215 Pacific Hwy; (02) 6652 4633; www.clogbiz.com
**Zip Circus** Novotel Pacific Bay Resort, cnr Pacific Hwy & Bay Dr;
(02) 6656 0768; Wed–Sun; www.zipcircus.com.au
**Muttonbird Island Natural Reserve & Bindarri National Park**
Dome Rd, Dorrigo; (02) 6657 2309; www.nationalparks.nsw.gov.au
**North Coast Regional Botanic Garden** Hardacre St; (02) 6648
4188; botanicgarden.coffsharbour.nsw.gov.au
**Solitary Island Marine Park** 32 Marine Dr; (02) 6652 3977;
www.mpa.nsw.gov.au
**Pet Porpoise Pool** Orlando St; (02) 6652 2164; www.
petporpoisepool.com

## Tours

**East Coast Surf School** Diggers Beach; (02) 6651 5515 or
0412 257 233; www.eastcoastsurfschool.com.au

Whitewater rafting on the Nymboida River

**Solitary Island Marine Park** 32 Marine Dr; (02) 6652 3977; www.mpa.nsw.gov.au/simp-contact.html

**Liquid Assets Adventure Tours** Sea-kayaking, surf rafting and whitewater rafting. 38 Marina Dr; (02) 6658 0850.

## Where to eat

**Fisherman's Co-op** 💲 Watch out for tourist traps on this marina, while you safely enjoy their fantastic cheap fish and chips. 69 Marina Dr; (02) 6652 2811; daily 9am–6pm.

**Julie's Galley at the Marina** 💲 Locals adore this place and you will too. Marina Dr; (02) 6650 0188; daily 8am–6.30pm.

**Riva** 💲💲 If you want to find the local cool kids, look no further than this hang out. Treat yourself to a glass of wine and some tapas. 384a Harbour Dr; (02) 6650 0195; dinner daily.

## Pubs

**Plantation Hotel** This popular pub has a bit of everything including live bands and a great bistro. 88 Grafton St (Pacific Hwy); (02) 6652 3855; Sun–Thur 10am–2.30am, Fri–Sat 10am–3.30am; www.plantationhotel.com.au

**Coffs Ex-Services Club** The cheap drinks on offer means this is the start of many a rowdy pub crawl. Cnr Pacific Hwy & Vernon St; (02) 6652 3888; Sun–Thur 9am–11.30pm, Fri–Sat 9am–1am; www.cex.com.au

## Nightclub

**Xtreme** If you're up for a night out, head here after 11pm. 15 High St Mall; (02) 6652 6426; Thurs–Sat 7pm–5am.

## Where to stay

**Hoey Moey Backpackers** ★★ Dorm $22, double or twin $46 Ocean Pde; (02) 6651 7966; www.hoeymoey.com.au

**Coffs Harbour YHA Backpackers Resort** ★★ Dorm $28.50–$31.50, double or twin $73.50–$83.50 51 Collingwood St; (02) 6652 6462.

**Aussietel** ★★ Dorm from $30, double or twin $65 312 High St; (02) 6651 1871.

**Caribbean Motel** ★★★ Single $89, double or twin $99–$135 353 High St; (02) 6652 1500; www.stayincoffs.com.au

## Events

**International Buskers & Comedy Festival** Eight days of fantastic street theatre from all over the world. Most performances are free, so you'll be able to tip your busker handsomely. Sept–Oct.

## ❹ Lennox Head (1–2 days)

Surf's up! Lennox Head is a great stopover as you continue north to Byron Bay. It's casual, everything is a short stroll from where you're standing and it's just gorgeous. Surfers have been flocking here for years; Lennox Point has one of the best right-hand breaks in the world. Hang-gliders are in on the action, launching themselves off the 65 m cliffs of these headlands.

Tucked behind the sand dunes, Lake Ainsworth is a freshwater lake with fantastic camping and is a great place to learn how to windsurf. Don't be alarmed at the colour of the water – it's stained with tannin from the tea trees hugging the shores. You should also visit Pat Morton Lookout for spectacular views of Seven Mile Beach reaching up towards Broken Head and Byron, as well as the whales that visit twice a year in June and July, and again in September and October. Dolphins can be viewed most mornings as they frolic and 'fish' about 15 m offshore.

## Further information

**Lennox Head Markets** Saturated with everything from local art to the best local produce, this market is not to be missed. Lake Ainsworth; (02) 6672 2874; 2nd & 5th Sun every month.

## Tours

**Summerland Surf School** 9 Evans Rd, Evans Head; (02) 6682 4393; www.summerlandbeachhouse.com.au

**Lennox Head Surf Coaching (one on one) – Max Perrot** (02) 6687 5066 or 0427 875 066.

**Lennox Head Hang-Gliding School** 0427 257 699.

**Akuna Seaplanes** 0423 874 939.

## Where to eat

**Lennox Head Pizza** 💲 Join the surfers for fantastic cheap pasta, pizza and salad. Ballina St; (02) 6687 7080; Wed–Sun from 5.30pm.

**Mi Thai** 💲 Divine Thai. 2/76 Ballina St; (02) 6687 5820; Wed–Sun from 5.30pm.

**Mavis's Health Food Store** 💲 Delicious pit stop for lunchtime nourishment. 3/62 Ballina St; (02) 6687 7129; daily 8am–5pm.

**Seven Mile Cafe Restaurant** 💲💲/💲💲💲 **TOP TREAT!!** Delicious dining with stunning water views. 41 Pacific Pde; (02) 6687 6210; Tue–Sat 6pm–9pm, Sun lunch from noon.

## Where to stay

**Lennox Head Beachouse YHA** ★★ Pick up service from Ballina. Dorm $28.50–$31.50, double or twin $68.50 3 Ross St; (02) 6687 7636.

**Lake Ainsworth Caravan Park** ★★ Site powered $30, site unpowered $25, basic cabin $78 Pacific Pde; (02) 6687 7249; www.bscp.com.au/lakeains/

**Lennox Lodge** ★★★ Single $70–$80, double $80–$90 20 Byron St; (02) 6687 7210; www.lennoxlodge.com.au

## Events

**All Girls Surf Showdown** Not as violent as it sounds, this is the largest women's surf competition in Australia (and possibly the world). Jun.

## [5] Byron Bay (3–4 days)

Bewitching Byron is home to 30 km of uninterrupted beaches and a relaxed town of hippies and surfies, together with uber-cool posers, celebs and tourists. It's a fantastic cross-section of counter-culture freedom and mainstream commercialism. Everything is on offer here, from yoga to day spas and New Age encounters, diving and sea-kayaking to surf lessons, to skydiving and gliding.

Head for the easternmost point on mainland Australia at Cape Byron with sweeping views, complete with a lighthouse. For peace and surf, there are Clarkes and Wategos beaches. Broken Head Nature Reserve rainforest hides other secluded beaches and there's more good surf at Cosy Corner and Broken Head. A must do is Cods Hole, an extensive underwater cave and home to large moray eels, as well as plenty of other marine life. Diving here is best between April and June. You can also take yourself off to Julian Rocks Aquatic Reserve, protector of 450 underwater species, which promises a diving experience more diverse than the Great Barrier Reef (seriously!).

### Further information

ⓘ **Byron Bay Tourist Information Centre** 80 Jonson St; (02) 6680 9271; www.visitbyronbay.com
**Byron Bay.com** Check out their fantastic blog. (02) 6680 7722; www.byron-bay.com/blog/
**Byron Bus & Backpacker Centre** Next door to information centre; (02) 6685 5517.
**Earth Car Rentals** Shop 6, 14 Middleton St; (02) 6685 7472; www.byron-bay.com/earthcar
**Airport bus: Byron Bay Airbus** Operates thrice daily to and from local airports. (02) 6684 3232; www.byron-bay.com/airbus

### Tours

**Byron Bay Walking Tours** (02) 6687 1112; walknorth@mullum.com.au
**Rockhoppers Adventure Company** 0500 881 881.
**Byron Bay Motorcycle Tours** (02) 6685 6762; soundwav@norex.com.au
**Byron Bay Sea Kayaks** (02) 6685 5830; www.byronbayadventureco.com
**Mick's Bay to Bush Tours** (02) 6685 6889.
**Byron Bay Dive Centre** 9 Marvell St; (02) 6685 8333 or 1800 243 483; www.byronbaydivecentre.com.au
**Baysail** 0418 656 160; www.baysail.com.au
**Blackdog Surfing** The Plaza, Jonson St; (02) 6680 9828; www.blackdogsurfing.com
**Yoga Arts** 1st floor, 6 Byron St; 130 Jonson St; (02) 6680 8684; www.yogarts.com.au
**Wicked Travel** 91 Jonson St; 1800 555 339; www.wickedtravel.com.au
**Peterpan Adventures** 87 Jonson St; 1800 252 459; www.peterpan.com
**A Real Surf Journey** 1800 828 888; www.arealsurfjourney.com
**SkyDive Byron Bay** 1800 800 840; www.skydivebyronbay.com

Byron Bay beach

### Where to eat

**Citrus Deli on Jonson** [$]/[$$] Fresh tangy meals using the best produce. Shop 1, 130 Jonson St; (02) 6680 7040; Mon–Fri 9.30am–6pm, Sat 9.30–4pm.
**Hulala Cafe** [$]/[$$] Hankering for a trip to Hawaii? This place takes 'Pacific Rim' eating to a whole new level with its Cajun fish tacos, Thai chicken tortillas and vegetable frijoke enchiladas! Bangalow Rd; (02) 6685 5577; Tue–Sat from 6pm.
**Zula Cafe** [$]/[$$] Tranquil, divine location for lingering lunches and dinners. Lot 1, Skinners Shoot Rd; (02) 6680 8038; daily 8am–9pm.
**Cafe Viva** [$]/[$$] Funky cafe feasts. Carlyle St, opposite Woolworths; (02) 6685 7871; Mon–Sat 9am–3pm.
**The Piggery Supernatural Food** [$] A vegetarian feasting spot set in the open, airy space that was originally a meatworks. You'll have the last laugh too at this popular noshery. Arts Factory, Skinners Shoot Rd, (02) 6685 5833; daily from 8am.
**Dish** [$$$] **TOP TREAT!!** Nestled in a rainforest garden, with a fantastic wine list and sublime seafood. A real treat. Cnr Jonson & Marvell sts; (02) 6685 7320; dinner Tue–Sun.

### Pubs

**Beach Hotel** A gigantic and beautiful beer garden with some free live music rounded off with a spectacular view of the Main Beach. Cnr Jonson & Bay sts; (02) 6685 6402; daily 10am–12.30am.
**The Cheeky Monkey** Hang out with all the other backpackers for cheap grub, loud music and the ecstatically happy hour that kicks in after 10pm. 115 Jonson St; (02) 6685 5886; Thur–Sat 7pm–3am.

Yoga on the beach at Byron Bay

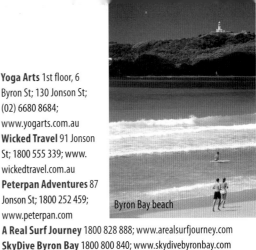

**Great Northern Hotel** A bit of everything served up to satisfy everyone: blokey bar, pool tables and a fancy space out the back for some of the best live Australian music. Jonson St; (02) 6685 6454; Mon–Thur 10am–1am, Fri–Sat 10am–3am, Sun noon–midnight.

## Nightclubs

**Cocomangas** Loud and outrageous bar and nightclub with an equally gaudy restaurant downstairs. 32 Jonson St; (02) 6685 8493; Mon–Sat 8pm–3am; www.cocomangas.com.au

**La La Land** Head upstairs to experience this groovy night spot with heaps of couches to sink into. 6 Lawson St; (02) 6680 7070; daily 7pm–3am; www.lalaland.com.au

**C-Moog** All betas, funk and hip-hoppers will be thrilled with this late-night boogie spot, peppered with tracks from visiting DJs. The Plaza, Jonson St; (02) 6680 7022; Tue–Sat 7pm–3am; www.c-moog.com.au

## Where to stay

**Aquarius Backpackers Motel** ★★★ Dorm $28, double or twin $70 16 Lawson St; 1800 028 909; www.aquarius-backpackers.com.au

**Arts Factory Backpackers Lodge** ★★ Dorm $90, double or twin $180 Shoot Rd; (02) 6685 7709; www.artsfactory.com.au

**Backpackers Holiday Village** ★★ Dorm $28, double or twin $75 116 Jonson St; 1800 350 388.

**J's Bay YHA** ★★ Dorm $31.50–$36.50, double or twin $73.50 7 Carlyle St; (02) 6685 8853; www.byron-bay.com/jsbay

**Belongil Beach House** ★★★ Dorm from $25, double or twin from $55 Childe St; (02) 6685 7868; www.belongilbeachouse.com

**Cape Byron YHA Hostel** ★★★ Dorm $31.50–$33.50, double or twin from $63.50 Cnr Middleton & Byron sts; (02) 6685 8788; www.yha.com.au

## Events

**East Coast Blues and Roots Festival** Join the hordes flocking to listen to R'n'B music. Easter.

**Splendour in the Grass** Camp out and listen to the hottest new bands at this hugely popular festival. Jul.

**Byron Bay Writers' Festival** Mingle with the local literati. Aug.

# 6 Nimbin (2–3 days)

Infused with Aboriginal history, Nimbin was originally the site of healing and initiation for the Bundjalung people and the resting place of Warrajum, the mighty Rainbow Serpent. It was a sleepy village until the tie-dyed, psychedelic 1973 Aquarius Festival resurrected the Rainbow Serpent spirit, establishing Nimbin as the alternative-culture capital of Australia. With tourist facilities advertising hours such as 'whenever', it takes the word 'laidback' to a whole new level. The focus of this colourful area is on good vibes and freedom of expression. Perhaps the easiest way to sum this place up is to call it Amsterdam in the Bush, so good luck if you're not keen on inhaling.

Nimbin street art

Nimbin Museum is dedicated to hippy culture and Aboriginal heritage and is worth a visit. Take a wander through Nightcap National Park, a lush World Heritage-listed forest with easy to difficult bushwalks (you'll need a map and compass). You can also see Nimbin Rocks, the spectacular remains of an ancient volcano and a sacred initiation site for the Bundjalung people (for this reason, viewing is from the road only).

## Further information

**Nimbin Tourist Connection** (02) 6689 1764.

**Nimbin Tourist Hotline** (02) 6689 1222.

**Nimbin Museum** Cullen St; (02) 6689 1123; www.nimbinaustralia.com

**Shuttle service: Nimbin Shuttle** Ex Byron Bay; (02) 6680 9189.

## Tours

**Jim's Alternative Tours** (02) 6685 7720; www.byron-bay.com/jimstours

**Nimbin Explorer Tours** (02) 6689 1577.

## Where to eat

**Rainbow Cafe** $ Multi-coloured features and great food 64a Cullen St; (02) 6689 1997; breakfast, lunch & dinner.

## Where to stay

**Rainbow Retreat** ★★★ Dorm $20, double or twin $40–$60, triple $60, hippy bungalow $60, camping $13 75 Thorburn St; (02) 6689 1262; www.rainbowretreat.net

**Nimbin Rox YHA** ★★Dorm $31.50, double or twin $57.50 74 Thorburn St; (02) 6689 0022.

## Events

**Aquarius Fair Markets** Pick up bargains while indulging in fantastic people watching. 3rd & 5th Sunday each month.

**Mardi Gras Festival** The usual Mardi Gras but with a Nimbin difference: it's organised by the Nimbin HEMP (Help End Marijuana Prohibition) Embassy. May.

**Winter Solstice Celebration** Its' all about the season and the vibe . . . man. Jun.

**Summer Solstice Celebration** As above with warmer weather. Dec.

For more detail
see maps
207, 213 & 214

# Snowy Mountains
# Magic mountains

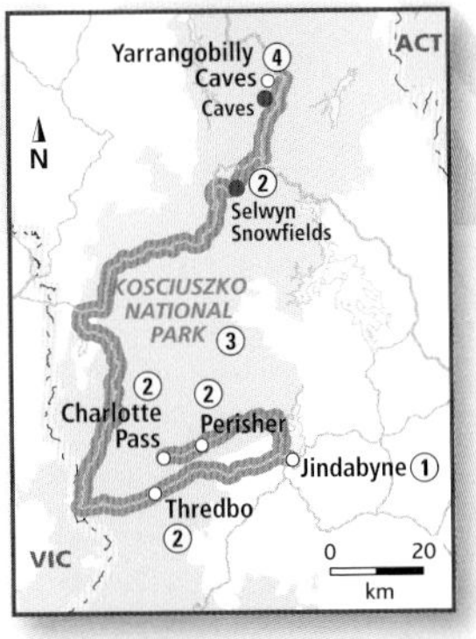


The Snowy Mountains are the ultimate perennial destination for adventurers. This spectacular region is bursting with life and character, and activities are simply divided according to the seasons. In winter, there are all the snow sports, while in autumn, spring and summer, there's cycling, whitewater rafting, bushwalking, mountain biking, canoeing, hiking, horseriding, cave tours, wildflowers, fishing . . . the list goes on and on.

**Number of days to spend in this region: 3–10 days**

## Getting here

Transport to the Snowy Mountains is excellent. For fantastic deals, check out www.snowymountains.com.au/By_Air_Rail_or_Coach.html

There are various flights to the Snowy Mountains (Cooma Airport). REX offer great daily budget deals from Sydney. If you're flying to Canberra, transfers from Canberra airport are available through SkiBus/Snowy Mountains Hire Cars.

Countrylink runs daily trains from Sydney to Canberra with a connecting coach to Cooma. Make sure you check the timetable as times differ from day to day.

Also check out Clippers Skibus Xpress, which will effortlessly get you from Sydney to snowfields.

**REX** 13 1713; www.rex.com.au

**SkiBus/Snowy Mountains Hire Cars** (02) 6456 2957.

**Countrylink** 13 2232; www.countrylink.info

**Clippers Skibus Xpress** 1300 361 156; www.clippertours.com.au

**Summit Coaches** Head straight for Thredbo from Canberra via Jindabyne and Cooma. 1800 608 008.

**Skitube** If you're heading for Perisher/Smiggens from Jindabyne, this is the mode for you. (02) 6456 2010.

**Adaminaby Bus Service** Runs between Jindabyne and Selwyn Snowfields in winter – make sure you book. (02) 6454 2318.

## 1 Jindabyne (1–2 days)

Jindabyne is nestled just beneath the snowline alongside Kosciuszko National Park. Amazingly, this town was moved from its original location on the banks of the Snowy River to make way for the ingenious Snowy Mountain Hydro-electric Scheme. You'll spot some of the surviving buildings at their final resting place when you visit Lake Jindabyne, best explored on foot or by bike from Banjo Paterson Park to Snowline Caravan Park. The lake is overflowing with rainbow trout that don't mind all the waterskiing that goes on in summer. Head for Snowy Valley Lookout for enviable views of the lake, or catch a ski-tube from Bullocks Flat around to flashy Perisher Blue. A more lengthy ramble can be had on the Alpine Way, 111 km of beauty threading its way through the mountain pass of Dead Horse Gap. Jindabyne is definitely quieter than its rowdy snowtown brothers, but it will be adored by your wallet.

### Further information

[i] **Snowy Region Visitor Centre** Kosciuszko Rd, Jindabyne; (02) 6450 5600; winter daily 8.30am–5.30pm, summer 8.30am–5pm; www.nationalparks.nsw.gov.au

**Ski & Save Snow Holidays** Shop 6a, Razorback Plaza; 1800 020 622; www.snowholidays.com.au

### Tours

**Snowy Wilderness Ingebyra** Offers various tours including hiking, horseriding, quad biking and wild brumby-watching. Barry Way, Jindabyne; (02) 6457 8300; www.snowywilderness.com.au

### Where to eat

**Cafe Susu** [S] From breakfast to burgers and everything in between

– drop by for sushi and tempura on Friday nights. 7–8 Gippsland St;
(02) 6456 1503; Mon–Sat 10am–9pm, Sun 8am–2pm (closed Sat
during summer).

**Sundance Bakehouse & Tea Rooms** $ Gorgeous little spot for a
hot bevvie and a sumptuous snack. Shop 13, Nuggets Crossing;
(02) 6456 2951; daily 6.30am–6pm.

**Bits & Pizzas** $ Dedicated to creating the cheapest mountain meals
– try their Vegemite pizza! Petamin Plaza, off Kosciuszko Rd; 1800 046
275; daily noon–3pm & 6pm–9pm.

Thredbo snowfields

Skier jumping mid-air

## Pubs

**Clancy's Cocktail Bar** You'll discover
everything you need for a fantastic night
out here. If cocktails aren't your speed,
duck into Muster's – the public bar at
this sprawling inn. Cap off a great night
out at their nightclub, Banjos. Banjo
Paterson Inn; 1 Kosciuszko Rd;
(02) 6456 2372; daily 10pm – 2am;
www.banjopatersoninn.com.au

## Where to stay

**Jindy Inn** ★★ Dorm $50–$340 (peak
season), twin or double $70–$440
(peak season) 18 Clyde St; (02) 6456
1957; www.jindyinn.com

**Banjo Paterson Inn** ★★★ Room,
including breakfast from $50 (summer
rate), twin budget room $144 (winter rate) 1 Kosciuszko Rd; 1800 046
275; www.banjopatersoninn.com.au

**Snowy Mountains Backpackers** ★★ Dorm $30–$42 (peak
season), double or single $90–$120 (peak season) 7–8 Gippsland St;
1800 333 468; www.snowybackpackers.com.au

## ❷ Snow Towns (3–4 days)

### Thredbo

Thredbo's snaking streets and European-style lodges will charm you
into thinking you're somewhere in the Swiss Alps. This is the area's main
snow village, with 480 ha of skiable terrain and boasting the longest
ski runs in Australia. The only hassle is everyone else knows this too so
you're staring down the barrel of busy tracks. The least crowded times
are first thing in the morning, lunchtime and, of course, weekdays.
Although alpine adventurers needn't worry: the scary trails are far less
populated.

No strong intermediate skier should leave without going on the
Dead Horse Gap run. Make sure you find someone who knows the way,
and on a clear day it's the ultimate skiing and scenic experience. Hitch a
ride with the chairlift to the top of Karels, investigate Ramshead Range,

ski along the ridge and through the gorgeous snow gums to Dead Horse
Gap. Brilliant.

If you're in town in July and August, night skiing is a must. But if
skiing's not your game, take a plunge down the 700 m luge-style track
on a bobsled, or indulge in some in-line skating on one of the several
paths threading through town. When your legs are begging to be set
free from the skis, there is loads to do away from the slopes. The cafes,
restaurants and bars are worth every cent.

### Charlotte Pass

Charlotte Pass twinkles from its cloistered setting deep within the
Snowy Mountains, tucked away past Perisher Valley. It's so fantastically
remote you can't drive here: the road is swallowed by snow. Drivers
must park their cars at Bullocks Flat (there's no overnight parking at
Perisher), take the Skitube to Perisher and then overland transport will
ferry you to Charlotte Pass.

Charlotte Pass is a beautiful escape from the city-like bustle of
Perisher. It's also the highest snow town, making for fantastic snow
quality. About 80 per cent of the slopes are geared for intermediate
skiers, but there are also good beginner runs. Lunch and lifts are about
the same price as a Perisher Blue day ticket, and if you stay overnight,
you'll enjoy the novelty of being able to ski in and out of your lodgings.
The only downside is that all this tranquil isolation makes Charlotte
Pass popular with both families and adventure skiers keen to escape
rowdy pranksters, so don't expect to have boozy nights out here.

### Perisher Blue

Perisher is a jam-packed smorgasbord of cruisey skiing. Despite shorter
runs, the altitude provides dependable snow cover and field heaven for
those who prefer to coast, rather than constantly doing gymnastics off
mountaintops. However, adrenalin junkies will still get their fix; have
a go at the Devil's Playground or Kamikaze at Blue Cow. Cross-country
skiers will also be grinning their way through this fantastic terrain.

Perisher's areas are Smiggen Holes, a Smurfs-sounding name
perfect for families and beginners and a great base; Perisher Valley,
the main region with a maze of lifts, loads of downhill runs and some
longer trails; Blue Cow, available during the day only and inaccessible
by car (adrenalin junkies should have a go at it); and Guthega, a little

lodgings and skiing base tucked away at the farthest point on the mountains.

Transport here is easy. There are lifts and ski trails linking you up with everything on offer, and don't forget the Skitube if you're heading from Perisher to Blue Cow. The carpark is at Bullocks Flat, located on the Alpine Way between Jindabyne and Thredbo.

## Selwyn Snowfields

Selwyn is a day-only snow area dominated by a friendly attitude to everything: slopes, prices and service. It's adored by visiting families and beginners. You can stay in nearby towns like Adaminaby and Talbingo, or even further away at Cooma or Tumut. Head for Selwyn armed with your skis and perhaps a picnic (there aren't many choices come lunchtime). Major attractions here are toboggans and snow tubes, and 12 chair lifts waiting to take you to great downhill runs. Cross-country skiing never felt so good, with a 45 km network of well-maintained tracks linking Selwyn to Dry Dam. If you're an experienced walker, Selwyn is also the starting point for a fantastic overnight hike into the national park.

## Further information

*ℹ️* **Thredbo Resort Centre** Friday Dr; (02) 6459 4100; www.thredbo.com.au
*ℹ️* **Charlotte Pass** (02) 6457 5458; www.charlottepass.com.au
*ℹ️* **Perisher Blue** 1300 655 811; www.perisherblue.com.au
*ℹ️* **Selwyn Snowfields** 1800 641 064; www.selwynsnow.com.au
**Ski school**: **Outdoor Adventure School** Thredbo; (02) 6459 4044.

## Where to eat

**The Pub Bistro** 💲 A proper country-style pub, with beer, spectacular snacks and and curry on Saturday nights. (02) 6459 4200; daily from 10.30am, food noon–2.30pm & 6pm–9pm.
**Alfresco Pizzeria** 💲💲 Bona fide pizzeria with the atmosphere to back up its big, Italian-hearted authenticity. You'll love everything about this well-priced gem. Lower Concourse, Thredbo Alpine Hotel; (02) 6457 6327; daily noon–9pm.
**TBar Restaurant** 💲💲 Steak and seafood to satisfy your tastebuds, including a bit of kangaroo, if you're keen. Dimity Walker, Village Square, Thredbo; (02) 6457 6355; daily from 6pm.
**The Mountain House** 💲/💲💲 Stews, soups and everything else needed to keep you warm for a day on the slopes. Cruiser Quad Chair, Valley Terminal, Thredbo; (02) 6457 6084; daily 8am–4.30pm.
**Ullr Bar & Grill** 💲💲 Cook your own

Mountain-biking around Thredbo

grub on the grill or check out the fantastic bar snacks. This place has everything from steak to sushi. Plus, there's karaoke later ... Thredbo Village; (02) 6457 6210; 2 sittings 6pm & 7.45pm.
**Credo Restaurant** 💲💲💲 **TOP TREAT!!** This award-winning establishment is stuffed full of spectacular modern Australian dishes, and is surrounded by great views of Thredbo River, snowfields and mountains. Best of all, it's not snooty: the atmosphere is just the right side of casual, so you can relax while you enjoy every cent you spend. Riverside Cabins, Thredbo Village; (02) 6457 6844; daily from 6pm.

## Pubs and bars

**Apres Bar** Completely remodelled, this Thredbo institution boasts a gleaming onyx bar. Denman Hotel, Diggins Tce, Thredbo Village; (02) 6457 6222; daily from 4pm in winter; www.thedenman.com.au
**Schuss Bar** There's nothing quiet about this popular nightspot. Schanpps anyone? Alpine Hotel, Friday Dr, Thredbo Village; (02) 6459 4200; daily from 4pm, happy hour daily 4–5pm; live music daily from 10pm.
**Clancy's At The Man Bar** Fantastic atmosphere at this great bar – don't be put off by the up-market restaurant next door. It has brilliant bar snacks if you're peckish. The Man, Perisher Valley; (02) 6457 5234; daily from 4pm.

## Nightclubs

**Keller Bar** You can't come to Thredbo without shaking your tail feather here. Thredbo Alpine Hotel, Friday Dr; (02) 6459 4200; DJs from 10pm daily.

## Where to stay

**Candlelight Lodge** ★★★ Dorm $85 (winter), single $85 (summer), double or twin $115–$120 32 Diggins Tce, Thredbo Village; (02) 6457 6318; www.candlelightlodge.com.au
**Thredbo YHA Lodge** ★★★ Dorm $29.50, double or twin $63.50–$73.50 8 Jack Adams Path; (02) 6457 6376; www.yha.com.au
**Pygmy Possum Lodge** ★★ Self-help lodge $44–$82.50 (peak season) Charlotte Pass; (02) 8715 6255; www.ski.com.au/pygmypossum
**Khancoban Backpackers & Fisherman's Lodge** ★ Single $19 Alpine Way, Khancoban; (02) 6076 9471.
**Ski Rider** ★★★ Dorm $115–$147 (peak season), double or twin $151–186 (peak season) PMB 10, Kosciuszko Rd, Kosciuszko National Park; (02) 6456 1100; www.skirider.com.au

## Events

**Thredbo Blues Festival** Fantastic three-day celebration of blues and roots music. Jan.

**Thredbo Jazz Festival** A weekend jazz extravaganza set in the magnificent mountain surrounds. May.

**Snowyfest International Film Festival** Over 50 short and feature films, acting workshops and seminars. Jun.

**Snowy River Festival** A delicious taste of Snowy River life – make sure you catch the 'Champion Snowy River Stockman's Challenge'. Apr.

## ❸ Kosciuszko National Park (1–2 days)

If the idea of 'being at one with nature' makes you want to sprint straight back to the city clutching your latte, this is the place for you. Kosciusko National Park will transform even the most uninterested into a nature rambler. New South Wales' largest national park has 690 000 ha of valleys, glacial lakes, woodlands, fields and the highest mountain in the country. It also protects rare and unusual wildlife species, including the gorgeous pygmy possum. All of New South Wales' snowfields are part of the park too (see Snow Towns above).

When the snow melts, the activities on offer range from whitewater rafting, climbing and 4WD touring, to a mountain bike experience called Cannonball Run, which requires participants to pass an initiation first, before you hurtle for 4.2 km. Horseriding is a real must – this is The Man from Snowy River country, after all – and most tours include a proper cooked breakfast in the bush.

The undisputed jewel in the crown of this park is Mount Kosciuszko. Standing at 2228 m above sea level, it's not to be sniffed at. They don't call this 'the roof of Australia' for nothing. Views from the summit are simply spectacular, particularly at sunrise. The easier option to the top is the Kosciuszko Express Chairlift. You can take a 45 min walk to the lookout, but if you actually want to reach the summit, be warned: there will be a 6.5 km walk to the top (2.5 hrs). The tougher option is the Summit Walk from the Charlotte Pass (9 km, 3.5 hrs). Guided walks are highly recommended.

There are various walks in the park, so your return journey need not be 'back the way we came'. If you have the energy and are keen to escape the crowds, treat yourself to the Main Range Track to Charlotte Pass (12.5 km, 4.5 hrs). It's worth every second of awe-inspiring beauty as you make your way back down from 'the roof of the world'.

## Further information

🛈 **Cooma Visitors Centre** Centennial Park; 1800 636 525; www.visitcooma.com.au

🛈 **NPWS Khancoban** Scott St; (02) 6076 9373; daily 8.30am–noon & 1–4pm (extended hours during peak times); www.nationalparks. nsw.gov.au

Kosciuszko National Park in summer

## Tours

**Raw NRG Mountain Bike Centre** Valley Terminal, Thredbo; (02) 6457 6282; www.rawnrg.com.au

**Upper Murray Whitewater Rafting** 7 North St, Cooma; (02) 6452 7998; www.raftingsnowymountains.com.au

**Reynella Kosciuszcko Rides – Horseriding** (02) 6454 2386; www.reynellarides.com.au;

**Kosciuszko Alpine Guided Walks** Lake Crackenback Resort, 1650 Alpine Way, Crackenback; 1800 020 524; www.novotellakecrackenback.com.au/walks

**Snowy Wilderness – 4WD, quad biking and much more** Barry Way, Ingebyra, via Jindabyne; 1800 218 171; www.snowywilderness. com.au

## Where to stay

**Bunkhouse Motel** ★ Dorm $30, double or twin $55 28–30 Soho St, Cooma; (02) 6452 2983; www.bunkhousemotel.com.au

**Snowline Caravan Park** ★★ Backpacker bunks $17–$42.50 Junction of Alpine Way & Kosciuszko Rd, Jindabyne; (02) 6456 2099; www.snowline.com.au

## ❹ Yarrangobilly Caves (1 day)

Yarrangobilly Caves needs to be written in bold lettering on your itinerary with arrows – whatever it takes – to make sure you don't get all snowed up and forget about visiting this world-class nature spot. This string of 70 limestone caves is extravagantly decorated. Six caves are open for viewing and the highlights are incredible: underground pools, frozen waterfalls and a weird web of limestone formations open to interpretation. There is also a lovely picnic area, which may only sound perfect for the Addams Family, but is so incredible you'll happily rename yourself Fester and settle down for a bite to eat. Just when you think nature can't do any better than this, you'll discover the naturally formed thermal pool where you can bathe in 27°C water.

## Further information

🛈 **NPWS Yarrangobilly Caves** Snowy Mts Hwy; (02) 6454 9597; daily 9am–5pm; www.nationalparks.nsw.gov.au

# Hunter Valley
# Quaffing and coastline

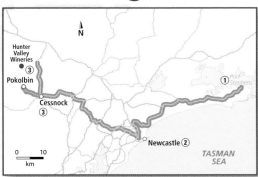

The Hunter is known as one of Australia's top wine-producing regions. You'll hear about 'Upper' and 'Lower' Hunter, and the Lower Hunter is undoubtedly the better of the two, perhaps because the Upper region has various large operations, missing out on the irresistible charisma of family-owned and -run estates. But grapes are only a small part of what this stunning landscape has to offer. The rest of the Hunter region is a playground of adventure, including dolphins, surf and rainforest.

**Number of days to spend in this region: 2–6 days**

## Getting here

If you prefer a quick flight to the Huntery Valley, there are daily flights from Sydney to Cessnock Airport with Qantas.

But it is pretty easy to just hop on a Cityrail train, which winds from the CBD to the Hunter Valley. Stations are Maitland, Newcastle or Morisset, with connecting buses found at Maitland and Newcastle.

Alternatively, Rover Coaches offer daily transfers from Central Station

to Cessnock. Port Stephens Buses bound for Port Stephens operate transfers from Newcastle and Sydney.

**Cityrail** 13 1500; www.cityrail.com.au

**Rover Coaches** (02) 4990 1699; www.rovercoaches.com.au

**Port Stephens Buses** (02) 4982 2940; www.psbuses.nelsonbay.com

## ❶ Port Stephens (1–2 days)

Don't be fooled by the tranquillity of the this blue-watered haven cluttered with pure, white sandy beaches and surrounded by glorious bushland. There's still loads of action here, from exploring the dunes on the back of a quad bike, camel or horse, to a 4WD tour along Stockton Beach, a toboggan ride at Toboggan Hill Park, or the excellent surf of Zenith, Fingal Bay and One Mile Beach. You'll also discover clusters of curious koalas in the branches of trees at Tilligerry Habitat, and over 100 bottlenosed dolphins are in permanent residence in the unspoilt waters. Migrating humpback and minke whales also visit this stunning slice of paradise from June to July and September to October.

Jetty at Port Stephens

### Further information

❶ **Port Stephens Visitor Information Centre** Victoria Pde, Nelson Bay; (02) 4980 6900; www.portstephens.org.au

**Toboggan Hill Park** Aquatic Cl, Nelson Bay; (02) 4984 1022.

**Tilligerry Habitat** Foreshore, Port Stephens; (02) 4982 4441.

### Tours

**Imagine Cruises** Dolphin- and whale-watching. Dock C, d'Albora Marina, Nelson Bay; (02) 2984 9000; www.imaginecruises.com.au

**Quad Bike King** Taylors Beach; (02) 4919 0088 or 0427 846 475; www.quadbikeking.com.au

**Moonshadow 4WD Tours** Shop 3, 35 Stockton St, Nelson Bay; (02) 4984 4760; www.moonshadow4wd.com.au

### Where to eat

**Holberts Oyster Supplies** 💲💲 Port Stephens is perfect for oysters, and this place with great water views has them shucked fresh daily. 51–52 Diemars Rd, Salamander Bay; (02) 4982 7234; daily 8am–4pm; www.holbertsoysterfarm.com

**Cruise In and Takeaway** $ Straightforward food plus it sells souvenirs. 40 Victoria Pde, Nelson Bay; (02) 4984 1262.
**Incredible Edibles** $ A great deli. Cnr Donaldson & Stockton sts, Nelson Bay; (02) 4981 4511.

## Where to stay
**Sahara Trails & Horseriding & Farmstays** ★★★ $25–$180 per night per couple 9 Port Stephens Dr, Anna Bay; (02) 4981 9077.
**Samurai Beach Bungalows – Port Stephens YHA** ★★ Dorm $28.50, double or twin $81.50, triple $108.50, quad $131.50 Cnr Frost Rd & Robert Connell Cl, Anna Bay; (02) 4982 1921 or 0409 327 502; www.samuraiportstephens.com
**Forster Dolphin Lodge YHA** ★★ Dorm $28.50, single $48.50, double or twin $65.50 43 Head St, Forster; (02) 6555 8155.

## ② Newcastle (1–2 days)
Australia's second-oldest city was founded as a penal colony in 1804. Today it's the perfect alter ego to the elegance of wine tasting in the Hunter. Head to Darby Street, the fabulous bohemian part of town.

For the best beaches, take a jaunt along Bathers Way, a 5 km coastal walk from Nobbys Lighthouse to Mereweather Beach. Have a paddle in Mereweather Ocean Baths, the largest ocean baths complex in the Southern Hemisphere. You should also go to jail – Maitland Gaol, just so we're clear – or you can see more of Newcastle's convict history by visiting Australia's first man- and convict-made ocean pool, Bogey Hole.

Blackbutt Reserve is surging with natural beauty, home to kangaroos, wombats and koalas. There's also the Wetlands Centre, which has transformed urban wasteland into a swamp home for over 200 bird and animal species. If you've some time, catch a ferry across to Stockton and meander along Shipwreck Walk.

## Further information
ⓘ **Newcastle Visitor Centre** 361 Hunter St; (02) 4974 2999; www.newcastletourism.com
**Darby Street Precinct** Darby St, Cooks Hill; (02) 4929 6883 or 0412 767 147; www.darbystreet.com.au
**Maitland Gaol** 6–18 John St, East Maitland; (02) 4936 6482; www.maitlandgaol.com.au
**Wetlands Centre** Sandgate Rd, Shortland; (02) 4951 6466; www.wetlands.org.au

## Where to eat
**Bogey Hole Cafe** $ It serves breakfasts to die for. Cnr Hunter & Pacific sts; (02) 4926 1790; breakfast, lunch & dinner daily.
**Big Al's** $/$$ Think *Goodfellas*: a themed restaurant with generous portions. Cnr King & Brown sts; (02) 4929 2717; lunch & dinner daily.

**Serious Sausage** $/$$ All organic. 76 Darby St; (02) 4929 2278; breakfast, lunch & dinner Mon–Fri, breakfast & lunch Sat–Sun.
**LongBench** $/$$ A funky interior, buckets of coffee and divine food. 161 Darby St; (02) 4927 8888; daily 8am–10pm.

## Pubs
**Queens Wharf Brewery** Beer overlooking the water. 150 Wharf Rd; (02) 4929 6333; Sun–Thur 10.30am–midnight, Fri–Sat 10.30am–3am; www.qwb.com.au
**The Beach Hotel** Spectacular. The view is pretty great too. Cnr Frederick & Ridge sts; (02) 4963 1574; Mon–Sat 11am–midnight, Sun noon–10pm; www.thebeachhotel.com.au
**Finnegans Irish Pub** The real Irish deal. 21–23 Darby St; (02) 4926 4777; Sun–Thur 11am–midnight, Fri–Sat 11am–3am; www.irishpub.com.au

## Live music
**Cambridge Hotel** The best place to get a taste of the hottest local bands. 789 Hunter St; (02) 4962 2459; Mon–Tue 11am–7.30pm, Wed–Sat 11am–4am, not open on Sun unless a band is playing.

## Where to stay
**Newcastle Beach Backpackers YHA** ★★ Dorm $29.50, double or twin $74.50 30 Pacific St; (02) 4925 3544; www.yha.com.au
**Backpackers by the Beach** ★★ Dorm $25; double or twin $57 34 Hunter St; (02) 4926 3472; www.backpackersbythebeach.com.au
**Backpackers Newcastle & Guesthouse** ★ Room from $18 (seasonal prices) 42–44 Denison St, Hamilton; (02) 4969 3436 or 0418 269 226; www.newcastlebackpackers.com

## Events
**Surfest** Australia's oldest surf comp. Mar.
**Newcastle Jazz Festival** Three-day festival attracting jazz artists and enthusiasts from across the country. Aug.
**Darby Street Fair** A funky way to celebrate the arrival of spring. Oct.

## ③ Hunter Valley wineries (1–2 days)
Cradled in the heart of the Hunter Valley, Pokolbin has no town of its own to speak of, but is home to a ravishing mix of large and small wineries, lovely accommodation and eateries. Vineyards radiate out into

Queens Wharf, Newcastle

Hunter Valley vineyard

the horizon, with the Brokenback Range providing breathtaking vistas. The nearest town is Cessnock, which is refreshingly down to earth. Attractions are limited, but its accommodation and food options are cheaper than around Pokolbin.

## Further information

[i] **Vintage Hunter Wine Country & Visitors Centre** 455 Wine Country Dr, Pokolbin; (02) 4990 4477; www.winecountry.com.au
**Hunter Valley Gardens** Broke Rd, Pokolbin; (02) 4998 7600; www.hvg.com.au
**Bicycle hire: Grapemobile Bike Hire** Cnr McDonalds Rd & Palmers La, Pokolbin; 0418 404 049.
**Taxis: Cessnock Radio Cabs** (02) 4990 1111.

## Tours

**Local Wine Tours** 1800 801 012; www.rovercoaches.com.au
**Shadows Wine Tours** 43 Congewai St, Kearsley; (02) 4990 7002.
**Hunter Vineyard Tours** (02) 4991 1659 or 1418 497 451; www.huntervineyardtours.com.au
**Hunter Valley Aviation** Terminal Bld, Cessnock Airport, Main Rd, Pokobin; (02) 4991 6500; www.huntervalleyaviation.com
**Hunter Valley Ballooning** Cessnock; (02) 8755 3100 or 1300 791 793; www.adrenalin.com.au
**Pokolbin Trail Rides** Hunter Resort, Hermitage Rd, Pokolbin; 0411 110 126.

## Wineries and breweries

**Bimbadgen Estate** Winner of the 2007 Tourism Australia Wineries award. 790 McDonalds Rd, Pokolbin; (02) 4998 7585; daily 10am–5pm; www.bimbadgen.com.au
**Small Winemakers Centre** Supporting 10 local winemakers who don't have their own cellar doors. McDonalds Rd, Pokolbin; (02) 4998 7668; daily 10am–5pm; www.smallwinemakerscentre.com.au
**Allandale Winery** Try its excellent chardonnay as you drink in the fantastic views of the Brokenback Range. Lovedale Rd, Pokolbin; (02) 4990 4526; Mon–Sat 9am–5pm, Sun 10am–5pm; www.allandalewinery.com.au
**Drayton's Family Wines** If you're after something laidback with a lovely family feel, you'll love it here. Oakley Creek Rd, Pokolbin; (02) 4998 7513; Mon–Fri 8am–5pm, Sat–Sun 10am–5pm; tours Mon–Fri 11am; www.draytonswines.com.au
**Hermitage Road Cellars & Winery** A bit impersonal, but the biggest commercial winery in the area. The advantage of tasting here is the informative wine tour, plus a 'wine school'. Hunter Resort, Hermitage Rd, Pokolbin; (02) 4998 777; daily 9am–5pm; tours daily 9am, 11am & 2pm; wine school daily 9am; www.hunterresort.com.au
**Lindemans** One of the best-known names and most established wineries in the region, plus it has a museum. McDonald's Rd, Pokolbin; (02) 4998 7766; daily 10am–5pm; www.lindemans.com
**Tyrrell's Family Vineyard** Near the Brokenback Range is the oldest of the family-run vineyards. Broke Rd, Pokolbin; (02) 4998 7509; Mon–Sat 8am–5pm; tours Mon–Sat 1.30pm; www.tyrrells.com.au
**Bluetongue Brewery** Hunter Resort Country Estate, Hermitage Rd, Pokolbin; (02) 4998 7777; daily 10am–late; www.bluetonguebrewery.com.au

## Where to eat

**The Hoot Cafe** [S] Listen to soul music in this sun-drenched cafe. Great food and coffee. 115 Vincent St, Cessnock; (02) 4991 2856; Mon–Fri 8am–4pm, Sat 8am–1pm.
**Amicos** [S] You won't be disappointed with its cheap, delicious meals. 138 Wollombi Rd, Cessnock; (02) 4991 1995; daily from 6pm.
**Gold Rock Cafe** [S][S] Light meals; decide for yourself whether they make 'the best coffee in the Hunter Valley'. Oakvale Wines, 1596 Broke Rd, Polkobin; (02) 4998 7088; Thur–Mon 10am–4pm.
**Cafe Enzo** [S][S] Set in a cosy courtyard, this is the perfect pit stop for coffee and a snack. Peppers Creek Antiques, Broke Rd, Pokolbin; (02) 4998 7233; Wed–Sun 10am–5pm.
**Il Caccitore** [S][S][S] **TOP TREAT!!** Superior northern Italian nosh to soak up the magnificent wine … and we haven't even mentioned their chocolate pasta! Hermitage Lodge, cnr McDonalds & Gilliards rds; (02) 4998 7639; lunch Sat–Sun, dinner daily.

## Where to stay

**Hunter Valley YHA** ★★ Dorm $28.50–$31.50, double or twin $73.50 100 Wine Country Dr, Nulkuba; (02) 4991 3278.
**Caledonia Hotel** ★★ Single $35, double or twin $55 110 Aberdare Rd, Cessnock; (02) 4990 1212.
**Belford Country Cabins** ★★ 2-bedroom cabin (weeknights) $50 659 Hermitage Rd, Pokolbin; (02) 6574 7100; www.belfordcabins.com.au

## Events

**Hunter Valley Vintage Festival** Ecstatic gathering to sample the best fermented grapes. Feb.
**Opera in the Vineyards** Exactly what it sounds like, only better. Oct.
**Jazz in the Vines Festival** Great opportunity for non opera lovers to experience music among the vineyards. Oct.

# QUEENSLAND

## CONTENTS

Brisbane 44

TOP REGIONS:

Gold Coast and the hinterland 54

Cairns, the Tropics and the
   Great Barrier Reef 58

Sunshine Coast 63

Fraser Island and the coast 66

### Visitor information

Tourism Queensland
(07) 3535 3535; www.tq.com.au

*i*

## FAST FACTS

**Length of coastline** 6973 km

**Number of islands** 1955

**Sunniest town** Townsville (average
   300 days of sunshine per year)

**Most remote town** Birdsville

**Major industries** sugar and mining

**Best beach** Whitehaven Beach,
   Whitsunday Island

**Local beer** XXXX

**Most famous person** Steve Irwin the 'Crocodile Hunter'

As a holiday destination, you don't get much better than the sun-filled utopia that is Queensland. Its tropical coastal lands offer a series of resplendent beaches, exuding a relaxed charm that will leave you desperately craving to call this place home. Winding its way up the rich coast is the brilliant underwater landscape of the Great Barrier Reef, which no photo or TV footage can really do justice. Hinterland areas protect World Heritage forests, while inland, great tracts of farm and grazing land dominate the state's outback. The Gold Coast has a vibrant beachside community, while Brisbane is a great mix of cosmopolitan living, urban landscapes and historic buildings. The tourism campaign really did get it right – 'Where else but Queensland?'

## Top region highlights

### Great Barrier Reef

The world's largest reef has brilliant coral seascapes, a vast population of sea creatures and around 900 islands, 22 of which cater to visitors. p. 61

### Surfers Paradise

The pulsating heart of the Gold Coast is strewn with high-rise buildings and a festive party atmosphere all year round. p. 55

### Australia Zoo

Made famous by the 'Crocodile Hunter', Steve Irwin, this zoo is now over 20 ha, showcasing many of Australia's native animals. p. 63

### Daintree National Park

One of the most revered parks in Australia, with rainforest-clad mountains creating a tropical wonderland to explore. p. 62

### Fraser Island

A World Heritage island with massive sand dunes, lakes and rainforests; nearby Hervey Bay plays host to masses of humpback whales migrating from Antarctica each spring. p. 66

## Other regions worth a look

### Whitsunday Islands

With 74 islands – only 8 of which are inhabited – this tropical paradise is very close to heaven on earth. A great place for walking, scuba diving and sailing.

### Townsville

Queensland's second-largest city is a thriving urban centre with some impressive dining, nightlife and museums.

### Cape York

One of Australia's final frontiers, the cape is home to some of the country's finest Aboriginal rock art, while the national park wildlife is spectacular.

### South Burnett

This comfortable slice of rural Queensland invites you along the scenic Barambah Wine Trail. Go to Nanango or Kilkivan to fossick for gold and see historic timber towns like Blackbutt and Yarraman.

### Darling Downs

This agricultural district has some of the most picturesque gardens in all of Australia. National parks preserve a native landscape of eucalypt forests and granite outcrops.

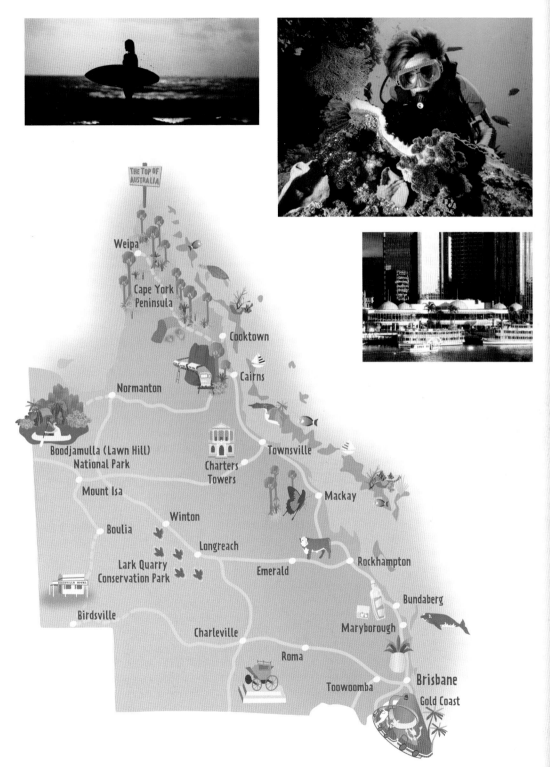

THE TOP OF
AUSTRALIA

Weipa

Cape York
Peninsula

Cooktown

Normanton

Cairns

Boodjamulla (Lawn Hill)
National Park

Townsville

Charters
Towers

Mount Isa

Mackay

Winton

Boulia

Longreach

Lark Quarry
Conservation Park

Emerald

Rockhampton

Bundaberg

Birdsville

Maryborough

Charleville

Roma

Brisbane

Toowoomba

Gold Coast

# Brisbane

Surrounded by lush, subtropical vegetation with gorgeous weather and a tranquil ambience, you might be surprised that Brisbane is also a cultural mecca brimming with diversity. The city offers a fantastic live music scene and a vibrant market culture, for those who love to pick up a bargain. There are also spectacular views of Brisbane River and numerous waterside activities, including South Bank (where else can you find a beach right in the centre of a city?) If you want it, Brisbane's got it.

## Visitor information centre

Brisbane Visitor Information Centre Cnr Albert & Queen sts, Queen Street Mall; (07) 3006 6200 or (07) 3006 6290; www.ourbrisbane.com

## Climate

Queensland isn't called the 'Sunshine State' for nothing. With an average of 300 days of sunshine each year, the south-east corner has (according to many) the most liveable climate in the country. Summers are hot and steamy in the high 20s or low 30s; make sure you pack a hat and sunscreen, as Australia's sun is much harsher than in other areas of the world. The hot days often build up to spectacular thunderstorms, and Brisbane's annual rainfall of approximately 1400 mm occurs mostly in summer. In winter the average temperature is 21°C, although evenings can be a bit cool, so make sure you pack at least one warm top.

# Top attractions

## Conrad Treasury Casino
At the top end of Queen Street Mall is Conrad Treasury Casino, one of Brisbane's most spectacular buildings. It was built as the Treasury Building between 1885 and 1928, but is now a top nightspot housing restaurants, bars and live bands nightly. Perhaps it is the popularity of this casino that has lead to a local name for the city – Brisvegas. George St; daily 24 hrs; admission free.

## ANZAC Square
Located at the other end of Queen Street Mall, ANZAC Square is a magnet for office workers eating their lunch and the pigeons who subsequently devour the leftovers. The square's main attraction, the Shrine of Remembrance, honours Australian soldiers who died in World War I. A World War II shrine (open Monday–Friday), in the pedestrian tunnel behind the square, displays unit plaques, honour rolls and a mosaic made from hand-cut glass enamels and soils taken from official WW II cemeteries. Ann & Adelaide sts, opposite Post Office Square.

## Museum of Brisbane (MoB)
Located on the ground floor of Brisbane City Hall, the Museum of Brisbane (or 'MoB') is relatively new on the scene, but is nothing short of spectacular. The museum has five exhibition spaces incorporating Brisbane's history, design, craft and the visual arts. The MoB Store is a good spot to pick up something created by one of Brisbane's talented writers, artists or musicians. Ground floor, Brisbane City Hall, King George Square, between Ann & Adelaide sts; daily 10am–5pm; general admission free.

## St John's Cathedral
This striking example of Gothic Revival architecture has the only fully stone-vaulted ceiling in Australia, as well as extensive woodcarvings by Queensland artists, fossiliferous marble 350 million years old and beautiful stained-glass windows. Next to the cathedral is the Deanery, built in 1850 and formerly the residence of Queensland's first governor, Sir George Bowen. Free tours are conducted Monday–Saturday 10am–2pm and most Sundays at 2pm. 373 Ann St; (07) 3835 2248; daily 9.30am–4.30pm.

## Customs House
Built in 1889 and beautifully restored, this magnificent building served as the city's Customs House for almost a century. Now part of the University of Queensland, it is set right on the edge of the Brisbane River and includes an art gallery and brasserie with waterfront tables. There are free guided tours on Sundays 10am–4pm. 399 Queen St; (07) 3365 8999; Mon–Fri 9am–4pm; admission free.

## Eagle Street Pier
On the riverfront just south of the Riverside Centre, Eagle Street Pier has some of Brisbane's best restaurants. If you prefer something more casual, grab some fish and chips and sit on the boardwalk, enjoying the spectacular views of the river and the landmark Story Bridge, the largest steel cantilever bridge in Australia (for information on climbing Story Bridge, see Tours and activities). On Sundays the Eagle Street Pier Markets, together with the Riverside Markets, create a vibrant atmosphere (for more information, see Markets).

## QUT Gardens Cultural Precinct
Queensland University of Technology's Gardens Cultural Precinct encompasses Old Government House, the QUT Arts Museum and the Gardens Theatre.

Old Government House was home to the Queensland governor for most of the state's first 50 years. This graceful sandstone building, built in 1860, is open Monday–Friday and guided tours are available; phone (07) 3864 8005.

QUT Arts Museum is housed in a 1930s Neoclassical building and exhibits a permanent collection and changing contemporary works. Pieces by QUT students are also displayed. The Arts Museum is open Tuesday–Friday 10am–5pm, Wednesday 10am–8pm and Saturday–Sunday noon–4pm. General admission is free.

The cultural venue of the Gardens Theatre has shows by QUT students and visiting international and Australian theatre companies. 2 George St; visit www.precinctshows.qut.edu.au for details of what's on.

## Roma Street Parkland
The world's largest subtropical parkland includes landscaped gardens, Queensland's largest public art collection and hundreds of unique plants. Meander through the parkland on the network of pathways (brochures for self-guided themed walks available) or take up a game of frisbee on the open Celebration Lawn. There's a cafe and barbecue facilities. 1 Parkland Blvd; Spectacle Garden open dawn–dusk.

## Streets Beach, South Bank
This sandy beach right in the centre of Brisbane has a crystal-clear lagoon that contains enough water to fill an Olympic swimming pool five times over. Surrounded by tropical palms, the area is patrolled by qualified lifesavers. Barbecue and covered picnic areas have views over the Brisbane River to the CBD.

Streets Beach

## Lone Pine Koala Sanctuary
Lone Pine is the world's largest koala sanctuary with over 130 koalas. Visitors can hold these cuddly cuties; hand-feed kangaroos and emus; and view wombats, Tasmanian devils and other species in their natural environment. There are informative

## Getting around

Brisbane's public transport is comprehensive and efficient. Trains, buses and ferries cater for all needs and a couple of bus routes are designed specifically for visitors (see below). A boat trip on the Brisbane River is a must. Plenty of tours are available to riverside tourist attractions and there is an excellent commuter ferry and catamaran (CityCat) service. You can buy a daily ticket and travel on the CityCats all day, from the University of Queensland in St Lucia to Brett's Wharf downriver. The Cats travel at high speed; standing on the deck with the wind in your hair is the best way to see Brisbane!

For drivers, Brisbane has well-signed, well-maintained roads, but it's not an easy city for the first-time visitor to negotiate. The city's phenomenal growth in recent times has resulted in a criss-crossing network of major motorways on the doorstep of the city centre and some significant new roadwork projects. In the centre itself, there are many one-way streets. To make matters more confusing, the Brisbane River twists its way through the city and suburbs. An up-to-date road map and some careful route planning at the beginning of each day is a good idea.

Public transport TransInfo (bus, ferry, CityCat and rail) 13 1230

Motoring organisation RACQ 13 1905; roadside assistance 13 1111

Car rental Avis 13 6333; Budget 13 2727; Hertz 13 3039; Thrifty 1300 367 227

Bus tours City Sights bus tours and The Loop (free bus circling the CBD) 13 1230

Taxis Black and White Cabs 13 1008; Yellow Cabs 13 1924

Bicycle hire Brisbane Bicycle Sales and Hire (07) 3229 2433, 87 Albert St; Valet Cycle Hire 0408 003 198, delivery to your hotel; Riders (07) 3846 6200, Shop 9, Little Stanley St, South Bank

talks daily, when you might get the chance to hold a snake, and a sheep dog show. The sanctuary is accessible by bus, or you can catch Mirimar's Wildlife Cruise (see Tours and activities). Jesmond Rd, Fig Tree Pocket; daily 8.30am–5pm; admission fee applies.

## Other attractions worth a look

**Commissariat Stores** Visit one of Brisbane's oldest buildings that was built by convicts. 115 William St; (07) 3221 4198; museum open Tue–Sun; admission fee applies.

**City Botanic Gardens** Chill in these lush surrounds, right in the heart of the CBD. Gardens Point, Alice St.

**Parliament House** Tour the inner sanctum of Queensland politics. Cnr George & Alice sts; (07) 3406 7562; tours daily Mon–Fri 9am–4.15pm; admission free.

**Old Windmill** Brisbane's oldest convict-built structure, overlooking the gorgeous Roma Street Parkland. Wickham Tce; not open to the public.

**Queensland Performing Arts Centre** Catch an opera, see experimental theatre, or visit the QPAC museum. Stanley St, South Bank; visit www.qpac.com.au for details of what's on; (07) 3840 7444 for details of guided tours; admission to gallery free.

**Queensland Museum** Check out the extensive natural history collection, or have fun at the interactive Sciencentre experience. Cnr Grey & Melbourne sts, South Bank; (07) 3840 7555; daily 9.30am–5pm; general admission free.

**Queensland Maritime Museum** Everything and anything you wanted to know about the Queensland seas – relics, memorabilia and exhibits galore. Sidon St, South Bank; daily 9.30am–4.30pm; admission fee applies.

**Grey Street Precinct** A majestic tree-lined boulevard, between South Bank and South Brisbane, full of exhibition halls, cafes and a cinema complex.

**Newstead House** Brisbane's oldest residential building. Feel the true essence of the quintessential Australian home in the 1850s. Newstead Park, Breakfast Creek Rd, Newstead; Mon–Fri 10am–4pm, Sun 2pm–5pm; admission fee applies.

**XXXX Brewery** The classic Australian icon. Take the tour and sample some of the country's best beer. Cnr Black & Paten sts, Milton (just off Milton Rd); (07) 3361 7597; Mon–Fri 10am–4pm, additional tour Wed 6pm; admission fee applies (bookings for tours are recommended).

## Where to eat

**Eagle Street Pier** Elegant fine dining and classic river views.
Our favourite: **Cha Cha Char** 😊😊😊 TOP TREAT!! ♡ Internationally renowned, Cha Cha Char is one of Brisbane's finest restaurants and, as the name suggests, it is one of the best places in Australia to get a steak. Shop 5, Plaza Level, Eagle Street Pier; (07) 3211 9944; lunch Mon–Fri 11.30am–5pm; dinner daily 5–11pm; www.chachachar.com.au

**East End** Centred on Adelaide Street, with some of the city's best and most innovative restaurants.
Our favourite: **Ciccio's Pasta Bar** 😊😊 ♡ For some simple and delicious Italian dishes without the hefty price tag, look no further. Great pizza, pasta and chicken. 471 Adelaide St; (07) 3831 9499; Tue–Fri noon–3pm & 6–10pm, Sat 6–10pm, Sun 6am–6pm.

**South Bank Parklands** Contemporary fine dining, outdoor cafes and easy takeaways in superb surrounds.
Our favourite: **River Canteen** 😊😊 ♡ More of an up-market eatery specialising in Modern Australian cuisine with spectacular views along the Brisbane River. If you're on a budget, hit this place at breakfast time among the birds and fresh riverside air. The Boardwalk, South Bank Parklands; (07) 3846 1880; Mon–Sat 11am–10pm, Sun 7.30am–10pm; www.rivercanteen.com.au

Eagle St Pier

**West End** Perfect for brunch, cosmopolitan dishes and delicious cocktails. Our favourite: **The Forest** 🟢 🌸 Travelling doesn't have to mean eating junk food (if you don't want it to). Regenerate your body with some organic and vegan food using only Australia's freshest produce. Sample some organic wine and beer while you're at it. 124 Boundary St; (07) 3846 6181; Tue–Wed & Sun 11am–10pm, Thur–Sat 11am–late; www.theforest.com.au

## Other places to eat
**Queen Street Mall Food Court** 🟢 ♡ From noodles to sushi to kebabs, pick up a cheap eat for under $10. Queen Street Mall; Mon–Thur 9am–5.30pm, Fri 9am–9pm, Sat 9am–5pm, Sun 10am–5pm.
**Pancakes at the Manor** 🟢 ♡ The perfect pick-me-up after a long night of partying. Sweet and savoury pancakes, chicken crepes, and even burgers and steaks. 18 Charlotte St; (07) 3221 6433; daily 24 hrs; www.pancakemanor.com.au
**Teppanyaki Time** 🟢 ♡ Very cheap Japanese cuisine at its best. QUT Gardens Point Campus, Level 3, 2 George St; (07) 3864 1487; Mon–Fri 10am–6.30pm.
**Bar Merlo** 🟢 ♡ The perfect place for a quick coffee and a cheap sandwich, panini or gourmet pizza. Bar Merlo has three other locations: at Market Street, Queen Street and at QUT. 239 George St; (07) 3221 8789; Mon–Fri 6.30am–6pm.
**Sultan's Kitchen** 🟢🟢 🌸 Arguably the best Indian cuisine in town, this establishment places a high emphasis on authenticity, spicy meats and delectable curry dishes. Try the Lamb Rogan Josh, or hit up the vindaloo. 163 Given Tce, Paddington; (07) 3368 2194; lunch Fri noon–2pm; dinner daily 6–10pm; www.sultanskitchen.net.au
**Breakfast Creek Hotel** 🟢🟢 🌸 The Creek is known for one thing – steak. Part of the 'Brekky Creek experience' is to line up and select your own superbly tender, aged fillet from the chilled cabinet and

have it char-grilled in an open kitchen in front of you. 2 Kingsford Smith Dr, Albion; (07) 3262 5988; lunch Mon–Wed 11.30am–2.30pm, Thur–Sun 11.30am–3pm; dinner Mon–Fri 5.30–9.30pm, Sat 5–9.30pm, Sun 5–8.30pm; www.breakfastcreekhotel.com

# Out and about
## Cinemas
**Brisbane City Myer Centre** The Myer Centre, Cnr Elizabeth & Albert sts; (07) 3027 9999.
**Brisbane City Regent** 167 Queen St; (07) 3027 9999.
**Dendy George Street** (art house selection) 346 George St; (07) 3211 3244.
**Dendy Paradise** (art house selection) Hercules St, Hamilton; (07) 3137 6000.
**Eldorado Indooroopilly** (Brisbane landmark) 141 Coonan St, Indooroopilly; (07) 3878 4993.
**Australian Cinematheque, Gallery of Modern Art** (international, art house selections) Stanley Pl, South Bank; (07) 3840 7303.
**South Bank 5 Cinema Complex** 167 Grey St, South Brisbane; (07) 3846 0289.
**AMC Redcliffe** Peninsula Fair Shopping Centre, 272 Anzac Ave, Redcliffe; (07) 3889 3722.

## Live music
**Tongue and Groove** The basement bar offers a vast range of live, local, interstate and international acts. An eclectic mix of reggae, jazz, blues, funk and urban beats will gets your hips shaking and your soul soaring. 63 Hardgrave Rd, West End; (07) 3846 0334; Tue 5.30pm–late, Wed–Sun 7am–late; www.tng.net.au
**Fridays Riverside** What better way to spend a balmy evening in Brissy town than sucking down an amber ale, listening to a great local band on the riverside, with the picturesque Story Bridge as your backdrop? A great mesh of live local acts and DJs spinning everything from acid jazz to urban grooves. 123 Eagle St;

(07) 3832 2122; restaurant Mon 5pm–late, Tue 5–10pm, Wed 7am–midnight, Thur–Sat 7.30am–midnight, Sun 7.30am–midnight; bar generally open later; www.fridays.com.au
**Brisbane Jazz Club** Formed in 1972, this club provides opportunities for amateur and professional jazz musos to get together and jam. Traditional and mainstream jazz is featured on Saturday nights, and big band dance music on Sunday nights. Watch out for the sloping dance floor, which used to be a boat ramp. Cover charge from around $15. 1 Annie St, Kangaroo Point; (07) 3391 2006; Fri–Sat 6.30–11.30pm, Sun 5–10pm; www.brisbanejazzclub.com.au
**Jazz & Blues Bar** One of Brisbane's best jazz joints lies on the ground floor of the Holiday Inn hotel. A mixed crowd of oldies and younger types. If you love your jazz, this is the place to be. Local and international acts perform seven nights a week. It only seats 30 people, so don't dawdle. Ground floor, Holiday Inn, Roma St; (07) 3238 2222; Wed, Thur, Sat 6pm–late, Fri 4pm–late.

## Pubs and bars

**Belgian Beer Cafe Brussels** The ideal place for a lazy afternoon, or maybe a place to recover after a long day's walk around the city. A wide range of boutique and imported beers that will quench whatever ails ya (pardon the pun!). Cnr Mary & Edward sts; (07) 3221 0199; daily noon–10pm; www. belgianbeercafebrussels.com.au

**Greystone Bar and Cellar** Greystone is a modern bar set in the heart of South Bank's vibrant cafe precinct. Enjoy outstanding views of the parklands as you sip on a cocktail. 166 Grey St (Little Stanley St); (07) 3846 6990; daily noon–late; www.greystonebar.com.au

**Lychee Lounge** This Asian-themed bar and restaurant is fitted with all the trimmings, the most impressive being a samurai-inspired bar. The mixologists take their job very seriously, and offer cocktails drawing on fresh ingredients, exotic spirits and stunning flavour combinations. 2/94 Boundary St, West End; (07) 3846 0544; daily 3pm–2am; www. lycheelounge.com.au

**The Exchange Hotel** With a young, urban, university vibe, the Exchange Hotel offers

much in the way of fine drinking. Rare wines, premium beers and specialised spirits are the highlights. 131 Edward St; (07) 3229 3522; Sun–Wed 10am–9pm, Thur 10am–2am, Fri–Sat 10am–late; www.theexchange. com.au

**One Degree Bar and Dining** If you feel like treating yourself, grab a cocktail at this swish, up-market bar. Try the unique 'Kiss the Boys Goodbye' concoction, a $14 cocktail made with Rémy Martin V.S. Grand Cru cognac, Gordon's sloe gin, lemon juice and shaken with egg white. Yum! Lower Level Eagle Street Pier, 1 Eagle St; (07) 3229 9915; Mon–Fri 7am–1am, Sat 5pm–1am, Sun 8am–1am; www.onedegree.net.au

**The Paddington Tavern** A quieter space for those who actually like to have a conversation. With a beer garden and live music, the 'Paddo' is perfect for a chilled night out. Located next to the Sit Down Comedy Club, if you feel like a laugh. 186 Given Tce, Paddington; (07) 3369 0044; Sun–Thur 10am–10pm, Fri–Sat 10am–late.

**The Caxton** This pub is one of the oldest licensed establishments in all of Queensland, dating back to 1884. Enjoy jazz on Sundays, or the rugby on the TV screens on Monday nights. 38 Caxton St, Petrie Terrace; (07) 3369 5544; Sun–Thur 10am–2am, Fri–Sat 10am–5am; www.caxton.com.au

**Gilhooley's Irish Pub** The original Irish-themed pub in Brisbane. With pine furniture scattered all over the joint, and traditional Irish music in the background, you'll be hard-pressed not to order a Guinness. Football and pizza on Monday nights. Cnr Albert & Charlotte sts; (07) 3229 0672; meals Mon–Fri 10am–6pm, Sat–Sun 11am–7pm; pub open late; www.gilhooleys.com

**Girder Bar** With postmodern designs and one of the best wine lists in town, Girder is a hip place to visit if you feel like escaping the city's hustle and bustle. Be prepared to pay a little more for the quality wines. 36 Vernon Tce, Teneriffe; (07) 3257 0402; Tue–Fri 4pm–midnight, Sat 2pm–midnight, Sun 2–10pm; www.girder.com.au

**The Regatta** This huge, recently renovated riverside pub offers various bars, as well as a restaurant area. The CityCat stops right at its doors, so transport back to the city is easy. 543 Coronation Dr, Toowong; (07) 3871 9595; Mon–Wed 7am–10pm, Thur–Sat 7am–3am, Sun 7am–midnight; www.regattahotel. com.au

**The Island Party Boat** Enjoy the sights of the city as you down margaritas on the party deck, along with finger food and a good old barbecue. Bookings essential. 1 Riverside Rd, Queensland Culture Centre cruise terminal; (07) 3255 3455; www.theisland.net.au

## Nightclubs

**Chibar** Chibar is a sensory explosion, a dual-level bar/nightclub where your fantasies become reality. Dance the night away as you watch the rooms magically morph into a different colour. A major trip! 383 Adelaide St; (07) 3831 7529; Sat–Sun 9pm–5am; www.chibar.com.au

## Where to shop

**Queen Street Mall, City** Brisbane's major shopping precinct, with ten malls and arcades including the Myer Centre department store, Brisbane Arcade, MacArthur Central and Wintergarden. Everything you'll ever need for retail therapy.

**Little Stanley Street, South Bank** Edgy designer fashion, homewares and gifts.

**Paddington** Antiques and boutique homewares on Latrobe and Given terraces.

**Toowong Shopping Centre** Medium-sized mall with a department store, specialty shops and fresh-food market.

**Indooroopilly Shopping Centre** Enormous mall with over 250 specialty shops, major department stores, a gym and a 16-cinema complex.

**Stones Corner** Factory outlets only 15 minutes south of the CBD.

**Chermside Shoppingtown** Huge mall in Brisbane's north with a department store, a 16-cinema complex and hundreds of specialty shops.

**Livewire Bar** More for an older crowd, Livewire is a party that never sleeps. Open 24 hours a day, seven days a week, the club boasts free live entertainment that will surely please those who love tunes from the 80s and 90s. Level 1, Treasury Casino, Queen St; (07) 3306 8888; daily 24 hrs; www.conrad.com.au/treasury/bars/livewire_default.htm

**Jorge** This place can best be described as a funky but friendly cocktail lounge. A stand-out feature is the Sugar Suite, a restored ballroom now equipped with a marble bar and stunning ottomans. 183 George St; (07) 3012 9121; Tue–Fri 11am–late, Sat–Sun 4pm–late; www.jorge.com.au

**Uber** This opulent dance club has a huge range of cocktails. Explosive live performances in the front room, and free entry. 100 Boundary St, West End; (07) 3846 6680; Wed–Sun 4pm–late; www.uber.net.au

## Performing arts

**Brisbane Powerhouse** 119 Lamington St, New Farm; (07) 3358 8622.
**La Boite Theatre Company Roundhouse**

Theatre, 6–8 Musk Ave, Kelvin Grove (box office, Mon–Fri 10am–4pm); (07) 3007 8600.
**Metro Arts** Level 1, Metro Arts, 109 Edward St; (07) 3002 7100.
**QUT Gardens Theatre** 2 George St (next to the City Botanic Gardens); (07) 3138 4455.
**Opera Queensland** Queensland Conservatorium, 16 Russell St, South Bank; (07) 3735 3030.
**Queensland Ballet** Thomas Dixon Centre, Cnr Drake St & Montague Rd, West End; (07) 3013 6666.
**Queensland Performing Arts Centre** Cnr Grey & Melbourne sts; (07) 3840 7444.
**Queensland Theatre Company** 78 Montague Rd, South Brisbane; (07) 3010 7600.
**The Queensland Orchestra** 53 Ferry Rd, West End; (07) 3377 5000.
**Brisbane Arts Theatre** 210 Petrie Tce; (07) 3369 2344.

## Sport

Brisbane's weather is perfect for sport, and Brisbane's stadiums are state-of-the-art. If AFL (Australian Football League) is your passion, you can't miss the Brisbane Lions at their home ground, the Gabba. In summertime, cricket fans can watch the Bulls defend the state's cricketing honour. You'll find the Gabba (known formally as the Brisbane Cricket Ground) in the suburb of Woolloongabba, south of Kangaroo Point.

Rugby League is a way of life in Queensland, culminating in the explosive State of Origin series (May–June). You can watch the Brisbane Broncos, the city's Rugby League team, at the redeveloped Lang Park (also known as Suncorp Stadium), in Milton. Ticket holders enjoy free public transport on match days.

Show your true colours by supporting the Reds, Queensland's Rugby Union team, at their matches, also at Lang Park.

If you're addicted to the speed and excitement of basketball, watch the Brisbane Bullets, the state's National Basketball League team, take on the nation at their home stadium in South Bank's Brisbane Convention and Exhibition Centre.

If you prefer horseracing, check out the venues at Doomben and Eagle Farm. Or for car racing at its loudest and most thrilling, head south for the Gold Coast Indy in October.

## Where to stay

**For further information and reviews on these hostels, please visit www. bugaustralia.com, www.hostelaustralia. com or www.hostelz.com**

**Brisbane City Backpackers** ★★★ Dorm $17–$26, single $59–$85, double $68–$88 380 Upper Roma St; (07) 3211 3211; www.citybackpackers.com

**Palace Embassy** ★★★ Dorm $27, single $75, double $75 Cnr Elizabeth & Edward sts; (07) 3211 2433; www.palacebackpackers. com.au

**Tinbilly** ★★★ Dorm $25–$28, double $89, deluxe king $99 446 George St (cnr Herschel St); 1800 446 646; www.tinbilly.com

**Brisbane City YHA** ★★ Dorm $27.50, double $63.50 92 Upper Roma St; (07) 3236 1004; www.yha.com.au

**Banana Bender Backpackers** ★★ Dorm $25–$27, double or twin $60 118 Petrie Tce; (07) 3367 1157; www.bananabenders.com

**Brisbane Backpackers Resort** ★★ Dorm $23–$27, double or twin $71 110 Vulture St, West End; (07) 3844 9956; www.brisbanebackpackers.com.au

**Brisbane's Homestead** ★★ Dorm $19–$22, double $60 57 Annie St, New Farm; (07) 3358 3538

**Cloud 9 Backpackers Resort** ★★ Dorm $17–$26, single $65, double $69 350 Upper Roma St; 07 3236 2300; www.cloud9backpackers.com.au

**Moreton Bay Backpackers** ★★ Dorm $20, single $55, double $70 45 Cambridge Pde (cnr Stratton Tce), Manly Harbour, Moreton Bay; (07) 3396 3824; www.moretonbaylodge.com.au

**Palace Backpackers** ★★ Dorm $25–$27, single $45, double $65 Cnr Ann & Edward sts; (07) 3211 2433; www.palacebackpackers. com.au

**Somewhere To Stay** ★★ Dorm $19–$25, single $39, double $49 47 Brighton Rd (cnr Brighton Rd & Franklin St), Highgate Hill; (07) 3844 6093; www.somewheretostay.com.au

**Brisbane Holiday Village** ★★★ **TOP TREAT!!** Beautiful holiday villas and cosmopolitan cabins at brilliant rates. Holiday Villa $110–$130, Cosmo Cabin $167–$187 10 Holmead Rd, Eight Mile Plains; (07) 3341 6133; www.brisbaneholiday.com.au

## Tours and activities

**Story Bridge Adventure Climb** For the ultimate panoramic views, take a safe but challenging adventure climb at dawn, during the day, or at night. Climb leaders also offer interesting commentary. Bookings 1300 CLIMBS. www.storybridgeadventureclimb. com.au

**Brisbane River City Cruise, South Bank** Hop aboard the MV *Neptune* for an hour and a half cruise around the city, including commentary on convicts, settlers and present

day landmarks. Bookings 0428 278473. www.rivercitycruises.com.au

**Balloons Over Brisbane** See the sun rise over Brisbane city at dawn from a hot-air balloon, followed by a champagne breakfast. Bookings (07) 3844 6671. www.balloonsoverbrisbane.com.au

**City Sights Bus Tours** Hop on and off these buses, and the CityCat ferry, to see the cultural and historic attractions of Brisbane. There are also City Nights tours departing 6.30pm from City Hall to Mount Coot-tha Lookout. Bookings 13 1230 or collect tickets and brochures from the visitor centre.

**Ghost Tours** Scare yourself silly on one of a variety of serious ghost tours, exploring Brisbane's haunted history led by local horror

historian Jack Sim. Bookings are essential (07) 3344 7265. www.ghost-tours.com.au

**Brisbane CityWalk** Explore Brisbane's green heart on this leisurely, self-guided walking tour that takes in the CBD's highlights via its three main parkland areas – the City Botanic Gardens, South Bank Parklands and Roma Street Parkland. Brochures available from the visitor centre.

**Brisbane Heritage Trails** Take a trip back in time with any one of the Brisbane City Council's Heritage Discovery Walks – excellent self-guided tours of historic districts in the city and its surrounds. Brochures available from the visitor centre and Brisbane City Council (07) 3403 8888.

# Outside the city: Fortitude Valley

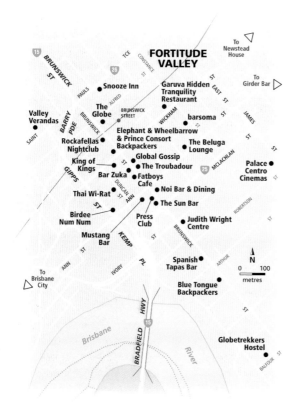

Known simply as the Valley, this cosmopolitan area of inner-city Brisbane is a fascinating mix of seedy history, stylish restaurants, great nightlife and alternative chic. First settled in 1849 by 256 'free' settlers, who arrived aboard the *Fortitude*, the Valley still retains much of its 19th-century heritage. Amid the old buildings and renovated Queenslanders are brand-new high-rise apartment blocks and fashionable inner-city residences, particularly in the riverside precinct of Teneriffe.

Brunswick Street Mall is where crowds flock on weekends for the bohemian Valley Markets. Free bands play in the mall on some Friday and Saturday nights, and the vibe is busy but always relaxed. Enjoy alfresco dining at any time of day here.

James Street, the newest development in the Valley, runs parallel to Brunswick Street and stretches to the neighbouring suburb of New Farm. It is a perfect example of urban renewal, having undergone a transformation from an industrial zone dotted with old houses and the odd church to a vibrant (and some say Brisbane's hottest) lifestyle district.

The Valley also has its own Chinatown, full of wonderful smells, bright colours and delicious food. Elements of feng shui were used in the design of Chinatown Mall on Duncan Street and you can expect to see peaceful tai chi practitioners on weekends.

The Valley is also Brisbane's alternative and artistic hub, home to many private art galleries, artist studios and live music joints. In January 2007, US magazine *Billboard* ranked Brisbane as one of the world's top five 'unlikely' cities to have an exciting music scene. Many Australian greats have had their time in the Valley, including Powderfinger, Pete Murray, and Regurgitator. So, make sure to check out a couple of gigs, because you never know who those musicians will become tomorrow.

## Getting to Fortitude Valley

Fortitude Valley is only 1 km north-east of the CBD, so your best bet is to walk. You can also catch a local bus or train to Brunswick Street Railway Station.

## Where to eat

**Brunswick Street** Stylish restaurants, relaxed pubs, tapas bars, street cafes and food from the world over.
Our favourite: **Fatboys Cafe** 💲 ♡ For a hearty breakfast, it's hard to look past the $4 plate of eggs, bacon, sausage, tomato and toast. And don't be afraid to come back and recharge the batteries with a cheap lunch or dinner of pizza, pasta, seafood or salads galore. 323 Brunswick St; (07) 3252 3789; Sun–Thur 6am–midnight, Fri–Sat daily 24 hrs.

**Emporium** A range of fine-dining options from the relaxed Wagamama to the exotic Mecca Bah.
Our favourite: **Mecca Bah** 💲💲 ♡ A pleasant fusion of Moroccan and other Middle Eastern flavours, you can't go past this delight

for price and something a little different. Great for a group, so you can sample a few different mains and get a true taste of the Middle East in Brisbane 19–21/1000 Ann St; (07) 3252 5299; daily 11am–11pm; www.meccabah.com/bris/

**Central Brunswick** Spanish, Mexican, Indian and Thai cuisine.
Our favourite: **Spanish Tapas Bar** 💲💲 ♡ Experience the culinary delights of Spain at this reasonably priced eatery, serving mouth-watering montaditos and hefty combination platters, which may be too much for one person. Shop 10, 455 Brunswick St; (07) 3257 3138; Sun–Thur 5.30–11pm, Fri–Sat noon–2.30pm & 5.30pm–2am; www.spanishtapasbar.com.au

**Chinatown** Pan-Asian restaurants that are good, cheap and open late, with even better yum cha.
Our favourite: **Thai Wi-Rat** 💲 ♢ This restaurant is proof that cheap prices don't always equate to bad food. For those who like offal, you're in for a treat. If not, there are plenty of other options, including mild soy-braised pork, coconut prawns and a great selection of noodles. TC Beirne Building, Shop 48, 20 Duncan St; (07) 3257 0884; daily 10am–9pm.

**James Street Precinct** Outdoor cafes, restaurants and bars to satisfy appetites for good coffee, fine-dining and innovative cocktails. Definitely a yuppie's heaven.
Our favourite: **The Purple Olive** 💲💲 ♡ This bright, cheerful eatery specialises in

southern European cuisine. Choose your own pasta sauce, or dive into one of the many scrumptious risotto dishes. Set menus also available, as is alfresco dining. 79 James St, New Farm; (07) 3254 0097; Tue–Thur 5.30–10.30pm, Fri–Sun noon–10.30pm.

## Other places to eat in the Valley

**King of Kings** 💲 ♡ With a huge dining hall (200 seats), this place has been serving classic yum cha to the good people of Brisbane for over 20 years. You can also make it a quick and cheap experience by grabbing an entree for as little as $3 or a main for $11. 169 Wickham St, Fortitude Valley; (07) 3852 1122; daily lunch & dinner.
**Birdee Num Num** 💲 ♢ Located in the Bunk Backpackers hostel, this relaxed cafe/bar is a cheap alternative for travellers on the go. Delicious gourmet pizzas from $4. 608 Ann St; (07) 3257 3644; Mon–Wed 2pm–3am, Thu–Fri 2pm–5am, Sat 11.30am–5am, Sun 11.30am–3am; www.birdeenumnum.com.au
**Elephant and Wheelbarrow** 💲💲 ♡ This spacious British-themed pub serves local and imported ales and a bevy of hearty meals fit for a king. Burgers, salads, quiches, schnitzels, all under $15. 230 Wickham St; (07) 3252 4136; daily Sun–Thur 11am–1am, Fri–Sat 11am–3am.
**Garuva Hidden Tranquility Restaurant** 💲💲 ♢ The name of this eccentric eatery hints at its elusive location (look for the big, black double doors and small post-it note). Once inside, enjoy delightful yakitori chicken skewers or Thai beef salad at low communal tables. 324 Wickham St; (07) 3216 0124; Sun–Thur 6pm–midnight, Fri–Sat 6pm–2am (weekend bookings essential); www.garuva.com.au

## Out and about
### Cinemas

**Palace Centro Cinemas** (art house selection) 39 James St; (07) 3852 4488.
**The Globe** (cult films) 220 Brunswick St; (07) 3844 4571.

Fortitude Valley street sign

布蘭斯威克街
BRUNSWICK ST
335–271

**Nissan Moonlight Cinema** (outdoor cinema, Nov–Feb, new release and classic films) New Farm Park, 119 Lamington St, New Farm (next to Brisbane Powerhouse); 1300 551 908

## Live music

**The Zoo** From rock to jazz to reggae, this icon of the Brisbane music scene has played an integral part in developing the careers of the some of the best local talent. Arrive early to avoid the queues. 711 Ann St, Fortitude Valley; (07) 3854 1381; Wed–Thur 8pm–late, Fri–Sat 8.30pm–late; www.thezoo.com.au

**Rics Bar** An absolute Brisbane institution. This soulful joint has live music acts almost every night, from grunge and sweaty alternative acts to sweet balladeers. The place also attracts a very diverse crowd. 321 Brunswick St; (07) 3854 1772; daily 10am–5am; www.ricsbar.com.au

**Tivoli Theatre** The luxurious Art Deco interior makes the Tivoli an inspired venue to see international and high-profile local bands. Catering for all music styles, with two levels of viewing offering optimal vantage points for all. 52 Costin St; (07) 3852 1711; see gig guide for opening hours; www.thetivoli.net.au

**The Troubadour** Right in the middle of the Brunswick Street Mall, this intimate venue is perfect place to chill on the comfy couches with a Corona in hand, as the local acts blow your mind. Level 2, 322 Brunswick St; (07) 3252 2626; see gig guide for opening hours; www.thetroubadour.com.au

**The Globe** During the week, The Globe

The Zoo

screens some of the best classics and cult films. On the weekend, it transforms into a rocking band venue with some of the best local and interstate acts. Enjoy popcorn while watching live music! 220 Brunswick St; (07) 3844 4751; Wed–Fri 7pm–1am, Sat–Sun 8pm–1am; www.globetheatre.com.au

## Pubs and bars

**Press Club** This sleek, up-market venue is home to an attractive yet diverse crowd, and cocktails that will make you weak at the knees. Try this place on a Sunday night, a typically dead time of the week for the Valley. 339 Brunswick St; (07) 3852 1216; Tue–Thur & Sun 5–10pm, Fri–Sat 5pm–5am.

**Fringe Bar** Usually packed on Friday and Saturday nights, this trendy bar is a little more casual than some of the up-market places in the area, and not too pricey either. Six unique rooms and great music. Cnr Ann & Constance sts; (07) 3252 9833; Wed noon–1am, Thur noon–3am, Fri noon–5am, Sat–Sun 3pm–5am; www.fringebar.net

**Bar Zuka** One of the newer cocktail bars in the area, Zuka is fast becoming one of the best nightspots in the Valley. Enjoy the drink specials and joyful ambience. TCB Valley Mall; (07) 3854 0944; Mon–Thur 7am–5pm, Fri–Sun 7am–1am; www.barzuka.com.au

**The Beluga Lounge** On the ground floor of the GPO Hotel, this funky lounge has great decor and an upbeat vibe, perfect for any occasion. 740 Ann St; (07) 3252 1322; Fri 4pm–5am, Sat 7pm–5am; www.gpohotel.com.au

**The Jubilee** The Jubilee Hotel is a unique, heritage-listed pub/bar. With four different rooms, including what they call a 'journo bar' featuring news memorabilia on its walls,

**Where to shop in the Valley**

**Brunswick Street Mall** For up-and-coming designer fashion and innovative chic, collectibles and books, art and trendy homewares, adventure gear and trinkets.

**James Street Precinct** Homeware and furniture stores cater to cashed-up, new inner-city residents.

**TCB** A new shopping precinct that links Chinatown and Brunswick Street Mall, with cutting-edge fashion, a multi-level bar and an energetic 24-hour eatery area called 'Licorice Lane'.

**Emporium** Over 35 specialty retailers offering luxury brand-label fashion, jewellery, wine and food.

**The Valley Markets** Brisbane's alternative markets, with vintage clothing, tarot readings, gifts, old books and an exciting atmosphere. Brunswick St & Chinatown malls; Sat 8am–4pm, Sun 8am–5pm.

**James Street Market** Fresh food and produce along with flowers, nuts and juices. New Farm; Mon–Fri 8.30am–7pm, Sat–Sun 8am–6pm.

grab yourself a pot and sit back and enjoy. 470 St Pauls Tce; (07) 3252 4508; Mon 10am–8pm, Tue 10am–9pm, Wed 10am–10pm, Thur 10am–midnight, Fri 10am–3am, Sat 10am–4am, Sun noon–6pm; www.jubileehotel.com.au

**Mustang Bar** This sports bar is perfect for Yankee travellers feeling a little homesick. Diner-style menus and Budweisers available. 633 Ann St; (07) 3257 4439; Fri 4pm–5am, Sat 2pm–5am; www.mustangbar.com.au

**Dooley's** A classic Irish pub with pool tables and good live music (Irish bands and DJs). If you feel too inebriated to move by the end of the night, they also have accommodation. 394 Brunswick St; (07) 3252 4344; Sun–Thur 11am–10pm, Fri–Sat 11am–late.

**The Sunbar** Formerly the *Daily Sun* newspaper office, the Sunbar is now a modern eatery and bar with retro designs and a sophisticated ambience. There are various rooms with sunken lounges, playing jazz and chilled-out grooves. 367 Brunswick St; (07) 3257 4999; Tue–Fri noon–2am, Sat–Sun 5pm–2am; www.thesunbar.com

**barsoma** In an interesting loft setting, this lush bar caters to all types of clientele. Enjoy the resident DJ playing ambient tunes and dance music. 22 Constance St; (07) 3252 9550; Wed–Sat 6pm–late.

## Nightclubs

**Family** This award-winning nightclub is undoubtedly Brisbane's most popular. Offering four individually styled floors and three genres of dance music, it's an entrancing experience for even the most experienced clubber. 8 McLachlan St; (07) 3852 5000; Fri–Sun 9pm–5am; www.thefamily.com.au

**Monastery** This spacious dance venue has a lot going for it, from its curved wooden bar and leather couches to the stained glass windows lit from behind. Oh, and the DJs clearly know their stuff. 621 Ann St; (07) 3257 7081; Thur–Sun 9pm–5am; www.monastery. com.au

**The Beat** Brisbane's oldest gay nightclub actually attracts gay, lesbian and heterosexual revellers. It must be the great music and casual atmosphere – and the live acts! Arrive before 10.30pm for free entry, and stay long into the night. 677 Ann St; (07) 3852 2661; Mon–Tue, Sun 9pm–5am, Wed–Sat 8pm–5am; www.thebeatmegaclub.com.au

**Empire Hotel** Three levels for three different types of clubbers. The top level has funky raps and beats, the middle level has hardcore house, and the bottom bar has more of a pub feel for those that want some time out. 339 Brunswick St; (07) 3852 1216; Fri–Sat 9pm–4am; www.empirehotel.com.au

**Rockafellas Nightclub** Offering multiple levels of the best club music in town. Check out the 'Temple of Techno' and 'The Hype Room'. 239 Brunswick St; (07) 3252 3177; Mon–Wed 11am–9pm, Fri–Sat 11am–3am, Sun 11am–10pm.

## Performing arts

**Judith Wright Centre** 420 Brunswick St; (07) 3872 9000.

## Where to stay

**Bunk Backpackers** ★★★ Dorm $25–$28, single $70, double or twin $85, triple $100, double deluxe $110, apartment $140–$160 Cnr of Ann & Gipps sts; 1800 682 865; www. bunkbrisbane.com.au

**Prince Consort Backpackers** ★★ Dorm $21–$27, double $60 230 Wickham St; (07) 3257 2252; www.princeconsort.com.au

**Blue Tongue Backpackers** ★★ Dorm $17, double $36 515 Brunswick St; (07) 3254 1984; www.bluetonguebackpackers.com.au

**Valley Verandas** ★★ Dorm $20–$22, single $39, double $60 11 Grenier St, Spring Hill; (07) 3252 1820; www.valleyverandas. com.au

**Kookaburra Inn** ★★ Single $40, double or twin $60 41 Phillips St, Spring Hill; (07) 3832 1303; www.kookaburra-inn.com.au

**Globetrekker's Hostel** ★★ Dorm $19, double or twin $40 35 Balfour St; (07) 3358 1251; www.globetrekkers.net

**Snooze Inn** ★★★ TOP TREAT!! Beautiful B&B style rooms at affordable prices. Single $105, double $125, twin $135 383 St Pauls Tce; 1800 655 805; www.snoozeinn.com.au

## Other suburbs worth visiting

**Milton** Home to the famed XXXX Brewery and legendary sportsground Lang Park.

**Eagle Farm** If you're a bit of a punter or just like the horses, visit the Eagle Farm racecourse.

**Hamilton** Home to some of Queensland most beautiful turn-of-the-century homes. Take a stroll along Bretts Wharf.

**Paddington** A quiet, hilly suburb brimming with some excellent cafes and shopping.

**Redcliffe** A thriving coastal town only 30 minutes north-east of Brisbane.

**Toowong** An eclectic mix of modern apartments and classic old Queenslanders.

**Mount Coot-tha** Forest Park View the superb tropical plants that make up Brisbane Botanic Gardens.

## Visitor information

### Brisbane Airport

Brisbane's international airport is conveniently located approximately 15–20 minutes from the CBD by car.

**Bus** Coachtrans operates bus services between Brisbane Airport and Brisbane Transit Centre, and to the door of all CBD hotels. $9.00 per person to the Transit Centre and $11.00 per person to the hotel door. Bookings (07) 3238 4700 or www.coachtrans.com.au

**Train** Airtrain offers a quick and easy 22-minute trip from Brisbane Airport to the main city area ($12). It also offers scenic rides to the Gold Coast. Bookings (07) 3216 3308 or www.airtrain.com.au

**Taxi** While a more expensive option, a taxi will take you anywhere you want to go. A trip from Brisbane Airport to the CBD will cost you approximately $35.

### Internet cafes

**The HUB** 125 Margaret St, Brisbane; (07) 3229 1119.

**Grand Orbit** Shop 16/17, Level 1, Eagle Street Pier; (07) 3236 1384.

**dotZero** 5/217 Hawken Dr, St Lucia; (07) 3871 0082.

**Global Gossip** 312 Brunswick St, Fortitude Valley; (07) 3229 4033.

**Noi Bar and Dining** (free wireless access) 350 Brunswick St, Fortitude Valley; (07) 3252 4349.

### Hospitals

**For all emergencies, including police, fire, or hospital, dial '000'.**

**Royal Brisbane and Women's Hospital** Cnr Butterfield St & Bowen Bridge Rd, Herston; (07) 3636 8111.

**Princess Alexandria Hospital** 199 Ipswich Rd, Woolloongabba; (07) 3240 2111.

For more detail
see maps
209, 220 & 221

Brisbane

# Gold Coast and the hinterland
## Fun in the sun

From some of the world's best beaches, to hidden hinterland gems, the Gold Coast is undoubtedly Queensland's coastal playground. Highlighted by Surfers Paradise, a tourist holy land, and five thrilling theme parks, once you get here you won't want to leave.

**Number of days to spend in this region: 6–10 days**

## Getting here

The Gold Coast is centrally located and very easy to get to via aeroplane to Gold Coast Airport in Coolangatta. You can organise transport to your specific destinations at the airport.

There are a number of coach services that travel to the Gold Coast with regular services from Brisbane, Byron Bay, Sydney and other major centres. All coaches will arrive at the Surfers Paradise Transit Centre.

If you're travelling from Brisbane, you can catch a Citytrain to Nerang and Robina, and then hop on a Surfside Busline which will take you to Surfers Paradise. The service is also a tourist shuttle.

**Gold Coast Airport** (07) 5589 1201; www.goldcoastairport.com.au

**Surfers Paradise Transit Centre** Cnr Beach & Cambridge rds; (07) 5584 3700.

**Citytrain** (07) 3606 5555; www.citytrain.com.au

**Surfside Buslines** 13 1230; www.surfside.com.au

## ❶ Coolangatta and Burleigh Heads (1–2 days)

If you think you've seen beaches, think again. Coolangatta and Burleigh Heads boast some of the most glorious beaches in the Southern Hemisphere. For surfing, the Snapper Rocks 'Superbank' is one of the world's longest point breaks. It can get crowded at times, but also attracts some world-class surfers.

If you're looking to be one with nature, go no further than the Burleigh Heads National Park. Walk along the 2.8 km Oceanview circuit and take in the wonderous coastal vegetation, rainforest and mangroves. Check out Tumgun Lookout to watch for dolphins and humpback whales (migrating along the coast during winter and spring).

Also in the area is the Currumbin Wildlife Sanctuary, a 20 ha reserve owned by the National Trust. You can see animals roaming free, as well as some sharp teeth at the Crocodile Wetlands.

### Further information

ℹ️ **Coolangatta Visitor Information Centre**
Cnr Griffith & Warner sts; (07) 5536 7765; Mon–Fri 8.30am–5.30pm, Sat–Sun 8am–2pm.
**Burleigh Heads National Park** Gold Coast Hwy (entrance near Tallebudegera Bridge); (07) 5535 3032.
**Currumbin Wildlife Sanctuary** Tomewin St, Currumbin; (07) 5534 1266; www.currumbin-sanctuary.org.au General admission tickets around $30.

### Where to eat

**Eat 'n' Sea Pizza** 💲💲 Award-winning pizza joint with arguably the best Italian pie in Queensland. Dine in or go alfresco and breathe in the fresh sea air. Showcase on the Beach, Marine Pde, Coolangatta; (07) 5536 3477; daily noon–close of dinner; www.earthnseapizza.com.au

### Where to stay

**Coolangatta/Kirra Beach YHA Hostel** ★★ Dorm $25.50, twin or double $55.50 230 Coolangatta Rd, Bilinga; (07) 5536 7644; www.yha.com.au
**Sunset Strip Budget Resort** ★★ Single $50, twin or double $66 199–203 Boundary St, Coolangatta; (07) 5599 5517; www.sunsetstrip.com.au

### Events

**Quiksilver Pro Surfing Championship** The best surfers in the world compete at Snapper Rocks. Mar.
**A La Carte On The Beach** A multicultural food and wine festival on the beach with great cuisine and music. Aug.
**Wintersun** Rock 'n' roll nostalgia fest with Elvis shows and classic cars. Jun.

## ❷ Broadbeach (1 day)

Not far north of Coolangatta is the incomparable Broadbeach. If you've got some room to spare in your backpack (trust me, you'll need it), head to

QUEENSLAND

Pacific Fair, Australia's largest shopping centre. For sand and surfing lovers, mosey on down to Mermaid Beach, the main focus of this small suburb. If you happen to be around for the 1st and 3rd Sunday of each month, you may also want to visit the beachfront markets at Kurrawa Park.

Your visit to Broadbeach could not be complete without taking in the dazzling landmark that is Conrad Jupiters Casino. Even if you're not much of a gambler, visit to experience the awesome, super-charged atmosphere that this 24-hr goliath has to offer.

## Further information
**Conrad Jupiters Casino** Broadbeach Island; (07) 5592 8100; open daily 24 hrs; www.conrad.com.au/jupiters

## Where to shop and eat
**Pacific Fair Shopping Centre** Hooker Blvd; (07) 5581 5100; Mon–Wed, Fri–Sat 9am–5.30pm, Thur 9am–9pm, Sun 9am–5pm; www.pacificfair.com.au

**Oasis Shopping Centre** Broadbeach's main shopping hub and the perfect place to recharge your batteries with a cheap meal. Peruse the cafes on the ground floor, particularly Charlie's and Mario's Italian Restaurant. Broadbeach Mall, Victoria Ave (opposite Jupiters Casino); (07) 5592 3900; daily 7am–midnight; www.oasisshoppingcentre.com

**Kurrawa Park** Old Burleigh Rd; market 1st & 3rd Sun each month.

## Where to stay
**A'Montego Mermaid Beach Motel** Single $90–$100, double $100–$150 2395 Gold Coast Hwy, Mermaid Beach; (07) 5575 1577; www.mermaidbeachmotel.com.au

## Events
**Blues On Broadbeach** Five-day blues music festival attracting some of the best local jazz and blues artists. May.

## ❸ Lamington National Park (1–2 days)
About 35 km west of Broadbeach and Surfers Paradise, this World Heritage-listed national park is definitely worth the detour. At over 20 500 ha, it is renowned for its lush rainforests, picturesque waterfalls and prolific birdlife, crisscrossed by 150 km of well-maintained walking tracks. You can also go abseiling or ride the flying fox at Binna Burra, or take the Tree Top Walk at Green Mountains, along a series of suspension bridges. There are picnic areas if you want to bring your own food, and camping and walking areas at Green Mountains and Binna Burra (camping at the latter organised through Binna Burra Mountain Lodge).

## Further information
ℹ️ **Green Mountain park ranger** PMB4 via Canungra; (07) 5544 0634; Mon–Fri 9am–11am & 1pm–3.30pm.

ℹ️ **Binna Burra park ranger** Beechmont via Nerang; (07) 5533 3584.

**QPWS Smart Service** (for camping bookings) 13 13 04; www.qld.gov.au/camping

**Binna Burra Mountain Lodge** Bookings 1800 074 260; www.binnaburralodge.com.au

**Bus transfer: Allstate Scenic Tours** Level 3, 151 Roma St, Brisbane; (07) 3003 0700. One-way ticket for around $40 from Brisbane.

## Tours
**Bushwacker Ecotours** Departing from Brisbane and the Gold Coast, exciting and educational day and overnight tours. 1300 559 355 or (07) 3871 0057; www.bushwacker-ecotours.com.au

## ❹ Surfers Paradise (3–4 days)
A stone's throw north of Broadbeach is the epicentre of the Gold Coast. 'Surfers' is a utopia characterised by breathtaking beaches, towering apartment buildings and an electricity in the air.

The city is centred around Cavill Avenue Mall, an effervescent pedestrian locale filled with countless cafes and tacky souvenir shops, not to mention a plethora of tourists (if you're not a fan of crowds, stay away in November–December, when drunken final year schoolkids come to let off steam during 'Schoolies Week').

A lingering, early morning stroll on the main beach's golden sands is absolute heaven, followed by alfresco breakfast at one of the open-air eateries. At night, take a stroll down Orchid Avenue, then head to some of the nightclubs, or breeze down The Esplanade and just listen to the gentle waves breaking on the shore.

## Further information
ℹ️ **Surfers Paradise Visitor Information Centre** Cavill Ave; (07) 5538 4419.

**Scooters and moped hire: Moped City** 103 Ferny Ave; (07) 5592 5878; mopedcity.com.au

**Queensland Coastal Car & Bus Rentals:** 3030 Gold Coast Hwy; (07) 5592 0227.

## Activities
**Bungy Australia** A thrilling 14-storey bungee experience. 19 Palm Ave; (07) 5570 4833; www.bungyaustralia.com

**Adrenalin Park** Amusement park with rides including the Slingshot, Vomatron and Skydiver. Cnr Palm Ave & Gold Coast Hwy; (07) 5570 2700; www.funtime.com.au

Beach volleyball at Surfers Paradise

Girl with surfboard at Surfers Paradise

**Cheyne Horan School of Surf** Learn from an Australian surfing champion and other qualified instructors. 1800 227 873; www.cheynehoran.com.au

**Learn to Surf Gold Coast** Fun and safe surfing experience. 0414 393 900; www.australiansurfer.com

**Skydive** Jump from a helicopter, take in the views, and don't have a heart attack! (07) 55462877; www.skydivequeensland.com.au

**JetBoat** Hop aboard one of Gold Coast's most extreme high-speed boats. Titanium Bar, 30–34 Ferny Ave; (07) 5538 8890; www.jetboatextreme.com.au

**Adventure Duck** An icon of Surfers Paradise. See the sights from land and sea in the one vehicle. (07) 5557 8869; www.adventureduck.com

## Where to eat

**Chateau Beachside 💲** Start your day here if you like unlimited bacon, eggs and sausage for only $12.90. That's right, Chateau's famous buffet smorgasbord is bound to fill you with energy for the big day ahead. Cnr The Esplanade & Elkhorn Ave; (07) 5538 1022; daily 7am–10am, noon–8.30pm; www.chateaubeachside.com.au

**Raptis Plaza Food Court 💲** Just off the famed Cavill Avenue Mall, the Raptis Plaza food court has cheap sushi, burgers, or even Thai food. A replica of Michelangelo's David watches over you as you eat. Raptis Plaza, The Esplanade.

## Pubs and bars

**Berlin** This funky, modern bar is a little less busy then some of the other hot spots, which will be a pleasant change. A sophisticated ambience with great local DJs spinning the best tracks. Cnr Cavill Ave & The Esplanade; (07) 5592 5600; Fri–Sun 9pm–5am; www.berlinlounge.com.au

**Cocktails and Dreams** An institution for the travelling backpacking fraternity. Shop 60–62, The Mark, 5–15 Orchid Ave; (07) 5592 1955; Thur–Sun 9pm–5am.

**Shooters** Another favourite for backpackers, this bar really gets fired up when the Indy car racing event comes to the Gold Coast in October. 46 Orchid Ave; (07) 5592 1144; Sun–Wed 5pm–midnight, Thur–Sat 5pm–5am.

## Where to stay

**Sleeping Inn** ★★★ Dorm $25, single, twin or double $66–$76 26 Peninsular Dr; (07) 5592 4455; www.sleepinginn.com.au

**Islander Backpackers Resort** ★★★ Dorm $28, single and double $85 Cnr Beach Rd & Surfers Paradise Blvd; (07) 5538 8000;

www.islander.com.au/backpackers.htm

**Backpackers in Paradise** ★★ Dorm $19–27, double $68 40 Peninsular Dr; (07) 5538 4344; www.backpackersinparadise.com

**Sun 'n' Surf Beachside Backpackers** ★★ Dorm $26, double $70 3323 Gold Coast Hwy; (07) 5592 2363; www.surfnsun-goldcoast.com

**Cheers Backpackers** ★★ Dorm $26, double $68 8 Pine Ave; 1800 636 539; www.cheersbackpackers.com.au

**Surfers Paradise Backpackers Resort** ★★ Dorm $26, apartment $30, double or twin $34 2837 Gold Coast Hwy; (07) 5592 4677; www.surfersparadisebackpackers.com.au

**Couple O' Days Backpackers** ★★ Dorm $22, single $48, double or twin $56, triple $84 18 Peninsular Dr; 1800 646 586; www.coupleodays.com.au

## 5 Southport (1–2 days)

A few kilometres up the road from Surfers is a more hushed beachside spot that is still a hub for fishing, windsurfing, sailing and jet skiing. Southport is also home to Sea World. There are daily dolphin feedings and thrilling rollercoaster rides (the 'Corkscrew' is not recommended for the fainthearted). For those with a current Diving Certificate, you can dive with the sharks at the Shark Bay Reef Lagoon for $90 (20 minutes in water, all equipment provided).

## Further information

**Sea World** Seaworld Dr, Main Beach; (07) 5588 2205; daily 10am–5.30pm; www.seaworld.com.au

## Where to eat

**Goldsteins Bakery and Pie Shop 💲** Grab a classic Aussie meat pie from this award-winning bakery. Cnr Ferry & Benowa rds; (08) 5532 0762; www.goldsteinsbakery.com.au

## Where to stay

**Trekkers Backpackers** ★★★ Dorm $24, twin and double $64 22 White St; (07) 5591 5616; www.trekkersbackpackers.com.au

**Aquarius Backpackers** ★★ Dorm $26–$30, single and twin $65–90 44 Queen St; (07) 5527 1300; www.aquariusbackpackers.com.au

**Surfers Paradise YHA** ★★ Dorm $26.50, twin or double $68.50 70 Seaworld Drive, Main Beach; (07) 5571 1776; www.yha.com.au

## Events

**Gold Coast Big Day Out** National travelling music festival attracting the world's biggest rock bands. Jan.

**Indy Car 300 Grand Prix** The town comes alive for four days as the Indy Cars race around. Oct.

## 6 Mount Tamborine (1–2 days)

Tamborine Mountain is a 552 m plateau that lies on the Darlington

Range. Tamborine National Park comprises 17 small areas, one being Witches Fall. You'll also find nearby villages full of galleries, cafes, antique stores and craft shops.

Not far north is Tamborine Mountain Distillery, one of Australia's smallest distilleries that produces fine-quality alcohol for sale in exquisite hand-painted bottles. You can also visit Mount Tamborine Coffee Plantation, a family owned boutique coffee plantation.

## Further information

ⓘ **North Tamborine Information Centre** Doughty Park, North Tamborine; (07) 5545 1171.

**Tamborine Mountain Distillery** 87–91 Beacon Rd, North Tamborine; (07) 5545 3452; Wed–Sat 10am–3pm; www.tamborinemountaindistillery.com

**Mount Tamborine Coffee Plantation** 64 Alpine Tce, Mount Tamborine; (07) 5545 3856; Sun–Thur 10am–4pm; www.mtcp.com.au

## ❼ Oxenford and Coomera (2–3 days)

Enter the fantasy realm. Get a Gold Coast theme parks pass if you're planning to visit more than one (see information below).

For the serious thrill seekers, Dreamworld should be first on your list. It has what is known as the 'Big 5', five of the most exhilarating and terrifying rides that are sure to make your stomach churn. The Tower of Terror reaches speeds of 160 km/h as you plunge 38 storeys downward. Yikes!

Not to be ignored is Wet 'n' Wild Water World, Australia's premier water theme park. This place gives the word 'waterslide' a whole new meaning.

In stiff competition is Whitewater World, which opened next to Dreamworld in 2006. It has the latest technology in theme park water rides and boasts all four of the 'world's best' water slides.

Last on the list is Warner Bros Movie World, or 'Hollywood on the Gold Coast'. This is Australia's only movie-related theme park, and while the movie star impersonators roaming the grounds can be a bit much, the rides are something special. Don't leave the park without trying the Superman Escapes rollercoaster.

Often lost in the theme park maze is Paradise Country, home of the ultimate Australian farm experience. Feed a kangaroo, cuddle a koala, or watch a whip cracking demonstration.

## Further information

**Dreamworld** Dreamworld Parkway, Coomera; 1800 073 300 or (07) 5588 1111; daily 10am–5pm; www.dreamworld.com.au
**Wet 'n' Wild Water World** Pacific Motorway; Oxenford; (07) 5556 1610; daily 10am–5pm (summer), 10am–4pm (winter); www.wetnwild.com.au
**Whitewater World** Dreamworld Parkway, Coomera; 1800 073 300 or (07) 5588 1111; daily 10am–5pm; www.whitewaterworld.com.au
**Warner Bros Movie World** Pacific Motorway, Oxenford;

(07) 5573 8485; daily 10am–5pm; www.movieworld.com.au
**Paradise Country** Entertainment Rd, Oxenford; (07) 5573 8270; daily 9.30am–4.30pm (depending on different tours); www.paradisecountry.com.au
There are a range of theme park passes available that give you unlimited entry to various parks for a specified time. These passes can be purchased at each park, or online at the websites above, www.theme-parks.com.au or www.ticketmaster.com.au

## Activities

**Zorb Gold Coast** Ever wondered what it would be like to be stuck in the middle of a PVC ball and rolled down a hill? Well, someone did and now we have zorbing on the Gold Coast. Choose between the harness zorb (when you are strapped to the inside of the ball) or the hydro zorb (leaving you free in the middle of the ball with 40 lt of water). It's a weird and wonderful experience that you just have to try. Free transfers from Dreamworld or Coomera Train Station. 232 Old Pacific Hwy, Pimpama; (07) 5547 6300; daily 10am–5pm; www.australia.zorb.com

## ❽ South Stradbroke Island (2 days)

Just over 10 km north of Surfers Paradise is this sandy, somewhat underdeveloped piece of land (a real contrast with the glistening high-rise buildings that typify the Gold Coast). South Stradbroke Island has something different to offer, namely an opportunity to relax in peace and quiet.

At only 22 km long and 2.5 km wide, the island is covered in tropical bushland. No cars are permitted, so you can either walk or cycle to the western side of the island, which is ideal for swimming and watersports, or head east with your surfboard for some impressive swells.

Wildlife is also in abundance, and if you're lucky you may catch a glimpse of a golden wallaby, a marsupial unique to the region.

## Further information

ⓘ **Stradbroke Island Visitor Centre** Ferry Terminal Dunwich; North Stradbroke Island; (07) 3409 9555: daily Mon–Fri 8.30am–4.30pm, Sat–Sun 8.30am–2pm.
**Ferry: Runaway Bay Marina** 247 Bayview St, Runaway Bay; (07) 5577 1400; www.runawaybaymarina.com.au
**Bike hire: Couran Cove Island Resort** John Lund Dr, Hope Harbour; (07) 5509 3000; www.couran-cove.com.au
**Camping** South Stradbroke Island has some great camping areas surrounded by beautiful native fauna and the deep, blue Pacific Ocean. For information on campsites, visit www.gctp.com.au/sthstradbroke/

Zorbing

For more detail see maps 225 & 226

# Cairns, the Tropics and the Great Barrier Reef

# A tropical wonderland

This middle section of Queensland is a region of ancient rainforest, remote islands and a coastline that faces one of the world's natural wonders – the Great Barrier Reef. National parks form part of the World Heritage Wet Tropics, and offer extensive opportunities for fishing, walking and wildlife exploring. At the heart of the area is Cairns, a city with a balanced blend of old Queensland style and modern development.

**Number of days to spend in this region: 12–18 days**

## Getting here: Cairns

Being a large tourist town with an airport, Cairns is fairly easy to reach by plane. Greyhound and Premier Motor Service operate coach services daily from Brisbane. Train services also run from Brisbane through Queensland Rail. Coral Reef Coaches run regular services between Cairns and Port Douglas, Daintree, Cape Tribulation and Cooktown, and is the best and cheapest way to explore the area. A hire car is also a great option, allowing greater flexibility when wanting to tour more remote areas.

**Cairns Airport** (07) 4052 3888 (through Cairns Port Authority); www.cairnsairport.com

**Premier Motor Service** 13 34 10; www.premierms.com.au

**Queensland Rail** 13 16 17; www.qr.com.au

**Coral Reef Coaches** (07) 4098 2800; www.coralreefcoaches.com.au

## [1] Mission Beach (2 days)

Named for the Aboriginal mission established in the area in 1914, this 14 km-long strip of golden sand is fringed by coconut palms and World Heritage-listed wet tropics. Take a stroll on the Ulysses Link Walking Trail, a 1.2 km pathway along the foreshore that features local history, sculptures and mosaics. The Porter Promenade, right near the visitor centre, has woodcarving exhibitions, a rainforest arboretum, and is home to a market on the first Saturday and third Sunday of each month. It'll be hard to ignore the inviting blue water, so hire a kayak (from $50 a day) and paddle out to the nearby islands. You can also go on whitewater rafting tours of the Tully River from here (see information under Wooroonooran National Park below).

### Further information

ℹ **Mission Beach Wet Tropics Visitor Information Centre** Porter Promenade; (07) 4068 7099; daily 9am–5pm; missionbeachtourism.com

**Kayak hire: Coral Sea Kayaking** 2 Wall St, South Mission Beach; (07) 4068 9154; www.coralseakayaking.com

### Where to eat

**Oceania Bar and Grill** $ Hugely inventive dishes and some of the coast's best seafood. You really can't miss with this place. Enjoy the art displays at the main bar while sipping a cocktail. The weekends get lively with DJs and beach parties. 52 Porter Promenade; (07) 4088 6222; Mon,Thur 4pm–late, Fri–Sun 3pm–late.

### Where to stay

**Treehouse YHA** ★★ Dorm $24, double $53 Frizelle Rd (off Bingil Bay Rd), Bingil Bay; (07) 4068 7137; www.yha.com.au

**Mission Beach Backpackers Lodge** ★★ Dorm $18, twin and double $38 28 Wongaling Beach Rd; 1800 688 316; www.missionbeachbackpacker.com

**Sanctuary Retreat at Mission Beach** ★★ Dorm $32.50, single $60.50, twin or double $65 72 Holt Rd, Bingil Bay; 1800 777 012; www.sanctuaryatmission.com

## [2] Wooroonooran National Park: whitewater rafting (1–2 days)

Part of the Wet Tropics World Heritage area, Wooroonooran National Park boasts the two highest mountains in Queensland, wild rivers and spectacular waterfalls.

If you're in the area between April and July, whitewater rafting down the North Johnstone River is an awesome experience, where rapids up to Grade 5 rush with extreme force. Rafters are flown to the starting point by helicopter and traverse the lush wilderness for four days. When

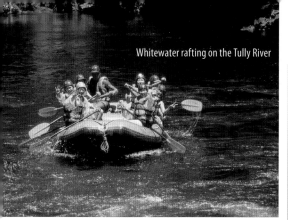
Whitewater rafting on the Tully River

you're not focusing on scary descents, given names like 'Mineshaft' and 'Scary White-faced Monster', you can admire the river, which travels through a gorge at one point and is lined with enormous ferns at another. There might also be stops to visit hidden waterfalls along the way. To preserve the national park, tour numbers are restricted, so make sure to book in advance.

There are also various walking tracks, including one to the spectacular Josephine Falls, and a campground in the Palmerston section (camping permits required and no facilities are provided).

## Further information

ℹ️ **QPWS Cairns Information Centre** 5B Sheridan St, Cairns; (07) 4046 6600; www.epa.qld.gov.au

ℹ️ **QPWS Innisfail Information Centre** Flying Fish Point Rd; (07) 4061 5900; www.epa.qld.gov.au

**Whitewater rafting: RnR Rafting** Experience four unforgettable days of whitewater madness. (07) 4041 9444; www.raft.com.au

### Other whitewater rafting options in the region

**Tully River** Famous for having Australia's highest rainfall, which makes for some pretty ferocious river rapids. It has more than 45 individual rapids up to Grade 4.

**Barron River** Rafting down the Barron River is a half-day expedition, passing through Barron Gorge. The waters have rapids up to Grade 3.

**Russell River** From nail-biting to gentle rapids, the Russell River covers it all.

**Raging Thunder Adventures** Full-day Tully and half-day Barron rafting tours. 52–54 Fearnley St, Portsmith, Cairns; (07) 4030 7990; www.ragingthunder.com.au

**Foaming Fury Tours** Half-day tours of the Barron and Russell rivers. 19–21 Barry St, Cairns; (07) 4031 3460; www.foamingfury.com.au

A specular example is Curtain Fig Tree, near Yungaburra, with aerial roots in a curtain-like formation.

You'll also be blown away by the volcanic lakes and waterfalls, namely Millaa Falls and Zillie Falls. If you're not averse to a bit of darkness and claustrophobia, enter the Crystal Caves, an underground chamber of tunnels lined with crystals, fossils and fluorescent minerals. Head in to the town of Atherton for a bit of culture by hitting the Hou Wang Temple and Chinatown.

If you need a pick-me-up and are happy to take a detour, The Australian Coffee Centre at the Skybury Coffee Plantation, 10 km from Mareeba, is sure to lift your senses. The recently renovated centre features a 54-seat cinema, plantation tours, coffee laboratory and restaurant.

## Further information

ℹ️ **Atherton Tableland Information Centre** 95 Main St; (07) 4091 4222; daily 9am–5pm.

**Crystal Caves** 69 Main St, Atherton; (07) 4091 2365; Mon–Fri 8.30am–5pm, Sat 8.30am–4pm, Sun 10am–4pm; www.crystalcaves.com.au

**Hou Wang Temple and Chinatown** 86 Herberton Rd, Atherton; (07) 4091 6945; daily 10am–4pm.

**The Australian Coffee Centre** Skybury Coffee, Ivicevic Rd, Paddys Green, Mareeba; (07) 4093 2190; daily 9am–5pm; www.skybury.com.au

## Tours

**On The Wallaby** This backpacker hostel offers wildlife canoeing and waterfall tours. They also help you make your own didgeridoo. (07) 4050 0650; www.onthewallaby.com

## Where to stay

**Atherton Travellers Lodge** ★★★ Dorm $20, single $35 and double $45 37 Alice St, Atherton; (07) 4091 3552; athertontravellerslodge.com.au

**On the Wallaby (also runs various tours)** ★★★ Dorm $20, camping $10, double $50 34 Eacham Rd, Yungaburra; (07) 4050 2031; www.onthewallaby.com

## Events

**Yungaburra Folk and Frog Festival** Massive festival celebrating music and cultural understanding. Jam sessions and ethnic food. Oct.

## ❸ Atherton Tableland (1–2 days)

Journeying a little inland from the coast, the Atherton Tableland is something you don't want to miss. The 900 m-high tableland is a productive farming district, thanks to high rainfall in the area. It is this subtropical climate that nurtures the unfortunate yet remarkable strangler fig, which subsumes its host, sending down a curtain of roots.

## ❹ Cairns (3–4 days)

This tropical destination is the proud custodian of one of the world's natural treasures – the Great Barrier Reef. Cairns is also a vibrant, cosmopolitan city, brimming with cafes, shops and some great nightlife. Near the heart of the city is the Flecker Botanical Garden, 38 ha of lush greenery, housing plants that you can't find anywhere else in Australia.

For those who don't mind heights, try the popular Skyrail Rainforest Cableway, offering amazing panoramic views over Cairns and the beautiful Barron Falls, which drops you right on the doorstep of Kuranda, a small village packed with restaurants, shopping and art galleries (check out the New Kuranda Markets Aboriginal Art Gallery). For another charming ride through the region, try the Kuranda Scenic Railway.

Cairns is steeped in Aboriginal history, making the Tjakupai Cultural Park a must-see. Here you can learn about the local Indigenous people's culture and art, throw a boomerang, play a didgeridoo or attend a corroboree by night. If markets are your thing, head to Rusty's Bazaar. For the daredevil in you, Cairns also has an unrivalled selection of danger sports, from bungee jumping to rapids kayaking.

## Further information

ℹ️ **Cairns Information Centre**; (07) 4031 4784; daily 9am–5pm; www.cairnsvisitorcentre.com

ℹ️ **Tourism Tropical North Queensland** 51 The Esplanade; (07) 4051 1766; daily 8.30am–6.30pm; www.tropicalaustralia.com.au

ℹ️ **Kuranda Visitor Information Centre** Centenary Park (top end of Coondoo St; (07) 4093 9311; daily 10am–4pm; www.kuranda.org

ℹ️ **The Accommodation Centre** Cnr Grafton & Shields sts; (07) 4051 1766; daily 9am–5pm; www.accomcentre.com.au

**Flecker Botanical Gardens** Collins Ave, Edge Hill; (07) 4044 3398; Mon–Fri 7.30am–5.30pm, Sat–Sun 8.30am–5.30pm.

**Cairns Skyrail Rainforest Cableway** Cnr Captain Cook Hwy & Cairns Western Arterial Rd, Smithfield; (07) 4038 1555; daily 8.15am–5.15pm; www.skyrail.com.au

**New Kuranda Markets Aboriginal Art Gallery** 23 Coondoo St; (07) 4093 9736; daily 9.30am–3.30pm.

Palm Cove beach, Cairns

**Kuranda Scenic Railway** Cairns Railway Station, Bunda St; (07) 4036 9333; tours run daily, leaving Cairns 8.30am & 9.30am, returning 2pm & 3.30pm; www.kurandascenicrailway.com.au

**Tjakupai Aboriginal Cultural Park** Kamerunga Rd, Smithfield; (07) 4042 9900; daily 9am–5pm (special shows commence 7.30pm); www.tjapukai.com.au

**Rusty's Bazaar** Between Grafton & Sheridan sts; Fri 5am–6pm, Sat 6am–3pm, Sun 6am–2pm; www.rustysmarkets.com.au

## Activities

**AJ Hackett Bungee Jump** McGregor Rd, Smithfield; (07) 4057 7188; www.ajhackett.com.au

**Skydive Cairns** (07) 4031 5466; www.skydivecairns.com.au

## Where to eat

**Hog's Breath Cafe** 💲 While the name may not be too appealing, the food is. A menu packed with burgers, wraps, steaks and ribs. You won't leave this place with anything but a full stomach. 64 Spence St; (07) 4031 7711; daily 11.30am–2.30pm, 5.30pm–late; www.hogsbreath.com.au

**Lillipad Cafe** 💲 This funky eatery specialises in vegetarian dishes, complemented by the famous Mungali Creek dairy products. Focaccias and sandwiches also available. 72 Grafton St (next to City Arcade); (07) 4051 9565; daily 7am–2pm.

**Green Ant Cantina** 💲💲 Affordable Mexican restaurant and bar. Good live music and great chicken burgers. Two-for-one meal deals on Tuesday nights. 183 Bunda St; (07) 4041 5061.

## Pubs and bars

**Gilligan's** This backpacker hostel is one of the most popular in all of Cairns. With a beer deck, beer hall and Pure Nightclub, it's no wonder that all the backpackers and locals flock here at weekends. 57–89 Grafton St; (07) 4041 6566; nightclub open Fri–Sun 10pm–late; www.gilligansbackpackers.com.au/bars

**Mad Cow Tavern** More of a local haunt if you want to get away from the same backpacking travellers you see everywhere. Great drink specials. 25–27 Spence St; (07) 4051 8846; Sun–Thur 8pm–3am, Fri 8pm–5am, Sat 8pm–5am.

## Where to stay

**Caravella Cairns City Backpackers** ★★★ Dorms $22, single $42, twin or double $57 77–81 The Esplanade; (07) 4051 2159; 149 The Esplanade; (07) 4051 2431; www.caravella.com.au

**Dreamtime Travellers Rest** ★★★ Dorm $22, twin and double $48 Cnr Bunda & Terminus sts; (07) 4031 6753; www.dreamtimetravel.com.au

**Gilligan's Backpacker Hostel and Resort** ★★★ Dorm $36, deluxe hotel suites $180 57–89 Grafton St; (07) 4041 6566;

Diving, Great
Barrier Reef

www.gilligansbackpackers.com.au

**Tropic Days** ★★★ Dorm $24, single $40, double $55 26–28 Bunting St; (07) 4041 1521; www.tropicdays.com.au

**Calypso Inn** ★★ Dorm $24, twin or double $54 5–9 Digger St; (07) 4031 0910; www.calypsobackpackers.com.au

**Cairns Girls Hostel** ★★ Dorm $18, twin $44 147 Lake St; (07) 4051 2016; www.cairnsgirlshostel.com.au

## Events

**Festival Cairns** A Cairns cultural bonanza, with food and wine events coupled with great local and international music performances. Sept.

**Palm Cove Fiesta** Outdoor food and wine festival with iron man races, sailing regattas and war planes. Oct.

## ❺ Great Barrier Reef (3–4 days)

It's difficult to sum up in words the sheer beauty that is the Great Barrier Reef. This vast, breathtakingly beautiful marine environment features over 900 tropical islands (only 22 of which cater to visitors), aquamarine waters, rare and brilliantly coloured corals, seagrass beds, fish, and sea-going mammals and birds. It is considered one of the world's great destinations for diving, sailing, fishing, swimming, windsurfing and kayaking. Scientists believe that coral bleaching, a result of global warming, is slowly having an impact on the reef, so you better see it now while it's still thriving. Be aware that it is illegal to take coral from the reef – look but don't touch!

## Further information

ℹ️ **Great Barrier Reef Marine Park Authority** (07) 4750 0700; www.gbrmpa.gov.au

## Getting here

The convenience of the Great Barrier Reef is that you can access it from many locations in North Queensland (spanning from Bundaberg to Cooktown). The reef can be reached by private charter, daily cruises, seaplane or helicopter. Taking a tour is usually the best way to access the island, as transfers are often included in your tour package.

## Tours

It's recommended that you research what tours suit your interests, budget and location. Most tours will cost you a bit of money, but to see the splendour of the reef, it's worth every penny. Here are some tour suggestions:

**Cairns Dive Centre** Offers some of the best value diving and snorkelling daytrips. A one-day tour will only set you back $75. 121 Abbott St, Cairns; (07) 4051 0294; www.cairnsdive.com.au

**Calypso Dive (from Mission Beach)** See some of the most spectacular outer reef sites the east coast has to offer. Suitable for beginners and experienced divers. Wongaling Beach Rd, Mission Beach; (07) 4068 8432; calypsodive.com

**Vagabond Dive n Sail** Amazing diving adventures, including night dives. D Finger 16, Marlin Jetty, Cairns; (07) 4059 0477; www.vagabond-dive.com

**Wavelength Reef Snorkelling** Snorkel the reef with a marine biologist as your guide. 38–42 Wharf St, Port Douglas; (07) 4099 5031; www.wavelength-reef.com.au

**Great Barrier Reef Dive and Snorkel Adventures** Cruises, scuba diving, helicopter trips and scenic flights. 100 Abbott St, Cairns; (07) 4031 7217; www.reeftrip.com

**Big Cat Cruises**\* Cruise to Green Island before hitting the reef with your snorkel. Then have a leisurely lunch on the white sandy beaches, or explore the emerald rainforest of the island itself. Day and half-day cruises available ($66–$99 packages). Reef Fleet Terminal, 1 Spence St, Cairns; (07) 4051 0444; www.bigcat-cruises.com.au

\*Book this tour and other reef or Queensland tours through Caravella Backpackers Resorts to receive 5% off. www.caravella.com.au/discount.html

## ❻ Port Douglas (2 days)

Looking at Port Douglas today, it's hard to believe that it was once a sleepy fishing town. Lying on the serene waters of a natural harbour, the port is now an internationally renowned tourist destination, with an aura of sophistication coupled with a laidback attitude. Four Mile Beach is a great place to feel the sand in your toes, although watch out for marine stingers in the summer months if you have a dip in the water. If you haven't seen enough Australian wildlife, the Rainforest Habitat Wildlife Sanctuary is your ticket, with over 1600 animals in four different habitats. Anzac Park is a spot for great fishing, and every Sunday it is host to a bustling market filled with fresh fruit and veggies, as well as arts and crafts. Try a coconut cocktail!

## Further information

ℹ️ **Port Douglas Tourist Information Centre** 23 Macrossan St; (07) 4099 5599.

**Rainforest Habitat Wildlife Sanctuary** Port Douglas Rd; (07) 4099 3235; daily 8am–5.30pm; www.rainforesthabitat.com.au

**Anzac Park Market** Macrossan St; Sun 8.30am–1.30pm.

## Where to eat

**Soul 'n' Pepper** ❺ Wildly popular joint, mainly for its huge cooked breakfast served in the pan, and its location right on Dickson Inlet. Packed on Sundays. 8/2 Dixie St; (07) 4099 4499; daily 7.30am–late.

## Pubs and bars

**Watergate Lounge** A torch-lit path leads you into this comfy lounge, where you can order anything from a Bluetongue beer to a cosmopolitan. 5/31 Macrossan St; (07) 4099 6665; daily 4pm–midnight.

## Where to stay

**Port O' Call** ★★ Dorm $27.50, double $72.50 Cnr Port St & Craven Cl; (07) 4099 5422; www.portocall.com.au
**Parrot Fish Lodge** ★★ Dorm $25–$33, double $85–$95
37–39 Warner St; (07) 4099 5011; www.parrotfishlodge.com
**Dougie's Backpackers** ★★ Dorm $25, twin and double $70
111 Davidson St; (07) 4099 6200; www.dougies.com.au

## Events

**Reef and Rainforest Carnivale** A massive street carnival with performances, parades and a fireworks spectacular. May.

## ⑦ Daintree National Park (1–2 days)

Not far north of Port Douglas lies Daintree National Park, incorporating two separate sections: the Mossman Gorge section stretching north-west from Mossman, and the smaller Cape Tribulation section.

The Mossman Gorge area features impenetrable mountain ranges and lush rainforest, the oldest rainforest area on earth at approximately 400 million years. Tours take visitors into the rainforest's green and shady heart via an easy, 2.7 km walk to the fabulous Mossman River. The Cape Tribulation section is a rich mix of coastal rainforest, mangroves, swamp and heath. Camping is available in this part of the rainforest at Noah Beach. There is also a small town area nearby with a few shops.

Another highlight, aside from the gorgeous rainforest surrounds, is Cape Trib Exotic Fruit Farm, where you can sample some of the strangest sounding fruits in the world (try the wax jambu, the sapodilla, and a red berry simply called Miracle Fruit). Then maybe head down to one of the glorious beaches, and go horseriding as you take in the surrounds.

## Daintree
### Further information

ⓘ **Daintree Tourist Information Centre** 5 Stewart St, Daintree; (07) 4098 6133; daily 9am–5pm.
ⓘ **Mossman Gorge park ranger** Level 1, Centenary Building, 1 Front Street, Mossman; (07) 4098 2188.
**QPWS Smart Service** (for camping bookings) 13 13 04; www.epa.qld.gov.au

Daintree rainforest

**Bus transfer: Coral Reef Coaches** 35 Front St, Mossman; (07) 4098 2800; www.coralreefcoaches.com.au One-way ticket for $40 from Port Douglas to Cape Tribulation.

## Tours

**Daintree Tranquility Tours** Half-day tours through the Daintree wilderness. Bring a camera! Upper Daintree Rd; Daintree; (07) 4098 6000; www.tranquilitytours.com.au
**Mason's Tours** Excellent 4WD safari and bushwalking tours. Cape Tribulation Rd, Cape Tribulation; (07) 4098 0070; www.masonstours.com.au
**Daintree Tour and Forest Tours** A range of day and night wilderness tours. (07) 4098 9126; www.ccwild.com

## Cape Tribulation
### Further information

ⓘ **Cape Tribulation Information Office** Cape Tribulation Rd, Cape Tribulation; (07) 4098 0052.
**Cape Trib Exotic Fruit Farm** This accomodation offers beach horseriding tours twice a day. Lot 5 Nicole Dve, Cape Tribulation; (07) 4098 0057; tours from 2pm (bookings essential); www.capetrib.com.au

## Tours

**Rainforest Hideaway** Beach horseriding tours twice daily. Lot 19 Camelot Cl, Cape Tribulation; (07) 4098 0108; www.rainforesthideaway.com

## Where to stay

**Cape Trib Beach House Resort** ★★★ Dorm $25, double cabin $79
7 Rykers Rd; (07) 4098 0030; www.capetribbeach.com.au
**PK's Jungle Village** ★★★ Dorm $25–$28, double $110
Cape Tribulation Rd; (07) 4098 0040; www.pksjunglevillage.com.au

# Sunshine Coast
# Slice of heaven

With near-perfect weather all year round, the Sunshine Coast is home to some of Queensland's premier holiday destinations. Noosa, Caloundra and Mooloolaba are lined with beautiful beaches, and offer travellers a bevy of diverse activities, from golf and bushwalking to just lazing about in a hammock. Journey inland to see the forested beauty of the Glass House Mountains. Feel free to have Dave Dobbyn's *Slice of Heaven* playing on your iPod the entire time.

**Number of days to spend in this region: 10–12 days**

## Getting here

The Sunshine Coast airport is located in Maroochydore, with flights from all over Australia landing there. Greyhound, Premier Motor Service and Suncoast Pacific are coach services that operate daily from Brisbane and travel to most of the region, and are your best and cheapest mode of travel. The typical trip to Noosa will take approximately 3 hours. A hire car is a good way to reach the Glass House Mountains and Nambour.

Suncoast Pacific (07) 5443 4180; www.suncoastpacific.com.au

## ① Glass House Mountains (1–2 days)

Named by Captain Cook during his epic voyage along the east coast, the Glass House Mountains are not particularly tall – at up to 556 m – but are very distinctive, being completely separate from each other and surrounded by rugged vegetation. They are the remaining plugs of extinct volcanoes, some 20 million years old, and you can hike to the top of three of the peaks: Mount Beerwah, the highest, Mount Tibrogargan and Mount Ngungun (only experienced climbers should attempt walking to any of the summits). Walking tracks in the area range from Class 2 to Class 5. The Glass House region is also a great place for some abseiling and rock climbing.

### Further information

🛈 QPWS Maleny 61 Bunya St, Maleny; (07) 5494 3983; Mon–Fri 7.30am–4pm; www.epa.qld.gov.au
🛈 Glass House Mountains Visitor Information Van Bus services operate regularly between the Sunshine Coast and Glass House Mountain area. Matthew Flinders Park, Steve Irwin Way; daily 9am–4pm.

### Tours

**Rainforest Rob's Explorer Tours** Walks, rockpool swimming and spectacular waterfalls. 0409 496 607.
**Pinnacle Sports** Also hires out rock climbing and abseiling gear. (07) 3368 3335; www.pinnaclesports.com.au
**Rock climbing** There aren't many tours or rock climbing equipment hire places in the area, so you must you organise this before you come

to the park. It is also a dangerous endeavour, so make sure you're experienced enough to handle the different peaks. Do not climb during or immediately after rain as slippery surfaces become extremely difficult to manage.

**Half- and full-day rock climbing and abseiling tours can be booked through: Glass House Mountains Ecolodge** 198 Barrs Rd; (07) 5493 0008; www.glasshouseecolodge.com

### Where to stay

**Glass House Mountains Ecolodge** Twin and double $80 198 Barrs Rd; (07) 5493 0008; www.glasshouseecolodge.com

## ② Beerwah: Australia Zoo (1 day)

The ultimate zoo experience is on offer at this sanctuary, made famous by Steve 'The Crocodile Hunter' Irwin, who was tragically killed by a stingray in 2006. But the zoo is still running strong, thanks to his wife Terri Irwin, and a passionate and animal-loving staff known as the

Glass House Mountains

'khaki collective'. There is so much to see and do at this enormous park, including live shows with koalas, otters, elephants and foxes. Take in the Wildlife Warriors adventure show (daily 11am and 2pm). The Tiger Temple boasts the Southern Hemisphere's only underwater viewing of tigers and cheetahs, while Elephantasia has daily feedings.

## Further information

**Australia Zoo** Steve Irwin Way, Beerwah; (07) 5436 2000; daily 9am–4.30pm; www.australiazoo.com.au Admission to the park is $49 for adults and $38 for students.

**Courtesy bus** A courtesy bus is a free way to travel to and from Australia Zoo. Bookings are essential. Bus departs 8.30am from the Noosa Heads Bus Stop in Noosa Parade. (07) 5436 2000; www.australiazoo.com.au/visit-us/how-to-get-here/

## ❸ Caloundra (2 days)

Now a vibrant mix of old and young, the Caloundra coast is scattered with magnificent beaches that offer a variety of watersports – Golden Beach is particularly popular with windsurfers. The Queensland Air Museum is a fascinating look at Australia's aviation history, with a vast collection of memorabilia, including old fighter planes and bombers. For something with a more relaxed tone, take a cruise or grab a kayak down the ever blue Pumicestone Passage.

## Further information

ℹ️ **Caloundra Visitors Centres** 7 Caloundra Rd; (07) 5420 6240; 77 Bulcock St; (07) 5420 8718; daily 9am–5pm; www.caloundratourism.com.au **Queensland Air Museum** 7 Pathfinder Dr; (07) 5492 5930; daily 9am–6pm; www.qam.com.au **Kayak hire: Blue Water Kayak** (Pumicestone Passage) (07) 5494 7789; www.bluewaterkayaktours.com **Windsurfing hire: Golden Beach Hire** Pumicestone Passage (opposite Gregory St); (07) 5492 4344; www.goldenbeachhire.com

## Where to eat

**Quarterdeck Restaurant** 💲 Enjoy this eatery's food with beautiful views over the Pumicestone passage. Woorim Park, The Esplanade, Golden Beach; (07) 5492 1444; daily, lunch noon–2pm, dinner Sun–Thur 5.30pm–8pm, Fri–Sat 5.30pm–8.30pm; www.caloundrapowerboat.com.au

## Pubs and bars

**Tonic Bar and Lounge** One of Caloundra's newer nightspots, Tonic offers contemporary live entertainment including bands, circus acts and DJs spinning dance tunes. Cocktails and beers aplenty. 66 Bulcock St; (07) 5492 5924; Thur 10pm–3am, Fri–Sat 9pm–3am; www.tonic-lounge.com.au

## Where to stay

**Caloundra City Backpackers** ★★ Dorm $22, twin $46, double $55 84 Omrah Ave; (07) 5499 7655; www.caloundracitybackpackers.com.au

## Events

**Woodford Folk Festival** Six-day festival of outstanding local and international acts encompassing music, dance, theatre, comedy and various workshops. Worth the trip inland. Dec–Jan.

## ❹ Mooloolaba (2 days)

This sleepy town is renowned as a holiday hub, thanks to its perfect beaches, nightlife and resort-style shopping. Mooloolaba Harbour is a good place for parasailing, fishing or a cruise.

While you're there, journey to Scuba World. This is a unique scuba diving experience with the opportunity to swim with grey nurse sharks. On the marine theme, you don't want to miss UnderWater World. This complex has a fantastic 80 m walkway through seawater 'ocean', displays of the Great Barrier Reef, and underwater creatures.

## Further information

ℹ️ **Maroochy Tourism** Cnr Sixth Ave & Melrose St; (07) 5479 1566; Mon–Fri 8am–5.30pm, Sat–Sun 8am–5pm; www.maroochytourism.com **Scuba World** Sharks dives $99–$165. The Wharf, Parykn Parade; (07) 5444 8595; www.scubaworld.com.au/ **UnderWater World** The Wharf, Parkyn Pde; (07) 5444 8488; www.underwaterworld.com.au

## Where to eat

**Zink Bar** 💲 Grab a bite at this funky, modern bar. With brilliant ocean views, it caters for everything from light brunches to tasty seafood mains. 77 The Esplanade; (07) 5477 6077; summer Mon–Thur, Sun 10am–midnight, Fri–Sat 10am–2am; winter Tue–Wed 4–11pm, Thur noon–midnight, Fri–Sat noon–2am; www.zinkbar.com.au

## Pubs and bars

**The Wharf Tavern** Easily the most popular bar/club in the Mooloolaba area. River Esplanade (cnr Parkyn Pde); (07) 5444 8383; daily noon–late; www.thewharftavern.com.au

## Where to stay

**Mooloolaba Beach Backpackers** ★★ Dorm $26–$29, double $70 75 Brisbane Rd; (07) 5444 3399; www.mooloolababackpackers.com

## ❺ Nambour: The Big Pineapple (1 day)

About 15 km west of Mooloolaba, this small town is known around Australia for The Big Pineapple and Macadamia Nut Factory! The 16 m fibreglass pineapple is a tourist icon, and an absolute must-see for any traveller in the region. There are a plethora of activities and you'll see koalas, kangaroos and wallabies at the Australia Wildlife Garden.

## Further information

**The Big Pineapple and Macadamia Nut Factory** Nambour Connection Rd, Woombye; (07) 5442 1333; daily 9am–5pm; www.bigpineapple.com.au

The Big Pineapple

## ⑥ Noosa (3 days)

The Sunshine Coast's most popular destination. With golden beaches and lush parklands, it has remained relatively untouched thanks to residents who have valiantly fought against development.

Most of the action happens around Noosa Heads where cosmopolitan Hastings Street displays a relaxed cafe lifestyle, and is in close proximity to all the town's natural attractions, including Noosa National Park. If you head down to the beaches, you'll see a host of sunbaking beauties, surf lifesavers and surfers out on the waves. Take a surfing lesson and hit some great breaking beaches along the coast, the pick of the lot being Sunshine Beach. Coral Sea and other inland waterways have a range of activities, including kite surfing and high-speed boating.

For a lively market experience, look no further than the Eumundi Markets, open every Wednesday and Saturday. Walk through the towering fig trees which droop over the 500 plus stalls.

## Further information

ℹ️ **Noosa Information Centre** Hastings St, Noosa Heads; (07) 5447 4988; daily 9am–5pm; www.tourismnoosa.com.au
**Noosa National Park** Park Rd, Noosa Heads; (07) 5447 3243; www.epa.qld.gov.au
**Eumundi Markets** Memorial Dr, Eumundi; (07) 5442 7106; Wed 8am–1pm, Sat 6.30am–2pm; www.eumundimarkets.com.au
**Bus to Eumundi: Sunbus** 131230 (timetable info); www.sunbus.com.au
**Surfing lessons and board hire: Learn to Surf** 19 Waterside Crt, Noosaville; 0418 787 577; www.learntosurf.com.au
**Noosa Surf Lessons** 9 Lake Weyba Dr, Noosaville; 0412 330 850;

www.noosasurflessons.com.au
**Motorbike hire: Aussie Riders** (03) 9383 5759; www.aussierider.com
**Scooter hire: Scooter Style** (07) 5455 5249; www.scooterstyle.com.au
**Bike hire: Koala Bike Hire** (07) 5474 2733.
**Kite surfing: GoActiv Kiteboarding** Boreen Point; 0400 404 040; www.goactiv.com.au

## Where to eat

**Cafe Noosa** $ A pizza and pasta joint with a casual ambience. Shop 2/1 Sunshine Beach Rd, Noosa Heads; (07) 5447 3949; Mon–Thur 4pm–midnight, Fri–Sun 1pm–midnight; www.noosapizza.com
**Massimo's** $ This gelateria is home to the best ice-cream in Noosa. Brain freezes expected. 75 Hastings St; (07) 5474 8022.
**Berardo's on the Beach** $$ Have a splurge at one of Noosa's finest restaurants. On the Beach, Hastings St; (07) 5448 0888; daily 8am–late.

## Pubs and bars

**Koala Bar** Drink specials, theme nights every Tuesday, and always a party atmosphere. One of Noosa's most popular nightspots. 44 Noosa Dr, Noosa Heads; (07) 5447 3355; daily 5pm–late; www.koala-backpackers.com.au
**Noosa Heads Surf Lifesaving Club** Enjoy a few beers at the local surf club. Great karaoke midweek. 69 Hastings St; (07) 5474 5688; Mon 11am–10pm, Tue–Fri 11am–midnight, Sat–Sun 7am–midnight.

## Where to stay

**Halse Lodge** ★★★ Dorm $31.50, double and twin $70 2 Halse La, Noosa Heads; (07) 5447 3377; www.halselodge.com.au
**Dolphins Beach House** ★★ Dorm $24, double $60 14–16 Duke St, Sunshine Beach
**Noosa Backpackers Resort** ★★ Dorm $24, double or twin $55 9–13 William St, Noosaville; (07) 5449 8151; www.noosabackpackers.com

## Events

**Noosa Festival of Surfing** Surfing and social events under the sun. Mar.
**Noosa Jazz Festival** A celebration of hot food and cool jazz, with over 150 national and international artists. Aug–Sept.

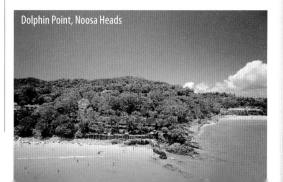
Dolphin Point, Noosa Heads

For more detail
see maps
221 & 223

Brisbane

# Fraser Island and the coast
# Island paradise

Along with Uluṟu and the Great Barrier Reef, Fraser Island stands as one of Australia's most precious World Heritage sites. The largest sand island in the world, it is a place of sheer beauty with long, uninterrupted white beaches, coloured sand cliffs and freshwater lakes. Nearby is Hervey Bay, a quiet resort town, while the northern town of Rockhampton, the beef capital of Australia, offers some amazing outback adventures, giving you a true taste of Oz.

**Number of days to spend in this region: 8–10 days**

## Getting here

Your best bet for getting to the Fraser Coast is by coach. Greyhound and Premier Motor Service run buses to Hervey Bay from Brisbane via Noosa and Rainbow Beach. To get to Fraser Island itself, you will need to catch a ferry. There are a few ferry options to various parts of Fraser Island.

**Fraser Island Ferry** (07) 4194 9222.

**Kingfisher Bay Ferry** 1800 072 555.

## ❶ Great Sandy National Park (2–3 days)

This enormous park encompasses two sections: Fraser Island and the Cooloola coastline. Both are excellent places for bushwalking, canoeing, fishing and camping.

Fraser Island is famous for its giant sand dunes and yellow, brown, orange and red-coloured sandy cliffs. It is also the only place in the world where you'll see vibrant and healthy rainforests growing out of the sand – extraordinary because sand is infertile.

Over 100 freshwater lakes hold some of the purest water in the world, including the amazingly blue Lake McKenzie. Make sure not to wear sunscreen when swimming in these lakes, as most are isolated from streams that can flush out contaminants that visitors bring in. Other than standing in awe of this incredible island paradise, there is plenty to see and do here. Fraser is a major 4WD beach driving destination, and there are adventure activities including sandboarding and sailing. You can relax on the long surf beaches or beside the hundreds of creeks that wind into the Pacific Ocean. An amazing relic of history beached just north of Happy Valley is the *Maheno*, a shipwrecked liner that landed on the beach after a cyclone in 1935.

The Cooloola coastline has a varied landscape highlighted by the magnificent Teewah Beach, home to uniquely coloured sandy cliffs that are around 40,000 years old. It is thought that oxidation or decay has caused the colouring; Aboriginal legend attributes it to the slaying of a rainbow serpent. Heading inland is a section of the Noosa River that has been dubbled The Everglades because the water is stained red-black by tree tannins, creating crystal-clear reflections of the riverbank. The best way to see the area is to hire a canoe and slowly make your way up the coast. For those wanting to try hang gliding, Rainbow Beach is a popular spot.

Before visiting, contact QPWS Tewantin for permits and information on walks and picnic areas.

### Further information

ℹ **QPWS Great Sandy Information Centre** 240 Moorindil St, Tewantin; (07) 5449 7792; www.epa.qld.gov.au

Sand dunes, Fraser Island

ℹ **Cooloola Regional Development Bureau** 24 Bruce Hwy, Lake Alford, Gympie; 1800 444 222.
**Smart Service (for camping bookings)** 13 13 04; www.qld.gov.au/camping
**Canoe hire: Elanda Point** (07) 5485 3165; www.elanda.com.au

### Fraser wildlife

The famous Fraser dingoes are genetically pure, unlike those on the mainland that have interbred with domestic dogs. Beware: Fraser dingoes are wild and can be dangerous, so don't get too close. In 2001, a dingo killed a nine-year-old boy who was treating it like a pet. For this reason, park rangers will fine anyone seen feeding dingoes. Also lock up any food containers and don't litter.

## Tours

**Cool Dingo Tours** Backpacker 4WD tour options, includes meals and accommodation. Great value. PMB 1, Urangan, Hervey Bay; (07) 4120 3333; www.cooldingotour.com
**Goanna Adventures** Another great backpacker tour company, with jeep-riding and sandboarding. Departs from Brisbane and Gold Coast. (07) 3422 1133; www.goannaadventures.com.au
**Koala Backpacker Adventures** Koala self-drive 4WD tours available. (07) 4946 6446; www.koalaadventures.com
**Beaches Backpackers** Camping safaris for backpackers. Really amazing value. 195 Torquay Tce, Hervey Bay; (07) 4124 1322; www.beaches.com.au
**Sail Shayla** Offers half-day and longer adventure sailing tours around the gorgeous Lake McKenzie. (07) 4125 3727; www.shaylacruises.com.au
**Footprints on Fraser** Walk where the 4WDs can't go. (07) 4125 6295; www.footprintsonfraser.com.au
**Fraser Island Company** One, two and three-day tours of the island, including camping adventures. (07) 4125 3933; www.fraserislandco.com.au
**Fraser Experience** Build your own tour options. (07) 4124 4244; www.fraserexperience.com

## 4WD hire

**Sunrover Expeditions** Fraser Coast Holiday Centre, 463 Esplanade, Hervey Bay; (07) 4124 9685; www.4wdfraser.com
**Aussie Trax 4WD Hire** 56 Boat Harbour Dr; Hervey Bay; 1800 062 275; www.fraserisland4wd.com.au
**Fraser Magic 4WD Hire** 5 Kruger Ct, Hervey Bay; (07) 4125 6612; www.fraser4wdhire.com.au

## Fishing

Fraser Island has long been renowned for its excellent fishing. From silver bream on the east coast, to the barramundi and garfish of the Great Sandy Strait and flathead and whiting on the Cooloola coast. A fishing licence is not required when fishing in these parts, but size and bag limits apply.
**Queensland Fisheries** (07) 3225 1843; www.dpi.qld.gov.au/fishweb

## Hang gliding and paragliding

**Rainbow Beach Hang Gliding** (through Amaroo Beach House Retreat) One-day courses and tandem flights. (07) 5486 8888.
**Rainbow Paragliding** 0418 754 157; www.paraglidingrainbow.com
**Epic Horizon** Offer paragliding courses and tours. 0428 185 727; www.epic-horizon.com

## Where to stay

**Eurong Beach Resort** ★★ Dorm $17–$28, units $140 and up Eurong; (07) 4127 9122; www.eurong.com
**Frasers at Cathedral Bay** ★★ Campsite $18, cabins $110 Cathedral Beach, Fraser Island; (07) 4127 9177; www.fraserislandco.com.au/accommodation.asp
**Camping** The park has some goergeous camping areas, including Central Station, Dundubara and Waddy Point on Fraser, and Fig Tree Point, Harrys Hut and Freshwater on the Cooloola coast. Bookings can be made through the information centre or by calling 13 1304 (24 hrs).

## ❷ Hervey Bay: Whale-watching (2 days)

This coastal centre, pronounced 'Harvey' Bay, is renowned for its natural features, soothing waters that are great for swimming, and relaxed lifestyle. The winter months are a popular time to visit, not only for the perfect climate, but also for the migrating humpback whales that frolic in the bay's warm waters between July and November (but you should not swim with the whales). The bay is also a popular point from which to visit nearby Fraser Island. For a bit of history on the town, pop in to the Hervey Bay Historical Museum, or for some performing seals, check out Neptune's Reefworld, a natural aquarium. For a bit of R&R, take a stroll along the Esplanade Track for some great views.

## Further information

ℹ **Hervey Bay Visitor Information Centre** 262 Urraween Rd; 1800 811 728; daily 9am–5pm.

Humpback whale, Hervey Bay

**Hervey Bay Historical Village and Museum** 13 Zephyr St; (07) 4128 4804; Fri–Sun (winter 1pm–4.30pm, summer 1pm–5pm); herveybaymuseum.museum.com
**Neptune's Reefworld** Pulgul St, Dayman Park, Urangan; (07) 4128 9828; daily 9.30am–5pm.

## Whale-watching

These amazing beasts can be viewed between July and November. There are a number of half- and full-day whale-watching tours (from $95).
**Spirit of Hervey Bay Whale Watching** (07) 4125 5131; www.spiritofherveybay.com
**Mikat Whale Watch Safari (includes buffet lunch)** (07) 4125 1522; www.mikat.com.au
**Blue Dolphin Marine Tours** 4 Alpsea Ave, Urangan; (07) 4124 9600; www.bluedolphintours.com.au
**Tasman Venture Whale Watching** Great Sandy Straits Marina; (07) 4124 3222; www.tasmanventure.com.au
**Quick Cat II** (07) 4128 9611; www.herveybaywhalewatch.com.au

## Tours and activities

**M.V Daytripper** Fishing daytrips. 0401 804 205; www.mvdaytripper.com
**MV Fighting Whiting** Fishing daytrips. (07) 4124 6599.
**Krystal Klear Aquatic Nature Tours** Snorkelling, reef watching and fish feeding. (07) 4124 0066; www.krystalkleer.com.au
**Susan River Homestead Resort** Offers horseriding, parasailing and waterskiing adventures. (07) 4121 6846; www.susanriver.com
**Hervey Bay Skydivers** Thrills aplenty. (07) 4183 0119; www.skydivefraser.com
**Hervey Big Air Adventures** Enjoy the passenger seat in a Tiger Moth. You get to wear a leather jacket and goggles! (07) 4124 9313.
**Hervey Bay Trike and Bike Tours** A fantastic way to tour the Fraser coast. (07) 4128 7221.

## Where to eat

**Cafe Salt** [$] A perfect place to enjoy great food and stunning ocean views. Choose from an eclectic mix of modern Australian cuisine. Shop 5, 569 Esplanade, Peppers Pier Resort, Urangan; (07) 4124 9722; daily from 7am; www.saltcafe.com.au
**Le Cafe de la baie** [$] Voted the best cafe in the region. Genuine alfresco dining, along with backpacker specials. 352a Esplanade, Scarness; (07) 4128 1793; daily 6.45am–9.30pm.

## Pubs and bars

**Blazing Saddles** With country style décor straight out of a Western movie, this is a great place to down a beer and put your feet up. 140 Freshwater Rd, Torquay; (07) 4125 5466; Mon–Fri 11am–late, Sat–Sun 4pm–late.

## Where to stay

**The Friendly Hostel** ★★★ Dorm $20, single $45, twin and double $48–$65 182 Torquay Rd; (07) 4124 4107; www.thefriendlyhostel.com
**Next Backpackers** ★★★ Dorm $22–$28, single or double $65 10 Bideford St, Torquay Beach; (07) 4125 6600; www.nextbackpackers.com.au
**Woolshed Backpackers** ★★ Dorm $18–$20, twin and double $44–$54 181 Torquay Rd; (07) 4124 0677; woolshedbackpackers.com
**Koala Beach Resort** ★★ Dorm $25, double $67 408 The Esplanade; (07) 4125 3601; www.koala-backpackers.com
**Fraser Roving (also camping and 4WD trips)** ★★ Dorm $20–$28, double $50–$65 412 The Esplanade; (07) 4125 6386; www.fraserroving.com

## Events

**Hervey Bay Whale Festival** A celebration of the town's most popular attraction, with great food and music. Aug.

## 3 Bundaberg (1 day)

Surrounded by sugarcanes, not much has changed over the years in this typical country town. Bundaberg is the southernmost access point for the Great Barrier Reef, and has glorious parks and gardens. The flat landscape is highlighted by the Botanic Gardens, a scenic mixture of beautiful gardens and historic houses. Every Sunday you can hop on the restored steam train and take a ride around the lakes. Bundaberg is also home to Bundaberg Rum Distillery, which runs tours daily (with lots of tastings included). For another industry insight, visit Fairymead House Sugar Museum.

Just east of Bundaberg is the Mon Repos Turtle Rookery. Between November and February, you can watch female sea turtles come ashore to lay up to 120 leathery-shelled eggs, which they return to protect several times during the season. From mid-January to March, the hatchlings emerge at night and make a dash to the relative safety of the sea to begin life unaided. In the periods when the turtles are not hatching, popular activities include snorkelling and exploring the rockpools. You can also visit the Mon Repos information centre to discover more about the area's turtles.

For keen divers, one of the cheapest places to do a course is 16 km east of Bundaberg. With some rocky coastline and an abundance of colourful hard and soft corals, the Woongarra Marine Park offers some of the state's most accessible shore diving.

Turtle hatching in water, Mon Repos

Bundaberg Rum Distillery

## Further information

ⓘ **Bundaberg City Visitor Information Centre** 186 Bourbong St, Bundaberg; (07) 4153 8888; Mon–Fri 8.30am–4.45pm, Sat–Sun 1am–1pm; www.bundabergregion.info

**Bundaberg Botanic Gardens** (07) 4153 2377; daily 6am–6pm.

**Bundaberg Rum Distillery** Whittred St, East Bundaberg; (07) 4131 2900; tours run on the hour, Mon–Fri 10am–3pm, Sat–Sun 10am–2pm; www.bundabergrum.com.au

**Fairymead House Sugar Museum** Botanic Gardens, Thornhill St; (07) 4153 6786; daily 10am–4pm.

**QPWS Mon Repos** 141 Mon Repos Rd; (07) 4159 1652; daily Nov–late Mar 7pm–midnight (best time to view hatchlings).

**Woongarra Marine Park** (07) 4131 1600.

**Diving: Bundaberg Aqua Scuba** (07) 4153 5761; www.aquascuba. com.au

**Salty's Dive Centre** (07) 4125 2343.

## Tours

**Footprint Adventures Turtle Tours** Nocturnal adventure tours to watch the loggerhead turtles nest and hatch. (07) 4152 3659; www.footprintsadventures.com.au

## Where to eat

**Spices Plus** Ⓢ A culinary feast of hot spices and the best Indian cuisine. This place is no secret, so bookings are advised. Cnr Quay & Targo sts; (07) 4154 3320; Mon–Fri 11.30am–2pm & 5.30pm–9.30pm, Sat–Sun 5.30pm–9.30pm.

## Where to stay

**Federal Backpackers** ★★ Dorm $23, twin or double $46 221 Bourbong St; (07) 4153 3711; www.federalbackpackers.com.au

**Grand Backpackers** ★★ Dorm $22 12 Queen St; (07) 4154 1166.

**Bundaberg Backpackers & Travellers Lodge** ★★ Dorm $21 2 Crofton St; (07) 4152 2080.

**Feeding Grounds Backpackers (runs turtle tours)** ★★ Dorm $23 4 Hinkler Ave, North Bundaberg; (07) 4152 3659; www.footprintsadventures.com.au

## ④ Rockhampton (1–2 days)

You can't go anywhere in Rockhampton without being greeted by cow figurines. No, you're not in a bad sequel to the *House of Wax*, but rather the beef capital of Australia. This prosperous city on the banks of the Fitzroy River still retains many of its stone buildings and churches amidst flowering bauhinia and brilliant bougainvilleas. Visit Quay Street, Australia's longest National Trust-classified streetscape, with over 20 heritage buildings charmingly set on the banks of the river. Watch out for the bent-wing bat exodus in summer and the summer solstice light spectacular in early December to mid-January.

The Rockhampton Art Gallery is one of the best regional galleries in Queensland, and has free entry. Being a beef town, you don't want to miss out on an overnight stay at Myella Farm Cattle Station. This is as 'Aussie outback' as you can get, with activities ranging from horseback riding to cow milking. The Beef 'n' Reef Adventure tour, led by Dave the bush tucker man, is another unique tour of the Queensland outback. Watch Dave dance with snakes – it's a real treat!

## Further information

ⓘ **Rockhampton Tourist Information Centre** Customs House, 208 Quay St; 1800 805 865; Mon–Fri 8.30am–4.30pm, Sat–Sun 9am–4pm; www.rockhamptoninfo.com.au

**Rockhampton Art Gallery** 62 Victoria Pde; (07) 4927 7129; Mon–Fri 10am–4pm, Sat–Sun 11am–4pm.

**Myella Farmstay Australia** Meals included. Bookings essential. Pick up from Rockhampton at around 6.30am; return from farmstay at around 7pm the next day. Baralaba; (07) 4998 1290; www.myella.com

**Beef 'n' Reef Adventures** 1800 753 786 (bookings essential); capricorndave.com.au

## Where to eat

**Daltons Bistro** ⓈⓈ Splurge at one of Rockhampton's finest restaurants. An amazing a la carte menu worth the price. Cnr East & Williams sts; (07) 4921 4900; Mon–Fri 9am–3pm, Wed–Sat 6pm-late; www.daltonhospitality.com.au

## Pubs and bars

**The Criterion Hotel** Wet your whistle at this classy pub, featuring live entertainment Wednesday and Thursday nights. Get on the Friday night drink specials. Cnr Quay & Fitzroy sts; (07) 4922 1225; daily, lunch noon–2pm, dinner 6–9pm; bar 11am-late; www.thecriterion.com.au

## Where to stay

**Ascot Backpackers** ★★ Dorm $20, twin and double $40 177 Musgrave St, North Rockhampton; (07) 4922 4719; www.ascothotel.com.au

**Rockhampton YHA** ★★ Dorm $22, twin or double $50 60 MacFarlane St; (07) 4927 5288; www.yha.com.au

# VICTORIA

# CONTENTS

Melbourne 72

TOP REGIONS:

Great Ocean Road and the Grampians 84

Dandenongs and the Yarra Valley 89

Phillip Island and Gippsland 92

Goldfields and Spa Country 96

## Visitor information

Tourism Victoria 13 2842; www.visitvictoria.com
www.backpackvictoria.com

## FAST FACTS

**Wettest place** Weeaproinah (1900 mm per year), Otway Ranges

**Most famous beach** Bells Beach, Torquay

**Tons of gold mined** 2500 (2 per cent of world total)

**Estimated tons of gold left** 5000

**Litres of milk produced on Victorian dairy farms per year** 7 billion

**Famous people** Germaine Greer, Barry Humphries, Kylie Minogue

**Original name for the Twelve Apostles** The Sow and Piglets

**Local beer** Victoria Bitter

Victoria is probably Australia's most diverse state. In an hour's drive from Melbourne you might be surrounded by mist-laden mountain ranges and ferny gullies, or sunbaking on an awesome beach. For a bit of history, you can't go past Ballarat, the place responsible for turning Victoria around after the first gold nugget was unearthed in 1851. The Twelve Apostles and the Great Ocean Road will capture you for at least a week with incredible scenery and great surf, while everyone loves a trip to Phillip Island to see the little penguins. If you're more of a food and wine lover, be careful you don't end up with the Australian version of a Heathrow injection in the Dandenongs and Yarra Valley. Finally, Melbourne may be Australia's second-largest city, but it's a great place to spend some time checking out the many bars and pubs, seeing stellar sporting events, taking in cultural highlights or going shopping (even Sydneysiders admit they come to Melbourne to fill their wardrobes).

## Top region highlights

### Penguins on Phillip Island

Witness cute fairy penguins waddling across Summerland Beach en masse in their nightly 'Penguin Parade'. p. 92

### Great Ocean Road

Legendary surf, historic lighthouses, rainforest walks and resort towns, plus the blockbuster Twelve Apostles. Take your camera. p. 84

### Sovereign Hill

Step back in time (but not into fancy dress – leave that to the staff) at this re-created, 19th-century gold-rush town that's authentic in every detail. p. 96

### The Grampians

Great bushwalks in a timeless mountain landscape, as well as wildlife and Aboriginal rock art. p. 88

### Yarra Valley

Over 50 wineries in a drop-dead-gorgeous valley, just over an hour's drive from Melbourne. p. 90

## Other regions worth a look

### Mornington Peninsula

Summer retreat with classy towns like Sorrento and Portsea, along with vineyards, great food and beaches.

### Bellarine Peninsula

Spend a few lazy days at wineries and quiet coastal towns on this peninsula east of Geelong before taking on the Great Ocean Road.

### Mallee Country

Sparse country where beauty is in small details – wildflowers, pink salt lakes and stunning night skies. Camp out in a national park.

### Mildura and the Murray River

Ride on paddlesteamers on this major river and experience outback oases – if you're after fruit-picking work, Mildura is the place to be.

### High Country

There is skiing in winter and great bushwalking in summer. The scenery is classic Australian – pristine rivers, old cattlemen's huts in remote valleys, and gnarled snow gums defying gravity on the mountaintops.

Mildura

Murray-Sunset
National Park

Swan Hill

Echuca

Wodonga

Alpine
National Park

Bright

Little Desert
National Park

Horsham

Bendigo

Ballarat

Melbourne

Lakes Entrance

Cann River

Croajingolong
National Park

Grampians
National Park

Geelong

Sale

Portland

Warrnambool

Phillip Island

Wilsons
Promontory
National Park

# Melbourne

Melbourne may not have a host of star attractions, but this is the ultimate city to hang out in. Renowned as Australia's cultural capital, you can be sure to find great art, music and theatre around every corner. Melbourne is also known for its love of sport, and a footy or cricket match at the MCG is an absolute must. The CBD's intersecting main streets are straight and easy to navigate, presenting Gothic cathedrals, much-loved department stores, as well as some of the most modern architecture you've seen. Within this mesh of straight lines are vibrant laneways given over to cafes, hidden bars, nightclubs, boutique shops and contemporary 'laneway art' – it's worth taking the time to discover it all. The city has as much diversity as it has suburbs, from beach-loving St Kilda to alternative Fitzroy.

## Top attractions

### Federation Square

Completed in 2002, 'Fed Square' was the biggest building project to occur in Melbourne in decades, if not in actual size, then at least in terms of its public significance and architectural ambition. The blocky buildings come together like an angular 3D jigsaw puzzle, surrounded by an intricate design of cobblestones made with sandstone from Western Australia's Kimberley region. The central piazza is a great place to hang out, with frequent free concerts and major sporting events showing on the massive TV screen. There is also a lively hub of galleries, cafes, restaurants and bars, with plenty of outdoor tables.

Amongst the various attractions, your first stop should be the Ian Potter Centre: NGV Australia gallery, home to many works by well-known Australian artists and a fantastic Indigenous art collection. Next door, the Australian Centre for the Moving Image (ACMI) is a showcase of new media, with cinemas and darkened galleries screening films and screen-based art. Computer geeks will love the Games Lab. There's also the National Design Centre, showcasing the latest in local design, with exhibition spaces and a shop, and Champions: Australian Racing

### Visitor information centre

Federation Square Cnr Flinders & Swanston sts; (03) 9658 9658; www.visitvictoria.com, www.backpackvictoria.com

### Climate

'Four seasons in one day' is a familiar phrase to all Melburnians. It might reach 38°C in the morning then drop to 20°C in the afternoon – and the weather the next day is anyone's guess. Generally though, winter is cold (daytime temperatures of 11–12°C are not unusual) and spring is wet. January and February are hot, with temperatures anywhere between the mid 20s and high 30s. The favourite season of many locals is autumn, when the weather is usually dry and stable.

Museum, holding interactive horseriding displays. Ian Potter Centre: NGV Australia (03) 8620 2222, Tue–Sun 10am–5pm, Thur until 9pm, general admission free (also visit NGV International at 180 St Kilda Rd); ACMI (03) 8663 2200, daily 10am–6pm, general admission free; National Design Centre (03) 9654 6335, Mon–Sat 10am–5pm, Sun noon–5pm, general admission free; Champions: Australian Racing Museum, 1300 139 407, daily 10am–6pm, admission fee applies.

### Hidden laneways and arcades

A part of Melbourne lives in its narrow, darkened, edgy and arty laneways. From Flinders Street Station to Bourke Street Mall, you can slip through a world of cafes, shoe shops, fashion boutiques and jewellers. Shopping or not, these laneways are worth it for the walk alone.

The Atrium at Fed Square

Fed Square at night

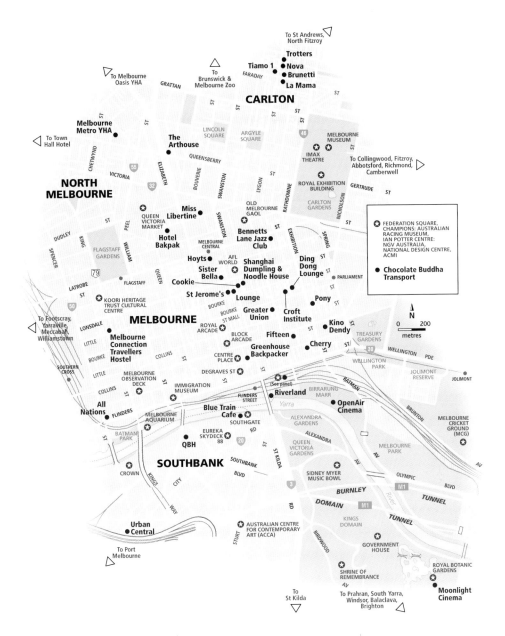

To St Andrews,
North Fitzroy

**Trotters**
**Tiamo 1** • **Nova**
• **Brunetti**
• **La Mama**

To Melbourne
Oasis YHA

To
Brunswick &
Melbourne Zoo

FARADAY

GRATTAN

**CARLTON**

ST

ST

LINCOLN
SQUARE

ARGYLE
SQUARE

46

**MELBOURNE
MUSEUM**

**Melbourne
Metro YHA**

To Town
Hall Hotel

**The
Arthouse**

QUEENSBERRY

LINCOLN

ELIZABETH

CHETWYND

VICTORIA

55

32

**IMAX
THEATRE**

**ROYAL EXHIBITION
BUILDING**

GERTRUDE

To Collingwood, Fitzroy,
Abbotsford, Richmond,
Camberwell

**NORTH
MELBOURNE**

PEEL

DUDLEY

KING

SPENCER

WILLIAM

BOUVERIE

SWANSTON

LYGON

RATHDOWNE

NICHOLSON

SPRING

CARLTON
GARDENS

ST

ST

**FEDERATION SQUARE,
CHAMPIONS: AUSTRALIAN
RACING MUSEUM,
IAN POTTER CENTRE:
NGV AUSTRALIA,
NATIONAL DESIGN CENTRE,
ACMI**

**QUEEN
VICTORIA
MARKET**

**Miss
Libertine**

OLD
MELBOURNE
GAOL

**Hotel
Bakpak**

FLAGSTAFF
GARDENS

MELBOURNE
CENTRAL

**Bennetts
Lane Jazz
Club**

EXHIBITION

**Chocolate Buddha
Transport**

79

FLAGSTAFF

QUEEN

**Hoyts**

AFL
WORLD

**Shanghai
Dumpling &
Noodle House**

**Ding
Dong
Lounge**

PARLIAMENT

**Sister
Bella**

**Cookie**

**St Jerome's**

**Lounge**

**Pony**

**KOORI HERITAGE
TRUST CULTURAL
CENTRE**

**MELBOURNE**

BOURKE

BOURKE
ST MALL

**Greater
Union**

**Croft
Institute**

To Footscray,
Yarraville,
Meccabah,
Williamstown

LONSDALE

LITTLE

BOURKE

LATROBE

ST

50

60

ROYAL
ARCADE

BLOCK
ARCADE

**Fifteen**

**Kino
Dendy**

TREASURY
GARDENS

N

0        200

metres

**Melbourne
Connection
Travellers
Hostel**

COLLINS

ST

CENTRE
PLACE

**Greenhouse
Backpacker**

**Cherry**

30

WELLINGTON

PDE

SOUTHERN
CROSS

LITTLE

DEGRAVES ST

WELLINGTON
PARK

JOLIMONT
RESERVE

JOLIMONT

COLLINS

ST

**MELBOURNE
OBSERVATION
DECK**

**IMMIGRATION
MUSEUM**

BIRRARUNG
MARR

**All
Nations**

FLINDERS

FLINDERS
STREET

**Riverland**

Yarra

**OpenAir
Cinema**

BRUNTON

**Blue Train
Cafe**

SOUTHGATE

**MELBOURNE
AQUARIUM**

ALEXANDRA
GARDENS

**MELBOURNE
CRICKET
GROUND
(MCG)**

BATMAN
PARK

**EUREKA
SKYDECK
88**

20

RD

ALEXANDRA

QUEEN
VICTORIA
GARDENS

ST KILDA

MELBOURNE
PARK

**QBH**

**SOUTHBANK**

SOUTHBANK

AV

AV

CROWN

KINGS

CITY

BLVD

**SIDNEY MYER
MUSIC BOWL**

OLYMPIC

BLVD

3

**BURNLEY**

M1

WAY

RD

**DOMAIN**

M1

**TUNNEL**

KINGS
DOMAIN

**TUNNEL**

**Urban
Central**

STURT

**AUSTRALIAN CENTRE
FOR CONTEMPORARY
ART (ACCA)**

BIRDWOOD

**GOVERNMENT
HOUSE**

To Port
Melbourne

**SHRINE OF
REMEMBRANCE**

AV

**ROYAL BOTANIC
GARDENS**

**Moonlight
Cinema**

To
St Kilda

To Prahran, South Yarra,
Windsor, Balaclava,
Brighton

---

You can access Degraves Street via a grungy subway from Flinders Street Station. The furthest section of Degraves Street is closed to cars and full of cafes spilling out onto the paved street. Degraves Espresso (23 Degraves Street) is the old favourite here, with its worn theatre seating, dim lighting and great coffee.

More clothes shops and tiny cafes, some only with crates for seating, are found in the next laneway, Centre Place. As you walk in, look up and see the beautiful Spanish-style Majorca Building.

Cross Collins Street to sophisticated Block Arcade, with its Italian-imported mosaic floors. Follow the arcade into the laneway

that joins onto Little Collins Street, an artery of yet more cafes.

Over Little Collins Street is Royal Arcade, Australia's oldest surviving arcade. Black-and-white chequered tiles give this place interest and elegance, and if you're a chocolate lover, head straight to Koko Black, which makes its own chocolates on-site.

# Getting around

Melbourne has tram, train and bus services, which are all covered by one ticket system. Tickets are called Metcards and the price depends on which of the two 'zones' you need to travel in (Zone 1 covers the inner suburbs). Two-hour tickets are also available. Metcards are available at train stations, on trams (for coin purchases only), on buses and at shops – usually newsagents – displaying a Metcard flag.

Trams are probably the best way of getting around the city, which you board from the centre of the main road or a designated tram stop. The City Circle tram is free, running along Spencer, La Trobe, Spring and Flinders streets, and extending to Docklands. Trams depart every 12 minutes between 10am and 6pm and run in both directions (with extended hours during daylight saving time to 9pm on Thursdays, Fridays and Saturdays). Paid services head out into the suburbs, with especially good coverage of the eastern, south-eastern and northern suburbs. A map of the different services can be found inside most trams.

Trains are generally a faster option if you're travelling to the suburbs. There are five stations in the city, three of them underground; the main one is Flinders Street. Details of services can be found at each one.

Buses tend to cover the areas that trains and trams don't. Details of bus routes (and also of tram and train routes) can be found at www.metlinkmelbourne.com.au or on some buses.

For drivers, the much-talked-about feature of Melbourne's roads is the hook-turn, a process of moving to the left of the road in order to turn right, and therefore getting out of the way of trams. Details of this rule can be found in the Melway street directory. If you wish to use the CityLink tollway, then either an e-TAG or a Day Pass is required (there are no tollbooths, but day passes can be purchased over the phone up to 24 hours after making a journey).

Public transport Tram, train and bus information line (Metlink) 13 1638

Tollway CityLink 13 2629

Motoring organisation RACV 13 1903; roadside assistance 13 1111

Car rental Avis 13 6333; Budget 1300 362 848; Hertz 13 3039; Thrifty 1300 367 227

Taxis 13CABS 13 2227; Embassy 13 1755; Northern Suburban 13 1119 Silver Top 13 1008; West Suburban (03) 9689 1144

Water taxi Melbourne Water Taxis (Yarra River) (03) 9686 0914

Tourist bus Melbourne on the Move 1300 558 686

Bicycle hire Hire a Bike (Waterfront City, Docklands) 0417 339 203; Bike Now (South Melbourne) (03) 9696 8588; St Kilda Cycles (03) 9534 3074

## Bird's-eye views

Melbourne's two tall towers both offer fantastic 360-degree views over the city and across to Port Phillip. The tallest is the 300 m Eureka Tower, where you can take a lift in 40 seconds to Eureka Skydeck 88 on the 88th floor. Pay extra to enter a glass cube that projects out of the building, giving you city views beneath your feet (not for those who experience vertigo). Melbourne Observation Deck is in Melbourne's original skyscraper, Rialto Towers, and still has great views from its 55th floor. Both have food and drink facilities. Eureka Skydeck 88, 76 City Rd, Southbank, (03) 9693 8888, daily 10am–10pm, admission fee applies; Melbourne Observation Deck, 525 Collins St, (03) 9629 8222, daily 10am–late, admission fee applies.

## Queen Victoria Market

This iconic market is spread across seven hectares under the shelter of giant sheds. At the Elizabeth Street end is a building containing meat, fish and deli produce, while outside, all manner of fruit and vegetable stalls extend up the hill. On weekends, Saturdays

Hanging sausages, Queen Victoria Market

in particular, the aisles are crammed with shoppers from all over Melbourne. As well as stocking up for the week, they treat the Vic Market as a social event, strolling around with their takeaway coffees and lining up for the ever-popular spinach and cheese boreks or kranksy sausages with sauerkraut. The other sections of the market are full of cheap clothing and souvenirs (including plenty of clip-on koalas for your token Aussie souvenirs). Tours of the markets are available (see Tours and activities below).

If you are in Melbourne during summer, come on Wednesday night for the Night Market. More a festival than a market, there is live music, alternative clothing, arts and crafts and food from around the globe. Cnr Elizabeth & Victoria sts; (03) 9320 5822; Tues, Thurs 6am–2pm, Fri 6am–6pm, Sat 6am–3pm, Sun 9am–4pm; admission free.

## Southgate and Crown

Stretching along the south of the Yarra River are these two modern shopping and dining precincts. To many locals, Crown is more of an anti-attraction – a symbol of excess with its casino, water walls along the riverfront that spew fireballs at night (and have killed a few passing pigeons in their time), restaurants where you can pay over $100 for a steak, and fashion salons where items regularly top $1000. Less cashed-up visitors might opt for a meal in the food court or maybe at Automatic Cafe, a similar set-up to Blue Train Cafe at Southgate (see Where to eat below).

Altogether less offensive, Southgate is a small, multi-level complex. There's a food court on the ground floor selling yummy Trampoline ice-cream, and a handful of shops, including one of Melbourne's Suga stores, where candy-making has been transformed into an art form. Shops, bars and

Block Place

restaurants become increasingly high-end as you make your way to the top — you'll find gifts, clothes, glassware, art and jewellery.

### Royal Botanic Gardens

If the best public gardens effortlessly combine several different functions, then this one is a high achiever. Within the Botanic Gardens and surrounding parkland, you'll find the sombre Shrine of Remembrance, honouring Australians killed in war; Government House, the official residence of the governor; Sidney Myer Music Bowl, a venue for raucous summer concerts; and in summertime, Moonlight Cinema offers an outdoor flick fest. A 3.8 km track called The Tan encircles the Botanic Gardens — Melbourne's favourite exercise track, constantly full of fitness freaks. But if it's a lazy day you're after, then pack a picnic and a frisbee, and wander deeper into the lush greenery, where you can feed

MCG footy match

the ducks. There are also some great spots for a barbecue or a picnic beside the Yarra. To really get to know the gardens, you can join an Aboriginal Heritage Walk (see Tours and activities). Birdwood Ave, South Yarra; (03) 9252 2300; Nov–Mar 7.30am–8.30pm, Apr, Sept–Oct 7.30am–6pm, May–Aug 7.30am–5.30am; general admission free.

### Royal Exhibition Building and Melbourne Museum

The Royal Exhibition Building was Australia's first man-made structure to achieve World Heritage status. A vast hall topped with a central dome, it is considered an enduring monument to the international exhibition movement that began in the mid-19th century. You can get inside the building to view this impressive space and its intricate frescoes on a tour run by Melbourne Museum, the spaceship-like structure next door.

Melbourne Museum is the famous home of Phar Lap, Australia's champion racing horse, standing proud and tall in a dimly lit room that harks back to the museums of old. Other exhibits are decidedly more upbeat. Bunjilaka is an impressive Indigenous cultural centre, and the museum also has dinosaur skeletons, a living rainforest, and impressive displays on science, the body and the mind. Located in the same building is the IMAX Theatre, screening films in 2D and 3D (see Cinemas below). Melbourne Museum, Carlton Gardens, 13 1102, daily 10am–5pm; admission fee applies; daily tours to see the Royal Exhibition Building (bookings required, 13 1102).

### Melbourne Cricket Ground (MCG)

Seeing a footy match amongst a capacity crowd of 100 000 mad fans at the MCG would have to be one of Melbourne's top experiences. Cricket matches are great too, but AFL madness seems to grip the city for longer (the season runs from March to September). Make sure you pick a team to 'barrack for', get into the loud and proud spirit, and dine on a hearty meal of beer, a meat pie and hot chips.

If you simply can't get enough sport in

## Markets

Prahran Market Australia's oldest continually running market, with everything from glistening seafood to gourmet potatoes and handmade chocolates. 163–185 Commercial Rd, South Yarra; Tues dawn–5pm, Thurs–Fri dawn–6pm, Sat dawn–5pm, Sun 10am–3pm.

South Melbourne Market Produce, deli items, clothing and homewares. Cnr Coventry & Cecil sts, South Melbourne, Wed 8am–4pm, Fri 8am–6pm, Sat–Sun 8am–4pm.

Collingwood Children's Farm Farmers' Market Victorian produce, from free-range eggs to fresh fruit and vegetables, in a lovely setting on the Yarra. St Heliers St, Yarra Bend; 2nd Sat each month 9am–5pm.

CERES Market Old-style breads and organic produce on a community-run property. 8–10 Lee St, Brunswick East; Wed & Sat 9am–2pm.

Camberwell Market Melbourne's best trash and treasure event. Carpark behind 515 Riversdale Rd, Camberwell; Sun 7am–12.30pm.

St Andrews Community Market Laidback market with alternative crafts, foods, music and clothing, an hour from the city. St Andrews, via Eltham; Sat 8am–2pm.

See also Queen Victoria Market above.

## Where to shop

Bourke Street Mall, City With department stores Myer and David Jones as well as the elegant GPO complex.

Collins Street, City Glamorous shopping strip with the big names. Check out the boutique-style shopping on adjacent Flinders Lane and Little Collins Street too.

Melbourne Central and QV, City These two modern centres on either side of Swanston Street are a shopper's paradise.

DFO Southern Cross Station, City Shopping mall of factory outlets for bargain hunters.

Southgate, Southbank A classy range of clothing, art and gifts.

Bridge Road, Richmond Back-to-back factory outlets and designer warehouses.

Chapel Street, South Yarra Where shopping is an event to dress up for. Find some of the best fashions in Australia on this trendy strip.

Collingwood and Fitzroy Sports stores and factory outlets along the top end of Smith Street, and many boutiques on Brunswick Street.

your system, then take a tour of the 'G'. Tours run on every non-event day, on the hour between 10am and 3pm (subject to availability). The tour includes a walk on the legendary ground. Brunton Ave, Richmond; tours leave from Gate 3 in the Olympic Stand; (03) 9657 8879.

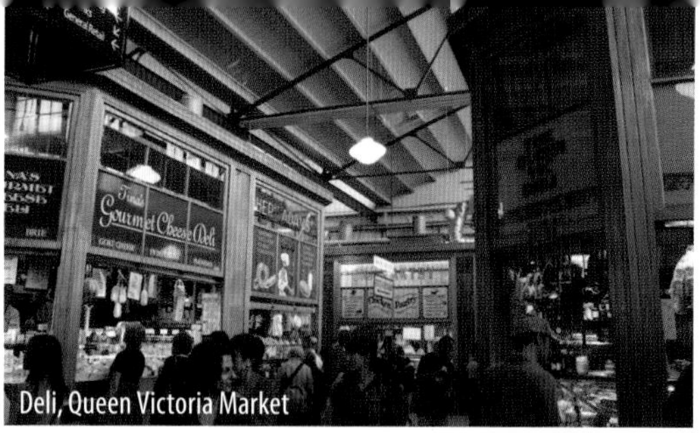
Deli, Queen Victoria Market

### Melbourne Zoo

A single iron-barred enclosure stands as a testimony to the fact that this is Australia's oldest zoo, established in the days when animal rights were rather low-profile. Today things are different – just look at the elephants, who slosh about in a giant plunge pool amid a re-creation of an Asian rainforest. A perennial favourite is the Butterfly House, where butterflies are happy to land on you as you walk through. You can also expect the full range of Australian animals wandering around an 'outback' area. During January and February the zoo runs a popular program of open-air jazz sessions called Zoo Twilights. Elliot Ave, Parkville; (03) 9285 9300; daily 9am–5pm; admission fee applies.

## Other attractions worth a look

**Old Melbourne Gaol** Setting for the execution of some of early Victoria's most notorious criminals, including Ned Kelly. Wander the cells and corridors or join a candle-lit Hangman's Night Tour. Russell St, between Victoria & Latrobe sts; (03) 9663 7228; daily 9.30am–5pm, plus evening tours; admission fee applies.

**Melbourne Aquarium** The creatures of the Southern Ocean take the limelight. See a surreal display of jellyfish and head to the 'fishbowl' for a close encounter with sharks (you can also arrange to dive with them). Cnr Queens Wharf Rd & King St; (03) 9620 0999; daily 9.30am–6pm; admission fee applies.

**AFL World** If seeing a game at the MCG isn't enough, this is the ultimate journey into the thick of footy culture. Learn about the players, see if you can kick one of the game's six most famous goals, and take over hosting *The Footy Show*, the local, Thursday-night program for the footy-mad. Swanston St; daily 10am–6pm; admission fee applies.

**Immigration Museum** Migration to Australia has been constant since the first days of European settlement. This museum is about tumultuous journeys and follows the waves of people who have brought new cultures and traditions to this land. 400 Flinders St; (03) 9927 2700; daily 10am–5pm; admission fee applies.

**Koorie Heritage Trust Cultural Centre** Learn about the Aboriginal people of Victoria and the violent and irreversible changes perpetrated on their 40 000-year-old culture. There are also changing exhibitions by local Aboriginal artists. 295 King St; (03) 8622 2600; daily 10am–4pm; entry by gold coin donation.

**Australian Centre for Contemporary Art (ACCA)** The Australian and international exhibitions shown within this rusted steel building veer towards confronting and interactive rather than conservative and traditional. The annual NEW exhibition, held around March/April, is a portal into the best and latest Australian art. 111 Sturt St, Southbank; (03) 9697 9999; Tue–Fri 10am–5pm, Sat–Sun 11am–6pm; admission free.

## Where to eat

**City and Southgate** Melbourne's CBD proves that it's Australia's top food city (never mind any Sydneysiders who argue the point). Why else would Jamie Oliver open the fourth restaurant in his international Fifteen chain here? (If you feel the urge to check out Fifteen, you'll find it in the basement of 115–117 Collins St; enter via George Pde.) Our favourites: **Pellegrini's** $ ♡ Prop up at the bar for traditional pasta, espresso or crème caramel, just as people have been doing since 1954. Gruff service is part of the experience. 66 Bourke St; (03) 9662 1885, Mon–Sat 8am–late, Sun noon–8pm.

**Shanghai Dumpling and Noodle House** $ 💎 Hidden down a laneway, this restaurant is popular with students. The decor isn't anything special, but the delicious steamed and fried dumplings and Shanghai noodles keep the crowds coming back. 25 Tattersalls La; (03) 9663 8555; Mon–Fri 11am–10pm.

**Riverland Cafe and Bar** $/$$ 💎 This modern establishment has a great riverside location. It's the ideal place for breakfast or an afternoon beer in summer, and the outdoor barbecue is smokin'. After dark, the crowds pile in for a good night out. 1–9 Federation Wharf, under Princes Bridge; (03) 9662 1771; daily 7am–midnight; www.riverlandbar.com

**Blue Train Cafe** $$ ♡ An old face in the ever-changing scene of Southgate. Blue Train is large, loud and fast, and aims to be everything to everyone. Dishes like golden dhal or the hot-rock pizzas are always good. Mid level, Southgate; (03) 9696 0440; Mon–Sat 7am–late, Sun 8am–late.

**Chocolate Buddha** $$$ **TOP TREAT!!** ♡ Perched in an elevated corner with views over Fed Square and Flinders Street Station, Chocolate Buddha is great for afternoons in the sun with a wine or beer. Inside, the restaurant is Japanese diner-style with one wall lined with Buddha statues. Start with edamame – salted fresh soy beans – and move on to great tempura, noodle soup or sashimi. Federation Sq; (03) 9654 5688; daily noon–late.

**Brunswick Street, Fitzroy** has everything from stalwart breakfast hubs like Mario's (303 Brunswick St), to Greek, to Afghan, to awesome vegetarian. After your meal, skip dessert and head to the Spanish chocolate wonderland of Chocolateria San

Churro (277b Brunswick St).

Our favourites: **Vegie Bar** 💲 💟 You might want to base yourself in Fitzroy just to be near the Vegie Bar, with its lively interior and walls covered in posters. Have a roti wrap one night, a perfect stir-fry the next, and wood-fired pizza the one after that. 378 Brunswick St; (03) 9417 6935; Mon–Fri 11am–late, Sat–Sun 9am–late.

**Babka** 💲 💟 Small bakery cafe where you might have to wait for a seat. The menu runs from sandwiches, pastries and salads to dishes proudly hailing from Russia and Eastern Europe, such as cottage cheese blintzes, borscht, and mushroom dumplings. Save room for some beautiful cake. 358 Brunswick St; (03) 9416 0091; Tue–Sun 7am–7pm.

**Bimbo Deluxe** 💲 💟 Some of Melbourne's cheapest and best pizzas are to be had in this moody, grungy ex-pub, where you can eat at a table or – if you're quick – on a couch. Enjoy Bimbo's own infused vodkas all night. There's a sister restaurant in Windsor called Lucky Coq (cnr Chapel & High sts, (03) 9525 1288). 376 Brunswick St; (03) 9419 8600; daily noon–2.30am.

**Moroccan Soup Bar** 💲 🍴 Head north across Alexandra Parade to find this gem, where the food is not strictly soup but is all vegetarian. The waitresses verbally impart the menu, and a good option is the banquet – under $20 for three courses, usually featuring a delicious creamy/crunchy dish of chickpeas and pita bread. Head to a nearby bar while you wait for a table. 183 St Georges Rd, Fitzroy North; (03) 9482 4240, Tue–Sun 6pm–10pm.

**Prahran and Windsor** Rivalling Fitzroy with their global flavours and alternative atmosphere. Make sure you pay a visit to Lucky Coq (see Bimbo Deluxe in Fitzroy above). The nightclub Revolver also has a surprisingly good Thai restaurant (see Out and about).

Our favourites: **Globe** 💲💲 💟 The crowd can sometimes be a bit too south-of-the-Yarra fashion conscious, but the food is fantastic, especially the global and/or vegetarian dishes

like Indonesian gado gado, the tofu burger on homemade cheese bread with crunchy Asian salad, and the quesadilla. There's also all-day breakfast, pastas, steak sandwiches and soups, and enormous cakes. 218 Chapel St, Prahran; (03) 9510 8693; Mon–Fri 8am–late, Sat–Sun 9am–late.

**Grill'd** 💲 💟 This chain of burger joints trumpets the 'healthy' fast food card. But don't let that turn you off – they make some mean burgers, from the Mighty Melbourne lean beef burger, to Moroccan lamb, chicken and vegetarian burgers. 157 Chapel St, Windsor; (03) 9510 2377; Sun–Thur 11.30am–10pm, Fri–Sat 11.30am–11pm; www.grilld.com.au

## Other areas to eat out

**Victoria St, Abbotsford** Like a mini Saigon with Vietnamese grocers, butchers and fishmongers all spilling onto the street and creating some rather pungent aromas. Choose from dozens of cheap, quick eateries.

**Lygon Street, Carlton** is Melbourne's mafia strip, full of pasta and pizza joints although not all of them are great. Worthy establishments are Tiamo 1 (303 Lygon St) and Trotters (400 Lygon St). For sweets, head to Brunetti (194–204 Faraday St).

**Sydney Road, Brunswick** Becoming the new Brunswick Street, as Fitzroy inevitably becomes more mainstream. Highlights are breakfasts at Ray (332 Victoria St), old-fashioned cakes at Green Refectory (115 Sydney Rd) and modern Asian at Tom Phat (184 Sydney Rd).

**Docklands** Modern waterfront precinct that lacks personality and tends to be pricey. But still, there are a few gems like Mecca Bah (55a Newquay Promenade) for mezze and Middle Eastern-style pizzas and, let's face it, great water views.

## Out and about
### Cinemas

**Hoyts On3** Entertainment Floor, Melbourne Central, cnr Swanston & La Trobe sts; (03) 8662 3555.

**Greater Union** 131 Russell St; (03) 9654 8133.

**Kino Dendy** (art house selection) 45 Collins St; (03) 9650 2100.

**Nova** (popular and art house selection) 380 Lygon St, Carlton; (03) 9347 5331.

**Village Jam Factory** 500 Chapel St, South Yarra; 1300 555 400.

**Moonlight Cinema** (outdoor cinema in summer) Royal Botanic Gardens; www.moonlight.com.au

**Open Air Cinema** (Feb–Mar) Birrarung Marr, behind Federation Sq; www.stgeorgeopenair.com.au

## Live music

Pick up a copy of street publications *Beat* or *Inpress*, or buy *The Age* on Friday for the 'EG' liftout with details of gigs around town.

Ding Dong Lounge Small space but an underground favourite featuring local and visiting rock and roll acts. The DJs play rock tunes too. Level 1, 18 Market La; (03) 9662 1020; Wed–Sat 7pm–late; www.dingdonglounge.com.au

Bennetts Lane Jazz Club Enter this small den and discover a world completely dedicated to jazz, featuring many local and international performers. 25 Bennetts La; (03) 9663 2856; daily from 8.30pm; www.bennettslane.com

Corner Hotel The dark carpet has soaked up many spilt beers, but who really cares when the music's the main focus. There is also a rooftop restaurant with views of the city and an outdoor area for summer, which serves better-than-average pub food. 57 Swan St, Richmond; (03) 9427 9198; Tue–Thur 4pm–late, Fri–Sun noon–late; www.cornerhotel.com

Night Cat Reggae, funk, Afro, Cuban or soul bands set up in the middle of the large

lamp-lit room and people boogie all around. When you need a rest and a drink, there are plenty of couches. Always a fun night out and no dancing skills are required – there's no judgement here. 141 Johnston St, Fitzroy; (03) 9417 0090; Thur–Sun 9pm–late; www.thenightcat.com.au

The Arthouse The hostel upstairs and grungy interiors guarantee a crowd of travellers and young music lovers. There are bands most nights of the week playing rock, punk and metal, and open stage nights on Mondays for any poets, musicians or comedians waiting to burst out. 616 Elizabeth St; (03) 9347 3917; Mon, Wed–Sun 7pm–late; www.thearthouse.com

## Pubs and bars

Cookie Stylish warehouse space with massive wall collages and polished wood floors. Cookie attracts after-work crowds, especially on Fridays, but you still might find yourself a nook. The middle of the day is quieter and there is seating on the sunny balconies. Beer service follows the sophisticated Belgian routine of dunk-in-a-water-bath and scrape-with-a-knife, so don't expect bargain prices. You can feast on some of Melbourne's best Thai food in the adjoining dining area. Level 1, 252 Swanston St; (03) 9663 7660; daily noon–late; www.cookie.net.au

St Jeromes The reputation of this place far exceeds its size. DJs play in the back courtyard that other establishments would only consider for bin storage. Tables and chairs are flung together from milk crates and other items. Beers are cheap, and St Jerome's even has its own laneway festival once a year, adding to the cult. If you can't make it past the bouncer, head to the 'sister' establishment called Sister Bella (end of Sniders Lane, off Drewery Lane, off Lonsdale Street near Swanston Street, whew). Caledonian La; Mon–Fri 8pm–late, Sat–Sun 11am–late.

Lounge Grungy upstairs space with pool tables, DJs, art exhibitions on the wall and cheap pub meals. Get yourself a table on the balcony overlooking Swanston Street.

1st Floor, 243 Swanston St; (03) 9663 2916; daily mid-morning–late; www.lounge.com.au

Transport A pub in the middle of Fed Square. The concrete and steel design can make the bar area seem cold and Star Trek-ish, but take your drink to the outside tables or into the room facing Flinders Street Station. There are over 100 beers to choose from. Two levels up is a cosier, more intimate space called Transit Lounge, with killer views over the Yarra. Federation Sq; (03) 9654 8808; daily 11am–late; www.transporthotel.com.au

The Workshop The Workshop is a refuge that knows how to make the industrial cool. As a converted motorcycle workshop, the raw interior, oil stains and graffiti walls culminate in an ideal place to mingle with a few drinks early in the evening or dance to some funk and hip-hop beats later at night. Lunch is available daily until 4.30pm. Level 1, 413 Elizabeth St; (03) 9326 4365; Mon–Tue 10am–late, Wed–Thur 10am–2am, Fri 10am–3am, Sat 1pm–3am, Sun 1pm–midnight; www.theworkshop.com.au

**Gin Palace** This glamour puss was one of the first back-alley bars in a city now crazy with them, and is still one of the best. Take your pick from a long list of martinis and sip while lounging on the velvet sofas. 10 Russell Pl; (03) 9654 0533, daily 4pm–3am.

**Belgian Beer Cafe** This place swarms in summer, when an outdoor bar and takeaway food area becomes the focal point of a giant beer garden. A historic bluestone building houses the main bar and a cosy dining area. There is live music on Sundays. 557 St Kilda Rd, Prahran; (03) 9529 2899; daily 11am– late; www.belgianbeercafemelbourne.com

**Sentido Funf** Brocade wallpaper and gilded mirrors give this bar, formerly known as Yelza, a touch of the Baroque. Out the back is one of Melbourne's best beer gardens in a greenhouse. 243–245 Gertrude St, Collingwood; (03) 9416 2689; Wed–Fri 4pm– late, Sat–Sun 2pm–late; www.sentidofunf. com.au

**Bar Open** Grungy Fitzroy hangout with lounges and tables downstairs. Upstairs is a small stage where experimental and up-and-coming bands play most nights of the week. 317 Brunswick St, Fitzroy; (03) 9415 9601; daily 1pm–late; www.baropen.com.au

**Windsor Castle** This lime green pub is tucked away in a back street, but worth the journey. Lounge about in the retro interior with a fire crackling in winter; in summer, head straight for the tropical beer garden. Lots of young people make a beeline here on Friday nights. The kitchen serves meals with Middle Eastern flair. 89 Albert St, Windsor; (03) 9525 0239; daily 11am–late.

**Mothers Milk** This funky bar has the power to transform from a relaxed lounge to a buzzing night spot, purely depending on the crowd and particular night. Afternoons and weeknights tend to be quieter, when the various couches get some good seat impressions, but come Friday and Saturday nights, an eclectic crowd fills this place right back to the private room. 17 Chapel St, Windsor; (03) 9521 4119; daily 3pm–late; www.mothers-milk.com.au

**Town Hall Hotel** The eclectic clutter, ranging from music memorabilia to empty bottles, will keep you entertained as you tuck into quality drinks and meals. There is live music, a fantastic beer garden showing films and – wait for it – Wednesday night betting on sumo wrestling matches that are screened on the pub's TVs. 33 Errol St, North Melbourne; (03) 9328 1983; Mon–Thur 4pm–1am, Fri noon–1am, Sat 10am–1am, Sun 10am–11pm.

## Nightclubs

**Cherry** No-fuss rock 'n' roll and soul club; in fact, dress down rather than up. DJs play to packed dance floors until the wee hours. 103–105 Flinders La, enter via AC/DC La; (03) 9639 8122; Tue–Sat 5pm–late.

**Croft Institute** The entry via a grimy alley off Chinatown, and all the laboratory and hospital equipment inside is meant to freak you … Once you get over that, this might become your favourite watering hole. It's set over three floors – bar downstairs, memorable loos on the second floor, dance floor on top. DJs play roots, reggae and drum and bass. 21–25 Croft Alley; (03) 9671 4399; Mon–Fri 5pm–late, Sat 8pm–late; www.thecroftinstitute.com.au

**Miss Libertine** An old pub given new life, Miss Libertine glides effortlessly from drinks venue for city workers to late-night DJ club on Fridays and Saturdays. The crowd is said to be a slightly more sophisticated version of Revolver's (see below). The kitchen does good pizzas. 34 Franklin St; (03) 9663 6855; Mon–Fri 10am–late, Sat noon–late; www.misslibertine.com.au

**Pony** Scruffy rock pub open to 7am on Friday and Saturday nights. Alternative bands play, then pass the baton to DJs. Feel free to sink into one of the well-loved couches and enjoy the music. 68 Little Collins St; (03) 9662 1026; Tue–Sun 4pm–late; www.pony.net.au

**Revolver** Steep stairs lead up from Chapel Street into a seedy hallway, perhaps not the most welcoming vision. But don't be deterred – off to the side is a room with a stage where bands and DJs play, and along the hallway is a large lounge with colourful lampshades and couches. Revolver is open 24 hours on weekends and DJs do recovery sessions from 7am. Unexpectedly, Revolver also has a good Thai restaurant. Revolver Upstairs, 229 Chapel St, Prahran; (03) 9521 5985; daily noon–late; www.revolverupstairs.com.au

**First Floor** Hip hop, roots and R'n'B acts play until around midnight, when the DJs take over. The people here really shake it on the dance floor. 393 Brunswick St, Fitzroy; (03) 9419 6380; Wed–Sun 9pm–late; www.firstfloor393.com.au

**Boutique** The most fashionable club in Melbourne – the kind of place where Paris Hilton goes when she's in town. Make sure you look fabulous. 134 Greville St, Prahran; (03) 9525 2322; Thur–Sat 9pm–late; www.boutique.net.au

**QBH** A HUGE club venue that attracts large crowds (expect to wait in a line before being let in). With four bars, lounge areas and great DJs, you're guaranteed an equally HUGE night out. 1 Queensbridge St, South Melbourne; (03) 9686 2944; Fri 10.30pm–5am, Sat 10pm–7am, check website for other events; www.queensbridge.com.au

## Performing arts

**Victorian Arts Centre** 100 St Kilda Rd; (03) 9281 8000.

**Malthouse Theatre** 113 Sturt St, Southbank; (03) 9685 5100.

**La Mama** (small theatre not afraid of the experimental) 205 Faraday St, Carlton; (03) 9347 6142.

VICTORIA

## Where to stay

For further information and reviews on these hostels, please visit www.bugaustralia.com, www.hostelaustralia.com or www.hostelz.com

**Greenhouse Backpacker ★ ★ ★** Dorm $27, double or twin $70 228 Flinders La; 1800 249 207; www.friendlygroup.com.au

**Melbourne Metro YHA ★ ★ ★** Dorm $29.50, double or twin $85 78 Howard St, North Melbourne; (03) 9329 8599; www.yha.com.au

**Urban Central ★ ★ ★** Dorm $23, double with ensuite $89 334 City Rd, Southbank; 1800 631 288; www.urbancentral.com.au

**Hotel Bakpak ★ ★** Dorm $24, double or twin $75 167 Franklin St; 1800 645 200; www.hotelbakpak.com

**Melbourne Oasis YHA ★ ★** Dorm $30.50, double $72 76 Chapman St, North Melbourne; (03) 9328 3595; www.yha.com.au

**Melbourne Connection Travellers Hostel ★ ★** Dorm $24, twin or double $80 205 King St; (03) 9642 4464; www.melbourneconnection.com

**The Nunnery ★ ★** Dorm $26, double $85 116 Nicholson St, Fitzroy; 1800 032 635; www.nunnery.com.au

**Chapel Street Backpackers ★ ★** Dorm $26, twin $68 22 Chapel St, Windsor; (03) 9533 6855; www.csbackpackers.com.au

**All Nations ★** Dorm $23, twin $70 Cnr Flinders & Spencer sts; 1800 222 238; www.allnations.com

**Adelphi Hotel ★ ★ ★ TOP TREAT!!** This hotel is all about modern, architectural, minimalist style with bright splashes of yellow. The rooftop pool, which is perched over the city laneway, has a clear perspex floor to give you a view of the people below while you swim. 187 Flinders La; (03) 9650 7555; www.adelphi.com.au

## Tours and activities

*Neighbours* **Tour** Visit the real Ramsay Street – if you're lucky, you might see some filming in action. Pay a little extra to meet the stars. Tours run daily. Bookings (03) 9629 5866. www.neighbourstour.com.au

**Lanes and Arcades Tour** Focusing on the city's hidden laneways full of innovative fashion, art, design and great food. Tours run Wednesdays, Fridays and Saturdays. Bookings (03) 9329 9665. www.hiddensecretstours.com

**Haunted Melbourne Ghost Tours** Get the adrenalin pumping as you traipse down dark alleys and enter city buildings that the ghosts of early Melbourne are known to haunt. Tours run Saturdays. Bookings (03) 9670 2585. www.haunted.com.au

**Chocoholic Tours** A range of tours to get you drooling, taking in Melbourne's best chocolatiers, candy-makers, ice-creameries and cafes. Tours run Fridays and Saturdays. Bookings (03) 9686 4655. www.chocoholictours.com.au

**Harley Davidson Tours** Take the 'Introduction to Melbourne Tour' over the West Gate Bridge with the wind whistling through your hair. Tours run daily. Bookings 1800 182 282. www.harleyrides.com.au

**Aboriginal Heritage Walk** With an Aboriginal guide and a gum leaf for a ticket, stroll through the Royal Botanic Gardens and learn about the bush foods, medicines and traditional lore of the Boonerwrung and Woiwurrung people, whose traditional lands meet here. Tours run Thursdays, Fridays and alternate Sundays. Bookings (03) 9252 2429. www.rbg.vic.gov.au

**Foodies' Tours, Queen Victoria Market** Get tips on picking the best fresh produce, meet the specialist traders and taste samples from the deli. Tours run Tuesdays and Thursdays–Saturdays. Bookings (03) 9320 5835. www.qvm.com.au

**Capital City Trail** Hire a bike at the Docklands and take this 29 km loop through suburban bushland. It follows the Yarra River past Crown and Southbank to Collingwood Children's Farm and Studley Park. Stop for lunch at Lentil as Anything in the old convent next to the children's farm (see St Kilda below), or at the cafe at Studley Park Boathouse. From here the path heads north along Merri Creek, west through Fitzroy North and Carlton, and back to Docklands. Trail information www.bv.com.au. Rentabike @ Docklands 0417 339 203.

**Ferry to Williamstown** From Southbank, take a ferry to Williamstown, a suburb with the feel of a maritime village. There's a great beach and plenty of cafes. On weekends a ferry service also runs between Williamstown and St Kilda. Ferries run hourly between 9.30am–4.30pm (to 5.30pm during daylight saving time), (03) 9506 4144. www.williamstownferries.com.au

St Kilda foreshore

# Outside the city: St Kilda

St Kilda began life as a seaside holiday destination, so separate from the city that on the sandy track that was then St Kilda Road, travellers ran the risk of a run-in with a bushranger. Today it has the feeling of a city within a city. Fitzroy Street is a long line of shoulder-to-shoulder cafes, restaurants, bars and pubs. Straight ahead is the palm-lined foreshore and beach, and the much-loved St Kilda Pier. The path along the foreshore goes to Port Melbourne in the north and beyond Brighton in the south, and is almost always busy with cyclists, rollerbladers and walkers.

Near the pier, St Kilda Sea Baths is a swanky relaxation and fitness complex, dating back to the days when people opted for saltwater baths overlooking the sea rather than swimming in the open ocean.

On the other side of Luna Park (see below), Acland Street flaunts a buzzy strip of cafes, restaurants and ice-cream shops, as well as the run of continental cake shops that originally made the street famous.

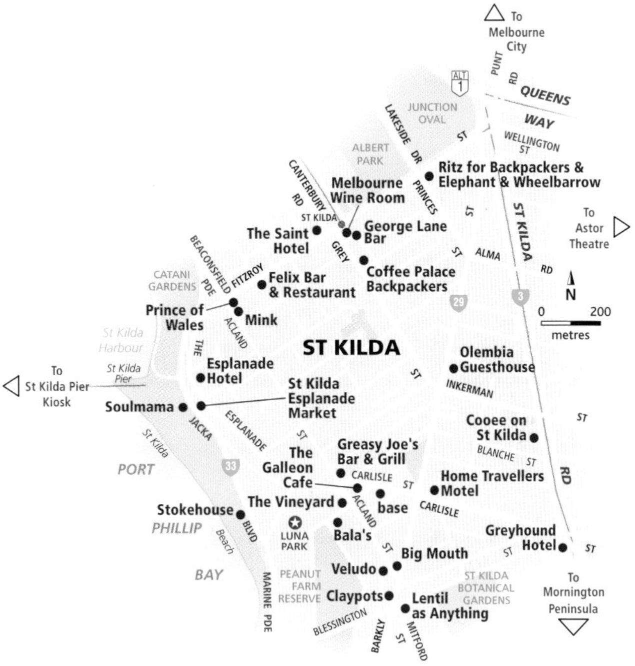


> ## Getting to St Kilda
>
> Trams are the easiest way to get from the city to St Kilda. The most direct option is tram #96 (East Brunswick to St Kilda East), which travels down Bourke Street and Spencer Street then becomes light rail to St Kilda. Other options are tram #16, which takes Swanston Street and St Kilda Rd, and tram #112, which takes Collins and Spencer streets and goes via South Melbourne and Albert Park.

## Top attractions

### Luna Park

While now appropriately modernised, Luna Park still feels like a chunk of the early 20th century, when a walk through the Palais de Folies (the Palace of Giggles) was a big night out, and live entertainment involving animals and midgets was perfectly acceptable. Since it opened in 1912, many things about the park live on, including the huge, famous and much-renovated face that forms its entrance – it's either laughing or screaming, depending on how you see it. A stroll through Luna Park is free, but let yourself be tempted by a ride on the ghost train or rollercoaster (or, if it's your cup of tea, the Shock Drop or G Force). Lower Esplanade; (03) 9525 5033; Sept–Apr Fri 7pm–11pm, Sat 11am–11pm, Sun 11am–6pm; Apr–Sept Sat–Sun 11am–6pm; daily in school holidays; general admission free.

## Where to eat

### St Kilda Pier Kiosk $/$$ ♡

Take the long promenade up the pier to this quaint building, which locals hold dear to their hearts. After being destroyed by fire in 2003, this St Kilda icon was rebuilt with the same old-fashioned kiosk serving quick and tasty morsels, and a more modern cafe out back. Snag yourself a spot on the deck for lazy afternoon beers overlooking the harbour. Pier Rd, off Jacka Blvd; (03) 9525 5545; kiosk daily 8am–4pm, Little Blue Cafe Mon–Tue 12pm–4pm, Wed–Fri 12pm–late, Sat–Sun 8am–late (tapas menu only on Sun nights).

### Soulmama $$ ♡

A vegetarian restaurant in the St Kilda Sea Baths with bay views. The food is glorified bain marie-style: take a ticket for a small, medium or large bowl and fill it with your choice of curries, salads, pastas and the like – these might not go together, but you might not mind. Save room for dessert. St Kilda Sea Baths, Jacka Blvd; (03) 9525 3338, lunch & dinner daily; www.soulmama.com.au

### Lentil as Anything [?] 💎

A novel concept – a pay-as-you-feel restaurant where you decide what the meal is worth. Everything is vegetarian and prepared to order. Highlights include the okonomiyaki (Japanese pancake) and curries with roti bread. There are now other

Lentil establishments at 113 Sydney Road, Brunswick, and in a beautiful old convent at 1 St Heliers Street, Abbotsford. But the St Kilda restaurant is the original. This place is for people with a conscience, so don't be nasty when your donation is requested. 41 Blessington St; (03) 9534 5833; daily noon–10 pm; www.lentilasanything.com

**Bala's** 🅂 Some of the dishes are cooked to order, some are steaming hot and waiting for you in the bain marie, but none are stodgy. Expect fabulously fragrant curries and stir-fries, along with nice touches like a choice between white or brown rice. Shakespeare Gve; (03) 9534 6116; daily noon–10 pm.

**Greasy Joe's Bar & Grill** 🅂🅂 ♡ Nothing about this place is subtle or elegant – it's all about giant burgers, steaks and beer (although that said, you can find a tofu or fish burger among the meat-with-extra-meat options if you insist). Greasy Joe's also does breakfast, and if it's love at first sight then you can take home a Greasy Joe's T-shirt. 64 Acland St; (03) 9525 3755, daily 7am–late; www. greasyjoes.com.au

**The Galleon Cafe** 🅂 ♡ Like a second lounge room for the St Kilda neighbourhood. Grab one of the Laminex tables, spread out a newspaper, and settle in for a lazy breakfast or lunch. There are great vegetarian options. 9 Carlisle St; (03) 9534 8934, daily 7am–5pm.

**Stokehouse** 🅂🅂 ♡ If someone was to shake out their towel on St Kilda Beach, outdoor tables here might get a small dusting of sand. That's how 'beachfront' this restaurant is. Stay downstairs for cheaper dishes like pizza, pasta or veal scaloppine. Head upstairs for a pricier white tablecloth experience and a memorable meal. 30 Jacka Blvd; (03) 9525 5555; lunch & dinner daily; www.stokehouse.com.au

**Claypots** 🅂🅂🅂 **TOP TREAT!!** 💎 Raucous seafood restaurant that is now also found at 153 Gertrude St, Fitzroy. If you don't want to blow your budget, then stick to a humble claypot dish or a cheaper fish special

like leatherjacket. Otherwise, go all out with a shellfish platter or a whole baked fish dish (these might seem expensive, but aren't usually when split between a few people). 213 Barkly St; (03) 9534 1282; lunch & dinner daily.

See also Esplanade Hotel below.

## Out and about
### Cinemas

**Palace George** 135 Fitzroy St; (03) 9534 6922.

**Astor Theatre** (re-runs of classics and recent releases) 1 Chapel St, St Kilda East; (03) 9510 1414.

### Pubs, bars and nightclubs

**Esplanade Hotel** 'The Espy' is a Melbourne icon, standing white and bright along The Esplanade. There are pool tables and three rooms for live music from rock to hip hop (the best room is the Gershwin Room, once an opulent dining room). The kitchen serves up old-school chicken parmigianas, smaller mezze dishes and breakfasts. 11 The Esplanade; (03) 9534 0211; Mon–Wed, Sun noon–1am, Thur–Sat noon–3am; www.espy.com.au

**Prince of Wales** Downstairs is a grungy public bar where locals like to hang out. Upstairs, the band room presents a diverse selection of local and visiting acts, maybe hip hop, electronic or roots. The best usually play Friday nights. On Saturday nights the room becomes a nightclub. 29 Fitzroy St; (03) 9536 1168; daily noon–late; www.princebandroom.com.au

**Mink** If you manage to get past the notorious bouncers, then you'll arrive in a slinky basement space with velvet chairs, dim lighting and plenty of private alcoves, as well as an enormous list of infused vodka cocktails.

2 Acland St, beneath The Prince of Wales Hotel; (03) 9536 1199; daily 6pm–late.

**Elephant and Wheelbarrow** Favourite backpacker pub, not least because *Neighbours* stars visit on Monday nights (tickets cost $35 and bookings are essential). Other nights feature poker, trivia and bands. 169 Fitzroy St; (03) 9534 7888, daily 11am–late; www.elephantandwheelbarrow.com.au

**The Saint Hotel** Is it a pub, a nightclub (DJs play on Fridays and Saturdays), or a cocktail lounge? The Saint dabbles in a little bit of everything and has a good beer garden. 54 Fitzroy St; (03) 9593 8333; Wed–Fri 5pm–late, Sat–Sun 2pm–late; www.thesainthotel.com

**Veludo** Cafe/restaurant downstairs, bar upstairs. DJs play Friday and Saturday nights. If you can, nab a seat by the window looking out over Acland Street. 175 Acland St; (03) 9534 4456; daily 8am–late; www.veludo.com.au

**George Lane Bar** The hidden alleyway location – like all of Melbourne's best city bars – maintains George Lane Bar's exclusivity. The interior recreates an antique parlour with white murals of animals. Great wines and cocktails. 1 George La, behind 129 Fitzroy St; (03) 9593 8884; Tue–Sun 4pm–1am.

**Melbourne Wine Room** Trendy reinvented pub that packs out with the after-work crowd on Friday nights, when things turn loud and boisterous. Even at other times it

has the feeling that this is where the party's at. There's an excellent wine list (surprise, surprise). 125 Fitzroy St; (03) 9525 5599; Mon–Thu 3pm–late, Fri–Sun noon–late.
**Vineyard** This place is packed out on Friday and Saturday nights when live bands play. At other times the low lighting makes it a funky place to sip a drink. During summer weekends, the outside area facing Luna Park is the place to mingle with a beer in hand. 71a Acland St; (03) 9534 1942; daily 8am–10pm; www.thevineyard.com.au
**Felix Bar & Restaurant** A slick, modern bar that gets a range of clientele. If you need a feed before a big night out, there's a $10 chicken parmigiana night on Mondays and $13.90 steak deal on Tuesdays. 43 Fitzroy St; (03) 9525 3744; Sun–Thur 6pm–1am, Fri–Sat 6pm–3am; www.felixbar.com
**Big Mouth** This multi-faceted venue is set over two levels with a cafe area downstairs, and a lounge and restaurant area upstairs. Get in early if you want to score one of the soft couches for a night of stress-free drinking. Cnr Acland & Barkly sts; (03) 9534 4611; Sun–Thur 6.30pm–midnight, Fri–Sat 6.30am–3am; www.bigmouthstkilda.com.au

## Where to stay

**base** ★ ★ ★ Dorm $24, double $95 17 Carlisle St; (03) 8598 6200; www.basebackpackers.com
**Home Travellers Motel** ★ ★ ★ Dorm $20, double or twin $80 32 Carlisle St; 1800 008 718; www.hometravellersmotel.com.au
**Coffee Palace Backpackers** ★ ★ Dorm $20, double or twin $50 24 Grey St; 1800 654 098; www.coffeepalacebackpackers.com.au
**Cooee on St Kilda** ★ ★ Dorm $25, twin or double $99 333 St Kilda Rd; 1800 202 500; www.cooeeonstkilda.com
**Ritz for Backpackers** ★ ★ Dorm $20–$29, double or twin $65 169 Fitzroy St; (03) 9525 3501; www.ritzpackpackers.com
**Olembia Guesthouse** ★ ★ Dorm $26, single $50, double or twin $75–$80, triple $90 96 Barkly St; (03) 95371412; www.olembia.com.au

## Other suburbs worth visiting

**South Melbourne** Clarendon Street is a long strip of shops, cafes and restaurants. One block behind is the South Melbourne Market and more cafe gems such as Q Eleven (303 Coventry St).
**Port Melbourne** Stroll along the waterfront, perhaps with an ice-cream or a bag of hot chips, and see where the *Spirit of Tasmania* docks. Bay Street is choc-a-block pubs, cafes and restaurants.
**Balaclava** Carlisle Street is where kosher butchers and bagelries mix with retro clothing stores and new cafes; Wall Two 80 (rear 280 Carlisle St) and Las Chicas (203 Carlisle St) are favourites – expect to wait for a table, particularly on weekends.
**Brunswick** Sydney Road is the main artery, renowned for its Middle Eastern shops. While old shops close, new cafes move in, and there are also many hidden in residential streets. Worth a stroll for its diversity.
**Williamstown** More like a small seaside town than a suburb, Williamstown oozes history. Picnic on the grass in front of the wharf and watch the yachts bobbing up and down in the harbour, or visit Scienceworks museum. You can get to Williamstown by ferry (see Tours and activities above).
**Brighton** The demographic is rather wealthy, so you'll find plush cafes and food stores. The beach appears in many photographs because of its long line of coloured bathing boxes, and there are views of the city.
**Footscray** An even grittier version of the Vietnamese hub that is Victoria Street, Abbotsford. Restaurants serve Vietnamese pho and bakeries sell egg tarts. There are also great African restaurants and the large Footscray Market.
**Yarraville** A gem tucked away in the largely dull and industrial sweep of western suburbs. Tiny streets make you feel like you're in the country; there are cafes, restaurants and a fantastic Art Deco cinema.

## Visitor information

### Melbourne Airports
Melbourne's major airport is **Tullamarine**, which is 20–30 minutes drive north of the city centre. A small domestic airport, **Avalon**, is located between Melbourne and Geelong servicing the airline Jetstar (some Jetstar flights also go to Tullamarine).
**Bus** From Tullamarine, the **Skybus** goes to Melbourne's Southern Cross Station every 15 minutes during the day and half hourly or hourly throughout the night. You don't need to book. Smaller shuttle buses can take you from Southern Cross to your hotel. (03) 9335 2811 or www.skybus.com.au
At Avalon, **Sunbus** services meet every flight to take passengers to Melbourne's Southern Cross Station ((03) 9689 6888 or www. sunbusaustralia.com.au) or Avalon **Airport Shuttle** goes to Geelong and the Great Ocean Road. Bookings (03) 5278 8788 or www. avalonairportshuttle.com.au
**Taxi** A taxi from Tullamarine to the CBD will cost around $40–$45 one way.

### Internet cafes
**The Lab** 490 Elizabeth St; (03) 9639 7500.
**e55** Basement, 55 Elizabeth St; (03) 9620 3899.
**eLounge** Level 1, 9 Elizabeth St; (03) 9629 3188.
**Kat Bahloo** 107 Acland St, St Kilda; (03) 9593 8855.
**World Wide Wash** 361 Brunswick St, Fitzroy; (03) 9419 8214.

### Hospitals
**For all emergencies, including police, fire, or hospital, dial '000'.**
**Royal Melbourne Hospital** Grattan St, Parkville; (03) 9342 7000.
**Alfred Hospital** Commercial Rd, Prahran; (03) 9276 2000.
**St Vincents Hospital** Victoria Pde, Fitzroy; (03) 9807 2211.

For more detail
see maps
206, 211 & 212

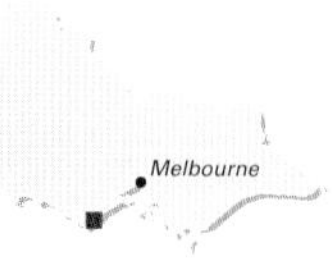


# Great Ocean Road and the Grampians

# From the ocean to the bush

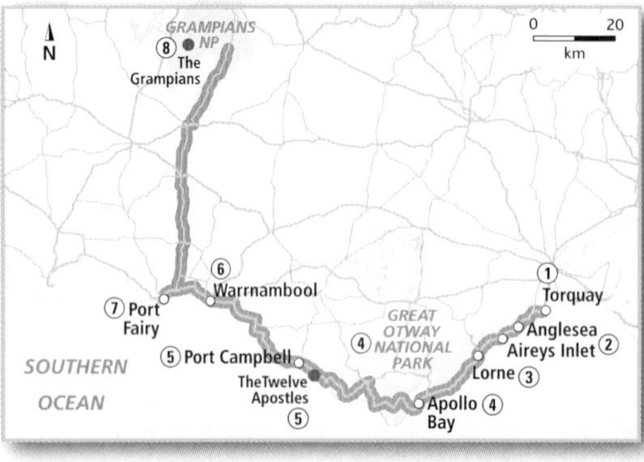


Victoria's south-west coast is one of the country's great scenic destinations, with the Great Ocean Road connecting a number of must-visit locations. The winding band of bitumen passes wild surf beaches, towering forests, rugged cliffs and limestone formations. Stop at Torquay for its thumping surf, Lorne for its lively resort atmosphere, Apollo Bay for a jaunt into the forests, and Port Campbell for scenery that is way more impressive than any photograph. To the north is the iconic mountain scenery of the Grampians, protecting significant Aboriginal rock art.

**Number of days to spend in this region: 10–20 days**

## Getting here

**V/Line** trains run frequently between Melbourne and Geelong. From Geelong, a bus service travels the Great Ocean Road as far as Apollo Bay several times a day. A service continues on from Apollo Bay to Warrnambool via Lavers Hill and Port Campbell on Mondays, Wednesdays and Fridays.

**V/Line** 13 6196; www.vline.com.au

Another option is to take a train from Melbourne to Warrnambool via Geelong and Colac. Regular buses run between Warrnambool and Port Fairy.

To get to the Grampians, daily bus services run from Melbourne to Halls Gap. It is also possible to get from Warrnambool to Halls Gap on a bus service that runs three times a week.

## 1 Torquay (2 days)

Torquay itself is nothing remarkable, but it's the thumping waves offshore that make it south-west Victoria's surfing mecca. Winds push the swells up along the coast, aided by low-pressure systems from the Southern Ocean, while the reefs, headlands and beaches help shape the waves into reef breaks, point breaks and beach breaks. The best surf is between April and September.

The signature break around Torquay is Bells Beach, around 5 km to the town's south-west. It has a rock shelf coming right to the shore, and a steady incline means waves break consistently, whatever the size of the swell. On a good day, distinct swell lines can be seen forming hollow, 3–4 m waves. Bells hosts the Rip Curl Pro during Easter. Another classic surf beach is Winkipop, while beaches like Jan Juc are good for beginners. If you want to learn how to surf, a few schools operate in the area.

To deck yourself out with gear, or just to soak up surfing culture, head to Surf City Plaza in the centre of town. Torquay is the birthplace of the major brands Rip Curl and Quiksilver, which still have large outlets here, as do many other names. You'll also find the Surfworld Museum, holding memorabilia from the early 1900s through to today, a surfer hall of fame and a theatre screening surf flicks.

### Further information

ℹ **Torquay Visitor Centre** Surf City Plaza, Beach Rd; (03) 5261 4219; daily 9am–5pm; www.visitsurfcoast.com

**Surfworld Museum** Surf City Plaza, Beach Rd; (03) 5261 4606; daily 9am–5pm; www.surfworld.org.au

**Surf school: Westcoast Surf School** (03) 5261 2241; www.westcoastsurfschool.com

### Where to eat

**Flippin' Fresh Seafoods** $ Above-par fish and chips. 33 Surfcoast Hwy; (03) 5261 6146; daily 10.30am–8pm.

**Growlers** $$ Eggs for breakfast, through to hearty dishes from around the globe for lunch and dinner. Overlooks the beach. 23 The Esplanade; (03) 5264 8455; Wed–Fri noon–late, Sat–Sun 10am–late (extended days/hours in summer).

**Imperial Rhino** $ Stir-fries, sushi, noodles and salads. 3 Bell St; (03) 5261 6780; daily 8am–3pm & 5–9pm.

### Where to stay

**Bells Beach Lodge** ★★ Dorm $25, double or twin $65 51–53 Surf Coast Hwy; (03) 5261 7070; www.bellsbeachlodge.com.au

## Events

Rip Curl Pro The world's top surfers converge for 10 days of competitions. A music festival is held over the long weekend. Easter.

# 2 Anglesea and Aireys Inlet (2–3 days)

You might choose to do what most visitors do – that is, speed past Anglesea and Aireys Inlet en route to Lorne. But if you have more time, you can pleasantly while away a few days in both towns, and hit the Anglesea Golf Club, renowned for its resident kangaroos.

Surrounding the town is bushland known as the Anglesea Heath. Minor vehicle tracks double as walking trails, passing spring orchids (details and maps available from Parks Victoria). Other Anglesea walks include the boardwalks through the wetlands of Coogoorah Reserve on the Anglesea River (behind the boatsheds on the river); the beach towards Torquay; or the extended Surf Coast Walk that runs between Jan Juc and Moggs Creek.

Aireys Inlet is marked by the red-capped Split Point Lighthouse, also signalling the beginning of Fairhaven Beach. At 6 km long, this is one of the longest beaches on the Great Ocean Road. The road above it runs for its entire length, making it easy to access the beach at all sections (however, only an area near the lifesaving club is patrolled in summer). There's also the option for horseriding along the beach and into the bush.

## Further information

[i] Anglesea Golf Club Golf Links Rd; (03) 5263 1951; www.angleseagolfclub.com.au

Anglesea Heath Parks Victoria 13 1963; www.parkweb.vic.gov.au

Surf Coast Walk www.anglesea-online.com.au/surfcoastwalk

## Horseriding

Blazing Saddles Aussie cowboy-style riding tours. (03) 5289 7322; www.blazingsaddlestrailrides.com

## Where to stay

Anglesea Backpackers ★ Dorms $23, ensuite $70 40 Noble St, Anglesea; (03) 5263 2664.

Aireys Inlet Holiday Park ★ Ensuite cabin from $85 19–25 Great Ocean Rd, Aireys Inlet; 1800 668 866; www.aicp.com.au

# 3 Lorne (2–3 days)

At the height of summer, the beach at Lorne can seem just as crowded and fashion-conscious as Sydney's Bondi Beach. But Lorne's beach is wide and long, so you should be able to find your own patch of sand. A smattering of historic hotels gives the town an English air, and there are great eating and accommodation options, all the mod-cons and plenty of young people here to have fun. The Falls Festival, held every New Year's Eve, is a major drawcard for young, music-loving campers. For a

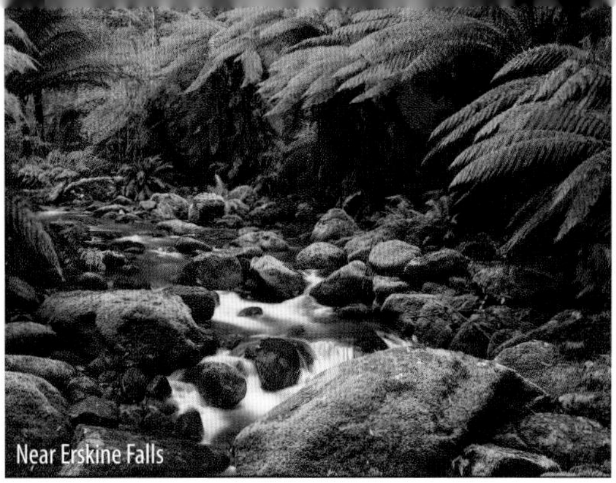

Near Erskine Falls

nature experience, Erskine Falls is around 10 km from Lorne, with water plummeting 30 m into a ferny gully. You can get there either by car or, if you're in the mood for a hike, walk along the river from town.

A few hours could also be spent visiting Qdos, a funky art gallery and studio surrounded by bush. January through to Easter sees a busy program of indoor and outdoor exhibitions. A giant on-site kiln is fired by ceramic artists twice a year, and there's a cafe open Friday to Monday.

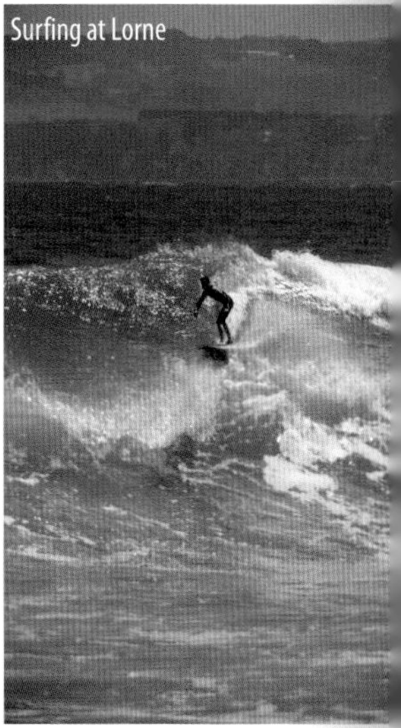

Surfing at Lorne

## Further information

[i] Lorne Visitor Centre 15 Mountjoy Pde; 1300 89 11 52; daily 9am–5pm; www.visitsurfcoast.com

Qdos 35 Allenvale Rd; (03) 5289 1989; daily 10am–5.30pm (closed Tue outside holiday periods); www.qdosarts.com

## Where to eat

Moons Espresso and Juice Bar $ Wholesome cafe fare. 108 Mountjoy Pde; (03) 5289 1149; daily 8am–5pm.

Reif's $$ An institution for breakfast, creeping into the up-market category for lunch and dinner. 84 Mountjoy Pde; (03) 5289 2366; daily 8.30am–late (reduced hours May–Sept).

The Lorne Ovenhouse $$ Pizzas cooked in a wood oven, along with a more expensive menu of Greek-inspired mains. 46a Mountjoy Pde; (03) 5289 2544; lunch & dinner daily, breakfast Sat–Sun.

ba ba lu bar $$ Choose between excellent Spanish tapas or more traditional mains, or come just for a drink. 6a Mountjoy Pde; (03) 5289 1808; daily 9am–late.

## Live music

The Lorne Hotel 176 Mountjoy Pde; 1800 633 2200; bands on Saturday nights.

## Where to stay

Great Ocean Road Backpackers (YHA) ★★★ Dorm $23.50, double or twin $53.50 10 Erskine Ave; (03) 5289 1809; www.yha.com.au

## Events

Falls Festival Rock festival with major bands playing over two nights, staged in a valley near Erskine Falls. Dec.

Pier to Pub Swim Popular open-water swimming event. Jan.

## 4 Apollo Bay and Great Otway National Park (3–4 days)

Apollo Bay is less adulterated by the tourist trade than Lorne, although accommodation is often booked solid in summer, and the town and beach can be crowded. But underneath it all, you can still see the town for the rugged fishing outpost it is. Stroll down to the wharf to see local fleet and their bright stacks of craypots and floats. The Apollo Bay Fishermen's Co-op sells whatever happens to be hauled in each day.

South and west of town is the bulk of Great Otway National Park. The main attraction is Otway Fly, a steel-trussed walkway through the trees, 25 m above ground. Tickets are expensive, but if your budget doesn't extend so far, there are other places where you can get close to the trees, if not in the actual treetops. Around 15 minutes west of Apollo Bay on the road to Lavers Hill, Maits Rest has a 20-minute walk through ferns and moss-covered trees. More of this scenery can also be found beyond Lavers Hill at Melba Gully, but you should definitely plan to visit the gully at night – the forest floor is lit up with twinkling glow worms.

Other park highlights are Cape Otway Lighthouse, the oldest on mainland Australia, and Lake Elizabeth near the town of Forrest. This tranquil lake was created by a landslide in 1952 and is home to platypus. Otway Eco Tours run guided canoe trips to see the platypus, claiming a 95 per cent strike rate.

The Great Ocean Walk runs through Great Otway National Park between Apollo Bay and Glenample Homestead near Port Campbell. The track covers 91 km in total, taking anywhere from five to eight days. Walkers ramble over deserted beaches and cliffs, and through coastal heath and rainforest. There are walker-dedicated campsites en route, or you can choose to do just a short section of the walk.

## Further information

ℹ Great Ocean Road Visitor Information Centre Great Ocean Rd, Apollo Bay; (03) 5237 6529; daily 9am–5pm; www.greatoceanrd.org.au

Great Otway National Park 13 1963; www.parkweb.vic.gov.au

Cape Otway Lightstation (03) 5237 9240; www.lightstation.com

Otway Fly Beech Forest; 1800 300 477; daily 9am–5pm; www.otwayfly.com

Great Ocean Walk www.greatoceanwalk.com.au

## Tours

Otway Eco Tours Guided platypus tours at Lake Elizabeth. (03) 5236 6345; www.platypustours.net.au

Apollo Bay Fishing and Adventure Tours Tours ranging from scenic excursions down to Cape Otway or to a nearby seal colony, through to deep-sea shark fishing adventures. (03) 5237 7888; www.apollobayfishing.com.au

Apollo Bay Surf and Kayak Paddle out to the seal colony or learn to surf. 0405 495 909; www.apollobaysurfkayak.com.au

## Where to eat

Bay Leaf Cafe $ A casual favourite doing breakfasts, toasted sandwiches and simple but delicious mains. 131 Great Ocean Rd, Apollo Bay; (03) 5237 6470; breakfast & lunch daily, dinner Nov–April.

La Bimba $$ Apollo Bay's fine-diner with views over the ocean from its first-floor location. 125 Great Ocean Rd, Apollo Bay; (03) 5237 7411; daily 8am–late.

The Ice-Cream Tub $ Great, locally made ice-cream and gelati. 89 Great Ocean Rd, Apollo Bay; (03) 5237 6430; daily 10am–6pm, later in summer.

## Where to stay

Eco Beach (YHA) ★★★ Dorm $31.50, double or twin $73.50 5 Pascoe St, Apollo Bay; (03) 5237 7899; www.yha.com.au

Apollo Bay Backpackers ★★ Dorm $20, double or twin $50 47 Montrose Ave, Apollo Bay; 1800 113 045; www.apollobaybackpackers.com.au

Bimbi Park ★ Campsites as well as cabins from $60 near Cape Otway lighthouse. Also offers horseriding tours. 90 Manna Gum Dr, Cape Otway; (03) 5237 9246; www.bimbipark.com.au

## Events

Apollo Bay Music Festival Major event with a wide range of acts, from country to rock to roots. Apr.

## 5 The Twelve Apostles and Port Campbell (2 days)

The Great Ocean Road's star attraction is the Twelve Apostles. While gradually dwindling in number (the most recent apostle to topple did so in 2005), these craggy peaks marooned just off the coast are still an awesome sight. Surging seas and salt-laden winds blasting in from the

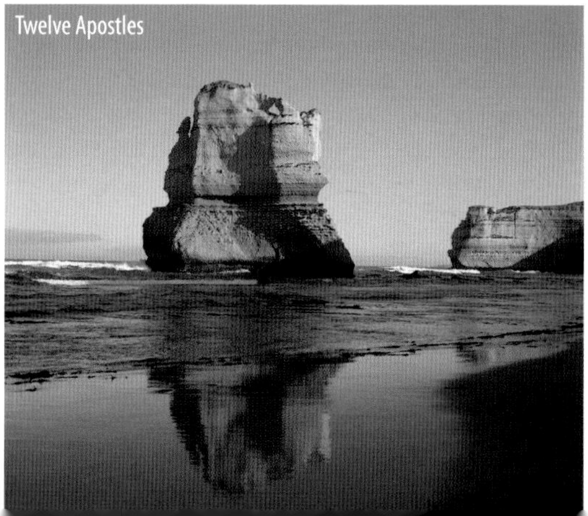

Twelve Apostles

Antarctic have shaped these limestone rocks, which are formed from layer upon layer of marine creature skeletons. A large carpark leads to a viewing area, or you can climb down Gibsons Steps for a view from the beach.

For perhaps an even greater sense of the region's beauty, isolation and history, head to nearby Loch Ard Gorge. The small beach tucked into the cliffs is where young Tom Pearce and Eva Carmichael swam ashore when their ship, the *Loch Ard*, sank in 1878. The wild weather proved treacherous for many sailing ships, giving the region its name of the 'Shipwreck Coast'. However, on a warm and sunny day this beach can feel like a private paradise (the sea is best left for paddling as it slopes away severely). West of Port Campbell are more impressive formations, such as London Bridge and the Bay of Islands.

Port Campbell is the best place to base yourself when exploring this part of the coast. It's a small fishing and (these days) tourist town with a lovely little beach. The highly informative interpretive centre nearby is also worth visiting for further information on the coastline's many caves, arches and blowholes.

## Further information

*i* **Port Campbell Visitor Information Centre** 26 Morris St; (03) 5598 6089; daily 9am–5pm.

## Where to stay

**Port Campbell Hostel** ★★ Dorms $22, doubles or twins $60 18 Tregea St, Port Campbell; (03) 5598 6305; www.portcampbellhostel.com.au
**Ocean House Backpackers** ★ Dorms $25 Cairns St, Port Campbell; (03) 5598 6223.

## ⑥ Warrnambool (2 days)

While this regional city is large and in some ways uninspiring, it definitely has a few drawcards. With a natural setting on a long beach, southern right whales visit Warrnambool yearly during winter. These huge sea creatures have suffered badly from harpooning over the last few centuries – they were considered the 'right' whale to hunt, being slow-moving, floating to the surface when killed, and yielding plenty of blubber. Today, around 1000 southern right whales visit Australian waters each year. In the past they have arrived at Warrnambool's Logans Beach around June to give birth to their calves, and linger until September. A large lookout platform has been built into the tall dunes. However, check for the best sighting spots, as recent seismic testing in the area has encouraged many whales to move further up the coast.

The town's other attraction is Flagstaff Hill Maritime Museum, a reconstructed 19th-century port town that presents the history of the 'Shipwreck Coast'. At night, a sound and light show re-enacts the *Loch Ard* tragedy (see the Twelve Apostles and Port Campbell above).

Warrnambool's university has bolstered the town's nightlife, which centres around the southern end of Liebig Street. Bands play at various venues on Friday and Saturday nights.

## Further information

*i* **Warrnambool Visitor Information Centre** Flagstaff Hill, Merri St; (03) 5564 7837; daily 9am–5pm; www.warrnamboolinfo.com.au
**Flagstaff Hill Maritime Museum** Merri St; 1800 556 111; daily 9am–5pm; www.flagstaffhill.com

## Where to eat

**Fishtales** $ Service can be slow in this colourful cafe with a courtyard. But when your felafel burger arrives, you'll probably forgive them. Also on the massive menu are pastas, curries and fish and chips. 63–65 Liebig St; (03) 5561 2957; daily 7.30am–late.
**Bojangles** $$ Best pizza in town, especially from the wood-fired menu. 61 Liebig St; (03) 5562 8751; daily 5pm–late.
**Kermonds** $ Local burger institution, still decked out in 1950s diner-style. 151 Lava St; (03) 5562 4854; daily 9am–10pm.
**Nonna Caslinga** $$ Authentic Italian with a touch of city class. 69 Liebig St; (03) 5562 2051; lunch & dinner Mon–Fri, dinner Sat.
**Hotel Warrnambool** $$ Local favourite – cosy and laidback with quality meals from the bar. Cnr Koroit & Kepler sts; (03) 5562 2377; daily 10am–late, Sun from 11am.

## Nightlife

**The Loft** 58 Liebig St; (03) 5561 0995; bands Wed–Sat nights.

## Where to stay

**Warrnambool Beach Backpackers** ★★ Dorm $23, double or twin $65 17 Stanley St; (03) 5562 4874; www.beachbackpackers.com.au

## ⑦ Port Fairy (2 days)

Almost every city dweller dreams of escaping to somewhere just like Port Fairy – small, quaint, with a sense of history and a great beach. Cafe culture has followed on the heels of burgeoning real estate, and some locals even think the town has grown too big for its boots. But Port Fairy is still a charming place to spend a few days, strolling along the beach and historic wharf, and enjoying the cafes and restaurants. A good short walk is out to the lighthouse on Griffiths Island. If you're here between late September and April, then watch for flocks of short-tailed shearwaters, which return to their burrows on the island each night.

## Further information

*i* **Port Fairy Visitor Information Centre** Railway Place, Bank St; (03) 5568 2682; daily 9am–5pm.

## Where to eat

**Rebecca's** $ Friendly cafe with homemade cakes, plus the Rebecca's ice-cream shop next door. 70 Sackville St; (03) 5568 2533; daily 7am–6pm.

**Wishart's at the Wharf** 💲💲 Seafood is the speciality, including takeaway fish and chips. Port Fairy Wharf; (03) 5568 1884; daily 11am–8pm.

**Time and Tide Gallery Cafe** 💲 Out of town towards Portland, this is a local favourite for lunches, cakes and ocean views. 21 Thistle Pl; (03) 5568 2134; Thur–Mon 9.30am–5pm.

**Dublin House Inn** 💲💲 Hearty European fare in a gorgeous old-world dining room. 57–59 Bank St; (03) 5568 2022; daily 6pm–late.

## Where to stay

**Port Fairy Hostel (YHA)** ★ ★ Dorm $24.50, double or twin $58.50
8 Cox St; (03) 5568 2468; www.portfairyhostel.com.au

## Events

**Port Fairy Folk Festival** HUGE event running for over three decades with local and international performers. Some free events in the street. Mar.

## 8 The Grampians (4 days)

The Grampians are an ancient landscape of mountains that soar abruptly from the flat agricultural plains, with caves and overhangs protecting Aboriginal art. These craggy mountains were formed by an upsurge of rock some 400 million years ago. Evocative names like Wonderland Range, Ladys Hat and Fallen Giant hint at their grandeur and drama.

The main mountains are protected within Grampians National Park. The best place to base yourself is in the small town of Halls Gap, in the middle of the park, or Dunkeld to the south. There are also many campsites scattered throughout.

This is one of the state's best places for bushwalking, with over 200 km of walking trails. There are short strolls to the magnificent MacKenzie Falls or the rocky perch known as The Balconies (once called Jaws of Death), or more challenging hikes up remote peaks such as Mount Difficult, Mount Stapylton and the Major Mitchell Plateau.

Brambuk Aboriginal Cultural Centre gives an insight into the area's rich Indigenous heritage and includes a great bush tucker cafe. Visitors can also get information about the seven rock-art sites that are open to the public, including Bunjils Shelter and Billimina.

Aboriginal rock art, Grampians National Park

If you're hankering to see wildlife (a third of Victoria's native animal species live here), head to Zumstein picnic ground north-west of Halls Gap, where kangaroos regularly graze. Also keep your eyes peeled for koalas, echidnas and birds by day; possums, gliders and bandicoots by night.

## Further information

ℹ️ **Halls Gap Visitor Information Centre** Grampians Rd; 1800 065 599; www.visitgrampians.com.au

ℹ️ **Dunkeld Visitor Information Centre** Parker St; (03) 5577 2558; www.visitgrampians.com.au

**Brambuk – the National Park and Cultural Centre** Halls Gap; (03) 5361 4000; www.brambuk.com.au

## Tours

**Grampians Mountain Adventure Company** Rock climbing and abseiling in The Grampians and nearby Mount Arapiles. (03) 5383 9218; www.grampiansadventure.com.au

**Hangin' Out** Rock climbing and adventure bushwalking. (03) 5356 4535; www.hanginout.com.au

**Grampians Personalised Tours and Adventures** 4WD tours, night wildlife walks, bushwalks, rock climbing and scenic flights. (03) 5356 4654; www.grampianstours.com.au

**Grampians Pyrenees Tours** Tours to nearby wine regions, including a half-day tour to the historic wine town of Great Western. (03) 5352 5075; www.grampianspyreneestours.com.au

## Where to eat

**Kookaburra Restaurant** 💲💲 Longstanding Grampians favourite. 125–127 Grampians Rd, Halls Gap; (03) 5356 4222; lunch & dinner daily.

**Mount Zero Olives** 💲 Weekend cafe set among olive groves, north of Grampians National Park. Winfield Rd, Laharum; (03) 5383 8280; Sat–Sun 10am–5pm.

**Royal Mail Hotel** 💲💲💲 TOP TREAT!! Some of country Victoria's finest food is served in the restaurant of this renovated hotel. More humble meals are offered in the bistro and bar. Glenelg Hwy, Dunkeld; (03) 5577 2241; breakfast, lunch & dinner daily.

## Where to stay

**Grampians Eco Hostel (YHA)** ★ ★ ★ Dorm $27.50, double or twin $65.50 Cnr Grampians & Buckler rds, Halls Gap; (03) 5356 4544; www.yha.com.au

**Tim's Place** ★ ★ Dorm $25, double or twin $60 42 Grampians Rd, Halls Gap; (03) 5356 4288; www.timsplace.com.au

**Camping** There are campgrounds at Boreang, Borough Huts, Buandik, Rosea, Smiths Mill and Strachans. All campgrounds are accessible by car, all have toilets and most have water (only Borough Huts has drinking water). Campsites cannot be booked and a site fee applies, payable at each ground. Bush camping is permitted in some areas.

# Dandenongs and the Yarra Valley
## Forest and a valley full of vino

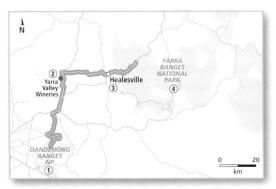

*Melbourne*

The tourist brochures have photographs of soft green vines unfurling under picturesque pastel skies – and the Yarra Valley actually is this handsome. It produces some of Australia's best cool-climate wines, so expect oodles of cellar doors, but also fantastic restaurants, cafes, galleries and Australia's largest wildlife sanctuary. The Dandenong Ranges nearby has expansive European gardens and villages bulging with craft shops and tearooms amid the misty native forests.

**Number of days to spend in this region: 1–4 days**

## Getting here

To get to the Dandenongs, trains run from the city to Belgrave, with connecting buses (#694) heading to the Dandenongs, stopping at Sassafras and Olinda.

To get to the Yarra Valley by public transport, take a train from the city to Lilydale and a bus on to Yarra Glen and Healesville. Buses also run from Lilydale to Warburton.

## ① The Dandenongs (1 day)

The Dandenong Ranges are less than an hour's drive from Melbourne. The main mountain towns are Sassafras and Olinda, with their many art and craft shops, cafes and quaint village atmosphere. On weekends, teams of bike riders pedal up the mountain and then reward themselves with coffee and cake.

The Dandenongs have many beautiful areas to explore, a fact that becomes easily recognisable as you pass towering forests of mountain ash and fern glades surrounding the roads. In spring the area is known for its rhododendrons, while deciduous trees blaze yellow, red and orange in autumn. For a stroll, and perhaps a picnic, the Alfred Nicholas Gardens in Sherbrooke has an ornamental lake, a waterfall, wooden bridges and a boathouse. Near Olinda, William Ricketts Sanctuary uniquely displays ceramic sculptures of Aboriginal people among the native foliage. The pieces were created by artist William Ricketts, who spent years living with Indigenous people in central Australia. Within Dandenong Ranges National Park there are a number of bushwalking tracks, including the 9 km Sherbrooke Trail to Sherbrooke Falls, which are especially beautiful during winter and spring. Keep your eyes and ears open for lyrebirds – the males have a trail of plumes that look like a lyre (a harp-like instrument) when in display. These birds are difficult to spot and their impressive ability to mimic other sounds means you can't pick them by their voices. Nevertheless, a good place to try is south of these falls.

If you're only up for a lazy day that doesn't involve much walking, you can see the area from the popular and beloved Puffing Billy, a restored steam train that runs daily between Belgrave and Gembrook via Emerald Lake. The journey takes about one and a half hours each way. Time your trip for the local craft and produce markets at Gembrook Station (4th Sunday of the month) or Emerald Lake (3rd Sunday of the month).

### Further information

ℹ **Dandenong Ranges and Knox Visitor Information Centre**
1211 Burwood Hwy, Upper Ferntree Gully; 1800 645 505;
www.dandenongrangestourism.com.au

William Ricketts Sanctuary

Alfred Nicholas Gardens Sherbrooke Rd, Sherbrooke; 13 1963; daily 10am–5pm; www.parkweb.vic.gov.au Bus #694 from Belgrave Station stops near the front gate.

William Ricketts Sanctuary Mount Dandenong Tourist Rd, 3 km north of Olinda; 13 1963; daily 10am–4.30pm; www.parkweb.vic.gov.au Buses run from Croydon Station (Lilydale line).

Puffing Billy Belgrave; (03) 9754 6800; train runs daily 10.30am–5pm; www.puffingbilly.com.au

## Where to eat

Miss Marple's Tea Room $ People crowd into ye olde tea room to feast on hearty soups, cottage pies, ploughman's lunches, and of course, the ultimate Devonshire tea experience – a pot of tea with scones, homemade raspberry jam and cream. Miss Marple was an Agatha Christie character and the menu runs to theme. This place is amazingly popular, so expect to wait before you can get a table. 382 Mount Dandenong Tourist Rd, Sassafras; (03) 9755 1610; daily 11am–4.30pm; www.missmarples.com.au

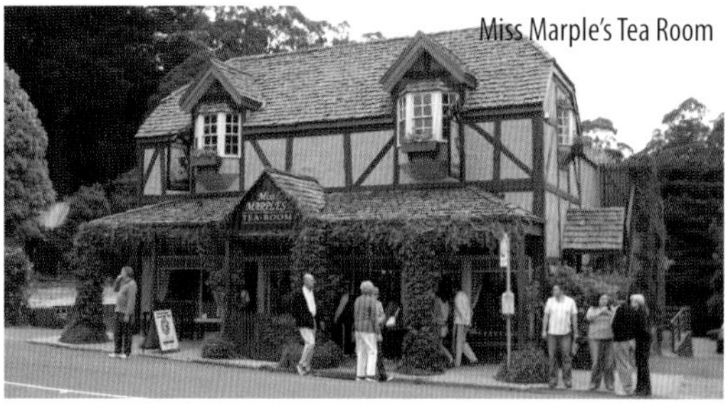
Miss Marple's Tea Room

Pie in the Sky $ For those moments when a good vegetable Cornish pastie or beef and burgundy pie is all you want. Just ignore the bakery's cheesy name. 43 Olinda–Monbulk Rd, Olinda; (03) 9751 2128; daily 10am–5pm.

Ripe – Australian Produce $$ Ripe is set back from the street and without signage, but any local can tell you where to find it. Inside is a dark, wood-panelled space with a large communal table by the fireplace, floor-to-ceiling shelves of preserves and wines, and a large deck out the back. There are soups, pastas and more substantial dishes. The cake display is very hard to ignore and the hot chocolates made with Lindt are legendary. 376–378 Mount Dandenong Tourist Rd, Sassafras; (03) 9755 2100; daily 8.30am–6.30pm.

## Where to stay

Emerald Backpackers ★★ Dorm $20, double $50 2 Lakeview Crt, Emerald; 0412 458 227; www.emeraldbackpackers.com.au

# 2 Yarra Valley wineries (1 day)

With over 50 wineries and picturesque scenery, the Yarra Valley is a great area in which to do some cellar door hopping. A number of companies run winery tours from Melbourne, so you'll be dropping words like 'body', 'legs' and 'mouthfeel' before you know it.

Two of the best-known wineries are De Bortoli and Domaine Chandon; the latter makes fantastic sparkling wines that can be enjoyed in a glass-walled tasting room overlooking the vines ($15 tastings include four glasses from the sparkling wine range and something to eat).

Yering Station makes excellent shiraz viognier and pinot noir, and is also the site of a produce store, a restaurant/wine bar, and the Yarra Valley Regional Farmers' Market held on the 3rd Sunday of the month in an old barn.

To combine wine with art, head to TarraWarra Estate for its chardonnay and pinot noir and its architect-designed gallery that holds exhibitions of works by many Australian greats, from Arthur Boyd to Peter Booth.

## Further information

ℹ Yarra Valley Visitor Information Centre
Old Courthouse, Harker St, Healesville; (03) 5962 2600; daily 9am–5pm; www.visityarravalley.com.au

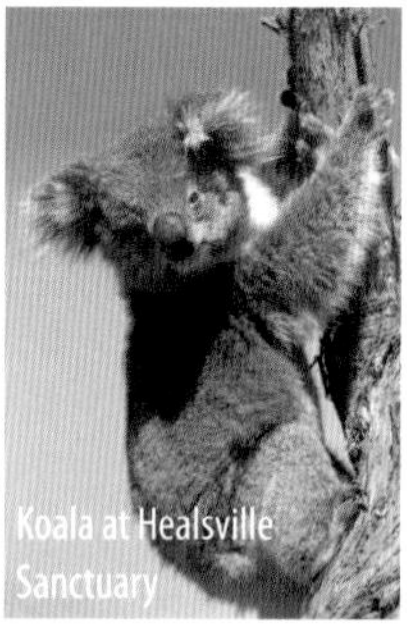
Koala at Healsville Sanctuary

De Bortoli Pinnacle La, Dixons Creek; (03) 5965 2271; www.debortoli.com.au

Domaine Chandon Maroondah Hwy, Coldstream; (03) 9738 9200; www.greenpointwines.com.au

Yering Station 38 Melba Hwy, Yarra Glen; (03) 9730 0100; www.yering.com

TarraWarra Estate 311 Healesville–Yarra Glen Rd, Yarra Glen; (03) 5962 3311; www.tarrawarra.com.au

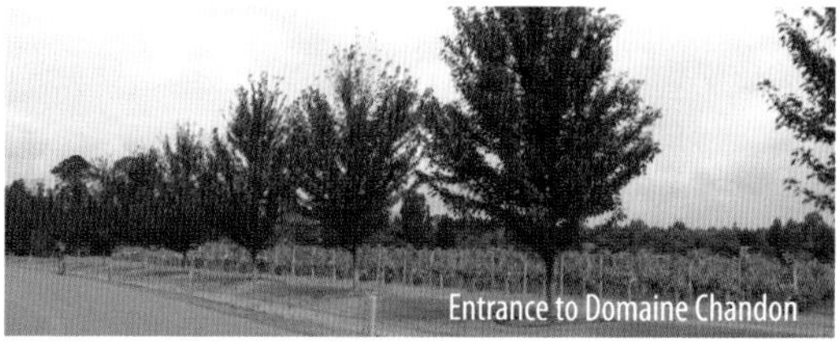
Entrance to Domaine Chandon

## Tours

Backpacker Winery Tours (03) 9419 4444; www.backpackerwinerytours.com.au

Yarra Valley Winery Tours (03) 5962 3870; www.yarravalleywinerytours.com.au

## Where to eat

Bella Vedere $$ Set in a farmhouse among vines, you can stop here for breakfast, lunch or a budget-breaking degustation dinner on Friday or Saturday nights. The restaurant has its own bakery plus a vegetable garden out the back door. This is slow food at its best – risottos, soups, slow-cooked meat dishes and pastries. If you can't

indulge, then come at least for a takeaway loaf of bread.
874 Maroondah Hwy, Coldstream; (03) 5962 6161; Wed–Sun
8am–5pm, dinner Fri–Sat; www.bellavedere.com.au

**Oakridge** $$ The menu at this day-only winery keeps it simple with platters to share, prepared with care and using good produce.
864 Maroondah Hwy, Coldstream; (03) 9739 1920; daily 10am–5pm; www.oakridgeestate.com.au

## Events

**Yarra Valley Grape Grazing Festival** Variety of events including music and food to celebrate the harvest, held throughout the valley. Feb.

## 3 Healesville (1 day)

Once again, Healesville has many great cafes and art, craft and antique shops. The township sprang up near the site of a major Aboriginal mission, Corranderrk, which ran from 1863 to 1924. The mission cemetery contains the grave of well-known tribal leader William Barak. Visit Galeena Beek Living Cultural Centre to learn about the local Aboriginal culture, and maybe even catch a traditional dance performance.

However, Healesville's main attraction is definitely Healesville Sanctuary. Spread across 32 ha of bushland, the sanctuary has over 200 species of native Australian animals, most of them roaming in natural settings. Highlights include the birds of prey flight presentation, the platypus enclosure and watching the koalas jump from tree to tree (if you're lucky enough to see them awake). Allow at least half a day to fully explore the sanctuary with the extra options of visiting the animal hospital or going on a keeper tour.

To get to Healesville Sanctuary via public transport, you can take a train to Lilydale station and then hop on McKenzie's Bus Lines.

## Further information

**Galeena Beek Living Cultural Centre** 22–24 Glen Eadie Ave, opposite Healesville Sanctuary; (03) 5962 1119.
**Healesville Sanctuary** Badger Creek Rd; (03) 5957 2800; daily 9am–5pm: www.zoo.org.au
**McKenzie's Bus Lines** (03) 9853 6264; www.mckenzies.com.au

## Where to eat

**Bodhi Tree Cafe** $ Loveable New Age cafe with basic offerings like nachos and carbonara pasta, through to some good global and vegetarian meals. Regular live music. 317 Maroondah Hwy; (03) 5962 4407; Wed–Fri 5.30pm–late, Sat–Sun noon–late; www.bodhitreecafe.com.au
**Giant Steps/Innocent Bystander** $$ An amazingly modern winery and foodie heaven like you've never seen before, with a cellar door, cafe, bakery and cheese room in one large, light-filled space. You can pick up baked treats like Portuguese tarts, but stopping for a meal is highly recommended. Everyone working here is young, so you won't feel surrounded by stuffy wine freaks. 336 Maroondah Hwy;

1800 661 624; Mon–Fri 10am–10pm, Sat–Sun 8am–10pm; www.giant-steps.com.au/winery/
**Healesville Hotel** $$$ TOP TREAT!! Great for a special occasion, combining old-fashioned decor with modern food like chorizo and muscatel-stuffed local quail, or asparagus and pea risotto with sorrel and witlof-apple salad. The Healesville Harvest Produce Store next to the restaurant is a relaxed daytime cafe with especially good doughnuts. 256 Maroondah Hwy; (03) 5962 4002; daily lunch and dinner; www.healesvillehotel.com.au

## Where to stay

**Badger Creek Holiday Park** ★ Cabin from $70 419 Don Rd; 1800 009 225; www.badgercreekholidays.com.au

## 4 Yarra Ranges National Park (1 day)

Compared to the Dandenongs, the Yarra Ranges are more pristine. Rare and endangered species such as the Leadbeater's possum live here – these mini marsupials are just 30 cm long (half of this being their tail) and they inhabit hollows in old mountain ash trees. Like this possum, many animals in these forests are nocturnal.

Some of the best forest vistas are along the steep and winding roads through the ranges, such as Black Spur, the road linking Healesville and Narbethong and on to Marysville. For full enjoyment, get someone else to drive!

Mount Donna Buang is a prominent peak in the south of the park and the closest mountain to Melbourne to receive snow in winter. In summer, daytrippers flock here for picnics and 360-degree views from the summit lookout tower. In winter, they come to glimpse the white stuff. You can hire a toboggan, build a snowman, or just simply throw snow around (more serious skiing and snowboarding happens at other mountains off to the east and north like Mount Buller and Mount Hotham).

Halfway up (or down) Donna Buang is the Rainforest Gallery, where you can step into a cool, dark world of mountain ash, ferns and the burbling Cement Creek via the Skywalk. If you're feeling energetic, there's a walk from here to the summit (around 3 hrs return).

## Further information

ⓘ **Marysville Information Centre** 11 Murchison St, Marysville; (03) 5963 4567; daily 9am–5pm; www.marysvilletourism.com

## Tours

**Eco Adventure Tours** Night tours of the forest to see gliders, owls and other species. (03) 5962 5115; www.ecoadventuretours.com.au

## Where to stay

Camping is available in the adjacent Upper Yarra Reservoir Park.
Bookings 13 1963; www.parkweb.vic.gov.au

For more detail
see maps
211 & 213

Melbourne

# Phillip Island and Gippsland
# Penguins and the Prom

Phillip Island is so packed with attractions it's almost a nature-based theme park where visitors can experience Australian fauna such as penguins, seals and koalas in their natural surrounds. Further away to the east, Gippsland beckons with good food and magnificent national parks. At the top of the list is Wilsons Promontory, with its trademark white beaches and giant boulders stained with orange lichen. This is one of the state's favourite spots to camp.

Number of days to spend in this region: 6–14 days

## Getting here

A V/Line bus service runs to Phillip Island (terminating at Cowes) from Dandenong train station several times a day. The same service can also take you to Inverloch. (To get to French Island, see the French Island entry.)

To get to Wilsons Promontory, V/Line buses run to Foster, the nearest town, en route to Yarram at least once a day.

To get to Gippsland, V/Line trains runs to Traralgon via Warragul, Moe and Morwell roughly every hour.

There is no public transport to Walhalla, however tour company Mountain Top Experience can provide transport from Morwell on their regular runs (about twice a week). For details, see information on Walhalla below.

V/Line 13 6196; www.vline.com.au

## ① Phillip Island (3 days)

Phillip Island, around 2 hours' drive from Melbourne, attracts an astronomical 3.5 million visitors every year. Its popularity has much to do with the colony of small, furry penguins that live on Summerland Beach. These are the world's smallest penguins at around 33 cm tall. Each night they waddle across the sand to their burrows after a day of fishing, with numbers reaching 4000 at the height of breeding season. You can see them on show from a viewing platform at the Penguin Parade (bookings recommended, particularly during summer and Easter; bookings essential for viewing boxes or beach tours).

Before your twilight penguin experience, spend some time at the western tip of the island. There are views of the outcrops known as The Nobbies as well as of Australia's largest colony of fur seals on Seal Rocks. The Nobbies Centre features high-powered cameras, including

an underwater one, that allow you to zoom in and out on the seals, and houses displays on the local marine life including sharks and dolphins. When you've had your fill of sea creatures, walk around the coast to see The Blowhole and hear the thunderous noise of huge waves travelling through this sea cave.

The final item in Phillip Island's wildlife hat-trick is the Koala Conservation Centre south of Cowes. Boardwalks into the treetops allow you meet and greet the koalas, and a visitor centre will tell you everything you want to know about these eucalypt lovers. The mothers and their young are adorable, while the old males can be positively boarish.

At Cape Woolamai, south of Newhaven, a range of walking tracks takes in beaches and rock formations, and surfers come for world-class breaks. From late September to around May, watch for dark masses of birds returning to their burrows in the headland at night – these are short-tailed shearwaters, once called muttonbirds, which were killed and boiled down for their fat. Even when they're not around you can detect their strong, fatty odour.

The northern coastline of Phillip Island is gentler than the southern and is generally a safer option for swimming. North of Newhaven you can walk across the bridge to Churchill Island and explore the old homestead and restored farm, and walk or ride around the island itself. A farmers' market is held here on the 4th Saturday of every month.

If you thought these attractions weren't enough, there's even more

Phillip Island penguins

wildlife on show at Wildlife Wonderland. This place is not on Phillip Island itself, but on the Bass Highway near the turn off. It's easy enough to spot – just look for the giant earthworm. Visitors can get up close with kangaroos, wombats, wallabies, dingoes and more koalas.

## Further information

ℹ **Phillip Island Visitor Information Centre** 895 Phillip Island Tourist Rd, Newhaven; 1300 366 422; daily 9am–5pm; www.visitphillipisland.com
**Penguin Parade** Private viewing boxes or guided tours onto the beach also available. Near western tip of island; (03) 5951 2800; www.penguins.org.au
**Nobbies Centre** Free entry. Western tip of island; (03) 5951 2816; www.penguins.org.au
**Koala Conservation Centre** Phillip Island Rd, 3 km south of Cowes; (03) 5951 2800; www.penguins.org.au
**Wildlife Wonderland** Bass Hwy before turn off to San Remo; (03) 5678 2222; www.wildlifewonderland.com
**Surf school: Island Surfboards** (03) 5952 2578; www.islandsurfboards.com.au

## Where to eat

**White Salt Gourmet Fish & Chippery** $ All that beach walking around Cape Woolamai should work up an appetite. This fish and chippery pays attention to small details, such as hand-cutting local potatoes for their chips. 7 Vista Place, Cape Woolamai; (03) 5956 6336; lunch & dinner daily.
**Island Food Store** $ Salads, quality pies, cakes, muffins and good coffee. Also bread, cheeses and other ingredients if you want to put together an impromptu hamper. Shop 2, 75 Chapel St, Cowes; (03) 5952 6400; daily 9.30am–5pm, closed Sun in winter.
**Harry's on The Esplanade** $$ Local fish, crayfish and beef feature on the menu, as well as dishes reflecting the chef's German heritage. Great bay views. 17 The Esplanade, Cowes; (03) 5952 6226; lunch & dinner Tue–Sun, breakfast Sat–Sun.
**Chicory** $$ Intimate dining room with a modern, Asian menu. 115 Thompson Ave, Cowes; (03) 5952 2655; lunch & dinner Thur–Tue.

## Where to stay

**Amaroo Park YHA** ★★ Dorm $26.50, double or twin $63.50 97 Church St, Cowes; (03) 5952 2548; www.yha.com.au

## Events

**World Superbike Championship** Factor this and the next two events in when planning your trip to Phillip Island – they're eagerly anticipated by some, but for others a good reason to steer clear. Mar.
**Australian Motorcycle Grand Prix** Oct.
**V8 Supercar Championship** Nov.

## ❷ French Island (2 days)

French Island is like Phillip Island's lost and lonely cousin. With less than 100 permanent residents and no bridge connecting it to the mainland, it's thoroughly off the tourist radar, save for a few bushwalkers and nature enthusiasts. But it makes for a great, low-key getaway, despite rumours that Kylie Minogue has purchased a property here.

In 1802 French Island was circumnavigated by a party of French explorers sent to sea by Napoléon Bonaparte. Their journey along the west and south coasts of Australia was an important scientific expedition and a naming frenzy. It seems that every man on *Le Geographe* and *Le Naturaliste* ended up with his name on the map – Tasmania's Freycinet Peninsula is named after the team's cartographer and Western Australia's Peron Peninsula follows the zoologist. When they reached French Island, perhaps they ran out of inspiration.

Two-thirds of the largely flat island is national park, and residents generate their own electricity (increasingly by solar and wind) and collect rainwater. There are heaps of animals around, including renowned birdlife, the rare long-nosed potoroo and Victoria's most significant koala population. Although introduced here, these koalas are isolated from disease and reproduce so rapidly that over 200 are moved off the island each year to recolonise the mainland.

At only 30 km across, the best way to get around the island is by bike (there are no made roads). For a two-night visit, you might pitch a tent at Fairhaven campsite, north of the ferry terminal, on the first night. The next day, ride to the other side of the island and stay at McLeod Eco Farm, a reform prison until 1975. The old cells are now carpeted bunkhouses, and meals are made with organic produce from the farm. The property also has a beachside camping area.

## Further information

ℹ **Peninsula Visitor Information Centre** 359 Point Nepean Road, Dromana; 1800 804 009; www.visitwesternport.com.au
**French Island National Park** (03) 5980 1294; www.parkweb.vic.gov.au
**Ferry: Inter Island Ferries** 2–4 services per day from Stony Point (Mornington Peninsula) to Tankerton jetty; (03) 9585 5730; www.interislandferries.com.au
**Bike hire: French Island general store and bike hire** (03) 5980 1209.

## Tours

**French Island Tours** (03) 5980 1214; www.frenchislandtours.com.au
**French Island Eco Tours** 1300 307 054; www.frenchislandecotours.com.au
**French Island Llama Experience** Ok, this may be a little daggy and more for the older generation, but how often can you get a llama to carry your lunch (sorry, no rides included)? Your hosts pick you up from Tankerton jetty, take you on a walking tour through the island and produce a real feast for morning tea and lunch. (03) 5980 1287; www.fillamas.com.au

## Where to stay

Tortoise Head Lodge ★ Double $85 Tankerton; (03) 5980 1234; www.tortoisehead.net

McLeod Eco Farm ★ Twin bunk room $59 McLeod Rd, French Island; (03) 5980 1224; www.mcleodecofarm.com

Camping There is one national park campsite at Fairhaven, north of the ferry terminal on the west coast.

## ❸ Walhalla and Baw Baw National Park (2 days)

Walhalla is a perfectly preserved, 19th-century goldmining town, and was only hooked up to electricity in 1998. Tucked away in a steep, narrow valley – so steep that some cemetery graves have been dug horizontally into the hillside – you could easily spend a couple of hours wandering around the historic buildings. There are daily tours of Long Tunnel Gold Mine and rides on the old Walhalla Goldfields Railway, departing from Thomson Station on Wednesdays, Saturdays and Sundays.

Baw Baw National Park has lots for the active and adventurous. Although a less popular skiing destination than Mount Buller or Mount Hotham to the north, Mount Baw Baw is relaxed and affordable. The slopes are ideal for beginners, and there are some good runs for intermediates and a 10 km network of cross-country trails. In summertime, head here for bushwalking across plateaus covered in wildflowers and excellent whitewater canoeing downstream of Thomson Dam.

The park also encompasses Mount St Gwinear, a day area only with no accommodation or food available. Toboggans and skis can be hired in Erica, but don't expect ski lifts at St Gwinear. The only way up is a 3.5 km slog that has been compared to walking up Melbourne's Rialto Tower (in summer the same track is a walking trail). But once at the top, there is cross-country terrain, and you can even ski across to Mount Baw Baw.

Mount Baw Baw can be accessed via the Yarra Valley or north from Moe, and Mount St Gwinear can be accessed from Walhalla.

## Further information

ⓘ Walhalla Visitor Information www.visitwalhalla.com

Long Tunnel Gold Mine Tours Mon–Fri 1.30pm, Sat–Sun noon, 2pm and 3pm. (03) 5165 6259.

Walhalla Goldfields Railway (03) 9513 3969; www.walhallarail.com

Mount Baw Baw National Park (03) 5165 3204; www.parkweb.vic.gov.au

Skiing: Mount Baw Baw Skiing Information 1300 651 136; www.mountbawbaw.com.au

St Gwinear Skiing Information 13 1963; www.stgwinear.info

## Tours

Mountain Top Experience 4WD tours around Walhalla area, as well as transport to Walhalla and Mount Baw Baw. (03) 5134 6876; www.mountaintopexperience.com

Adventure Canoeing Whitewater canoe trips down the Thomson River in Baw Baw National Park. (03) 9844 3323; www.adventurecanoeing.com.au

## Where to eat

GreyHorse Cafe $ Next door to the Star Hotel, there are homemade pies and cakes for lunch. Walhalla; (03) 5165 6262; lunch daily.

Star Hotel $$ This verandah-front, two-storey hotel looks historic, but was actually built in 1999 as a replica of the original Star. The dinner menu might feature duck or roast lamb. Walhalla; (03) 5165 6262; dinner daily.

## Where to stay

Alpine Hotel ★ Dorm $45 Mount Baw Baw; 1300 651 136.

Camping There are campsites with basic facilities at Aberfeldy River camping area and Eastern Tyres camping area. Bush camping is also allowed on the Baw Baw Plateau.

## ❹ Gippsland (2–3 days)

Central Gippsland is home to the La Trobe Valley, hinging on the towns of Moe, Morwell and Traralgon. This valley produces a massive 85 per cent of Victoria's electricity through one of the world's largest brown coal deposits. But away from the open-cut mines, Gippsland is rather picturesque, characterised by the green Strzelecki Ranges. The area broadly circling Warragul has been dubbed Gippsland Gourmet Country because of its luscious milks and cheeses, and a healthy smattering of berry farms and wineries. Foodies can get onto the website and plot a route from farm gates to cellar doors and restaurants.

Along the coast on either side of Wilsons Promontory are plenty of laidback coastal villages and quiet beaches. Cape Paterson has good surf, and some of the state's best snorkelling and diving in the park-protected waters. The town is linked to Inverloch via the 14 km Bunurong Coastal Drive, where you can get out of the car to explore cliffs, coves and rockpools.

Past Inverloch, the town of Venus Bay is tucked into the dunes and boasts five surf beaches, creatively called One to Five. Cape Liptrap is a mecca for windsurfing and has views to the Prom and Sandy Point. East of the Prom, Port Albert has old maritime buildings harking back to the town's major port days during Victoria's gold-rush era. You can explore the town's history at Port Albert Maritime Museum, complete with a lighthouse, restored boats and artefacts from shipwrecks.

Between Port Albert and the La Trobe Valley is Tarra–Bulga National Park, where mountain ash trees reach for the sky and moss-covered myrtle beech, southern sassafras and 40 fern species rest in the sheltered gullies. The unsealed and incredibly scenic Grand Ridge Road skirts along the northern boundary of the park, leading from Mirboo North and looping up to Traralgon. Short walks include the Tarra Valley Rainforest Walk to Cyathea Falls, and Corrigan's Suspension Bridge Walk over the rainforest.

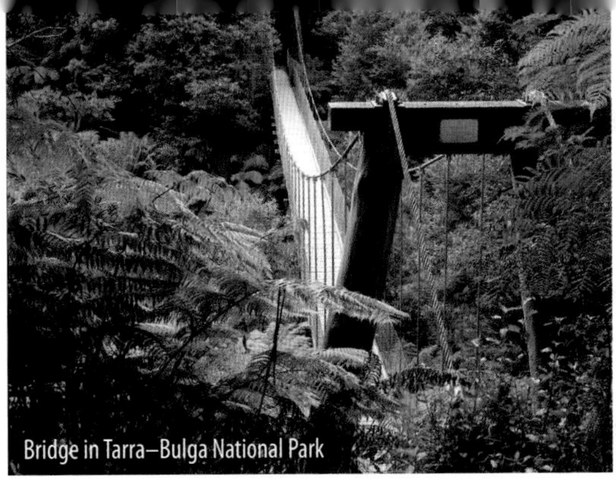
Bridge in Tarra–Bulga National Park

## Further information

ⓘ Inverloch Visitor Centre A'Beckett St; (03) 5674 2706; www.gippslandtourism.com.au
ⓘ Yarram Visitor Centre 9 Rodgers St (close to Port Albert); (03) 5182 6553; www.gippslandtourism.com.au
Gippsland Gourmet Country www.gippslandgourmetcountry.com A highlight is Grand Ridge Brewery, Main St, Mirboo North; (03) 9778 6996; daily 11am–late; www.grand-ridge.com.au
Port Albert Maritime Museum Tarraville Rd; (03) 5183 2520; daily 10.30am–4pm (weekends only June–Aug).
Tarra–Bulga National Park (03) 5172 2111; www.parkweb.vic.gov.au

## Tours

Outthere Snorkelling, surfing and kayaking in south Gippsland, including snorkelling in Bunurong Marine Park (03) 5956 6450; www.outthere.net.au

## Where to eat

Koonwarra Fine Food and Wine Store $$ Koonwarra is a fantastic stopover on the way to Wilsons Prom, or you could make it the destination itself. The store doubles as the community's post office and is decked out in friendly country style. Come for breakfast or lunch, and cakes like grandma makes. South Gippsland Hwy, Koonwarra; (03) 5664 2285; daily 9am–5pm.

# 5 Wilsons Promontory National Park (4 days)

'The Prom' is only 200 km from Melbourne and is extremely popular with bushwalkers and campers, yet still feels remote. It originally formed part of a land bridge to Tasmania over 15 000 years ago; some of the scenery is similar to the Apple Isle, with mountains sweeping down to the sea and white beaches strewn with massive lichen-mottled boulders. Inland are rainforests and creeks. The Prom's exquisite beauty is kept in check by controlled development, with only one road and one main campground. The best time to visit is February and March, when the weather is generally sunny and holidaymakers are back at work.

Tidal River has the one campground, with 450 campsites beneath trees, as well as a range of hut and cabin accommodation. (Campsite bookings are required during holiday periods, when you join a ballot, and bookings are required for huts and cabins at all times). It never takes long to get acquainted with the resident wombats and the ubiquitous crimson rosellas. For more wildlife, especially birdlife, head to the north of the park.

Tidal River – the river itself – is picture-perfect with sculptural boulders jutting out of the twisted tea trees, reflected in the still water. The waves along adjacent Norman Beach are great for beginner surfers and bodysurfing. Other beaches in the area, connected via a coastal walking trail, are Squeaky Beach, so called because of the quartz sand that squeaks under your feet, and Whisky Bay.

The first bushwalk to check off your list is the popular hike up Mount Oberon (2 hrs return), offering views that extend north and south over the bays and headlands. Other routes to consider are Lilly Pilly Gully from the campground, traversing coastal heath and rainforest dominated by lilly pilly and tree ferns. Longer treks include the walk east across the Prom to secluded Sealers Cove (full day return), and the overnight trek to the lighthouse at South East Point, where you can book a lighthouse cottage for the night (operated by the national park).

## Further information

ⓘ Tidal River Visitor Centre 1800 350 552; www.parkweb.vic.gov.au

## Tours

Bunyip Bushwalking Tours (03) 9650 9680; www.bunyiptours.com
Wildlife Coast Cruises Half- and full-day cruises along parts of Wilsons Promontory coastline inaccessible by road. Get off the boat for some walking or snorkelling, and see seals and other marine life. 1300 763 739; www.wildlifecoastcruises.com.au
Meridian Kayak Sea kayaying adventures around the Prom. 1300 656 433; www.meridiankayak.com.au

## Where to stay

Tidal River accommodation Campsite $21.50, four-bed hut $59, eco-cabin (for 2 people) $154 1800 350 552; www.parkweb.vic.gov.au
Prom Coast Backpackers (YHA) ★★ Can arrange transport to Wilsons Promontory. Dorm $25, double $58.50 40 Station St, Foster; (03) 5682 2171; www.yha.com.au
Lighthouse Cottage Contact the Tidal River Visitor Centre for information on staying at a lighthouse cottage.

Wilsons Promontory
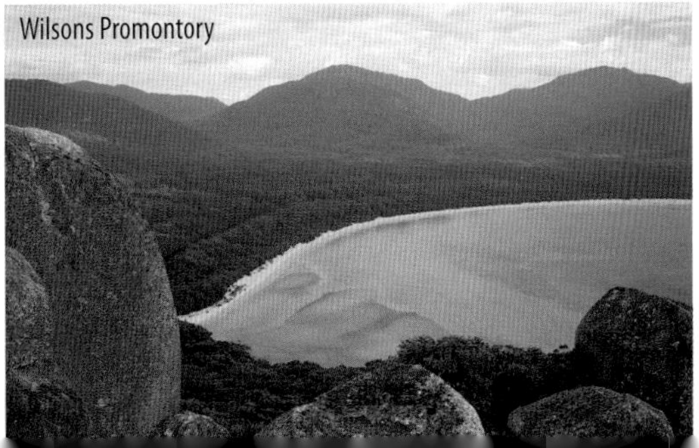

For more detail see maps 206, 211, 212 & 215

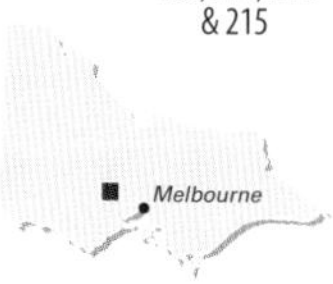
Melbourne

# Goldfields and Spa Country
# Filthy rich in history and luxury

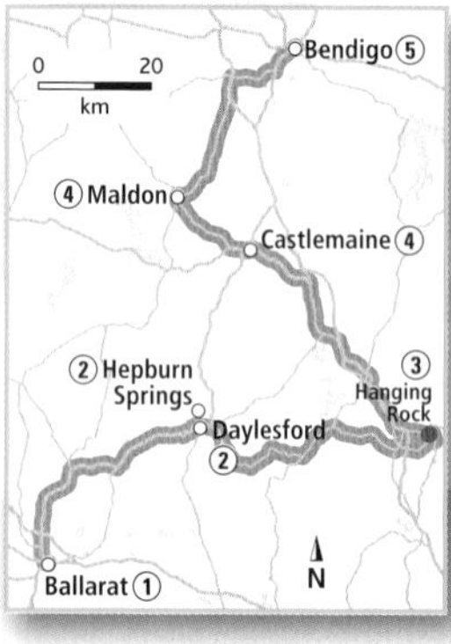
0
20
km
Bendigo ⑤
④ Maldon
Castlemaine ④
② Hepburn Springs
③ Hanging Rock
Daylesford ②
Ballarat ①
N

The discovery of gold in the 1800s transformed the Ballarat and Bendigo district into a rowdy and fantastically wealthy goldmining frontier. Grand public buildings and backstreets full of miners' cottages signify this past, while Ballarat's Sovereign Hill lets you step right back into the thick of this history. Closer to Melbourne is Daylesford and Hepburn Springs, renowned destinations for luxury pampering (perfect for easing a sore back after months of lugging around a heavy backpack).

**Number of days to spend in this region: 1–4 days**

## Getting here

V/Line has regular train services to Ballarat and Bendigo (the Bendigo line runs via Woodend and Castlemaine). A bus service between Ballarat and Bendigo stops in Castlemaine, Maldon and Daylesford.

To get directly from Melbourne to Daylesford, a train runs to Woodend with connecting buses to Daylesford.

V/Line 13 6196; www.vline.com.au

## 1 Ballarat (2–3 days)

Gold was first discovered in Ballarat in 1851, and within two years a deluge of 20 000 prospectors had descended on the town. At first, miners were practically scraping gold off the earth's surface, but the hunger for more soon pushed them underground. Instant wealth was glorious – more French champagne was consumed in Ballarat during the late 1800s than in the rest of the world combined!

Today, Ballarat is Victoria's largest inland city, featuring elaborate, multi-storey buildings that are evidence of its historic prosperity. To go with the architecture are some fine botanic gardens and the adjacent Lake Wendouree, a man-made lake.

The number one attraction is Sovereign Hill, a re-created village showing Ballarat as it was in its first decade of gold mining. You can ride in a horse and cart, pan for gold, tour underground mines, and see blacksmiths in their workshops. At night, Sovereign Hill leaps into full drama with a re-enactment of the Eureka Rebellion, in a sound and light show called Blood on the Southern Cross (bookings essential).

Across from Sovereign Hill is the Gold Museum (free with entry to Sovereign Hill). This fascinating museum displays artefacts and photographs on the significance of gold in the area, as well as the history of gold from the times of the Egyptians and the Incas.

Ballarat's other important museum is the Eureka Centre, focusing on the Eureka Stockade miners' rebellion that gave the city its special place in Australian history. Multimedia displays let you relive the event.

Other attractions include Ballarat Wildlife Park, with Australian animals and various weekend shows between 1.30pm and 3.30pm including snake and wombat shows, and the Ballarat Fine Art Gallery, which holds the original, tattered Eureka flag and displays permanent and touring artworks. Kirrit Barreet Aboriginal Art and Cultural Centre has local Indigenous art and offers cultural talks, didgeridoo shows and boomerang painting sessions (entry is free).

### Further information

[i] Ballarat Visitor Information Centre Eureka Centre, cnr Eureka & Rodier sts; 1800 446 633; www.visitballarat.com.au

Sovereign Hill Bradshaw St; (03) 5337 1100; daily 10am–5pm; www.sovereignhill.com.au

Gold Museum Bradshaw St; (03) 5337 1107; daily 9.30am–5.20pm; www.sovereignhill.com.au

Eureka Centre Cnr Eureka & Rodier sts; (03) 5333 1854; daily 9am–4.30pm; www.eurekaballarat.com

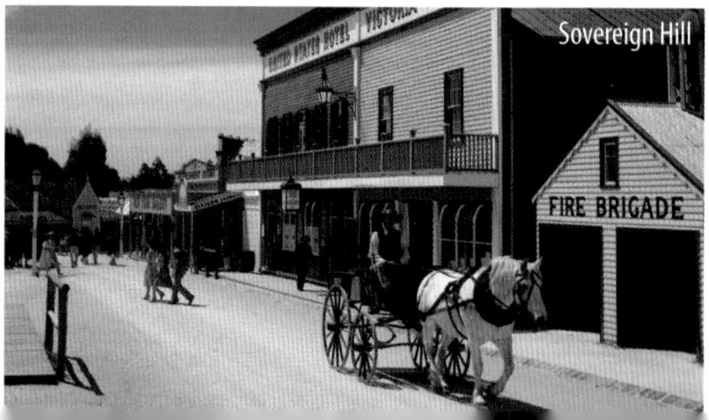
FIRE BRIGADE
Sovereign Hill

Ballarat Wildlife Park Cnr York & Fussell sts; (03) 5333 5933;
daily 9am–5pm; www.wildlifepark.com.au

Ballarat Fine Art Gallery 40 Lydiard St North; (03) 5320 5858;
daily 9am–5pm; www.balgal.com

Kirrit Barreet Aboriginal Art and Cultural Centre
407 Main Rd; (03) 5332 2755; daily 10am–5pm;
www.aboriginalballarat.com.au

Eureka Passes, covering entry to Sovereign Hill, the Gold Museum, the
Eureka Centre and Ballarat Fine Art Gallery, are available for purchase at
any of the four attractions.

## Where to eat

L'Espresso ⓢ Ballarat's best coffee with great breakfast options and
Italian-inspired lunches. The establishment began as a music store,
so you can also pick up a CD on your way out. 417 Sturt St; (03) 5333
1789; daily 7am–6pm, dinner Fri.

Mason's Cafe and Foodstore ⓢ A homely space with wooden
tables, floorboards and an open fire in winter. Go for lunch, for
wholesome sandwiches, pasta or quesadillas. 32 Drummond St North;
(03) 5333 3895; Mon–Fri 9am–6pm, dinner Fri.

Cafe Companis ⓢ Attached to Ballarat's art gallery and run by a
renowned local chef, sweet tooths will find some of the best cakes and
tarts around. Risottos, soups and other dishes are on offer for lunch.
40 Lydiard St North; (03) 5320 5798; daily 10.30am–5pm, dinner Fri.

Tozers at the Ansonia ⓢⓢ A flash place for dinner in a city that
gets full points for its daytime cafes, but lacks a little in the evening
department. You'll find white tablecloths and luscious food with Middle
Eastern inspiration. 32 Lydiard St South; (03) 5338 8908; lunch Tue–Fri,
dinner Mon–Sat.

Boatshed Restaurant ⓢⓢ Run-of-the-mill bistro food in a
gorgeous waterfront location. Another good option for dinner.
Lake Wendouree; (03) 5333 5533; daily breakfast, lunch & dinner.

## Entertainment

Karova Lounge Premier live music venue with rock, alternative and
blues bands and many others. Cnr Field & Camp sts; (03) 5332 9122;
Wed–Sat 9pm–late; www.karovalounge.com

Her Majesty's Theatre Open since 1875, it's worth checking out
what's showing, as you might stumble on a great Aussie performance.
17 Lydiard St South; (03) 5333 5800; www.hermaj.com.

## Where to stay

Sovereign Hill Lodge YHA ★★ Dorm $25.50, twin $57 Magpie St;
(03) 5337 1159; www.yha.com.au

Peter Lalor Hotel ★ Single $35, double $45 331 Mair St;
(03) 5331 1702.

## Events

Begonia Festival Large celebration with a parade, music and
horticultural events. Mar.

## ② Daylesford and Hepburn Springs (2–3 days)

The region is dubbed the Spa Country because of the area's natural
mineral springs, which have led to a proliferation of places offering spa
treatments, massages and many other related indulgences.

In a food sense, the Spa Country also has a taste for the finer side
of life with excellent local producers, restaurants and cafes. The area is
known for its bull boar sausages, Australia's first entry on the Slow Food
Ark of Taste, an international register of unique foods in danger of being
lost. These sausages hark back to the region's Swiss–Italian settlers and
continue to be made to a closely guarded recipe (if you want to try them,
Newstead Butchers north of Daylesford is a good place).

For a spa treatment, the original 1895 Hepburn Springs spa house,
now called Hepburn Spa, is still going strong. Even if you're not after a
treatment, you should still visit the reserve and walk along the paths
to the various springs featuring old hand pumps. The water from each
spring differs in taste.

To fill in the time between meals and spa treatments, activities in
Daylesford include going for a stroll around picturesque Lake Daylesford
or up to Wombat Hill Botanic Gardens (the original name for Daylesford
was Wombat), or looking at art in the Convent Gallery.

For a delectable experience just outside Daylesford, you can watch
exquisite chocolates being made at the Chocolate Mill. Associations with
Willy Wonka are so strong that a sign on the window looking into the
factory reads, 'Do not lick the glass'. You should be able to resist by heading
to the cafe and shop for hot chocolate or individual chocolate delicacies.

## Further information

ⓘ Daylesford Regional Visitor Information Centre 98 Vincent
St; (03) 5321 6123; www.visitdaylesford.com

Newstead Butchers 23 Lyons St, Newstead; (03) 5476 2217.

Hepburn Spa 1 Mineral Springs Reserve, Hepburn Springs; (03) 5348
8888; Sun–Fri 10am–6pm, Sat 9am–7pm; www.hepburnspa.com.au

Wombat Hill Botanic Gardens Central Springs Rd, Daylesford;
(03) 5348 3616.

Relaxing in
Hepburn Springs

Convent Gallery Daly St, Daylesford; (03) 5348 3211; daily 10am–5pm; www.conventgallery.com.au
Chocolate Mill 5451 Midland Hwy, Mount Franklin; (03) 5476 4208; Tue–Sun 10am–4.45pm; www.chocmill.com.au

## Where to eat

Cliffy's $ The interior is like an olden-day general store with a full range of local products and fresh fruit and veggies for sale. The menu includes soups, pies and omelettes. 30 Raglan St, Daylesford; (03) 5348 3279; daily 9am–5pm, dinner Sat.
Himalaya Bakery $ A bakery and cafe where everything is vegetarian but big on goodness and flavour. Buy a loaf of bread or a pie takeaway, or dine in on soup or focaccia. 73 Vincent St, Daylesford; (03) 5348 1267; Wed–Mon 9.30am–5pm.
Red Star $ Friendly cafe with a wall of books to browse. A local favourite for breakfast. 115 Main Rd, Hepburn Springs; (03) 5348 2297; daily 8am–5pm, dinner Fri–Sat.
La Trattoria $ The scene could not be more picturesque – an old brick farmhouse and outbuildings surrounded by fields of lavender, olive trees, chestnut trees and grape vines. Dine in the old barn on a simple dish of bread, oil and the farm's own olives, or on a wood-fired meat dish, and finish with Italian dessert. Lavandula Swiss Italian Farm, 350 Hepburn–Newstead Rd, Shepherds Flat; (03) 5476 4393; daily 10.30am–5.30pm, closed Aug.
Farmers Arms Hotel $$ Great place for a drink (maybe a beer brewed in nearby Woodend) and a suave place for a meal in the dining room tucked behind the bar. The menu is an exciting read, drawing from the Middle East and the Mediterranean. 1 East St, Daylesford; (03) 5348 2091; lunch Sat–Sun, dinner daily.
Lake House $$$ TOP TREAT!! Regarded as one of Victoria's very best restaurants. The white, light-filled space is split across several levels overlooking Lake Daylesford, and the menu might feature local yabbies, free-range pork or hare, as well as dishes that tip their hat to the chef and owner's Russian heritage. King St, Daylesford; (03) 5348 3329; daily breakfast, lunch & dinner; www.lakehouse.com.au

## Where to stay

Wildwood YHA ★★ Dorm $27–$32, double or twin $64 42 Main Rd, Hepburn Springs; (03) 5348 4435; www.yha.com.au
Daylesford Victoria Caravan Park ★ Cabin from $58 Ballan Rd, Daylesford; (03) 5348 3821.

## Events

Swiss–Italian Festa Singing, dancing and feasting. Apr/May.

# 3 Hanging Rock (1 day)

This small reserve near the town of Woodend is a popular daytrip from Melbourne, or a good place to stop on the way to Daylesford or the Goldfields.

Despite its name, the rock is in fact a hill with scrubby slopes of gum trees and a strange garden of stones perched on top. On days of low-lying cloud, the 'rock' can seem suspended in the mist when viewed from a distance. The visitor centre interprets the geology and history of the rock.

The ideal way to experience this area is to pack a picnic and take the short walk to the top of the rock, where the views extend over the agricultural plains. Stones tower overhead like giants, making it easy to feel lost as you walk between, through and around them. The area is famously connected with Joan Lindsay's novel *Picnic at Hanging Rock*, which relates a mythical story of some schoolgirls vanishing here in 1900. The book was turned into a well-known Australian film under the same name.

## Further information

Hanging Rock South Rock Rd, Woodend; 1800 244 711; www.hangingrock.info

## Events

New Year's Day Races Popular event on the adjacent racetrack (races are also held on Australia Day in Jan and Labour Day in Mar).
The Age Harvest Picnic The best of Victoria's food and wine come together surrounded by gum trees. Feb.

# 4 Castlemaine and Maldon (1–2 days)

Castlemaine and Maldon are two much smaller hamlets in Victoria's Goldfields region. They have plenty of charm, and lovely shops and cafes to keep you mesmerised for a couple of days. When you're out browsing, look for Castlemaine Rock, confectionery sold in distinctive yellow tins and made in Castlemaine since 1853.

Castlemaine is known for its fine public buildings, botanic gardens and arts community, including painters, potters and instrument makers. Check out the renowned Castlemaine Art Gallery & Historical Museum, a great place to see both traditional and contemporary works by Australia-born artists. Buda Historic Home and Garden is also worth a visit. Originally the residence of silversmith and jeweller Ernest Leviny and his family, this beautiful house is furnished more or less as they left it.

Maldon is known for having one of Australia's most intact historic streetscapes. The best thing to do is simply go for a stroll along its verandah-fronted main street and wander into the backstreets, which are full of miners' cottages. Pick up a brochure detailing the town's most notable buildings from the visitor centre.

## Further information

ℹ Castlemaine Visitor Information Centre Market Building, 44 Mostyn St; (03) 5470 6200.
ℹ Maldon Visitor Information Centre Shire Gardens, High St; (03) 5475 2569; www.maldoncastlemaine.com

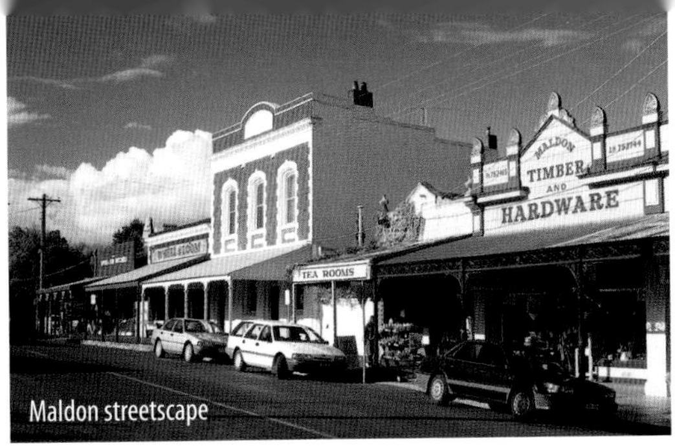

Maldon streetscape

Castlemaine Art Gallery & Historical Museum 14 Lyttleton St; (03) 5472 2292; Mon–Fri 10am–5pm, Sat–Sun noon–5pm; www.castlemainegallery.com.au
Buda Historic Home and Garden 42 Hunter St, Castlemaine; (03) 5472 1032; Wed–Sat noon–5pm, Sun 10am–5pm; www.budacastlemaine.org

## Where to eat

Togs Place $ Castlemaine's favourite for coffee, breakfast and lunch. There's a fireplace inside and a rooftop deck. 58 Lyttleton St, Castlemaine; (03) 5470 5090; daily 9am–5pm, dinner Fri–Sat.
Empyre Hotel $$ Superbly renovated hotel made exactly like it was in its heyday, but better . . . if only you could also afford to stay here. Cutting-edge food and a simpler cafe next door. 68 Mostyn St, Castlemaine; (03) 5472 5166; cafe daily 9am–5pm, dinner Thur–Sat.
Penny School Gallery and Cafe $ This old schoolhouse set among gum trees has views across Maldon and beyond. There is a changing program of Australian art and a daytime cafe with outdoor tables. 11 Church St, Maldon; (03) 5475 1911; Mon–Thur 11am–5pm, Fri–Sun 11am–10pm.

## Events

Maldon Folk Festival Bush music festival that's been running for over three decades. Nov.

# 5 Bendigo (2 days)

Bendigo is Ballarat's sister metropolis, with its own dazzling suite of ornate Victorian buildings (in fact, Bendigo's are known to be more impressive). Gold was discovered here in the same year and miners tapped into incredibly rich quartz reefs, digging 1400 m underground – a world record at the time. Compared to Ballarat, however, there aren't as many blockbuster attractions.

Central Deborah is an old mine offering guided tours. Visitors can plunge 85 m below ground level in a miner's cage, pan for gold or inspect the old-time machinery. Various structures around Bendigo also indicate the important role the Chinese played in goldfields life here, as elsewhere in Victoria. There is a Chinese Joss House, which still receives a trail of curious tourists, and the Golden Dragon Museum, displaying the history and culture of the Chinese in Bendigo. The centrepieces are the dragon exhibit and the authentic Yin Yuan Gardens based on Beijing's Imperial Palace.

One way to link some of Bendigo's sights is to take a tour on a vintage tram. There are daily tours running from Central Deborah Gold Mine, along the historic boulevard of Pall Mall, and on to the Chinese Joss House.

North of town is Bendigo Pottery, dating back to 1858. You can inspect heritage kilns and see potters at work. Within the complex you'll also find Living Wings and Things, a wildlife park with butterflies, birds and reptiles.

When you are eating out in Bendigo and the wider Goldfields, scan wine lists for the local reds. Heathcote and Bendigo shiraz, in particular, make wine lovers go weak at the knees.

## Further information

[i] Bendigo Visitor Centre Old post office, cnr Pall Mall & Williamson St, 1800 813 153; daily 9am–5pm; www.bendigotourism.com
Central Deborah Gold Mine Cnr High & Violet sts; (03) 5443 8322; daily 9.30am–5pm; www.central-deborah.com
Chinese Joss House Finn St, Emu Point; (03) 5442 1685.
Golden Dragon Museum 5–11 Bridge St; (03) 5441 5044; daily 9.30am–5pm; www.goldendragonmuseum.org
Bendigo Tramways (03) 5442 2821; www.bendigotramways.com
Bendigo Pottery Midland Hwy, Epsom; (03) 5448 4404; daily 9am–5pm; www.bendigopottery.com.au

## Where to eat

The Green Olive $ A Bendigo institution, doubling as a deli, serving good coffee and Italian cafe food. 11 Bath La; (03) 5442 2676; Mon–Fri 7am–5.30pm, Sat 7am–3.30pm.
Bridge Hotel $$ Refurbished historic hotel with a lavish dining room and a Mediterranean-influenced menu. Cheaper meals can be had in the bar. 49 Bridge St; (03) 5443 7811; daily lunch & dinner.
Shamrock Hotel $$ One of Bendigo's architectural gems – more palace than pub. No doubt you'll feel the urge to go in, even if just for a drink. Cnr Pall Mall & Williamson St; (03) 5443 0333; Mon–Sat breakfast, lunch & dinner, Sun breakfast & lunch.
GPO $$ Contemporary place attracting the young and stylish. Choose from small tastes, pizzas or mains. 60–64 Pall Mall; (03) 5443 4343; daily lunch & dinner.

## Where to stay

Bendigo YHA ★★ Dorm $24.50, double or twin $59 33 Creek St South; (03) 5443 7860; www.yha.com.au
Ironbark Bush Cabins ★★ Dorm $25, double $60 Watson St; (03) 5448 3344; www.bwc.com.au/ironbark

## Events

Bendigo Easter Festival First held in 1871, the Chinese community soon joined in, parading an imperial dragon. The dragons are still the highlight. Easter.

# NORTHERN TERRITORY

## CONTENTS

Darwin 102
TOP REGIONS:
Kakadu and Arnhem Land 111
Red Centre 115

### Visitor information ⓘ

Travel NT 13 6768; www.travelnt.com

## FAST FACTS

**Hottest place** Aputula (Finke), 48.3°C in 1960
**Longest road** Stuart Highway (approximately 2000 km)
**Strangest place name** Humpty Doo
**Quirkiest festival** Henley-on-Todd Regatta with boat races in the dry river bed, Alice Springs
**Most impressive sight** Electrical storms in the build-up to the wet season, Darwin
**Favourite food** Barramundi
**Local beer** NT Draught
**Interesting fact** Some 50 per cent of the Northern Territory is either Aboriginal land or land under claim

The Northern Territory is Australia's least settled state or territory, with vast tracts of desert around Central Australia and the tropical woodlands of Kakadu National Park. But to regard this country as empty is to do it a major disservice; Aboriginal people have lived and travelled across the Territory for thousands of years, and their spiritual connection with the land is still strong. One of the country's most iconic natural attractions, Uluru, will not only take your breath away, but is also a sacred site for local Indigenous groups. Visitors can learn about this unique culture, be it through the rock art, by visiting Aboriginal-owned Arnhem Land, or listening to Dreamtime stories. Moving across to the Territory's capital city, Darwin is a multicultural country meets boomtown, with plenty of sights, sounds and flavours to soak in. It's safe to say that the Northern Territory is the most unique destination that Australia has to offer.

## Top region highlights

### Uluru

This stunning, iconic rock has to be seen to be believed. Its most beautiful feature is its colour, which changes according to the weather, ranging from a palette of reds and oranges to purples and browns. p. 119

### Kakadu National Park

This World Heritage-listed park is nature at its most pure and creative. Gorgeous landscapes, roaring waterfalls and lily-strewn billabongs, not to mention the world's largest collection of Indigenous rock art. p. 111

### Darwin

The vibrant, multicultural epicentre of the Territory has sightseeing galore, along with great restaurants and a buzzing nightlife. The Mindil Beach Sunset Markets are a must. p. 102

### Alice Springs

'The Alice' is a cultural wonderland smack bang in the middle of the desert, with plenty of unique sights. p. 115

## Other regions worth a look

### Katherine

Home to towering Katherine Gorge, a cavernous gorge carved by the Katherine River through ancient sandstone. The town itself has some interesting sights, as well as great arts and crafts shopping.

### Tennant Creek

A former gold-mining town, this friendly place is steeped in Aboriginal culture. Nearby, the Devils Marbles are sacred Indigenous relics, believed to be the eggs of the Rainbow Serpent, a creature from Dreamtime stories.

### Tiwi Islands

Bathurst and Melville islands form the Tiwi Islands, 80 km offshore from Darwin. They belong to the Tiwi people, whose unique culture results from their long isolation. The locals are renowned for their arts and crafts.

### Gulf of Carpentaria

This shallow sea, which separates Australia from Papua New Guinea, is a hot spot for fishing and 4WD enthusiasts out to explore new frontiers.

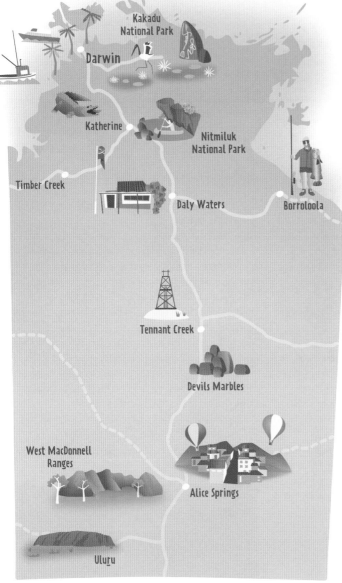

Kakadu
National Park

Darwin

Katherine

Nitmiluk
National Park

Timber Creek

Daly Waters

Borroloola

Tennant Creek

Devils Marbles

West MacDonnell
Ranges

Alice Springs

Uluṟu

# Darwin

Regarded as Australia's northern outpost, Darwin is a classically tropical and humid city that retains the feel of a big country town. It has been largely rebuilt after devastation by cyclone Tracy over 30 years ago and exudes a natural beauty through its harbour, swaying palm trees and tropical parks. Over 50 ethnic groups live together harmoniously here – this diversity stretches back to the early days of Darwin's development, when Aboriginal, European and Chinese people worked side by side. The city's population is also a relatively young one, with 37 per cent aged 24 years and under. All of this ensures a relaxed lifestyle and booming nightlife, making Darwin one of the most attractive and hassle-free cities in the world.

## Top attractions

### The Esplanade and Darwin Deckchair Cinema

Much of Darwin's up-market accommodation is built along The Esplanade, with balconies and windows looking out over Darwin Harbour. There are many Australian and American wrecks at the bottom of the harbour, sunk by Japanese bombers that struck without warning in February 1942. Memorial sites all around the harbour record the hundreds of bombing raids that were made on the city during WW II. Beautiful Bicentennial Park runs the length of The Esplanade and a walking/cycling track goes from Doctors Gully in the north to the Wharf Precinct in the south. A branch of the track goes past Lameroo Beach and the Darwin Deckchair Cinema. Seeing a current or popular film 'under the stars' here is a necessary Darwin experience. Films screen every night during the dry season. On the corner of Knuckey Street, at the southern end of The Esplanade, is Old Admiralty House, which shows off tropical design and living standards before the city was devastated in 1974. Further north, Lyons Cottage is the former British Australian Telegraph (BAT) headquarters for the Overland Telegraph. It now houses an excellent chronology of early Darwin life. Darwin Deckchair Cinema, end of Jervois Rd, off Kitchener Dr, Wharf Precinct, (08) 8941 4377, 18 Apr – 11 Nov daily 6.30pm, admission fee applies; Old Admiralty House, Cnr Knuckey St & The Esplanade; Lyons Cottage, cnr The Esplanade & Knuckey St, daily 10am–4.30pm, admission free.

### Parliament House

Parliament House is a large, white rectangular building with one of the finest views of Darwin Harbour. Opened in 1994, this modern, imposing edifice also houses the Northern Territory Library and a cafe that opens out to an area of lawn, a large fountain and a great view. People

## Visitor information centre

Tourism Top End Darwin City Centre Beagle House, Cnr Knuckey & Mitchell sts; (08) 8936 2499; www.tourismtopend.com.au

## Climate

Darwin has a constant temperature of around 30°C and the weather is always warm and humid – just how humid depends on the time of year. Most people visit during the dry season, which extends from May to the end of September. The 'build-up' period (between October and December) is famous for hot, stifling weather and massive electrical storms. During the wet season (which can last until late April), the Asian monsoon drops over Darwin, often bringing days of cleansing rain. When the inevitable cyclone comes, the city streets and surrounding landscape become waterlogged and flood-bound. The wet season may be uncomfortable, but this is when the landscape is green and lush. At the end of the season, native trees burst into flower and attract thousands of birds.

are encouraged to look through the grand hall that displays art and photographic exhibitions. State Sq; (08) 8946 1434; daily 8am–6pm; free guided tours depart from foyer Sat 9am & 11am, also May–Sept Wed 10.30am; Northern Territory Library Mon–Fri 10am–6pm, Sat–Sun 1–5pm; admission free.

### Supreme Court, Government House and Survivors Lookout

Across the wide courtyard at the front of Parliament House is the Supreme Court building, constructed in 1990. High ceilings and an atmosphere of modern grandeur are its major features – the spectacular foyer has a giant mosaic floor designed by Aboriginal artist Norah Napaljarri Nelson and a permanent exhibit of Arnhem Land burial poles. Next to the Supreme Court is an open, grassed area called Liberty Square, which also separates the court from Government House, an elegant, colonial-style building that has survived the cyclone and bombings. The building is open to the public once a year and is the venue for formal government occasions and ceremonies. Further down, Survivors Lookout surveys the Wharf Precinct and Darwin Harbour to East Arm Port and the terminus of the historic train The Ghan. The lookout also marks a spot where WW II battles were witnessed by journalists and photographers. Supreme Court, State Sq, daily 8am–5.30pm, admission free; Government House, 29 The Esplanade, (08) 8999 7103, admission free.

Deckchair Cinema

To Rapid Creek, East Point & Fannie Bay

To Framed: The Darwin Gallery, Litchfield National Park, Palmerston & Casuarina Airport

To Gecko Lodge

To Winnellie & Charles Darwin National Park

DASHWOOD CRES

Nirvana

To Cullen Bay

Elkes Backpackers

Banyan View Lodge

CAVENAGH

WOODS

DALY ST

SMITH

PEARY ST

MCLACHLAN ST

SHEPHERD ST

LINDSAY ST

Frogshollow Lodge & Backpackers

MCMINN

Fisherman's Wharf Eatery

Lizards Outdoor Bar & Grill

GULLY RD

MITCHELL

Wilderness Lodge

DOCTORS

AQUASCENE

Globe Trotters Bar & Lodge & Darwin YHA Backpackers Hostel

Discovery & Lost Arc

Ducks Nuts Bar & Grill & Tzars Vodka Bar

FRANCES

LITCHFIELD ST

Hogs Breath Cafe & Fox 'n' Fiddle

THE

Youth Shack

Trinity Nightclub & Squires Tavern

Tim's Surf & Turf

BAY

Shenannigans

ST

The Tap

Throb Nightclub

AUSTIN ST

The Cavenagh

DRIVE

Jabiru Bar

Melaleuca On Mitchell

ST

Saville Park Suites

ESPLANADE

Chilli's Backpackers

KNUCKEY

WEST

Rendezvous Cafe

The Roma Bar

LYONS COTTAGE

Victoria Hotel

DARWIN

THE ESPLANADE

OLD ADMIRALTY HOUSE

Lewinsky's & Go Sushi

LA

CHURCH LA

Lameroo Beach

ST

The Deck Bar

OLD POLICE STATION & COURTHOUSE

DR

INDO PACIFIC MARINE & AUSTRALIAN PEARLING EXHIBITION

BICENTENNIAL PARK

PARLIAMENT HOUSE & NT LIBRARY

SUPREME COURT

DARWIN DECKCHAIR CINEMA

SURVIVORS LOOKOUT

WORLD WAR II OIL STORAGE TUNNELS

Darwin Harbour

GOVERNMENT HOUSE

KITCHENER

N

0        150
metres

WHARF PRECINCT

STOKES HILL WHARF

Fort Hill Wharf

## Indo Pacific Marine

Here local coral ecosystems can be viewed without dipping a toe in the water. Find out what lies in Darwin Harbour, from deadly stonefish that can inflict terrible pain and even death, to the beautiful coral that lies hidden in the Top End's sometimes murky waters. Indo Pacific Marine is one of the few places in the world that has been able to transfer a living ecosystem from the water into a land-based exhibition. Also on show are creatures endemic to the Top End, such as the deadly box jellyfish. If you're up for some special night-time activities, 'Coral Reef by Night' tours and seafood dinners are offered on Wednesdays, Fridays and Sundays from 7pm. While you are dining, the lights are turned off so that you can see these marine creatures glowing in the dark.

Kitchener Dr, near the entrance to Stokes Hill Wharf; Apr–Oct daily 10am–5pm, Nov–Mar Mon–Fri 9am–1pm, Sat–Sun 10am–5pm; admission fee applies.

## Stokes Hill Wharf

Once catering to sailing vessels and steamers, Stokes Hill Wharf is now a berth for international cruise ships and a place for restaurants, bars and shops. When the fish are biting, the wharf is also one of the best places in Darwin to fish. During the build-up to the wet season, head here to watch one of the city's magnificent storms as it gathers across the harbour and travels towards Darwin. These storms are the city's most spectacular – and free – natural shows.

## Aquascene

This is one of Darwin's most popular attractions, where visitors can hand-feed fish that live in Darwin Harbour. Opening times depend on the high tide, but Aquascene publishes feeding times every day in the *Northern Territory News* and weekly timetables can be found at Tourism Top End. Aquascene is not only a chance to interact with the marine life of the harbour, but also an opportunity to learn about northern Australian creatures through informative talks. 28 Doctors Gully Rd; (08) 8981 7837; feeding times change monthly; admission fee applies.

## Australian Aviation Heritage Centre

Darwin was the first port of call for many early aviators – Sir Charles Kingsford Smith touched down in present-day Parap on his historic flight between Britain and Australia. The Australian Aviation Heritage Centre houses an American B-52 bomber and the wreckage of a Japanese Zero shot down over Darwin in 1942. The city's rich aviation history is detailed at the centre, along with superbly restored exhibits. 557 Stuart Hwy, Winnellie; (08) 8947 2145; daily 9am–5pm; admission fee applies.

## Crocodylus Park

If you're fascinated by crocodiles, get your fix of the huge saltwater variety that inhabits waters around Darwin at Crocodylus Park. The park is a research centre as well as a tourist attraction, with other animals on show, including monkeys and tigers. Crocodiles emerge from the murky waters at feeding times to take pieces of meat that are dangled over the side of their enclosures. Well-trained guides will allow you (under supervision) to handle baby crocodiles with their jaws taped shut to avoid any sharp teeth. Work by scientists at Crocodylus Park helped establish the Northern Territory's ground-breaking policies on crocodile preservation. End of McMillans Rd, past the airport, near the Police Centre; (08) 8922 4500; daily 9am–5pm; feedings and tours 10am, noon & 2pm; admission fee applies.

## Other attractions worth a look

**World War II Oil Storage Tunnels** Creep through the underground halls and view historic displays of the war years. Kitchener Dr; (08) 8985 6333; May–Sept daily 9am–4pm, Oct–Apr Tue–Sun 9am–1pm; admission fee applies.

**Australian Pearling Exhibition** Housed in the same building as Indo Pacific Marine, this exhibition gives a detailed history of pearling in northern Australia, with beautiful displays of South Sea pearls, the largest pearls in the world. Kitchener Dr; (08) 8999 6573; daily 10am–5pm; admission fee applies.

**Myilly Point Heritage Precinct** Pre-WW II houses that managed to survive cyclone Tracy. Beautiful architecture and gardens. North of Cullen Bay Marina; buildings open to the public at different times, check with the National Trust (08) 8981 2848.

**East Point Military Museum** Sitting in the shadow of two huge, cement gun emplacements, the museum highlights the role of Darwin in WW II and the parts played by service personnel in the defence of northern Australia. Alec Fong Lim Dr, East Point; (08) 8981 9702; daily 9.30am–5pm; admission fee applies.

**Charles Darwin National Park** Excellent views of the city from a lookout. The park also incorporates one of the most pristine

### Getting around

Darwin is easy to get around. City streets are laid out in a grid, traffic is rarely heavy and most attractions are within walking distance. A regular public bus service covers many of the suburbs, as well as the satellite town of Palmerston (the city terminus is on Harry Chan Avenue). Private minibuses can be found near the northern end of Smith Street Mall and taxis are available at either end of the mall. The Tour Tub is an open-air bus service to the city's top sights, departing every hour from the northern end of Smith Street Mall. Darwin's network of bicycle paths extends from the city out to the northern suburbs, and bikes can be hired from many backpacker lodges, most of which can be found on Mitchell Street.

Public transport **Buses** (08) 8924 7666

Motoring organisation **AANT** (08) 8981 3837, **roadside assistance** 13 1111

**Police road report** 1800 246 199 (a good source of information for travel outside Darwin, particularly in the wet season)

Car rental **Avis** 13 6333; **Britz Camperdown Rentals** 1800 331 454; **Budget** 13 2727

**Four-wheel drive hire service** (08) 8947 2736; Hertz 13 3039

Taxis **City Radio Taxis** 13 1008 or (08) 8981 3777

**Tour Tub** (08) 9895 6322

Bicycle and scooter hire **Darwin Scooter Hire** (bikes and scooters) (08) 8941 2434

Crocodylus Park

mangrove areas in northern Australia – great for fishing.

**Nightcliff Foreshore** Provides an excellent cliff-top walkway that runs from Nightcliff boat ramp to a bridge over Rapid Creek, on to Casuarina Beach Parks.

**Framed – the Darwin Gallery** One of the oldest art galleries in Darwin, with some of the best Aboriginal and Torres Strait Islander arts and crafts in northern Australia. 55 Stuart Hwy; (08) 8981 2994; Mon–Sat 9am–5.30pm, Sun 11am–4pm; admission free.

**Darwin Crocodile Farm** Just 40 km south of Darwin lies Australia's largest crocodile farm, housing over 36 000 saltwater crocs. Stuart Hwy; (08) 8988 1491; daily 9am–4pm; admission fee applies.

# Where to eat

**City Centre** Good restaurants with a strong emphasis on Asian dining. Plenty of variety for any mood.
Our favourite: **Rendezvous Cafe** 💲 ♡ This intimate cafe serves up some of the town's best Malaysian and Thai cuisine, including the best laksa in Darwin by a country mile. The Mall, Shop 6, 32 Smith St; (08) 8981 9231; Mon–Sat 10.30am–2.30pm, Tue–Sat 5.30–9pm.

**The Wharf Precinct** A range of eat-in or takeaway cafes and restaurants make this one of Darwin's most eclectic and scenic dining areas.
Our favourite: **Fisherman Wharf's Eatery** 💲 ♨ While a little bit out of the way, this wharf eatery has some scrumptious barramundi, and is arguably the best fish and chips joint in town. Frances Bay Dr; (08) 8981 1113; Mon–Sat 6am–8pm, Sun 10.30am–8pm.

**Cullen Bay** Contemporary fine-dining with a choice of spectacular views over the Cullen Bay Marina or the Timor Sea.
Our favourite: **Yots** 💲💲 ♡ This award-winning cafe is the best waterfront eatery this side of Alice Springs. Dishes range from

marinated quail to goat cheese and leek tarts. Simple wood-fired pizzas and casual breakfasts are also available. Marina Blvd; (08) 8981 4433; Tue–Sun 8am–1am.

## Other places to eat

**Hogs Breath Cafe** 💲💲 ♡ For all things meat, this is the place to come. Dine alfresco or grab a seat at the bar and enjoy their wide selection of cocktails. 85 Mitchell St; (08) 8941 3333; daily 11.30am–11pm; www.hogsbreath.com.au

**The Roma Bar** 💲 ♡ Open since the 70s, this place attracts a mixed bag of people. There's an interesting and cheap lunch menu with rendang beef parcels and mozzarella fritters. An ideal spot for breakfast. 9–11 Cavenagh St; (08) 8981 6729; Mon–Fri 7am–4pm, Sat–Sun 8am–2pm; www.romabar.com.au

**Ducks Nuts Bar & Grill** 💲💲 ♡ Modern Australian food is fused with Asian cuisine right on busy Mitchell Street. Sit outside and soak up the city bustle while enjoying Thai duck leg with banana curry. 76 Mitchell St; (08) 8942 2122; daily 7–11.30am, noon–3pm & 6–10pm.

**Go Sushi** 💲 ♡ Cheap and easy Japanese grub. If you miss out on a spot at the sushi train, don't fret – there are plenty of bento boxes, udon noodles and teriyaki dishes available. Shop 5, 28 Mitchell St; (08) 8941 1008; Mon 10am–3pm, Tue–Fri 10am–3pm

& 5.30–9pm, Sat 10am–4pm & 5.30–9pm.
**Tim's Surf 'n' Turf** 💲 ♨ Tucked down a laneway, this fun, atmospheric restaurant prides itself on big, juicy steaks and the freshest seafood. Tim even does magic tricks! 10 Litchfield St; (08) 8981 1024; Mon–Fri 11.30am–2pm, daily 5.30–9pm.

**Prickles** 💲💲 ♨ Arguably the best Tex Mex in the country with a wide selection of burritos and barbecue ribs. 9 Parap Pl; (08) 8981 2641; Tue–Sun 6–11pm.

**Lewinsky's** 💲💲💲 TOP TREAT!! This ultra-modern restaurant takes the freshest seafood and combines it with classical modern Australian cooking. You can't go

Stokes Hill Wharf

past the seafood platter for two. It's money well spent. 28 Mitchell St; (08) 8941 8666; Mon–Fri noon–3pm, Mon–Sat 6–10pm; lewinskysdarwin.com.au

# Out and about
## Cinemas

**Greater Union Cinema** 76 Mitchell St; (08) 8981 5999.

**Casuarina Square** 247 Trower Rd, Casuarina; (08) 8945 7777.

**Deckchair Cinema** (outside cinema, with old-fashioned seats and both classic and popular films) End of Jervois Rd, off Kitchener Dr; (08) 8981 0700.

## Live music

**Nirvana** Dedicated to live jazz and blues, this dim-lit joint with classic leather couches has jam sessions every Tuesday night. If you have a saxophone handy and can play a bit, bring it along. A great wine and cocktail list make this music venue a must-visit. 6 Dashwood Cr; (08) 8981 2025; daily 6.30pm–1am.

# Pubs and bars

**Shenannigans Irish Pub** With Guinness flowing like water and nightly entertainment, this is one of the most popular nightspots in Darwin, packed with travellers and locals alike. Anyone who downs 100 pints of Guinness (no, not all at once) has their name immortalised on the '100 Pint Board'. 69 Mitchell St; (08) 8981 2100; daily 11am–2am; www.shenannigans.com.au

**Victoria Hotel** Another favourite with backpackers, this place has something for everyone – a downstairs bar, an outside courtyard and a nightclub upstairs. Always a vibrant ambience with some great Aussie beers on tap. 27 Smith St; (08) 8981 4011; daily 1pm–4am; www.thevichotel.com

**Squires Tavern** Women need not apply to this joint. This blokey pub, situated right next to a strip club, can get very rowdy when there's rugby or the V8 Supercar Championship on the tube. Plenty of pool tables and pokie machines to entertain, and, well, if the boys get bored, there is always next door. 3 Edmunds St; (08) 8981 9761; Mon–Sat 11am–4am, Sun 7pm–3am.

**Lizards Outdoor Bar and Grill** This popular drinking spot has a fantastic, leafy outside area, which will make you think you're in one of the Top End's glorious national parks. Great local beers on tap, live bands and a tasty selection of pub grub if you get a little peckish. Top End Hotel, Daly St, cnr Mitchell St; (08) 8981 6511; daily 10am–2am.

**Fox 'n' Fiddle** This British-themed pub offers 15 beers on tap, as well as a diverse selection of cocktails. With trivia and karaoke nights, the pièce de résistance is the nightly hermit crab races. Yes, you read correctly – hermit crab races! 85 Mitchell St; (08) 8942 1844; daily noon–2am.

**The Tap on Mitchell** The owners here encourage guests to enjoy the warm weather and surrounds of the alfresco beer garden. Plenty of beers on tap (hence the name), or try the Midori, Cointreau, vodka, lime and pineapple juice cocktail served in a large

fishbowl. 58 Mitchell St; (08) 8981 5521; daily 10am–midnight; www.thetap.com.au

**Jabiru Bar** The self-proclaimed 'Cocktail Capital of Darwin'. Have a few of their delectable concoctions amid the lush indoor forest decor. They also have crab races during the dry season. Maybe they can team up with the Fox 'n' Fiddle and have a crustacean Olympics. Novotel Atrium Hotel, 100 The Esplanade; (08) 8941 0755; daily 5pm–3am.

**Globe Trotter's Bar and Lodge** Another quality pub/bar with a section for the chilled-out lounge-types and the other for the heavy partiers. 97 Mitchell St; (08) 8981 5385; daily noon–2am.

**Lost Arc** The front part of Discovery Nightclub (see below) has a bar where weary clubbers can have a bit of respite. Live bands appear

## Markets

**Palmerston Night Market** A community event with arts and crafts for sale. Frances Mall; May–Oct Fri 5.30–9.30pm.

**Rapid Creek Markets** Asian food, Top End craft and excellent fresh produce. Rapid Creek Business Village, 48 Trower Rd, Milner; Fri 3pm–late, Sun 6.30am–1pm.

**Nightcliff Markets** These markets are focused on relaxed Sunday mornings – visitors can drink coffee and read the newspapers – all in an outdoor setting. Nightcliff Shopping Centre, Sun 8am–2pm.

regularly. 89 Mitchell St; (08) 8942 3300; Sat–Thur 6pm–4am, Fri 2pm–4am.

**The Deck Bar** This place truly gets kicking on the weekend. The spacious indoor area and gorgeous deck are perfect for both diners and drinkers. 22 Mitchell St; (08) 8942 3001; daily noon–10pm.

**Tzars Vodka Bar** This bar is located inside Duck Nuts Bar & Grill and is a posh night spot where you can enjoy the DJs and strengthen your vodka palate. 76 Mitchell St; (08) 8942 2122; Thur–Sat 10pm–2am; www.ducksnuts.com.au

## Nightclubs

**Discovery Nightclub** This uber-club is home to all those who love glow sticks and jaegarbombs. This is the ultimate clubbing experience in Darwin, with four levels and international DJs. 89 Mitchell St; (08) 8942 3300; Fri–Sat 9.30pm–4am; discoverynightclub.com

**Trinity** This club is for lovers of hardcore techno, attracting some of the best DJs in the country. 3 Edmunds St; (08) 8981 9761; Fri–Sat 11pm–4am.

## Performing arts

**Darwin Entertainment Centre** 93 Mitchell St; (08) 8980 3333.

**Darwin Theatre Company ArtsNT** Small Meeting Room, First Floor 9–11 Cavenagh St; (08) 8924 4184.

**Brown's Mart Community Arts** Cnr Smith St & Harry Chan Ave; (08) 8981 5522.

**Darwin Symphony Orchestra** Ground

Floor Building 17, Charles Darwin University; (08) 8946 6488.

# Where to stay

For further information and reviews on these hostels, please visit www. bugaustralia.com, www.hostelaustralia. com or www.hostelz.com

**Melaleuca on Mitchell** ★★★ Dorm $22–$30, double $85 52 Mitchell St; (08) 8941 7800; www.momdarwin.com

**Chilli's Backpackers** ★★★ Dorm $25, twin and double $56 69a Mitchell St; (08) 8941 9722; www.chillis.com.au

**Banyan View Lodge** ★★★ Dorm $20–$25, single $55, twin and double $65 119 Mitchell St; (08) 8981 8644; www.banyanviewlodge.com.au

**Youth Shack** ★★★ Dorm $25, twin and double $58 69 Mitchell St; (08) 8923 9790; www.youthshack.com.au

**Gecko Lodge** ★★ Dorm $18–$24, single, twin and double $50–$75 146 Mitchell St; (08) 8981 5569; www.geckolodge.com.au

**Darwin YHA Backpackers Hostel** ★★ Dorm $24.50, double $75.50 97 Mitchell St; (08) 8981 5385; www.yha.com.au

**The Cavenagh** ★★ Dorm $16–$27, single and double $70 12 Cavenagh St; (08) 8941 6383; www.thecavenagh.com

**Wilderness Lodge Backpackers** ★★ Dorm $22, twin and double $50 89 Mitchell St; (08) 8981 8363; www.wildlodge.com.au

**Frogshollow Lodge and Backpackers** ★★ Dorm $20, single, twin and double $54–$64 27 Lindsay St; (08) 8941 2600; www.frogs-hollow.com.au

**Elkes Backpackers Darwin** ★★ Dorm $22–$29, single, twin and double $55–$115 112 Mitchell St; (08) 8981 8399; www.elkesbackpackers.com.au

Waterskiing around Fannie Bay

**Saville Park Suites Darwin** ★★★ **TOP TREAT!!** Luxury rooms from $189 88 The Esplanade; (08) 8943 4333; www.savillehotelgroup.com.au

# Tours and activities

**Sunset cruises** Take a cruise on a charter boat from Cullen Bay Marina to see the sun slip below the horizon over the Timor Sea. Operators include City of Darwin Cruises 0417 855 829, Darwin Cruises and Charters (08) 8942 3131, and Spirit of Darwin (08) 8981 3711.

**Ferry to Mandorah** Cast a line off the Mandorah Jetty and enjoy the views of Darwin. It's 130 km by road, but only a 20-minute ferry ride from Cullen Bay Marina. Mandorah Ferry Service (08) 8941 1991. See also the Tour Tub (Getting around, above).

**Rock climbing** Hit The Rock to practise your moves before hitting some of the Northern Territory's great climbing areas. Doctors Gully Rd; (08) 8941 0747.

**Darwin Harbour Diving** Explore the underwater world of the Top End. Cullen Bay Dive (08) 8981 3049 and Coral Divers (08) 8947 4525.

**Darwin Tours** Tours to Crocodylus Park and fishing on the Darwin Harbour. Bookings (08) 8985 6333. www.darwintours.com.au

**Aussie Adventure Tours** Take a Tiwi tour and become familiar with the Aboriginal culture. Bookings (08) 8923 6523. www. aussieadventure.com.au

**The 'Discovering Trails' Walks** Eight self-guided walks, including the Wharf Precinct, The Esplanade, the city centre, the northern suburbs, East Point and Fannie Bay. Brochure available from the visitor centre.

**Heritage Carriage tour** A relaxed tour of the CBD in a horse-drawn carriage. Bookings 0417 813 112.

**George Brown Darwin Botanic Gardens Walks** Self-guided walks through different habitats. Pamphlets are available from the visitor centre at the Geranium Street entrance. A guide can be organised if you book ahead. (08) 8981 1958.

# Outside the city: Fannie Bay

Fannie Bay is a picturesque coastal community located just north-west of Darwin's city centre, surrounded by the suburbs of Parap and The Gardens. This effervescent suburb with fresh sea breezes has a few good attractions and a tranquil ambience. During the day, visit the Museum and Art Gallery of the Northern Territory for a bit of culture and take a stroll through the botanic gardens. At night, one of the great pleasures of visiting Darwin is being able to enjoy a meal by the beach as the sun sets over Fannie Bay. There are several popular dining venues, such as the deck of the Darwin Sailing Club, but just about anywhere is good for a beer and some rest and relaxation.

## Getting to Fannie Bay

Fannie Bay is in very close proximity to Darwin's CBD. Local buses run daily to the Fannie Bay area, but it's only a few kilometres to walk if you're up to it.

## Top attractions

### Museum and Art Gallery of the Northern Territory

This institution houses one of the finest Aboriginal art collections in Australia, which is enhanced every year with the work of entrants in the Aboriginal and Torres Strait Islander Art Award. There's also a spine-tingling cyclone Tracy gallery detailing what happened during and after that fateful Christmas in 1974, and an excellent natural history display of fauna and flora of the Top End and South East Asia. The Maritime Boatshed, a vast room filled with all sorts of vessels that have travelled to northern Australia over the years, is impressive in its size and in the diversity of its exhibits, from tiny jukung to the large fishing vessels that limped to Australian shores overloaded with refugees. Nearby Territory Craft Darwin exhibits the work of local artists and craft producers. Conacher St, Bullocky Point; (08) 8999 8264; Mon–Fri 9am–5pm, Sat–Sun 10am–5pm; general admission free.

### Fannie Bay Gaol Museum

This is one of Darwin's most interesting destinations. It served as Darwin's prison between 1883 and 1979. Located barely 300 m from the Darwin Sailing Club, the gaol housed some of Darwin's most desperate criminals. The cells and gallows provide a sobering display for visitors, but are sometimes used as a backdrop for dinner parties and social events. East Point Rd; (08) 8999 8264; daily 10am–4.30pm; admission free.

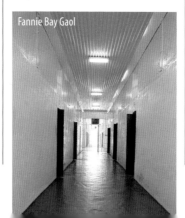
Fannie Bay Gaol

### SKYCITY

A short walk from the Fannie Bay precinct is SKYCITY casino. As well as the attraction of gambling, the casino frequently holds concerts on its lawns. With the beach only metres away, this is a fantastic way to spend an afternoon or evening. There are several restaurants in the casino, and the complex becomes the hub of the horseracing scene in August when a gala ball is held on the lawns. Gilruth Ave, Mindil Beach; (08) 8943 8888; daily 24 hrs.

### George Brown Darwin Botanic Gardens

These botanic gardens have paths that wind through one of the best collections of tropical plants in Australia. Established in the 1870s, the gardens cover an area of 42 ha and contain an extensive collection of tropical orchids and palms, and a self-guided Aboriginal

Where to shop
in Fannie Bay

**Mindil Beach Sunset Markets** This market is Darwin's most popular tourist attraction. Set up on 1–2 km of wide footpaths, starting at the CBD, they attract up to 10 000 people enjoying food from more than 30 nations and wandering between stalls that offer everything from Aboriginal arts to tarot-card readings, massages and kangaroo sausages. Live performances by theatrical and singing troupes are spiced up with whip cracking and poetry readings. Bands play at night and there is an occasional offshore fireworks display. At sunset, people often walk over the sand dunes to the beach to experience a quintessential Darwin moment. Off Gilruth Ave; last week of Apr – end of Oct Thur 5–10pm, Sun 4–9pm.

**Parap Market** This market is about waking up to the splendours of Asia. Colourful flowers, frozen-fruit ice-cream, silk-screened sarongs, Asian food, relaxing massages and exotic, blended drinks are all on offer. Parap Shopping Centre; Sat 8am–2pm.

**Parap Shopping Centre** Specialty shops and a great selection of food outlets.

plant-use trail. A guide can be arranged if you book ahead (see Tours and activities above). Geranium St, The Gardens; (08) 8981 1958; daily 7am–7pm; Orientation Centre Mon–Fri 8.30am–4pm, Sat–Sun 8am–4pm.

**Fannie Bay Racecourse**
Enjoy the sport of kings at Darwin's main horseracing venue. This is the home of the Darwin Cup Carnival, which runs from

Mindil Beach Sunset Market

July to August and sees horses competing for over $1.3 million in prize money and trophies. There are also general racing meets throughout the year. Dick Ward Dr.

# Where to eat
**Cee Cea's Bistro** 💲💲 ♡ This no-frills bistro offers top-quality grub with scenic views of the Arafura Sea. Enjoy the decadent seafood dishes as you watch the sunset. Darwin Trailer Boat Club, Atkins Dr; (08) 8941 6688; daily noon–2.30pm & 5.30–10pm.

**Cool Spot** 💲 💎 The name alone is an attraction when the temperatures soar in the summer months. Tuck into one of Cool Spot's famous banana splits, milkshakes or something off the varied breakfast menu. 1 Keith La; (08) 8981 8428; Mon–Thur 7am–11pm, Fri–Sat 7am–midnight, Sun 7am–10pm; www.coolspot.com.au

**Fannie Bay Super Pizza** 💲 ♡ Having been around for years, this stalwart of Italian cuisine is a no-fuss eatery that serves good and filling food. Shop 4, Fannie Bay Pl; (08) 8981 7324; Sun–Thur 5–11pm, Fri–Sat 5pm–midnight.

**Waterfront Bistro** 💲💲 ♡ With million-dollar views and a relaxed atmosphere, look no further than this fantastic restaurant. Located at the Darwin Sailing Club, it has great contemporary meals at good prices. The Darwin Sailing Club, Atkins Dr; (08) 8981 1700; daily noon–3pm, 5.30–9pm.

**Cyclone Cafe** 💲 ♡ This legendary cafe is constructed from debris left after cyclone Tracy and serves a mean cup of java coffee. Be wary, the joint gets packed on Saturdays thanks to the bustling market crowd. 8 Urquhart Street, Parap; (08) 8941 1992; Mon–Fri 7.30am–3pm, Sat–Sun 8.30am–1pm.

**Evoo Restaurant** 💲💲 Situated right in the SKYCITY casino complex is this elegant restaurant with dishes that'll knock your socks off, like chicken & pistachio roulade served with potato fondant. It tastes just as good as it sounds. SKYCITY Casino, Floor 3, Gilruth Ave, Larrakeyah; (08) 8943 8888; Fri noon–3pm, daily 6–10pm; www.skycitydarwin.com.au

Events in Fannie Bay

**Darwin Cup Carnival** The city's premier horseracing carnival. Jul–Aug.

**National Aboriginal Art Award** Exquisite Aboriginal art at the Museum and Art Gallery of the Northern Territory. Aug–Oct.

**Pee Wee's at the Point** 💲💲💲 **TOP TREAT!!** Situated in the East Point Nature Reserve, you can eat your meal here amid swaying palms, with the Timor Sea lapping the shore below. Meals combine Asian and Australia flavours. Alec Fong Lim Dr, East Point Reserve; (08) 8981 6868; daily 5pm–12.30am; www.peewees.com.au

# Out and about
## Pubs and bars
**Darwin Sailing Club** With beautiful waterfront views, this place is perfect to visit on a warm summer's night. Order some hot chips and a Crown Lager, and sit back to watch the sun set. Fannie Bay; (08) 8981 1700; Sun–Thur 10am–noon, Fri–Sat 10am–2am; www.dwnsail.com.au

**Darwin Ski Club** Another picturesque outdoor venue, with live acoustic performances every Friday and Saturday. 20 Conacher St; (08) 8981 6630; Mon–Thur noon–11.45pm, Fri–Sun noon–1am.

**Buzz** Frozen mango daiquiris and tacky, novelty decor – what more could you want from a waterfront bar? Even the bathrooms have avant-garde furnishings. 48 Marina Blvd, Larrakeyah; (08) 8941 1141; daily 10am–2am.

**Bar Aqua** You'll understand the meaning behind the bar's name when you view the large aquarium upon entry. Come for the fishies, stay for the wines, boutique beers, cognac and premium whiskys. SKYCITY Casino, Gilruth Ave, The Gardens; (08) 8943 8949; daily 8am–2am; www.skycitydarwin.com.au

# Where to stay
**Capricornia Motel** ★★ Rooms from $66–$130 3 Kellaway St; (08) 8981 4055

## Other suburbs worth visiting

**Karama** Excellent walking trails through the Holmes Jungle Nature Park.

**Nightcliff** Has a magnificent foreshore cliff-top walkway.

**Casuarina** Boasts some pristine, white, sandy beaches.

# Daytrip: Litchfield National Park

Given Darwin's small size, a daytrip outside the capital city can be easily organised. Just 100 km south-west of Darwin lies Litchfield National Park, a diverse landscape that takes in most Top End habitats. Named after European explorer Frederick Litchfield, the park's magnificent spring-fed waterfalls flow from a plateau, creating beautiful – and crocodile-free – swimming holes. The most impressive falls are Florence, Wangi and Tjaynera falls, each possessing rockpools that you should definitely bring your swimmers to try out. Buley Rockhole, Tjaetaba Falls and Surprise Creek Falls are also great spots. Please note that swimming is prohibited in Reynolds River.

On the outside edges of the park, weathered rocks rise from the grassy plains, which are dotted with massive magnetic termite mounds. These oddly shaped mounds look like something out of *Lord of the Rings*, and you can stroll around them on a boardwalk complete with information panels. Of the park's prolific wildlife, orange leafnosed-bats, pythons, sugar gliders and red-tailed black-cockatoos are all common sights.

The area is also terrific for bushwalking. One of the best walks is among the sandstone pillars of the Lost City, a series of freestanding, unusual rock towers. Wangi Falls has a beautiful walk, which leads around the pool via the top of the falls. For the hardcore walker, the Tabletop Track is a 39 km circuit that links many of the park's attractions and can be accessed at Florence Falls, Greenant Creek, Wangi Falls and Walker Creek. There are also guided walks daily between May and October. For information on guided walks, call (08) 8999 4555.

## Further information
🟢 **PWCNT Batchelor** (08) 8976 0282; www.nt.gov.au

## Tours
**Albatross Helicopters** See the park from the sky. (08) 8988 5081; www.albatrosshelicopters.com.au
**Kakadu Dreams** Rolling Thunder and Wildlife and Waterfalls day tours. (08) 8981 3266; www.kakadudreams.com.au

## Where to stay
**Banyan Tree Caravan and Tourist Park** ★★★ Budget room $49–$59, cabin $99, unit $129 Litchfield Park Rd, Batchelor; (08) 8976 0330; www.banyan-tree.com.au

## Visitor information

### Darwin Airport
Darwin's international airport is conveniently located approximately 13 km from the CBD.
**Bus** The **Darwin City Shuttle Bus** operates daily between Darwin International Airport and Darwin city accommodation. Other locations are available upon request. 1800 358 945 or (08) 8981 5066.
**Taxi** A taxi zone is located right at the front of the airport terminal. It's a quick but more expensive alternative.

### Internet cafes
**Global Gossip** 44 Mitchell St; (08) 8942 3044.
**Internet Outpost Darwin** 69 Mitchell St; (08) 8952 8855.
**Northern Territory Library** (free internet) Parliament House; (08) 8999 7177.

### Hospitals
For all emergencies, including police, fire, or hospital, dial '000'.
**Royal Darwin Hospital**
Rocklands Dr, Casuarina; (08) 8922 8888.

**Batchelor Resort**★★★ Camping $12–$29, ensuite cabins $115 37–39 Jungle Rum Rd, Batchelor; (08) 8976 0123; www.batchelor-resort.com
**Camping** Wangi Falls, Buley Rockhole and Florence Falls all have managed campsites. During the dry season, there are 4WD campsites at Tjaynera Falls, Surprise Creek Falls, and just downstream from Florence Falls. There's also a walk-in campsite at Walker Creek during the dry season.

Magnetic termite mounds

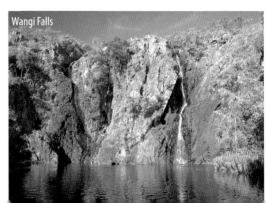
Wangi Falls

For more detail
see maps
236–237

111

*Darwin*

NORTHERN TERRITORY

# Kakadu and Arnhem Land
# Insights into a
# unique culture

The ancient Arnhem Land escarpment meanders 500 km from north to south, separating Kakadu National Park in the west from Aboriginal-owned Arnhem Land in the east. The largest national park in Australia, Kakadu National Park is a place of rare beauty and grand landscapes, abundant flora and fauna, impressive rock art and ancient mythology. Before European settlement this was one of the most intensely populated areas on the continent. Today the traditional owners showcase their culture through excellent guided tours and displays at the on-site cultural centres. Arnhem Land is the traditional home of a number of language groups, and is one of Australia's most remote and least-traversed regions. Permits are required for approaches by road.

**Number of days to spend in this region: 6–12 days**

## Getting here

Most of the region is fairly remote, so the best way to explore is by bus, car or on a tour. Greyhound offer bus passes, as well as daily services from Darwin. Darwin and Kakadu National Park have plenty of vehicle-hire outlets.

Those interested in travelling by vehicle in Arnhem Land must obtain a permit from the Northern Land Council beforehand and allow two weeks for processing. Alternatively, Qantas flies to Gove Airport in the east from Cairns and Darwin.

**Bargain Wheels Car Rentals** Jabiru; 1800 115 111; www.bargainwheels.com.au

**Top End 4WD and Car Hire** 1300 360 339; www.topend4wd.com.au

**Northern Land Council** 9 Rowling St, Casuarina; (08) 8920 5100; www.nlc.org.au

## Kakadu National Park (2–5 days)

World Heritage-listed Kakadu National Park is by far the most spectacular environmental wonder in all of Australia. The wide-ranging habitats, from arid sandstone hills, savannah woodlands and monsoon forests, to freshwater floodplains, thundering waterfalls and tidal mudflats, support an immense variety of wildlife – some rare, endangered or endemic. The park also has the world's largest and possibly oldest Aboriginal rock-art collection, depicting now extinct creatures, spirit figures embodied in Indigenous

### When to go

Most people visit the Kakadu region during the dry season, which extends from May to the end of September. The wet season, which is at its peak from December to late April, can bring monsoonal-like weather, with harsh rains, winds and flooding. While the park's vegetation is lush and green at this time, it is a very uncomfortable time to travel.

mythology and even the first contact with Europeans. All of this makes for a place of immense spirituality, with a cultural heritage that reflects the unique relationship between the Aboriginal custodians and the land itself.

### Jim Jim Falls

You may recognise these majestic falls from the countless images of them in television commercials and calendars. But to see this area is something very different. Access to Jim Jim Falls is by 4WD only, and your vehicle will require a snorkel to cross Jim Jim Creek. From the carpark, a 1 km walk (involving some rock-hopping) will lead you to Jim Jim Plunge Pool, one of the most beautiful swimming areas in Kakadu. Although generally considered safe, swimmers are warned that there is still some threat of travelling crocs (see the Crocodile information box). The pool is surrounded by 150 m-high cliffs that change colour as the sun changes position. The falls are a fury of white

Jim Jim Falls

water during the wet season, but stop flowing during the dry season. Nearby, Budjmi Lookout Walk (1 km, 45 min) is a dry-season trail that starts at Jim Jim camping area and involves a moderate-grade climb to the top of a rocky outcrop for expansive views of the Arnhem Land escarpment.

Only a short boat ride away is Twin Falls, another spectacular waterfall that is surrounded by gorgeous sandy beaches. Swimming is not allowed because of crocodiles, but experienced walkers can take the difficult Twin Falls plateau trail (6 km, 3–4 hrs), which climbs the cliffs above the falls.

### Crocodiles

Many visitors to Australia harbour a fear of crocodiles, but there is no need to panic if you travel sensibly. In Kakadu National Park, all plunge pools and gorge areas are surveyed for estuarine crocodiles before park rangers open the areas for the dry season. However, there remains some risk of saltwater crocs venturing into these areas, so make sure you look for crocodile warning signs and consider all information before taking a dip.

**Boat shuttle** The boat shuttle is the only way to access Twin Falls Gorge. The service departs every half hour between 7.30am–4.30pm. Tickets should be purchased prior to the day of travel from the visitor centre in Darwin or Kakadu National Park, or Garnamarr or Mardugal campgrounds (inside the park). For more information, contact Bowali Visitor Centre (08) 8938 1120.

**Jim Jim Falls tours: Lord's Kakadu and Arnhem Land Safaris**
Offers small group 4WD tours of the falls. (08) 8948 2200; www.lords-safaris.com

**Kakadu Gorge and Waterfall Tours** Day trips to Jim Jim and Twin falls. (08) 8979 0145.

**Yellow Water Cruises** A scenic cruise down Yellow Water Billabong, located at the end of Jim Jim Creek. (08) 8979 0145; www.yellowwatercruises.com

## Nourlangie Rock

Nourlangie Rock is located on an outlying area of the Arnhem Land escarpment and is one of Kakadu's main rock-art areas. It's difficult to know exactly how long these glorious examples of rock-drawings have been around, although shell and animal-bone fragments suggest occupation over the past 6000 years. The most visited site in the area is the Anbangbang Gallery, which contains artwork by Najombolmi, who decorated the walls in 1964 in an effort to preserve his Indigenous

culture. Walking trails will take you to see different styles of Aboriginal rock-painting, including what is known as 'X-ray' art, illustrating in depth the anatomy of humans and animals.

There are six walking trails in the Nourlangie area, ranging from shorter, more brisk outings to longer, difficult treks. The Nanguluwur Art Site Walk (3.4 km, 2 hrs) leads through open savannah woodlands to a small gallery displaying most of the rock-art styles found in Kakadu. The Nawurlandja Lookout Walk (1.2 km, 40 min) is shorter but steeper, giving panoramic views of the escarpment and the Anbangbang Billabong. For a longer trail, the Barrk Walk (12 km, 6–8 hrs) traverses sandstone country, passing the Nanguluwur gallery along the way.

## Ubirr

Aboriginal people once camped in the rock shelters at Ubirr, another marvel housing some of the most intriguing rock art in Kakadu. This area consists of over 120 rock-art sites, with large, naturalistic portrayals of extinct animals, simple stick figures with large headdresses, and animated and ornamented figures in motion. One of the most striking sites has a frieze depicting an animated group of hunters and spear throwers with goose-wing fans – thought to hark back to a period when Indigenous tribes hunted geese in the vast freshwater wetlands. Other art displays to look out for include the Namarrgran Sisters, who are represented as crocodiles, and the Rainbow Serpent, a creation ancestor and one of the oldest artistic symbols in the world. A 1 km circuit covers all of the rock-art areas, and another 500 m track takes a steep climb to a rocky vantage point with sensational views over the Nardab floodplain. Sunsets from here are spectacular.

## East Alligator area

Encompassing the Ubirr art sites, the East Alligator area is definitely worth a visit, mainly for a cruise down the splendiferous East Alligator River. Cruises take in an abundance of unique flora and fauna, as well as saltwater crocodiles, several bird species and beautiful water lilies. During February and March, you can also take a cruise down Magela Creek, where you'll experience vast pine forests, lillipad billabongs and gorgeous freshwater mangroves. If the water isn't your thing, there are some walking trails in the area, and if you're into fishing, East Alligator River is a great spot. Just don't clean your fish too close to the water's edge – the crocs are always hungry.

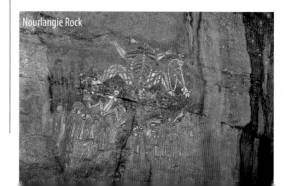

Nourlangie Rock

**East Alligator tours and activities: Guluyambi on the East Alligator** The ultimate East Alligator River cruise experience, with Aboriginal guides and breathtaking scenery. (08) 8979 2411; May–Oct; www.guluyambi.com.au

**Fishing** A boat ramp is located upstream and downstream of Cahills Crossing for anglers. For more information on fishing and boating visit www.environment.gov.au

## Further information

ⓘ **Bowali Visitor Centre** (08) 8938 1120; daily 8am–5pm; www.environment.gov.au

ⓘ **Warradjan Aboriginal Cultural Centre** Cooinda; (08) 8979 0145; daily 9am–5pm.

## Kakadu tours

**Aussie Adventure Tours** Two- to four-day tours of Kakadu in all its glory. (08) 8923 6523; www.aussieadventure.com.au

**Kakadu Animal Tracks** Explore the native wildlife and gather your own bush tucker. (08) 8979 0145; www.animaltracks.com.au

**Gecko Canoeing** Kayaking and adventure tours. (08) 8972 2224; www.geckocanoeing.com.au

**Wilderness 4WD Adventures** Three- to five-day camping tours including rock climbing. (08) 8941 2161; www.wildernessadventures.com.au

**Wayward Bus Tours** Three-day camping excursion of the park. (08) 8410 8833; www.waywardbus.com.au

**Australia Wilderness Tours** 1300 661 229 or (02) 6587 7188; www.awtours.com.au

**Kakadu Dreams** (08) 8981 3266; www.kakadudreams.com.au

**AAT Kings** (03) 9915 1500; www.aatkings.com

## Where to eat

**Barra Bistro** 💲💲 Large buffet meals and live entertainment from May to November. Kakadu Hwy, Jim Jim; (08) 8979 0145; daily 10am–9pm.

Kakadu National Park

## Where to stay

**Lakeview Park YHA** ★★★ Dorm $30.50, twin and double $84.50–$106.50 Lakeview Dr, Jabiru; (08) 8979 3144; www.yha.com.au

**Kakadu Lodge** ★★ Dorm $36, budget room (4 people) $141 Jabiru Dr, Jabiru; (08) 8979 2422.

**Gagudju Lodge YHA** ★★ Dorm $32.50, double $73.50 Kakadu Hwy, Cooinda; (08) 8979 0145; www.yha.com.au

**Wirnwirnmila Mary River Road House** ★★ Dorm $17–$30, twin and double $90 Kakadu Hwy, Mary River; (08) 8975 4564.

**Gagudju Crocodile Holiday Inn** ★★ TOP TREAT!! This NT icon is a 250 m crocodile-shaped building that really only resembles a crocodile from the air. The reception area is designed to represent a billabong and accommodation is in the belly of the beast. The thrill of staying here is mostly for the novelty factor (and a bit of luxury in a private room). Room $160–$310 Flinders St, Jabiru; 1800 669 562; www.holidayinn.com.au

**Camping** Campsites are numerous and are listed by area. Garnamarr Campground caters for about 200 people and is located beside the Jim Jim Falls access road, about 50 km from the Kakadu Highway. Bookings are allocated on a 'first come, first serve' basis. Muirella Park near Nourlangie Rock has a camping area with toilets, showers and a generator. In the East Alligator area, Merl camping area has showers, toilets and access to a generator. For vacancies, contact the Bowali Visitor Centre (08) 8938 1120.

# Arnhem Land (3–8 days)

Arnhem Land is the largest Aboriginal reserve in Australia and is home to many Indigenous groups still living according to traditional laws and practices. Land ownership is held by the Yolngu people, who have lived in north-east Arnhem Land for over 40 000 years. The only current exception to this title is the mining lease that the town of Nhulunbuy is located on.

From the early 1600s, the Yolngu traded and mingled with Indonesian seafarers, known as Macassans. It was only from the 1930s that Yolngu people had steady contact with Balanda (white people), which explains how their culture has remained intact. Aside from producing beautiful bark paintings and other arts and crafts, the Yolngu people live on the custodial lands of Australia's most famous Indigenous instrument, the didgeridoo (or yidaki). The Yolngu are known for being excellent traditional musicians, and most of the members of Australia's most prominent Indigenous band, Yothu Yindi, are of Yolngu descent.

There are plenty of things to see and do when visiting this region. Nhulunbuy is east Arnham Land's town centre, a small place with a few recreational activities available, including golf and tennis. You can also take a 4WD tour to pristine beaches, including Nanydjaka (Cape Arnhem), or go snorkelling or scuba diving around the islands. Please note that recreational permits are required from Dhimurru Land Management in Nhulunbuy for access to these areas.

Not far from the township is the Gayngaru Wetlands, a natural lagoon teeming with native plants and wildlife, including 200 bird species. The interpretive walk provides information on native plants and animals, and their importance to the Yolngu for food and bush medicine. There are also two viewing platforms and a bird hide, so that visitors can view the wildlife without disturbing it.

The other must-see is Buku-Larrnggay Mulka Centre, a renowned community-based art museum, which was opened to educate visitors in the local law and culture of the Yolngu people. The artists of the Yirrkala were actually the first Indigenous Australians to see their artistic creations as a political tool. The famous church panels, on display at the gallery's museum, were painted as a statement of Aboriginal solidarity in relation to a proposed plan to mine bauxite nearby in 1962. This is one of your best chances to buy guaranteed authentic Indigenous art, some of which is reasonably priced and can be shipped back home.

On the western side of Arnhem Land, Garig Gunak Barlu National Park on the Cobourg Peninsula has some brilliant fishing spots, green vegetation and turquoise waters.

## Further information

ⓘ **Nhulunbuy Visitor Information Centre** (08) 8987 1111; Mon–Fri 9am–5pm; www.ealta.org

ⓘ **Bark Hut Tourist Centre** (08) 8978 8988; Arnhem Hwy, Annaburroo; daily 6am–late.

ⓘ **PWCNT Black Point** (Garig Gunak Barlu National Park) (08) 8979 0244; www.nt.gov.au

**Dhimurru Land Management** Opposite Captain Cook Shopping Centre, Nhulunbuy; (08) 8987 3992; www.dhimurru.com.au

**Buku-Larrnggay Mulka Centre** Yirrkala; (08) 8987 1701; Mon–Fri 8am–4.30pm, Sat 9am–noon; www.yirrkala.com

## Tours

**Venture North Australia** Comprehensive 4WD tours of Arnhem Land and the Cobourg Peninsula, covering everything from art and fishing to spotlighting for turtles and crocodiles on the beach after dark. (08) 8927 5500; www.northernaustralia.com

**Lord's Kakadu and Arnhemland Safaris** Award-winning 4WD tour operators. (08) 8948 2200; www.lords-safaris.com

**Cape Don Experience** Fishing and eco-tours. (08) 8979 0030; www.capedon.com.au

**Cobourg Adventures** Tours, cruises and fishing in the wondrous Cobourg Peninsula. (08) 8979 0455; www.cobourgbeachhuts.com.au

**Birds Bees Trees and Things** Tranquil lagoons, birdwatching, spear fishing and Aboriginal culture. (08) 8987 1814; www.birdsbeestreesandthings.com.au

## Where to eat

**Macassans** 💲💲 This no-fuss eatery located at the Arnhem Club has the freshest seafood platters and beef dishes. Every Friday lunch is a carvery buffet. Hit the bar after for a few quiet frothies. 1 Franklyn St, Nhulunbuy; (08) 8987 0600; daily noon–2.30pm & 6–9.30pm; www.thearnhemclub.com.au

## Where to stay

**Bark Hut Tourist Centre** ★★★ Camping $14–$22, single $45, twin $60  Arnhem Hwy, Annaburroo; (08) 8978 8988.

**Point Stuart Wilderness Lodge** ★★ Budget room (2 people) $85, ensuite room $145  Off Port Stuart Rd; (08) 8978 8914; www.pointstuart.com.au

## Events

**Garma Festival** The largest and most vibrant celebration of the Yolngu Aboriginal people, with didgeridoo master classes, art, spear-throwing demonstrations and academic forums. Aug.

**Gove Bush Golf Classic** A unique golf charity day. This 9-hole golf course actually covers 120 km. Oct.

### Aboriginal native title

In recent times, native title has been a controversial political issue between the Australian Government and Aboriginal and Torres Strait Islander people. Since European settlement, Australian soil has been under the government's control, but many groups feel a strong need and right to fight for what once belonged to them. Land is vitally important to Indigenous people, not only territorially, but also culturally and spiritually.

The Yolngu people of Arnhem Land played a pivotal role in the birth of the land rights movement, when in 1963 they protested against the government's decision to excise part of the land for a bauxite mine. They signed a petition on bark and sent it to the Australian House of Representatives. This act attracted national and international attention; the bark still hangs in the hallowed halls of Parliament House in Canberra.

But it wasn't until 1992 that the Aboriginal native title movement had its first major breakthrough. The Mabo case saw the High Court of Australia reject the assumption that Australia was terra nullius, or empty land, when first settled. Ownership of Murray Island in the Torres Strait was granted to its Indigenous residents.

There are still many native title claims being negotiated today. It's an issue that will be talked about for many years to come.

Aboriginal children in Arnhem Land

# Red Centre
# Rock on in the desert

With spectacular landforms, deserts, blue skies and a monumental sense of scale, the Red Centre has become a powerful symbol of Australia's ancient grandeur. The mythic heart of this land is Uluru (previously known as Ayers Rock), the world's

second-largest single rock, and an extremely sacred site for local Aboriginal groups. The surrounding wonders are equally impressive, including the sandstone walls of Kings Canyon and Ormiston Gorge's soaring orange cliffs. Alice Springs is the region's small town centre, a modern oasis in the middle of this uninhabited desert. This country is large and vast, but the Red Centre is one region that you don't want to leave without experiencing to the max.

**Number of days to spend in this region: 8–10 days**

## Getting here

Alice Springs is the Red Centre's central hub. There are daily flights to and from Alice Springs Airport, and daily bus services run by Greyhound. Alternatively, you could hop on one of the country's most famous trains, the *Ghan*. It departs twice weekly from Adelaide in South Australia, stopping in

Alice Springs before finishing its journey in Darwin. There is a range of travel options onboard, from day seats to sleeper cabins, but all have astounding scenery out of the window. Car hire is another option, and a quicker method of getting to the more remote wilderness locations.

**The *Ghan*** 13 2147; www.gsr.com.au

## Red Centre tours

**Adventure Tours** From overnight to longer 4WD safari tours. (08) 8132 8230; www.adventuretours.com.au

**Alice Springs Holidays** Day tours to Palm Valley and the West MacDonnell Ranges, or longer tours of Alice Springs and Ayers Rock. (08) 8953 1411; www.alicespringsholidays.com.au

**Backpacker Adventure Tours** Ten-day tours from Sydney and Adelaide to Alice Springs. (08) 8356 5501; www.battours.com.au

**Alice Wanderer Centre Sightseeing** Excursions to West MacDonnell

National Park, Palm Valley and Hermannsburg available. 1800 722 111; www.alicewanderer.com.au

**Ossie's 4WD Tours** Half- to 14-day 4WD tours of the outback. The Afternoon 4WD Sunset Tour takes you to Owen Springs Station, then to Rainbow Valley to enjoy the sunset with some champagne. (08) 8952 2308; www.ossies.com.au

**Northern Territory Tours and Travel** (08) 8981 3833; www.northernterritoryholidays.com.au

**Aussie Adventures** (08) 8923 6523; www.aussieadventure.com.au

## When to go

Most people visit the Red Centre during the dry season, from May to the end of September. It can be hot and dry during the day, but generally becomes cool at night – make sure you bring warm clothes. The wet season (October–April) isn't a pleasant time to travel around the region, with uncomfortably hot and humid temperatures and monsoonal rains.

## ❶ Alice Springs (2–3 days)

'The Alice', as it is colloquially known, is a modern civilisation smack bang in the middle of harsh desert terrain. It's made all the more likeable by not taking itself too seriously (as some of its annual events testify).

In the town centre is the Royal Flying Doctor Service, which was the world's first aero-medical organisation and still acts as Australia's angel of the sky. Tours of the base cover the radio communication centre and audiovisual presentations, leaving you to peruse the interactive museum. To see the largest collection of reptiles in the Territory, including perentie goannas, frill-neck lizards and thorny devils, mosey on down to the Alice Springs Reptile Centre. If art is more your style, the Aboriginal Art & Cultural Centre offers some amazing Indigenous art that you can actually afford (a hand-painted platypus for $50 – bargain).

You should also wander down to the cultural precinct, which is home to some of the town's most fascinating attractions. There are tickets available that cover entry to each attraction. The Araluen Centre has four separate galleries of Aboriginal art, with an emphasis on work from the central desert, and a magnificent stained-glass window by local artist Wenten Rubuntja. The Museum of Central Australia offers an insight into the Red Centre's geological and natural history, with interpretive displays and impressive fossils. Also in the area is the Central Australian Aviation Museum, displaying historic aircraft and aviation memorabilia, and the Yeperenye Sculpture, a public artwork depicting a Dreamtime caterpillar.

Alice Springs Desert Park, 8 km west of town, is a combined nature area, zoo and interpretive centre that invites visitors to explore the arid lands. The park has a spectacular nocturnal house with native marsupials such as the bilby, and there are free-flying birds of prey in daily shows.

For a bit of shopping and entertainment in the town centre, hit the relaxing markets at Todd Mall on a Sunday. In the evening, grab a bite and then purchase tickets to the Sound of Starlight Theatre. This sound excursion takes audiences on a journey through the Red Centre, with the pulsating sound of didgeridoos sure to give you goosebumps.

## Further information

[i] **Central Australian Tourism Visitor Information Centre** 60 Gregory Tce; (08) 8952 5800; Mon–Fri 8.30am–5.30pm, Sat–Sun 9am–4pm.

**Royal Flying Doctor Service** 8–10 Stuart Tce; (08) 8952 1129; Mon–Sat 9am–5pm, Sun 1–5pm; www.flyingdoctor.net

**Alice Springs Reptile Centre** 9 Stuart Tce; (08) 8952 8900; daily 9.30am–5pm; www.reptilecentre.com.au

**Aboriginal Art & Cultural Centre** 125 Todd St; (08) 8952 3408; Mon–Fri 9am–5pm, Sat 9am–noon; www.aboriginalaustralia.com

**Alice Springs Cultural Precinct** Cnr Larapinta Dr & Memorial Ave; (08) 8951 1120; attractions generally open daily 10am–5pm; www.nt.gov.au/nreta/museums/ascp

**Alice Springs Desert Park** Larapinta Dr; (08) 8951 8788; daily 7.30am–6pm; www.alicespringsdesertpark.com.au

**Todd Mall Markets** Sun, every 2 weeks after Jan and weekly during Jul; contact the City Council for more information (08) 8950 0500.

**Sound of Starlight Theatre** Performances run April–Nov Tue, Fri & Sat 8–9.30pm. Bookings can be made via phone or the website. Dinner packages and transfers also available. 40 Todd Mall; (08) 8953 0826; www.soundsofstarlight.com

## Tours

**Alice Wanderer Centre Sightseeing** See all of The Alice's attractions. As well as guided tours, the company has a shuttle service that runs an hourly circuit, stopping at all the major tourist attractions. Phone for bookings and enquiries. (08) 8952 2111; www.alicewanderer.com.au

**Aboriginal Dreamtime and Bushtucker Tours** A hands-on

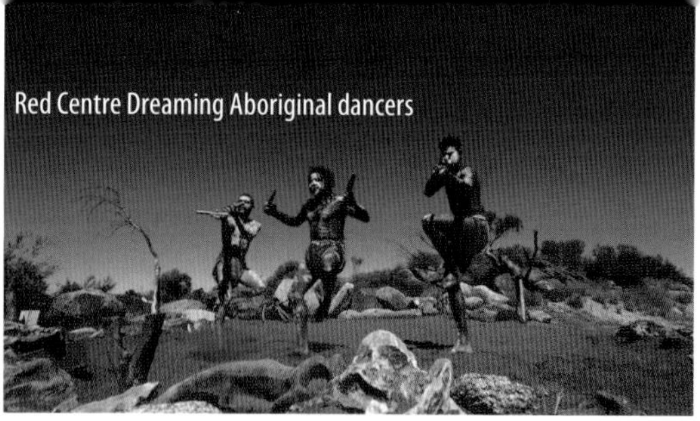

Red Centre Dreaming Aboriginal dancers

learning experience about the local Aboriginal culture. Boomerang and spear throwing on offer, as well as samples of traditional bush tucker. (08) 8955 5095; rstours.com.au

**The Original Outback Bush BBQ** At the foot of the East MacDonnell Ranges you can experience a traditional outback bash. See boomerang demonstrations, sing classic Australian campfire songs, and eat your weight in meat and potatoes. (08) 8952 1731; www.tailormadetours.com.au

**Camel to Dinner** Enjoy a 1 hr sunset camel ride along the banks of the Todd River, then dig in to a homemade three-course meal at the Camel Farm Restaurant. Breakfast camel trips also available. 1300 134 044; www.alicespringsresort.com.au

**Outback Quad Adventures** Get the red dust in your face on a quad motorcycle ride around The Alice. Overnight tours are available, which allows for camping under the stars. (08) 8953 0697; www.outbackquadadventures.com.au

**Just The Alice Helicopter Flight** A short but breathtaking 10-minute chopper flight over Alice Springs. (08) 8952 9800; www.alicespringshelicopters.com.au

## Where to eat

**Bar Doppio** $ A favourite among the locals, with wholesome, cheap food. Sit back with a coffee and enjoy the cool ambience. 89 Todd Mall, Fan Arcade; (08) 8952 6525; Mon–Sat 8am–4pm, Sun 10am–3pm.

**Hanuman** $$ The exotic and sophisticated flavours of Asia are not lost in the desert. Lunch and dinner menus include some amazing seafood dishes and curries. Guaranteed not to disappoint. Crown Plaza, 82 Barrett Dr; (08) 8953 7188; Mon–Fri noon–2.30pm, daily 6–10pm; www.hanuman.com.au

**Keller's Swiss, Indian and Australian Restaurant** $$ How could Swiss, Indian and Australian cuisines possibly co-exist? At Keller's they do, with a wide variety of mouth-watering meals, from Swiss cheese fondue to beef vindaloo. Takeaway is available as a cheaper option. Diplomat Hotel, Shop 1, 20 Gregory Tce; (08) 8952 3188; Mon–Sat 5.30–10pm; www.kellers.com.au

**Overlanders Steakhouse** $$$ **TOP TREAT!!** 'More than just a steakhouse' is an apt slogan for Overlanders. This restaurant dares diners to try the 'Drover's Blowout', a multi-course meal of soup, emu, crocodile, camel, barramundi, beef, kangaroo and dessert. If you're not up for the challenge, there's also an à la carte menu. The bar area features bar-top cowboy dancers, à la the American film *Coyote Ugly*, who will guide you through Australia's favourite bush songs. 72 Hartley

St; (08) 8952 2159; daily 6pm–late (last food orders 9.45pm); www.overlanders.com.au

## Pubs and bars

**Melanka Party Bar** Do you need more than a place called the 'Party Bar'? Next door to Melanka Backpackers, this place is always a riot, with DJs, live bands, daily happy hours and nightly backpacker party games. 94 Todd St; (08) 8952 4744; daily 5pm–4am; www.melanka.com.au

**Firkin and Hound** A traditional English pub right in the middle of the Australian desert. Enjoy the relaxed outback setting and happy-go-lucky locals. 21 Hartley St; (08) 8953 3033; daily 11.30am–1am.

**Todd Tavern** A traditional Aussie pub with a bistro and a bottle shop. 1 Todd Mall; (08) 8952 1255; Sun–Tue 10.30am–10pm, Wed–Fri 10.30am–midnight, Sat 10.30am–late, meals daily noon–9pm; www.toddtavern.com.au

## Where to stay

**Annie's Place** ★★★ Dorm $16, twin and double $50–$60 4 Traeger Ave; (08) 8952 1545; www.anniesplace.com.au

**Alice's Secret Travellers Inn** ★★★ Dorm $19–$22, single $40, twin $52, double $60 6 Khalick St; (08) 8952 8686; www.asecret.com.au

**Heavitree Gap Outback Lodge** ★★★ Dorm $25, kitchen and lodge room $79–$99 Palm Circuit; (08) 8950 4444; www.auroraresorts.com.au

**Todd Tavern** ★★★ Room from $50 1 Todd Mall; (08) 8952 1255; www.toddtavern.com.au

**Alice Springs YHA** ★★ Dorm $23.50–$25.50, twin and double $61.50 Cnr Parsons St & Leichhardt Tce; (08) 8952 8855; www.yha.com.au

**Toddy's Resort** ★★ Dorm $18–$20, single, twin and double $55–$85 39–41 Gap Rd; (08) 8952 1322; www.toddys.com.au

**Melanka Backpackers** ★★ Dorm $20, twin and hotel $90 Gregory Tce; (08) 8952 2233; www.melanka.com.au

**Alice Lodge Backpackers** ★★ Dorm $20–$24, twin and double $58 4 Mueller St; (08) 8953 0804; www.alicelodge.com.au

## Events

**Bangtail Muster** Street parade down Todd Mall and various sporting events. May.

**Finke Desert Race** Australia's fastest desert race for bikes, cars and buggies. Speed, speed, dust and more speed! Jun.

**Beanie Festival** Yes, a festival of beanies. See unique designs, from emu beanies to border collie tea cosies. Jun–Jul.

**Imparja Camel Cup Carnival** Famous camel race with great food and drink stalls, and entertainment. Jul.

**Alice Springs Rodeo** Saddle bronc, bareback brahman bull riding and a ladies' barrel race. Aug.

**Henley-on-Todd Regatta** Head to the banks of the Todd River for the Alice's most iconic event, with the Oxford Tubs race. Aug.

**Alice Desert Festival** Cultural festival of film, theatre, literature and music. Sept.

## ❷ West MacDonnell National Park (1–2 days)

The majestic MacDonnell Ranges, once higher than the Himalayas, were formed over 800 million years ago. Over time these ancient peaks have been dramatically eroded, leaving spectacular gorges, hidden waterholes, remnant rainforests and abundant native flora and wildlife.

Standley Chasm is an inspirational site to visit. A deep, red crevice crowded on either side by slopes rising 80 m high is the result of millions of years of flooding. The best time to visit is around noon, when the sun strikes the walls and lights up the chasm to a dramatic, bright orange. The park's other jewel is Ormiston Gorge, a picturesque area with a near-permanent waterhole for swimming (though the water might be cold) and some brilliant walking trails.

Other attractions in the park include Serpentine Gorge, a desert oasis and waterhole with an easy, well-marked trail leading to a lookout. There are also some brisk trails around Ellery Creek Big Hole, a beautiful place to swim, picnic and view birdlife. Ochre Pits is a natural quarry where, for thousands of years, Aboriginal people gathered ochre from the banks of the creek for medicinal and cultural purposes.

The park is part of the Larapinta Trail, a 223 km hike lasting several weeks, which has been touted as one of the best trails in the world. It runs along the backbone of the West MacDonnells and is divided into 12 sections. Those with basic bushwalking experience can easily traverse the first section from Alice Springs to Simpsons Gap. Around Simpsons Gap are other short, well-marked trails, including the Cassia Hill Walk (1.5 km, 1 hr), with views over the gap, and the Woodland Trail (17 km), leading to Bond Gap, a narrow chasm with an ice-cold pool. Another lengthy walk departs from Redbank Gorge to Mount Sonder (16 km, 6–7 hrs).

If you're more interested in cycling, a great place to ride is the sealed bike path off Larapinta Drive, opposite Reverend John Flynn's grave; he played a major role in establishing the Royal Flying Doctor Service. The 17 km path finishes at Simpsons Gap and is suitable for beginner cyclists.

## Further information

🛈 **PWCNT Alice Springs** South Stuart Hwy; (08) 8951 8211; www.nt.gov.au

**Standley Chasm** (08) 8956 7440; daily 8am–6pm (no entry after 5pm); www.standleychasm.com.au

## Tours

**Glen Helen Resort Tours** Half- to two-day tours covering West MacDonnell National Park, Palm Valley and Hermannsburg, plus Larapinta Trail transfers. (08) 8956 7489; www.glenhelen.com.au

Ghost Gum in West MacDonnell Ranges

**Tailormade Tours** Morning bus tours around the best of the park. (08) 8952 1731; www.tailormadetours.com.au

**West MacDonnell Wilderness Flight** It will cost a pretty penny, but this half-day chopper trip over the West MacDonnell wilderness is an unforgettable experience. (08) 8952 9800; www.alicespringshelicopters.com.au

## Where to stay

**Glen Helen Resort ★★** Dorm $20, camping (2 people) $25, motel $130–$160 Namatjira Dr, West MacDonnell Ranges; (08) 8956 7489; www.glenhelen.com.au

**Camping** The best campsites are at Ellery Creek Big Hole and Redbank Gorge, which have toilets, drinking water and fireplaces. Ormiston Gorge also has full camping facilities and caravan sites. Serpentine Chalet and 2 Mile (reached by 4WD) only have basic facilities.

## ❸ Hermannsburg (Ntaria) (1 day)

Hermannsburg Mission Station was established in 1877 by Lutheran missionaries. In 1982 the land was returned to its traditional owners and is now called Ntaria. Visitors are more than welcome to visit this historic area, but are asked to respect the privacy of the residents. The historic precinct comprises of 13 main buildings, mostly made out of stone and dating back 130 years. Strehlows House contains local artwork and the Kata-Anga Tearoom is famous for its apple strudel. A gallery houses works by local Indigenous artist Albert Namatjira, who is famous for his classic watercolour landscapes of the area with its dramatic ghost gums. An old schoolhouse and the Old Colonists House display items from the missionary era. You can also visit the Hermannsburg Potters, who are internationally renowned for their unique terracotta pots. Their collection of amazing ceramics and paintings is open for viewing by appointment only.

## Further information

Hermannsburg is small with very limited amenities: a supermarket and petrol station. For information, contact the Hermannsburg Historical Precinct (08) 8956 7402; daily 9am–4pm.

**Hermannsburg Potters** Hermannsburg Rd; (08) 8956 7414; by appointment only; www.hermannsburgpotters.com.au

## Tours

**Emu Run Tours** Day tour hits the historic Hermannsburg Mission,

before a 4WD through Palm Valley. (08) 8953 7057; www.emurun.com.au

## ❹ Finke Gorge National Park (1 day)

The main attraction of this 46 000 ha park is Palm Valley, where the graceful shapes of red cabbage palms are silhouetted against bright blue sky. This oasis has over 3000 palms, found nowhere else in the world, which extend through the gorges of the Finke River and its tributary, Palm Creek. The park is also a refuge for hundreds of animal species and birds. Rock-wallabies are common but very shy, while smaller mammals tend to come out at night when temperatures are cooler. Pelicans, black swans and black-necked storks (jabirus) fly around.

There are some magnificent walking trails through the arid landscape. Kalaranga Lookout Walk (1.5 km, 45 min) is an easy climb to a beautiful view of a natural amphitheatre. Mpaara Walk (5 km, 2 hrs) provides scenic views over Arrernte lands, while the Arankaia (2 km, 1 hr) and Mpulungkinya (5 km, 2 hrs) walks take you through Palm Valley.

A 4WD track begins just east of Hermannsburg, taking in Boggy Hole where you can swim and fish. Call the park for advice before undertaking the drive.

## Further information

ℹ **PWCNT Finke Gorge** (08) 8956 7401; www.nt.gov.au

## Tours

**Palm Valley Tours** 4WD tours incorporating Finke Gorge, West MacDonnell National Park and Hermannsburg. (08) 8952 0022; www.palmvalleytours.com.au

## Where to stay

**Camping** There are two main camping areas. Palm Valley has a ranger station, toilets, drinking water, picnic tables, showers and fireplaces. Boggy Hole only has basic bush camping with no facilities.

## ❺ Watarrka National Park (1 day)

At the western end of the George Gill Range, Watarrka National Park is a landscape of rugged ranges, isolated rock holes and cavernous gorges. The most imposing gorge is Kings Canyon, a massive cut of red sandstone that towers 100 m high. Other natural wonders include the

Kata Tjuṯa

Lost City, a maze of tiny weathered domes and rock shelters, and the Garden of Eden, home to a chain of pools and shady tree spots.

This is one park that should be seen on foot, and the Kings Canyon Rim Walk (6 km, 3–4 hrs) is by the far the best trail. The loop scales the side of the canyon and leads past the Lost City's beehive formations to the Garden of Eden. If you prefer easier walks, the Kathleen Springs Walk (2.6 km 1½ hrs) leads to a beautiful waterhole, while the Kings Creek Walk (2.6 km, 1 hr) passes fallen boulders and vegetation.

## Further information

ℹ **PWCNT Watarrka** (08) 8956 7460; www.nt.gov.au

## Tours

**Kings Canyon Resort Tours** Offers Kings Canyon rim walks, camel rides and helicopter tours. (08) 8956 7442; www.kingscanyonresort.com.au
**The Stockcamp** Run through Kings Creek Station, this exciting tour includes animal handling demonstrations and whip cracking (not done concurrently). (08) 8956 7474; www.kingscreekstation.com.au

## Where to stay

**Kings Canyon YHA** ★★★ Dorm $38.60, twin and double $93.50 Ernest Giles Rd; 1300 139 889; www.yha.com.au
**Kings Canyon Resort** ★★★ Camping $9–$13, budget quad $39, twin and double $100 Luritja Rd; (08) 8956 7442; www.kingscanyonresort.com.au
**Kings Creek Station** ★★ Camping $14–$19, single $85, twin $126 PMB 164, Alice Springs; (08) 8956 7474; www.kingscreekstation.com.au

## ❻ Uluṟu–Kata Tjuṯa National Park (2–3 days)

The ancient forms of Uluṟu and Kata Tjuṯa lie geographically, spiritually and symbolically at the centre of the continent. These unique formations are some of the most photographed natural wonders on earth.

Uluṟu, or Ayers Rock as it was formerly known, is the ultimate outback icon, and a significant site for many Aboriginal groups. The rock's most stunning feature is that its colour changes according to the weather; in the sun it is a fierce red, while during rain its grooves host spontaneous waterfalls and it appears a more pensive purple-brown. The best times to view it are at sunrise and sunset (many tours ensure you arrive in time). During the day, you can visit caves around the base that are decorated with rock paintings. Unfortunately, many have deteriorated due to weather and the flocks of tourists.

Uluṟu's sister formation, Kata Tjuṯa, comprises 36 magnificently domed and coloured shapes covering around 35 sq km. The domes are intersected by canyons and passages, the eroded remains of a monolith many times the size of Uluṟu. The Valley of the Winds walk (7.4 km, 3 hrs) winds through these, while the shorter Walpa Gorge Walk (2.6 km, 1 hr) reveals some rare and magnificent flowers.

## Climbing Uluṟu

The decision whether or not to climb Uluṟu is up to the discretion of each individual. However, the traditional owners prefer visitors to refrain from climbing the rock, and there are countless tales of a curse befalling those who take home a piece of the rock as a souvenir. The climb can also be difficult and dangerous for unfit individuals.

Those who choose to respect the traditional owners' wishes should not feel that they are missing out, as there are a number of great walks around Uluṟu's base. The **Mutitjulu Walk** (1 km, 45 min) takes you to rock-art sites, while the **Mala Walk** (2 km, 1 hr) is an easy trail passing several caves and ending at Kantju Gorge. Signage on this walk gives explanations of Aboriginal creation times. The longer **Base of Uluṟu** walk (9.8 km, 3–4 hrs), which you are asked to complete in a clockwise direction, takes in both of the shorter trails and allows visitors to appreciate the immensity of Uluṟu. Contact the cultural centre for more information on walking trails.

## Further information

ℹ **Uluṟu–Kata Tjuṯa Cultural Centre** (08) 8956 1128; daily 7am–6pm, information desk 8am–noon & 1–5pm; www.environment.gov.au

## Tours

**Wayoutback Desert Safaris** Three-day 4WD safari tours of Uluṟu and its surrounds. (08) 8952 4324; www.wayoutback.com.au
**Mulga's Adventures** Inexpensive three-day tour of Uluṟu. (08) 8952 1545; www.mulgas.com.au
**Wayward Bus Touring Company** Three- to five-day hiking and camping tours. (08) 8410 8833; www.waywardbus.com.au
**Uluṟu Camel Tours (Anangu Tours)** What better way to see the rock than by camel? (08) 8950 3030; www.ananguwaai.com.au
**Uluṟu Motorcycle Tours** Helmets on and Harleys away! (08) 8956 2019

Tours to and around Uluṟu and Kata Tjuṯa can be booked through the **Ayers Rock Resort** 1300 134 044 or www.ayersrockresort.com.au

## Where to stay

**Outback Pioneer Hotel & YHA Lodge** ★★ Dorm $33.20–$40.40 Ayers Rock Resort; 1300 139 889; www.yha.com.au
**Ayers Rock Resort** ★★ Camping (2 people) $17, village tent (2 people) $90, cabin $150 Yulara Dr; (08) 8296 8010; www.ayersrockresort.com.au

Uluṟu

# WESTERN AUSTRALIA

## CONTENTS

Perth 122
TOP REGIONS:
Rottnest Island 131
The South-west 133
Outback Coast and the Mid-west 138
The Kimberley 143
Esperance and the Nullarbor 148

### Visitor information

Western Australian Visitor Centre
1300 361 351; www.tourism.wa.gov.au

## FAST FACTS

**Length of coastline** 12 889 km
**Number of islands** 3747
**Largest constructed reservoir** Lake Argyle
(storage volume 10 760 million cubic metres)
**Most remote town** Warburton
**Strangest place name** Walkaway
**Most famous person** Rolf Harris
**Quirkiest festival** Milk Carton Regatta,
Hillarys Boat Harbour

If there is one thing that defines Western Australia, it is its size. At 2.5 million sq km, it covers one-third of the Australian continent. Yet for all this space, its population of just two million is mostly concentrated around the capital city of Perth. Around here you'll find vineyards, wildflowers, forests of huge karri trees and a stunning coastline offering top-class leisure opportunities. Equally spectacular is the remote northern coastline where attractions include the wild Monkey Mia dolphins and the 350 million-year-old Bungle Bungle Range.

Travelling in Western Australia requires time and, in remote regions, care. After driving for hours along empty highways, you'll get a true feeling for the state's vastness. But when you reach your destination, you'll be amply rewarded with some precious natural features.

## Top region highlights

### Fremantle
Just 19 km south-west of Perth, 'Freo' is a historic maritime settlement with great restaurants and cafes, heritage buildings and impressive museums. p. 128

### Rottnest Island
This tiny island of sandy coves and heritage sites retains a peaceful holiday atmosphere despite hosting thousands of visitors a year. p. 131

### Margaret River and the South-west
This famous corner of WA features world-class wineries, tall timber forests and great opportunities for fishing, diving and surfing. p. 133

### Monkey Mia and Ningaloo Reef
A major snorkelling and diving destination, there are dolphins aplenty at Monkey Mia, part of World Heritage-listed Shark Bay. Further north is Ningaloo Reef – the only place in the world where awesome whale sharks reliably appear. p. 140

### Broome and the Kimberley
Broome claims a balmy winter climate and one of the world's most beautiful beaches, while inland is an ancient semi-arid landscape of rock domes and gorges. p. 143

## Other regions worth a look

### Darling Range and Swan Valley
Just out of Perth, you'll find hills covered with jarrah forest and Australia's oldest wine region.

### The Goldfields
Steeped in history, the Goldfields are a source of mining wonder, both old and new.

### Great Southern
Centred around the historic town of Albany are mist-encircled mountain peaks, cool-climate wineries and a rugged coastline.

### The Heartlands
Boasting surf beaches along the coast and wildflowers inland, there's also the extraordinary limestone sentinels of the Pinnacles Desert.

### The Pilbara
Turquoise rockpools, deep gorges and tumbling waterfalls provide dramatic scenery in this resource-rich, ochre-hued landscape.

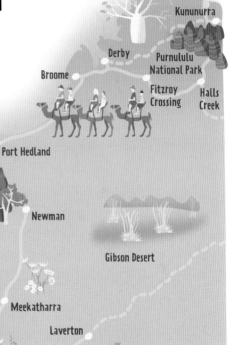

Kununurra

Derby

Purnululu
National Park

Broome

Fitzroy
Crossing

Halls
Creek

Port Hedland

Ningaloo Reef

Newman

Karijini
National Park

Gibson Desert

Carnarvon

Meekatharra

Laverton

Geraldton

90 MILE
STRAIGHT

Kalgoorlie–Boulder

Eucla

Perth

Norseman

Bunbury

Esperance

Albany

# Perth

Set on the banks of the majestic Swan River, Perth's Mediterranean climate gives the city a relaxed, easy-going charm. The city's skyscrapers overlook the bushland and botanic garden of Kings Park, while just a short drive west is the Indian Ocean and its endless white-sand beaches. At the mouth of the Swan is the historic port city of Fremantle, renowned for its maritime history, creative community and street-cafe culture. As you'd expect, Perthites love the outdoors.

## Top attractions

### Kings Park and Botanic Garden

You can't visit Perth and not visit Kings Park, with its fantastic views of the Swan River from the ANZAC Memorial on top of Mount Eliza. The park itself is a huge, 400 ha natural bushland reserve with landscaped gardens, restaurants and cafes. The Lotterywest Federation Walkway – a combination of on-ground pathways, an elevated walkway and a spectacular steel-and-glass bridge – provides a snapshot of WA's famed flora. At ground level you'll pass boabs, boronias and tuart trees, while the walkway through the treetops takes you close to karri, marri, tingle and jarrah trees. In spring the annual Kings Park Wildflower Festival attracts over 50 000 visitors. Fraser Ave; (08) 9480 3600; daily; free guided walks from the visitor centre daily 10am & 2pm; admission free.

### Swan Bells

At the river end of Barrack Street is the spaceship-shaped bell tower that houses the Swan Bells. Twelve of the 18 bells, given to WA in 1988 by the British government, come from London's St Martin-in-the-Fields church. Watching people pulling on bell ropes isn't everyone's idea of a good time, but the views from the top of the controversial $6 million tower are excellent. Barrack Sq, intersection of Barrack St & Riverside Dr; (08) 9218 8183; daily 10am–5pm; full bell ringing Mon, Tue, Thur, Sat & Sun noon–1pm; admission fee applies, except on the first Tue of the month.

Inside the Swan Bells tower

## Climate

Perth is Australia's sunniest capital, with an annual average of 8 hours of sunshine per day. All this sunshine gives Perth a Mediterranean climate of hot, dry summers and mild, wet winters. In summer, the average maximum temperature is 31°C; however, heatwaves with temperatures in the high 30s and low 40s are not unusual. Fortunately, an afternoon sea breeze affectionately known as 'the Fremantle Doctor' helps beat the heat.

## Perth Cultural Centre

Just across the walkway from Perth Railway Station in Northbridge is the Perth Cultural Centre. First stop is the Art Gallery of Western Australia, where overseas visitors can feast their eyes on an outstanding collection of Indigenous art. Regarded as one of Australia's finest, it sits alongside comprehensive exhibitions of Western Australian art, craft and design.

A little further north is the Western Australian Museum, where you can see a 25 m whale skeleton, the 11 ton Mundrabilla meteorite, and the enormous 'Megamouth', a rare species of shark. There are also exhibitions about the origins of the universe, as well as various animal galleries.

Commonly referred to by its acronym, PICA, the Perth Institute of Contemporary Arts is the third cultural hot spot in Northbridge. Showcasing the latest in visual and performance art, it provides an ever-changing program of exhibitions. Art Gallery of WA, James St Mall, Northbridge, (08) 9492 6600, daily 10am–5pm, general admission free, free guided tours available; WA Museum, James St Mall, Northbridge, (08) 9427 2700, daily 9.30am–5pm, admission by donation, free guided tours available; PICA, James St Mall, Northbridge, (08) 9227 6144, Tue–Sun 11am–6pm, general admission free.

## Perth Mint

The Perth Mint is a superb example of gold-boom architecture. Inside you can marvel at the world's largest collection of natural gold specimens, including the 'Golden Beauty', a huge 11.5 kg nugget that'll have those with 'shiny object syndrome' in fits. You can also watch gold being poured, mint your own coins and hold a 400 oz gold bar. No, you can't take it home. 310 Hay St, cnr Hill St; (08) 9421 7277; Mon–Fri 9am–4pm, Sat–Sun 9am–1pm; admission fee applies.

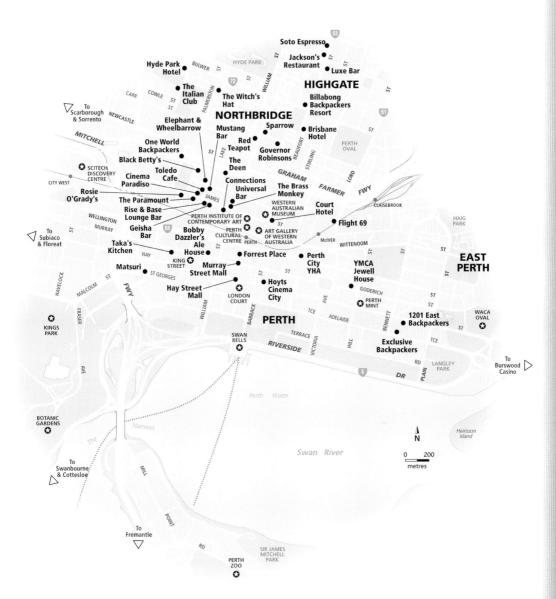

## Burswood International Resort Casino

If you're cashed up and feeling lucky, hit the Burswood International Resort Casino. The casino's Atrium Lobby has a Las Vegas-style, 47 m-high pyramid of shimmering glass complete with tropical garden and waterfall. Great Eastern Hwy, Burswood; (08) 9362 7777; daily 24 hrs.

## Perth Zoo

Perth Zoo is just a short ferry ride from the city. Visit the Australian Walkabout for a close-up look at native animals in a bush setting. Other exhibits include the Penguin Plunge, African Savannah, Reptile Encounter and Rainforest Retreat. 20 Labouchere Rd, South Perth; (08) 9474 0444; daily 9am–5pm; admission fee applies.

## Subiaco

One of Perth's oldest suburbs, 'Subi' is an enclave of trendy cafes, bars, restaurants and up-market shops, all centred on the village-style main street, Rokeby Road (pronounced 'Rock-a-bee'). AFL football at Subiaco Oval draws another crowd entirely, but the two worlds mix happily in after-match moments. If seeing a black swan – WA's faunal emblem – is on your to-do list, then head to nearby Lake Monger in Leederville.

### Getting around

Perth is compact and easy to explore. A free bus service known as the CAT (Central Area Transit) System operates regular services, every 5–10 minutes, around central Perth. The blue CAT runs in a north–south loop, the red CAT operates in an east–west loop, and the yellow CAT travels to the city centre from East Perth. A CAT bus also services Fremantle. Travel is free on Transperth buses and trains within the Free Transit Zone in Perth's city centre, but only on trips that start and finish within the zone.

Trains run from the city out to the northern suburbs and down to Fremantle. The new Southern Suburbs Railway, which opened in late 2007, links Perth to Mandurah.

Ferries and cruise boats depart regularly from Barrack Street Jetty to various destinations, including Fremantle, Rottnest Island and the Swan Valley wine region.

With its largely flat landscape, Perth is also excellent for cycling; maps of the city's 700 km bike network are available at bike shops and from the Department for Planning and Infrastructure, 441 Murray Street, Perth, (08) 9216 8000.

Public transport Transperth (bus, ferry and train) 13 6213

Motoring organisation RAC of WA (08) 9301 3113 or 13 1703

Car rental Avis 13 6333; Budget 13 2727; Hertz 13 3039; Thrifty 1300 367 227

Taxis Black and White Taxis 13 1008; Swan Taxis 13 1330

Swan River ferries and cruises Captain Cook Cruises (08) 9325 3341; Boat Torque Cruises (08) 9421 5888; Oceanic Cruises (08) 9325 1191

Bicycle hire About Bike Hire (08) 9221 2665

## Beach side

With pristine white-sand beaches stretching forever northwards up the coast, swimming and surfing are central to the Perth way of life. Cottesloe Beach, a local favourite, is distinguished by its towering Norfolk Island pines and the Indiana Tea House, a neo-colonial building of grand proportions; Scarborough is a top spot for surfers and sailboarders. These and several other stunning beaches – including Swanbourne (a nude bathing beach), City, Floreat and Sorrento – are not far from the city. You'll find plenty of cafes, restaurants and bars scattered along these beachfronts, but you can't go past fish 'n' chips while the sun sets into the Indian Ocean.

## Aquarium of Western Australia (AQWA)

It's a 15 km trip up the coast involving both train and bus to get to AQWA, but it's well worth it. The highlight is a jaw-dropping 98 m underwater tunnel aquarium, surrounded by approximately three million litres of the Indian Ocean. Here you'll see thousands of marine creatures including sharks, stingrays, seals, crocodiles, sea dragons and turtles. You can even snorkel or dive with the sharks. 91 Southside Dr, Hillarys Boat Harbour; (08) 9447 7500; daily 10am–5pm; admission fee applies.

## Other attractions worth a look

**Western Australian Cricket Ground** (WACA) Offers cricket memorabilia and tours of the grounds. Gate 2, Nelson Cres, East Perth; tours run Tue–Thur 10am & 1pm; Mon–Fri 9.30am–3pm, except on match

days; admission fee applies.

**King Street** 1890s gold-boom architecture housing more modern pursuits. Check out Creative Native at 32 King Street for Aboriginal art, artefacts and didgeridoo lessons. Between Hay & Wellington sts.

**Scitech Discovery Centre** This interactive science and technology centre has more than 160 hands-on exhibits. City West, cnr Sutherland St & Railway Pde, West Perth; Mon–Fri 9.30am–4pm, Sat–Sun 10am–5pm; admission fee applies.

## Where to eat

**City** Living in the shadow of Northbridge, the city still holds a few culinary gems. Our favourites: Taka's Kitchen 🟢 💠 Taka's busy little eateries offer fresh Japanese food at very reasonable prices. 397 Murray St; (08) 9324 1234; lunch & dinner; 150 Barrack St, cnr Wellington St; (08) 9221 4771; lunch & dinner daily.

**Bobby Dazzler's Ale House** 🟢🟢 ♡ Step into Bobby Dazzler's Australiana-inspired decor for a great range of local and imported tap beers and good pub grub, covering everything from all-day breakfasts to Malaysian beef curry or crocodile, emu and pork sausages. 300 Murray St; (08) 9481 0728; breakfast, lunch & dinner daily.

**Matsuri** 🟢🟢 ♡ The set munis (salad, rice and soup included with sashimi or sushi for around $20) are highly recommended. QV1 Bld, 250 St Georges Tce; (08) 9322 7737; Mon–Fri noon–2.30pm & 6–10pm.

**Northbridge** Cuisine to suit all tastes and budgets. Our favourites: Toledo Cafe 🟢 ♡ Backpackers flock to this friendly pizza and

Snorkelling with marine life at AQWA

City from Barrack Square

pasta joint for all-you-can-eat pizza from Thursdays to Sundays 6–8pm for just $10. 35 Lake St, Northbridge; (08) 9227 9222; lunch & dinner Tue–Sun.

**Sparrow** $ ♡ The rare combination of cheap, quality food and cheerful service keeps this humble Indonesian eatery flying high. 434 William St, Northbridge; (08) 9328 5660; lunch Fri 11.30am–2.30pm, dinner Mon–Thur 5–8.30pm, Fri–Sat 5–9pm.

**Red Teapot** $ ♨ How could you not love a place with a signature dish called Prosperous Fragrant Chicken? Book ahead for this Cantonese gem. 413 William St, Northbridge; (08) 9228 1981; Mon–Sat 11.30am–3pm & 5.30–10pm.

**Oxford Street, Leederville** Offers interesting 'alternative' eateries.
Our favourite: **Retro Betty's Burger Cafe** $$ ♡ Old-fashioned American-style diner serving huge burgers, oven-baked pancakes and milkshakes. 127 Oxford St, Leederville; (08) 9444 0499; lunch & dinner daily.
**Subiaco** Street cafes, stylish pubs and fine restaurants draw the 'in' crowd on weekends.
Our favourite: **Chutney Mary's** $$ ♡ Colourful and cosmopolitan, this popular Indian restaurant is always busy, so book ahead. Try the achaar gosht (curried baby goat on the bone). 67 Rokeby Rd, cnr Hay St, Subiaco; (08) 9381 2099; lunch Wed–Sat noon–2.30pm, dinner daily 5.30–10pm.

**Beaufort St, Mount Lawley** Lots of fine restaurants and cafes.
Our favourites: **Soto Expresso** $ ♡ Serving what could possibly be Perth's best coffee. 507 Beaufort St, Mount Lawley; (08) 9227 7686; breakfast & lunch daily.
**Jackson's Restaurant** $$$ TOP TREAT!! ♡ Dress for a first-class culinary experience. The nine-course degustation menu is spectacular. 484 Beaufort St, Highgate; (08) 9328 1177; Mon–Sat 7pm–late; www.jacksonsrestaurant.com.au

## Out and about
### Cinemas
**Hoyts Cinema City** 580 Hay St; (08) 9325 2377.
**Cinema Paradiso** (art house selection) 164 James St, Northbridge; (08) 9227 1771.
**Luna Cinema** (art house selection) 155 Oxford St, Leederville; (08) 9444 4056.
**Astor Cinema** (art house selection) 659 Beaufort St, Mount Lawley; (08) 9370 1777.
**Moonlight Cinema** (outdoor cinema, summer only) Synergy Parklands, Kings Park and Botanic Garden; 1300 551 908.
**Somerville** (outdoor cinema, summer only) University of Western Australia, Nedlands; (08) 9380 2691.

### Live music
**For gig guides, pick up the free street publication *Xpress* or visit www.xpressmag. com.au. For jazz gigs, call Jazzline on (08) 9357 2807 or visit www.jazzwa.com**
**Mustang Bar** An American-style sports bar with a US diner menu and live entertainment most nights. 46 Lake St, Northbridge; (08) 9328 2350; Mon–Thur 11.30am–1am, Fri–Sat 11.30am–3am, Sun noon–midnight; www.mustangbar.com.au
**The Paramount** Combines live music downstairs with pumping dance music upstairs. 163 James St, Northbridge; (08) 9228 1344; Fri 9pm–6am, Sat 8pm–6am; www.paramountnightclub.com.au
**Hyde Park Hotel** The Hydey's front bar showcases local rock bands, while the lounge has jazz on Mondays, country rock on Wednesdays and cover bands on weekends. 331 Bulwer St, West Perth; (08) 9328 6166; Mon–Thur noon–midnight, Fri 11am–late, Sat 10am–late, Sun 11am–10pm; www.hydeparkhotel.com.au
**Universal Bar** 'The house of blues and jazz' features funky, soulful and smokin'

**Where to shop**
**Hay Street Mall, Murray Street Mall and Forrest Place, City** The CBD's main shopping precinct with brand-name fashion outlets and major department stores Myer and David Jones.
**King Street, City** High fashion, galleries and cafes with style.
**London Court, City** Mock-Tudor arcade with souvenir, jewellery and antique stores.
**Rokeby Road, Subiaco** Funky local designers sit alongside more established labels.
**Bay View Terrace, Claremont** Perth's up-market fashion hot spot.
**Napoleon Street, Cottesloe** Cafes, boutiques and designer homewares.

bands from Wednesday to Sundays nights at 5.30pm. 221 William St, Northbridge; (08) 9227 6771; Wed–Thur 5pm–1am, Fri 4pm–2am, Sat 5pm–2am, Sun 5pm–midnight; www.universalbar.com.au

### Pubs and bars
**Brass Monkey** Perhaps the most photographed hotel in WA, this pub offers a choice of main bar, sports bar or big beer garden. Sample the house stout, or choose from 22 ice-cold beers on tap. Pop upstairs to the BrassGrill if you're hungry, or next door to the Grapeskin if you fancy wine. Cnr James & William sts, Northbridge; (08) 9227 9596; Mon–Tue 11am–midnight, Wed–Thur 11am–1am, Fri–Sat 11am–2am, Sun 11am–10pm; www.thebrassmonkey.com.au
**Brisbane Hotel** The Brissy combines 1898 heritage with up-to-the-minute style and a beer garden that's all giant palms, ponds and umbrellas. 292 Beaufort St, cnr Brisbane St, Northbridge; (08) 9227 2300; Mon–Sat noon–midnight, Sun noon–10pm.
**Ocean Beach Hotel** The OBH is the place to down a middy as you watch the sun sink into the ocean. There's live entertainment on Friday nights, pool tables and four big-screen TVs. The Backpackers' Pool Comp on Wednesday nights could bring out the shark in you. Cnr Marine Pde & Eric St, Cottesloe; (08) 9384 2555; Mon–Sat 10am–midnight, Sun 10am–10pm; www.obh.com.au

**Cottesloe Beach Hotel** Another top spot for catching the magnificent Perth sunset over a couple of middies. The Back Bar has pool tables and a dance floor, while the beer garden is legendary for its Sunday Session. 104 Marine Pde, Cottesloe; (08) 9383 1100; Mon–Sat 11am–midnight, Sun noon–10pm; www.cottesloebeachhotel.com.au

**The Deen** Six bar areas easily accommodate both live music and DJs. Check out the backpackers' special Manik Mundaze from 5pm when there's a free barbecue, pool comp, limbo comp and a giant twister board. 84 Aberdeen St, Northbridge; (08) 9227 9361; Thur–Mon from 5pm; www.thedeen.com

**Elephant & Wheelbarrow** This self-proclaimed 'little piece of Britian' is the pub for homesick Brit backpackers. 53 Lake St, Northbridge; (08) 9228 4433; Mon–Wed 11am–midnight, Thur–Sat 11am–3am, Sun noon–midnight; www.northbridge. elephantandwheelbarrow.com.au

**The Flying Scotsman** Don't miss the Sunday session with live music and the $10 pizza and pint special. Wednesdays have cheap jugs and DJs. 639 Beaufort St, Mount Lawley; (08) 9328 6200; Mon–Thur 11am–midnight, Fri–Sat 11am–1am, Sun 11am–10pm.

**Llama Bar** The happening vibe of Llama Bar includes comedy and trivia on Tuesdays, live music on Wednesdays and Thursdays, and DJs on weekends. Wednesday is $9 steak night, with cheap(er) cocktails. 1/464 Hay St, cnr Rokeby Rd, Subiaco; (08) 9388 0222; Tue–Thur 5pm–1am, Fri–Sat 5pm–3am; www.llamabar.com

**Luxe** This up-market bar aims for the 'cocktail couture' crowd. Wednesdays and Thursdays are $11 cocktail nights. DJs play funk-infused tunes from Friday to Sunday nights. 446 Beaufort St, Mount Lawley; (08) 9228 9680; Wed–Sat 8pm–late, Sun 8pm–midnight; www.luxebar.com

**Rosie O'Grady's** Enjoy the craic with cheap pints, meal specials, live music and enough Irish sport to satisfy the most die-hard fan. Backpacker nights every Sunday and Tuesday. Cnr James & Milligan sts, Northbridge; (08) 9328 1488; Tue noon–midnight, Wed–Thur 11.30am–1am, Fri–Sat noon–2am, Sun 2–11pm; www.northbridge. rosieogradys.com.au

**Subiaco Hotel** The facade of this grand old building masks a contemporary, chic interior. Cnr Hay St & Rokeby Rd, Subiaco; (08) 9381 3069; Mon–Wed 7am–midnight, Thur–Sat 7am–1am, Sun 7am–10pm; www.subiacohotel.com.au

## Nightclubs

**Base Lounge Bar** Resident DJs play R'n'B tunes in this stylish yet unpretentious cocktail lounge. Entry is free, so expect long lines after midnight. Cnr Lake & James sts, Northbridge; (08) 9226 0322; Wed–Sat 9pm–late.

**Black Betty's** DJs, live bands and pool comps to keep you going till the wee hours. Wednesday is backpacker night with free giveaways. Free entry before 10pm. Cnr Aberdeen & Parker sts, Northbridge; (08) 9228 0077; Wed 9pm–late, Fri 10pm–late, Sat 9pm–late; www.blackbettys.com.au

**Geisha Bar** Local and international DJs spin the finest underground house in Perth's club scene. 135a James St, Northbridge; (08) 9328 9808; Fri–Sat 11pm–6am; www.geishabar.com.au

**Hip-E Club** With its neon kaleidoscope interior, the Hip-E has been at it for nearly 20 years. Tuesday's famous Backpacker and Student Night offers free entry, barbecues and a complimentary drink if you show up before 10pm. There's also a free bus service for hostels. Cnr Newcastle & Oxford sts, Leederville; (08) 9227 8899; Tue 8pm–late, Wed–Sun 10pm–late; www.hipeclub.com.au

**Rise** With its massive dance floor and podiums aplenty, Rise is built for those who want to party hard. 139 James St, Northbridge; (08) 9328 7447; Fri–Sat 10pm–6am; www.rise.net.au

## Performing arts

**Ticket sales and performance information is available at www.bocsticketing.com.au and in the *West Australian* newspaper.**

**His Majesty's Theatre** 825 Hay St; (08) 9265 0900.

**Playhouse Theatre** 3 Pier St; (08) 9323 3400.

**Perth Concert Hall** 5 St Georges Tce; (08) 9231 9900.

**Regal Theatre** 474 Hay St, Subiaco; (08) 9484 1133.

**Subiaco Arts Centre** 180 Hamersley Rd, Subiaco; (08) 9382 3385.

## Where to stay

For further information and reviews on these hostels, please visit www.bugaustralia.com, www.hostelaustralia.com or www.hostelz.com

**Exclusive Backpackers** ★★★ Dorm $22–$27, single $45, twin or double $65 158 Adelaide Tce; (08) 9221 9991; www.exclusivebackpackers.com

**One World Backpackers** ★★★ Dorm $20–$24, single $52–$61, double $57–$68 162 Aberdeen St, Northbridge; (08) 9228 8206; www.oneworldbackpackers.com.au

**Governor Robinsons** ★★★ Dorm $25, twin or double $70; double with ensuite $80 7 Robinson Ave, Northbridge; (08) 9328 3200; www.govrobinsons.com.au

**The Witch's Hat** ★★★ Dorm $24–$26, twin $58; double $68 148 Palmerston St, Northbridge; (08) 9228 4228; www.witchshat.com

**Ocean Beach Backpackers** ★★★ Dorm $21, twin or double $63 1 Eric St, Cottesloe; (08) 9384 5111; www.oceanbeachbackpackers.com

**Scarborough Backpackers** ★★★ Dorm $23–$26, single, twin or double $60–$70 190 West Coast Hwy, cnr Manning St, Scarborough; (08) 9245 3111; www.scarboroughbackpackers.com

**Perth City YHA** ★★ Dorm $29–$34, twin or double $80–$100 300 Wellington St; (08) 9366 3000; www.yha.com.au

**YMCA Jewell House** ★★ Single $39–$44, twin or double $50–$55 180 Goderich St, East Perth; (08) 325 8488; www.ymcajewellhouse.com

**1201 East Backpackers** ★★ Dorm $19–$22, single $37, twin $48, double $50 195 Hay St, East Perth; 1800 001 201; www.1201east.com.au

**Billabong Backpackers Resort** ★★ Dorm $20–$24, single, twin or double $63–$68 381 Beaufort St, Highgate; (08) 9328 7720; www.billabongresort.com.au

### Sport

**AFL (Australian Football League)** is Perth's most popular spectator sport, with crowds flocking to Subiaco Oval from April through September to support local teams the West Coast Eagles and the Fremantle Dockers.

Subiaco Oval is also home to Western Australia's **rugby** team, the Western Force, which plays in the Super 14 international rugby union competition.

**Cricket** takes up where footy leaves off, with the famous WACA hosting both interstate and international test matches in summer.

**Basketball** fans can catch the popular Perth Wildcats from September to February at Challenge Stadium in Mount Claremont. Their female counterparts, the Perth Lynx, play at Perry Lakes Stadium in Floreat.

In January, Perth's Burswood Dome hosts the Hopman Cup, a prestigious international **tennis** event.

**Horseracing** is a year-round sport, split between two venues: Ascot Racecourse in summer and Belmont Park in winter. Events such as the Perth Cup (held on New Year's Day), the Easter Racing Carnival and the Opening Day at Ascot draw huge crowds. There's night harness racing at Gloucester Park.

## Tours and activities

**Perth Walking Tours** Take a city orientation tour or learn about Perth's history and culture on a free guided tour. Tours leave from the City of Perth Information Kiosk, Murray Street Mall, near Forrest Place.

Sailboarding on the Swan River

**Perth Coffee Cruise** A leisurely 2-hour voyage from Perth to Fremantle and back, with full commentary. Bookings (08) 9325 1191.

**Spirit of the West** Saturday dinner or Sunday lunch aboard a Federation-era restaurant train from Perth to the Avon Valley. Bookings (08) 9328 8460. www.spiritofthewest.com.au

**Swan Brewery Tour** Check out this state-of-the-art brewery renowned for its Swan and Emu beers. Yes, and tastings are included. Bookings (08) 9350 0222.

**'Tram' Tours** Take in all the inner-city attractions aboard a replica of the city's first trams. The Tourist Trifecta is a full-day tour taking in Perth, Fremantle and a cruise on the Swan River. Bookings (08) 9322 2006.

**Swan Valley Wine Cruise** Spend the day cruising the Swan River to Swan Valley, where you can taste wine at Houghton's picturesque winery and tour the Margaret River Chocolate Factory. Bookings (08) 9325 1191.

### Markets

**Galleria Art and Craft Markets** Handcrafted items in the grounds of the Perth Cultural Centre. WA Museum concourse, Northbridge; Sat–Sun 9am–5pm.

**Subiaco Pavilion Markets** Art and craft stalls in a restored warehouse adjacent to station. Subiaco Pavilion, cnr Rokeby & Robert rds; Thur–Fri 10am–9pm, Sat–Sun 10am–5pm.

**Station Street Markets, Subiaco** Eclectic array of goods and live entertainment. 52 Station St, Subiaco; Fri–Sun 9am–5.30pm.

**Scarborough Fair Markets** Specialty stalls and a food hall on Scarborough Beach. Cnr Scarborough Beach Rd & West Coast Hwy; daily 10am–5pm.

Cottesloe Beach

# Outside the city: Fremantle

Although now linked to Perth by a sprawl of suburbs, the port city of Fremantle at the mouth of the Swan River is quite different in both architecture and atmosphere. 'Freo' has the old-world streetscape of a 19th-century port, with beautifully preserved buildings on every corner. Yet the artists and bohemians who have flocked to Freo have stamped it with an eclectic, creative feel. The influence of its strong Italian migrant community – pioneers of Freo's fishing industry – can be seen in its unique street cafe culture, centred around the famous cappuccino strip of South Terrace.

## Top attractions

### Historic Centre
This precinct is roughly bordered by Queen, Phillimore, Norfolk and Parry streets and Marine Terrace. The Town Hall, which now houses the Fremantle Tourist Bureau, is in the heart of the port city. Built in 1887, it can be easily distinguished by its clock tower. It is also the departure point for Tram Tours (see Getting to Fremantle). From here it is an easy walk to many historic buildings, galleries, museums and the cappuccino strip of South Terrace. The Fremantle Markets (see Where to shop in Fremantle), also along South Terrace, are one of the city's most popular attractions.

### Western Australian Maritime Museum
Perched on the waterfront, this museum showcases WA's many maritime endeavours. Outside the museum are the Welcome Walls, a series of engraved panels that list the names of thousands of migrants who have arrived in WA through the port of Fremantle. Next door you can visit the submarine HMAS *Ovens*. Victoria Quay; (08) 9431 8444; daily 9.30am–5pm; admission fee applies.

### Shipwreck Galleries
Although on a completely different site, the Shipwreck Galleries are also part of the Western Australian Maritime Museum. Here you can see salvaged items from really old shipwrecks. Don't miss the Batavia Gallery, with its reconstructed stern of a ship. Cliff St; (08) 9431 8444; daily, 9.30am–5pm; admission by donation.

### The Round House
Built in 1831 by the first settlers as a prison, this is the oldest public building in WA. At 1pm each day, the Round House's signal station fires a cannon – the time gun – and this activates a time ball (an instrument once used to give accurate time readings to vessels out at sea). 10 Arthur Head; (08) 9336 6897; daily 10.30am–3.30pm; admission by gold coin donation.

### Fremantle Prison
Huge, forbidding and full of history, the Freo Prison was in use until 1991. Experience it on a spooky guided tour, taking in the isolation chamber and the gallows. Enter via Fremantle Oval from Parry Street. 1 The Terrace; (08) 9336 9200; tours conducted half-hourly daily 10am–5pm; Tunnels Tours daily

and Torchlight Tours Wed & Fri (bookings essential); admission fee applies.

### Fremantle Arts Centre and History Museum
Built by convicts, the colony's first lunatic asylum now houses displays on the history of Fremantle, contemporary art exhibitions, a craft shop, a ghost walk and a garden area. 1 Finnerty St; (08) 9432 9555; daily 10am–5pm; admission to museum by donation.

### Fremantle Motor Museum
Rev-head heaven! Australia's foremost collection of veteran, vintage, classic and racing cars ranges from an 1894 Peugeot to the Williams driven by Formula One Grand Prix World Champion Alan Jones. B Shed, Victoria Quay; (08) 9336 5222; daily 9.30am–5pm; admission fee applies.

### Getting to Fremantle

**By car** 20–30 minutes from Perth, either via Stirling Highway on the north bank of the Swan River or via Canning Highway on the south.

**By train** 30-minute journey from Perth Railway Station, Wellington Street. Trains depart every 15 minutes on weekdays, less frequently on weekends.

**By bus** Many buses and routes link both cities. Timetables and route details from Transperth 13 6213. Once in Fremantle, look out for the free orange CAT bus, which runs regular services from Victoria Quay, through the city centre and down to South Fremantle.

**By ferry** Various ferry operators travel twice daily between Perth and Fremantle, departing Barrack Street Jetty, Perth. See Getting around above.

**Combined travel packages** For combined ferry, train and 'tram' tours of Perth and Fremantle, contact either Fremantle Tram Tours (08) 9339 8719 or Perth Tram Company (08) 9322 2006. 'Tram' tours in Fremantle depart hourly 10am–5pm from the Town Hall.

**Leeuwin Ocean Adventure**
Adventurers should check out *Leeuwin II*, a 55 m triple-masted barquentine, rated as the largest tall ship in Australia. Available for full-day, morning and twilight sails. B Shed, Victoria Quay; (08) 9430 4105.

## Where to eat

**South Terrace** Numerous cafes and restaurants line Fremantle's famous cappuccino strip.
Our favourites: **Sail & Anchor Pub Brewery** $$ ♡ This historic 1854 pub has an on-site brewery creating unique beers, including Chilli Beer. The downstairs bar and courtyard is more relaxed, while the upstairs area takes on a lounge feel with the Red Room Bar, displaying geisha artwork. 64 South Tce; (08) 9335 8433; Mon–Thur 11am–midnight, Fri–Sat 11am–1am, Sun 11am–10pm; www.sailandanchor.com.au
**Pizza Bella Roma** $ ♡ The queues outside at weekends indicate the popularity of this place, serving good pizzas and mussels with generous portion sizes. 14 South Tce; (08) 9335 1554; Tue–Fri 5pm–late, Sat–Sun noon–late.
**Old Shanghai Food Market** $ ♡ Inexpensive, mouth-watering Asian food. Favourites are the Siam Kitchen for great Thai food and Taka's next door. 6 Henderson St; (08) 9431 7234; lunch & dinner daily.
**Sala Thai** $$ ♡ Top-shelf Thai food in a beautiful setting with great service. A real treat. 22 Norfolk St; (08) 9335 7749 or (08) 9336 1939; daily 6–10.30pm.

**Fishing Boat Harbour** The place to go for fish 'n' chips and seafood.
Our favourites: **Little Creatures Brewing** $$ ♡ Set inside a massive converted boat shed, with the brewery on one side and the bar and restaurant on the other. Enjoy a pale ale, chow down on kebabs, wood-fired pizza and sharing serves of 'nosh', all while taking in the view of Fremantle Harbour. 40 Mews Rd; (08) 9430 5555; Mon–Fri 10am–midnight, Sat–Sun 9am–midnight; www.littlecreatures.com.au
**Cicerello's Fish & Chips** $$ ♡ The home of fish 'n' chips in Freo. Check out the amazing aquariums! 44 Mews Rd; (08) 9335 1911; daily 10am–8.30pm; www.cicerellos.com.au
**Kailis Fish Market Cafe** $$ ♡ Multi award-winning tourist restaurant specialising in super fresh seafood. 46 Mews Rd; (08) 9335 7755; daily 8am–late; www.kailis.com

**West End** Vietnamese, Indian and vegetarian fare are easy to find here.
Our favourites: **Bengal Indian Restaurant** $$ 💎 Located in the historic Old Fire Station, the Bengal serves great Indian cuisine. Also a great place for vegetarians. 18 Phillimore St; (08) 9335 2400; Mon–Sun 6pm–late; www.bengalindian.theguide.com.au
**Villa Roma** $$ ♡ The Freo icon that for 50 years was the Roma Restaurant has been reborn, with delicious Italian cuisine keeping the faith. 9 High St; (08) 9335 3664; lunch Tue–Fri, dinner Tue–Sat.

**East Fremantle** Head under the Queen Victoria Street and Stirling Highway bridges on Riverside Road for some good grub.
Our favourites: **The Left Bank Cafe, Bar and Restaurant** $$ ♡ Swanky restaurant upstairs, the food and drink is just as good downstairs. 15 Riverside Rd, East Fremantle; (08) 9319 1315; breakfast daily 7.30–11.30am, lunch & dinner Mon–Thur 11.30am–9pm, Fri–Sat noon–9pm, Sun noon–4pm, bar open later; www.leftbank.com.au
**The Red Herring Restaurant** $$$ **TOP TREAT!!** ♡ Magnificent setting right on the river with sensational seafood and prices to match. A real splurge. 26 Riverside Rd, East Fremantle; (08) 9339 1611; lunch & dinner Mon–Sat, breakfast, lunch & dinner Sun; www.redherring.com.au

## Out and about

### Cinemas

**Hoyts Queensgate** William St; (08) 9430 6988.
**Hoyts Millennium** Collie St; (08) 9430 6988.
**Luna on SX** (art house selection) 13 Essex St; (08) 9430 5999.

### Live music

**Kulcha** This well-known Freo venue is a haven for multicultural arts and music. 1st Floor, 13 South Tce, cnr Collie St, above the Dome Cafe; (08) 9336 4544; Thur–Sat 7.30pm–midnight, Sun 7.30–11pm (depends on gigs); www.kulcha.com.au
**Fly By Night Musicians Club** Musicians, actors, comedians and even circus performers get on stage here. Queen St, enter via Parry St; (08) 9430 5976; opening hours dependent on gigs; www.flybynight.org
**Mojo's Bar** If you like your music original, you can't go past Mojo's. 237 Queen Victoria St, North Fremantle; (08) 9430 4010; Mon–Thur 8pm–midnight, Fri–Sat 8pm–1am; www.mojosbar.com.au
**Navy Club** Jazz Fremantle meets at the Navy Club every Sunday afternoon. 64 High St; (08) 9336 3752; jazz Sun 4–7pm; www.navyclub.com.au/events

## Pubs and bars

See Sail & Anchor and Little Creatures Brewery under Where to eat.

**The Norfolk Hotel** Favourite beer garden of the Freo cool crowd. The Basement plays host to funky DJs on Friday and Saturday nights. 47 South Tce; (08) 9335 5405; Mon–Tue 11am–10pm, Wed–Sat 11am–midnight, Sun 8.30am–10pm.

## Nightclubs

**Metropolis Concert Club** A huge, three-level club with eight bars, worth a visit on a Saturday night – and entry is free! 58 South Tce, Fremantle; (08) 9336 1880; Fri–Sat 9pm–late; www.metropolisfremantle.com.au

## Performing arts

**Deckchair Theatre** 179 High St; (08) 9430 4771.

**Spare Parts Puppet Theatre** 1 Short St; (08) 9335 5044.

## Where to stay

**Sundancer Backpackers** ★★★ Dorm $23, single $45, double $55, double ensuite $70 80 High St; 1800 061 144;

www.sundancerbackpackers.com

**Old Firestation Backpackers** ★★★ Dorm $22, double $60 18 Phillimore St; (08) 9430 5454; www.old-firestation.net

**Australia Backpackers Fremantle** ★★ Dorm $20, single $35, twin $44, double $50 Cnr Beach & Parry sts; (08) 9433 2055; www.austbackpackers.com

**YHA Backpackers Inn Fremantle** ★★ Dorm $23–$32, single $40–$53, double or twin $57–$65 11–15 Pakenham St; (08) 9431 7065; www.yha.com.au

# Other suburbs worth visiting

**Leederville** More alternative than Subiaco, Leederville has a good mix of cafes, restaurants and funky fashion on Oxford Street.

**Mount Lawley** Just up from Northbridge is this cafe, pub and shopping strip.

**Hillarys** WA's aquarium, AQWA, is the main reason most tourists trek out here. However, there's also Sorrento Quay 'village' and The Great Escape, a leisure park with waterslides, miniature golf and trampolines.

**Yanchep** This coastal suburb, just under an hour's drive north of Perth, is home to Yanchep National Park, one of Perth's favourite recreation areas. Have your photo taken with a koala; see didgeridoo and Indigenous dance performances; or take a guided tour of Crystal Cave.

# Visitor information

## Perth Airport

Perth Airport is located near the suburb of Redcliffe. For more information, call (08) 9478 8888 or visit www.perthairport.com

**Bus** Perth Airport City Shuttle operates regular shuttle to the city. Bookings (08) 9277 7958; www.perthshuttle.com.au. Transperth bus #37 travels to the domestic airport from the City Busport every 30 minutes from 6.15am to 11.20pm, returning to the city from 5.30am to 11pm.

**Taxi** A taxi ride to the CBD will cost around $33, while Fremantle will be around $50.

## Internet cafes

**Backpackers Travel Centre** 246 William St; (08) 9228 1877.

**Traveller's Club** 137a William St; 1800 016 969.

**Travel Forever** Includes free luggage storage. 135 Barrack St; (08) 6267 0700.

**Internet Cafe** 9 Bannister St, Fremantle; (08) 9336 4900.

**Travel Lounge** Bargain tours, free internet (with bookings) and CD burning. 16 Market St, Fremantle; (08) 9335 8776.

## Hospitals

**For all emergencies, including police, fire, or hospital, dial '000'.**

**Royal Perth Hospital** Wellington St; (08) 9224 2244.

**Sir Charles Gairdner Hospital** Hospital Ave, Nedlands; (08) 9346 3333.

**Fremantle Hospital** Alma St, Fremantle; (08) 9431 3333.

*Perth*

# Rottnest Island
# Quokka country

Rottnest Island is Perth's private holiday playground. Just a short ferry or plane ride from the mainland, 'Rotto's' azure waters and white sandy beaches lure about half a million holidaymakers every year. But this is no glam resort destination: the vegetation is scrubby, the accommodation is basic and you have to walk or cycle to get around. Yet it's exactly this laidback atmosphere that gives Rotto its charm.

Some 11 km long and 4.5 km wide, the island boasts crystal-clear bays surrounded by fish-friendly reefs just perfect for a range of aquatic pleasures. On land there are heritage sites and the island's famous animal, the quokka, to discover. Limited bus services operate and a light railway takes visitors to Oliver Hill, in the centre of the island, for spectacular views. Daytrips are popular, but you really need to spend a couple of days to get the full Rotto experience.

**Number of days to spend in this region: 1–2 days**

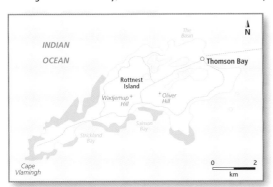

## Getting here

You can get to Rottnest in 15 minutes by aeroplane from Jandakot Airport, but the main access is via ferry from Fremantle (30 min), Perth (1½ hrs) or Hillarys Boat Harbour (45 min).

Rottnest Express (08) 9421 5888 or (08) 9335 6406;

www.rottnestexpress.com.au

Oceanic Cruises (08) 9325 1191 or (08) 9335 2666; www.oceaniccruises.com.au

Hillarys Fast Ferries (08) 9246 1039; www.hillarysfastferries.com.au

## Quokka country

There are about 10 000 quokkas living on Rottnest, so chances are you'll see a few of them. However, they are semi-nocturnal marsupials, so the best time of day for quokka-spotting is late afternoon when they wake up hungry after a good sleep. Don't feed them though – they're a protected species. Find the interpretive signs about 1 km south of Thomson Bay, just before Kingstown Barracks; if you don't see a quokka here, check 'em out at the viewing spots along the boardwalk at Garden Lake.

## Tours

**Rottnest Voluntary Guides** Free historical and nature tours. (08) 9372 9757.

## 63 beaches and 20 bays

The island's sparkling turquoise water invites any number of aquatic activities. The reef-protected Basin, wide Longreach Bay and the stunningly private Little Parakeet Bay are popular swimming spots, while surfers can catch the waves at Strickland Bay, Salmon Bay and Stark Bay (a guide to the island's surf breaks is available for purchase

from the visitor centre). The reefs surrounding the island provide snorkellers and divers with a stunning array of fish and coral to marvel at. Dive charters and snorkelling tours are popular; if you prefer not to get wet, enjoy the underwater scenery aboard a glass-bottomed boat.

## Tours

**Underwater Explorer** Two tour options are available: for those who want to remain dry, the Reef & Wreck Tour reveals the underwater world of fish – and maybe even dolphins – through a glass-bottomed boat; while snorkelling tours around West Kingston Reef pass shipwrecks on the way to discovering caves and the reef's hidden treasures. 0400 202 340; www.underwaterexplorer.com.au

**Rottnest Island Dive & Snorkel** Snorkelling and scuba diving tours. Thomson Bay; (08) 9292 5111; www.rottnestdiving.com.au

**Capricorn Seakayaking** Half-day tours around Rotto's coves, reefs and beaches. (08) 6267 8059; www.capricornseakayaking.com.au

**Glass-bottomed boat hire: Time-Out** Geordie Bay; 0413 181 322.

*Quokka*

## West End

The 'West End' of Rottnest can be reached on an 11 km bike ride along a sealed road, or on a bus tour. There are stunning ocean views from Cape Vlamingh (where you may also spot a humpback whale in winter) and a 1 km heritage trail where you can spot wedge-tailed shearwaters, fairy terns, quokkas and bottlenose dolphins.

## Island heritage

It's ironic that this idyllic island should have been named by a Dutch explorer who dismissed it as being nothing more than a 'rat's nest'. Willem de Vlamingh landed here in 1696 and, thinking the island's quokkas were large rats, called it Rotte-nest. After European settlement in 1831, the island became a prison for Indigenous Australians during 1838–1903, then an internment camp during WW I and a military post during WW II. Vincent Way in Thomson Bay is an original 1840s streetscape; Rottnest Lodge incorporates what was the 'Quod', an octagonal prison (1864); and the Oliver Hill Gun Battery (1930s) sits on Wadjemup Hill. The Rottnest Museum offers informative displays and historic photos. There's also the Salt Store Gallery and Exhibition Centre, one of the island's oldest buildings, displaying photographic and art exhibitions.

## Not-so-natural entertainments

When you've had enough cycling, swimming and relaxing, drop in to Brett Heady's Family Fun Park just past Rottnest Lodge, where you can get competitive with your mates on the 18-hole mini putt-putt course. There are also trampolines and amusement machines. Next door is the Rottnest Island Picture Hall, a wonderful time-warp experience. No raked seating, no posh armchairs, just you, the movie and a hall full of happy holidaymakers.

## Further information

ⓘ **Rottnest Island Visitor Centre** Located at the end of the Rottnest jetty; (08) 9372 9732; daily from 7.30am; www.rottnestisland.com

**Rottnest Museum** Behind the Thomson Bay Settlement shopping mall; (08) 9372 9732; daily 10.45am–3.30pm.
**Salt Store Gallery and Exhibition Centre** Thomson Bay Settlement; (08) 9432 9351.
**Brett Heady's Family Fun Park** Opposite Rottnest Lodge; (08) 9292 5156; summer daily 9am–8pm/9pm (times vary during school holidays); winter daily 9am–5pm.

Coastline at Rottnest Island

**Rottnest Island Picture Hall** Screening times available from the visitor centre.

## Transport

A free shuttle service around the island runs from 7.45am to 9.20pm, doing a circuit from the main bus stop in Thomson Bay before heading out to Kingstown and the airport. The separate Bayseeker Bus drops you off at the island's best beaches. All-day tickets are reasonably priced and are available from the visitor centre.
**Bike hire: Rottnest Bike Hire** Thomson Bay; (08) 9292 5105; 8.30am–5pm.

## Where to eat and drink

**Rottnest Bakery** 🅢 Great pies, bread and pastries – the cream buns are legendary – but the queues can be a killer at lunchtime. Thomson Bay Mall; (08) 9292 5023; breakfast & lunch daily.
**Rottnest Tearooms Bar and Cafe** 🅢🅢 Set on the beach, this casual eatery offers terrific views and hunger-busting food. Takeaways include fish 'n' chips, burgers, sandwiches, rolls, baguettes and focaccias. Thomson Bay; (08) 9292 5171; breakfast, lunch & dinner daily; www.rottnesttearooms.com
**Dome Cafe** 🅢/🅢🅢 Right on the beachfront at Thomson Bay, this is the only place to go to get your coffee fix. There are also cakes, a menu of modern favourites for more substantial meals and takeaway. Thomson Bay Mall; (08) 9292 5026; breakfast, lunch & dinner daily.
**Quokka Arms Hotel** 🅢/🅢🅢 Previously known as the Rottnest Hotel, the Quokka Arms has a beachside beer garden where the young and thirsty like to hang as the sun sinks into the sea. Thomson Bay; (08) 9292 5011; daily from 11am.

## Where to stay

**Rottnest Island Youth Hostel** ★★★ Dorm $21–$24, family room $49–$57. Kingstown; (08) 9432 9111.
**Allison Camping Area** ★ Gas barbecue facilities provided. Camping (site unpowered, guests must provide their own tent) $8.50 Thomson Bay; (08) 9432 9111.

## Events

**Rottnest Channel Swim** This swimming race from Cottesloe Beach to the island is the biggest event on the Rotto calendar. Feb.
**The Big Splash** Non-competitive swim event from Fremantle to Rotto. Mar.
**Rottnest Island Triathlon** Swim, run and cycle race around the island. Apr.
**Rottnest Marathon and Fun Run** A 42 km marathon for serious runners, with a 5 km and 10 km fun run/walk for everyone else. Oct.
**Rottnest Swim Thru** Annual 1600 m open water swim in the crystal-clear waters of Thomson Bay. Dec.

# The South-west
# Wild at heart

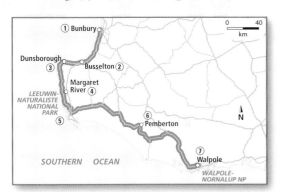

Perth

Renowned for its world-class wines, excellent surf breaks and towering old-growth forests, the South-west is the most visited corner of Western Australia. Here you'll find a wild and wonderful coastline, fantastic limestone caves and tall-timber forests of jarrah and karri. Scenic drives link historic towns, while national parks offer superb bushwalking. The Bibbulmun Track, a 963 km-long walking trail, passes through some of the state's most picturesque towns, including Pemberton and Walpole.

**Number of days to spend in this region: 8–14 days**

## Getting here

There are regular bus services operated by Transwa and South West Coach Lines between Perth, Bunbury, Busselton and Margaret River. Transwa also has a twice daily train service from Perth to Bunbury. Alternatively, the South-west is a great region to drive around.

Transwa 300 662 205; www.transwa.wa.gov.au

South West Coach Lines (08) 9754 1666; www.southwestcoachlines.com.au

## South-west tours

**WesternXposure** This reliable eco-based adventure tour company offers a three-day tour that takes in the Margaret River wine region, the tall trees of the South-west and the south coast as far as Albany. Tours depart Monday, Thursday and Saturday. 1800 621 200; www.westernxposure.com.au

**Planet Perth Tours and Active Safaris** Planet Perth Tours and Active Safaris merged in 2006, yet they still have separate websites spruiking their tours. Planet Perth offer a three-day South-west tour covering Margaret River, Pemberton and Albany. Tours depart Tuesday and Saturday. Active Safaris offer a two-day weekend tour between December and June that travels inland to Donnybrook, Manjimup and Pemberton before heading to Margaret River. (08) 9225 6622; www.planettours.com.au, www.activesafaris.com.au

**Easyrider Backpacker Tours** For time-pressed travellers, Easyrider offers one-day trips to Margaret River, leaving Perth every Tuesday and Thursday. Their 'Southern Curl' three-day tour takes in Margaret River, Pemberton and Albany. Tours depart Monday, Wednesday and Saturday between December and March; Wednesday and Saturday between April and May and September and November; Saturday only between June and August. If time isn't a concern, try a six-month 'Jump On, Jump Off' ticket, which allows you the flexibility to take a tour (one-day tours not included), get off where you want, stay as long as you like, then catch the bus when it passes through again. 224 William St, Northbridge; (08) 9227 0824; www.easyridertours.com.au

## ❶ Bunbury (1–2 days)

This busy town has a proud history, fine beaches and a good cafe strip on Victoria Street. One of Bunbury's drawcards is its Dolphin Discovery Centre. Take a 'Swim on the Wild Side' tour and experience the thrill of swimming alongside wild dolphins. Or go for the more laidback dolphin-spotting cruise. The centre also has an interpretive museum and big-screen video to get you primed with information.

### Further information

🛈 **Bunbury Visitor Centre** Old Railway Station, Carmody Pl; 1800 286 287; www.visitbunbury.com.au
**Dolphin Discovery Centre** Koombana Dr; (08) 9791 3088; Nov–May daily 8am–5pm, Jun–Aug daily 9am–3pm; www.dolphins.mysouthwest.com.au

## Where to eat

**Just One Thai** $\textcircled{\$}\textcircled{\$}$ Sensational Thai food well worth the wait. 109a Victoria St; (08) 9721 1205; lunch & dinner daily.

**Henrys** $\textcircled{\$}\textcircled{\$}$ All-day breakfasts, the best coffee in town and a great seafood selection make this a popular choice for the hungry hordes. 97 Victoria St; (08) 9721 6000; breakfast, lunch & dinner daily.

**Raang Mahal** $\textcircled{\$}\textcircled{\$}$ Delicious Indian food with $8 lunch specials and 15% off take-away orders. 27 Victoria St; (08) 9792 1555; lunch Tue–Fri, dinner daily.

## Where to stay

**WanderInn** ★★ Dorm $25, single $38, double $60 16 Clifton St; (08) 9721 3242; www.bunburybackpackers.com.au

**Dolphin Retreat  Bunbury YHA** ★★ Dorm $23.50, single $35.50, twin or double $53.50–$58.50 14 Wellington St; (08) 9792 4690; www.yha.com.au

## Events

**City of Bunbury Australia Day Fireworks** Including a big breakfast and a family concert, this is the biggest Australia Day Fireworks outside the metro area. Jan.

**Bunbury Carnaval** An eight-day program of horseracing, music, sporting and cultural events leading up to the Bunbury Cup. Mar.

**Bunbury International Jazz Festival** Weekend event with international and Australian jazz artists. Jun.

**Christmas Carnival** Day-long celebration with market stalls, a float parade, children's activities and live entertainment. Dec.

## ② Busselton (1–2 days)

Busselton, a popular spot for Perth holidaymakers, lies on the calm waters of Geographe Bay. The town's landmark is the 2 km-long Busselton Jetty – the longest wooden jetty in the Southern Hemisphere. A top spot for fishing, snorkelling and scuba diving, the jetty also boasts an Underwater Observatory at its seaward end, where you can go below the surface to see the explosion of sea life. At the beach end is an Interpretive Centre, packed with interesting information. If that's too tame for you, hit the Nautical Lady Entertainment World, a fun park with giant waterslide, flying fox, minigolf, skate park and racing cars.

## Further information

**ⓘ Busselton Visitor Centre** 38 Peel Tce; (08) 9752 1288; www.geographebay.com

**Busselton Jetty** Beachfront, Queen St; (08) 9754 0900; Underwater Observatory open Dec–Apr daily 8am–5pm, May–

Karri forest near Northcliffe

Sept daily 10am–4pm, Oct–Nov daily 9am–5pm; www.busseltonjetty.com.au

**Nautical Lady Entertainment World** Beachfront, Queen St; (08) 9752 3473; daily 10am–5pm (open 9.30am during summer holidays); www.nauticallady.com

## Where to eat

**Timeless Cafe** $\textcircled{\$}$ No-fuss dining with timeless favourites such as burgers, steaks and chicken parma. 105 Queen St; (08) 9752 3900; breakfast, lunch & dinner Wed–Mon, breakfast & lunch Tue.

**Vasse Bar Cafe** $\textcircled{\$}\textcircled{\$}$ Tasty pizza and pasta with your choice of draught beer. 44 Queen St; (08) 9754 8560; breakfast, lunch & dinner daily.

## Where to stay

**Busselton Backpackers** ★★ Dorm $23, double $45 14 Peel Tce; (08) 9754 2763.

## Events

**Busselton Beach Festival** A weekend beach party of activities on the foreshore with a fireworks display to finish. Jan.

**Festival of Busselton** This week-long celebration with markets, musical events and an outdoor cinema program culminates in the crowning of the Festival Queen. Jan.

**Southbound Concert** Busselton's version of the Big Day Out. Jan.

**Busselton Jetty Swim** A 3.8 km ocean swim competition around Busselton's famous jetty. Feb.

**Geographe Bay Race Week** The largest yachting regatta on the west coast. Feb/Mar.

**Naturaliste Bluewater Classic** Competition for fishing lovers. Mar.

**Busselton Agricultural Show** Dating back to 1861, this is one of WA's longest surviving country shows. Oct/Nov.

**Anaconda Adventure Race** The WA leg of this national race series includes a swim, paddle, cycle, trail run and beach run. Nov.

**Ironman Western Australia Triathlon** For the seriously fit, race day includes a 3.8 km swim, 180 km cycle and 42 km run. Dec.

## ③ Dunsborough (2 days)

Just 3 hours from Perth, Dunsborough used to be a sleepy little backwater but is now a thriving coastal town with pricey beachfront homes, up-market cafes and plenty of attractions.

Many nearby beaches, including Meelup, Eagle Bay and Bunker Bay, offer great swimming, snorkelling and fishing. Divers should check out the HMAS *Swan* wreck, the largest accessible dive wreck site in the Southern Hemisphere, which lies off Point Picquet south of Eagle Bay.

For a touch of Australiana, head to the popular Quindalup Fauna Park, home to kangaroos, wallabies, quokkas, wombats and dingoes, among other native animals.

## Further information

ⓘ **Dunsborough–Yallingup Information Centre**
Dunsborough Park Shopping Centre, Seymour Blvd; (08) 9755 3299;
www.geographebay.com
**Quindalup Fauna Park** Cnr Caves & Quindalup Siding rds;
(08) 9755 3933; daily 9.30am–5pm.

## Where to eat

**Simmo's Ice-creamery** 🅢 Boasts an ice-cream-eating emu, but the
frozen stuff is so good you won't want to feed it to the animals.
161 Commonage Rd; (08) 9755 3745; daily 10.30am–5pm;
www.simmos.com.au
**Cafe Mozza's** 🅢🅢 Popular with the locals, this all-day cafe offers
simple but tasty fare. Shop 4, Dunsborough Village; (08) 9756 7104;
breakfast, lunch & dinner daily.
**Shakes Diner** 🅢🅢 The place to go for a big breakfast or a good burger.
Shop 9, 34 Dunn Bay Rd; (08) 9755 3599; breakfast & lunch daily.

## Where to stay

**Dunsborough Beach House YHA** ★★★ Dorm $25.50–$27.50, single
$36.50–$43.50, twin or double $58.50–$63.50 201–205 Geographe Bay
Rd, Quindalup; (08) 9755 3107; www.dunsboroughbeachouse.com.au
**Dunsborough Beach Lodge** ★★ Dorm from $20, double from $50
13 Dunn Bay Rd; (08) 9756 7144; www.dunsboroughbeachlodge.com.au
**Dunsborough Inn** ★★ Single $30, twin or double $50 50 Dunn Bay
Rd; (08) 9756 7277; www.dunsboroughinn.com

## Events

**Dunsborough Market** Cnr Gibney St & Gifford Rd. 2nd Sat each month.

## ④ Margaret River (2–3 days)

Margaret River is one of the best-known towns in Western Australia,
and rightly so. It is the centre of a world-class wine region, with
cabernet sauvignon and chardonnay at the core of its reputation, and is
just 10 km from a bunch of top surf beaches and spectacular caves.
Stop at the Wine Tourism Showroom in the visitor centre for the
lowdown on more than 100 local wine producers. The region's most
famous winery is Leeuwin Estate – well worth the visit for its superb
wines and enormous lawn with gum tree backdrop that provides the
setting for the annual Leeuwin Estate Concert.

Fresh produce is also big in Margaret River. Chocoholics should head
to the Margaret River Chocolate Factory, while The Berry Farm, with its
quaint cottage and gardens, has jams, sauces and fruit wines for sale.

## Further information

ⓘ **Margaret River Visitor Centre** 100 Bussell Hwy;
(08) 9757 2911; www.margaretriver.com
**Margaret River Chocolate Company** Cnr Harmans Mill & Harmans

South rds, Wilyabrup; (08) 9755 6555; daily 9am–5pm;
www.chocolatefactory.com.au
**The Berry Farm** 222 Bessell Rd; (08) 9757 5054; cottage & cellar door
daily 10am–4pm; www.berryfarm.com.au

## Tours

**Wine for Dudes** With a name like that, it's no wonder these daily wine
tours attract a young crowd out to have fun and learn a little about
wine on the way. 0427 774 994; www.winefordudes.com
**Bushtucker Tours** The winery tour includes a winery lunch, visits to
chocolate and cheese companies and, of course, tastings at wineries.
The river tour takes a canoe trip up the Margaret River with a bush
tucker lunch. (08) 9757 1084; www.bushtuckertours.com
**South West Adventure Tours** Choose from half-day and full-day
wine tours or a scenic trail taking in some of the region's attractions,
including Mammoth Cave, Boranup Forest and the Augusta Lighthouse.
(08) 9758 7654 or 0416 295 795; www.swatmr.com.au

## Wineries

**Leeuwin Estate** Never mind that many consider Leeuwin Estate
makes Australia's most exquisite chardonnay, this place is worth visiting
purely for its grounds. A free art gallery displays works by the likes
of Arthur Boyd and Sir Sidney Nolan, as well as contemporary pieces.
Stevens Rd; (08) 9759 0000; daily 10am–4.30pm;
www.leeuwinestate.com.au
**Voyager Estate** With its Dutch architecture and elegant rose garden,
this is a beautiful place to taste a range of wines. Stevens Rd; (08) 9757
6354; daily 10am–5pm; www.voyagerestate.com.au
**Cape Mentelle** Together with Leeuwin and Voyager, Cape Mentelle
completes what Australian wine critic James Halliday has called the
'golden triangle'. Enjoy some fantastic chardonnay and semillon
sauvignon blanc. Wallcliffe Rd; (08) 9757 0888;
www.capementelle.com.au
**Vasse Felix** 'Felix' in Latin means 'luck', and this winery has been lucky
with its 'classic dry white' and 'dry red'; its best wine is the Heytesbury
cabernet. Cnr Caves Rd & Harmans Rd Sth, Cowaramup;
(08) 9756 5000; daily 10am–5pm; www.vassefelix.com.au
**Evans & Tate** This label is huge around the world and makes lovely
red wines. Cnr Caves & Metricup rds, Wilyabrup; (08) 9755 6244; daily
10.30am–4.30pm; www.evansandtate.com.au
**Cullen** For a splurge, the restaurant overlooking the vineyard makes
wonderful meals. Or come for a tasting of the flagship wines, including
sauvignon blanc semillon, chardonnay and Diana Madeline cabernet
sauvignon merlot. Caves Rd, Cowaramup; (08) 9755 5277; daily 10am–
4pm; www.cullenwines.com.au
**Ashbrook Estate** This label is one of Margaret River's secrets, with
excellent whites, including chardonnay, riesling, semillon and verdelho.
Harmans Rd Sth, Wilyabrup; (08) 9322 9914; daily 11am–5pm.

## Where to eat

**Chill-E-Cafe** $ Great burgers and internet. 111 Bussell Hwy; (08) 9758 7222; breakfast & lunch daily.

**Goodfellas Cafe** $$ A local institution, Goodfellas serves up pizza, pasta, steak and seafood. 97 Bussell Hwy; (08) 9757 3184; lunch & dinner daily.

**Sea Gardens Cafe** $$ After a swim or a surf, head to this beachfront cafe for its tasty tummy-fillers. Lot 99, Mitchell Dr, Prevelly Park; (08) 9757 2374; breakfast, lunch & dinner daily.

**Leeuwin Estate Restaurant** $$$ TOP TREAT!! Overlooking a meadow surrounded by a forest of karri trees, you'll dine on the freshest local produce. Marron, a freshwater crustacean, is its specialty – and a real treat. Stevens Rd; (08) 9759 0000; lunch daily, dinner Sat; www.leeuwinestate.com.au

## Where to stay

**Surfpoint Resort** ★★★ Dorm $25–$27, double $73–$86 Riedle Dr, Gnarabup; (08) 9757 1777; www.surfpoint.com.au

**Margaret River Lodge YHA** ★★ Dorm $24.50–$27.50, single $56.50, double $59.50 220 Railway Tce; (08) 9757 9532; www.mrlodge.com.au

**Inne Town Backpackers** ★★★ Dorm $25, single $60, double $65 93 Bussell Hwy; 1800 244 115; www.innetown.com

## Events

**Leeuwin Estate Concert** World-renowned outdoor concert sets internationally acclaimed musicians and entertainers against a majestic backdrop of karri forest. Feb.

**Margaret River Pro Surfing Event** The world's best surfers strut their stuff in this high-profile sporting event. Mar/Apr.

**Margaret River Wine Region Festival** A four-day festival of food, wine, art and entertainment. Nov.

## ❺ Leeuwin–Naturaliste National Park (1 day)

This long, thin park is the most visited national park in the state. It hugs the south-west coast of WA for 120 km between two prominent capes, Cape Naturaliste to the north and Cape Leeuwin to the south. Known as the Limestone Coast, it is a wild untamed landscape of crumbling cliffs and big surf.

Here the ultimate bushwalking experience is the 140 km Cape to Cape Walk, which takes in some exceptional coastal scenery along the way. Don't worry if you can't spare the six to eight days needed to complete it; you can get a taste of it on one of its five shorter sections.

Cape Naturaliste has a lighthouse, museum and

Cape Leeuwin Lighthouse

Bunker Bay, Leeuwin–Naturaliste National Park

whale-watching platform (humpback whales linger offshore Sept–Nov). Guided tours of the lighthouse allow you to soak in the great views. At ground level there are a number of excellent walking tracks.

Another of the park's highlights is its magnificent limestone caves. South of Margaret River is Mammoth Cave, where the fossil remains of prehistoric animals have been unearthed. A few km further is the beautiful Lake Cave with a reflective lake. Here you'll also find CaveWorks, which has displays on the geology of the caves. North of Augusta, Jewel Cave contains the longest straw stalactite found in any cave open to the public. Near Yallingup, Ngilgi Cave has amazing stalactite, stalagmite and shawl formations. Other caves can be accessed by adventurers.

The park has several campgrounds with basic facilities. Camping fees apply.

## Further information

ℹ **CALM Busselton** (Leeuwin–Naturaliste National Park) (08) 9752 1677; www.naturebase.net

## Tours

**Naturaliste Charters** Operating out of Dunsborough (Sept–Dec) and Augusta (June–Sept), these 3-hour eco-tours will have you cruising the high seas with migrating humpback, southern right and blue whales, and other aquatic friends. (08) 9755 2276 (Dunsborough office) or (08) 9758 0111 (Augusta office); www.whales-australia.com

**Cape Naturaliste Lighthouse Tours** Climb 123 m above sea level on a guided tour for awe-inspiring views of Geographe Bay and the surrounding national park. The tours cover the history and workings of this fully operational lighthouse. Cape Naturaliste Rd, Dunsborough; tours depart every half hour from 9.30am (9am during summer school holidays); (08) 9755 3955.

**Cave Tours** Of the many caves that lie underneath the Leeuwin–Naturaliste ridge, Lake Cave near Margaret River and Jewel Cave near Augusta can be explored on a guided tour, giving you an insight into the formation of these spectacular caves. Tours depart on the hour |from 9.30am in winter (every half hour during summer school holidays); (08) 9757 7411.

## ❻ Pemberton (half- to full-day)

Picturesque Pemberton is in the heart of the South-west's karri country. Surrounded by magnificent forests of tall timber, this is bushwalker heaven. More sedate, but still enjoyable, is a tram or steam train ride through the forest run by the Pemberton Tramway Company.

For something a little wilder, test your fearlessness at the Gloucester Tree in nearby Gloucester National Park. With 153 metal spikes spiralling upwards to a 61 m-high lookout – which sways in the wind! – this climb is not for the faint-hearted. The Dave Evans Bicentennial Tree in Warren National Park offers thrill-seekers more of the same.

Although much of the high-quality woodcraft at the Fine Woodcraft Gallery won't fit in your backpack, there are smaller items that will, such as bowls, boxes and puzzles. Foodies should tuck into the local specialties: rainbow trout, freshwater crayfish and cool-climate wines.

## Further information
*ℹ* **Pemberton Visitor Centre** Brockman St; 1800 671 133; www.pembertontourist.com.au
**Pemberton Tramway Company** Pemberton Train Station, Railway Cres; (08) 9776 1322; www.pemtram.com.au
**Fine Woodcraft Gallery** Dickinson St, (08) 9776 1399.

## Tours
**Pemberton Discovery Tours** Beach and forest off-road adventures in 4WD vehicles, national park tours, fishing safaris, wildflower tours, Pemberton wine tours … this company does it all. 48 Brockman St; (08) 9776 0484 or 0427 760 484.
**Pemberton Hiking & Canoeing Company** Eco-tours from 4 hrs to five days, walking through old-growth forest or canoeing through Warren National Park. (08) 9776 1559.

## Where to eat
**Pemberton Millhouse Cafe** 🟢 This tearoom serves generous lunches and a good selection of cakes. 14 Brockman St; (08) 9776 1122; breakfast & lunch daily.
**Fine Woodcraft Gallery & Gryphon's Garden Cafe** 🟢 After checking out the gallery, stop here for lunch or a cuppa. In winter, try the soup – it's always delicious and super-filling. Dickinson St; (08) 9776 1399; lunch daily.

## Events
**Autumn Festival** A main-street event celebrating local produce. May.
**Gloucester Tree Birthday** Free tree-climbing demonstrations, face painting and stalls over the long weekend. Sept/Oct.

## ➐ Walpole (1 day)
This tiny town is so unassuming you could easily drive straight through it. But don't. Walpole is surrounded by rugged coast, forests and wilderness areas that hold the most wonderful natural treasures.

Walpole–Nornalup National Park is renowned for its forest of

rare red tingle trees known as the Valley of the Giants. These are the most massive of all eucalypts and are unique to the Walpole area. The breathtaking 38 m-high Tree Top Walk through the forest canopy is a world-class tourist attraction. At ground level, the Ancient Empire interpretive boardwalk weaves its way through the veteran tingle trees. To the east of Walpole is the start of the Hilltop Drive, a 24 km loop drive to the Hilltop Lookout, the Coke-coloured swirling waters of Circular Pool and the Giant Tingle Tree. This tree, with its whopping 25 m circumference, is one of the ten largest living things on the planet.

Another Walpole 'treasure' is local legend Gary Muir, whose WOW Wilderness EcoCruises take you up the beautiful Walpole–Nornalup waterways. When Gary takes the cruise, you're in for a wildly enthusiastic and entertaining commentary on the stunning scenery that surrounds you.

## Further information
*ℹ* **Walpole–Nornalup Visitor Centre** Pioneer Cottage, South Coast Hwy; (08) 9840 1111; www.walpole.com.au
*ℹ* **CALM Walpole** (Walpole–Nornalup National Park) (08) 9840 1027; www.naturebase.net

## Tours
**WOW Wilderness EcoCruises** Walpole St; (08) 9840 1036; www.wowwilderness.com.au

## Where to eat
**Top Deck Cafe** 🟢🟢 Overlooking the Pioneer Park, the view from the Top Deck is spectacular, but you're really here for the local fish. 25 Nockolds St; (08) 9840 1344; breakfast & lunch daily.
**Wooz & Suz Cafe** 🟢🟢 Focaccias, burgers and steaks. Lot 13 Nockolds St; (08) 9840 1214; breakfast & lunch daily.
**Walpole Hotel Motel** 🟢🟢 Cheap and cheerful counter meals or if you're feeling flush, try the restaurant. South West Highway; (08) 9840 1023; lunch & dinner daily.
**Barb and Malcolm's Flaming Hot Takeaways** 🟢 Pizza, pasta, kebabs, burgers and fish 'n' chips. Vista St; (08) 9840 1440; Tue–Thur & Sun 11am–9pm, Fri–Sat 10am–10pm.

## Where to stay
**Walpole Lodge** ★★ Dorm $22, single $38, twin or double $55 Cnr Pier St & Park Ave; (08) 9840 1244; www.walpolelodge.com.au
**Tingle All Over YHA** ★★ Dorm $23.50–$25.50, single $41.50–$43.50, twin or double $57.50–$60.50 60 Nockolds St; (08) 9840 1041; www. yha.com.au
**Coalmine Beach Caravan Park** ★★ Campsite (2 people): unpowered $21, powered $24–$26 Knoll Dr; (08) 9840 1026; www.coalminebeach.com.au

For more detail see maps 228 & 234

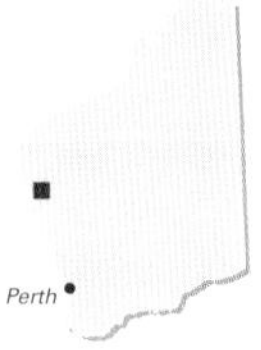
Perth

# Outback Coast and the Mid-west

# Reef to range

CAPE RANGE NP
Exmouth ⑦
NINGALOO MARINE PARK
Coral Bay ⑥
INDIAN OCEAN
0 120 km
Carnarvon ⑤
FRANCOIS PERON NP ④
Monkey Mia ③
KALBARRI NP
② Kalbarri
① Geraldton
N

From a coastline of secluded beaches, coral reefs and the most extraordinary diversity of marine life to spectacular limestone gorges and dazzling displays of wildflowers, this region is a traveller's treasure trove. It's also only a few days' drive north of Perth, so visitors pressed for time can get a taste of this vast state's awesome landscapes.

**Number of days to spend in this region: 10–14 days**

## Getting here

There are regional flights with Skywest to Geraldton, Kalbarri, Carnarvon, Monkey Mia and Exmouth. Alternatively, TransWA and Greyhound buses service the region, or you could hire a car.

**Skywest Airlines** 1300 660 088; www.skywest.com.au

**TransWA** (08) 9071 2330; www.transwa.wa.gov.au

## Outback Coast and the Mid-west tours

**WesternXposure** Four- to five-day tours departing from Perth to the Pinnacles, Kalbarri National Park, Monkey Mia, Coral Bay, Ningaloo Reef, Cape Range National Park and Exmouth. Two extra days required to get back to Perth. 1800 621 200 or (08) 9371 3695; www.westernxposure.com.au

**Planet Perth Tours** Also offers four- to five-day tours of the region's attractions. (08) 9225 6622; www.planettours.com.au

**Easyrider Backpacker Tours** For travellers with no deadlines to meet, there are six-month Jump On, Jump Off tickets, which allows you the flexibility to take a tour, get off where you fancy, stay as long as you want and then catch the bus when it passes through again (one-day tours not included). For everyone else, there's the four-day 'Monkey Mia Magic' or 'Exmouth Exposure' tours from Perth and back. 224 William St, Northbridge; (08) 9227 0824; www.easyridertours.com.au

Driving along the Big Lagoon, Francois Peron National Park

## 1 Geraldton (1–2 days)

Geraldton is a town blessed with constant warm days and good winds, making it one of the world's best spots for windsurfing. It is also surrounded by superb swimming and surfing beaches, and brilliant diving around the nearby Houtman Abrolhos Islands, so there's no shortage of aquatic activities to keep you happy.

If all that sunshine wears thin, then head to the Geraldton Museum for a bit of murder and mutiny. The shipwreck of the *Batavia* in 1629 is infamous for its bloody aftermath; get all the gory details and the stories of the many other ships that have foundered on this treacherous coastline.

A more recent naval tragedy is remembered on Mount Scott overlooking the town. The HMAS *Sydney* memorial commemorates the loss of the HMAS *Sydney* in 1941, which went down with 645 men on board somewhere between Geraldton and Carnarvon after an encounter with the German raider HSK *Kormoran*.

Architecture buffs can follow the Hawes Heritage Trail, which highlights the remarkable church buildings of architect-priest Monsignor John Cyril Hawes. One of Hawes' masterpieces is the Byzantine-styled St Francis Xavier Cathedral. Pick up a brochure from the visitor centre.

Lastly, a trip to Geraldton isn't complete without a tour of the crayfish processing plant, a fascinating part of the town's multi-million-dollar crayfishing industry.

### Further information

[i] **Geraldton Visitor Centre** Bill Sewell Complex, cnr Chapman Rd & Bayly St; 1800 818 881; www.geraldtontourist.com.au

**Geraldton Museum** 1 Museum Pl, Batavis Coast Marina; (08) 9921 5080; daily 9.30am–4pm.

## Tours

**Live Cray Factory Tours** Geraldton Fisherman's Co-operative; Fisherman's Wharf, Connell Rd; Nov–Jun Mon–Fri 9.30am.
**Abrolhos Island Charters** Get aboard the Rat Patrol with Captain Jay Cox for fishing, scuba, snorkelling or surfing adventure tours to the Abrolhos Islands. Geraldton Fisherman's Wharf; (08) 9964 9516; www.abrolhosislandcharters.com
**Geraldton Air Charter** Aerial tours of the Abrolhos Islands include landing at East Wallabi Island and snorkelling in Turtle Bay. Tours are also available to Kalbarri, Murchison River Gorges and Monkey Mia. (08) 9923 3434; www.geraldtonaircharter.com

## Where to eat

**Go Health Lunch Bar** [$] The name says it all: healthy food for lunch with fresh juices and good coffee. 122 Marine Tce; (08) 9965 5200.
**Skeetas Restaurant & Cafe** [$][$] With its great location just across from the beach, this is a popular spot for a meal. 101 Foreshore Dr; (08) 9964 1619; breakfast, lunch & dinner daily.

## Where to stay

**Foreshore Backpackers** ★★ Dorm $22, single $30, twin or double $50 172 Marine Tce, Geraldton; (08) 9921 3275.
**Geraldton Backpackers** ★★ Dorm $18, single $25, twin or double $42 Cnr Chapman Rd & Bayly St, Geraldton; (08) 9964 3001.

## Events

**Geraldton Windsurfing Festival** Weekend of competition windsurfing and partying. Jan.
**Mid-West Show & Shine** One-day car show for revheads. Sept.
**The Big Sky Writers' Festival** Weekend festival of readings, workshops and panel discussions with local and interstate guest writers. Sept.
**Geraldton–Greenough Sunshine Festival** Two-week community festival with food, wine, music, art, and sport, including everything from a pet parade to a sand sculpture competition. Oct.
**Blessing of the Fleet** Celebrations at Fisherman's Wharf for the town's fishing industry. Oct.

# 2 Kalbarri (1–2 days)

This popular holiday town at the mouth of the Murchison River makes a great base from which to explore the nearby Kalbarri National Park. When you're not checking out the park's impressive gorges, you can visit the Rainbow Jungle for an encounter with Australia's brilliant parrots and cockatoos, or the Seahorse Sanctuary, a fascinating aquaculture centre focused on the conservation of seahorses.

Only 1 km from Kalbarri, the vast 183 000 ha national park is best known for its 80 km of gorges carved out by the Murchison River. The views here are crying out to be photographed: there's the natural frame of 'Nature's Window' and the hold-on-tight views at Z Bend lookout, where the gorge plunges 150 m to the river below. Where the park hits the coast, you get panoramic ocean views and whale-watching lookouts. However, if you're into more extreme pleasures, then bushwalk, abseil, rock climb or go rafting. Don't overdo it though, as this is a day-visit park only; there are no camp sites and drinking water is not available, so carry your own supplies.

Road and dunes north of Coral Bay

## Further information

[i] **Kalbarri Visitor Centre** Grey St; 1800 639 468; www.kalbarriwa.info
[i] **CALM Geraldton** (Kalbarri National Park) (08) 9921 5955; www.naturebase.net
**Rainbow Jungle – The Australian Parrot Breeding Centre** Red Bluff Rd; (08) 9937 1248; Mon–Sat 9am–5pm, Sun 10am–5pm.
**Seahorse Sanctuary** Lot 582, Red Bluff Rd; (08) 9937 1124; Thur–Tue 10am–4pm; guided tours available on request; www.seahorsesanctuary.com.au

## Tours

**Kalbarri Wilderness Cruises** Lunchtime and sunset cruises up the Murchison River on the *Kalbarri River Queen* with commentary on the region's history and wildlife. (08) 9937 2259; www.kalbarricruises.com.au
**Kalbarri Adventure Tours** Popular all-day bushwalking and canoeing trips through Kalbarri National Park. (08) 9937 1677; www.kalbarritours.com.au
**Kalbarri Abseil** Experience the thrill of abseiling down Kalbarri National Park's gorges on half-day or full-day adventure tours. (08) 9937 1618; www.abseilaustralia.com.au

**Kalbarri Air Charter** Spectacular views of the Murchison River gorges and coastal cliffs from the air on 20 min scenic flights. Longer flights also available. 52 Grey St; (08) 9937 1130; www.kalbarriaircharter.com.au

## Where to eat
**Black Rock Cafe** 💲💲 Widely regarded as Kalbarri's best cafe. 80 Grey St; (08) 9937 1062; breakfast, lunch & dinner daily.
**Grass Tree Cafe and Restaurant** 💲💲 Asian-inspired cuisine with
a seafood focus. 94 Grey St; (08) 9937 2288; lunch & dinner daily.

## Where to stay
**Kalbarri Backpackers YHA** ★★ Dorm $25.50–$26.50, twin or double $31–$33.50 51 Mortimer St, Kalbarri; (08) 9937 1430.
**Murchison Caravan Park** ★★ Unpowered/powered site $20–$24, cabin $65–$85 29 Grey St, Kalbarri; 1300 851 555 or (08) 9937 1005.

## Events
**Kalbarri Canoe and Cray Carnival** Canoe races on the Murchison River combine with a two-day celebration of local produce. Jun.

## ❸ Monkey Mia (1–2 days)
It seems every visitor to WA knows about the daily shore visits by the wild bottlenose dolphins at Monkey Mia. Unfortunately, given its reputation and the great distance required to get there, expectation sometimes outweighs experience. Yes, the dolphins do swim right into the shallows to get a small feed of fish, giving you an extraordinary opportunity to see them up close and natural. However, don't expect this to be a mind-blowing interactive experience; it's more a gentle, back-to-nature viewing. Nevertheless, it is a special event. Keep in mind, as you stand in the shallows with the dolphins swimming near your feet, that these are wild creatures. Early morning is the best time to see them. To protect the dolphins, there are rules you must observe: don't wear sunscreen on your legs, as it irritates their eyes; look but don't touch; and always follow the ranger's instructions.

Monkey Mia itself might also not be what you expect. A resort complex rather than a town, its collection of places to sleep and eat have been built around the dolphin phenomenon. (You have to pay a $6 admission fee when you arrive, which goes towards dolphin research.) However, there are other things to do here, including snorkelling, sailing, taking a camel ride or a marine-wildlife cruise, learning about the dolphins and seeing them on DolphinCam at the Monkey Mia Visitor Centre, or simply soaking up the sun on the glorious beach. While there is no shortage of accommodation for all budgets, the food here is expensive so if you're travelling on a budget, get your groceries from Denham, 27 km away.

Monkey Mia dolphin

## Further information
ℹ **Shark Bay Tourist Bureau** 71 Knight Tce, Denham; (08) 9948 1253.
**Monkey Mia Dolphin Resort** 1800 653 611; www.monkeymia.com.au
**Shark Bay Information & Booking Office** 29 Knight Tce, Denham; 1300 135 887.
**Monkey Mia Visitor Centre** 27 Thornbill Loop; 1300 135 887; daily 7.30am–4pm.

## Tours
**Monkey Mia Yacht Charters** Spot dolphins, dugongs, sharks, turtles and other marine life aboard the *Aristocat II*. Choose from short hour-long trips to afternoon cruises; the Champagne Sunset Cruise is particularly appealing. (08) 9948 1446; www.monkey-mia.net
**Shotover** Short wildlife cruises aboard the *Shotover* catamaran take in the wonders of Monkey Mia's famous aquatic world. 1800 241 481.
**Wula Guda Nyinda** Aboriginal-guided cultural walks take you into the world of the local Malgana people, revealing the secrets of bush survival including bush tucker and bush medicine. 0429 708 847.

## Where to eat
**Monkey Bar** 💲 Located within the Dolphin Lodge, this backpacker bar offers light snacks to enjoy in the beer garden, cheap takeaway food and barbecues for cooking your own.
**Peron Cafe** 💲💲 Slightly more expensive than the Monkey Bar, this casual cafe serves light meals and takeaway food, including fish 'n' chips.

## Where to stay
**Monkey Mia Dolphin Lodge & Backpackers** ★★ Dorms from $24 1800 653 611.

## ❹ Francois Peron National Park (1–2 days)
Lying on the northernmost tip of the Peron Peninsula, this park is a 52 000 ha wilderness area edged by a coastline of low red cliffs, white-sand beaches and the azure waters of the Shark Bay Marine Park. A former sheep station, it is now part of the Shark Bay World Heritage Area. Here you can camp, swim, fish from the beach and watch for wildlife. Bush camping areas with toilets and gas barbecues are located at Big

Lagoon, Gregories, South Gregories, Bottle Bay and Herald Bight; only accessible by 4WD. Campers must be fully self-sufficient, bringing all supplies and water with them. To get to the park, take the turn-off 4 km from Denham on the Monkey Mia Rd; a further 6 km after this, you'll find the visitor centre at the old Peron Homestead. A hot-water artesian bore nearby is used for a hot tub that you're welcome to soak in.

### Further information

[i] **CALM Denham** (Francois Peron National Park)
(08) 9948 1208; www.naturebase.net, www.sharkbay.org

## 5 Carnarvon (1–2 days)

Carmen Miranda would be perfectly at home in this town. Plantations stretching for 15 km along the banks of the Gascoyne River grow a host of tropical fruits, including bananas, mangoes, avocados, pineapples, paw-paws and melons. Take a tour of Bumbaks Fresh Fruit Plantation, where they grow bananas, grapes and mangoes, and reward yourself at the end with a yummy fresh fruit chocolate-covered ice-cream.
For great views of Carnarvon, visit the huge 29 m wide reflector known as the Big Dish, part of the now redundant NASA station that guided early US space flights. Back in town, take a stroll through the Carnarvon Heritage Precinct and down the One Mile Jetty.

For a more thrilling sight, travel just over 70 km north of Carnarvon to the impressive Blowholes, where water forced through holes in the coastal rock shoots up to 20 m in the air. The huge sign nearby declaring 'King Waves Kill' is a blunt reminder that you should be careful where you stand, as over 30 people have been killed here by freak waves.

### Further information

[i] **Carnarvon Visitor Centre** Civic Centre, Robinson St; (08) 9941 1146; www.carnarvon.wa.gov.au
**Bumbaks Fresh Fruit Plantation** North River Rd; (08) 9941 8006; tours Mon–Fri 10am.

### Where to eat

**Cafe La Nez** $ Filling breakfasts and light lunches of focaccia, wraps and salads make this cafe a popular daytime diner. 16 Robinson St; (08) 9941 1252; breakfast daily, lunch Mon–Sat.
**Old Post Office Cafe** $$ This licensed cafe with a healthy takeaway service offers tasty casual meals. Pizza is its specialty. Park yourself on a verandah table and enjoy the night air. 10 Robinson St; (08) 9941 1800; dinner Tue–Sat.

### Where to stay

**Port Hotel** ★★ Single $35, twin $22 Cnr Robinson & Alexandra sts; (08) 9941 1704.
**Carnavon Backpackers** ★ Dorm $20, single $30, double $50 97–99 Olivia Tce; (08) 9941 1095.
**Coral Coast Tourist Park** ★★ Powered/unpowered site (2 people) $22/$19, unit $55–$95. 108 Robinson St; (08) 9941 1438.

### Events

**Carnafin Fishing Competition** One of the largest game fishing competitions in Australia. Jun.
**Xtreme Festival** A weekend of music and entertainment with live bands, workshops and markets. Jul.
**Carnarvon Festival and Rodeo** This weekend festival has a float parade, fireworks, rodeo – yeeha! – and ball. Aug.
**Gascoyne Dash** A 485 km, two-day outback motorcross race. Oct.

## 6 Coral Bay (2–3 days)

The tiny township of Coral Bay is known for one thing – its proximity to the Ningaloo Marine Park. At Coral Bay the coral gardens lie close to the shore, which makes access to the reef as easy as a gentle swim.

Ningaloo Marine Park protects the 260 km Ningaloo Reef, the longest fringing coral reef in Australia. What makes this reef so special is that it's really close to the shore. At just 100 m at its nearest and less than 7 km at its furthest, even novice snorkellers and children can enjoy the magnificent coral gardens and their marine inhabitants.

To say the marine life here is abundant is a massive understatement: there's some 500 fish species, 250 coral species, manta rays, turtles, the list goes on. Seasonal visitors include humpback whales, dolphins and whale sharks. The latter is the world's biggest fish species, reaching a colossal 12 m long and weighing more than 11 tons. From April–June you can snorkel with these gentle giants – a truly awesome experience. The whale sharks return to Ningaloo each year for another extraordinary event: the mass coral-spawning. This three-day event begins a week or so after the full moon in March and results in abundant food for the sharks.

Lying at the southern end of the Ningaloo Marine Park, Coral Bay is blessed with pristine beaches and a near-perfect climate: it is consistently warm and dry, regardless of the season, and the water temperature only varies from 18 to 28 degrees.

Swimming, snorkelling, scuba diving, and every kind of fishing imaginable (but only outside sanctuary areas) are available year-round.

Snorkelling near Exmouth

You can get a tour here for almost anything aquatic: glass-bottomed boat cruises, snorkel and dive tours, kayak tours, fishing charters and marine wildlife-watching tours to see whale sharks (April–June), humpback whales (June–Nov) and manta rays (all year).

## Further information
Coastal Adventure Tours Coral Bay Arcade, Robinson St; (08) 9948 5190.

## Tours
Coral Bay Adventures Provides a wide range of snorkelling and diving tours, including the popular whale shark snorkelling tour (Apr– June) and a humpback whale-watching tour. For those who don't want to get wet, there are scenic flights available and a glass-bottom boat tour. Robinson St; (08) 9942 5955; www.coralbayadventures.com.au
Ningaloo Reef Dive Options for getting up close and personal with the reef include snorkel tours, reef dives, manta ray interaction tours, and all-day North Reef Safaris. Dive courses also available. Shop 8, Coral Bay Arcade; (08) 9942 5824; www.ningalooreefdive.com

## Where to eat
Shades Restaurant $$ Open for takeaway lunches and bistro meals for dinner. It's popular, so make sure you book. Ningaloo Reef Resort; (08) 9942 5863.
Ningaloo Reef Cafe $$ The place to go for pizza. Bayview Holiday Village, Robinson St; (08) 9942 5882; dinner daily from 5pm.
Fins Cafe $$ A more up-market option with BYO alcohol. Internet access available. 4 Robinson St; (08) 9942 5900; breakfast, lunch and dinner daily.

## Where to stay
Ningaloo Club ★★ Dorm $22–$25, twin $70–$75, double $70–$95 (08) 9948 5100; www.coralbaywa.com/ningalooclub

## 7 Exmouth (1–2 days)
Not a big drawcard in itself, this ex-army town makes a good base to visit Ningaloo Marine Park or Cape Range National Park. This national park is a rugged landscape of arid rocky gorges softened by the stunning coastline of the Ningaloo Marine Park. Wildlife is abundant, so it's highly likely you'll stumble upon emus, euros, rock wallabies and red kangaroos. In late winter there is a beautiful array of wildflowers including the Sturt's Desert Pea and the superb bird flower. Here you can camp, swim and bushwalk.

On the eastern side of the park are Shothole Canyon, an impressive gorge, and Charles Knife Canyon, with spectacular views. To the west is Mangrove Bay, a sanctuary zone with a bird hide overlooking a lagoon, and Mandu Mandu Gorge where you can walk along an ancient riverbed. Yardie Creek is the only gorge in the area with permanent

water, fed from the ocean. Of the many beaches along the coastline, Turquoise Bay is one of the most popular for swimming and snorkelling. Campsites along the coast are limited and have minimal facilities.

The Milyering Visitor Centre, made of rammed earth and run by solar power, is 52 km from Exmouth on the western side of the park and offers information on both Cape Range and Ningaloo.

## Further information
🛈 Exmouth Visitor Centre Murat Rd; (08) 9949 1176; www.exmouthwa.com.au
🛈 CALM Exmouth (Cape Range National Park) (08) 9949 1676; www.naturebase.net
🛈 Milyering Visitor Centre (08) 9949 2808.

## Tours
Exmouth Diving Centre Exmouth's original dive centre offers the full range of diving and snorkelling options for the Ningaloo Reef. Payne St; (08) 9949 1201; www.exmouthdiving.com.au
Ningaloo Blue Ningaloo Blue offers deep-sea fishing charters, a wide range of snorkelling and diving options, coral viewing aboard a glass-bottom boat and whale shark tours (Apr–June). Cnr Thew & Kennedy sts; 1800 811 338; www.ningalooblue.com.au
Capricorn Kayak Tours Sea-kayak your way around the Ningaloo Reef on Capricorn's one-day Ningaloo Reef Eco tour (July–Oct). Serious kayakers can go to town on the five-day Ningaloo Safari, which will set you back quite a bit. (08) 6267 8059; www.capricornkayak.com.au
Ningaloo Safari Tours The full-day Top of the Range Safari includes a 4WD adventure into Cape Range National Park, a cruise up Yardie Creek, a snorkel on the Ningaloo Reef and finally a stop at Vlamingh Head Lighthouse for panoramic views. (08) 9949 1550; www.ningaloosafari.com
Yardie Creek Tours Operates 1 hr boat tours up this spectacular gorge in Cape Range National Park. (08) 9949 2659.

## Where to eat
Sea Urchin $$ Great fish 'n' chips, pasta and laksas – and it's BYO (bring your own grog)! 73 Maidstone Cres.
BJ's Takeaway and Pizza $$ Pizza you can trust, with a few gourmet additions. Exmouth Shopping Centre.

## Where to stay
Pete's Exmouth Backpackers ★★ Dorm $20–$22, twin $28–$32, double $48–$52 Cnr Truscott Cres & Murat Rd; (08) 9949 1101; www.exmouthvillage.com

## Events
Gamex Five days of serious fishing. Mar.
Whale Shark Festival Three days of displays, stalls and live music. May.

Perth

# The Kimberley
## The final frontier

Remote and rugged, the Kimberley is one of the world's great wilderness areas. Covering more than 420 000 sq km – that's three times the size of England – it is an ancient landscape of mighty ranges, spectacular gorges and arid desert. Along its coastline, pristine beaches fringe the turquoise waters of the Indian Ocean. While the coastal town of Broome is well known as a resort holiday destination, there are large tracts of the Kimberley that are completely inaccessible by road – or only accessible by 4WD. Travellers should familiarise themselves with prevailing conditions and carry adequate supplies.

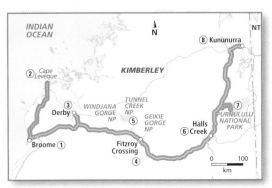

Number of days to spend in this region: 10–14 days

## Getting here

To get to Broome, the start of your Kimberley adventure, you can either fly with Qantas, Virgin Blue or Skywest Airlines, bus with

Greyhound or drive from Perth.

Skywest Airlines 1300 660 088; www.skywest.com.au

## When to go

The Kimberley has two distinct seasons: the Wet and the Dry. The Wet season extends from November to the end of March and is a time of swelteringly hot, humid days, when huge thunderstorms dump most of the annual rainfall on the region. Road closures at this time are common. The Dry season, from April to the end of October, is characterised by little rain, low temperatures and open roads – perfect for travellers. However, at all times of the year, travelling conditions are highly variable so it is best to check ahead.

## Kimberley tours

Easyrider Backpacker Tours Easyrider will take you from Perth as far north as Broome on their seven-day Broometime Tour with a handy 'Jump On/Off' option. 1800 247 848; www.easyridertours.com.au

Kimberley Wilderness Adventures This award-winning company works in partnership with the Kimberley Aboriginal people to offer exclusive safari camps near iconic regional attractions. 1800 675 222; www.kimberleywilderness.com.au

## ❶ Broome (2–3 days)

The gateway to the vast Kimberley region, Broome is a real getaway destination. Completely unique, the town manages to be both cosmopolitan and laidback, and is famous as much for its pearling industry as for the endless white sand and turquoise waters of nearby Cable Beach. Everywhere here you can see the influences of the melting pot of nationalities – Japanese, Malays, Koepangers and Chinese – that

flocked to this frontier town in the 1880s when pearling grounds were discovered offshore.

Immerse yourself in Broome's rich and fascinating history at the Broome Historical Society Museum. Visit two restored pearl luggers for tales of Broome's pearling history (admission is free), then see today's pearls on display in Chinatown. In the evening, take in a flick at Sun Pictures, the world's oldest operating outdoor cinema, which opened in 1916.

If you're in town from March to October, check dates and times at the visitor centre for the Staircase to the Moon, an optical illusion caused by a full moon reflecting off the exposed mudflats of Roebuck Bay at extremely low tides. Remains of Japanese fighter planes, known as the Flying Boat Wrecks, can also be seen 1 km from Town Beach at this time of year.

At the far end of Cable Beach is Gantheaume Point, where at very low tide you can see dinosaur footprints believed to be 130 million years old. If the tide's in, make do with a plaster cast of the tracks at the top of the cliff.

Cable Beach, Broome

To experience Australia's scaly wildlife, see crocodiles that have been caught after causing 'disturbances' in the wild at the Malcolm Douglas Broome Crocodile Park. Guided feeding tours are available. Malcolm is also planning to open a wilderness park and animal refuge for a range of animals, including kangaroos, wallabies and emus.

Gantheaume Point

## Further information

ℹ️ **Broome Visitor Centre** Cnr Bagot St & Broome Rd; (08) 9192 2222; www.broomevisitorcentre.com.au

**Broome Historical Society Museum** Saville St; (08) 9192 2075; Nov–May Mon–Fri 10am–1pm, Jun–Oct Mon–Fri 10am–4pm, Sat–Sun 10am–1pm.

**Pearl Luggers** 31 Dampier Tce; (08) 9192 2059; tours Mon–Fri 11am & 2pm, Sat–Sun 11am.

**Sun Pictures** Carnarvon St; (08) 9192 1077; daily from 6pm, 2 sessions per night.

**Malcolm Douglas Broome Crocodile Park** Cnr Cable Beach Rd & Sanctuary Dr; (08) 9192 1489; tours Apr–Nov Mon–Fri 10am–5pm, Sat–Sun 2–5pm, Dec–Mar daily 4.15–5.45pm; feeding Apr–Nov daily 3pm, Dec–Mar daily 4.30pm; www.malcolmdouglas.com.au

**Bike hire: Broome Cycles** 2 Hamersley St; (08) 9192 1871.

## Tours

**Beach Hut** Make like a local on Cable Beach! Just below the Broome Surf Lifesaving Club is this handy 'hut', where you can hire umbrellas, deckchairs, body boards, surfboards and wave skis.

**Red Sun Camels** The quintessential Broome experience of a camel ride on Cable Beach can be had on a 40-minute morning ride or 1 hr sunset ride. 1800 184 488; www.redsuncamels.com.au

**Astro Tours** Learn about the secrets of the Broome night sky with Astro Tours' powerful telescopes. (08) 9193 5362l; Apr–Dec Mon–Wed, Fri–Sat; www.astrotours.net

**Broome Aviation** Get a bird's-eye view of Broome's natural attractions with a 25-minute scenic flight. (08) 9192 1369; www.broomeaviation.com

**Lurujarri Songcycle Heritage Dreaming Trail** This 80 km trail through spectacular country around Broome follows part of a traditional Aboriginal song cycle that originated from the Dreamtime. Divided into six sections, each section is an easy day's walk. (08) 9192 3337; trails.heritage.wa.gov.au

## Where to eat and drink

**Matso's Cafe & Brewery** 💲💲 You've got to have at least one meal – and a beer – in this Broome institution. 60 Hamersley St; (08) 9193 5811; breakfast, lunch & dinner daily.

**Cable Beach Sandbar & Grill** 💲💲 Great seafood and steaks with an amazing view to top it off. Cable Beach Rd; (08) 9193 5090; breakfast, lunch & dinner daily.

**2 Rice** 💲 Sushi and Asian curries during the week, freshly baked breads on the weekend. 26 Dampier Tce; (08) 9192 1395; Mon–Fri 10am–3pm during the Wet, Mon–Fri 8am–5pm during the Dry, Sat 9am–1pm year-round.

## Nightlife

**Roebuck Bay Hotel** The raucous 'Roey' is an Aussie pub the way they should be. 45 Dampier Tce; (08) 9192 1221; Sun–Wed 10am– midnight, Thur 10am–1am, Fri–Sat 10am–2am.

**Tokyo Joe's** Backpackers love this joint. Beer, pool tables, dancin' tunes – what more do you need? 52 Napier Tce; (08) 9193 7222; open till late.

**Nippon Inn** Much the same as Tokyo Joe's but with an outdoor beer garden. Wednesday is backpacker night. Prizes for best beer gut. 27 Dampier Tce; (08) 9192 1941; open till late.

## Where to stay

**Kimberley Klub YHA** ★ ★ ★ Dorm $23.50–$27.50, twin or double $53.50–$88.50 62 Frederick St; 1800 004 345; www.kimberleyklub.com

**Cable Beach Backpackers** ★ ★ Dorm $23–$27, single $50–$55, double $65–$70 12 Sanctuary Rd; 1800 655 011; www.cablebeachbackpackers.com

## Events

**Broome Arts & Music Festival** Ten-day showcase of artists and musicians, both local and imported. Mar.

**Big Moon Rising Festival** Month-long cultural festival. Apr.

**Broome Race Round** Series of horseracing days over a three-month period, culminating in the Broome Cup. Jun–Aug.

**Worn Art** An art show that explores the human form in weird and wonderful ways. Sept.

**Shinju Matsuri** AKA the Festival of the Pearl, this is Broome's annual ten-day celebration of its pearling industry and its rich multiculturalism. Sept.

**Mango Festival** Three-day celebration for lovers of the king of fruits. Nov.

## ❷ Cape Leveque (2–3 days)

This remote, 4WD-only area north of Broome is the perfect destination for off-the-beaten-track adventurers. The 200 km unsealed route from Broome to Cape Leveque traverses open eucalypt country and Aboriginal reserve land. Within the reserve is the Sacred Heart Church at Beagle Bay, with a stunning pearl-shell altar. The Aboriginal community at Lombadina offers sightseeing, fishing and mudcrabbing tours.

### Where to stay

**Kooljaman at Cape Leveque** ★★★ Owned by the Aboriginal communities of One Arm Point and Djarindjin, Kooljaman is an award-winning wilderness camp 220 km north of Broome. Visitors to this remote location can sleep in traditional palm frond shelters on the beach or stay in rustic cabins. (08) 9192 4970; www.kooljaman.com.au

## ❸ Derby (1–2 days)

Apart from being the oldest town in the Kimberley, Derby's claim to fame is simply that it's the point of departure for a number of the region's attractions. It is at the western end of the 4WD-only Gibb River Road, a 649 km 'alternative' route from Derby to Kununurra/Wyndham that's impassable during the Wet. Even in the Dry it's only for the self-sufficient adventurer. From this road you can reach the western entrance of the Devonian Reef National Parks, with their spectacular gorges (see next page). Derby is also where you can charter a flight or cruise north to the remote, pristine islands of the Buccaneer Archipelago in King Sound, a place of spectacular scenery including whirlpools created by massive 11 m tides and the amazing Horizontal Waterfall.

### Further information

ℹ️ **Derby Visitor Centre** 2 Clarendon St; 1800 621 426; www.derbytourism.com.au

### Tours

**Buccaneer Sea Safaris** Fly-and-cruise adventure tours range from the four-day safari to the Horizontal Waterfall in the Buccaneer Archipelago to the 14-day tour from Derby to Wyndham. (08) 9191 1991; www.buccaneerseasafaris.com
**Derby Discovery Tours/Windjana Tours/West Kimberley Tours** Derby Bus Service runs Derby Discovery Tours – half- or full-day tours around Derby. Windjana Tours explores Windjana Gorge and Tunnell Creek, while West Kimberley Tours operates two- to

seven-day customised safari tours of the region. (08) 9193 1550; www.derbybus.com.au

### Where to eat

**Wharf Restaurant** 💲💲 With that gorgeous jetty location, it's only right that seafood should be big on the menu. Jetty Rd; (08) 9191 1195; Mon 4pm–late, Tue–Sun 11am–late.

### Where to stay

**West Kimberley Lodge and Caravan Park** ★★ Powered campsite (2 people) $24, single $45, double $65 Lot 100 Sutherland St; (08) 9191 1031.
**Spinifex Hotel** ★ Dorm $20, single $40–$60, double $65–$85 Clarendon St; (08) 9191 1233.

### Events

**King Tide Day** Day-long events celebrating highest tide in Australia. May.
**Mowanjum Festival** Weekend display of Indigenous art and culture. Jul.
**Boab Festival** This two-week party includes a mardi gras, mud football and the Stockmen and Bushies Weekend. Jul.
**Boxing Day Sports** Wild and wacky sports such as watermelon spitting and egg eating. Dec.

## ❹ Fitzroy Crossing (1 day)

While there's not much to see at Fitzroy Crossing, its proximity to Geikie and Windjana gorges makes it a stopping point for many travellers. As its name suggests, this tiny settlement lies where the Great Northern Highway crosses the Fitzroy River, so the area is prone to flooding – check road conditions from November to March. When you get into town, have a drink at the Crossing Inn and soak up the real outback atmosphere of the oldest pub in the Kimberley.

Lake Argyle

### Further information

ℹ **Fitzroy Crossing Visitor Centre** Cnr Great Northern Hwy & Flynn Dr; (08) 9191 5355.

### Where to stay

**Fitzroy River Lodge Motel, Hotel & Caravan Park** ★★ Camp/caravan site (2 people) $21–$24; safari tent $130 Great Northern Hwy; (08) 9191 5141.
**Crossing Inn** ★ Campsite (2 people) from $15; motel double $95 Skuthorpe Rd; (08) 9191 5080.
**Tarunda Caravan Park** ★ Camp/caravan site (2 people) $20–$23 Forrest Rd; (08) 9191 5330.

Driving near the Bungle Bungles

### Events

**Camp Drafting and Rodeo** Three-day event showcasing the skills of the outback's horse riders. Jul.
**Garnduwa Festival** A week-long series of sporting events. Oct.

## 5 Devonian Reef National Parks (1–3 days)

It's hard to imagine that these parks were once under water and that the gorges were once part of a reef. But 350 million years ago in the Devonian period, there was a gigantic inland sea in the West Kimberley. Now three national parks protect what is left of this reef.

Just north-east of Fitzroy Crossing is Geikie Gorge National Park. The spectacular sheer walls of Geikie Gorge, bleached by annual flooding, are best seen on a guided boat tour. Entry to the park is restricted during the Wet.

At Windjana Gorge National Park, look out for the primeval life forms fossilised within the gorge walls. To explore the 750 m-long cave that runs through the Napier Range at Tunnel Creek National Park, you'll need to wear sandshoes or sandals, carry a torch and be prepared to get wet. Nearby Pigeon's Cave was the hideout of an 1890s Aboriginal outlaw, Jandamarra, also known as 'Pigeon'.

### Further information

ℹ **CALM Broome** (Geikie Gorge National Park, Windjana Gorge National Park and Tunnel Creek National Park) (08) 9192 1036; www.naturebase.net

## 6 Halls Creek (1 day)

Lying 148 km to the south of Halls Creek is the Wolfe Creek Crater – the second-largest meteorite crater in the world and a place intrinsically linked with the rainbow snake of Aboriginal Dreaming. Scenic flights from Halls Creek are the best way to see the crater; you can also organise aerial tours of the Bungle Bungles from here. There's not much else to keep you in Halls Creek, except a collection of roadhouses that make for a good supply stop between Fitzroy Crossing and Purnululu National Park (see next entry).

### Further information

ℹ **Halls Creek Visitor Centre** Hall St; (08) 9168 6262.

### Tours

**Bungle Bungle Scenic Flights** 1300 136 629.
**Oasis Air** 1800 501 462.

## 7 Purnululu National Park (1–3 days)

A rough 50 km track off the Great Northern Highway between Halls Creek and Warmun leads to Purnululu National Park, which was added to the World Heritage List in 2003. It is home of the spectacular Bungle Bungle Range, a remarkable landscape of tiger-striped, beehive-shaped rock domes intersected by narrow, palm-lined gorges. Well-known to the Indigenous Kidja people, the Bungle Bungles were only 'discovered' in the 1980s. The national park was created in 1987, and the Bungle Bungles were added to the World Heritage list in 2003. A scenic flight from Halls Creek, Kununurra or Warmun is the best way to gain a perspective of the Bungle Bungles' massive size and spectacular scenery.

The most visited site in Purnululu is Cathedral Gorge, a fairly easy walk. A couple of days and a backpack allow you to explore nearby Piccaninny Gorge, camping overnight. If you do this, make sure you're well prepared and tell a ranger before setting out. On the northern side of the park is the easily accessible Echidna Chasm and Mini Palms, requiring a slightly longer walk.

Purnululu is only open from April to December, and is accessible by 4WD. The two campsites offer fresh water and toilets.

## Further information

**ⓘ CALM Kununurra** (Purnululu National Park) (08) 9168 4200; www.naturebase.net

## Tours

**East Kimberley Tours** These 'Bungle Bungle experts' offer an amazing array of tours to Purnululu. 1800 682 213; www.eastkimberleytours.com.au

**Alligator Airways** Choose from a 2 hr flight above the Bungle Bungles or a one-day Air & Ground Tour, which lets you see the Bungle Bungles from the air and then explore them on foot. 1800 632 533; www.alligatorairways.com.au

**Wilderness 4WD Adventures** Adventure is the name of the game on these camping safaris designed for fit, active people. See the Bungles on the five-day Kimberley Escape or the nine-day Kimberley Challenge. 1300 666 100 or (08) 8941 2161; www.wildernessadventures.com.au

## ⑧ Kununurra (2 days)

After the string of tiny outback towns that make up most of the Kimberley, Kununurra appears as an oasis of organisation to travel-weary backpackers. Purpose-built in the 1960s as the centre for the massive Ord River Irrigation Scheme – the town's name means 'meeting of big waters' – it is surrounded by attractions.

Nearby Mirima National Park, known to the locals as the 'mini-Bungles', features steep gorges, great views and those ungainly boab trees growing on rock faces. You can take a boat cruise on Lake Argyle to the south, the largest body of fresh water in Australia, which was created by damming the Ord River. (In a former life, the lake's islands were hills and ridges.) Over 100 km to the south is the Argyle Diamond Mine, which is both the world's largest diamond mine and the only producer of intense pink diamonds. Access by tour only.

## Further information

**ⓘ Kununurra Visitor Centre** Coolibah Dr; (08) 9168 1177; www.kununurratourism.com

## Tours

**Slingair Heliwork WA** Scenic flights over the Bungles and Lake Argyle or catch a helicopter ride when you're at the Bungles to get the full aerial impact. 1800 095 500; www.slingair.com.au

**Lake Argyle Cruises** These cruises range from a 2 hr morning tour on Lake Argyle to an all-day cruise that also takes in the Ord River. (08) 9168 7687; www.lakeargylecruises.com

**Big Waters Kimberley Canoe Safaris** This three-day, self-guided canoe safari will have you paddling from Lake Argyle to Kununurra along the Ord River, stopping at designated bush camps along the way. 1800 641 998; www.adventure.kimberley.net.au

## Where to eat and drink

**Valentine's Pizzeria** $ Offers a range of pizzas and Mexican food, all at reasonable prices. Cottontree Ave; (08) 9169 1167; daily 5pm–late.

**Stars in the Kimberley** $$ Good coffee in the outback, and some interesting eats to go with it.  4 Papuana St.

## Where to stay

**Kununurra Backpackers** ★★ Dorm $20–$22, double $52–$54 24 Knutwood Cres; 1800 641 998; www.adventure.kimberley.net.au

**Kimberley Croc YHA** ★★ Dorm $24.50–$25.50, twin or double $63.50–$73.50 257 Konkerberry Dr; (08) 9168 2702; www.yha.com.au

**Ivanhoe Village Caravan Resort** ★★★ Camp/caravan site (2 people) $12–$30; double cabin from $75 Cnr Ivanhoe Rd & Coolibah Dr; (08) 9169 1995; www.ivanhoevillageresort.com

**El Questro Wilderness Park** ★★★ TOP TREAT!! Lying 110 km west of Kununurra and extending 80 km into the heart of the Kimberley, this is one of the world's unique holiday destinations. Here you'll see rugged ranges, broad tidal flats, rainforest pockets, gorges and waterfalls. There are various accommodation options, ranging from the internationally acclaimed and super-expensive El Questro Homestead to camping along the Pentecost River for $15 a night (plus a $15 park permit). El Questro is open from April until the end of October. (08) 9169 1777; www.elquestro.com.au; www.elquestrohomestead.com.au

## Events

**Ord Valley Muster** Two-week festival featuring over 40 individual events and concluding with the award-winning Kimberley Moon Experience music concert. May.

**Lake Argyle Classic** A 10–20 km swim for solo, duo or quad teams in Lake Argyle. Jun.

Kimberley crocodile

For more detail
see maps
218 & 229

WESTERN AUSTRALIA

# Esperance and the Nullarbor
## Pleasure and plain

*Perth*

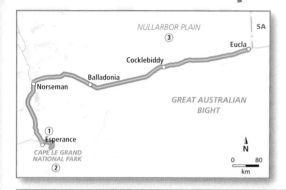

NULLARBOR PLAIN — SA
③
Eucla
Cocklebiddy
Balladonia
Norseman
GREAT AUSTRALIAN
BIGHT
① Esperance
CAPE LE GRAND
NATIONAL PARK
②
N
0    80
km

The coastline that surrounds the town of Esperance is among the most stunning in Australia. Here you'll find pristine beaches that are ideal for swimming, surfing, sailing and fishing. To the north-east lies the vast Nullarbor Plain – about as remote as you can get. Advanced bookings should be made for the limited accommodation en route, and travellers should observe basic outback travel precautions, such as ensuring adequate fuel and water supplies.

**Number of days to spend in this region: 5–7 days**

## Getting here

There are daily flights from Perth to Esperance with Skywest Airlines. Esperance Airport is 26 km from town. Car hire and a taxi service are both available from the airport. You can also take a bus with Transwa, operating from East Perth terminal to Esperance.

Skywest Airlines  1300 660 088; www.skywest.com.au

Taxi (08) 9071 1782.

Transwa  (08) 9071 2330; www.transwa.wa.gov.au

## ❶ Esperance (2–3 days)

Gaze at the sugar-white beaches edged by aquamarine waters and you'll understand why Esperance is a popular holiday spot. The Archipelago of the Recherche lies offshore, with a collection of 110 islands that provide a haven for seals and sea lions. Daily cruises take you to Woody Island, the only one you're allowed to land on; its safari huts offer a camping opportunity not to be missed.

The Great Ocean Drive, exploring the coastline west of Esperance, is 38 km of postcard-perfect scenery. Attractions include Australia's first wind farm, sheltered swimming at Twilight Cove and Pink Lake, rendered a lipstick-colour by algae. Stop at the many coastal lookouts and, if it's between June and October, you might see southern right whales out to sea.

### Further information
ⓘ **Esperance Visitor Centre** Museum Village, Dempster St; 1300 664 455 or (08) 9083 1555; www.visitesperance.com

Esperance coastline

### Tours

**McKenzies Island Cruises** This family-owned company offers half-day and full-day island wildlife tours cruising around the Recherche Archipelago aboard a 24 m catamaran. Daily transfers to Woody Island Sept–Apr. 71 The Esplanade; (08) 9071 5757; www.woodyisland.com.au

**Esperance Diving and Fishing** These are the folks to see if you want scuba or snorkelling tours, fishing charters, whale-watching tours or scenic cruises. Diving equipment is also sold and hired. 72 The Esplanade; (08) 9071 5111; www.esperancedivingandfishing.com.au

**Esperance 4WD & Dive Tours** All-day guided tours of the south coast for small groups include 4WD sightseeing, swimming, diving (if requested) and lunch. 11 Sampson St; (08) 9071 3357.

**Esperance Air Service** Take a 45-minute flight along Esperance's picturesque, sapphire-blue coastline for stunning views of Cape Le Grand, Lucky Bay and the Recherche Archipelago. (08) 9071 1467.

### Where to eat and drink

**Taylor Street Tearooms** 🟢🟢 You can eat inside, on the verandah or alfresco on the lawn. Big buffet breakfasts start the day, and it just keeps going. Licensed. Taylor St Jetty; (08) 9071 4317; daily 7am–10pm.

**Ocean Blues Cafe** 🟢🟢 Good for a big breakfast, a burger or focaccia for lunch, or an early dinner. 19 The Esplanade; (08) 9071 7107; Tue–Fri 9.30am–8.30pm, Sat–Sun 8am–8.30pm.

**Onshore Cafe** 🟢🟢 In addition to serving excellent coffee and light meals, Onshore has gifts, gourmet products and artwork for sale. 105 Dempster St; (08) 9071 7505; Tue–Fri 9.30am–8.30pm, Sat–Sun 8am–8.30pm.

## Where to stay

**Esperance Backpackers** ★★ Dorm $19, twin or double $48
14 Emily St; (08) 9071 4724.
**Blue Waters Lodge YHA** ★★ Dorm $23.50–$25.50, single $33.50–
$35.50, twin or double $53.50–$58.50 299 Goldfields Rd; (08) 9071
1040; www.yha.com.au
**Esperance Guesthouse** ★★★ Dorm $25, single $40, double $50
23 Daphne St; (08) 9071 3396; www.esperanceguesthouse.com.au

## Events

**Festival of the Wind** Biennial two-day event with food stalls,
concerts and family entertainment. Mar.
**French Weekend** A French-themed celebration including a bicycle
race, markets, movies and evening concerts. Jul.
**Esperance Annual Music Festival** Features local and interstate
musicians. Aug.
**Wildflower Show** A weekend of stunning wildflower displays. Sept.

## ❷ Cape Le Grand National Park (1–2 days)

Cape Le Grand is the first of two exquisite national parks east of
Esperance (the second, Cape Arid, is more remote). In summer the
beaches are close to paradise, with evocative names like Lucky Bay,
Hellfire Bay and Thistle Cove. This show-stopping trio of bays makes up
the 15 km, one-way Coastal Trail. If you start early, you'll have time for a
swim at each. Between the start at Le Grand Beach and the first stop at
Hellfire, walkers scale the 345 m granite outcrop of Mount Le Grand. You
will need to arrange a drop-off or pick-up from the start or the finish at
Rossiter Bay. There is camping at Lucky Bay and Le Grand Beach.

## Further information

ℹ **CALM Esperance** (Cape Le Grand National Park and Cape Arid
National Park) (08) 9071 3733; www.naturebase.net

## Tours

**Aussie Bight Expeditions** Full- and half-day 4WD safaris to secluded
beaches and bays around Esperance, including a half-day tour to Cape
Le Grand National Park and a full day tour to both Cape Le Grand and
Cape Arid national parks. (08) 9071 7778.
**Vacation Country Tours** Guided tours of Cape Le Grand National Park
and other scenic attractions within the Esperance area. 94 Pink Lake
Rd; (08) 9071 2227.

## ❸ The Nullarbor (4–5 days)

Covering 250 000 sq km, the Nullarbor Plain is the largest single piece of
limestone in the world. Although it can seem featureless, the country is
far from monotonous. The terrain is riddled with sinkholes, caverns and
caves, only some of which are open to the public. Murrawijinie Caves
include Koonalda Cave, containing rock art that dates back 20 000 years.

Crossing the Nullarbor is one of Australia's essential touring
experiences. This 2700 km rite of passage involves driving for days, so
make sure you have plenty of petrol and water. You can also travel on
the Trans Australia Railway, which crosses the Nullarbor further inland.

Attractions along the way include the town of Balladonia, which
made world headlines in 1979 when space debris from NASA's Skylab
landed nearby. The Cultural Heritage Museum, in the Balladonia Hotel
Motel, has displays on the crash-landing, local Indigenous culture, early
explorers and Afghan cameleers. Some 35 km east of Balladonia is a
signpost marking the 90-Mile Straight – the longest straight stretch
of road in Australia, and a great photo op! Once you pass Cocklebiddy,
visit the Eyre Bird Observatory for some birdwatching, bushwalking and
beachcombing. Twilight Cove, 32 km to the south, is a top fishing and
whale-watching spot with views overlooking the Great Australian Bight.
Your last stop before hitting the South Australian border is Eucla, the
largest settlement on the Nullarbor Plain. The much-photographed ruins
of a telegraph station lies in the sand dunes at the original townsite.

## Further information

ℹ **Norseman Visitor Centre** 68 Roberts St; (08) 9039 1071;
www.norseman.info
**Eyre Bird Observatory** Eyre Telegraph Station; (08) 9039 3450;
overnight stays available; www.eyrebirds.org

## Where to eat and drink

**Norseman-Eyre Hotel** 💲 Filling counter meals for a no-fuss feed.
90 Roberts St; (08) 9039 1130; lunch & dinner daily.
**Norseman Great Western Motel** 💲💲 The motel's licensed
restaurant serves up good home-style cooking. Prinsep St;
(08) 9039 1633; summer daily 6.30-8.30pm, winter daily 6-8pm;
www.norsemangreatwesternmotel.com.au

## Where to stay

**Lodge 101 Guest House & Backpackers** ★★ Dorm $20, single
$35, double $55 101 Prinsep St; Norseman; (08) 9039 1541.
**Balladonia Hotel Motel** ★★ Powered/unpowered site (2 people)
$21.90/$13, dorm $22.50, budget single/double $39/$85, motel
single/double $99/$106. Eyre Hwy; Balladonia; (08) 9039 3453.
**Cocklebiddy Roadhouse** ★ Powered/unpowered site (2 people)
$19/$13, single $82, double $99.50. Eyre Hwy; Cocklebiddy; (08) 9039 3462.
**Eucla Motor Hotel** ★★ Powered/unpowered site (2 people)
$20/$15, budget single/double $35/$60, motel single/double
$90/$105. Eyre Hwy; Eucla; (08) 9039 3468.

## Events

**Norseman Cup** Family day of racing, entertainment and two-up. Mar.
**Border Dash** Fundraising run from Border Village to Eucla. Oct.

# SOUTH AUSTRALIA

# CONTENTS

Adelaide 152
TOP REGIONS:
Barossa Valley and the Adelaide Hills 161
Kangaroo Island 165
Flinders Ranges 170
Limestone Coast 174

## Visitor information

South Australia Tourism Commission 1300 655 276 or (08) 8303 2220; www.southaustralia.com

## FAST FACTS

**Hottest place** 50.7°C – Australia's hottest recorded temperature – was reached in Oodnadatta in 1960

**Driest place** Lake Eyre is Australia's driest place with a mere 125 mm of rainfall per year

**Longest place name** Nooldoonooldoona, a waterhole in the Gammon Ranges

**Best discoveries and inventions** penicillin by Howard Florey; the wine cask by Tom Angove

**Best political stunt** Premier Don Dunstan wore pink hot pants into parliament to campaign for gay law reform in the 1970s

With the majority of this southern land arid and uninhabitable, South Australia often fails to attract visitors in the same way as Queensland's stunning beaches. But there is just as much to see and do here as any other state. Towards the coast, you can drive through gorgeous vineyards, see incredible underground cave scenery, get up close to a range of wildlife or hike through a national park. The capital city of Adelaide is small, but with enough nightlife to please the most fervent city tenant. And if you are interested in heading due west to the outback, the town of Coober Pedy is a unique, opal-mining town where inhabitants live underground. No two parts are the same in South Australia, and that's what makes it so much fun.

# Top region highlights

## Kangaroo Island

This unspoilt wildlife refuge is jam-packed with activities for visitors. You can watch cute penguins waddling in from the ocean, see unique national park landscapes, go adventure caving and sand dune surfing, or just relax on the island's beautiful northern beaches. p. 165

## Barossa Valley

Australia's best-known wine region offers vine-covered hills dotted with historic villages, stone cottages and old wine estates. Oh, and plenty of cellar doors for tastings. p. 161

## Flinders Ranges National Park

This ancient landscape of rippled outback terrain and exposed ridges culminates in the striking natural amphitheatre of Wilpena Pound. Startling colours and scenery will take your breath away. p. 172

## Coober Pedy

One of the most unique towns in all of Australia, and the site of the world's leading opal producer. Locals live mostly underground, due to scorching temperatures in summer. p. 170

## Naracoorte Caves

Over 60 caves can be found at Naracoorte, several of them open to the public. This is the perfect spot for some adventure caving – for those who don't mind a tight squeeze. p. 177

# Other regions worth a look

## Fleurieu Peninsula

This hugely popular and accessible destination won't leave you bored. It is known for its magnificent coastline, scenic hinterland, McLaren Vale wineries and gourmet produce.

## Yorke Peninsula

This long, boot-shaped peninsula is one of South Australia's most popular beachside holiday destinations. An ideal spot for some fishing, diving and surfing.

## Port Lincoln

Known as the seafood capital of Australia, this place oozes cozy, coastal town charm, with great beaches, gardens, parks and dining spots.

## Nullarbor Plain

The Nullarbor, Latin for 'treeless', is a plain of 250 000 sq km, resting on a massive area of limestone-riddled caves. Along the coast, sheer-faced cliffs drop suddenly into the waters of the Great Australian Bight.

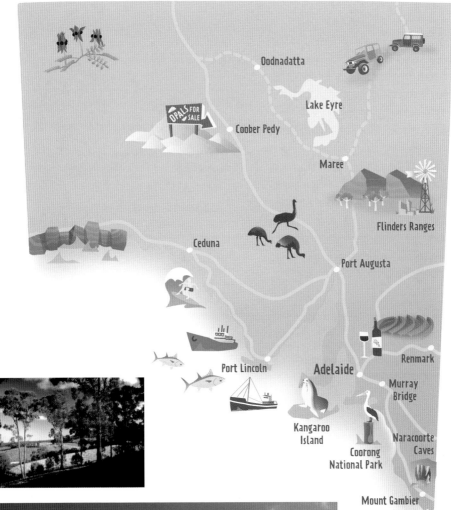

Oodnadatta

Lake Eyre

OPALS FOR SALE

Coober Pedy

Maree

Flinders Ranges

Ceduna

Port Augusta

Renmark

Port Lincoln

Adelaide

Murray Bridge

Kangaroo Island

Naracoorte Caves

Coorong National Park

Mount Gambier

# Adelaide

Let's face it, Adelaide is not known for being the most happening Australian city, but maybe the locals just like to keep it that way so that their fantastic pubs and bars don't get overcrowded. Small, cosmopolitan and with a touch of elegant panache, Adelaide features parklands and broad streets that rarely see a traffic jam. Bordered by the Mount Lofty Ranges and the gorgeous sandy beaches of Gulf St Vincent, this is a city that knows how to enjoy itself. Its restaurants are second to none, the bars are unique, the music scene is vibrant, and the arts culture is bustling (the best times to be around are during top events like the Adelaide Fringe Festival or WOMADelaide). Enjoy the good life in the City of Churches.

## Top attractions

### Government House and Parliament House

These impressive buildings sit at the intersection of North Terrace and King William Road. Government House, the oldest of its kind in Australia, is set on a sweep of manicured lawns and has two open days a year, in spring and autumn. Along with the War Memorial at the corner of Kintore Avenue, these buildings make an interesting walk. Phone (08) 8203 9800 for Government House open days; guided tours of Parliament House run on non-sitting days (Mon & Fri) 10am & 2pm; sitting days are published on www.parliament.sa.gov.au

### Migration Museum

This museum details immigrant life from pioneering days up to now. The building has a long history connected with refuge – it was once Adelaide's Destitute Asylum, where many of the city's aged, homeless and underprivileged lived (and died). The stories of the women and children who lived there from the mid-1800s to 1918 are told in the 'Behind the Wall' exhibition. 82 Kintore Ave; (08) 8207 7570; Mon–Fri 10am–5pm, weekends & public holidays 1–5pm; entry by donation.

Adelaide Fringe Festival

### Visitor information centre

South Australian Visitor and Travel Centre 18 King William St; 1300 655 276; www.southaustralia.com

### Climate

Adelaide's weather is described as temperate Mediterranean, with temperatures in summer rising to around 40°C on a number of days, and falling to a minimum near zero a couple of times during winter. The in-between seasons are near-perfect, with maximum temperatures in the mid 20s for much of March, April, September and October.

### South Australian Museum

For over a century, the South Australian Museum has had a crucial role in researching, documenting and displaying Aboriginal culture. The excellent Australian Aboriginal Cultures Gallery is the world's most comprehensive Aboriginal cultural exhibition. Traditional items include shields, canoes and boomerangs, while other displays explain about Aboriginal people today. The Origin Energy Fossil Gallery is a fascinating collection of opalised fossils, a distinctive part of South Australia's natural history – look up to see the impressive model skeleton of the Addyman plesiosaur, a marine animal over 100 million years old. North Tce; (08) 8207 7500; daily 10am–5pm; admission free.

### Tandanya – National Aboriginal Cultural Institute

The name of this vibrant meeting place translates to 'place of the Red Kangaroo' in the language of the Kaurna people, the traditional owners of the land on which Adelaide stands. Tandanya aims to exhibit the contemporary culture, art and lifestyles of Australia's Indigenous people, while still acknowledging the traditions these cultures are built on. In the gallery see exciting works by emerging artists, or taste modern versions of traditional bush tucker in the cafe. Indigenous tours are also offered, encompassing both the centre and the grounds. 253 Grenfell St; daily 10am–5pm; admission fee applies; tours by arrangement only.

### Adelaide Zoo

The zoo's 19th-century buildings and landscaped gardens have led many to call it the most attractive zoo in Australia. The Elephant House is a highlight of 1900s architecture – the enclosure's design was based on an Indian temple, and is now classified by the National Trust. The zoo also has a great bird collection, with native Australian birds at the Australian Rainforest Aviary and more exotic displays in the Amazon Aviary. Frome Rd; (08) 8267 3255; daily 9.30am–5pm; admission fee applies.

### JamFactory

Each year a rigorous process occurs to whittle down the applications of hopefuls keen on becoming a Design

LIGHT'S
VISION

To
Port Adelaide,
Parkside &
Semaphore

ADELAIDE ZOO

Moonlight
Cinema

ADELAIDE
OVAL

BOTANIC
PARK

MONTEFIORE

KING

FROME

PLANE     TREE     DR

Torrens

ADELAIDE
BOTANIC
GARDEN

To
Norwood

PIONEER
WOMEN'S
MEMORIAL
GARDEN

RD

Adelaide
University
Union
Cinema

WILLIAM

ADELAIDE
FESTIVAL
CENTRE

NATIONAL WINE
CENTRE OF
AUSTRALIA

To
Henley Beach, Hindmarsh
Thebarton, The Gov &
South Australian
Brewing Company

City Pie
Cart

PARLIAMENT HOUSE
& OLD PARLIAMENT
HOUSE

MIGRATION
MUSEUM

RD

GOVERNMENT
HOUSE

SOUTH
AUSTRALIAN
MUSEUM

Amalfi

TCE

LOCO

ADELAIDE

HQ
Complex

Fowlers
Live

NORTH

Mercury
Cinema

Swish

STATE LIBRARY OF
SOUTH AUSTRALIA

ART GALLERY
OF SOUTH
AUSTRALIA

Rhino
Room

Palace East
End Cinemas
& Sugar

RUNDLE
PARK

WEST

Worldsend
Hotel

Electric
Circus

Woolshed
on Hindley

Tatts
Backpackers

RUNDLE     MALL

Church

The Austral

RUNDLE     RD

Mojo
West

HINDLEY

GRAY

Enigma

ST

The
Apothecary

Red
Square

Blue Galah
Backpackers
Hostel

Nova
Cinema

Chocolate
Bean

Belgian
Beer Cafe

RYMILL
PARK

Moskva
Vodka
Bar

CURRIE

Greater
Union
Cinema

The Jerusalem
Sheshkabab
House

ST

GRENFELL

Jade
Monkey

Wallis
Academy
Cinema
City

ST

TANDANYA

The
Exeter

My Place Adelaide
Backpackers Hostel

WAYMOUTH

Tonic

Zhivago

Shakespeare
Backpackers
International
Hostel

KING

ST     PIRIE

ADELAIDE

Sumo
Station

FROME

HUTT

ST

Annie's
Place

Adelaide
Central YHA

City Pie Cart

ST

FLINDERS

PULTENEY

FRANKLIN

Sunny's Adelaide
Backpackers Hostel

Cannon Street
Backpackers

ST

VICTORIA
SQUARE

Backpack Oz

CARDWELL

ST

0          200

metres

GROTE

ST

WAKEFIELD

A21

Mars
Bar

Ky Chow

ST

ANGAS

GOUGER

MORPHETT

Crown &
Sceptre

ST

TCE

Directors Studios

Queens
Arms
Hotel

RUSSELL

WILLIAM

CARRINGTON

Citrus
Restaurant

ST

WRIGHT

ST

ST

Hawkers
Corner

HALIFAX

Adelaide
Travellers
Inn

To
Glenelg

ST

ST

To
Boho Bar

To
Mt Barker

N

ADELAIDE

Associate of the JamFactory. Only the best make it into this institution's training programs, which are split into ceramics, furniture, metal (including jewellery) and glass work. The pieces produced by each studio are said to be some of the most innovative craft in Australia. Changing exhibits of international and JamFactory works are displayed in the gallery, and many one-off designs are available for purchase in the store. 19 Morphett St; (08) 8410 0727; Mon–Sat 10am–5pm, Sun 1–5pm; admission free; tours of the studios Mon & Fri 10am.

### Historic Adelaide Gaol

This gaol was in operation as late as 1988. Today you can tour the cells and yards, and see an array of artefacts, including items confiscated from prisoners. The truly obsessed can take a night tour. 18 Gaol Rd, Thebarton; (08) 8231 4062; Mon–Fri & Sun 11am–5pm (last entry 3.30pm); bookings required for night tours; admission fee applies.

### Port Adelaide's dolphins

The thick mangroves, mud and mosquitoes didn't endear the Port Adelaide area to the early settlers; hence the name Port Misery. Today it is a haven for birdlife and a pod of playful bottlenose dolphins. You can drive along the Dolphin Trail to six hot spots where dolphins are commonly sighted (maps are available from the visitor centre) or take a cruise from Queens Wharf near the lighthouse – the dolphins often swim alongside the boat. For a special outing, book a cruise on one of the tall ships; the *One and All* or the *Falie*. Port Adelaide Visitor Centre, 66 Commercial Rd; (08) 8405 6560; several cruise companies operate on Sun; bookings advised for other days.

### Haigh's Chocolates

Australia's oldest chocolate-maker is located just south of Adelaide's CBD. The visitor centre includes a viewing area, displays of original factory machinery and a delightful, old-world shop with a tempting array of chocolates. 154 Greenhill Rd, Parkside; (08) 8372 7070; free tours Mon–Sat 11am, 1pm & 2pm (bookings essential).

## Getting around

Adelaide has a range of public transport. First there is the city's sole tram, which heads from Victoria Square in the city to the seaside suburb of Glenelg. Then there is the Adelaide O-Bahn, a kind of cross between a bus and a tram that forms the longest and fastest guided bus service in the world. It travels along Currie and Grenfell streets in the city, then heads out to Westfield Tea Tree Plaza in Modbury, in the north-eastern suburbs.

The City Loop and the Beeline are two free buses that operate around the city centre. The City Loop runs every 15 minutes and takes in North Terrace and Light, Hindmarsh and Victoria squares; while the Beeline runs every 5 minutes and includes Victoria Square, King William Street and the railway station. Both services operate during shopping hours.

Four train routes operate from the CBD to Adelaide's suburbs (to Gawler in the north, Outer Harbour in the north-west, Noarlunga in the south and Belair in the Adelaide Hills). There are also plenty of bus services operating around the suburbs. All public transport in Adelaide is covered by one ticketing system, and tickets can be purchased at train stations and on buses and trams.

Public transport Passenger Transport InfoLine 1800 182 160; Adelaide Metro InfoCentre, Cnr King William & Currie sts (08) 8210 1000

Motoring organisation RAA (08) 8202 4600, roadside assistance 13 1111

Car rental Avis 13 6333; Budget 13 2727; Hertz 13 3039; Thrifty 1300 367 227; Europcar 1300 131 390

Taxis Suburban Taxis 13 1008; Yellow Cabs 13 2227; Independent Taxis 13 2211

Tourist bus Adelaide Explorer (replica tram) (08) 8231 7172

Bicycle hire Contact Bicycle SA for operators (08) 8232 2644

# Other attractions worth a look

Art Gallery of South Australia Holds a comprehensive collection of Australian art, as well as European works by the likes of French sculptor Auguste Rodin. North Tce; (08) 8207 7000; daily 10am–5pm; general admission free.

State Library of South Australia A magnificent 19th-century building and the state's largest library. Visit the Bradman Collection to see cricket memorabilia belonging to the great Sir Donald Bradman. Cnr North Tce & Kintore Ave; 1800 182 013; Mon–Wed 10am–8pm, Thur–Fri 10am–6pm, Sat–Sun 10am–5pm; admission free.

Adelaide Botanic Garden Visit the Palm House and the Bicentennial Conservatory, lined with lush rainforest and native plants. North Tce; (08) 8222 9311; Mon–Fri from 7.15am, Sat–Sun from 9am (closing times vary throughout yr); general admission free (fee applies for Bicentennial Conservatory).

National Wine Centre of Australia South Australia is known for its wine, but if you can't make it to the Barossa, why not take in some history and sample some plonk here? Cnr Botanic & Hackney rds; (08) 8303 3355; daily 9am–5pm; admission free.

Adelaide Festival Centre Four large theatres make this the heart of arts in the city. King William Rd; (08) 8216 8600.

Lights Vision and Park Colonel William Light designed this park, which has great views of the city. Montefiore Rd & Ward St.

South Australia Maritime Museum Immerse yourself in everything water related. Look out for the striking lighthouse. 126 Lipson St, Port Adelaide; (08) 8207 6255; daily 10am–5pm; admission fee applies.

Ships Graveyard Take in this magnificent shipwreck, one of the few in Australia that you can view from land. Garden Island Bridge; for a closer look by kayak, tour with Blue Water Sea (08) 8295 8812.

South Australia Brewing Company Learn all about making beer, from the raw materials through to brewing, keg handling, canning and bottling. 107 Port Rd, Thebarton; (08) 8354 8744; tours Mon–Thur 10.30am & 1pm (bookings essential); admission fee applies.

# Where to eat

East End A lively precinct with good Greek food at Eros (277 Rundle St), great coffee from Al Fresco (260 Rundle St) and renovated pubs. Our favourite: Amalfi 🅢🅢 ♡ This place is littered with chefs in the early hours, so it must be doing something right. Home-style Italian cooking with excellent gourmet pizzas. 29 Frome St; (08) 8223 1948; Mon–Thur noon–2.30pm & 5.30–10.30pm, Fri noon–2.30pm & 5.30–11pm, Sat 5.30–11pm.

Hindley Street Lebanese and Italian are among the offerings. Our favourite: The Jerusalem Sheshkabab House 🅢 ♡ One of the best and cheapest Lebanese joints in town. While the decor may

South Australian Museum

not be fancy, the food is fantastic. Indulge in the Lebanese banquet – no need for breakfast the next day. 131b Hindley St; (08) 8212 6185; Mon–Sat noon–midnight, Sun 4–11pm.

**Gouger Street** For cultural variety and value-for-money.
Our favourite: **Ky Chow** 🟢 ♡ Not the prettiest place in the world, but the best salt and pepper squid ever. 82 Gouger St; (08) 8221 5411; Mon–Fri noon–2.30pm, Sat–Thur 5.30–10pm, Fri 5.30pm–midnight.

**Hutt Street** A belt of cafes that are a touch more up-market.
Our favourite: **Citrus Restaurant** 🟢🟢🟢 TOP TREAT!! ♡ Modern Australian cuisine with Italian influences. Try linguini with chilli and lemon rocket salad. 199 Hutt St; (08) 8224 0100; Mon–Fri 7–11.30am, noon–2.30pm & 6–9pm, Sat 7–11.30am & 6–9.30pm, Sun 7–11.30am; www.citrus.net.au

**Henley Square** Everything from fish and chips to Greek, Thai and Italian.
Our favourite: **Zootz Kitchen Bar** 🟢🟢 💠 On Henley Beach, the perfect place to relax while you're downing a hearty breakfast. Henley Sq, 257 Seaview Rd, Henley Beach; (08) 8235 9990; Mon–Thur 7am–9pm, Fri–Sun 7am–9.30pm; www.zootz.com.au

**O'Connell Street, North Adelaide** Pizza, pasta and coffee, and pubs with good atmosphere.
Our favourite: **Scuzzi Cafe** 🟢 ♡ Some of the best pizza and pasta in town. Interesting daily specials at affordable prices. 99 O'Connell St; (08) 8239 2233; daily 8am–3pm & 5–11pm.

**The Parade, Norwood** A range of cafes and a couple of good pubs.
Our favourite: **Paul's on Parade** 🟢🟢 ♡ This eatery is famous for its seafood. A great place on a hot summer's night. 218 The Pde, Norwood; (08) 8333 2633; daily 11.30am–

2.30pm, Mon–Thur & Sun 5–9.30pm, Fri–Sat 5–10pm.

## Other places to eat

**Chocolate Bean** 🟢 ♡ A chocolate paradise. Order the 'chocolate filth' – rich cake accompanied by shot glasses filled with cream, ganache and mousse. 18 Union St; (08) 8359 3399; Mon 11am–8pm, Tue–Thur 11am–10pm, Fri 11am–10.30pm, Sat noon–10.30pm.

**The Tap Inn** 🟢 💠 This bizarrely themed joint has an amazing tapas menu, great atmosphere and a golf driving range inside. Kent Town Hotel, 76 Rundle St; (08) 8362 2116; Birdies Restaurant daily noon–3pm & 6–9pm; www.tapinn.com.au

**Sumo Station** 🟢 💠 The sushi is scrumptious and meals are also available from the teppanyaki grill. All very cheap. 172 Pulteney St; (08) 8232 0188; Tue–Thur 6–10pm, Fri–Sat 6–11pm, Sun 6–10pm; www.sumostation.com.au

**Hawkers Corner** 🟢 ♡ A cheap-eats institution. The Malay seafood laksa is a highlight. 141 West Tce; (08) 8231 2676; Tue–Sat 5–10pm, Sun 11.30am–8.30pm.

**City pie carts** Every visitor should try a pie floater (a unique Adelaide creation featuring a meat pie floating in a bowl of pea soup). There are two regular carts: one outside the Railway Station on North Tce; the other on Victoria Sq near the GPO.

## Out and about
### Cinemas

**Mercury Cinema** 13 Morphett St; (08) 8410 0979.
**Wallis Academy Cinema** 10–20 Hindmarsh Sq; (08) 8223 5000.
**Greater Union Cinema** 128 Hindley St; (08) 8231 1100.
**Palace East End Cinemas** (art house selection) 274 Rundle St; (08) 8232 3434.
**Nova Cinema** (art house selection) 251 Rundle St; (08) 8232 3434.
**Wallis Piccadilly Cinema** 181 O'Connell St; (08) 8267 1500.

**Where to shop**

**Rundle Mall, City** The CBD's main shopping area, with major department stores as well as clothing, chocolates and much more.

**Melbourne Street, North Adelaide** Adelaide's most exclusive strip, with designer boutiques.

**The Parade, Norwood** Very cosmopolitan, with an array of stores and plenty of places to stop for a coffee, a meal or a drink.

**King William Road, Hyde Park** Hip fashion outlets sprinkled among cafes, and furniture and homeware stores.

**Harbour Town** This complex has seconds and discount stores.

**Magill Road, Stepney** For antiques and second-hand treasures.

**Mount Barker Cinemas** 17 Adelaide Rd, Mount Barker; (08) 8391 2777.
**Adelaide University Union Cinema** (cheap tickets for classic and modern films, every Thur 7pm) Level 5, Union Building, Adelaide University; (08) 8303 3410.
**Moonlight Cinema** (Nov–Feb, new releases and classic films) Plane Tree Dr, Adelaide Botanic Gardens; 1300 364 328.

### Live music

**HQ Complex** The premier live music venue in Adelaide. The complex transforms into a dance club on Friday and Saturday nights. Miami Nights on Fridays has the best Latino, R'n'B and reggae music around. 1 North Tce; (08) 8221 1245; Wed & Fri 8pm–3am, Sat 9pm–6am, open other nights for concerts and events; www.hqcomplex.com.au

**The Gov** The Governor Hindmarsh is Australian music at its best. See amazing local talent, as well as international treats. 59 Port Rd, Hindmarsh; (08) 8340 0744; Mon–Sat 11am–9pm; front bar and music area open later on weekends, times change depending on gigs; www.thegov.com.au

**Enigma** An alternative music venue that always pulls great crowds. You might see a lesser-known band before they hit it big. 173 Hindley St; (08) 8212 2313; Thur–Sat 7pm–late, occasional Sun show; www.enigmabar.com.au

## Sport

Adelaide has been passionate about cricket from its earliest beginnings. Until his death in 2001, Adelaide was the proud home of Australia's greatest cricketer, Sir Donald Bradman. The city is also home to the Adelaide Oval, regarded as one of the most beautiful sporting arenas in the world. The oval has a charming blend of historic and contemporary grandstand architecture and a scoreboard more than a century old. Adelaide's cricket test, usually in December, is a great event.

With two local AFL teams, Adelaide and Port Adelaide, football is the city's other sporting passion. Showdown is the twice-yearly match between the two teams. AAMI Stadium at West Lakes is the city's home of AFL.

In March there is a V8 motor race that takes over the city. Sections of the Clipsal 500 Adelaide track are run on Wakefield Road and East Terrace in the south-east of the city, finishing at Victoria Park Racecourse.

Also on the calendar is the AAPT Championships, the international tennis tournament held at Memorial Drive near the Adelaide Oval in early January. Adelaide United soccer team matches are held at Hindmarsh Stadium, and the NBL 36ers play basketball on their home court at Beverley.

Worldsend Hotel For some cool jazz in a pub setting, look no further then Worldsend. The Tuesday night jazz show is an Adelaide institution. 208 Hindley St; (08) 8231 9137; Mon–Fri 11am–late, Sat 4pm–late; www.worldsendhotel.com.au

Fowlers Live A former turn-of-the-century flour factory, now one of the most popular music venues. The atmosphere is crazy when this place is full. 68 North Tce; (08) 8212 0255; daily 10am–4am; www.fowlerslive.com.au

Jade Monkey A more intimate venue that's like watching a gig in your own lounge room. Mostly local acts. 29a Twin St; (08) 8232 0950; Thur–Sat 9pm–late.

## Pubs and bars

The Exeter A lively pub in the centre of Adelaide's East End. With front and lounge bars, as well as a beer garden, this is one of the more popular pubs in town. 246 Rundle St; (08) 8223 2623; daily 11am–late.

The Austral A casual mix of classic pub and trendy hangout. Come in for a pub meal. 205 Rundle St; (08) 8223 4660; daily 11am–late; www.theaustral.com

Belgian Beer Cafe A huge selection of local and international brews on hand. 27–29 Ebenezer Pl; (08) 8359 3400; Sun–Thur noon–9.30pm, Fri–Sat noon–10.30pm, bar open later; www.oostende.com.au

Woolshed on Hindley The only pub in town that has a mechanical bull on site. Try it! 94 Hindley St; (08) 8231 3023; daily 24 hrs; www.woolshedonhindley.com.au

Crown and Sceptre This bar is just too cool. It screams funk and has over 380 different beverages to choose from. 308 King William St; (08) 8212 4159; Mon–Wed 10am–1am, Thur 10am–2am, Fri 10am–3am, Sat 10am–5am, Sun noon–1am; www.sceptre.com.au

Mojo West This is an unassuming, very funky little bar that plays some of the best in hip-hop. 258a Hindley St; (08) 8221 5050; Thur 8pm–late, Fri–Sat 9pm–late; www.mojowest.net

The Apothecary An unusual yet graceful wine bar. This heritage-listed building is strewn with antique pharmacy cabinets. Come for a meal or just tapas. 118 Hindley St; (08) 8212 9099; Tue–Thur 4pm–late, Fri noon–late, Sat 4pm–late; www.theapothecary1878.com.au

Swish This part bar, part club, part lounge gets rocking every Friday and Saturday night, with free entry and great drink specials. Stamford Plaza Adelaide, 150 North Tce; (08) 8461 0860; daily 11am–late; swishbar.com

Boho Bar Carnival-inspired decor sets the scene for fortune tellers, Wednesday's 80s night and DJs and live bands on weekends. Half-priced lunches daily. 27 Unley Rd, Parkside; (08) 8271 0274; Mon–Thur noon–midnight, Fri–Sat noon–1am, Sun noon–11pm; www.bohobar.com.au

Botanic Bar Home to velvety sounds and extravagant cocktails. DJs play everything from African beats to garage. 310 North Tce; (08) 8227 0799; Mon 8.30pm–late, Tue–Fri noon–late, Sat 4pm–late; www.sahotels.com.au/botanicbar

## Top events

Schützenfest Traditional German folk festival with music, food, and frivolity. Jan.

Jacobs Creek Tour Down Under Bike riders descend on Adelaide for this race into the hills. Jan.

Adelaide Festival of Arts The city's defining event, and one of the world's highly regarded arts festivals. Feb–Mar (even-numbered yrs).

Adelaide Fringe Alongside the Festival of Arts, the edgy performances of this world-renowned festival are great entertainment. Feb–Mar.

WOMADelaide A huge festival of world music and dance in Botanic Park. Mar.

Clipsal 500 V8 supercars race on city streets; said to be Australia's best motor event. Mar.

Glendi Festival Greek culture, food, song and dance. Apr.

Tasting Australia International event celebrating food, wine and beer as well as chefs and writers. Oct (odd-numbered yrs).

Feast Festival One of the country's top gay and lesbian events, with theatre, film, dance and more. Nov.

LOCO This 24-hour party is Adelaide's newest and funkiest bar, with modern decor and a chilled-out vibe. SKYCITY Adelaide, Railway Station Bld, North Tce; (08) 8212 2811; daily 24 hrs; www.skycityadelaide.com.au

## Nightclubs

Sugar This place is many things – bar, cafe, even an art gallery. But it works best as a nightclub. Packed out on the weekends, Sugar is always the last to close. Level 1, 274 Rundle St; (08) 8223 6160; Mon–Fri 8pm–3am, Sat 8pm–4am; www.sugarclub.com.au

Tonic A stylish venue offering two rooms, a separate VIP lounge, and an outside area at the front. The place to go if you're into R'n'B. 63 Light Sq; (08) 8221 5145; Thur 5–10.30pm, Fri 5pm–3am, Sat 8pm–5am; www.tonicbar.com.au

Moskva Vodka Bar Dress up and come early to avoid the long lines. Once you get in, it's bliss. Even the female bathroom has a champagne bar and perfumery. 192 Hindley St; (08) 8211 9007; Fri–Sat 9pm–5am.

Electric Circus Don't be put off by the dingy stairway leading to this underground club

– the place is energy itself in nightclub form with the best DJs in town. There are tangy cocktails and comfy lounges. 17–19 Crippen Pl; (08) 8410 4844; Fri–Sat 10pm–5am; www.electriccircus.com.au

**Church** This place used to be a synagogue. With mile-high ceilings and funky decor, rooms on various levels cater for whatever type of music you're in the mood for. 9 Synagogue Pl; (08) 8223 4233; Fri–Sat 9pm–5am; www.churchthenightclub.com.au

**Rhino Room** This place has a double personality: as a hip-hop dance venue and laugh-out-loud comedy club. Level 1, 13 Frome St; (08) 8227 1611; Wed–Sat 9pm–3am.

**Zhivago** The chilled-out reggae vibe attracts plenty of cool cats. Friday nights sees a young crowd. 155 Waymouth St; (08) 8212 0569; Mon–Sun 9.30pm–late.

**Red Square** With multiple levels and some of the city's best DJs, Red Square has been proclaimed one of Adelaide's best clubs for R'n'B. 111 Hindley St; (08) 8221 5688; Fri 10pm–7am, Sat 5pm–10am; www.redsquarecomplex.com.au

## Performing arts

**Adelaide Festival Centre** King William Rd; (08) 8216 8600.

**State Theatre Company of South Australia** Adelaide Railway Station, Station Rd; (08) 8231 5151.

**The Bakehouse Theatre** 255 Angas St; (08) 8227 0505.

**Her Majesty's Theatre** 58 Grote St;

(08) 8216 8600.

**Holden Street Theatres** 34 Holden St, Hindmarsh; (08) 8223 1450.

**Nexus Multicultural Arts Centre** Lion Arts Centre, cnr North Tce & Morphett St; (08) 8212 4276.

**Patch Theatre Company** Lion Arts Centre, cnr North Tce & Morphett St; (08) 8218 8411.

**The Weimar Room** 27–29 Hindley St; (08) 8410 4700.

## Where to stay

**For further information and reviews on these hostels, please visit www.bugaustralia.com, www.hostelaustralia.com or www.hostelz.com**

**Backpack Oz** ★ ★ ★ Dorm $22, single $49, double $55 144 Wakefield St; (08) 8223 3551; www.backpackoz.com.au

**My Place Adelaide Backpackers Hostel** ★ ★ ★ Dorm $21, twin and double $58 257 Waymouth St; (08) 8221 5299; www.adelaidehostel.com.au

**Blue Galah Backpackers Hostel** ★ ★ ★ Dorm $23–$25, single, twin and double $70 Level 1, 62 King William St; (08) 8231 9295; www.bluegalah.com.au

**Adelaide Central YHA** ★ ★ ★ Dorm $26.50, twin and double $68.50 135 Waymouth St; (08) 8414 3010; www.yha.com.au

**Adelaide Travellers Inn** ★ ★ Dorm $22–$25, double $60–$70 220 Hutt St; (08) 8224 0753; www.adelaidebackpackers.com.au

**Tatts Backpackers** ★ ★ Dorm $16, twin and double $56 17 Hindley St; 1800 133 355.

**Shakespeare Backpackers International Hostel** ★ ★ Dorm $23, twin and double $66 123 Waymouth St; (08) 8231 7655; www.bluegalah.com.au/index_Shakeys.html

**Annie's Place** ★ ★ Dorm $20, double $60–$65 239 Franklin St; (08) 8212 2668; www.anniesplace.com.au

**Sunny's Adelaide Backpackers Hostel** ★ ★ Dorm $22, single $38, double $55 139 Franklin St; (08) 8231 2430; www.sunnys.com.au

**Cannon Street Backpackers** ★ ★ Dorm $19–$22, single $55, twin and double $57

Adelaide Central Market

110 Franklin St; (08) 8410 1218; www.cannonst.com.au

**Director's Studio Adelaide** ★ ★ ★ TOP TREAT!! Standard room from $89 259 Gouger St; (08) 8213 2500; www.savillehotelgroup.com

## Tours and activities

**Adelaide Oval Tours** Get an up-close view of this Adelaide sporting icon. Tours depart from the southern gate, Mon–Fri (on non-event days) at 10am. No bookings required. www.cricketsa.com.au

**Adelaide Food and Wine Tours** A range of tours, including following experts through Adelaide's famous Central Market, chocolate tours and a 'Grazing on Gouger' tour: five courses at five of Gouger Street's best

restaurants. Bookings (08) 8263 0265. www.topfoodandwinetours.com.au
**Adelaide Sightseeing** City tours and trips to Mount Lofty. Bus tour stops include Haigh's Chocolates, Glenelg Beach, Colonel Light's Lookout and Rundle Mall. Bookings (08) 8413 6199. www.adelaidesightseeing.com.au
**Enjoy Adelaide** Half-day city tours and further regional expeditions. See St Peters

Cathedral, the SA Museum, the Torrens River, and a heap more. Bookings (08) 8332 1401. www.enjoyadelaide.com.au
**City of Adelaide Historical Walking Trails** Pick up a brochure from the visitor centre and head out on one of a series of themed walks.
**Port Walks** Take a walk through historic Port Adelaide. Contact the Port Adelaide Visitor

Centre for details (08) 8405 6560.
**Yurrebilla Trail** Take in the magnificent bushland on Adelaide's doorstep on this 52 km trail that links Black Hill and Morialta conservation parks in the north with Belair National Park in the south. Walkers can also opt to do smaller sections. Contact the visitor centre for details. www.environment.sa.gov.au/parks/yurrebilla

# Outside the city: Glenelg

Glenelg is South Australia's best-known beach and its most developed piece of coastal real estate. Only 20 minutes from the CBD, it's brimming with shops and restaurants, and people strolling, sunbaking, cycling and rollerblading. Walking trails lead up and down the coast and the calm water is perfect for swimming, fishing and sailing. The suburb would not be complete without the long, iconic pier – an ideal spot to dine on fish and chips at sunset.

## Getting to Glenelg

You can get to and from Glenelg by tram from Victoria Street in the city centre. Trams depart every 15 minutes, and more frequently during peak hours. Local bus services also run from the CBD to Glenelg.

## Glenelg information centre

Tourist Information Building ,
The Foreshore; (08) 8294 5833;
Mon–Fri 9.30am–4.30pm, Sat 9.30am–3pm, Sun 10am–2pm.

## Top attractions

**Bay Discovery Centre**
Housed within the historic Glenelg Town Hall, this magnificent centre provides a detailed history of the town itself. There are some fascinating multimedia exhibitions, as well as a mezzanine gallery, and the Rodney Fox

Shark Experience, with photos and displays that reveal much about this fierce sea predator.

If this turns you into a *Jaws* lover, you can hop on board Rodney's vessel for a four- to five-day expedition in search of Great White sharks. After being attacked by a shark in 1963, Rodney decided to meet his attacker

and began running diving expeditions. You'll get as close as you ever will (want to) with a Great White inside a shark-proof cage. Tours depart from Port Lincoln. Bay Discovery Centre, Glenelg Town Hall, Moseley Sq, (08) 8179 9500 or (08) 8179 9508 (on weekends), daily 10am–5pm; Rodney Fox Shark Experience, (08) 8376 3373, www.rodneyfox.com.au

**Jetty Road** The epicentre of retail therapy in Glenelg. There is also some great historic architecture along this 1 km shopping hub with over 350 specialty shops.

**Holdfast Shores** Many boutique shops and restaurants, and a massive marina.

**Moseley Square** Market Right on the beach, this market offers a variety of unique products including mud drums, handmade jewellery, embroidery and knitted items. Moseley Sq; Oct–May Sat–Sun 9am–5pm.

## Heritage Trails

The Freedom Trail is a drive through Glenelg's past and present, including the iconic Old Gum Tree on McFarlane Street. The Proclamation Trail is suited for pedestrians and cyclists, and consists of eight historic sites in the Glenelg and Hodfast Bay area. Brochures for trails are available at the Bay Discovery Centre.

## HMS Buffalo

History is re-created along the foreshore where a replica of the HMS *Buffalo*, the ship that carried South Australia's first settlers, now stands. Unlike the original, it has an onboard restaurant offering fine seafood dining along with a small museum featuring logbooks, illustrations and other

memorabilia. Cnr Adelphi Tce & Anzac Hwy; (08) 8294 7000; daily 10am–5pm.

## Boomerang Art

This gallery specialises in authentic Aboriginal art from Central Australia, Arnhem Land, the Kimberley and South Australia. See the works of some of the best Indigenous artists in the country. 716 Anzac Hwy; (08) 8376 3921; by appointment only; www.boomerangart. com.au

## Where to eat

**Cafe Blu** $\$\$$ 🌿 This modern eatery is one of the affordable culinary highlights in town. The menu features Middle Eastern and Italian flavours, as well as seafood and pub grub. Oaks Plaza Pier Hotel, 16 Holdfast Prm; (08) 8350 3108; Mon–Thur 11am–3pm & 5–9pm, Fri–Sun 11am–10pm.

**Cafe Strand** $\$\$$ ♡ Touted as one of the best cafes in all of South Australia. While the setting is very casual and the prices very affordable, the dishes themselves are exquisite and complex. Try the kangaroo loin in a Moroccan marinade topped with pickled red cabbage. That's right, it's not a crime to eat an animal on the country's coat of arms. 108 Jetty Rd; (08) 8376 9222; daily 8.30am–10pm; www.cafestrand.com.au

**Salt Bar and Restaurant** $\$\$$ ♡ Salt is a classy restaurant with a touch of funk and gorgeous views of the marina. The menu is diverse, from the luscious confit duck legs to the extremely palatable pumpkin and blue cheese risotto. Lights Landing, Holdfast Shores Marina, Anzac Hwy; (08) 8376 6887; Mon–Thur noon–11.30pm, Fri noon–12.30am, Sat 9am–12.30am, Sun 9am–11.30pm; www.saltbarandrestaurant.com

**Simply Sushi** $\$$ 🌿 Affordable Japanese cuisine at its best. Enjoy pickings from the sushi train or partake in one of their famous bento boxes. 108 Jetty Rd;

(08) 8294 5514; daily noon–2pm & 6–9pm; www.simplysushi.com.au

**Montezuma's** $\$$/$\$\$$ ♡ Cheap and no-fuss Mexican food, including chilli, burritos, tacos and combination platters. Just warn your fellow hostel dwellers before bedtime. 2 Partridge St; (08) 8350 0111; lunch & dinner daily; www.montezumas.com.au

**Top of the World Revolving Restaurant** $\$\$\$$ TOP TREAT!! ♡ Hit the 12th floor of the Atlantic Tower and indulge in the seafood platter for two, or try the three-course set menu. This is an extravagance at around $50, but well worth it. Floor 12, Atlantic Tower Motel, 760 Anzac Hwy; (08) 8376 0050; Sun 11.30am–2.30pm, Tue–Sun 5.30–9pm; www.topoftheworld.net.au

## Out and about
### Cinemas

**Glenelg Cinema Centre** 119 Jetty Rd; (08) 8294 3366.

## Pubs and bars

**Sol Bar** Sol is the Roman god of the sun and this funky, beachfront bar has fully embraced it. With sun mosaics plastered across the walls and floor, Sol Bar offers a perfect mix of R'n'B, jazz, house and soothing cocktails. Enjoy sunset views and happy hour from 8–10pm every night. Oaks Plaza Pier Hotel, 16 Holdfast Prm; (08) 8350 3142; Fri–Sun 6pm–3am.

**Horizons Cocktail Lounge** A large range of cocktails, premium wines and beers, with panoramic views of the ocean. For the more refined, there are cigars and an array of single malt whiskys. Stamford Grand Adelaide,

**Glenelg Food and Wine Festival** Spectacular two-day festival with great food, music, and of course, wine. Oct.

**Adelaide Rock 'n' Roll Festival** A classic live music rock 'n' roll festival featuring local and interstate bands. Nov.

**Bay Sheffield Carnival** Spectacular carnival revolving around a 100 m dash. An iconic South Australian event. Dec.

Glenelg tram

Moseley Sq; (08) 8376 1222; daily 5pm–late.
**Dublin Hotel** If there was ever a place to watch sport in Adelaide, then this is the pub to do it. With plasma and 16 LCD screens, along with DJs and live bands, you won't want to leave. 11 Moseley St; (08) 8295 3966; Mon–Wed noon–1am, Thur & Sun noon–1.30am, Fri–Sat noon–2am; www.dublinhotel.com.au

**Pier One** Another casual, beachfront bar with superb cocktails and a care-free ambience. DJs man the deck on Friday and Saturday nights, while Sundays feature live bands. Oaks Plaza Pier Hotel, 16 Holdfast Prm; (08) 8350 3142; Mon–Thur noon–12.30am, Fri noon–1am, Sat 11am–2.30am, Sun 11am–3am.

**Holdfast Hotel** Your typical Australian pub with great music, drinks and packed crowds. 83 Brighton Rd; (08) 8295 2051; Mon–Wed & Sun noon–1am, Thur–Sat noon–2am; www.holdfasthotel.com.au

**The Grand Bar** Formerly known as the Pier and Pines, this Glenelg icon is an ambient pub/bar/club/whatever you want it to be. Enjoy Uni Nights on Thursdays, Electro on Fridays, and a massive party all weekend. Stamford Grand Adelaide, Moseley Sq; (08) 8376 1222; daily 11am–late; www.thegrandbar.com.au

## Where to stay

**Glenelg Beach Hostel** ★ ★ ★ Dorm $22, single $40, double $65 1–7 Moseley St; (08) 8376 0007; www.glenelgbeachhostel.com.au
**Comfort Inn Haven Marina** ★ ★ ★ TOP TREAT!! Standard room $108, corporate $118 6–10 Adelphi Tce, Glenelg North; (08) 8350 5199; www.haveninn.com.au

## Other suburbs worth visiting

**Port Adelaide** The biggest suburb outside the city, Port has a rich maritime history. Visit the wharf markets and antique shops, among other things.
**Henley Beach** A popular spot, especially on weekends. Restaurants, cafes and bars aplenty!
**Semaphore** Uninterrupted sea views and stunning heritage buildings.
**St Kilda** More of a village than a suburb. Walk the Mangrove Trail or visit the Tramway Museum.
**Thebarton** Home of the South Australian Brewing Company (see Other attractions worth a look).
**Norwood** Highlighted by the Parade, this is one of Adelaide's best shopping areas.

## Visitor information

### Adelaide Airport

Adelaide Airport is conveniently located approximately 15 minutes from the CBD by car.
**Bus** **Skylink Airport Shuttle** specialises in providing a regular scheduled bus service between Adelaide Airport, Keswick Interstate Railway Terminal and Adelaide CBD. It's around $7.50 from the terminal to the city. Bookings (08) 8332 0528 or www.skylinkadelaide.com
**Taxi** While a more expensive option, a taxi will take you anywhere you want to go. A trip from the terminal to the CBD will cost around $15.

### Internet cafes

**The Zone Internet Cafe** 238 Rundle St; (08) 8223 1947.
**Arena Internet Cafe** 264 Rundle St; (08) 8223 3481.
**Aztec Cyber Cafe** 96 Gouger St; (08) 8212 0282.
**Wireless Cafe** 53 Hindley St; (08) 8212 1266.

### Hospitals

For all emergencies, including police, fire, or hospital, dial '000'.
**Royal Adelaide Hospital** North Tce; (08) 8222 4000.

Glenelg Beach

# Barossa Valley and the Adelaide Hills
# Plonk for one and all

If you're into your plonk (that's wine, for those who aren't up with the lingo), then the Barossa Valley is the place for you. This is one of Australia's eminent wine regions and offers a landscape of vine-swept hills dotted with historic villages, stone cottages, grand buildings on old wine estates, and some excellent (but pricey) restaurants. A little further south, the Adelaide Hills have been influenced by German Lutheran settlers who first came here in the early 1800s. With an eclectic combination of Australian bushland and European farmland, there are more wineries, historic villages, gardens, museums and galleries. The region also contains the fantastic Cleland Wildlife Park, and Mount Lofty, with great views from the summit.

**Number of days to spend in this region: 3–5 days**

## Getting here

A hire car or bus is the best way to get to the Barossa Valley. There are a few coach companies, including Barossa Valley Coaches and Premier Stateliner, which run services direct from Adelaide to Tanunda (90 minutes). The region also has a 24 hr taxi service.

For the Adelaide Hills, a hire car will allow you to drive around and take in all of the gorgeous attractions. Regular bus services also run from Adelaide's central bus terminal to Hahndorf (70 minutes).

**Barossa Valley Coaches** (08) 8564 3022; www.bvcoach.com

**Premier Stateliner** 111 Franklin St, Adelaide; (08) 8415 5500; www.premierstateliner.com.au

**Barossa Valley Taxis** (08) 8563 3600.

**Bus SA – information service** (08) 8303 0822; www.bussa.com.au

## Barossa Valley tours

**Adelaide Sightseeing** Offers brilliant day tours taking you all over the Barossa region, from Cleland Wildlife Park to the Mount Lofty Ranges, and everything in between. (08) 8413 6199; www.adelaidesightseeing.com.au

**Discover Australia Holidays** Visit some of the region's best wineries, the German town of Hahndorf and delightful Bridgewater. 1800 73 2001; www.discoveraustralia.com.au

**Adelaide South Australia Tours** Offers wildlife, sightseeing, and wine-tasting tours of the region. (08) 8294 6042; www.adelaidesouthaustraliatours.com.au

## ① Tanunda (1–2 days)

At the heart of the Barossa Valley is the town of Tanunda, an Aboriginal word for 'watering hole' or 'many birds on a creek'. For history buffs who want to learn all about the region and its vast German history, the Barossa Historical Museum is your definitive pit stop. The town has numerous awe-inspiring churches, notable examples being the Tabor Lutheran Church and the Langmeil Lutheran Church. The Keg Factory is a quaint little stop where you can see handcrafted kegs, wine barrels and bars, and even take a tour of the workshop. For something straight off the good ol' Aussie farm, Norm's Coolies are performing sheep dogs like you've never seen before.

### Further information

**Barossa Historical Museum** 47 Murray St; (08) 8566 0212; Mon–Fri 1–5pm, Sat–Sun 2–5pm.

**The Keg Factory** St Halletts Rd; 0418 805 085; workshops & showroom Mon–Fri 8am–5pm, Sat 8.30am–5pm, Sun 9.30am–5pm (bookings essential).

**Norm's Coolies** Barossa Valley Way; (08) 8563 2198; performances Mon, Wed, Sat 2pm.

### Where to eat

**Maggie Beer's Restaurant** 💲💲 A television personality and an icon of the Australian food scene, stop at Maggie's eatery/shop and indulge in her all-day picnic fare menu, or grab some chutney to take home. 2 Keith St; (08) 8562 4477; daily 10.30am–5pm; www.maggiebeer.com.au

## Events

**Barossa Under the Stars** Enjoy a picnic in the day and stay for the huge concert and stars at night. Date changes yearly.

## ❷ Barossa Valley wineries (3–5 days)

The Barossa Valley is one of Australia's most famous wine-producing regions. Old, gnarled shiraz vines, planted as early as the 1840s, add character to the more recent vines and varieties. The best view of the thousands of hectares of vineyards is atop Menglers Hill. But we all know you didn't come to Barossa Valley for the view. Drop in on some of the Barossa's best wineries, including Penfolds, Yalumba and Seppelt. Free tastings allow you to sample different wines before you decide if you like any enough to buy a bottle (you can always get a crate shipped home, if you're worried about weighing down your backpack with booze). For some history on the Barossa and winemaking, the Jacob's Creek Visitor Centre has a gallery with displays next to its wine-tasting areas. Chateau Tanunda is also worth a visit, and has long been recognised as one of the valley's most picturesque spots. Then head to the Whispering Wall, south of Cockatoo Valley, for a truly trippy experience. The shape of this wall, retained from the Barossa Reservoir, enables a whispered message at one end to be heard 140 m away at the other end.

## Further information

ⓘ **Barossa Wine and Visitor Centre**
66–68 Murray St, Tanunda; 1300 852 982; daily 10am–4pm.

## Tours

**Cellar Door Pass** $99 pass that entitles you to free wine tastings and tours, as well as other perks. Also for use in Victoria and South Africa. Visit the website for more details. 1300 661 711; www.cellardoorpass.com

**Groovy Grape Getaways** Fun backpackers day tour of the region. The Big Rocking Horse is a highlight. 1800 661 177; www.groovygrape.com.au

**Barossa Valley Wine Tours** From private to shared, day and custom tours. 39 Basedow Rd, Tanunda; (08) 8563 3248; www.barossavalleytours.com

**Barossa Epicurean Tours** Full- and half-day tours of the valley and surrounding areas. Includes cheese tasting. (08) 8564 2191; www.barossatours.com.au

**Prime Mini Tours** An array of tours, from the simple to the more advanced tasting tours. (08) 8298 8146; www.primeminitours.com

**Barossa Trike Tours** Take a full-day tour of the region on a custom motorbike. 0438 623 342; barossatrike.com.au

**Barossa Helicopters** See the region from the air. Flights from 10 to 60 minutes. (08) 8524 4209; www.barossahelicopters.com.au

## Wineries

**Penfolds** A feature of the Barossa wine scene since 1911. Come here to sample some excellent wines, including their world-renowned Grange. Tanunda Rd, Nuriootpa; (08) 8568 9408; daily 10am–5pm; www.penfolds.com.au

**Yalumba** Officially part of the Eden Valley, Yalumba is the place to go for cabernet sauvignon and shiraz. Also try its viognier, an exotic variety that originates from the Rhone Valley in France and is now a Yalumba speciality. Eden Valley Rd, Angaston; (08) 8561 3200; daily 10am–5pm; www.yalumba.com

**Seppelt** A must-visit winery with its elegant bluestone buildings and gardens. Its range of fortified wines includes Spanish styles and classic tawnys – the jewel is Para Liqueur, a tawny released when it is 100 years old. 1 Seppeltsfield Rd, Seppeltsfield; (08) 8568 6217; Mon–Fri 9am–5pm, Sat–Sun 10am–4pm; www.seppelt.com.au

**Jacob's Creek Visitor Centre** Aside from the gallery, this is a very well-known label with four tiers to its range. Barossa Valley Way, Rowland Flat; (08) 8521 300; daily 10am–5pm; www.jacobscreek.com

**Peter Lehmann** The beautiful, rustic cellar door makes this well-known winery a great place to visit. The Eden Valley Reserve Riesling is its signature wine, but you can pick up a reasonably priced bottle of some other varieties. Off Para Rd, Tanunda; (08) 8563 2100; Mon–Fri 9.30am–5pm, Sat–Sun 10.30am–4.30pm; www.peterlehmannwines.com.au

**Rockford** With fantastic wines seldom seen in other Australian states. Krondorf Rd, Tanunda; (08) 8563 2720; daily 11am–5pm; www.rockfordwines.com.au

Cellar door in the Barossa Valley

Torbreck Vintners Offering excellent shiraz and shiraz viognier. Roennfeldt Rd, Marananga; (08) 8562 4155; daily 10am–6pm; www.torbreck.com

Chateau Tanunda A recently restored icon of the Barossa Valley, with breathtaking views of the valley and Barossa Ranges. 9 Basedow Rd, Tanunda; (08) 8563 3888; daily 10am–5pm; www.chateautanunda.com

Langmeil This small, family-run winery may not have a big name, but its cellar door is worth visiting to sample some premium Barossa wines. Cnr Langmeil & Para rds, Tanunda; (08) 8563 2595; daily 10.30am–4.30pm; www.langmeilwinery.com.au

### Where to stay

Barossa Doubles D'vine ★★★ Twin and double $50–$60 Cnr Barossa Valley Way & Nuraip Rd, Nuriootpa; (08) 8562 2260; www.doublesdvine.com.au

Barossa Valley Farmhouse YHA ★★ 16-bed mixed bunk house (for big groups) $103.50 Sandy Creek Conservation Park; (08) 8414 3001; www.yha.com.au

Barossa Valley Tourist Park ★★ Double from $45 Penrice Rd, Nurioopta; (08) 8562 1404; www.barossatouristpark.com.au

### Events

Barossa Music Festival One of the best classical musical festivals in the country. Oct.

Barossa Vintage Festival Everything's on offer from a parade to great food, vintage aircrafts and big band jazz. Apr (every odd-numbered year).

## 3 Mount Lofty Summit (1–2 days)

The Adelaide Hills are highlighted by Mount Lofty Summit, offering a window to much of the region's beauty. At approximately 727 m above sea level, the lookout area has amazing views from the hills to Kangaroo Island and all the way to the Yorke Peninsula. After taking in this panorama, head to Mount Lofty Botanical Gardens with its myriad of beautiful exotic plants, and plenty of walking trails to take it all in. Your next stop should definitely be Petaluma Cellar & Bridgewater Mill Restaurant. Built in 1860, this was the only flourmill in the state driven by water, and slowly became an icon of the area. It has now been renovated to house the cellar door for Petaluma Wines. Grapes from the Adelaide Hills vineyard are responsible for fantastic chardonnay and Croser sparkling white. On-site is also the famed Bridgewater Mill Restaurant, which is the place to go for a bit of a splurge. Not far from the Mount Lofty area, the National Motor Museum in Birdwood is an international centre that displays Australia's road transport history and an amazing assortment of cars, motorcyles, trucks and fire engines. The Holden Pavilion has the best collection.

### Further information

[i] Mount Lofty Summit Information Centre Summit Rd, Mt Lofty

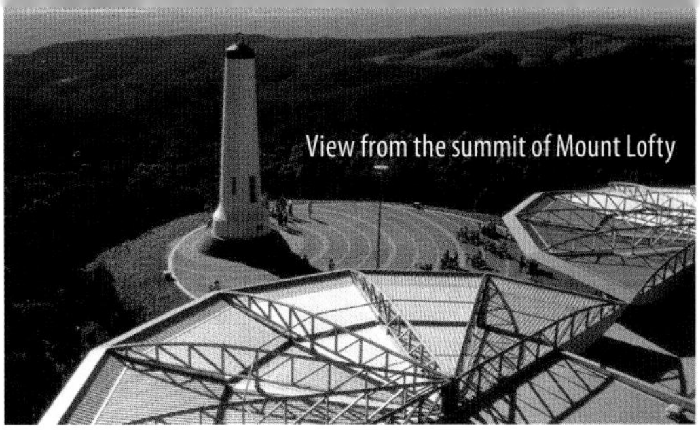
View from the summit of Mount Lofty

mtloftysummit.com

Mount Lofty Botanical Gardens Summit Rd or Piccadilly Rd; (08) 8370 8370; Mon–Fri 8.30am–4pm, Sat–Sun 10am–5pm (6pm daylight saving time); www.environment.sa.gov.au

Petaluma Cellar Door Bridgewater Mill, Mt Barker Rd, Bridgewater; (08) 8339 9222; daily 9am–5pm.

National Motor Museum Shannon St, Birdwood; (08) 8568 4000; daily 10am–5pm; www.history.sa.gov.au/motor

### Where to eat

Mount Lofty Summit Cafe $ Cheap cafe eats at over 700 m above sea level. A great breakfast menu, tasty foccacias and baguettes. Summit Rd, Mt Lofty Lookout; (08) 8339 2600; Mon–Tue 9am–5pm, Wed–Sun 9am–late; www.mtloftysummit.com

Bridgewater Mill $$$ TOP TREAT!! A culinary sensation and voted 2006 Restaurant of the Year by the *Adelaide Advertiser*. Incredible dishes from roast quail with coconut rice, green mango salad, crispy egg and red curry, to honey and soy glazed Kangaroo Island chicken breast with radish cake and teriyaki glaze. Mt Barker Rd, Bridgewater; (08) 8339 9200; Thur–Mon noon–2.30pm (weekend bookings essential); www.bridgewatermill.com.au

### Where to stay

Mt Lofty Cottage YHA ★ Room with 16 beds (for large groups) $73.50 Summit Rd; (08) 8414 3001; www.yha.com.au

Mount Lofty Railway Station ★★★ Double and twin from $95 2 Sturt Valley Rd, Stirling; (08) 8339 7400; www.mlrs.com.au

## 4 Cleland Wildlife Park (1 day)

Just 20 minutes from Adelaide within a protected wilderness area, this award-winning park allows its native animals to roam free, from yellow-footed rock-wallabies to Tasmanian devils. 'Koalas in Close Up' sessions run from 11am–noon and 2pm–4pm daily, giving you the chance to have a photo with these cute Aussie animals. Consult the park's website for further information on animal feeding times. If you're interested in a guided tour, the Yurridla Trail explains and retells fascinating local Aboriginal Dreamtime stories. On every third Friday of the month during summer, there are also guided night walks that shows off many nocturnal animals, and you may even be able to feed wild possums (bookings essential). Make sure you also visit the Ocean to Outback Interpretive Centre to learn more about the park via an interactive forum. There's a cafe in the centre, but for a an unforgettable picnic spot, find nearby Waterfall Gully.

## Further information

Cleland Wildlife Park Cleland Conservation Park; (08) 8339 2444; daily 9am–5pm; www.parks.sa.gov.au/cleland

## Tours

Yurridla Trail The coming together of Aboriginal culture and Australian wildlife. Bookings through Tauondi Cultural Agency (08) 8240 0300.

Nightlife @ Cleland See what happens when the lights go out. Observe nocturnal animals including bettongs and bandicoots. Only available in summer, 3rd Friday of the month. Bookings through the park.

# 5 Hahndorf (1–2 days)

In the heart of the Adelaide Hills is Australia's oldest German settlement, first inhabited by Prussian Lutheran refugees fleeing religious persecution in the 1830s. To this day it has retained its distinctly Germanic look, and many of the local businesses and attractions are operated by descendants of the original German pioneers. The best way to get acquainted with this charming town is by foot, where you'll see some significant historic buildings, like the Old Mill and St Michaels Lutheran Church. The Hahndorf Academy is a must-see art gallery in the old school, which showcases some great contemporary Australian art. Works by renowned Australian artist Sir Hans Heysen are housed in The Cedars Gallery, Heysen's former home – his studio still displays painting materials and sketches.

On the culinary side of things, you should in no way leave Hahndorf until you've bought jam from Beerenberg Strawberry Farm. These jams are so delicious that many of Australia's top hotels stock them. Since you've already booked a date with your dentist, you may as well head to the nearby town of Woodside and see how chocolate is made at Melba's Chocolate and Confectionery Factory (samples are available, of course). Also in the area is the Shaw + Smith Winery, if you're in the mood for some top-notch sauvignon blanc.

## Further information

[i] Adelaide Hills Visitor Information Centre 41 Main St; 1800 353 323; daily 10am–4pm; www.visitadelaidehills.com.au

Hahndorf Academy 68 Main St; (08) 8388 7250; daily 10am–5pm (4pm in winter); www.hahndorfacademy.org.au

The Cedars Gallery Heysen Rd; (08) 8388 7277; Tue–Sun 10am–4.30pm.

Beerenberg Strawberry Farm Mt Barker Rd; (08) 8388 7272; daily 9am–5pm; www.beerenberg.com.au

Melba's Chocolate and Confectionery Factory 22 Henry St, Woodside; (08) 8389 7868; daily 9am–4.30pm; www.melbaschocolates.com

Shaw + Smith Winery Lot 4, Jones Rd, Balhannah; (08) 8398 0500; Sat–Sun 11am–4pm; www.shawandsmith.com

## Tours

Australian Pacific Tours Half-day tours taking in everything this Bavarian town has to offer. 1300 655 965; www.australiasightseeing.com

## Where to eat

German Cake Shop $ Whilst known for automobiles and beer, the good people of Germany are also celebrated for their pastries. Try the traditional bienenstich, a yeast cake topped with honey and almonds and filled with cream, butter and custard. 2 Pine Ave; (08) 8388 7086; daily 8.30am–5.30pm.

German Arms Hotel $$ Pokies machines aside, this place reeks of the Deutschland. For those with an empty stomach, you can't go past the trio of German wurst – bockwurst, weisswurst and kransky served on a bed of sauerkraut with Hahndorf Beerenburg mustard. 69 Main St; (08) 8388 7013; daily 8am–9pm.

Zorro's $$ There aren't many places in Australia where you can sample some of the best in Balkan cuisine. While you may not be able to pronounce the names of the dishes, it's pretty simple in the end – sausages, kebabs and steaks. 60 Main St; (08) 8388 1309; Wed–Mon 6–10pm, Sat–Sun noon–3pm.

Hahndorf Hill Winery $$ Voted one of the best winery restaurants in Australia, this place is perfect for a weekend lunch. Complement your meal with a bottle of the winery's own sauvignon blanc. Pains Rd; (08) 8388 7512; Sat–Sun 10am–5pm; www.hahndorfhillwinery.com.au

## Where to stay

Adelaide Hills Wilderness Lodge ★★ Dorm $24–$30 Mylor; (08) 8388 5588; www.adelaidewilderness.com.au

Lavender Greene Cottage ★★ Single $80, double $95 Cromer Rd, Birdwood; (08) 8568 5361.

## Events

Heysen Festival Ten-day art celebrations, with exhibits, awards, food and wine. Sept–Oct.

Horse and cart, Hahndorf

# Kangaroo Island
## Much more than just roos

Australia's third-largest island is located in the remote Southern Ocean, 16 km off the tip of the Fleurieu Peninsula. Just a little warning to help you avoid disappointment – no, you will not be greeted by a family of hopping kangaroos on your arrival. Actually, famed explorer Matthew Flinders named the island in 1802 after he and his crew landed here and shot and cooked 31 kangaroos. Morbidity aside, Kangaroo Island is a premier destination that encompasses adventure, exploration, relaxation, and everything in between. From its large population of native creatures, to idyllic coves in the north and spectacular rugged surf beaches in the south, there isn't much you can't do here. Beauty comes in many forms, one of them being this hidden jewel.

**Number of days to spend in this region: 9–11 days**

## Getting here

The most popular and cheapest way to get to Kangaroo Island is by ferry. You can catch the SeaLink ferry from Cape Jervis to Penneshaw for around $40 return. There are also flights between Adelaide and Kingscote through Regional Express and Emu Airways, but they are the pricey options.

Once on the island, there are coach services running twice daily between Kingscote, American River and Penneshaw, connecting with SeaLink ferry service. A shuttle service operates between Kingscote Airport and Kingscote township. Bookings for both services are necessary. There is no taxi service on the island, so a hire car is a good alternative. Be careful driving on the roads, as many of them are unsealed and very gravelly.

While there is hostel accommodation in Penneshaw and Kingscote, it might be wise to invest in some camping gear for overnight stays in the wilderness. Also make sure you obtain your permits for the necessary parks.

SeaLink City Centre Travel , Shop 3, 75 King William St, Adelaide; 13 1301; www.sealink.com.au

Premier Stateliner 111 Franklin St, Adelaide; (08) 8415 5500; www.premierstateliner.com.au

Bus SA – information service (08) 8303 0822; www.bussa.com.au

Regional Express 13 1713; www.regionalexpress.com.au

Emu Airways General Aviation Terminal, Kel Barclay Ave, Adelaide Airport; (08) 8234 3711; daily 6am–7pm.

Airport Shuttle Service Bookings (08) 8553 2390.

## Kangaroo Island tours

Sahara Adventures The two-day Kangaroo Island Safari Adventure is ideal for budget travellers. (02) 8252 5333; www.saharaadventures.com.au

Australian Wildlife Walkabouts 4WD adventures, from one- to three-day tours. Emu Bay, Newland Service & Kingscote; (08) 8553 5350; www.australianwildlifewalkabouts.com.au

Escape Tours 4WD tours of the island. (08) 8553 5199; www.kangarooislandtours.com.au

Southern Cross Tours Day tours encompassing all the major sights, departing from Adelaide by plane and returning the same day. (08) 8374 0340; www.southerncrosstours.com

Kangaroo Island Tour Pass For only $45 you can purchase a pass that gives you unlimited access to all the main attractions on Kangaroo Island for 12 months. (08) 8559 7235.

## ❶ Penneshaw (1–2 days)

Your first port of call on Kangaroo Island will be Penneshaw, a small, Cornish-style town which overlooks the South Australian mainland. There are number of attractions, including Cape

Willoughby Lighthouse. This 75 m-tall structure is a town icon that was established in 1852, making it the oldest lighthouse in South Australia. Tours take you to the top of the lighthouse, where there are magnificent views of the Fleurieu Peninsula and

Backstairs Passage. The Penneshaw Maritime and Folk Museum is owned by the National Trust and has many interesting displays, information and artefacts depicting the history of the area. But it's the town's adorable resident penguins that people really come to see. The Penneshaw Penguin Centre brings you up close with these little waddlers as they emerge from the waters of Hog Bay Beach. You might even witness some romantic courtship displays – or some not so romantic territorial disputes. If you're visiting in the warmer months, Antechamber Bay has a beautiful beach that's ideal for swimming, bushwalking, fishing and camping.

## Further information

ℹ **Kangaroo Island Gateway Visitor Information Centre** Howard Dr; (08) 8553 1185; Mon–Fri 9am–5pm, Sat–Sun 10am–4pm.

**Cape Willoughby Lightstation** RSD via Penneshaw; (08) 8553 1191; daily 11am–2pm; www.parks.sa.gov.au/cape_willoughby

**Penneshaw Maritime and Folk Museum** Howard Dr; (08) 8553 1109; Sept–May Wed–Sun 3–5pm; www.communitywebs.org/PenneshawMaritimeMuseum

**Penneshaw Penguin Centre** Lloyd Collins Reserve; (08) 8553 1103; summer open 8pm, tours 8.30pm & 9.30pm; winter open 6pm, tours 7.30pm & 8.30pm.

## Tours

**Alkirna Nocturnal Tours** Night tours of Penneshaw with guaranteed sightings of penguins, tammar wallabies and owls. (08) 8553 7464; www.alkirna.com.au

**Kangaroo Island Outlook Tours** If you've got a bit of money saved, take a private tour of the island in a luxury 4WD. (08) 8553 1048; www.the-lookout.com.au

## Where to eat

**Fish** $ The *Australian* newspaper proclaimed this joint 'the best fish and chip shop in the world'. The endorsements don't get more ringing than that! King George whiting, garfish, lobster, scallops – you name it, they'll cook it. Their famous salt and pepper squid is exquisite and you can order beer-battered seafood with Coopers Sparkling Ale. Off SeaLink Ramp; (08) 8553 7406; Oct–May daily 4.30–8pm; www.2birds1squid.com

**Hog Bay Stores** $ Quality food in a chilled, comfortable atmosphere. With a choice of indoor or outdoor dining, it's the ideal place for a hearty breakfast or a quick coffee and cake for lunch. Cnr North Tce & Thomas Willson St; (08) 8553 1151; daily 8am–7pm.

**Old Post Office Restaurant** $$ This open restaurant is very homely, with hanging plants inside and a wood-burning stove right in the middle. As you'd expect, seafood is the specialty. North Tce; (08) 8553 1063; Thur–Mon from 5.30pm.

Diving around the island

## Where to stay

**Kangaroo Island YHA** ★★ Dorm $28.50, twin and double $68.50–$93.50 33 Middle Tce; (08) 8553 1344; www.yha.com.au

**Dudley Villa** ★★ Rooms from $100 Hog Bay Rd, near Charing Cross Cnr; (08) 8553 1331; www.dudleyvilla.com.au

**Seashells Penneshaw** ★★★ Rooms from $120 178 Karatta Tce; (08) 8553 1488; www.seashells-penneshaw.com.au

**Camping** Camping is available at Antechamber Bay. Permits can be obtained through self-registration at the campground. Facilities include toilets, gas barbecues, campfires and caravan access. Wood fires are permitted, except on days of total fire ban. For more information, contact the information centre.

## Events

**Penneshaw Easter Art Exhibition** The best in Kangaroo Island art on display. Apr.

# 2 Kingscote (2 days)

Kangaroo Island's largest town is situated on the Nepean Bay. A flagpole at Reeves Point indicates that Kingscote was the site of the state's first European settlement in 1836. A mulberry tree stands nearby, which was planted by the first immigrants and amazingly, still bears fruit. Kingscote's long pioneering history is presented at the excellent Hope Cottage Folk Museum, run by the National Trust. Amongst the relics are photographs, coin collections, an automobilia display, laundry display and an original cellar. At the KI Marine Centre, take the Discovering Penguins Tour, which run twice per night. The centre also has an enormous aquarium, as well as daily pelican feedings.

In and around Kingscote, there are a host of other places to check out. For a fascinating look at the world of honey and Ligurian bees, visit Island Beehive and Clifford's Honey Farm, the latter selling yummy honey ice-cream. Like much of Australia, Kangaroo Island's economic stability was, and still is, heavily dependent on the wool industry. Jumbuck Australiana is where you can see sheep shearing demonstrations and learn how to spin wool. Still on sheep, the Island Pure Sheep Dairy gives visitors a glimpse of the life of a sheep farmer, with daily milking exhibitions and cheese tastings. And you can't go home to your family and friends empty-handed, so hit up some unique gifts from the Emu Ridge Eucalyptus Oil Distillery & Craft Gallery. They also run tours of the distillery.

## Further information

*i* **Kangaroo Island Tourist Services** 69–77 Cygnet Rd; (08) 8553 2657; Mon–Fri 9am–5pm, Sat–Sun 10am–4pm.
*i* **National Parks & Wildlife Office** 39 Dauncey St; (08) 8553 2381; Mon–Fri 9am–5pm.
**Hope Cottage Folk Museum** Top of Centenary Ave; (08) 8553 2656; daily 1–4pm, Jan extended hours 10am–4pm, only open Sat in Aug; www.nationaltrustsa.org.au
**KI Marine Centre** The Wharf; (08) 8553 3112; penguin tours 8.30pm & 9.30pm (summer), 7.30pm & 8.30pm (all other times); www.kimarinecentre.com.au
**Island Beehive** 1 Acacia Dr; (08) 8553 0080; daily 9am–5pm; www.island-beehive.com.au
**Clifford's Honey Farm** Elsegood Rd, MacGillivray; (08) 8553 8295; daily 9am–5pm.
**Jumbuck Australiana** Cnr Hog Bay & American River rds; (08) 8553 7370; daily 9.30am–1.30pm.
**Island Pure Sheep Dairy** Gum Creek Rd, Cygnet River; (08) 8553 9110; daily 1–5pm.
**Emu Ridge Eucalyptus Oil Distillery** Wilson Rd, Macgillivray; (08) 8553 8228; daily 9am–2pm; www.emuridge.com.au

## Tours

**Kangaroo Island Marine Tours** Aquatic excursions, everything from sunset tours to great coastal adventures. 9 Chapman Tce, Kingscote; (08) 8553 0016; www.kimarinetours.com
**Island Trekker Tours and Charter** The Heartlands full-day tour hits all of the Kingscote hotspots, including Clifford's Honey Farm and the Eucalyptus Distillery. (08) 8553 2657; www.welcometoki.com

## Where to eat

**Ozone Seafront Hotel** $ At breakfast time, you can often see the dolphins gliding through the calm waters of Nepean Bay. You can also enjoy your eggs, bacon, tomato and toast special for $10. Hit this place on Wednesday – schnitzel day! The Foreshore; (08) 8553 2011; daily 7–9am, noon–2pm & 6–8.30pm; www.ozonehotel.com
**Kangaroo Island Fresh Seafood** $ Select from the island's largest range of fresh fish and seafood. Staff will cook anything for you with a side of chips or greens. The best spot to enjoy your meal is on the Kingscote foreshore watching the sunset. Telegraph Rd, Kingscote; (08) 8553 0177; daily 9am–8.30pm (cooking from 11am), closed Sundays May–Nov.
**Roger's Deli** $ A relaxed cafe ambience makes this eatery the perfect place for breakfast (served all day). The lunch menu includes fish, pasta, stir-fry and curry. 76 Dauncey St; (08) 8553 2053; Mon–Fri 8am–5.45pm, Sat 8.30am–4pm, Sun 9am–3pm (extended hrs during the summer months).
**Restaurant Bella** $ A veritable cornucopia of Mediterranean and Asian cuisine, as well as some spectacular seafood. Pizzas and grilled snacks are best enjoyed alfresco. 54 Dauncey St; (08) 8553 0400; daily 11am–late

## Where to stay

**Kangaroo Island Central Hostel** ★★ Dorm $20, twin and double $45 19 Murray St; (08) 8553 2787.
**Kangaroo Island Holiday Village** ★★ Rooms from $95 9 Dauncey St; (08) 8553 2366.
**Kingscote Tourist Park** ★★ Camping $20, cabins from $55 First St (cnr Third St), Brownlow; (08) 8553 2394; www.kingscotetouristpark.com.au
**Kingscote Central Lodge** ★★ Units from $78 16 Murray St; (08) 8553 2891.

## Events

**Kangaroo Island Cup Carnival** The island's premier horseracing event. Feb.

## ❸ North coast (1–2 days)

The island's stunning and seemingly untouched north coast has its own unique flavour and charm, highlighted by the spectacular Emu Bay. With a resplendent white beach framing the inviting water, it is a hotspot for swimming, fishing and boating year-round. Behind the long beach you'll find pristine sand dunes, which are home to a vast array of birdlife, and there are superb views of the entire bay from the western end of the beach. Stokes Bay is another stunning beach that's great for swimming. The Stokes Bay Bush Garden is worth a stop and offers visitors a chance to view over 150 Kangaroo Island plant species, including 70 different banksias. Snelling Bay, Western River Cove and King George Beach are some other terrific beach spots that you'll never want to leave.

## Further information

**Stokes Bay Bush Garden** Stokes Bay Rd; (08) 8559 2244; daily 10am–5pm.
**Fishing: Emu Bay Fishing Charter** Half- and full-day fishing charters available. (08) 8553 9084 or 0429 356 213; www.emubayfishing.com

## Tours

**Kangaroo Island Diving Safari** View over 270 species of fish, as well as seals and dolphins. (08) 8559 3225; www.kidivingsafaris.com

## Where to stay

**Emu Bay Holiday Homes** ★★★ Double $75, deluxe cabin from $95 Lot 7 Bayview Rd, Emu Bay; (08) 8553 5241; www.emubaysuperviews.com.au
**Waves and Wildlife Cottages** ★★★ Room from $95 Lot 1 North Coast Rd, Stokes Bay; (08) 8559 2232; www.wavesandwildlife.com.au

Remarkable Rocks

Emu Bay Sea Breeze ★★★ Room from $120 51 Hamilton Dr, Emu Bay; (08) 8553 9097.

## 4 Flinders Chase National Park (1–2 days)

The Remarkable Rocks are the most photographed feature of Flinders Chase National Park, located on the west coast of Kangaroo Island. These massive granite boulders, which are being weathered away from the inside, appear artfully placed on a domed cliff top at Kirkpatrick Point. The sheen of orange lichen makes them even more spectacular against the sea.

After visiting the rocks, head to Cape du Couedic, home to a sandstone lighthouse and a colony of New Zealand fur seals that can be seen from the boardwalk down to Admirals Arch, a wave-sculpted sea cave. You can also take a tour inside the famed 1858 Cape Borda Lighthouse. There is a small museum and historic cemetery that provides an insight into the hardships faced by the lighthouse keepers and their families.

Around the visitor centre and to the west of the park, there is a network of excellent walking trails to view wonderfully varied wildflowers (best seen in the spring). The easy Platypus Waterholes Walk (4.5 km, 2 hrs) leads to viewing platforms overlooking pools where platypus live. The Snake Lagoon Hike (3 km, 1.5 hrs) is a shorter expedition, taking you through mallee and sugar gums, then across Rocky River to the Southern Ocean. There is a steep trail at Cape Borda, known as Harveys Return Hike (1.5 km, 1 hr), which leads you down the haulage way where supplies for the lightkeepers were brought up from the shore.

### Further information

ℹ Flinders Chase Visitor Centre Rocky River; (08) 8559 7235; daily 9am–5pm; www.parks.sa.gov.au/flinderschase

### Tours

Cape Borda Lighthouse Tours to Cape Borda Lighthouse last for approximately 45 minutes, and occur five times a day (three times during the winter months). The cannon, which used to signal that a ship was in danger, is fired at 12.30pm every day. (08) 8559 7235.

### Where to eat

The Chase Cafe [$] Located in the visitors centre, this stock-standard cafe has sandwiches, foccacias and bakery goods sure to ease any appetite. Flinders Chase Visitor Centre, Rocky River; (08) 8559 7339; daily 9am–5pm.

### Where to stay

Cape Borda Lighthouse Keeper Heritage Accommodation ★★ Huts from $94 Playford Hwy, Cape Borda; (08) 8559 7268.

Flinders Chase Farm ★★ Dorm $27.50, double $66 West End Hwy; (08) 8559 7223.

For information and bookings regarding the following accommodation, call the accommodation manager at the visitor centre:

Postman's Cottage ★★ Bunk $23 ($16 extra for linen)

Karatta Lodge ★★ Double $144 (capacity 6 people)

Mays Homestead ★★ Double $112 (capacity 6 people)

Camping The main area for camping is the Rocky River Campground, located near the Flinders Chase Visitors Centre. These grounds provide visitors with access to water, showers, gas barbecues and a public telephone. Other campgrounds in the area are Snake Lagoon, West Bay and Harveys Return. Fees and bookings are required for all grounds. Phone the visitor centre for further information.

## 5 Hanson Bay Wildlife Sanctuary (1 day)

Nestled between the Kelly Hill Caves Conservation Park and Flinders Chase National Park is this wildlife sanctuary renowned for its abundant native birds and animal wildlife. Within the large, vibrant forests you'll find tammar wallabies, possums, kangaroos, echidnas, and the unforgettably cute koalas. The park even has a Koala Walk, which allows visitors to get up close and personal with these cuddly creatures. Nocturnal driving tours and guided walks of the sanctuary are also available. For a bit of rest and relaxation, there is plenty to choose from – swimming in the bay, surfing, fishing and diving for crayfish. But why choose one when you can do them all!

### Further information

Hanson Bay Wildlife Sanctuary Off South Coast Rd, between Kelly Hill Caves Park & Flinders Chase NP; (08) 8559 7344; daily 9am–5pm; www.hansonbay.com.au

## Tours

Koala Walk Take a leisurely stroll down the famous Koala Walk and observe these creatures relaxing in an avenue of shady eucalyptus trees.
Nature Trail With 83 fenced-off ha, walk freely amidst the beautiful vegetation, birdlife and animals. The trail itself should take 90 minutes to complete.
Nocturnal Walks Fully guided 90-minute walk to discover the creatures of the night. Bookings essential.
Nocturnal Driving Tours Why walk when you can drive? Take a spotlight drive into the darkness and look out for native animals.

# 6 Kelly Hill Caves Conservation Park (1 day)

Welcome to the seedy underbelly of Kangaroo Island! Well, it's not actually seedy, but rather a subterranean wonderland of unique limestone caves set amid a natural bush setting. The appeal of this 7000 ha park is undoubtedly bolstered by what's underneath it. The main show cave contains an impressive arrangement of pristine cave formations, including straws, stalactites, stalagmites and helictites (even if you're not exactly sure what that all means, just trust that they look astonishing). There is also adventure caving available, from beginner to advanced tours. For those who don't like it underground, there are some bush and wetland walks, as well as lovely picnic areas to just eat a sandwich and take it all in.

## Further information

Kelly Hill Caves Conservation Park (08) 8559 7231; www.environment.sa.gov.au

## Tours

Show Cave Tour Daily 10am–4.15pm (40 minutes). Bookings through the park.
Adventure Caving Experience the excitement of climbing through underground labyrinths. K9 tours and Mount Taylor Cave tours are also available, but previous caving experience is necessary. Bookings are essential.

# 7 Seal Bay Conservation Park (1 day)

Down on the southern tip of Kangaroo Island, and about 45 minutes from Kingscote, lies an amazing home to approximately 500 Australian sea lions. This is one of the only places in the world where these animals are tolerant of people, meaning you have the privilege of observing their natural behaviour up close. Watch as they feed their young and then go out on three-day fishing excursions. They return for some much needed rest for three more days, before starting all over again. The best way to view the sea lions is by taking a beach tour, which grants you access to the boardwalk, beach and the lookout vantage spots.

Surrounding Seal Bay is a huge variety of natural attractions. Visit the desolate and ancient sand dunes that make up Little Sahara, where you can climb to the top of the ridge and even hop on a board and surf your way down – it's *Lawrence of Arabia* meets *Point Break*. Speaking of sand, Vivonne Bay is undoubtedly one of the best beaches in Australia, with great rips for surfers and serene spots to just chill and work on your tan. You also do not want to bypass Murray Lagoon at Cape Gantheaume National Park, the island's largest freshwater lagoon with gorgeous wetland habitats supporting abundant birdlife.

## Further information

Seal Bay Conservation Park Guided beach, boardwalk and pre-sunset tours all available. The Kangaroo Island Tour Pass gives you entry to the beach and boardwalk tours. Bookings through the park. (08) 8559 4207; daily 9am–5pm, summer and school holidays 9am–7.45pm; www.parks.sa.gov.au/sealbay

## Tours

KI Outdoor Action Quad motorcycle tours, as well as sand board and body board hire. Yarraman Ridge, South Coast Rd, Vivonne Bay; (08) 8559 4296.

Kelly Hill Caves

## Where to eat

Vivonne Bay Store $ It's your classic Australian takeaway food joint. Indulge in the legendary KI Whiting Burger. South Coast Rd, Vivonne Bay; (08) 8559 4285; daily 8am–6pm.

## Where to stay

Kaiwarra Cottage ★★ Dorm $20–$25, double $50–$55 South Coast Rd, adjacent to Seal Bay Rd; (08) 8559 6115; www.kaiwarra.com.au

For more detail
see maps
216, 217 &
218–219

# Flinders Ranges
## The Aussie outback

The vast and varied region that is the Flinders Ranges covers around 70 per cent of South Australia, and includes some of the country's most legendary landscapes. The Ranges are rich in scenery and history, with magnificent gorges, watering holes, Aboriginal sites and evocative ruins indicating many failed attempts at European settlement. Coober Pedy, the opal capital of the world, is a quintessential outback town (just watch *Priscilla Queen of the Desert* for a preview), while Port Augusta is a prosperous port city with some excellent natural attractions.

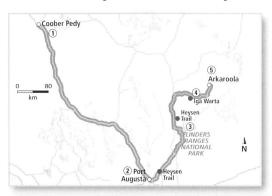

**Number of days to spend in this region: 8–10 days**

There are many tours of the region, which include transfers to and from various attractions. If you're making your own way, Premier Stateliner buses depart from Adelaide daily. A hire car is also a good option, or there are local bus services that run throughout the state. For a more expensive but fast option, Regional Express flies from Adelaide to Coober Pedy Airport.

Premier Stateliner 111 Franklin St, Adelaide; (08) 8415 5500; www.premierstateliner.com.au

Bus SA – information service (08) 8303 0822; www.bussa.com.au

Regional Express 13 1713; www.regionalexpress.com.au

## Flinders Ranges tours

**Wombatventures** Great four-day tours of the Flinders region. Ideal for backpackers. (08) 8395 5276; www.wombatventures.com.au

**Just Cruisin 4WD Tours** Offers various 4WD tours of the region. (08) 8323 9827; www.justcruisin4wdtours.com.au

**Wayward Bus** Excellent tours incorporating the Ranges, Coober Pedy and Iga Warta. 119 Waymouth St, Adelaide; (08) 8410 8833; www.waywardbus.com.au

**Aussie Heritage Tours** One- to three-day tours of the Ranges. See the park by bus, 4WD and scenic flights. (08) 8289 4191; www.aussieheritagetours.com.au

**Tom's Tours** Jam-packed, two-day tour of the Ranges, as well as two nights at Hornsdale Farm. 1800 618 876; www.tomstours.com.au

**Wallaby Track Adventure Tours** One- to five-day outback adventures in and around the Flinders Ranges. Guided bushwalks, mountain biking and boomerang throwing all included. (08) 8648 6655; www.users.bigpond.com/headbush

## ❶ Coober Pedy (2 days)

On 1 February 1915, a group of gold prospectors discovered opals in the area surrounding Coober Pedy. Little did they know that this area would become the biggest opal field in the world, producing over 90 per cent

of the world's opals. This is the place to come if you're looking for good deals on opal-related gifts.

Coober Pedy is as outback as Australia gets – arid, hot, and inhabited by friendly and eccentric locals. The town's name is derived from the Aboriginal phrase 'kupa piti', loosely translating to 'white man's hole in the ground'. This refers not only to opal mining, but also the town's unique underground style of living, which was first established by returning WW I soldiers who were used to trench life, and now suits locals who are keen to escape the harsh summer sun and cold winter nights. It is highly recommended that you experience 'dug out' life in underground accommodation and visit the underground art galleries, churches, opal shops and museums.

Umoona Underground Mine and Museum is an award-winning centre with free admission to its excellent museum covering the town's rich, detailed history. There is also an Aboriginal interpretive centre, animal fossils and on-site mine tours. If you can't get enough of the miner's world, make your way through the vast network of tunnels at Old Timers Mine. This former opal mine was accidently unearthed in 1968, and also has a museum and gift shop.

Above ground, Big Winch Lookout is one of Coober Pedy's most renowned landmarks, and gives you a bird's-eye view of the town. Just north of Coober Pedy, Moon Plain and the Breakaways is an amazingly coloured, rocky landscape once covered by an inland sea. The best time to visit this marvel is at sunset.

## Further information

ⓘ **Coober Pedy Visitor Centre** Hutchinson St; 1800 637 076; Mon–Fri 8.30am–5pm, Sat–Sun 10am–1pm; www.cooberpedy.sa.gov.au
**Umoona Underground Mine and Museum** Mine tours daily 10am, noon, 2pm & 4pm. Lot 14 Hutchison St; (08) 8672 5288; daily 8am–7pm; www.umoonaopalmine.com.au
**Old Timers Mine** Crowders Gully Rd; (08) 8672 5555; daily 9am–5.30pm; www.oldtimersmine.com
**Big Winch Lookout** Italian Club Rd.

## Tours

**The Mail Run Tour** Go on an overland adventure with Coober Pedy's mailman, past waterholes and through scenic landscapes, on his delivery run to Oodnadatta, William Creek and remote cattle stations. The mailman tells many fascinating stories along the way. Tours leave from the Underground Bookshop Mon & Thur 9am. (08) 8672 5226; www.desertdiversity.com
**Oasis Tour** Cheap, half-day bus tours of all the town's hot spots. Evening tours also available, including Moon Plain and the Breakaways. (08) 8672 5169.
**Opal Air** Although most of Coober Pedy's attractions are underground, there's still plenty to see from a plane in the sky. (08) 8672 3067; www.opalair.com.au
**Radeka's Downunder Stargazing Presentation** An unforgettable night under the southern sky. (08) 8672 5223; www.radekadownunder.com.au
**Radeka's Desert Breakaways Tours** Half-day bus excursions, offering visits to some of Coober Pedy's most interesting and unique sites, including Moon Plain and the Breakaways. (08) 8672 5223; www.radekadownunder.com.au

Brachina Gorge

Roadhouse Oodnadatta

## Where to stay

**Radeka's Underground Backpackers** ★★ Dorm $22, twin and double $55 Hutchinson St; (08) 8672 5223; www.radekadownunder.com.au
**Bedrock Bunkhouse (Opal Cave)** ★★ Dorm $19–$20 Hutchinson St; (08) 8672 5028; www.opalcavecooberpedy.com
**Desert Cave Hotel** ★★★ **TOP TREAT!!** The world's only underground hotel with a shopping complex and display gallery detailing the early hardships of the miners. Single, twin and double $198 Hutchinson St; (08) 8672 5688; www.desertcave.com.au

## Events

**Opal Festival** Unique art work, street parades, food and dancing. Apr.
**Coober Pedy Greek Glendi** A celebration of everything Greek in town. Jul.
**Coober Pedy Horseracing** Watch the horsies run around and soak up the atmosphere that is Coober Pedy racing at its finest. Aug.

## ② Port Augusta (1–2 days)

Port Augusta is the most northerly port in South Australia and is the point where many state roads intersect, giving it the name, 'Crossroads of Australia'. It is a thriving industrial city, as well as a major tourist and commercial hub. The award-winning Wadlata Outback Centre covers the Indigenous, natural and social history of the outback and Flinders Ranges. There are interpretive displays, audiovisual presentations and artefacts. You can discover the landscape of 15 million years ago in the Tunnel of Time, and hear ancient Dreamtime stories. The Australian Arid Lands Botanic Gardens has 200 ha of arid-zone vegetation that is fascinating to walk through. Meanwhile, don't forget to visit the Homestead Park Pioneer Museum, a farming and railway museum with a blacksmith's shop and old steam train, set amidst a 135-year-old homestead. If all this history isn't enough, follow in the footsteps of intrepid explorer Matthew Flinders and take a river cruise along the calm scenic waters of the Spencer Gulf.

## Further information

ⓘ **Port Augusta Visitor Information Centre – Wadlata**
41 Flinders Tce; (08) 8641 0793; Mon–Fri 9am–5.30pm, Sat–Sun 10am–4pm.

Wadlata Outback Centre 41 Flinders Tce; (08) 8642 4511; Mon–Fri 9am–5.30pm, Sat–Sun 10am–4pm; www.wadlata.sa.gov.au
Australian Arid Lands Botanic Gardens Stuart Hwy; (08) 8641 1049; gardens daily 7.30am–sunset, visitor centre & cafe Mon–Fri 9am–5pm, Sat–Sun 10am–4pm; www.australian-aridlands-botanic-garden.org
Homestead Park Pioneer Museum Elsie St; (08) 8642 2035; daily 9am–5pm.

### Tours

Augusta Water Cruises Two-hour cruises passing the port's gorgeous landscape. 3 Loudon Rd; 0438 857 001; www.augustawestside.com.au
Gulf Getaways Enjoy a short, three-hour eco-cruise along the Spencer Gulf. Evening and party cruises also available. (08) 8642 6827; www.gulfgetaways.net
Pichi Richi Camel Tour Not far from Port Augusta, in the town of Quorn, experience the true Australian bush from the back of a camel. Transfers can be arranged from Port Augusta to the Pichi Richi farm. (08) 8648 6640; www.pichirichicameltours.com

### Where to eat

Outback Tuckerbox $ Within the Wadlata Outback Centre is this comfortable and friendly cafe under a huge windmill. Winners include outback steaks, bushman's burgers, gourmet baguettes and Mars Bar cheesecakes. 41 Flinders Tce; (08) 8641 0755; Mon–Fri 9am–5.30pm, Sat–Sun 10am–4.30pm.

### Where to stay

Motel Pampas ★★ Room from $55 76 Stirling Rd; (08) 8642 3795.

## 3 Flinders Ranges National Park (2 days)

This park is one of the most loved in Australia, perhaps because of the sheer contrast between the Flinders Ranges and the surrounding open plains, or because of the amazing geology of Wilpena Pound at its heart. From the air, Wilpena Pound looks like a giant bird's nest or a hand forming the shape of a cup (the word 'wilpena' is thought to come from an Aboriginal word meaning 'place of bent fingers'). It is in fact a remnant valley, whose ridges are the eroded stumps of once large mountains. There are various walking trails starting from the lively campgrounds of Wilpena Pound Resort. North of the pound is mesmerising scenery along Bunyeroo Drive and the not-to-be missed Brachina Gorge Geological Trail, following Brachina Creek as it slices through three mountain ranges. The southern section of the park is ideal for rock climbing, with an extensive site at Moonarie near Arkaroo Rock. There are also some magnificent cycling tracks – the Mawson Trail is by far and away the best – as well as abseiling spots and walking trails throughout this majestic landscape.

4WD touring near Arkaroola

### Further information

ⓘ Flinders Ranges Visitor Centre Seventh St, Quorn; (08) 8648 6419; daily 9am–5pm; www.parks.sa.gov.au
ⓘ Wilpena Pound Visitor Information Centre Wilpena Pound Resort; (08) 8648 0048; daily 8am–6pm.

### Rock climbing and abseiling

Flinders Ranges National Park has some of the most challenging climbs in the country. There aren't many tours or rock climbing equipment hire places in the area, so you must organise this in advance. Climbing and abseiling around here can also be very dangerous, so make sure you're experienced enough to handle the different peaks.
Rock Solid Adventures (08) 8270 4244; www.rock-solid-adventure.com
DCXP Mountain Journeys This company specialises in rock climbing all over the world and is for serious climbers only. Their Australian tour package includes the Moonarie segment of Flinders Ranges National Park, Mount Arapiles in Victoria and the Blue Mountains in NSW. 208 Rundle St, Adelaide; (08) 8232 4433; www.dcxp.com

### Tours

Barking Gecko Tours A range of spirited mountain-bike tours around Flinders Ranges with informative guides. (08) 8648 6877; www.barkinggeckotours.com.au
Rawnsley Park Station Offers 4WD tours, scenic flights, mountain-bike hire and horseriding. (08) 8648 0030; www.rawnsleypark.com.au

### Where to stay

Rawnsley Park Station ★★ Camping $10–$17, on-site vans $38, park cabins $58 Wilpena Rd, via Hawker; (08) 8648 0030; www.rawnsleypark.com.au
Rawnsley Park Station YHA ★★ Single $41.50, double $59.50 (08) 8648 0008; www.yha.com.au
Willow Springs Station ★★ Camping (2 people) $15, hut $45, cottage $85 (08) 8648 0016; www.frabs.com.au/willowsprings.htm
Wilpena Pound Resort ★★ Camping $11–$18 Wilpena Pound; (08) 8648 0004; www.wilpenapound.com.au

## Heysen Trail (1–60 days)

The 1200 km Heysen Trail begins on the tip of the Fleurieu Peninsula and ends at Parachilna Gorge. It is one of the longest and most beautiful walks in the world, so not surprisingly, many walkers choose to experience it in small sections – perhaps the rolling hills and glittering coast of the Fleurieu, the Mount Lofty Ranges outside Adelaide, or the Barossa Valley. The entire track will take you around 60 days to complete, and will earn you a Friends of the Heysen Trail 'End to End' certificate. For those with less time, the most popular leg of the journey is the Flinders Ranges, where the track winds from Wilpena Pound to the classic river red gum scenery of the Aroona Valley, made famous by painter Sir Hans Heysen. Bring some sturdy walking shoes with you, and camping gear if you want to spend the night. The trail itself is open from 1 May – 31 October. It is closed during the hotter months because of the danger of fire.

## Further information

It's vitally important that you plan your walking treks along the Heysen Trail. Don't overestimate how far you can walk, and always take plenty of food, water and a kit (including sunscreen, insect repellent, bandages and skin adhesives). If an emergency occurs, dial 13 1400 or 000. For further information, visit www.heysentrail.sa.gov.au

## Tours

**Ecotour** Seven-day walking tour of easy to moderate difficulty. (08) 8346 4155; www.ecotrek.com.au

### ❹ Iga Warta (1 day)

Iga Warta is home to the Adnyamathanha people, or the 'stone people'. The Iga Warta Experience is a unique opportunity to discover their unique culture as they guide you along ancient creation paths, pointing out food and medicine plants, introducing you to engraving and painting sites, and sharing their traditional and contemporary stories. Prices include cultural tours, walks, campfires and night tours. Overnight stays are available, in either camping or motel facilities. Bookings are essential.

## Tours

**Iga Warta (Direct)** Iga Warta, Copley; (08) 8648 3737; www.igawarta.com
**Diverse Travel** 35–37 Stirling St, Thebarton; (08) 8303 3418; www.aboriginalaustralia.com.au

### ❺ Arkaroola (1–2 days)

Set in ranges dotted with precious mineral sites and waterholes nestled inside tall gorges, Arkaroola is one of South Australia's great wonders. The area is alive with many small earthquakes occurring year-round. Take the opportunity to explore this area via a Ridgetop Tour. Travelling in a specially constructed open-top 4WD through inspired red-granite mountains and golden-coloured hillsides will truly take your breath away. Just when you think that's enough, the Vulkathunha-Gammon Ranges National Park invites you to enjoy its distinctive scenery. Find

your way to the lush Weetootla Gorge, which is fed by a permanent spring, and the Italowie Gorge.

## Further information

ⓘ **NPWSA Balcanoona** (Vulkathunha-Gammon Ranges National Park) (08) 8648 4829 or 1800 816 078 (Desert Parks Hotline).

## Ridgetop tours

**Arkaroola Wilderness Sanctuary** Waterholes and astronomy tours also available. (08) 8648 4848; www.arkaroola.com.au/ridgetop.php
**4WD Aussie Outback Adventures** (08) 8289 4191; www.aussieheritagetours.com.au
**Swagabout Tours** 0408 845 378; www.swagabouttours.com.au
**Dingo Whoop Whoop Tours** (08) 8327 3402; www.dingowwtours.com

## Where to stay

**Greenwood Lodge** ★★★ Room $89 (08) 8648 4848; www.arkaroola.com.au
**Callitris Lodge** ★★★ Room $130 (08) 8648 4848; www.arkaroola.com.au
**Balcanoona Shearer's Quarters** Room from $220 (sleeps 18) (08) 8648 4829.

**For information and bookings for the following accommodation options, call the DEH Wilpena office (08) 8648 0049:**
**Grindells Hut** Hut from $90 (solar-powered)
**Nudlamutana Hut** Hut from $67
**Camping** There are many camping areas in Vulkathunha-Gammon Ranges National Park. Campsites with vehicle-based access and toilets are at Weetootla, Balcanoona and Grindells Hut. Camping areas without facilities are at Italowie Gorge in the south, Lochness Well and Mainwater Well in the centre of the park, and Arcoona in the west. There is water available for all campers at Grindells Hut and Nudlamutana. Bookings (08) 8648 0049.

View towards Arkaroola Rock near Wilpena

For more detail see maps 212 & 217

Adelaide

# Limestone Coast
# Attractions above and below ground

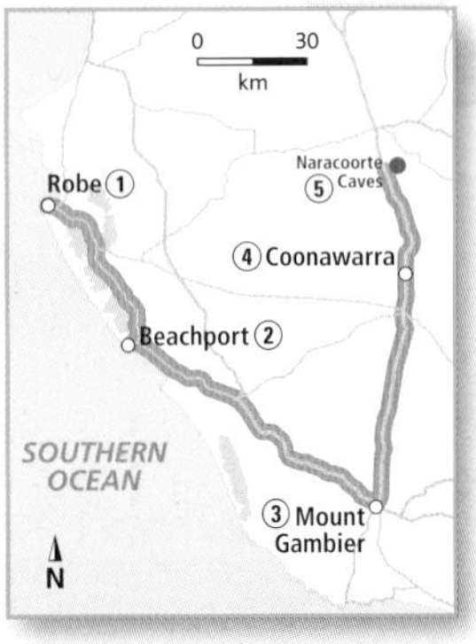
0
30
km
Robe ①
Naracoorte ⑤ Caves
④ Coonawarra
Beachport ②
SOUTHERN OCEAN
③ Mount Gambier
N

The south-east region of South Australia follows the coastline from Kingston S.E. to the Victorian border. This is one of South Australia's major holiday regions, featuring historic fishing villages, stunning beach scenery and the prestigious wineries of the Coonawarra. Impressive natural wonders are present above and below ground, including Mount Gambier's Blue Lake and the World Heritage-listed Naracoorte Caves. So whether you want to relax or suit up for some adventure caving, the Limestone Coast has you covered.

**Number of days to spend in this region: 7–8 days**

There are many tours of the region, which include transfers to and from the various sights and attractions. If you're making your own way, Premier Stateliner buses depart from Adelaide and other cities in South Australia daily. Regional Express also flies from Melbourne and Adelaide to Mount Gambier Airport.

**Premier Stateliner** 111 Franklin St, Adelaide; (08) 8415 5500; www.premierstateliner.com.au

**Regional Express** 13 1713; www.regionalexpress.com.au

**Bus SA – information service** (08) 8303 0822; www.bussa.com.au

## 1 Robe (1 day)

Guichen Bay and Robe's red-and-white-striped Obelisk at Cape Dombey would have been welcome sights to the thousands of Chinese immigrants who disembarked here to travel overland to Victoria's goldfields in the mid 1800s. Robe today is one of South Australia's oldest and best-preserved towns. It boasts a fine collection of stone cottages and shops, many of them classified by the National Trust. Visit the Customs House for Chinese artefacts and displays on explorers and significant governors. Guichen Bay is a marvellous stretch of coast with beautiful beaches, including Long Beach, a pristine beach for surfing and swimming, and one of the only beaches in the country that you can drive on (but be careful not to get caught by the tide). Lake Fellmongery, also known as the Ski Lake, is the place for waterskiing, while the Little Dip Conservation Park is worth exploring for its complex, moving sand dune system. You can drive or walk through native bush to beaches for surfing and beach-fishing.

Road sign near Robe

### Further information

ⓘ **Robe Visitor Information Centre** Mundy Tce; (08) 8768 2465; Mon–Fri 9am–5pm, Sat–Sun 10am–4pm.

**Customs House** Royal Circus; (08) 8768 2419; Tue & Sat 2–4pm, Jan Mon–Sat 2–4pm.

**Department of Environment and Heritage Mount Gambier** (Little Dip Conservation Park) 11 Helen St, Mt Gambier; (08) 8735 1177; www.parks.sa.gov.au

**Boogie board hire: Steve's Place Surf Shop** Also provides information on surf conditions and ideal locations for watersports. Victoria St; (08) 8768 2094.

### Where to eat

**Wild Mulberry Cafe** $ Serving breakfast and lunch, this cafe has cheap, simple meals

from caesar salad to lamb korma. Try some excellent regional wines while you're there. 46 Victoria St; (08) 8768 2488; daily 8am–5pm.
**The Caledonian Inn** $\$\$$ This classy hotel has a diverse menu, whether you're in the mood for a light snack or a filling dinner. The seafood basket and chicken parmas are some of the favourites. 1 Victoria St; (08) 8768 2029; daily noon–2pm, 6–8.30pm; www.robelifestyle.com.au

### Where to stay
**Lakeside Manor YHA** ★★★ Dorm $27.50, twin and double $68.50–$93.50 22 Main Rd; (08) 8768 1995; www.yha.com.au
**Bushland Cabins and Caravan Park** ★★ Cabin $18–$30, ensuite cabin $60–$80 Cnr Main Rd & Nora Creina; (08) 8768 2386; www.robe.sa.gov.au/bushland
**Longbeach Caravan Park** ★★ Cabin (2 people) $50–$58 The Esplanade; (08) 8768 2237; www.robelongbeach.com.au

### Events
Robe Village Fair Family music festival with great acts, food, and arts and crafts. Nov.

## ② Beachport (2 days)
Beachport is a seaside town with an air of elegance, and is a great place to unwind. If you're not one for relaxing, visit the Old Wool and Grain Store, now a National Trust museum with displays on the history of the town's shipping and whaling past. Nearby, the Pool of Siloam has salinity levels seven times that of the sea and is said to be a cure for all manner of ailments. It's the closest thing Australia has to Israel's Dead Sea, so yes, you can float on the surface and read the newspaper!

A bit out of the main town but well worth seeing is Beachport Conservation Park, a long succession of white beaches, sand dunes and rugged limestone coastline. Five Mile Drift, a beach on Lake George, is a good base for swimming, sailing and windsurfing. Canunda National Park is of a similar ilk, and a great place for those who love bushwalking and birdwatching. The park's Cape Buffon Walking Trail is a brisk, 2.5 km trek passing limestone cliffs and beautiful wildflowers. There are also interpretive signs along the way that explain the area's features. Lastly, don't forget the gorgeous Tantanoola Caves Conservation Park, on the Princess Highway, 29 km north-west of Mount Gambier. There are daily tours of the elaborate cave formations on show in one easily accessible cavern (tours run 10.15am, 11.15am, noon, 1.15pm, 2pm, 3pm, 4pm).

### Further information
ⓘ **Beachport Visitor Information Centre** Millicent Rd; (08) 8735 8029; Mon–Fri 9am–5pm, Sat–Sun 10am–4pm, winter 10am–1pm.
Old Wool and Grain Store Museum Railway Tce; (08) 8735 8029; Fri–Wed 10am–4pm, Sun 10am–2pm.
Pool of Siloam End of McCourt St.

**Department of Environment and Heritage Mount Gambier** (Beachport Conservation Park, Canunda National Park & Tantanoola Caves Conservation Park) 11 Helen St, Mt Gambier; (08) 8735 1177; www.parks.sa.gov.au

### Where to stay
**Beachport Motor Inn** ★★ Room from $75 13 Railway Tce; (08) 8735 8070.
**Beachport Southern Ocean Tourist Park** ★★ Cabin from $60 Somerville St; (08) 8735 8153.

Coastline at Robe

## ③ Mount Gambier (2 days)
The second-largest city in South Australia, Mount Gambier is set on an extinct volcano, boasting a fascinating network of volcanic craters above sea level and limestone caves beneath the surface. This place truly is a city in the heart of the country, with a mix of commercial developments and historic buildings, such as the Old Courthouse, which houses a local history museum and an art and craft gallery. Mount Gambier's nickname, Blue Lake City, stems from the town's absolute highlight, the Blue Lake. Every November to March, the colour of this spectacular body of water changes from a dull grey to a vibrant blue, a phenomenon yet to be explained by scientists. You may also want to visit Umpherston Sinkhole, also known as the Sunken Garden. This sinkhole was created when a cave chamber collapsed on itself, and now hosts a beautiful underground garden, perfect for a barbecue or a stroll on a sunny afternoon. The gardens are floodlit at night. For a bird's-eye view that will be etched in your memory forever, head to the top of Centenary Tower in the Crater Lakes area.

Surrounding Mount Gambier are further attractions. It's worth making the effort to trek to the top of Mount Schank, where you can descend down into the middle of the extinct volcano (note that the two summit walks are very steep). Piccaninnie Ponds is an absolute treat for snorkelling and diving enthusiasts, who can glide through the crystal-clear, water-filled sinkholes and see delicate plants, fish and eels.

SOUTH AUSTRALIA

Blue Lake near Mount Gambier

## Further information
ℹ️ **The Lady Nelson Visitor and Discovery Centre**
Jubilee Hwy East; (08) 8724 9750; daily 9am–5pm;
www.mountgambiertourism.com.au
**Old Courthouse and Heritage Centre** Bay Rd; 1800 087 127;
Sun–Fri 11am–3pm.
**Umpherston Sinkhole** Jubilee Hwy East; (08) 8724 9750.
**Centenary Tower** Crater Lakes; 0438 239 224; opening hrs vary,
usually open Sat–Sun & public holidays. Flag flying on top of the tower
indicates whether it's open to climb.
**Department of Environment and Heritage Mount Gambier**
(Mount Schank State Heritage Area & Piccaninnie Ponds Conservation
Park) 11 Helen St, Mt Gambier; (08) 8735 1177; www.parks.sa.gov.au
**Piccaninnie Ponds diving** Snorkel permits are required, and are
issued to any individual on an annual or a single snorkel basis. Diving
permits are also required, but are only issued to divers who are current
financial members of the Cave Divers Association of Australia (CDAA)
and are rated at sinkhole category. Proof of current CDAA membership
and categorisation will be supplied by the CDAA. Snorkel and dive
times range from 5am–midnight. For more information contact the
Department of Environment and Heritage Mount Gambier.

## Tours
**Aquifer Tours** Specialises in tours to the Blue Lake. Cnr Bay Rd & John
Watson Dr; (08) 8723 1199; www.aquifertours.com
**Lake City Taxis** Day tours to wineries and caves. (08) 8723 0000;
www.lakecitytaxis.com
**Lake City Tours** Half- and full-day tours of all Mount Gambier's sights.
(08) 8723 2991.

## Where to eat
**The Barn Steakhouse** 💲💲 It's not uncommon to hear someone
in town say that the best steak they ever tasted was at this place. Most
come here for aged, quality beef cooked to order over mallee coals, but

there's also a great range of seafood. Nelson Rd;
(08) 8726 8250; daily 6–10.30pm; www.barn.com.au
**Laughton Park Gardens** 💲 Ideal for afternoon tea on
a gorgeous spring day. They also sell jams for diabetics.
Brim Brim Rd; (08) 8725 0479; gardens daily 11am–
5pm, tea rooms Mon & Fri 1–5pm, Sat–Sun 10am–5pm
(excluding winter months); www.laughtonpark.com

## Pubs and bars
**The Gambier Hotel** The 'G' Bar at the hotel is always
bustling with locals and tourists. Comfy lounges, open
fires and great live music make it one of the best bars
in town. 2 Commercial St; (08) 8725 0611; Mon–Wed
7am–1am, Thur–Sat 7am–3am, Sun 7am–midnight;
www.gambierhotel.com.au

## Where to stay
**The Jail Backpackers** ★★ Dorm $20, twin and double $45
Old Gaol, Margaret St; (08) 8723 0032; www.jailbackpackers.com
**Blue Lake Holiday Park** ★★★ Cabin from $70, unit from $93,
bungalows from $124 Blue Lake; (08) 8725 9856;
www.bluelakeholidaypark.com.au

## Events
**Mount Gambier Winter Festival** Winter-themed activities,
including ice skating. Jul.

## ④ The Coonawarra (1–2 days)
Prominent wine professionals such as Wolf Blass damned the region
as a place that could never produce decent wine, but in the 1950s
companies like Penfolds and Yalumba finally recognised the value
of this 12 km-long and 2 km-wide stretch of terra rossa soil. Helped
by the cool climate, the Coonawarra soil produces some of the best
cabernet sauvignon in the country. Over 20 wineries offer cellar-
door tastings and sales. Balnaves of Coonawarra is a family-owned
winery, with award-winning cabernet sauvignon that can be sampled
while overlooking a pond surrounded by 900 rose bushes. Brand's of
Coonawarra has a diverse selection of wines to try, from fruity yet spicy
chardonnays to more reserved merlots. Majella has an excellent cellar
door and is famous for red varieties, particularly its sparkling shiraz,
while Zema Estate is worth a stop so that you can try the Cluny, a blend
of cabernet sauvignon, merlot, cabernet franc and malbec with a sweet
oak overtone.

## Further information
ℹ️ **Penola Coonawarra Visitor Information Centre** 27 Arthur St,
Penola; (08) 8737 2855; Mon–Fri 8.30am–5pm, Sat 10am–5pm, Sun
9.30am–4pm; www.coonawarra.org

Balnaves of Coonawarra Main Rd; (08) 8737 2946; Mon–Fri 9am–5pm, Sat–Sun 12pm–5pm; www.balnaves.com.au

Brand's of Coonawarra Riddoch Hwy; (08) 8736 3260; Mon–Fri 9am–4.30pm, Sat–Sun 10am–4pm.

Majella Lynn Rd; (08) 8736 3055; daily 10am–4.30pm; www.majellawines.com.au

Zema Estate Riddoch Hwy: (08) 8736 3219; daily 9am–5pm; www.zema.com.au

## Tours

Penola Coonawarra Tour Service (Limecoast Tours) The experts of the Coonawarra wine region. (08) 8723 9790; www.lcat.com.au

For Wine or Reason Tours to all regions of the state, including Coonawarra. 0438 388 883; www.forwineorreason.com.au

## Where to eat

Upstairs at Hollick 💲💲 A modern Australian bistro with a touch of class. Enjoy the freshest produce, as well as the chef's own home-grown herbs and veggies. Try a wood-fired pizza for lunch and the vegetable and cannellini stew for dinner, both with wine from Hollick's vineyard. Hollick Winery, Riddoch Hwy; (08) 8737 2752; lunch Tue–Sun noon–2.30pm, dinner Fri–Sat 6.30–8.30pm; www.hollick.com

## Where to Stay

Penola Caravan Park ★★ Cabins from $72 4 South Tce, Penola; (08) 8737 2381; www.penolacaravanpark.com.au

## 5 Naracoorte Caves (1 day)

For thousands of years these 26 caves have acted as a natural trap for animals. It was a simple process at work: the hidden openings surprised passing animals and they fell to their deaths. With just the right environment for fossilisation, 20 fossil deposits have been found – establishing an incredible record of Australia's evolution over the last 500 000 years. The Wonambi Fossil Centre holds some of the fossils retrieved from the caves, as well as life-size replicas of ancient animals and scientific displays that take visitors back in time.

Not all caves are open to the public, but there are some fantastic tour options. For the adventurer, there are caving activities available, complete with matching overalls and kneepads. There are also various walking trails, including the World Heritage Trail (1.2 km, 30 min) from the Wet Cave entrance to Victoria Fossil Cave, and then through dry red gum woodlands and savannah grassland to the Stoney Point picnic ground.

## Further information

Naracoorte Caves National Park (08) 8762 3412; www.parks.sa.gov.au/naracoorte

Wonambi Fossil Centre (08) 8762 2340; daily 9am–5pm.

## Tours

Victoria Fossil Cave Tour An introduction to Australia's ancient animal history. You will pass through several decorated chambers on the way to the Fossil Chamber.

Alexandra Cave Tour This 30-minute tour reveals beautiful decorations, with examples of stalactites, stalagmites, helectites and columns. A cluster of stalactites reflected in a pool of water is a highlight.

Bat Tour Takes you through Blanche Cave, where thousands of native bent wing bats cling to the ceiling. You will also visit the Bat Interpretive Centre where the bats can be viewed via infrared cameras.

Wet Cave Tour This is the only self-guided cave. Enjoy the motion-sensor light system and the dripping spelothems.

Adventure Caving Experience the thrill of squeezing through some tight spaces. The Blackberry and Sticky-Tomato tours are more appropriate for beginners, while the Starburst Chamber Tour and the Fox Cave Tour are for the experienced.

You Toucan Tours Four-day tour incorporating the Naracoorte Caves and Wonambi Fossil Centre. 0407 609 752; www.youtoucantour.com.au

## Where to stay

Naracoorte Backpackers ★★ Dorm $20, twin $25 pp 4 Jones St; (08) 8762 3835; www.goinsouth.com.au

Wirreanda Bunkhouse ★ Dorm $15 Naracoorte Caves National Park; (08) 8762 2340.

Camping There are ten powered camping areas throughout the national park. Power and laundry facilities and rainwater are available to campers. For more information on accommodation, consult the website or call (08) 8762 2340.

Naracoorte Caves

# TASMANIA

# CONTENTS

Hobart 180

TOP REGIONS:

The South-East 188

East Coast and the Mid-north 193

The North-west 198

## Visitor information

Tourism Tasmania 1300 655 145; www. discovertasmania.com.au, www.tastravel.com.au

## Tasmanian backpacker tours

Tasmanian Expeditions Will take you whitewater rafting, rock climbing, bushwalking, cycling and sea-kayaking. 1300 666 856 or (03) 6339 3999; www.tas-ex.com

Under Down Under Easy paced, fun adventure tours for small groups of travellers. (03) 6234 4951; www.underdownunder.com.au

Escape Tours Tasmania One- to five-day backpacker adventure tours all around the island. 1800 133 555; www.escapetourstasmania.com.au

Adventure Tours Australia Three- to seven-day guided adventure and nature tours for fun-loving, young travellers. 1300 654 604; www.adventuretours.com.au

Australia's southern island is a feast for travellers, offering mind-blowing coastal scenery, World Heritage-protected wilderness, incredible examples of the nation's earliest colonial history and some of the most relaxed and friendly people you'll ever meet. 'Tassie' is also the perfect place to kick back and indulge in cool-climate wines, fresh seafood, fruits and fine cheeses. The state's small size and quiet roads make it a great place for an extended driving holiday, and most visitors find that they can comfortably meander around the major attractions in ten days. But be warned: there are so many gorgeous distractions, you'll find yourself wanting more time to linger. Tasmania's superb network of bushwalking trails brings adventurers from around the world, and there's also whitewater rafting, awesome surfing and spectacular rock climbing and abseiling that will satisfy even the most passionate adrenalin seeker.

## Top region highlights

### Cradle Mountain–Lake St Clair National Park

These two iconic World Heritage features sit at either end of the eight-day Overland Track, regarded as one of the world's great bushwalks. p. 198

### Port Arthur Historic Site

This remarkable site preserves the ruins of what was once an extensive convict complex, established in 1830. Take a ghost tour to really get into its eerie character. p. 189

### Wineglass Bay

This tranquil bay surrounded by wilderness is the scenic centrepiece of the beautiful east coast. p. 194

### Tasmanian wineries

World-class cool-climate wines are to be found at boutique wineries along the Tamar River, near the historic city of Launceston. p. 197

### Tasmanian Devil Conservation Park

The island's most famous animal species is on show at this park — come at feeding time and hear the devils crunching on bones. p. 189

## Other regions worth a look

### Strahan and the Franklin

The west coast fishing village of Strahan leads to the Franklin River, one of the state's great wilderness experiences and a mecca for whitewater rafters.

### South-west Wilderness

An almost uninhabited land of fretted mountains, glacial lakes, wild rivers and dripping, ferny forests.

### Bass Strait islands

These low, windswept islands in Bass Strait's storm-lashed seas are the remains of the land bridge between Tasmania and mainland Australia. King and Flinders are the main islands, offering incredible beauty and activities including diving and game fishing.

Stanley

Marrawah

Burnie

Devonport

Scottsdale

St Helens

Deloraine

Launceston

Cradle Mountain–Lake St Clair
National Park

Queenstown

Miena

Ross

Bicheno

Strahan

Freycinet
National Park

Franklin–Gordon Wild Rivers
National Park

Strathgordon

New
Norfolk

Sorell

Hobart

Huonville

Port Arthur

Southwest
National Park

# Hobart

This tiny city is Australia's prettiest and most historic, where you could be caught in a 19th-century time warp. Around Sullivans Cove waterfront, historic warehouses are packed with galleries, restaurants, bars and cafes, while Hobart's low-rise shopping areas line narrow streets near the harbour. Life is relaxed here with everything in easy walking distance, if you don't mind a few hills. A key attraction is Salamanca Market, a lively arts, craft and fresh food market that's held each Saturday under plane trees along Salamanca Place. Nearby, Mount Wellington dominates Hobart's skyline: on a clear day the summit provides fantastic views, and in winter, a snow-capped playground.

## Top attractions

### Salamanca Place

The sandstone warehouses along Salamanca Place are probably Australia's most photographed Georgian buildings. Their interesting shops and galleries are worth exploring from end to end. There are also dozens of cafes, including the trendy Zum (29 Salamanca Place) and a couple of excellent pubs that are perfect for a hot coffee or cold beer. For 150 years, Salamanca's hotels catered for the whalers, ships' crews and 'riffraff' of the port: Knopwood's still does a roaring trade and is so popular on Friday nights that present day 'riffraff' spill onto the street. Nearby at the Salamanca Arts Centre, a free street party with a very danceable band is held every Friday from 5.30pm to 7.30pm. Hobart's famous Salamanca Market is held here every Saturday (see Markets).

### Tasmanian Museum and Art Gallery

Walking into this complex is like taking a step back in time. You'll see Australia's finest collection of colonial art, as well as fascinating displays on whaling and some gruesome convict history. The zoology galleries will introduce you to Tasmania's unique wildlife, including a glimpse of the extinct Tasmanian tiger or thylacine. 40 Macquarie St; (03) 6211 4177; daily 10am–5pm; general admission free; tours Wed–Sun 2.30pm.

Salamanca Market

### Maritime Museum of Tasmania

This museum brings Tasmania's rich maritime history to life with gear from the whaling era, and relics from shipwrecks. Cnr Davey & Argyle sts; (03) 6234 1427; daily 9am–5pm; admission fee applies.

### Elizabeth Mall

Surrounded by shops and cafes, 'The Mall' is busy most days. There's an information booth for travellers open on weekdays until 4.30pm and from 10am till 2pm on Saturdays. Underneath the mall, the once-pristine Hobart Rivulet is a reminder of why this spot was chosen for Hobart's settlement in 1804. You can still see it under the footpath next to the NAB building on the Liverpool Street corner.

### Constitution and Victoria docks

Constitution Dock and the neighbouring Victoria Dock are the heart of Sullivans Cove. They're working docks with the sights and smells to match. Several excellent seafood restaurants and dockside punts offering takeaway fish and chips complete the picture. At the end of the Sydney and Melbourne to Hobart yacht races in January, Constitution Dock is the centre of a three-day party.

### Battery Point

On the hill behind the wharves, Battery Point was built in colonial times to house the workers and merchants of the port. It's best to explore the area on foot, climbing up Kellys Steps from Salamanca Place. Hampden Road winds through the heart of Battery Point with handmade-brick workers' cottages on both sides. There is the wonderful Jackman and McRoss bakery cafe (57–59 Hampden Road), which has such exquisite tarts, flans and tasty breads that it has become a destination in itself. At the top of Runnymede Street, Arthurs Circus is an intact Georgian streetscape of 16 tiny workers' cottages nestled around a cute village green. A far grander house is Narryna, with tours that transport you into a 19th-century existence. At Trumpeter Street, stop in at The Shipwright's Arms Hotel, or 'Shippies', which has poured beer since 1846. The bar has a crazy nautical atmosphere with pictures of ships

To Claremont, Glenorchy & Moonah

To North Hobart

Soak @ Kaos

Lizbon Bar

PATRICK

ELIZABETH

ST

BRISBANE

MELVILLE

BATHURST

Ocean Child Inn

ST

CAMPBELL

ST

ARGYLE

To Government House, Royal Tasmanian Botanical Gardens, Lewisham & Sorell

To Rosny Park & Bellerive

Hollydene Lodge

ST

A6

New Sydney Hotel & Backpacker Inn

Shu Yuan Vegetarian Cafe

Rivulet

MURRAY

LIVERPOOL

ELIZABETH MALL

Montgomery's Pub, Private Hotel & YHA Backpackers

ST

Drunken Admiral

The Henry Jones Art Hotel

VICTORIA DOCK

HUNTER ST

Curly's

Cat & Fiddle Arcade

Halo Nightclub

TASMANIAN MUSEUM & ART GALLERY

Orizuru Sushi Bar

HARRINGTON ST

Vanny's Cafe & Takeaway

Centrepoint Shopping Centre

Central City Backpackers

MARITIME MUSEUM OF TASMANIA

FRANKLIN SQUARE

Lark Distillery

ST

CONSTITUTION DOCK

WHARF

The Shamrock Hotel

Hobart

Hadley's Hotel Lobby Bar

COLLINS

HOBART

Customs House Waterfront Hotel

FRANKLIN

ST

Fish Frenzy

Hobart Hostel

GOULBURN

BARRACK

Flamingos Dance Bar

Isobar

Elizabeth Street Pier

Narrara Backpackers

The Pickled Frog

Hobart Village Cinema & Gold Class

ST

SALAMANCA

PARLIAMENT HOUSE

LIVERPOOL

Transit Centre Backpackers

ST

Welcome Stranger Hotel

SANDY

BAY

ST DAVIDS PARK

SALAMANCA

Vietnamese Kitchen

CASTRAY

SALAMANCA PLACE

ESPL

To South Hobart & Mt Wellington

MACQUARIE

HAMPDEN

Retro Cafe

Irish Murphy's

RETREAT

Grape

SALAMANCA ARTS CENTRE

PL

DAVEY

Knopwood's Retreat & Syrup

Machine Laundry Cafe

ST

BATTERY POINT

PRINCES PARK

N

0    100

metres

Hotel Soho

RD

MONTPELIER

NARRYNA

KELLY

SOUTH

Jackman & McRoss

RD

To Kingston

B68

To Wrest Point Casino & Sandy Bay

and vessels. Narryna Heritage Museum, 103 Hampden Rd; (03) 6234 2791; Tue–Fri 10.30am–5pm, Sat–Sun 2–5pm; admission fee applies.

## Cadbury Schweppes Chocolate Factory

Cadbury's factory at Claremont makes, among other wicked delights, the 90 million Freddo frogs eaten every year by Australians. The factory dates back to 1921, so you can only imagine how much chocolate it has made in that time. Please note: you MUST book a tour, and make sure you have sensible shoes. Once there, you can soak up the sights, sounds and best of all, smells, of this magical place. Give in to temptation in the factory shop after the tour. Cadbury Rd, Claremont; Mon–Fri 8am–3.30pm; admission fee applies; tour bookings essential 1800 627 367.

## Cascade Brewery

Cascade's fine brews have been made here from local hops, barley, and mountain water since 1824. Several tours run daily (bookings essential and closed shoes must be worn) with samples included. You can also hang out at the bar and picturesque garden. 140 Cascade Rd, South Hobart; (03) 6224 1117; tours Mon–Fri 9.30am, 10am, 1pm & 1.30pm.

## Mount Wellington

With stunning views across the Derwent Valley and Storm Bay, Mount Wellington's often-snowy peak is just a 20-minute drive from the centre of Hobart. Pinnacle Road winds up through tall forest and alpine meadows, passing under the Organ Pipes' sheer cliffs before reaching

## Getting around

Public transport choices are limited in Hobart as there are no commuter trains or trams, but there are buses, and luckily, many of the city's attractions are in easy walking distance.

Metro buses are fairly regular around the city and suburbs at peak times, but less frequent on weekends. Timetables are displayed at most bus stops and are available from the Metro shop in the Hobart Bus Mall at the post office end of Elizabeth Street. An all-day ticket allows you to catch any number of buses after 9am, from Monday to Friday, and anytime on weekends.

Hobart's traffic is free-flowing and driving is easy, except for Hobart's many one-way streets, which can confound visitors – so keep a map or street directory on hand. Parking is rarely a problem with plenty of street spaces and multi-storey car parks in Argyle, Melville and Victoria streets.

On the river, commuter ferries operate from Brooke Street Pier to Bellerive on the eastern shore twice a day. Timetable information is available at the pier. There are also harbour cruises during the day (see Tours and activities below).

The 15 km Inter-City Cycleway runs alongside a rail track between Hobart's waterfront and the northern suburb of Claremont. With a paved surface and no hills, it's popular with commuters and recreational riders alike. The most scenic section links Hobart with Cornelian Bay and the Royal Tasmanian Botanical Gardens, running underneath the approaches to the Tasman Bridge. Bikes of all types can be hired from the Hobart end of the cycleway.

Public transport **Bus information line** 13 2201

Motoring organisation **RACT** 13 2722; **roadside assistance** 13 1111

Car rental **Autorent Hertz** (03) 6237 1111; **Avis** 13 6333 or (03) 6234 4222; **Budget** 1800 030 035; **Thrifty** 1800 030 730; **Europcar** 1800 030 118; **Look Selective Car Rentals** 1800 300 102

Campervan and 4WD rental **Britz** 1800 331 454

Taxis **Australian Taxi Service** 0411 286 780; **City Cabs** 13 1008; **Taxi Combined Services** 13 2227; **Yellow Cabs** 13 1924; **United Taxis** (03) 6278 2244

Ferry services **Captain Fells** (commuter service to Bellerive) (03) 6223 5893

Bicycle hire **Bike Hire Tasmania** (Appleby Cycles) (03) 6234 0400; **Derwent Bike Hire** (every day Nov–Mar) (03) 6260 4426

the summit. For explorers on foot, there are tracks into the forest or zigzagging up to the top. A visitor centre at the pinnacle offers shelter from the freezing winds. But if you enjoy the icy wind on your face, you can plummet down the road on a mountain bike, or arrange an abseil off one of the spectacular cliffs (see Tours and activities). Mount Wellington park ranger; (03) 6233 6680; www.parks.tas.gov.au

## Other attractions worth a look

**Parliament House** Built by convicts as a customs house. Between Salamanca Pl & Murray St; visitors gallery open on sitting days; tours Mon–Fri 10am & 2pm on non-sitting days; admission free.

**Franklin Square** City park of large trees, statues and lawns around an elegant fountain. Cnr Macquarie & Elizabeth sts.

**St Davids Park** Oasis of huge trees with the remains of its colonial gravestones still on display. Cnr Davey St & Sandy Bay Rd.

**Government House** One of the finest viceregal residences in the Commonwealth with Neogothic designs. Lower Domain Rd; (03) 6234 2611; open to the public one Sunday each year, usually in Feb; admission free.

**Royal Tasmanian Botanical Gardens** Started in 1818 and one of Australia's best gardens. Lower Domain Rd; (03) 6236 3075 or (03) 6236 3076; Apr & Sept 8am–5.30pm, May–Aug 8am–5pm, Oct–Mar 8am–6.30pm; admission fee applies for conservatory and discovery centre.

**Wrest Point Casino** Australia's first legal casino, opened in 1973. Sandy Bay Rd, Sandy

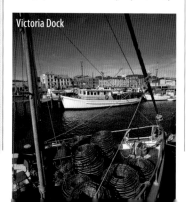
Victoria Dock

Bay; 1800 030 611; table gaming Mon–Thur & Sun 2pm–2am, Fri & Sat 2pm–4am; pokies daily 9am–5am; bars daily 10am–3am.

**Female Factory** Serving at various times as a rum distillery, contagious diseases hospital, home for 'imperial lunatics' and a fudge factory, this historic site was also a female prison for 50 years. Visitors can have morning tea with the Matron in her cottage. 16 Degraves St, South Hobart; (03) 6223 1559; Mon–Fri 9am–4pm; admission fee applies for morning tea with the Matron each Mon, Wed & Fri.

## Where to eat

**Sullivans Cove waterfront** Fish and chips from the punts in Constitution Dock is a yummy Hobart tradition not to be missed, or try one of the seafood cafes.

Our favourites: **Fish Frenzy** 💲💲 ♡ A breezy cafe serving paper cones of scrumptious fish and chips, salads, burgers and good wines by the glass. Tables inside and outside right next to the water. Elizabeth St Pier; (03) 6231 2134; Mon–Fri 11am–3pm & 5–9pm, Sat–Sun 11am–9pm.

**Orizuru Sushi Bar** 💲💲 ♡ Boxes of Japanese delicacies almost too pretty to eat, as well as miso soup, sushi and sashimi right next to the docks. Victoria Dock; (03) 6231 1790; lunch Mon–Sat noon–2.30pm, dinner daily 6–9.30pm.

**Drunken Admiral** 💲💲💲 TOP TREAT!! ♡ One of Hobart's favourite eateries. The maritime clutter is deliberately tacky (as is the salad bar) but worth putting up with for the sizzling Yachties seafood mixed grill. 17 Hunter St; (03) 6234 1903; dinner daily from 6pm; www.drunkenadmiral.com

**Downtown Hobart** Elizabeth Mall and Liverpool Street cafes are open during shopping hours. Cheap and cheerful food courts are in Centrepoint on Murray Street, and in Cat and Fiddle Arcade.

Our favourites: **Vanny's Cafe and Takeaway** 💲 ♡ Daggy decor, but the best Cambodian dishes. Be prepared to be asked, 'you want chilli?' – and Vanny means serious chilli. 181 Liverpool St; (03) 6234 1457;

## Markets

**Salamanca Market** Every Saturday come rain, hail or shine, Salamanca Place bursts into life with over 300 stalls selling craft, fresh produce and gourmet food from all over Tasmania. Salamanca Place; Sat 8.30am–3pm.

**Glenorchy Showgrounds** Sunday Market Tasmania's biggest trash and treasure market with craft, bric-a-brac and occasionally livestock. Royal Hobart Showgrounds, Glenorchy; Sun 8am–2pm.

**Island Market** Indoor market with craft, produce and new and second-hand goods. Gormanston Rd, Moonah; Thur–Sun 10am–4pm.

**Sorell Market** Produce, craft, and trash and treasure. Sorell Memorial Hall, Cole St, Sorell; Sun 8am–2pm (weekly in summer; fortnightly in winter; check with visitors centre for current schedule (03) 6265 6438).

lunch daily 11.30am–3pm, dinner Mon–Fri 5–9.30pm.
**Shu Yuan Vegetarian Cafe** ⓢ ♦ It offers tasty vegan stir-fries, soups and rice paper rolls based on odd ingredients like purple yam, black mushrooms and various meat substitutes. Shop 5/7, Bank Arcade, 64–68 Liverpool St; (03) 6231 1270; Mon–Fri 11am–3pm, Sat noon–3pm.

### Hampden Road, Battery Point
Casual and fine-dining restaurants, and counter meals in nearby pubs.
Our favourite: **Jackman & McRoss** ⓢ ♡ Pass the front counter's irresistible offerings of homemade bread, frittatas, flans and tarts, then settle in for some sweet and savoury delights with very good coffee. 57 Hampden Rd, Battery Point; (03) 6223 3186; daily 7.30am–5pm.

### Salamanca Place
A choice of restaurants, cafes, bistros and pubs.
Our favourites: **Machine Laundry Cafe** ⓢ ♦ This combined laundromat and chic cafe leaves no excuse to ignore that growing pile of festering laundry. Named one of the 'coolest places on earth' by *Arena* magazine. 12 Salamanca Sq; (03) 6224 9922; Mon–Sat

7.30am–5pm, Sun 8.30am–5pm.
**Retro Cafe** ⓢⓢ ♡ A Hobart institution and the place to be seen. It serves good breakfasts and takes its coffee very seriously. Bohemian atmosphere and arty crowd. 31 Salamanca Pl; (03) 6223 3073; Mon–Sat 8am–6pm, Sun 8.30am–6pm.
**Vietnamese Kitchen** ⓢ ♡ A red-hot favourite with locals. Keep the winter chill at bay with a steaming laksa or stir-fry with rice. Fast and tasty food that won't bust the budget. 61 Salamanca Pl; (03) 6223 2188; daily 10am–10pm.

### Sandy Bay
Loads of cheap eateries catering to uni students.
Our favourite: **Metz Restaurant Cafe Bar** ⓢ A favourite haunt for a loyal crowd not least because it has wonderful wood-fired pizzas. There are also good beers on tap and friendly service. 217 Sandy Bay Rd, Sandy Bay; (03) 6224 4444; daily 8am–late.

## Other areas to eat out
**Harrington & Collins streets corner** Some good, cheap takeaways, covering Thai, Indian and Balinese.
**Kingston** Beachside takeaways, pubs and a handful of shopping centre cafes.
**Moonah and New Town** The usual fast food outlets plus a couple of interesting cafes along the main road.
**Glenorchy** Look for the range of foodie franchises off Eady Street.
**Bellerive** A little cluster of cafes and bakeries around the foreshore boardwalk.

## Out and about
### Cinemas
**Hobart Village Cinema & Gold Class** 181 Collins St; (03) 6234 7288 or 1300 555 400.
**Eastlands Village Cinemas** Bligh St, Rosny Park; (03) 6245 1033.
**Glenorchy Village Cinema** Cnr Cooper & Eady sts, Glenorchy; (03) 6273 0444.

### Live music
**Hobart has a small but thriving live music**

## Where to shop

**Salamanca Place & Salamanca Square, Battery Point** Fine craft and Tasmanian art, books, outdoor clothes and travel gear.

**Elizabeth Street & Elizabeth Mall, City** Gifts, CDs, fashion, musical instruments, outdoor clothing, camping gear and antiques.

**Liverpool Street, City** Fashion, jewellery and a sci-fi specialist bookstore.

**Cat and Fiddle Arcade, City** Bargain fashion and sportswear.

**Centrepoint Shopping Centre, off Murray St, City** Fashion, sportswear, luggage, CD shops and bookstores around an internal plaza.

**Collins St, City** Electrical goods, jewellery and superb bookstores.

**Sandy Bay Road, Battery Point** Second-hand furniture, books, china and art.

**Sandy Bay Road, Sandy Bay** Stylish fashion, supermarkets and pharmacies.

**Eastlands Shopping Centre, Rosny Park** Hobart's largest undercover suburban mall housing most of the well-known department stores.

scene. Check out what's on in Thursday's Mercury newspaper and the *Tasmanian Gig Guide* at www.thedwarf.com.au
**New Sydney Hotel** Mainly local bands and always a packed dance floor. A large range of beers on tap, good pub food and a friendly crowd. 87 Bathurst St; (03) 6234 4516; bar Mon–Sat noon–midnight, Sun 4–9pm; live bands Tue & Fri–Sat 9pm–midnight, Sun 6–9pm; www.view.com.au/newsydney/contact.htm
**Lark Distillery** Nice, relaxed vibe in a long narrow venue with a smallish beer garden out the back. Mostly local folk musos or blues and roots bands. Lark Distillery, 14 Davey St; (03) 6231 9088; bar Mon–Wed & Sun 10am–6pm, Thur–Sat 10am–midnight; live music Thur–Fri 6pm–midnight, Sat 8pm–midnight; www.larkdistillery.com.au
**Curly's** The venue is modern and roomy and designed for clubbers, but they still rock on with live pub bands. There are long couches in the fire lounge, a heated beer garden, a chill-out room and a dance floor. 112 Murray St; (03) 6234 5112; Wed–Fri 4pm–5am, Sat 10pm–5am; www.curlysbar.com.au

## Pubs and bars

**Hotel Soho** Twenty beers on tap in this spacious, Art Deco pub with huge windows overlooking Hobart. Pub meals, live music and occasional DJs attract a mixed crowd. 124 Davey St; (03) 6224 9494; daily noon–late.

**Irish Murphy's** Enjoy 'the best craic in town' in a fake Irish pub. Bands on Friday and Saturday nights. 21 Salamanca Pl; (03) 6223 1119; Sun–Thur noon–midnight, Fri–Sat 11am–2am; www.irishmurphys.com.au

**Hadley's Hotel Lobby Bar** Stylish bar with a grand piano, leather armchairs and open fire. Good pub food, too. 34 Murray St; (03) 6223 4355; Mon–Fri noon–9pm, Fri–Sun 5–10pm; www.dohertyhotels.com.au

**Customs House Waterfront Hotel** Possibly the best site for a hotel in the whole of Australia. Gaming, a restaurant and live bands Wednesdays to Saturdays. 1 Murray St; (03) 6234 6645; Mon–Fri 7am–11pm, Sat 8am–late; www.customshousehotel.com

**Knopwood's Retreat Tavern & Wine Bar** Hobart's most famous waterfront pub and a tight squeeze on Friday nights. 39 Salamanca Pl; (03) 6223 5808; daily 11am–late.

**Montgomery's Pub** Big and busy pub with karaoke on Friday and Saturdays nights, pool tables, bands, DJs and a jukebox. 9 Argyle St; (03) 6231 2660; Mon–Thur 11am–10pm, Fri–Sat 11am–1am.

**The Shamrock Hotel** Unpretentious, small pub with really good meals. Busy with city folk. 195 Liverpool St; (03) 6234 3892; Mon–Thur 11am–10pm, Fri–Sat 11am–midnight.

**Grape** This place holds its own by doubling as a bottleshop and a narrow, trendy wine bar with distressed walls. 55 Salamanca Pl; (03) 6224 0611; daily 10am–11pm; www.grape.net.au

## Nightclubs

**Halo Nightclub** Fantastic venue to dance your adidas off. 37a Elizabeth Mall, entry off Purdys La; (03) 6234 6669; Wed & Fri–Sat 11pm–5am.

**Syrup** Hobart's funky dance club upstairs in Salamanca Place, with a mixed crowd and hits from past decades. 1st Floor, 39 Salamanca Pl, Hobart; (03) 6224 8249; Wed–Thur

### Gay and lesbian culture

Tassie has turned its old anti-gay reputation on its head and now has the most progressive anti-discrimination laws in the country. While the gay scene here isn't exactly thriving, there are cool bars and clubs if you know where to look. Try Soak bar in Elizabeth Street, North Hobart, for some sophisticated, velvet ambience with your Pimms, or Flamingos Dance Bar every Saturday from 10.30pm until late. Serious clubbers head to LaLaLand at Halo in Elizabeth Mall for a monthly fix of high-energy dance and partying.

**Soak@Kaos** 237 Elizabeth St; (03) 6231 5699; Mon–Thur noon–midnight, Fri–Sat noon–2am, Sun 10am–10pm; www.kaoscafe.com.au

**Flamingos Dance Bar** Level 2, 251 Liverpool St; Fri 5–10.30pm, Sat 9pm–late; www.flamingosbar.com

**Halo Nightclub** 37a Elizabeth Mall, entry off Purdys La; (03) 6234 6669; Wed & Fri–Sat 11pm–5am; www.clublala.net

### Sport

The Sydney to Hobart Yacht Race is Hobart's premier sporting event. Crowds gather to watch the first yacht take line honours, no matter what time of the day or night.

Australian Rules Football, or 'footy', is Tasmania's winter passion as in most of the rest of Australia. AFL team Hawthorn plays premiership season games at Aurora Stadium in Launceston and VFL games are played at Bellerive Oval – local Tasmanian team the Tassie Devils' home ground in the south. Bellerive Oval doubles as Hobart's premier cricket ground and Australia's most eye-pleasing venue to watch international and Pura Cup first-class domestic games.

There's an international-standard hockey centre at New Town, a premier tennis venue on the Domain and a spanking-new horseracing track at Tattersalls Park in Goodwood, north of the city. Swimmers can get their fill of laps at the Hobart Aquatic Centre in Davies Avenue.

9pm–2am, Fri–Sat 9pm–5am.

**Isobar** Live music in the downstairs bar, while DJs pump out the groove in the upstairs club. 11a Franklin Wharf; (03) 6231 6600; bar Fri 5pm–2am, Sat 7pm–5am; club Wed & Fri–Sat 10pm–5am; www.isobar.com.au

**Lizbon Bar** Cool nightclub with a huge selection of wines and spirits, and a low-light, smoochy atmosphere. 217 Elizabeth St; (03) 6234 9133; Tue 4pm–midnight, Wed–Sat 4pm–3am.

## Performing arts

**Theatre Royal** 29 Campbell St; (03) 6233 2299.

**The Backspace Theatre** Sackville St, behind Theatre Royal; (03) 6234 8561.

**Federation Concert Hall** 1 Davey St; 1800 001 190.

**Peacock Theatre Salamanca Arts Centre** 77 Salamanca Pl, Battery Point; (03) 6234 8414.

**Playhouse Theatre** 106 Bathurst St; (03) 6243 1077.

## Where to stay

For further information and reviews on these hostels, please visit

Cascade Brewery

Organ Pipes at Mount Wellington

Top events

**King of the Derwent** Maxi yachts take on each other and the Derwent Estuary to capture the crown. Jan.

**Royal Hobart Regatta** An old-fashioned family regatta and fireworks display since 1838. Feb.

**Australian Wooden Boat Festival** The Hobart docks are taken over with this biennial celebration of maritime history and visiting flotilla of every type of wooden boat imaginable. Feb (odd-numbered years).

**Southern Roots** A huge line-up of international and Australian rock, electronic and hip-hop at the Royal Hobart Showgrounds. Easter.

**Ten Days on the Island** An international sharing of 'island-ness' as Tasmania welcomes performances, music and art from the world's island cultures to its shores. Mar–Apr (odd-numbered years).

**Targa Tasmania** This exciting classic car rally circumnavigates the island. Apr–May.

**Antarctic Tasmania Midwinter Festival** Warms up midwinter with a celebration of snow, ice and long nights at the winter solstice. Jun.

**Sydney to Hobart and Melbourne to Hobart** yacht races. These two gruelling ocean races end with a dockside party, no matter what time of the day or night. Dec.

**Hobart Summer Festival** Hobart's streets sparkle with fun activities. Dec–Jan.

**Taste of Tasmania** Waterfront gourmet indulgence on a budget. Dec–Jan.

**The Falls Festival** Amp up into the New Year with a massive two-day festival of great bands and summer vibes. 30 Dec – 1 Jan.

www.bugaustralia.com, www.hostelaustralia.com or www.hostelz.com

**Central City Backpackers**★★★ Dorm $22, single $49, double or twin $62 138 Collins St; 1800 811 507; www.centralbackpackers.com.au

**Hobart Hostel**★★★ Dorm $17, double or twin $48 41 Barrack St; (03) 6234 6122.

**Narrara Backpackers** ★★★ Dorm $19, single $45, double or twin $48 (summer rates are higher) 88 Goulburn St; (03) 6231 3191; www.narrarabackpackers.com

**New Sydney Hotel & Backpacker Inn** ★★ Dorm $25 87 Bathurst St; (03) 6234 4516; www.newsydneyhotel.com

**Ocean Child Inn**★★★ Dorm $25 86 Argyle St; (03) 6234 6730; www.oceanchildinn.com

**The Pickled Frog**★★★ Dorm $22, single $55, double or twin $60 281 Liverpool St; (03) 6234 7977; www.thepickledfrog.com

**Transit Centre Backpackers**★★ Dorm $19, single $34 199 Collins St; (03) 6231 2400; www.salamanca.com.au/backpackers/

**Welcome Stranger Hotel** Dorm $22 Cnr Davey & Harrington sts; (03) 6223 6655.

**Montgomery's Private Hotel & YHA Backpackers**★★★ Dorm $23.50–$26.50, single $74.50, double $63.50 9 Argyle St; 1800 005 125; www.montgomerys.com.au

**Hollydene Lodge**★★ Dorm $25, double or twin $55 67 Liverpool St; (03) 6234 4981; www.hollydene.com.au

**Henry Jones Art Hotel**★★★ TOP TREAT!! Australia's only dedicated gallery hotel. Super-stylish luxury in historic waterfront warehouses. From $260 per night to $765 for the Peking Suite. 25 Hunter St; (03) 6210 7700; www.thehenryjones.com

# Tours and activities

**Blackaby's Sea Kayaks and Tours** Sea-kayak around the harbour at twilight, or for an extended paddle. Bookings 0418 124 072.

**Brake Out Cycling Tours** The Mount Wellington Downhill Tour takes you to the spectacular summit, where you hop on an 18-speed mountain bike for an exhilarating plummet down. Bookings (03) 6239 1080.

**Island Cycle Tours** See Tasmania from a bike. Tours include Mount Wellington Descent, East Coast Walking and Cycling combinations, and Tasmanian Training Rides. Bookings 1800 064 726. www.islandcycletours.com

**Aardvark Adventures Tasmania** Abseil Mount Wellington, Freycinet or the sheer wall of the spectacular Gordon River Dam – the world's highest commercial abseil. Suited to various levels. Bookings (03) 6273 7722. www.aardvarkadventures.com.au

**Mount Wellington Walks** Expertly guided ecotours winding through the forests of Hobart's fascinating Mount Wellington, or short walks in Mount Field, Freycinet or Cradle Mountain national parks. Gourmet lunches included. Bookings 0439 551 197.

**Wild Thing Adventures** An adrenalin rush by jet-boat to Storm Bay's amazing natural features, or circumnavigations of Bruny Island. Bookings (03) 6224 2021; www.wildthingadventures.com.au

**Derwent River Rafting** Starts with a tranquil journey through farmland, before encountering various rapids. Bookings (03) 6239 1080. www.raftingtasmania.com

**Lady Nelson** Join a bunch of hearty sailors for a cruise out on the Derwent in the square rigger, the *Lady Nelson*. Tours leave from Franklin Wharf. Bookings (03) 6234 3348.

**Hobart Historic Tours** Relive Hobart's colonial history with guided tours of the waterfront, Battery Point or its notorious pubs. Bookings (03) 6230 8233. www.hobarthistorictours.com.au

**The Peppermint Bay Cruise** Spend a day on this fully guided boat tour, taking in the D'Entrecasteaux Channel. There's lunch on board, followed by a stroll around Peppermint Bay (see p. 191). Brook St Pier; 1300 137 919; www.hobartcruises.com

# Outside the city: North Hobart

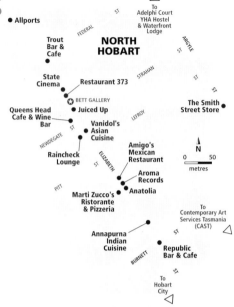

**NORTH HOBART**

To Adelphi Court YHA Hostel & Waterfront Lodge

Allports

Trout Bar & Cafe

State Cinema

Restaurant 373

BETT GALLERY

Juiced Up

The Smith Street Store

Queens Head Cafe & Wine Bar

Vanidol's Asian Cuisine

Amigo's Mexican Restaurant

Raincheck Lounge

Aroma Records

Anatolia

Marti Zucco's Ristorante & Pizzeria

To Contemporary Art Services Tasmania (CAST)

Annapurna Indian Cuisine

Republic Bar & Cafe

To Hobart City

N

0    50

metres

Just up the hill from Hobart city, North Hobart is an eclectic mix of shops, eateries and bars located along three blocks of Elizabeth Street. Once a dusty cart track to the colony's first farm at New Town, and later the working-class suburban home of the Redlegs (now Demons) footy team, this cosmopolitan restaurant strip has become a busy meeting place for locals away from the more touristy Sullivans Cove.

There's a nice ambience both day and night here, with Friday and Saturday nights bringing crowds of locals to eat, browse and party along both sides of the street. During the day, there are plenty of out-of-the-ordinary shops to poke around in, as well as fabulously cheap cafes and coffee shops, where you can linger over a cheap brekky or just watch the traffic negotiate the world's silliest roundabout.

## Top attractions

### Galleries

North Hobart has two of the city's most renowned galleries. Bett Gallery is where you'll find serious museum-quality contemporary art created by Tasmania's finest. Tucked away in nearby Tasma Street, CAST Gallery exhibits new works by Tasmania's most exciting young artists. Bett Gallery, 369 Elizabeth St, (03) 6231 6511, Mon–Fri 10am–6pm, Sat 10am–5pm, admission free; Contemporary Art Services Tasmania (CAST), 27 Tasma St, (03) 6233 2681, Wed–Sun noon–5pm, admission free.

## Where to eat

### Elizabeth Street, North Hobart

Bistros, takeaways, cafes, pubs and casual restaurants offering Asian, Italian, Indian and contemporary Australian food at affordable prices.

Our favourites: **Raincheck Lounge** $$ Hip cafe with a 70s vibe opens early for breakfast and doesn't shut its doors until late most nights. Lunch is soups, salads and focaccias, while dinner offerings include shareable starters and braised wallaby shanks. 392 Elizabeth St; (03) 6234 5975; Mon–Fri from 7.30am, Sat–Sun from 8.30am, dinner Wed–Sat; www.northhobart.com/raincheck

**Annapurna Indian Cuisine** $$ ♡ Fragrant and spicy meat and veggie curries served in metal bowls. Try the standout Cochin Fish, or if you've got an appetite, a thali platter. Lunch is a steal with curry and rice for $5.50. Wise to book on weekends. 305 Elizabeth St; (03) 6236 9500; lunch Mon–Fri noon–3pm, dinner daily 5.30–10pm; www.northhobart.com/annapurna

**Marti Zucco's Ristorante and Pizzeria** $ ♡ The best garlic pizza in Hobart and dead cheap, too. 364 Elizabeth St; (03) 6234 9611; lunch Thur–Sat, dinner daily 5.30pm–late; www.martizuccos.com.au

**Amigo's Mexican Restaurant** $$ ♡ Apart from dozens of different tortilla options, there is also good seafood and a rainbow of fruity margaritas. 329 Elizabeth St; (03) 6234 6115; dinner daily from 5.30pm; www.northhobart.com/amigos

**Vanidol's Asian Cuisine** $$ ♡ The first problem is to bag a table, followed by choosing from the scrumptious and overwhelming range of dishes. They have Thai, Indian and Indonesian, and all at good prices. Try the fragrant, yoghurty Nepalese

### Getting to North Hobart

Dozens of northern suburbs Metro bus routes travel from the city through nearby North Hobart along Elizabeth Street. From the city, hop on at the corner of Elizabeth and Liverpool streets.

lamb curry or their budget-priced dahl. Leave room for desserts like gulab jamun or gloy boid chee (poached bananas in coconut syrup). Book ahead, especially on weekends. 353 Elizabeth St, North Hobart; (03) 6234 9307; dinner Tue–Sun; www.northhobart.com/vanidols

**Juiced Up** $ ♡ Repair the damage you did last night with a serious upload of fruit and veggie vitamins, in the form of a crush or smoothie – so you don't even have to chew. 367 Elizabeth St; (03) 6231 1570; Mon–Fri 8am–5pm, Sat 9am–3.30pm.

**Anatolia** $ ♡ This traditional Turkish restaurant does a brisk trade in takeaway and budget meals. Homemade dips and pide bread is a steal at $5, and try their borek (Turkish pizza) or sis (skewered marinated grills). They have a belly dancer on Saturdays to add a little more spice to your meal. 321 Elizabeth St; (03) 6231 1770; dinner Tue–Sun;

www.northhobart.com/anatolia

**Restaurant 373** 💲💲💲 ♡ **TOP TREAT!!** A haunt for cashed-up hippies, this place gets rave reviews for its perfect cooking. Modern game and seafood predominate at just under $30, but it would be a sin to leave without dessert. While you decide, there's amuse-bouches (look it up!) to tickle your palate. 373 Elizabeth St; (03) 6231 9031; dinner Mon–Sat; www.restaurant373.com.au

**The Smith Street Store** 💲 ♡ One block off the main strip, this funky little coffee shop boasts the best coffee in Hobart. Upstairs you can get a massage or check your emails at Mouse on Mars. Cnr Argyle & Smith sts; (03) 6231 9955; Mon–Fri 7.30am–5pm, Sat–Sun 9am–4pm.

## Out and about
### Cinemas
**State Cinema** (art house and international films) 375 Elizabeth St; (03) 6234 6318.

### Live music, pubs, bars and nightclubs
**Republic Bar & Cafe** A Hobart icon that you won't beat for a night of great blues or rock. Local and touring acts perform Wednesdays to Saturdays. Even when it's crowded, it's still a cool place to listen to some great music. Cnr Elizabeth & Burnett sts; (03) 6234 6954; Mon 3pm–midnight, Tue–Sun noon–late; www.republicbar.com

**Trout Bar and Cafe** Head here for good, local, sweaty rock and roots in a scruffy pub, which gets a bit smoky when there's a full crowd of long-haired and black-jeaned revellers. Trout lines up local talent from Thursdays to Sundays. Gigs are mostly free or just $7. Cnr Elizabeth & Federal sts; (03) 6236 9777; daily noon–late.

**Queens Head Cafe and Wine Bar** This

---

**Where to shop in North Hobart**

**Aroma Records** Hobart's most laidback music store, where you can kick back with a good coffee while browsing and listening to their CDs, music DVDs and vinyl. 323a Elizabeth St; (03) 6231 9256.

---

pub does it all. There's a nice, long bar to lean on, gaming, a big dining area and irresistibly danceable swing, jazz, Latin, rock or soul music from Tuesdays to Sundays. They serve huge meals of modern pub fare for $14–$22. 400 Elizabeth St; (03) 6234 4670; daily 10am–late; www.northhobart.com/queenshead

## Where to stay
**Adelphi Court YHA Hostel** ★★★ Dorm $24.50–$27.50, single, double or twin $60.50–$67.50 17 Stoke St, New Town; (03) 6228 4829; www.yha.com.au

**Allport** ★★★ Dorm $22, single $50, double $60, twin $65 432 Elizabeth St; (03) 6231 5464.

**Waterfront Lodge** ★★ Dorm $20, double or twin $69 153 Risdon Rd, New Town; (03) 6228 4748; www.waterfrontnewtownbay.com

## Events
**Estia Greek Festival** Food, dancing, wine and more food make this event the year's best cultural celebration. Hobart's Greek community puts on two weeks of arts, sport, film, drama and exhibitions to celebrate Greek National Day on 25 March, then they let their hair down with a street party in Federal Street, where you can eat your fill of honey-soaked delicacies and test your Zorba dancing skills. Mar.

## Other suburbs worth visiting
**Taroona** Climb the dizzying heights of Taroona's 1870 sandstone Shot Tower, or swim at this leafy suburb's best-kept secret – the beautiful Hinsby Beach (access from Jenkins Street or along the foreshore from Taroona Beach).

**Bellerive** Take a relaxed stroll around this picturesque foreshore village or spend an hour at the fortress on Kangaroo Bluff. Incredibly scenic views across the Derwent to Hobart, with Mount Wellington behind.

**Clifton and South Arm** Fabulous, unspoilt beaches with the occasional swell kicking up some decent, surfable waves.

## Visitor information

### Hobart Airport
Hobart International Airport is just 17 km outside the CBD.

**Bus** The **Airporter Bus Service** meets all flights and drops travellers off to accommodation in the city and inner suburbs of Sandy Bay, Battery Point, North Hobart and New Town. Bookings are needed for hotel pick-ups on 0419 382 240 or 0419 383 462. www.hobartairpt.com.au/transport

**Taxi** This more expensive option will set you back around $45 for a trip to the CBD.

### Internet cafes
**Drifters Internet Cafe** Shop 9, 33 Salamanca Pl; (03) 6224 6286.

**Mouse on Mars Cyberlounge** 112 Liverpool St; (03) 6231 5421; www.mouseonmars.com.au

**The Pelican Loft Internet Cafe** 35a Elizabeth Mall; (03) 6234 2225.

**Outzone Computer Gaming & Internet Centre** 1st Floor, 66 Murray St; (03) 6224 0755.

**State Library** 91 Murray St; (03) 6233 7529.

**Service Tasmania** 134 Macquarie St; 1300 135 513.

### Hospitals
**For all emergencies, including police, fire, or hospital, dial '000'.**

**Royal Hobart Hospital** 48 Liverpool St; (03) 6222 8308.

**Calvary Hospital** 49 Augusta Rd, Lenah Valley; (03) 6278 5333.

**St John's Calvary Hospital** 30 Cascade Rd, South Hobart; (03) 6223 7444.

**Hobart Private Hospital** Cnr Collins & Argyle sts; (03) 6214 3000.

**St Helens Private Hospital** 186 Macquarie St; (03) 6221 6444.

For more detail see map 241

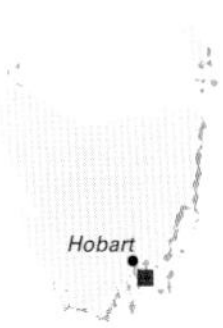
Hobart

# The South-east
# A great escape to the past

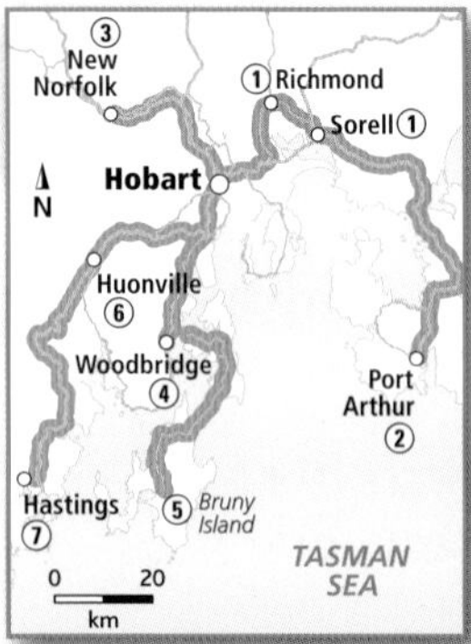
③ New Norfolk
① Richmond
Sorell ①
N
Hobart
Huonville ⑥
Woodbridge ④
Port Arthur ②
Hastings ⑦
⑤ Bruny Island
TASMAN SEA
0 20
km

Rivers, sea and mountains dominate the landscape of this extraordinarily scenic touring region. The coastline fronting the Tasman Sea is a long, ragged and spectacularly beautiful strip of peninsulas, islands, inlets and channels. Imposing mountains shadow the coast in scenes more reminiscent of the seasides of Europe. A leisurely pace of development over the last 200 years has kept much of the natural landscape intact. After passing small towns and national parks, you'll reach the arresting sandstone ruins of Port Arthur. This is the region's star attraction, a reminder of Australia's convict years.

**Number of days to spend in this region: 5–6 days**

## Getting here

Despite its name, there are no international flights to Hobart International Airport. Domestic carriers Qantas, Virgin Blue and Jetstar fly into Hobart from Melbourne, Sydney and Brisbane.

Tassielink's East Coast service passes through Richmond, and the Richmond Tourist Bus operates two services daily from Hobart. For the rest of the south-east region, Hobart Coaches run daily between Hobart and Kettering (two services connect with the Bruny Island ferry) and Cygnet. Tassielink has services from Hobart to Kingston and Geeveston, a summer service to Mount Field National Park, and a daily service to Port Arthur during school terms.

**Tassielink** 1300 300 520; www.tassielink.com.au

**Richmond Tourist Bus** 0408 341 804.

**Hobart Coaches** 13 22 01; www.hobartcoaches.com.au

## South-east tours

**Bottom Bits Bus** Runs day tours from Hobart to the Huon Valley, Mount Field National Park and Port Arthur. 1800 777 103; www.bottombitsbus.com.au

**Adventure Island Tours** Full-day tours of outdoor adventure and history around Port Arthur, Richmond and Eaglehawk Neck. (03) 6244 7080; www.adventureislandtours.com

## 1 Richmond and Sorell (half-day)

For those with their own transportation, stop in Cambridge on your way from Hobart to Richmond for some good food and wine experiences. Gorgeous Meadowbank Estate winery is set in a modern building with a beautiful fireplace that will warm you up during winter. Try the riesling and Grace Elizabeth chardonnay. Frogmore Creek is making a splash with organic wines; its cellar door is incorporated with Hood Wines. If you're into slurping oyster, Barilla Bay runs tours of its oyster farm on weekends. Samples are included, or you can splurge on a meal at their restaurant.

Richmond is Tasmania's most important historic town, with neatly restored cottages, pubs, churches and manor houses (several with their own resident ghosts) dating back to the 1800s. The much-photographed Richmond Bridge is the oldest surviving freestone bridge in Australia, built by convicts under appalling conditions in 1823. The situation was so bad that one convict committed suicide by throwing himself off the bridge and other convicts beat and killed an overseer who was known for his cruelty; legend has it that his ghost still haunts the bridge. You can steep yourself in more convict history at Richmond Gaol, once the abode of convict Ikey Solomon, the inspiration for Dickens' Fagin. You can also lose your mates in Richmond Maze and enjoy Devonshire tea once you find each other.

The town of Sorell has its roots in agriculture and there's a fruity abundance of pick-your-own farm produce in season, including apricots, cherries, peaches and berries too numerous to list. Sorell Fruit Farm also has free fruit wine and liqueur tastings. Nearby on the east

One of the many named houses in Doo Town

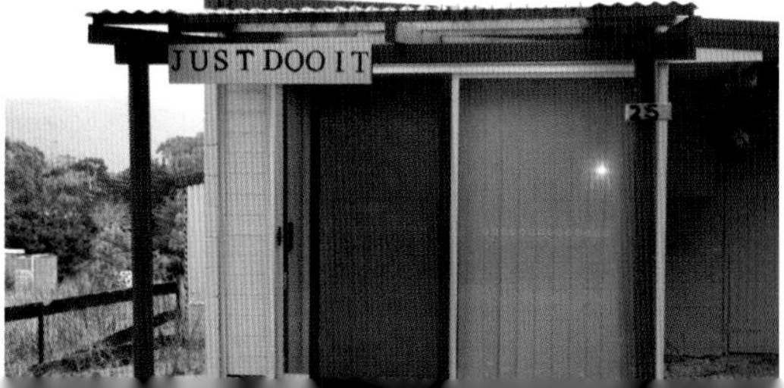
JUST DOO IT
25

coast, Marion Bay hosts The Falls music festival, bringing thousands of fans to the dunes each New Year.

## Further information

**Meadowbank Estate** 699 Richmond Rd, Cambridge; (03) 6248 4484; daily 10am–5pm; www.meadowbankwines.com.au
**Hood Wines** 208 Denholms Rd, Cambridge; (03) 6248 5844; Sat–Sun 10am–5pm; www.hoodwines.com.au
**Barilla Bay** 1388 Tasman Hwy, Cambridge; (03) 6248 5458; tours Sat–Sun noon & 4pm, extra tour Dec–Feb Wed noon; www.barillabay.com.au
**Richmond Maze & Tea Rooms** 13 Bridge St, Richmond; (03) 6260 2451; Mon–Fri & Sun 9am–5pm, Sat 10am–5pm; www.sullivanscove.com
**Richmond Gaol** 37 Bathurst St, Richmond; (03) 6260 2127; daily 9am–5pm.
**Sorell Fruit Farm** Buy or preferably pick your own fresh fruit and berries. 174 Pawleena Rd, Sorell; (03) 6265 2744; Oct–May daily 8.30am–5pm; www.sorellfruitfarm.com/harvest

## Tours

**Day and Night Tours of Richmond** Off Bridge St, Richmond; 0409 935 139.

## Where to eat

**Ashmore on Bridge Street** $ Enjoy good coffee and scrumptious Devonshire tea in a corner store with big, paned windows and a cosy open fire in winter. 34 Bridge St, Richmond; (03) 6260 2238; breakfast, lunch & afternoon tea daily; www.ashmoreonbridge.com.au

## Events

**Richmond Village Colonial Fair** This quaint village fair features many stalls, as well as butter churning and shingle splitting displays. Mar.
**The Great Tasmanian Oyster Riot** Food, wine and entertainment, all paying homage to the wonderful oyster. Hosted by Barilla Bay Restaurant. Oct.
**The Falls Festival** Marion Bay hosts the Siamese twin of the namesake music festival in Lorne, Victoria. Dec–Jan.

# 2 Port Arthur (1 day)

Eaglehawk Neck is the spectacular narrow entrance to the Tasman Peninsula, and was once a natural prison gate for the Port Arthur convict settlement, guarded by soldiers and a line of ferocious tethered dogs. Tasman National Park's striking scenery makes it clear why this coastline was the perfect deterrent for aspiring escapee prisoners. Tasman Blowhole, Tasmans Arch and Devils Kitchen are cavernous blowholes in the area's massive cliffs, creating awesome swells as the sea rushes in and out. The natural tile formation of the Tessellated Pavement is also in the

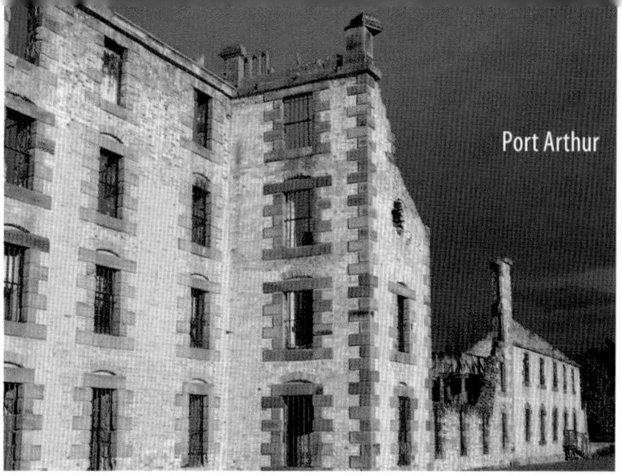

Port Arthur

area, but this is somewhat of a letdown on sight. If you have a head for heights take the trail to Tasmans Arch, Waterfall Bay and Patersons Arch, or a longer walk from Eaglehawk Neck to Fortescue Bay.

Offshore, this area has a huge diversity of dive sites. Attractions include the spectacular formations of Sisters Rocks, the 25 m-high giant kelp forests, the seal colony at Hippolyte Rock, the SS *Nord* shipwreck and amazing sea cave systems. There's good surfing at Pirates Bay, Maingon Bay and Roaring Beach, and some of the best adrenalin-pumping climbs and abseiling you'll find anywhere.

On your way to or from the area, take a detour to Doo Town, a small town where most of the houses bear names with variations of 'doo', like 'Just Doo It' and the crude Aussie slang term, 'She'll Doo'. It's a bit of fun.

At Taranna, a visit to the Tasmanian Devil Conservation Park is an absolute must. Get close enough to growl at a Tasmanian devil or watch them being fed – you'll hear their sharp teeth crunching on the bones of their unfortunate lunch. Then head to the Federation Chocolate and Heritage Museum, on the opposite side of the road, for some chocolate tastings.

The highway ends at Port Arthur, hell on Earth for most of its 12 000 convicts. An entry ticket lets you explore the grounds at your leisure and on a guided historical walking tour, and gives you access to the visitor centre, interpretation gallery, museum and a harbour cruise in summer. Spooky lantern-lit historical ghost tours depart at dusk and there are cruises to the Isle of the Dead just offshore. Scenic flights are another way to see the site and its stunning surrounds. Port Arthur Memorial Garden is a recent addition, dedicated to the victims of the 1996 tragedy at the site in which 35 people were killed by a gunman.

## Further information

[i] **Tasman Peninsula Visitor Information Centre** Officers Mess, 443 Pirates Bay Dr, Eaglehawk Neck; (03) 6250 3635
[i] **PWS Seven Mile Beach** (Tasman National Park) (03) 6214 8100; www.parks.tas.gov.au
[i] **Port Arthur Historic Site Visitor Information Centre** Port Arthur Historic Site, Port Arthur; (03) 6250 2363; www.portarthur.org.au
**Tasmanian Devil Conservation Park** Port Arthur Hwy, Taranna; (03) 6250 3230; daily 9am–5pm, devil feedings 10am, 11am, 1.30pm & 5pm (4.30pm in winter); www.tasmaniandevilpark.com
**Federation Chocolate and Heritage Museum** 2 South St, Taranna; (03) 6250 3435; Mon–Sat 9am–5pm.

## Tours

**Eaglehawk Dive Centre Tours** 178 Pirates Bay Rd, Eaglehawk Neck; (03) 6250 3566; www.eaglehawkdive.com.au
**Blackaby's Sea Kayaks & Tours** Sea-kayaking tours around Port Arthur and the Tasman Peninsula. 0418 124 072 or 0438 671 508.
**Sealife Experience Cruises** Pirates Bay Jetty, Eaglehawk Neck; 0428 300 303; www.sealife.com.au
**Port Arthur Historic Ghost Tours** Lantern-lit walking tours of Port Arthur – be prepared to freak out when you get to the autopsy room. Packages available with daytime entry. 1800 659 101; www.portarthur.org.au
**Tasmanian Seaplanes** Port Arthur Historic Site; (03) 6250 1077.

## Where to eat

**Officers Mess** $ Fish and chips or superb seafood salad rolls right on the beach. They've got Tassie's excellent scallop pies as well. 433 Pirates Bay Dr, Eaglehawk Neck; (03) 6250 3635; daily 9am–5pm.
**Mussel Boys** $$ Fresh and modern food with local seafood, including mussels, a specialty. 5927 Arthur Hwy, Taranna; (03) 6250 3088; daily 10am–late.
**Felons Restaurant** $$/$$$ **TOP TREAT!!** Forget salt meat and coarse gruel. Enjoy fine food in the visitor centre's à la carte restaurant, then watch out for nocturnal wildlife as you leave. Port Arthur Historic Site, Port Arthur; 1800 659 101; dinner daily (bookings required); www.portarthur.org.au

## Where to stay

**Roseview Youth Hostel** ★★★ Dorm $22.50, double or twin $51 Champ St, Port Arthur (right next to the historic site); (03) 6250 2311.
**Eaglehawk Neck Backpackers** ★ Dorm $18 92 Old Jetty Rd, Eaglehawk Neck; (03) 6250 3248; www.backpackers.eaglehawkneck.com
**Port Arthur Caravan and Cabin Park** ★★ Dorm $15 Garden Point; (03) 6250 2340; www.portarthurcaravan-cabinpark.com.au

# 3 New Norfolk (1–2 days)

New Norfolk is a National Trust-classified town renowned for its beauty and thriving hops industry. Enjoy a beer in Australia's oldest continuously licensed hotel, the Bush Inn, and visit the museum at the Oast House, showing all you ever wanted to know about hops and how they're processed. The Old Colony Inn is another museum, with antique furniture, dolls houses and a restaurant.

New Norfolk is surrounded by a natural adventure wonderland. You can hit the Derwent River in a jet-boat for some whitewater rapids at 80 km/h, or walk among giant swamp gums at the Styx Big Tree Reserve. Australia's tallest living tree – a whopping 97 m – is now protected here. Other forest giants are not so lucky and Tasmania's timber industry is an ongoing contentious issue.

At Mount Field National Park, you'll be awestruck by giant swamp gums, alpine tarns, snow-covered mountains and caves. Russell Falls is the state's most gorgeous waterfall, while Lake Dobson is home to platypus that you might see in the afternoon on the Pandani Grove Nature Walk (40 min). If you've got good all-weather gear, hike up to Mawson Plateau for some awesome alpine scenery.

## Further information

[i] **New Norfolk** (03) 6261 2333; www.newnorfolk.org
[i] **Mount Field National Park Visitor Centre** 66 Lake Dobson Rd; (03) 6288 1149; www.parks.tas.gov.au
**Bush Inn** 49–51 Montagu St; (03) 6261 2256; daily until midnight; www.thebushinn.com.au
**Oast House** Lyell Hwy; (03) 6261 1322; daily 9am–6pm; www.newnorfolk.org/~oast_house/
**Old Colony Inn** 21 Montagu St; (03) 6261 2731; daily 10am–5pm; www.newnorfolk.org/~old_colony_inn
**Styx Big Tree Reserve** Styx Valley Rd, Maydena; (03) 6233 7453; www.tasforestrytourism.com.au

## Tours

**Tasmanian Devil Jet Tours** The Esplanade; (03) 6261 3460; www.deviljet.com.au

## Where to stay

**The Bush Inn** ★★ Bed & breakfast $37.50 49 Montague St; (03) 6261 2256; www.thebushinn.com
**National Park Hotel** ★ Bed & breakfast from $40 Gordon River Rd, Mount Field NP; (03) 6283 1103.
**Celtic Dawn Accommodation** ★★ Single $25, double $70 2400 Gordon River Rd, Mount Field NP; (03) 6288 1058; www.celticdawn.com.au
**Base Camp Tasmania** ★★ Dorm $30 959 Glenfern Rd, Glenfern; (03) 6261 4971.
**Camping** Land of the Giants Caravan Park and Campground near the Mount Field National Park Visitor Centre has powered sites, toilets, showers, washing machines, dryers and barbecues. There's self-registration at the park entrance and fees apply. For more information, call (03) 6288 1319.

Russell Falls, Mount Field National Park

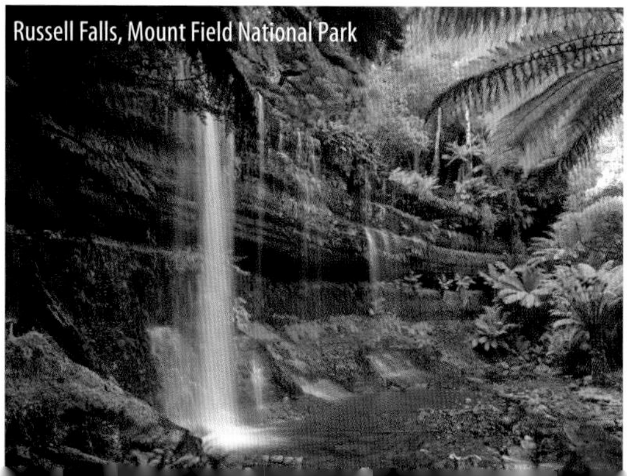

## 4 Woodbridge (1 day)

Between the Hartz Mountains and the deep-blue D'Entrecasteaux Channel lies a world's-end coast of tiny towns in sheltered coves. Take a dip in Conningham at a good swimming beach or try a pretty 1.5 hr walk to Snug Falls. Kettering is principally the launching point to Bruny Island (see next entry), but there are also ocean-kayak tours around sheltered coves. The area's most famous attraction is Peppermint Bay, a modern complex with a cafe, outdoor sculptures and art gallery that are great to walk around. You can also visit the light-filled restaurant for one of the best food experiences in the state. At Woodbridge Hill Handweaving Studio add weaving to your skills base.

### Further information

**Woodbridge Hill Handweaving Studio** Woodbridge Hill Rd; (03) 6267 4430; daily 10am–1pm & 2pm–5.30pm.

### Tours

**Roaring 40s Ocean Kayaking** Oyster Cove Marina, Ferry Rd, Kettering; (03) 6267 5000; www.roaring40skayaking.com.au

### Where to eat

**Peppermint Bay** $$/$$$ **TOP TREAT!!** One of the best meals you'll ever eat, showcasing farm produce, seafood and herbs picked from the on-site garden near the entrance. 3435 Channel Hwy, Woodbridge; (03) 6267 4088; lunch daily, dinner Sat; www.peppermintbay.com.au

**Pear Ridge Gardens & Restaurant** $$ Sit on the sun-drenched deck looking over the restaurant's potager garden and enjoy fine local dishes. 1683 Channel Hwy, Margate; (03) 6267 1811; lunch & dinner daily.

## 5 Bruny Island (1 day)

Bruny Island is largely undeveloped, having been occupied by local Indigenous people until sealers decimated the population. Of those who survived, Truganini is the most famous.

Today Bruny Island is a bushwalker's heaven with spectacular coastal scenery. The Neck is a thin band of dunes between the north and south islands, and home to penguins and shearwaters (locals call them muttonbirds). At the southern tip, South Bruny National Park has several walking tracks, lagoons and surf beaches that give way to fluted cliffs and wild seas. The rainforest at Mavista Falls is another breathtaking spot, as is Cape Queen Elizabeth.

From Adventure Bay, or with bus connections from Kettering or Hobart, you can also take one of the state's top attractions, a great eco-cruise around Fluted Cape. The 3-hour cruise takes in the seal colonies, penguins, dolphins, humpback whales and abundant birdlife of the area, as well as Australia's highest sea cliffs.

To get to the island, take the car ferry from Kettering. You'll need to organise your own vehicle transport on Bruny, unless you take a tour.

### Further information

ℹ **Bruny D'Entrecasteaux Visitors Centre** 81 Ferry Rd, Kettering; (03) 6267 4494; www.tasmaniaholiday.com

### Tours

**Bruny Island Charters** 915 Adventure Bay Rd, Adventure Bay; (03) 6293 1465; www.brunycharters.com.au

**Bruny Island Ventures** 6 Amarina Crt, Kingston; 1300 653 633.

**Bruny Island Scenic Farm Tours** 18 Wisbys Rd; (03) 6260 6258.

**Inala Nature Tours** Tours with an expert biologist. 320 Cloudy Bay Rd; (03) 6293 1217.

**Ol' Kid Fishing Charters** 786 Adventure Bay Rd, Adventure Bay; (03) 6293 1128.

### Where to eat

**Get Shucked, Hothouse Cafe** $ They could be the best oysters you've ever tasted. Freshly plucked 'n' shucked. Morella Island Retreats, 46 Adventure Bay Rd; (03) 6293 1131; breakfast, lunch & dinner daily; www.getshucked.com.au

## 6 Huonville (half-day)

Nowhere is Tasmania's nickname, the 'Apple Isle', more appropriate than in the Huon Valley, which produces more than half of Tasmania's apples, as well as cherries, plums, pears, berries and hops. If you're in the area during the picking season (April–May) there's work for backpackers. Otherwise, pick something up at the Huonville Market.

Huonville is the largest town in the valley and offers a variety of fun, aquatic activities. Boost your adrenalin with an exciting 35-minute jet-boat ride along the Huon River rapids, or quietly explore the river on a pedal boat or aquabike. You can also learn how to build your own watercraft at the Wooden Boat Centre in Franklin. For fishing enthusiasts, the Snowy Range Trout Fishery hires out rods. When you've caught your stream-fed trout or salmon, they'll clean it for you.

If you're starting to feel parched, get acquainted with the art of cider making at Welcome Swallow Cyderworks in Pethcheys Bay. Wine lovers can head to Hartzview Wine Centre, known for pinot noir, ports and liqueurs. There are also lovely beaches at Gardners Bay, Randalls Bay, Egg and Bacon Bay and Verona Sands, while Nine Pin Point Marine Nature Reserve offers some fantastic reef diving in deep, dark waters.

### Further information

ℹ **Huon Visitor Centre** Huon Jet/Boatshed Cafe; (03) 6264 1838; daily 9am–5pm.

**Fruit picking** Contact huonvalley@tassie.net.au

**Huonville Market** Websters carpark, Cool Store Rd; 2nd & 4th Sun each month.

**Wooden Boat Centre** Main St, Franklin; (03) 6266 3586; daily 9.30am–5pm; www.woodenboatcentre.com

**Snowy Range Trout Fishery** Denison River, via Judbury; (03) 6266 0243; daily 9am–5pm; www.snowyrangetrout.com.au
**Welcome Swallow Cyderworks** 113 Sunday Hill Rd, Petcheys Bay; (03) 6295 1214; summer Wed–Mon 11am–3pm, winter Sat–Sun 11am–3pm; www.southcountrycyder.com
**Hartzview Wine Centre** 70 Dillons Rd, Gardners Bay; (03) 6295 1623; daily 10am–5pm; www.hartzview.com.au
**Boat hire: Huon Jet and Huon River Pedal Boats** (03) 6264 1838; www.huonjet.com

## Tours

**Huon 4WD Bushventures** Esplanade; (03) 6264 1838; www.huonjet.com/trips/bushvent.html
**Huon Valley Horse Trekking** 179 Judds Creek Rd, Judbury; (03) 6266 0343.
**MV *Southern Contessa* Huon River Cruises** Esplanade; (03) 6264 1838; daily from 10am.

## Where to eat

**Boat House Cafe** 💲 Old-fashioned, homemade burgers and seafood. The staff here are also masters of the humble milkshake. Esplanade; (03) 6264 1133; lunch & dinner Wed–Sun.
**Petty Sessions Cafe & Gallery** 💲💲 Modern, light food and good coffee near an open fire. Meals predominantly incorporate fresh, local produce, and the abalone soup is a winner. 3445 Huon Hwy, Geeveston; (03) 6266 3488; lunch daily, dinner Fri–Sun.

## Where to stay

**Huonville Grand Hotel** ★★ Single $50 2 Main St; (03) 6264 1004.
**Nomads Huon Valley Backpackers** ★★ 4 Sandhill Rd, Cradoc; (03) 6295 1551; www.nomadsworld.com

## Events

**Taste of the Huon** A two-day showcase of the Huon Valley, D'Entrecasteaux Channel and Bruny Island's fabulous food, wine, entertainment and art. Venue changes towns yearly, so check visitor centre for details. Mar.
**Huon Agricultural Show** One of the best old-time country shows. Nov.

## ❼ Hastings (half-day)

Before reaching Hastings, make sure you stop around Geeveston. This town, on the cusp of the enormous Southwest National Park, is driven by timber and forestry industries. The Forest & Heritage Centre offers a comprehensive look at forest practices, with computer games and a wood-turning viewing area, together with a gallery and a craft shop. Nearby, Tahune Forest AirWalk is one of the longest and highest canopy walks in the world. The walk goes through the treetops of the Tahune Forest Reserve, giving a bird's-eye view of rainforest and the Huon and

Picton rivers below.

Hastings is known for the stunning dolomite caves to the west of town. Newdegate Cave, formed more than 40 million years ago, has stalactites, stalagmites, columns, shawls, flowstone and the more unusual helictites that make it one of Australia's most beautiful caves. Tours include a 3–6 hour adventure tour of King George V Cave (bookings essential). And don't pass up a swim at the nearby Hastings Thermal Springs, which stays at a balmy 28°C year-round.

## Further information

**Forest & Heritage Centre** Church St, Geeveston; (03) 6297 1821; daily 9am–5.30pm; www.forestandheritagecentre.com
**Tahune Forest AirWalk & Visitor Centre** Tahune Forest Reserve; (03) 6297 0068; daily 9am–5pm; www.tasforestrytourism.com.au
**Hastings Caves & Thermal Springs** 754 Caves Rd, Hastings; (03) 6298 3209; May–Aug daily 10am–4pm, Sept–Dec & Mar–Apr daily 9am–5pm, Jan–Feb 9am–6pm; www.parks.tas.gov.au

## Tours

**Geeveston Highlands Salmon and Trout Fishery** Learn the mysteries of fly fishing at the world's first catch-and-release Atlantic salmon fishery. 172 Kermandie Rd, Geeveston; (03) 6297 0030.
**Eagle Hang Gliding** Take a 400 m cable hang gliding flight. Tahune Forest Reserve; 0419 311 198; www.cablehanggliding.com.au
**Aardvark Adventures** Abseiling tours off the Tahune Forest AirWalk, descending from the forest canopy to the understorey of ferns. (03) 6273 7722; www.aardvarkadventures.com.au
**Entrance Cave Tours** Tours May–Aug 11am & 3pm, Sept–Dec & Mar–Apr 10am & 4pm, Jan–Feb 10am & 5pm. Book at Hastings Caves & Thermal Springs Centre, (03) 6298 3209.

## Where to stay

**Far South Wilderness Lodge** ★★★ Dorm $25 247 Narrows Rd, Dover; (03) 6298 1922; www.farsouthwilderness.com.au
**Bob's Bunkhouse Geeveston Backpackers** ★★ Dorm $20 4870 Huon Hwy, Geeveston; (03) 6297 1069; www.bobsbunkhousegeevestonbackpackers.com.au
**Geeveston Forest House** ★ Dorm $20 24 Arve Rd, Geeveston; (03) 6297 1844.

## Events

**Tasmanian Forest Festival** A forest-industry showcase sponsored by the local timber industry in Geeveston. Mar.

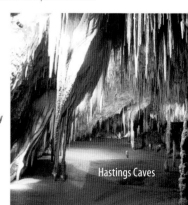
Hastings Caves

# East Coast and the Mid-north
## Days of wine and beaches

The east coast is Tasmania's prettiest and most varied region. It boasts a mild, sunny climate, some of Australia's most exquisite coastal scenery, historic sites, gourmet produce, and a hinterland of peaks, gorges, waterfalls and forests. You can ramble up the coast, stopping off for a night here and there in a low-key fishing and holiday village. But don't think that it's all relaxed – the region is jam-packed with activities such as rock climbing, bushwalking, diving and wildlife-watching.

In the heart of Tassie's mid-north, Launceston is a food and wine lover's delight (and a beer lover's, if you're interested in a tour of Boag's brewery). From here you can explore the Tamar Valley, including Beaconsfield's historic buildings, established during the gold-mining boom. The valley has a climate similar to the south of France and is Tasmania's most productive wine region.

**Number of days to spend in this region: 3–9 days**

## Getting here

If you prefer to fly straight to the centre of Tasmania, Qantas, Jetstar and Virgin Blue all fly to Launceston Airport.

Redline and Tassielink have bus services between Launceston and Bicheno, while Tassielink runs between Hobart and Swansea, and Bicheno and St Helens.

From Bicheno on the coast, Suncoast has services to St Helens, Derby and Scottsdale, and Peake runs to Derby and St Marys. Bicheno Coach Services runs a shuttle to Freycinet National Park.

The Maria Island Ferry leaves Triabunna daily, but check services beforehand as only limited services run during winter months.

Redline 1300 360 000; www.tasredline.com.au

Tassielink Coaches 1300 300 520; www.tassielink.com.au

Suncoast Bus Service (03) 6376 3488.

Peake (03) 6372 5390.

Bicheno Coach Service (03) 6257 0293.

Maria Island Ferry 0428 666 650 or (03) 6227 8900.

## ① Maria Island (1 day)

Maria Island is a blissfully quiet place with only a few buildings interrupting the rugged landscape and wildlife – look out for pademelons, long-nosed potoroos and echidnas. It is virtually two islands joined by an isthmus, with the larger northern section dominated by 709 m Mount Maria.

For mountain-bike riders, there are 30 km of gravel roads and – the best part – no cars. There is also a great range of walking trails. From the old convict settlement of Darlington you can walk to the Fossil Cliffs, which contain masses of dark grey bivalve fossils from an ancient polar sea. You can either walk or ride to the spectacular Painted Cliffs that display circular orange and white patterns.

For those with a head for heights, the Mount Maria walk (6 hrs return) involves lots of climbing, but rewards with views of Mount Wellington, on a clear day, and the Tasman Peninsula. The Bishop and Clerk summit track (5 hrs return) has some hair-raising rock hopping near the 630 m summit, which once again lead to stunning scenery.

The Maria Island ferry leaves from the visitor information centre at Triabunna. Nearby is the quiet fishing village of Orford, the centre of Tasmania's scallop and abalone industries. The town's Gateway Cafe, just off the main road, is a good place to stop for provisions or breakfast before heading out to the island. Between the two towns, you can sink your toes into the white sands of Spring Beach in summer and marvel at the dramatic backdrop created by Maria Island.

### Further information
ℹ️ Triabunna Visitor Information Centre Cnr Charles St & Esplanade; (03) 6257 4772; daily 10am–4pm; www.springbay.net/tourist-info/

### Tours
**Once Upon Maria** A one-day tour including a cruise passing the Painted Cliffs, as well as a guided walk around the island, discovering wildlife and historic sites. Tours leave from Hobart. There is also a four-

Maria Island

day hike organised by the same company. (03) 6227 8900;
www.mariaisland.com

## Where to eat

**Gateway Cafe** $/$$ This bright cafe is a great pit stop with a range of breakfast and lunch options, including awesome pancakes. Shelves with provisions showcase Tasmania's top produce. 1 Charles St, Orford; (03) 6257 1539; daily 7am–6pm.

## Where to stay

**Penitentiary Accommodation Units** ★ Dorm $9, unit (sleeps 6) $22 Darlington, Maria Island; (03) 6257 1420 www.parks.tas.gov.au
**Udda Backpackers** ★★ Dorm $20, double or twin $47 12 Spencer St, Triabunna; (03) 6257 3439.
**Camping** There are three campsites on Maria Island: at Darlington (water, tables, barbecue and firewood), Frenchs Farm (limited water, fires not permitted) and Encampment Cove (tables, fireplaces, firewood and a small cabin).

## Events

**Triabunna Festival** The Lions Club hosts a celebration of local food and craft on the Triabunna marina. Easter.

## ❷ Freycinet National Park (1–2 days)

Freycinet National Park is a long, narrow paradise that is world renowned for its stunning coastal scenery, challenging rock climbs, abundant wildlife, walking tracks and water activities. A peaceful base from which to explore the area is Coles Bay, a small village of 150 residents that became Australia's first plastic bag-free town in 2003. In the first year alone they stopped the use of 350,000 plastic supermarket check-out bags.

The jewel of Freycinet National Park is undoubtedly Wineglass Bay, voted one of the world's ten best beaches. Most people content themselves with a view from the lookout, accessed by a 30-minute climb up the hills called The Hazards. From a rocky perch, visitors can gaze down over the perfect crescent of white sand and calm aquamarine water that gradually becomes a deeper blue. The walk to the actual beach is at least 1 hr, but means that you might have this ideal swimming spot all to yourself.

Accessible by car are other highlights, like the tiny impression that is Honeymoon Bay, just south of Coles Bay. Honeymoon Bay and Sleepy Bay,

on the other side of the peninsula, are great spots for snorkelling. The long stretch of Friendly Beaches is where visitors can camp, fish and surf.

Perched on Great Oyster Bay, the town of Swansea looks out across turquoise waters to Freycinet Peninsula. There's not too much here, but you might like to stop at the Swansea Bark Mill & Museum, with a tree mill, displays on life in the 1820s and tavern.

Also in the area are some great wineries, including Freycinet Vineyard, making stunning pinot noir, and the gorgeous stable cellar door for Spring Vale Vineyards.

## Further information

ⓘ **Freycinet Visitor Centre** (03) 6256 7000; www. freycinetcolesbay.com
**Swansea Bark Mill & Museum** 96 Tasman Hwy, Swansea; (03) 6257 8382; Sept–May daily 9am–5pm, Jun–Aug daily 9am–6pm; www.swanseabarkmill.com.au
**Freycinet Vineyard** 15919 Tasman Hwy; (03) 6257 8574; daily 10am–5pm; www.freycinetvineyard.com.au
**Spring Vale Vineyards** 130 Spring Vale Rd, Cranbrook; (03) 6257 8208; Mon–Fri 10am–5pm; www.springvalewines.com

## Tours

**All 4 Adventure** Various tours around Freycinet National Park, including a 4WD tour, or experience the thrill of riding a four-wheel motorbike to secluded beaches. The Esplanade, Coles Bay; (03) 6257 0018; www.all4adventure.com.au
**The Freycinet Paddle** Sea-kayak around the national park. Freycinet Dr, Coles Bay; (03) 6257 0500 www.freycinetadventures.com.au
**The Grape Escape** Visit award-winning wineries around the Freycinet, Coles Bay and Bicheno area. (03) 6257 0344.

## Where to eat

**Kate's Berry Farm** $ Not just fresh berries! Kate makes ice-cream, jams and fruit wine such as a strawberry dry table wine and a strawberry-riesling blend from the berries she grows on her farm, perched high on the coastline. Addison St (3 km south of Swansea); (03) 6257 8428; daily 8.30am–5.30pm.
**Freycinet Marine Farm** $ Try some delicious, fresh oysters born and raised in this gorgeous region. 88 Flacks Rd, Coles Bay; (03) 6257 0140; daily 9am–6pm; farm tours daily 10am; www.freycinetmarinefarm.com

Wineglass Bay

## Where to stay

**Swansea Backpackers** ★★★ Dorm \$28–\$34, double or twin \$65–\$75 Tasman Hwy, Swansea; (03) 6257 8650; www.swanseabackpackers.com.au

**Coles Bay YHA** ★★ Dorm \$13.50, room from \$53.50 Freycinet National Park; (03) 6234 9617; www.yha.com.au

**Iluka Backpackers YHA** ★★ Dorm \$25.50, single, double or twin \$58.50 Esplanade, Coles Bay; (03) 6257 0115; www.yha.com.au

## Events

**Freycinet Challenge** Two-day running, sea-kayaking, road-bike and mountain-bike racing event. Oct.

# 3 Bicheno and St Helens (1–2 days)

The coastline between Bicheno and St Helens boasts excellent fishing, surfing, stunning beaches and gorgeous little towns. Bicheno has some of the best scuba diving in Tasmania and one of the best temperate dive locations in the world. Just offshore is Governor Island Marine Reserve where, beneath clear waters, granite outcrops create cliffs, caves and deep fissures, providing a home for diverse marine communities. The town's other major attraction is its little fairy penguins, which you can watch as they waddle up the coast in groups every night. Just north of Bicheno, Douglas-Apsley National Park has stunning gorges, waterfalls and safe swimming spots.

The popular resort of St Helens is renowned for its crayfish and scalefish, which help maintain a thriving restaurant industry. The surrounding hills and warm sea breezes create a mild climate year-round, and the nearby beaches have pristine white sand dunes. The Bay of Fires, north of St Helens, is a wilderness coastline with seemingly endless white beaches and sand dunes unfolding into turquoise seas. Its dramatic name came from Captain Furneaux, who saw Aboriginal campfires burning along the shore as he sailed past in 1773. It could equally be a reference to the granite boulders that rim the beaches, stained with fiery orange lichen.

## Further information

[i] **St Helens Visitor Information Centre** 61 Cecilia St; (03) 6376 1744.

**Coastline near Bicheno Wildlife Service** (Douglas–Apsley National Park) 1300 135 513; www.parks.tas.gov.au

Coastline near Bicheno

## Tours

**Bicheno Dive Centre Tours** 2 Scuba Crt, Bicheno; (03) 6375 1138; www.bichenodive.com.au

**Bicheno Penguin Tours** Evening small-group tours will get you closer than ever to fairy penguins waddling up the shore to find their burrows for the night. Tasman Hwy, Bicheno; (03) 6375 1333; www.bichenopenguintours.com.au

**Johno's " Quicky " 4WD Tas Tours** From a 1½ hr 'quicky' 4WD tour to a five-day East Coast tour, taking in the Bay of Fires. St Helens; (03) 6376 3604; www.johnos4wdtours.com.au

## Where to eat

**Mount Elephant Pancake Barn** [$] Choose from the amazing range of mouth-watering treats, considered by some to be the best pancakes in Australia. Enjoy forest and ocean views while you eat. Elephant Pass, south of St Marys; (03) 6372 2263; daily 8am–6pm; www.mount-elephant-pancakes.com.au

**Captains Catch** [$] If you prefer eating fish rather than wrangling big game onto the back of a boat, Captain's Catch is one of the best fish and chip shops in Tasmania, specialising in only the freshest east-coast seafood. Marine Parade, St Helens; (03) 6376 1170; daily 10am–6.30pm.

## Pubs and bars

**Pub in the Paddock** Venture 28 km west to the Pyengana Valley, where the Pub in the Paddock has been licensed since 1880 and is infamous for its beer-swilling pig. St Columba Falls Rd, Pyengana; (03) 6373 6121; lunch daily, bar daily 11am–late.

## Where to stay

**Bicheno Backpackers Hostel** ★★★ Dorm \$20–\$23, double or twin \$55 11 Morrison St, Bicheno; (03) 6375 1651; www.bichenobackpackers.com

**St Helens Backpackers** ★★ Dorm \$20, double or twin \$55–\$70 9 Cecilia St, St Helens; (03) 6376 2017.

## Events

**St Helens Regatta and Seafood Festival** A perfect day of music, races, craft stalls, not to mention sideshow alley. Jan.

**The Bay of Fires Festival** A seafood and wine feast that includes the Great Abalone Bakeoff. Feb.

**Suncoast Jazz Festival** Tasmania's biggest jazz event is held in St Helens over three days each year. Jun.

**Winter Solstice Festival** Situated between Bicheno and St Helens, the town of St Marys celebrates the shortest day of the year with fire, lanterns and music. Jun.

# 4 Launceston (2 days)

Launceston is a quaint city, perhaps with more charm than the capital of Hobart. It reputedly has the highest concentration of 19th-century buildings in Australia, and its magnificent parks and gardens have earned it the nickname of Tasmania's Garden City.

The big question every local asks is whether you have been to Launceston's top natural attraction, Cataract Gorge. The single-span chairlift offers the best views of the area, but walking tracks will also lead you around the spectacular gorge to an elegant Victorian park with peacocks and a restaurant. You can also visit the gorge at night when it is lit in spectacular fashion.

Around the city centre, there is free admission to the Queen Victoria Museum & Art Gallery, located at two venues and considered one of the best regional museums in the country. There are permanent exhibits on Aboriginal and convict history, and a section for the Launceston Planetarium, showing astronomy displays on its projector. The Design Centre of Tasmania has a fantastic museum collection of contemporary wood furniture, including pieces made from Tasmania's unique Huon pine, all created by the state's top caftspeople. The Old Umbrella Shop is the only genuine Victorian shopfront in Launceston with a museum and gift shop showcasing beautiful and unusual antique umbrellas. If you'd prefer a tasty experience, Boag's Centre for Beer Lovers has self-guided or guided tours of its brewery and museum with tastings included.

Just south of Launceston, the tiny historic towns of Evandale and Longford have streets lined with beautiful buildings. Longford is home to Woolmers Estate, regarded as Australia's most significant colonial property.

## Further information

ⓘ **Launceston Visitor Information Centre** Cornwall Sqr, 12–16 St John St; (03) 6336 3133; Mon–Fri 9am–5pm, Sat 9am–3pm, Sun 9am–noon.
**Queen Victoria Museum & Art Gallery** 2 Wellington St; Invermay Rd; (03) 6323 3777; daily 10am–5pm; Launceston Planetarium Tue–Fri 3pm, Sat 2pm & 3pm; www.qvmag.tas.gov.au
**Design Centre of Tasmania** City Park, cnr Tamar & Brisbane sts; (03) 6331 5505; Mon–Sat 9.30am–5.30pm, Sun 10.30am– 3.30pm; designcentre.com.au
**Boag's Centre for Beer Lovers** 39 William St; (03) 6332 6300; tours Mon–Fri 8.45am–4.30pm; www.boags.com.au
**Old Umbrella Shop** 60 George St; (03) 6331 9248; Mon–Fri 9am–5pm, Sat 9am–noon.

## Tours

**Cataract Gorge Cruise** Home Point; (03) 6334 9900; www.tamarrivercruises.com.au
**Cable Hang Gliding** Trevallyn Dam; 0419 311 198; www.cablehanggliding.com.au
**Launceston City Ghost Tours** Get chills down your spine as you learn about Launceston's convict past. 14 Brisbane St; 0421 819 373; www.launcestoncityghosttours.com

Boag's Brewery tastings

**Boag's Brewery Tours** This brewery tour is a must if you're a beer lover, and you'll enjoy it even if you just like a bit of history. 39 William St; (03) 6332 6300; www.boags.com.au

## Where to eat

**Star Bar Cafe** 💲💲 A bright and modern place serving satisfying lunches and dinners, including wood-fired pizza and pasta. 113 Charles St; (03) 6331 9659; Mon–Sat 11am–late, Sun noon–10pm; www.starhotel.net.au
**Dockside Cafe Winebar** 💲💲 A wide timber boardwalk separates you from the river's edge as you tuck into your satay chicken and mango pizza, or perhaps the vegetarian pizza topped with eggplant, artichokes and roasted pumpkin. Seaport; (03) 6331 0711; lunch daily, dinner Mon–Sat; www.dockside.net.au
**Stillwater River Cafe** 💲💲💲 TOP TREAT!! Set in an 1830s flour mill overlooking the Tamar River, this is the best restaurant in town. Meals marry Australian and Asian flavours to create some amazing flavours, all based on the freshest produce. Come here for a sunny breakfast or lunch outdoors if you want to pay a little less. Ritchies Mill, 2 Bridge Rd; (03) 6331 4153; daily 8.30am–4pm & 6pm–midnight; www.stillwater.net.au
**Novaro's Restaurant** 💲💲💲 TOP TREAT!! Try Novaro's if you're feeling extravagant and fancy some very good Italian food. Enjoy the intimate, provincial atmosphere while you read the tome-like wine list. 28 Brisbane St; (03) 6334 5589; dinner Mon–Sat 6–10pm.

## Pubs and bars

**Metz** This cosmopolitan-style cafe/wine bar has simple, good food. Cnr St John & York sts; (03) 6331 7277; Mon–Fri 8am–late, Sat–Sun 9am–late.
**Royal Oak** Nothing fancy here, but if you enjoy a cold drink and some live music in an unpretentious atmosphere give the Oak a try. Monthly jazz gigs are held on the last Tuesday of the month. Cnr Brisbane & Tamar sts; (03) 6331 5346; daily noon–late.

## Where to stay

**Launceston Backpackers** ★★★ Dorm $18–$20, double or twin $24–$60 103 Canning St; (03) 6334 2327; www.launcestonbackpackers.com.au
**Metro Backpackers** ★★★ Dorm $22, double or twin $65 270 Brisbane St; (03) 6334 7321; www.pennyroyalbackpackers.com.au

**Lloyds Hotel Backpackers** ★★ Dorm $21, single $50, double $68, twin $70, triple $75 23 George St; 1300 858 861 or (03) 6231 9906; www.backpackers-accommodation.com.au
**Backpacker Hub & Bar** ★★ Dorm $23, twin and double $27, single $47 1 Tamar St; (03) 6334 9288; www.backpackerhub.com.au
**Highview Lodge YHA** ★★ Dorm $23.50, double or twin $50.50 8 Blake St, Deloraine; (03) 6362 2996; www.yha.com.au

## Events

**Festivale** Three days of food, wine and entertainment in City Park. Feb.
**Ten Days on the Island** Biennial celebration of island culture and the arts. Mar–Apr.
**Agfest** Tasmania's premier agricultural event in Carrick with pavilions for local food, wine and crafts. May.
**Tasmanian Craft Fair** Discover hundreds of stalls and craftspeople in the picturesque township of Deloraine, west of Launceston. Nov.

# 5 Tamar Valley (2 days)

There is so much to explore in the beautiful Tamar Valley. Villages and wineries hug the banks of the River Tamar and the superb quality of the wines has much to do with the dry, warm autumn. If you have a car, take some time to drive around and sample a few wines.

The area's most well-known label is Pipers Brook, whose cellar door offers tastings of excellent pinot noir, chardonnay, gewürztraminer, and Kreglinger and Ninth Island varieties. The on-site cafe makes delicious cottage pies and afternoon teas, which can be enjoyed in the outdoor courtyard during summer. Next door, the Jansz cellar door is a modern architectural building with an interpretive centre. The label is dedicated to producing sparkling wines following the French 'méthode champenoise'. Bay of Fires has young and friendly staff who will take you through a long list of tasting options under the two labels, Bay of Fires and Tigress. Other cellar doors worth visiting include Tamar Ridge, particularly for its riesling, and Clover Hill for sparkling wines.

Also in the area, Beaconsfield became the wealthiest gold town in Tasmania, with over 50 companies vying for a slice of its riches after gold was discovered at Cannage Tree Hill in the 1870s. Modern-day Beaconsfield is very different, but mining still continues as the world learned after news coverage of the amazing rescue of two trapped miners in 2006. One of the old, closed shafts now houses the Grubb Shaft Gold and Heritage Museum, offering tours of the mine and displaying a collection of old steam engines.

Not far from Beaconsfield is Beauty Point, near the mouth of the River Tamar. This is a popular spot for fishing and boating, and is home to some excellent wildlife attractions that are focused on protecting and studying local creatures. Fantastic tours of Seahorse World provide an insight into the seahorse breeding process (a baby seahorse is only the size of a newborn child's little finger). Platypus House lets you get up close with this unique Australian creature in an indoor setting.

## Further information

[i] **Tamar Visitor Centre** Main Rd, Exeter; 1800 637 989; www.tamarvalley.com.au
**Pipers Brook** 1216 Pipers Brook Rd, Pipers Brook; (03) 6382 7527; daily 10am–5pm; kreglingerwineestates.com
**Jansz** 1216b Pipers Brook Rd, Pipers Brook; (03) 6382 7066; daily 10am–4.30pm; www.jansz.com.au
**Bay of Fires** 40 Baxters Rd, Pipers River; (03) 6382 7622; daily 10am–5pm; www.bayoffireswines.com.au
**Tamar Ridge** 653 Auburn Rd, Kayena; (03) 6394 1114; daily 10am–5pm; www.tamarridge.com.au
**Clover Hill** 60 Clover Hill Rd, Lebrina; (03) 6395 6286; daily 10am–5pm; www.taltarni.com.au
**Grubb Shaft Gold and Heritage Museum** West St, Beaconsfield; (03) 6383 1473; Sept–Apr daily 9.30am–4.30pm, May–Aug daily 10am–4pm; www.beaconsfieldgold.com.au/GrubbShaftMuseum.html
**Seahorse World** Inspection Head Wharf, 200 Flinders St, Beauty Point; (03) 6383 4111; daily 9.30am–4.30pm (last tour 3.30pm); www.seahorseworld.com.au
**Platypus House** Inspection Head Wharf, 200 Flinders St, Beauty Point; (03) 6383 4884; summer daily 9.30am–4.30pm, winter daily 10.30am–3.30pm; www.platypushouse.com.au

## Tours

**Valleybrook Wine Tours** Various tours leaving from Launceston. (03) 6334 0586; www.valleybrook.com.au
**Tamar River Cruises** Home Point Cruise Terminal; (03) 6334 9900; www.tamarrivercruises.com.au

## Events

**Tamar Valley Folk Festival** Three days of music, dancing, workshops and children's activities in historic George Town. Jan.
**Beaconsfield Gold Festival** Draws a large crowd with street theatre, children's activities, arts and crafts, food and wine. Dec.

Tamar Valley vineyards

For more detail
see map
240

Hobart

TASMANIA

# The North-west
# Edge of the world

Wild, rugged and with a climate to match, north-west Tasmania is the place to head if you're a keen bushwalker or someone who likes to get off the beaten track. The dramatic dolomite peaks and still lakes of Cradle Mountain–Lake St Clair National Park set the scene for one of the word's best wilderness treks, the Overland Track. Along the north coast, the Bass Highway passes small towns that are worth discovering. Once you get to the west coast, a sign for 'The End of the World' indicates that from here the Southern Ocean extends all the way to Argentina. Make sure you take a cruise on the moody Arthur and Pieman rivers, which tumble through gorges and rainforest to a coastline of rolling breakers and dangerous headlands.

Number of days to spend in this region: 2–5 days

## Getting here

The most exciting way to get to this region is taking the overnight *Spirit of Tasmania* ferry from Melbourne to Devonport. There's an option to take a vehicle with you on the ship.

If you prefer to fly, Rex Regional Express has services from Melbourne to Burnie, and Qantas flies to Devonport.

Redline and Tassielink buses operate shipside to Launceston and Hobart or west to Cradle Mountain–Queenstown–Strahan.

Maxwells runs a taxi and bus service to Cradle Mountain and Walls of Jerusalem national parks.

*Spirit of Tasmania* 1800 634 906; www.spiritoftasmania.com.au

Rex Regional Express 13 17 13; www.rex.com.au

Redline 1300 360 000; www.tasredline.com.au

Tassielink Coaches 1300 300 520; www.tassielink.com.au

Maxwells Cradle Mt–Lake St Clair Taxi & Bus Service (03) 6492 1431 or 0418 584 004.

## ① Cradle Mountain–Lake St Clair National Park (1–3 days: 6 if doing the Overland Track)

Almost every feature of this park's landscape was formed in the ice ages. While the dolomite mountain caps remained above the ice, moving glaciers shaped the slopes beneath. The park's vegetation has also evolved to give the scenery an 'otherworldliness'.

Over 9000 bushwalkers flock here every year to tackle the 65 km Overland Track, taking six days to complete (or longer with side trips to other lakes and peaks). The trail covers one of the world's most scenic alpine landscapes of deep glacial lakes, alpine moors and forests dripping with moss. There are guided tours available with catering and accommodation in luxury huts, or you can brave the wilderness alone. Summer is the peak season and bookings are required between November and May. Autumn days are often still and sunny, but the nights are very cold. Winter is only for experienced walkers, with severe weather conditions and short days. Fees apply to complete the track.

If you don't have six days to spare, there are good day walks, too. In the north, the Enchanted Walk (20 min) circles around the rainforest

leaving from the Cradle Mountain visitor centre, while the Dove Lake Loop Track (6 km, 2 hrs) skirts around the edge of the lake, passing through the Ballroom Forest. There's also the Cradle summit track (6 km, 4 hrs), which is a hard, uphill climb. In the south near Lake St Clair, the Larmairremener Tabelti is an Aboriginal cultural walk (1 hr) with information on the local Indigenous people. The Woodlands Nature Walk extends to the summit of Mount Rufus (6 hrs).

### Further information
ⓘ **Cradle Mountain Visitors Centre** 1110 Cradle Mountain Rd; (03) 6492 1110; www.parks.tas.gov.au
ⓘ **Lake St Clair Visitor Information Centre** Lake St Clair; (03) 6289 1137.
**Overland Track Bookings** (03) 6233 6047; Mon–Fri 9am–5pm; www.overlandtrack.com.au

### Tours
**Craclair Tours** Specialists in guided walking tours of the Cradle Mountain–Lake St Clair National Park. Launceston; (03) 6339 4488;

www.craclairtasmania.com
**Cradle Mountain Helicopters** Cradle Mountain; (03) 6492 1132; www.adventureflights.com.au
**Pure Tasmania** Cradle Mountain canoeing, trout fishing and wildlife spotlight tours. 1800 420 155; www.puretasmania.com.au
**Cradle Mountain Huts** A guided tour of the Overland Track, staying in luxury accommodation. (03) 6391 9339; www.cradlehuts.com.au

## Where to eat
**Cradle Mountain Wilderness Cafe** 🟢🟢 Wide variety of takeaways, as well as cheap cafe fare. There aren't many alternative places to eat. Cradle Mountain Rd; (03) 6492 1018; lunch & dinner daily.
**Hungry Wombat Cafe** 🟢 Huge servings to fight off the chill outside. Ignore the band of wombats watching you from the counter. Caltex Service Station, Lyell Hwy, Derwent Bridge; (03) 6289 1125; winter daily 9am–5pm, summer daily 8am–7pm.

## Where to stay
**Cosy Cabins Cradle Mountain** ★★★ Dorm $25  3832 Cradle Mountain Rd; 1800 068 574 (bookings essential).
**Lakeside St Clair Backpacker Hostel** ★★ Dorm $25 Derwent Bridge; (03) 6289 1137.
**Derwent Bridge Wilderness Hotel** ★★ Dorm $23 Lyall Hwy, Derwent Bridge; (03) 6289 1144.
**The Bronte Park Highland Village** ★★ Cottage (2 people) from $90 Marlborough Hwy, Bronte Park; (03) 6289 1126; www.bronteparkvillage.com.au
**Cradle Mountain Lodge Cabins** ★★★ **TOP TREAT!!** Cabin from $115 Cradle Mountain Rd; 1300 134 044 or (03) 6492 1303; www.cradlemountainlodge.com.au

## ❷ Devonport to Marrawah (2 days)
Devonport is the terminal for the *Spirit of Tasmania* ferry linking Tasmania and Victoria across the Bass Strait. Most travellers are quick to head out of town, but it's worth visiting the Tiagarra Aboriginal Culture Centre and Museum, where you see Aboriginal rock carvings and over 2000 artefacts in the adjoining art centre. Once you're on the Bass Highway, there is spectacular scenery between Ulverstone and Stanley. A good pit stop is the aptly named village of Penguin for evening tours of the local penguins. Historic Stanley is dominated by the 152 m-high volcanic Circular Head (known as The Nut), Tasmania's version of Uluru. A steep stairway and a chairlift go to the cliff-top, where a 40-minute circuit walk offers spectacular views. At Dismal Swamp, you can freak out on a 110 m slide down a giant slippery-dip into a sinkhole full of gloomy forest and swampy wildlife.

Down the west coast, tiny Marrawah is famous for its huge surf breaks, which host the Rip Curl West Coast Classic in March. There's also a friendly local pub and important Aboriginal rock-art sites at Mount

Cameron West, recognised for holding some of the most intricate examples of hunter/gatherer art in the world. Keep travelling down the coast to Gardiner Point to find a sign marking 'The End of the World' (good photo opportunity). Your final trip into the unknown could be a cruise through the dense forest on the Arthur and Pieman rivers.

## Further information
ℹ **Devonport Visitors Centre** 92 Formby Rd, Devonport; (03) 6424 8176; daily 7.30am–5pm, 7pm when ferry arrives.
ℹ **Penguin Visitor Information** Main St; (03) 6437 1421.
ℹ **Stanley Information Centre** 45 Main Rd, Stanley; 1300 138 229; www.stanley.com.au
ℹ **Backpackers Barn** Lockers, outdoor gear hire and advisory service for backpackers. 10 Edward St, Devonport; (03) 6424 3628; Mon–Fri 9am–5.30pm, Sat 9am–noon; www.backpackersbarn.com.au
**Tiagarra Aboriginal Culture Centre & Museum** Bluff Rd, Devonport; (03) 6424 8250; daily 9am–4.30pm.
**Dismal Swamp** West of Smithton; (03) 6456 7199; summer daily 9am–5pm, winter daily 10am–4pm; www.dismalswamp.com.au

## Where to stay
**Formby Road Hostel** ★★★ Dorm $16, double $38 16 Formby Rd, Devonport; (03) 6423 6563.
**Formby Hotel** ★★ Dorm $20, double $75 82 Formby Rd, Devonport; (03) 6424 1601; www.goodstone.com.au

## Tours
**Arthur River Canoe and Boat Hire** Arthur River; (03) 6457 1312; www.smithton.tco.asn.au
**Arthur River Cruises** Cruises into the Arthur Pieman Conservation Area. 1414 Arthur River Rd, Arthur River; (03) 6457 1158; Sept–Jun; www.arthurrivercruises.com
**Pieman River Cruises** Corinna; (03) 6457 1225.

## Events
**Henley-on-the-Mersey Regatta** Beer-can boat races and pig and ferret racing. Jan.
**Rip Curl West Coast Classic** Tasmania's premier surfing comp, in the Marrawah area. Mar.

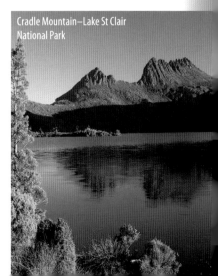
Cradle Mountain–Lake St Clair National Park

| Approximate Distances AUSTRALIA | Grafton | Horsham | Kalgoorlie–Boulder | Katherine | Kununurra | Longreach | Mackay | Meekatharra | Melbourne | Mildura | Moree | Mount Gambier | Mount Isa | Newcastle | Perth | Port Augusta | Port Hedland | Port Lincoln | Port Macquarie | Renmark | Rockhampton | Sydney | Tamworth | Tennant Creek | Toowoomba | Townsville | Wagga Wagga | Warrnambool |
|---|---|---|---|---|---|---|---|---|---|---|---|---|---|---|---|---|---|---|---|---|---|---|---|---|---|---|---|---|
| Adelaide | 1845 | 433 | 2184 | 2712 | 3224 | 2098 | 2670 | 3055 | 733 | 394 | 1567 | 452 | 2706 | 1553 | 2700 | 307 | 3921 | 647 | 1804 | 250 | 2336 | 1414 | 1534 | 2043 | 1921 | 2862 | 948 | 649 |
| Albany | 4177 | 3095 | 886 | 4114 | 3602 | 4357 | 4932 | 1159 | 3395 | 2916 | 3829 | 3114 | 4754 | 3930 | 410 | 2355 | 2025 | 2289 | 4136 | 2772 | 4598 | 3936 | 3866 | 4091 | 4183 | 5121 | 3470 | 3311 |
| Albury | 1184 | 531 | 3009 | 3537 | 4049 | 1748 | 2029 | 3880 | 313 | 571 | 926 | 721 | 2383 | 704 | 3525 | 1132 | 4746 | 1472 | 942 | 715 | 1695 | 565 | 893 | 2868 | 1280 | 2419 | 145 | 567 |
| Alice Springs | 3052 | 1970 | 3107 | 1175 | 1687 | 1804 | 2451 | 3978 | 2270 | 1791 | 2704 | 1989 | 1169 | 2805 | 3623 | 1230 | 3264 | 1570 | 3011 | 1647 | 2486 | 2811 | 2741 | 531 | 2852 | 2061 | 2345 | 2186 |
| Ayers Rock/Yulara | 3093 | 2011 | 3148 | 1618 | 2130 | 2247 | 2894 | 4019 | 2311 | 1832 | 2745 | 2030 | 1612 | 2846 | 3664 | 1271 | 3707 | 1611 | 3052 | 1688 | 2929 | 2852 | 2782 | 949 | 3099 | 2504 | 2386 | 2227 |
| Bairnsdale | 1397 | 577 | 3194 | 3722 | 4234 | 2084 | 2365 | 4065 | 277 | 825 | 1262 | 697 | 2719 | 917 | 3710 | 1317 | 5100 | 1657 | 1155 | 969 | 2031 | 759 | 1186 | 3053 | 1616 | 2755 | 481 | 534 |
| Ballarat | 1544 | 192 | 2809 | 3337 | 3849 | 1965 | 2369 | 3680 | 111 | 460 | 1294 | 309 | 2600 | 1116 | 3325 | 932 | 4546 | 1272 | 1354 | 604 | 2035 | 977 | 1233 | 2668 | 1620 | 2759 | 550 | 174 |
| Bathurst | 825 | 997 | 3242 | 3455 | 3967 | 1538 | 1681 | 4113 | 779 | 804 | 578 | 1187 | 2173 | 338 | 3758 | 1365 | 4979 | 1705 | 565 | 948 | 1347 | 211 | 457 | 2836 | 956 | 2071 | 321 | 1052 |
| Bega | 1069 | 905 | 3522 | 3880 | 4392 | 1963 | 2106 | 4393 | 605 | 956 | 1003 | 1025 | 2598 | 589 | 4038 | 1645 | 5259 | 1985 | 827 | 1100 | 1772 | 431 | 858 | 3261 | 1357 | 2496 | 402 | 862 |
| Bendigo | 1420 | 218 | 2824 | 3352 | 3864 | 1841 | 2245 | 3695 | 146 | 402 | 1141 | 433 | 2476 | 1017 | 3340 | 947 | 4561 | 1287 | 1255 | 546 | 1911 | 878 | 1109 | 2683 | 1496 | 2635 | 426 | 298 |
| Bordertown | 1719 | 159 | 2458 | 2986 | 3498 | 2107 | 2544 | 3329 | 459 | 417 | 1482 | 186 | 2742 | 1427 | 2974 | 581 | 4195 | 921 | 1665 | 269 | 2210 | 1288 | 1408 | 2317 | 1795 | 2871 | 822 | 383 |
| Bourke | 808 | 1067 | 2910 | 2886 | 3398 | 969 | 1544 | 3781 | 978 | 870 | 441 | 1324 | 1604 | 768 | 3426 | 1033 | 4647 | 1373 | 859 | 1014 | 1210 | 780 | 589 | 2267 | 795 | 1733 | 711 | 1170 |
| Brisbane | 330 | 1841 | 3832 | 3092 | 3604 | 1175 | 968 | 4175 | 1676 | 1654 | 481 | 2098 | 1810 | 821 | 4348 | 1955 | 5181 | 2295 | 584 | 1798 | 634 | 966 | 573 | 2473 | 127 | 1358 | 1262 | 1933 |
| Broken Hill | 1404 | 599 | 2295 | 2823 | 3335 | 1584 | 2159 | 3166 | 842 | 294 | 1056 | 856 | 2219 | 1157 | 2811 | 418 | 4032 | 758 | 1363 | 438 | 1825 | 1169 | 1093 | 2154 | 1410 | 2348 | 848 | 829 |
| Broome | 4975 | 4701 | 2338 | 1556 | 1044 | 3473 | 4120 | 1467 | 5001 | 4522 | 4608 | 4720 | 2838 | 5111 | 2230 | 3961 | 601 | 4149 | 5150 | 4378 | 4155 | 5222 | 4880 | 2225 | 4521 | 3730 | 5076 | 4917 |
| Bunbury | 4402 | 3320 | 779 | 3905 | 3393 | 4582 | 5157 | 950 | 3620 | 3141 | 4054 | 3339 | 4979 | 4155 | 187 | 2580 | 1816 | 2514 | 4361 | 2997 | 4823 | 4161 | 4091 | 4316 | 4408 | 5346 | 3695 | 3536 |
| Cairns | 2033 | 3145 | 4988 | 2489 | 3001 | 1109 | 735 | 5444 | 3033 | 2948 | 1838 | 3402 | 1207 | 2341 | 5504 | 3111 | 4578 | 3451 | 2287 | 3092 | 1069 | 2479 | 2110 | 1870 | 1705 | 345 | 2619 | 3278 |
| Canberra | 911 | 879 | 3241 | 3658 | 4170 | 1741 | 1884 | 4112 | 661 | 803 | 781 | 1069 | 2736 | 431 | 3757 | 1364 | 4978 | 1704 | 669 | 947 | 1550 | 292 | 700 | 3039 | 1199 | 2274 | 249 | 987 |
| Carnarvon | 5083 | 4001 | 1460 | 2939 | 2427 | 4856 | 5503 | 627 | 4301 | 3822 | 4735 | 4020 | 4221 | 4836 | 904 | 3261 | 850 | 3195 | 5042 | 3678 | 5504 | 4842 | 4772 | 3608 | 5089 | 5113 | 4376 | 4217 |
| Ceduna | 2287 | 1205 | 1412 | 2870 | 3382 | 2467 | 3042 | 2283 | 1505 | 1026 | 1939 | 1224 | 2864 | 2040 | 1928 | 465 | 3149 | 399 | 2246 | 882 | 2708 | 2046 | 1965 | 2201 | 2293 | 3231 | 1580 | 1421 |
| Charleville | 1069 | 1520 | 3363 | 2433 | 2945 | 516 | 1091 | 4234 | 1431 | 1323 | 702 | 1777 | 1151 | 1205 | 3879 | 1486 | 4522 | 1826 | 1244 | 1467 | 831 | 1233 | 974 | 1814 | 615 | 1280 | 1164 | 1623 |
| Coober Pedy | 2362 | 1280 | 2417 | 1865 | 2377 | 2494 | 3141 | 3288 | 1580 | 1101 | 2014 | 1299 | 1859 | 2115 | 2933 | 540 | 3954 | 880 | 2321 | 957 | 3176 | 2121 | 2051 | 1196 | 2368 | 2751 | 1655 | 1496 |
| Darwin | 3733 | 3459 | 4140 | 314 | 826 | 2231 | 2878 | 3269 | 3759 | 3280 | 3366 | 3478 | 1836 | 3869 | 4032 | 2719 | 2403 | 3059 | 3908 | 3136 | 2913 | 3980 | 3638 | 983 | 3279 | 2488 | 3834 | 3675 |
| Dubbo | 651 | 987 | 3048 | 3250 | 3762 | 1333 | 1476 | 3919 | 822 | 800 | 373 | 1244 | 1968 | 404 | 3564 | 1171 | 4785 | 1511 | 610 | 944 | 1142 | 416 | 340 | 2631 | 727 | 1866 | 408 | 1067 |
| Esperance | 3698 | 2616 | 407 | 4233 | 3721 | 3878 | 4453 | 1278 | 2916 | 2437 | 3350 | 2635 | 4275 | 3451 | 738 | 1876 | 2144 | 1751 | 3657 | 2293 | 4119 | 3457 | 3387 | 3612 | 3704 | 4642 | 2991 | 2832 |
| Eucla | 2782 | 1700 | 917 | 3365 | 3877 | 2962 | 3537 | 1788 | 2000 | 1521 | 2434 | 1719 | 3359 | 2535 | 1433 | 960 | 2654 | 894 | 2741 | 1377 | 3203 | 2541 | 2471 | 2696 | 2788 | 3726 | 2075 | 1916 |
| Geelong | 1542 | 278 | 2895 | 3423 | 3935 | 2016 | 2367 | 3766 | 72 | 546 | 1264 | 365 | 2651 | 1086 | 3411 | 1018 | 4632 | 1358 | 1324 | 690 | 2033 | 947 | 1231 | 2754 | 1618 | 2757 | 527 | 185 |
| Geraldton | 4601 | 3519 | 978 | 3409 | 2897 | 4781 | 5356 | 541 | 3819 | 3340 | 4253 | 3538 | 4691 | 4354 | 422 | 2779 | 1320 | 2713 | 4560 | 3196 | 5022 | 4360 | 4290 | 4078 | 4607 | 5545 | 3894 | 3735 |
| Grafton | | 1638 | 3699 | 3419 | 3931 | 1502 | 1298 | 4570 | 1473 | 1451 | 367 | 1895 | 2137 | 491 | 4215 | 1822 | 5436 | 2162 | 254 | 1595 | 964 | 638 | 311 | 2800 | 431 | 1688 | 1059 | 1718 |
| Horsham | 1638 | | 2451 | 3145 | 3657 | 2036 | 2463 | 3322 | 300 | 305 | 1360 | 257 | 2671 | 1235 | 3133 | 740 | 4188 | 1080 | 1462 | 428 | 2129 | 1096 | 1327 | 2476 | 1714 | 2800 | 644 | 230 |
| Kalgoorlie–Boulder | 3699 | 2451 | | 3826 | 3314 | 3879 | 4454 | 871 | 2917 | 2438 | 3351 | 2636 | 4276 | 3452 | 582 | 1877 | 1737 | 1811 | 3658 | 2294 | 4120 | 3458 | 3388 | 3613 | 3705 | 4643 | 2992 | 2833 |
| Katherine | 3419 | 3145 | 3826 | | 512 | 1917 | 2564 | 2955 | 3445 | 2966 | 3052 | 3164 | 1282 | 3556 | 3718 | 2405 | 2089 | 2745 | 3594 | 2822 | 2599 | 3666 | 3324 | 669 | 2965 | 2174 | 3520 | 3361 |
| Kununurra | 3931 | 3657 | 3314 | 512 | | 2429 | 3076 | 2443 | 3957 | 3478 | 3564 | 3676 | 1794 | 4067 | 3206 | 2917 | 1577 | 3257 | 4106 | 3334 | 3111 | 4178 | 3836 | 1181 | 3477 | 2686 | 4032 | 3873 |
| Longreach | 1502 | 2036 | 3879 | 1917 | 2429 | | 791 | 4750 | 1947 | 1839 | 1135 | 2293 | 635 | 1638 | 4395 | 2042 | 4006 | 2342 | 1677 | 1983 | 682 | 1749 | 1407 | 1298 | 1048 | 764 | 1680 | 2139 |
| Mackay | 1298 | 2463 | 4454 | 2564 | 3076 | 791 | | 5325 | 2298 | 2276 | 1103 | 2720 | 1282 | 1606 | 4970 | 2577 | 4653 | 2917 | 1552 | 2420 | 334 | 1744 | 1375 | 1945 | 970 | 390 | 1884 | 2543 |
| Meekatharra | 4570 | 3322 | 871 | 2955 | 2443 | 4750 | 5325 | | 3788 | 3309 | 4222 | 3507 | 4237 | 4323 | 763 | 2748 | 866 | 2682 | 4529 | 3165 | 5524 | 4329 | 4259 | 3624 | 4576 | 5129 | 3863 | 3704 |
| Melbourne | 1473 | 300 | 2917 | 3445 | 3957 | 1947 | 2298 | 3788 | | 548 | 1195 | 420 | 2582 | 1017 | 3433 | 1040 | 4823 | 1380 | 1255 | 692 | 1964 | 878 | 1162 | 2776 | 1549 | 2688 | 458 | 257 |
| Mildura | 1451 | 305 | 2438 | 2966 | 3478 | 1839 | 2276 | 3309 | 548 | | 1173 | 562 | 2474 | 1159 | 2954 | 561 | 4175 | 901 | 1397 | 144 | 1942 | 1020 | 1140 | 2297 | 1527 | 2603 | 554 | 535 |
| Moree | 367 | 1360 | 3351 | 3052 | 3564 | 1135 | 1103 | 4222 | 1195 | 1173 | | 1627 | 1770 | 503 | 3867 | 1474 | 5088 | 1814 | 542 | 1317 | 769 | 641 | 272 | 2433 | 354 | 1493 | 781 | 1449 |
| Mount Gambier | 1895 | 257 | 2636 | 3164 | 3676 | 2293 | 2720 | 3507 | 420 | 562 | 1627 | | 2928 | 1425 | 3152 | 759 | 4373 | 1099 | 1663 | 455 | 2386 | 1584 | 1895 | 2495 | 1971 | 3057 | 901 | 197 |
| Mount Isa | 2137 | 2671 | 4276 | 1282 | 1794 | 635 | 1282 | 4237 | 2582 | 2474 | 1770 | 2928 | | 2273 | 4792 | 2399 | 3371 | 2739 | 2312 | 2618 | 1317 | 2384 | 2042 | 663 | 1683 | 892 | 2315 | 2774 |
| Newcastle | 491 | 1235 | 3452 | 3556 | 4067 | 1638 | 1606 | 4323 | 1017 | 1159 | 503 | 1425 | 2273 | | 3968 | 1575 | 5189 | 1915 | 249 | 1303 | 1272 | 158 | 289 | 2936 | 788 | 1996 | 605 | 1271 |
| Perth | 4215 | 3133 | 582 | 3718 | 3206 | 4395 | 4970 | 763 | 3433 | 2954 | 3867 | 3152 | 4792 | 3968 | | 2393 | 1629 | 2327 | 4174 | 2810 | 4636 | 3974 | 3904 | 4129 | 4221 | 5159 | 3508 | 3349 |
| Port Augusta | 1822 | 740 | 1877 | 2405 | 2917 | 2002 | 2577 | 2748 | 1040 | 561 | 1474 | 759 | 2399 | 1575 | 2393 | | 3614 | 340 | 1781 | 417 | 2243 | 1581 | 1511 | 1736 | 1828 | 2766 | 1115 | 956 |
| Port Hedland | 5436 | 4188 | 1737 | 2089 | 1577 | 4006 | 4653 | 866 | 4823 | 4175 | 5088 | 4373 | 3371 | 5189 | 1629 | 3614 | | 3548 | 5395 | 4031 | 4688 | 5195 | 5125 | 2758 | 5054 | 4263 | 4729 | 4570 |
| Port Lincoln | 2162 | 1080 | 1811 | 2745 | 3257 | 2342 | 2917 | 2682 | 1380 | 901 | 1814 | 1099 | 2739 | 1915 | 2327 | 340 | 3548 | | 2121 | 757 | 2583 | 1921 | 1851 | 2076 | 2168 | 3106 | 1455 | 1296 |
| Port Macquarie | 254 | 1462 | 3658 | 3594 | 4106 | 1677 | 1552 | 4529 | 1255 | 1397 | 542 | 1663 | 2312 | 249 | 4174 | 1781 | 5395 | 2121 | | 1541 | 1218 | 396 | 270 | 2975 | 630 | 1942 | 843 | 1509 |
| Renmark | 1595 | 428 | 2294 | 2822 | 3334 | 1983 | 2420 | 3165 | 692 | 144 | 1317 | 455 | 2618 | 1303 | 2810 | 417 | 4031 | 757 | 1541 | | 2086 | 1164 | 1284 | 2153 | 1671 | 2747 | 698 | 652 |
| Rockhampton | 964 | 2129 | 4120 | 2599 | 3111 | 682 | 334 | 5524 | 1964 | 1942 | 769 | 2386 | 1317 | 1272 | 4636 | 2243 | 4688 | 2583 | 1218 | 2086 | | 1410 | 1041 | 1980 | 636 | 724 | 1550 | 2209 |
| Sydney | 638 | 1096 | 3458 | 3666 | 4178 | 1749 | 1744 | 4329 | 878 | 1020 | 641 | 1584 | 2384 | 158 | 3974 | 1581 | 5195 | 1921 | 396 | 1164 | 1410 | | 427 | 3047 | 926 | 2134 | 466 | 1132 |
| Tamworth | 311 | 1327 | 3388 | 3324 | 3836 | 1407 | 1375 | 4259 | 1162 | 1140 | 272 | 1584 | 2042 | 289 | 3904 | 1511 | 5125 | 1851 | 270 | 1284 | 1041 | 427 | | 2705 | 499 | 1765 | 748 | 1407 |
| Tennant Creek | 2800 | 2476 | 3613 | 669 | 1181 | 1298 | 1945 | 3624 | 2776 | 2297 | 2433 | 2495 | 663 | 2936 | 4129 | 1736 | 2758 | 2076 | 2975 | 2153 | 1980 | 3047 | 2705 | | 2346 | 1555 | 2851 | 2692 |
| Toowoomba | 431 | 1714 | 3705 | 2965 | 3477 | 1048 | 970 | 4576 | 1549 | 1527 | 354 | 1971 | 1683 | 788 | 4221 | 1828 | 5054 | 2168 | 630 | 1671 | 636 | 926 | 499 | 2346 | | 1360 | 1135 | 1794 |
| Townsville | 1688 | 2800 | 4643 | 2174 | 2686 | 764 | 390 | 5129 | 2688 | 2603 | 1493 | 3057 | 892 | 1996 | 5159 | 2766 | 4263 | 3106 | 1942 | 2747 | 724 | 2134 | 1765 | 1555 | 1360 | | 2274 | 2933 |
| Wagga Wagga | 1059 | 644 | 2992 | 3520 | 4032 | 1680 | 1884 | 3863 | 458 | 554 | 781 | 901 | 2315 | 605 | 3508 | 1115 | 4729 | 1455 | 843 | 698 | 1550 | 466 | 748 | 2851 | 1135 | 2274 | | 724 |
| Warrnambool | 1718 | 230 | 2833 | 3361 | 3873 | 2139 | 2543 | 3704 | 257 | 535 | 1449 | 197 | 2774 | 1271 | 3349 | 956 | 4570 | 1296 | 1509 | 652 | 2209 | 1132 | 1407 | 2692 | 1794 | 2933 | 724 | |

**Approximate Distances AUSTRALIA**

| | Grafton | Horsham | Kalgoorlie–Boulder | Katherine | Kununurra | Longreach | Mackay | Meekatharra | Melbourne | Mildura | Moree | Mount Gambier | Mount Isa | Newcastle | Perth | Port Augusta | Port Hedland | Port Lincoln | Port Macquarie | Renmark | Rockhampton | Sydney | Tamworth | Tennant Creek | Toowoomba | Townsville | Wagga Wagga | Warrnambool |
|---|---|---|---|---|---|---|---|---|---|---|---|---|---|---|---|---|---|---|---|---|---|---|---|---|---|---|---|---|
| Adelaide | 1845 | 433 | 2184 | 2712 | 3224 | 2098 | 2670 | 3055 | 733 | 394 | 1567 | 452 | 2706 | 1553 | 2700 | 307 | 3921 | 647 | 1804 | 250 | 2336 | 1414 | 1534 | 2043 | 1921 | 2862 | 948 | 649 |
| Albany | 4177 | 3095 | 886 | 4114 | 3602 | 4357 | 4932 | 1159 | 3395 | 2916 | 3829 | 3114 | 4754 | 3930 | 410 | 2355 | 2025 | 2289 | 4136 | 2772 | 4598 | 3936 | 3866 | 4091 | 4183 | 5121 | 3470 | 3311 |
| Albury | 1184 | 531 | 3009 | 3537 | 4049 | 1748 | 2029 | 3880 | 313 | 571 | 926 | 721 | 2383 | 704 | 3525 | 1132 | 4746 | 1472 | 942 | 715 | 1695 | 565 | 893 | 2868 | 1280 | 2419 | 145 | 567 |
| Alice Springs | 3052 | 1970 | 3107 | 1175 | 1687 | 1804 | 2451 | 3978 | 2270 | 1791 | 2704 | 1989 | 1169 | 2805 | 3623 | 1230 | 3264 | 1570 | 3011 | 1647 | 2486 | 2811 | 2741 | 531 | 2852 | 2061 | 2345 | 2186 |
| Ayers Rock/Yulara | 3093 | 2011 | 3148 | 1618 | 2130 | 2247 | 2894 | 4019 | 2311 | 1832 | 2745 | 2030 | 1612 | 2846 | 3664 | 1271 | 3707 | 1611 | 3052 | 1688 | 2929 | 2852 | 2782 | 949 | 3099 | 2504 | 2386 | 2227 |
| Bairnsdale | 1397 | 577 | 3194 | 3722 | 4234 | 2084 | 2365 | 4065 | 277 | 825 | 1262 | 697 | 2719 | 917 | 3710 | 1317 | 5100 | 1657 | 1155 | 969 | 2031 | 759 | 1186 | 3053 | 1616 | 2755 | 481 | 534 |
| Ballarat | 1544 | 192 | 2809 | 3337 | 3849 | 1965 | 2369 | 3680 | 111 | 460 | 1294 | 309 | 2600 | 1116 | 3325 | 932 | 4546 | 1272 | 1354 | 604 | 2035 | 977 | 1233 | 2668 | 1620 | 2759 | 550 | 174 |
| Bathurst | 825 | 997 | 3242 | 3455 | 3967 | 1538 | 1681 | 4113 | 779 | 804 | 578 | 1187 | 2173 | 338 | 3758 | 1365 | 4979 | 1705 | 565 | 948 | 1347 | 211 | 457 | 2836 | 956 | 2071 | 321 | 1052 |
| Bega | 1069 | 905 | 3522 | 3880 | 4392 | 1963 | 2106 | 4393 | 605 | 956 | 1003 | 1025 | 2598 | 589 | 4038 | 1645 | 5259 | 1985 | 827 | 1100 | 1772 | 431 | 858 | 3261 | 1357 | 2496 | 402 | 862 |
| Bendigo | 1420 | 218 | 2824 | 3352 | 3864 | 1841 | 2245 | 3695 | 146 | 402 | 1141 | 433 | 2476 | 1017 | 3340 | 947 | 4561 | 1287 | 1255 | 546 | 1911 | 878 | 1109 | 2683 | 1496 | 2635 | 426 | 298 |
| Bordertown | 1719 | 159 | 2458 | 2986 | 3498 | 2107 | 2544 | 3329 | 459 | 417 | 1482 | 186 | 2742 | 1427 | 2974 | 581 | 4195 | 921 | 1665 | 269 | 2210 | 1288 | 1408 | 2317 | 1795 | 2871 | 822 | 383 |
| Bourke | 808 | 1067 | 2910 | 2886 | 3398 | 969 | 1544 | 3781 | 978 | 870 | 441 | 1324 | 1604 | 768 | 3426 | 1033 | 4647 | 1373 | 859 | 1014 | 1210 | 780 | 589 | 2267 | 795 | 1733 | 711 | 1170 |
| Brisbane | 330 | 1841 | 3832 | 3092 | 3604 | 1175 | 968 | 4703 | 1676 | 1654 | 481 | 2090 | 1810 | 821 | 4348 | 1955 | 5181 | 2295 | 584 | 1798 | 634 | 966 | 573 | 2473 | 127 | 1358 | 1262 | 1593 |
| Broken Hill | 1404 | 599 | 2295 | 2823 | 3335 | 1584 | 2159 | 3166 | 842 | 294 | 1056 | 856 | 2219 | 1157 | 2811 | 418 | 4032 | 758 | 1363 | 438 | 1825 | 1169 | 1093 | 2154 | 1410 | 2348 | 848 | 829 |
| Broome | 4975 | 4701 | 2338 | 1556 | 1044 | 3473 | 4120 | 1467 | 5001 | 4522 | 4608 | 4720 | 2838 | 5111 | 2230 | 3961 | 601 | 4149 | 5150 | 4378 | 4155 | 5222 | 4880 | 2225 | 4521 | 3730 | 5076 | 4917 |
| Bunbury | 4402 | 3320 | 779 | 3905 | 3393 | 4582 | 5157 | 950 | 3620 | 3141 | 4054 | 3339 | 4979 | 4155 | 187 | 2580 | 1816 | 2514 | 4361 | 2997 | 4823 | 4161 | 4091 | 4316 | 4408 | 5346 | 3695 | 3536 |
| Cairns | 2033 | 3145 | 4988 | 2489 | 3001 | 1109 | 735 | 5444 | 3033 | 2948 | 1838 | 3402 | 1207 | 2341 | 5504 | 3111 | 4578 | 3451 | 2287 | 3092 | 1069 | 2479 | 2110 | 1870 | 1705 | 345 | 2619 | 3278 |
| Canberra | 911 | 879 | 3241 | 3658 | 4170 | 1741 | 1884 | 4112 | 661 | 803 | 781 | 1069 | 2736 | 431 | 3757 | 1364 | 4978 | 1704 | 669 | 947 | 1550 | 292 | 700 | 3039 | 1199 | 2274 | 249 | 987 |
| Carnarvon | 5083 | 4001 | 1460 | 2939 | 2427 | 4856 | 5503 | 627 | 4301 | 3822 | 4735 | 4020 | 4221 | 4836 | 904 | 3261 | 850 | 3195 | 5042 | 3678 | 5504 | 4842 | 4772 | 3608 | 5089 | 5113 | 4376 | 4217 |
| Ceduna | 2287 | 1205 | 1412 | 2870 | 3382 | 2467 | 3042 | 1505 | 1026 | 1939 | 1224 | 2864 | 2040 | | 1928 | 465 | 3149 | 399 | 2246 | 882 | 2708 | 2046 | 1965 | 2201 | 2293 | 3231 | 1580 | 1421 |
| Charleville | 1069 | 1520 | 3363 | 2433 | 2945 | 516 | 1091 | 4234 | 1431 | 1323 | 702 | 1777 | 1151 | 1205 | 3879 | 1486 | 4522 | 1826 | 1244 | 1467 | 831 | 1233 | 974 | 1814 | 615 | 1280 | 1164 | 1623 |
| Coober Pedy | 2362 | 1280 | 2417 | 1865 | 2377 | 2494 | 3141 | 3288 | 1580 | 1101 | 2014 | 1299 | 1859 | 2115 | 2933 | 540 | 3954 | 880 | 2321 | 957 | 3176 | 2121 | 2051 | 1196 | 2368 | 2751 | 1655 | 1496 |
| Darwin | 3733 | 3459 | 4140 | 314 | 826 | 2231 | 2878 | 3269 | 3759 | 3280 | 3366 | 3478 | 1596 | 3869 | 4032 | 2719 | 2403 | 3059 | 3908 | 3136 | 2913 | 3980 | 3638 | 983 | 3279 | 2488 | 3834 | 3675 |
| Dubbo | 651 | 987 | 3048 | 3250 | 3762 | 1333 | 1349 | 4913 | 822 | 800 | 373 | 1244 | 1968 | 404 | 3564 | 1171 | 4785 | 1511 | 610 | 944 | 1142 | 416 | 340 | 2631 | 727 | 1866 | 408 | 1067 |
| Esperance | 3698 | 2616 | 407 | 4233 | 3721 | 3878 | 4453 | 1278 | 2916 | 2437 | 3350 | 2635 | 4275 | 3451 | 738 | 1876 | 2144 | 1751 | 3657 | 2293 | 4119 | 3457 | 3387 | 3612 | 3704 | 4642 | 2991 | 2832 |
| Eucla | 2782 | 1700 | 917 | 3365 | 3877 | 2962 | 3537 | 1788 | 2000 | 1521 | 2434 | 1719 | 3359 | 2535 | 1433 | 960 | 2654 | 894 | 2741 | 1377 | 3203 | 2541 | 2471 | 2696 | 2788 | 3726 | 2075 | 1916 |
| Geelong | 1542 | 278 | 2895 | 3423 | 3935 | 2016 | 2367 | 3766 | 72 | 546 | 1264 | 365 | 2651 | 1086 | 3411 | 1018 | 4632 | 1358 | 1324 | 690 | 2033 | 947 | 1231 | 2754 | 1618 | 2757 | 527 | 185 |
| Geraldton | 4601 | 3519 | 978 | 3409 | 2897 | 4781 | 5356 | 541 | 3819 | 3340 | 4253 | 3538 | 4691 | 4354 | 422 | 2779 | 1320 | 2713 | 4560 | 3196 | 5022 | 4360 | 4290 | 4078 | 4607 | 5545 | 3894 | 3735 |
| Grafton | | 1638 | 3699 | 3419 | 3931 | 1502 | 1298 | 4570 | 1473 | 1451 | 367 | 1895 | 2137 | 491 | 4215 | 1822 | 5436 | 2162 | 254 | 1595 | 964 | 638 | 311 | 2800 | 431 | 1688 | 1059 | 1718 |
| Horsham | 1638 | | 2451 | 3145 | 3657 | 2036 | 2463 | 3322 | 300 | 305 | 1360 | 257 | 2671 | 1235 | 3133 | 740 | 4188 | 1080 | 1462 | 428 | 2129 | 1096 | 1327 | 2476 | 1714 | 2800 | 644 | 230 |
| Kalgoorlie–Boulder | 3699 | 2451 | | 3826 | 3314 | 3879 | 4454 | 871 | 2917 | 2438 | 3351 | 2636 | 4276 | 3452 | 582 | 1877 | 1737 | 1811 | 3658 | 2294 | 4120 | 3458 | 3388 | 3613 | 3705 | 4643 | 2992 | 2833 |
| Katherine | 3419 | 3145 | 3826 | | 512 | 1917 | 2564 | 2955 | 3445 | 2966 | 3052 | 3164 | 1282 | 3556 | 3718 | 2405 | 2089 | 2745 | 3594 | 2822 | 2599 | 3666 | 3324 | 669 | 2965 | 2174 | 3520 | 3361 |
| Kununurra | 3931 | 3657 | 3314 | 512 | | 2429 | 3076 | 2443 | 3957 | 3478 | 3564 | 3676 | 1794 | 4067 | 3206 | 2917 | 1577 | 3257 | 4106 | 3334 | 3111 | 4178 | 3836 | 1181 | 3477 | 2686 | 4032 | 3873 |
| Longreach | 1502 | 2036 | 3879 | 1917 | 2429 | | 791 | 4750 | 1947 | 1839 | 1135 | 2293 | 635 | 1638 | 4395 | 2002 | 4006 | 2342 | 1677 | 1983 | 682 | 1749 | 1407 | 1298 | 1048 | 764 | 1680 | 2139 |
| Mackay | 1298 | 2463 | 4454 | 2564 | 3076 | 791 | | 5325 | 2298 | 2276 | 1103 | 2720 | 1282 | 1606 | 4970 | 2577 | 4653 | 2917 | 1552 | 2420 | 334 | 1744 | 1375 | 1945 | 970 | 390 | 1884 | 2543 |
| Meekatharra | 4570 | 3322 | 871 | 2955 | 2443 | 4750 | 5325 | | 3788 | 3309 | 4222 | 3507 | 4237 | 4323 | 763 | 2748 | 866 | 2682 | 4529 | 3165 | 5524 | 4329 | 4259 | 3624 | 4576 | 5129 | 3863 | 3704 |
| Melbourne | 1473 | 300 | 2917 | 3445 | 3957 | 1947 | 2298 | 3788 | | 548 | 1195 | 420 | 2582 | 1017 | 3433 | 1040 | 4823 | 1380 | 1255 | 692 | 1964 | 878 | 1162 | 2776 | 1549 | 2688 | 458 | 257 |
| Mildura | 1451 | 305 | 2438 | 2966 | 3478 | 1839 | 2276 | 3309 | 548 | | 1173 | 562 | 2474 | 1159 | 2954 | 561 | 4175 | 901 | 1397 | 144 | 1942 | 1020 | 1140 | 2297 | 1527 | 2603 | 554 | 535 |
| Moree | 367 | 1360 | 3351 | 3052 | 3564 | 1135 | 1103 | 4222 | 1195 | 1173 | | 1627 | 1770 | 503 | 3867 | 1474 | 5088 | 1814 | 542 | 1317 | 769 | 641 | 272 | 2433 | 354 | 1493 | 781 | 1449 |
| Mount Gambier | 1895 | 257 | 2636 | 3164 | 3676 | 2293 | 2720 | 3507 | 420 | 562 | 1627 | | 2928 | 1425 | 3152 | 759 | 4573 | 1099 | 1663 | 455 | 2386 | 1286 | 1584 | 2495 | 1971 | 3057 | 901 | 197 |
| Mount Isa | 2137 | 2671 | 4276 | 1282 | 1794 | 635 | 1282 | 4237 | 2582 | 2474 | 1770 | 2928 | | 2273 | 4792 | 2399 | 3371 | 2739 | 2312 | 2618 | 1317 | 2384 | 2042 | 661 | 1683 | 892 | 2315 | 2774 |
| Newcastle | 491 | 1235 | 3452 | 3556 | 4067 | 1638 | 1606 | 4323 | 1017 | 1159 | 503 | 1425 | 2273 | | 3968 | 1575 | 5189 | 1915 | 249 | 1303 | 1272 | 158 | 289 | 2936 | 788 | 1996 | 605 | 1271 |
| Perth | 4215 | 3133 | 582 | 3718 | 3206 | 4395 | 4970 | 763 | 3433 | 2954 | 3867 | 3152 | 4792 | 3968 | | 2393 | 1629 | 2327 | 4174 | 2810 | 4636 | 3974 | 3904 | 4129 | 4221 | 5159 | 3508 | 3349 |
| Port Augusta | 1822 | 740 | 1877 | 2405 | 2917 | 2002 | 2577 | 2748 | 1040 | 561 | 1474 | 759 | 2399 | 1575 | 2393 | | 3614 | 340 | 1781 | 417 | 2243 | 1581 | 1511 | 1736 | 1828 | 2766 | 1115 | 956 |
| Port Hedland | 5436 | 4188 | 1737 | 2089 | 1577 | 4006 | 4653 | 866 | 4823 | 4175 | 5088 | 4573 | 3371 | 5189 | 1629 | 3614 | | 3548 | 5395 | 4031 | 4688 | 5195 | 5125 | 2758 | 5054 | 4263 | 4729 | 4579 |
| Port Lincoln | 2162 | 1080 | 1811 | 2745 | 3257 | 2342 | 2917 | 2682 | 1380 | 901 | 1814 | 1099 | 2739 | 1915 | 2327 | 340 | 3548 | | 2121 | 757 | 2583 | 1921 | 1851 | 2076 | 2168 | 3106 | 1455 | 1296 |
| Port Macquarie | 254 | 1462 | 3658 | 3594 | 4106 | 1677 | 1552 | 4529 | 1255 | 1397 | 542 | 1663 | 2312 | 249 | 4174 | 1781 | 5395 | 2121 | | 1541 | 1218 | 396 | 270 | 2975 | 630 | 1942 | 843 | 1509 |
| Renmark | 1595 | 428 | 2294 | 2822 | 3334 | 1983 | 2420 | 3165 | 692 | 144 | 1317 | 455 | 2618 | 1303 | 2810 | 417 | 4031 | 757 | 1541 | | 2086 | 1164 | 1284 | 2153 | 1671 | 2747 | 698 | 652 |
| Rockhampton | 964 | 2129 | 4120 | 2599 | 3111 | 682 | 334 | 5524 | 1964 | 1942 | 769 | 2386 | 1317 | 1272 | 4636 | 2243 | 4688 | 2583 | 1218 | 2086 | | 1410 | 1041 | 1980 | 636 | 724 | 1550 | 2209 |
| Sydney | 638 | 1096 | 3458 | 3666 | 4178 | 1749 | 1744 | 4329 | 878 | 1020 | 641 | 1286 | 2384 | 158 | 3974 | 1581 | 5195 | 1921 | 396 | 1164 | 1410 | | 427 | 3047 | 926 | 2134 | 466 | 1132 |
| Tamworth | 311 | 1327 | 3388 | 3324 | 3836 | 1407 | 1375 | 4259 | 1162 | 1140 | 272 | 1584 | 2042 | 289 | 3904 | 1511 | 5125 | 1851 | 270 | 1284 | 1041 | 427 | | 2705 | 499 | 1765 | 748 | 1407 |
| Tennant Creek | 2800 | 2476 | 3613 | 669 | 1181 | 1298 | 1945 | 3624 | 2776 | 2297 | 2433 | 2495 | 661 | 2936 | 4129 | 1736 | 2758 | 2076 | 2975 | 2153 | 1980 | 3047 | 2705 | | 2346 | 1555 | 2851 | 2692 |
| Toowoomba | 431 | 1714 | 3705 | 2965 | 3477 | 1048 | 970 | 4576 | 1549 | 1527 | 354 | 1971 | 1683 | 788 | 4221 | 1828 | 5054 | 2168 | 630 | 1671 | 636 | 926 | 499 | 2346 | | 1360 | 1135 | 1794 |
| Townsville | 1688 | 2800 | 4643 | 2174 | 2686 | 764 | 390 | 5129 | 2688 | 2603 | 1493 | 3057 | 892 | 1996 | 5159 | 2766 | 4263 | 3106 | 1942 | 2747 | 724 | 2134 | 1765 | 1555 | 1360 | | 2274 | 2933 |
| Wagga Wagga | 1059 | 644 | 2992 | 3520 | 4032 | 1680 | 1884 | 3863 | 458 | 554 | 781 | 901 | 2315 | 605 | 3508 | 1115 | 4729 | 1455 | 843 | 698 | 1550 | 466 | 748 | 2851 | 1135 | 2274 | | 724 |
| Warrnambool | 1718 | 230 | 2833 | 3361 | 3873 | 2139 | 2543 | 3704 | 257 | 535 | 1449 | 197 | 2774 | 1271 | 3349 | 956 | 4579 | 1296 | 1509 | 652 | 2209 | 1132 | 1407 | 2692 | 1794 | 2933 | 724 | |

# ROAD ATLAS of AUSTRALIA

| INTER CITY ROUTES | | DISTANCE | TIME |
|---|---|---|---|
| Sydney–Melbourne via Hume Hwy/Fwy | | 881 km | 12 hrs |
| Sydney–Melbourne via Princes Hwy/Fwy | | 1037 km | 15 hrs |
| Sydney–Brisbane via New England Hwy | | 1001 km | 14 hrs |
| Melbourne–Adelaide via Western & Dukes hwys | | 733 km | 8 hrs |
| Melbourne–Adelaide via Princes Hwy | | 906 km | 11 hrs |
| Melbourne–Brisbane via Newell Hwy | | 1676 km | 20 hrs |
| Darwin–Adelaide via Stuart Hwy | | 3026 km | 31 hrs |
| Adelaide–Perth via Eyre & Great Eastern hwys | | 2700 km | 32 hrs |
| Adelaide–Sydney via Sturt & Hume hwys | | 1417 km | 19 hrs |
| Perth–Darwin via Great Northern Hwy | | 4032 km | 46 hrs |
| Sydney–Brisbane via Pacific Hwy | | 966 km | 14 hrs |
| Brisbane–Darwin via Warrego Hwy | | 3406 km | 39 hrs |
| Brisbane–Cairns via Bruce Hwy | | 1703 km | 20 hrs |
| Hobart–Launceston via Midland Hwy | | 200 km | 3 hrs |
| Hobart–Devonport via Midland & Bass hwys | | 286 km | 4 hrs |

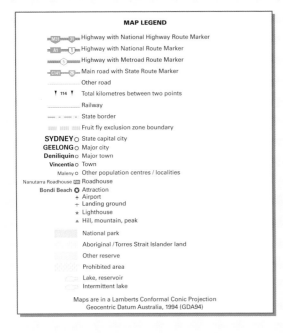

**MAP LEGEND**

Highway with National Highway Route Marker
Highway with National Route Marker
Highway with Metrod Route Marker
Main road with State Route Marker
Other road
114  Total kilometres between two points
Railway
State border
Fruit fly exclusion zone boundary
**SYDNEY**○ State capital city
**GEELONG**○ Major city
**Deniliquin**○ Major town
**Vincentia**○ Town
Maleny○ Other population centres / localities
Nanutarra Roadhouse RH Roadhouse
Bondi Beach ✪ Attraction
+ Airport
+ Landing ground
★ Lighthouse
▲ Hill, mountain, peak
National park
Aboriginal / Torres Strait Islander land
Other reserve
Prohibited area
Lake, reservoir
Intermittent lake

Maps are in a Lamberts Conformal Conic Projection
Geocentric Datum Australia, 1994 (GDA94)

**232-233**

Derby

Broome○    Fitzroy
            Crossing

Port Hedland○

○ Karratha

*WESTERN*

*AUSTRALIA*

Exmouth○

Tom Price○

Paraburdoo○  ○Newman

**234**

Carnarvon ○

Denham○         Meekatharra ○

**230-231**

Leinster
○

Kalbarri ○

Leonora
○

Geraldton○

Dongara-○
Denison

Kalgoorlie-
Boulder
○

Coolgardie ○

○Moora    Southern        ○Kambalda
          Cross

Yanchep○  Northam ○Merredin

Norseman
○

**PERTH**○  Mundaring

Mandurah○

**227**          Bunbury○   ○Narrogin
                    Collie
                    ○Kojonup        Esperance
Busselton○
           ○Manjimup
Augusta○
           ○Albany

**228-229**

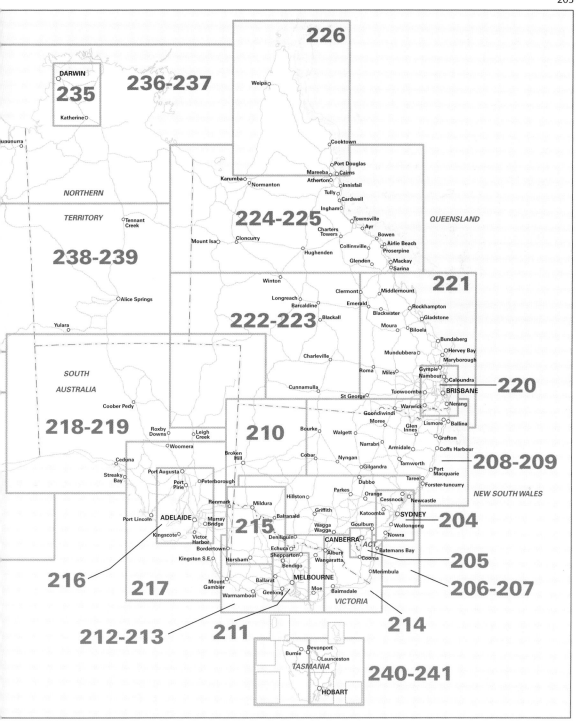

**226**

Weipa ○

**235** DARWIN ○
Katherine ○

**236-237**

ᵘnununurra ○

**NORTHERN**

**TERRITORY** Tennant ○ Creek

**238-239**

Alice Springs ○

Yulara ○

**SOUTH**

**AUSTRALIA**

Coober Pedy ○

**218-219**

Roxby ○ Downs
Woomera ○

Ceduna ○

Streaky ○ Bay

Cooktown ○
Port Douglas ○
Mareeba ○ ○ Cairns
Karumba ○ Atherton ○
Normanton ○ Innisfail ○
Tully ○
Cardwell ○
Ingham ○
Townsville ○ **QUEENSLAND**

**224-225** Charters ○ Ayr ○
Towers Bowen ○
Mount Isa ○ Cloncurry ○ Collinsville ○ ○ Airlie Beach
Hughenden ○ Proserpine
Glenden ○ ○ Mackay
○ Sarina

Winton ○

**221**
Clermont ○ Middlemount ○

Longreach ○ Emerald ○ Rockhampton ○
Barcaldine ○ Blackwater ○ Gladstone ○
**222-223** Blackall ○ Moura ○ ○ Biloela

○ Bundaberg
Mundubbera ○ ○ Hervey Bay
Charleville ○ ○ Maryborough
Roma ○ Miles ○ Gympie ○
Nambour ○ ○ Caloundra
Cunnamulla ○ Toowoomba ○ **BRISBANE** **220**
St George ○ Nerang ○
Warwick ○
Goondiwindi Lismore ○ Ballina
Moree ○ Glen ○ ○
Bourke ○ Walgett ○ Innes Grafton ○
Narrabri ○ Armidale ○ Coffs Harbour ○
Gilgandra ○ Tamworth ○ **208-209**
Cobar ○ Nyngan ○ Port ○
Macquarie
Dubbo ○ Taree ○ **NEW SOUTH WALES**
Forster-tuncurry ○

**210**
Broken ○
Hill

Port Augusta ○
Port ○ Peterborough ○
Pirie

Renmark ○ Mildura ○

Port Lincoln ○ **ADELAIDE** ○
Murray ○
Bridge
Kingscote ○ Victor ○
Harbor
Bordertown ○
Kingston S.E. ○

**216**

**217**

Mount ○
Gambier
Warrnambool ○

**212-213**

**215**

Hillston ○
Parkes ○ Orange ○ Cessnock ○ Newcastle ○
Balranald ○ Griffith ○ Katoomba ○ **SYDNEY** ○ **204**
Wagga ○ Goulburn ○ Wollongong ○
Wagga Nowra ○
Deniliquin ○ **CANBERRA** ○ **ACT**
Echuca ○ ○ ○ Batemans Bay **205**
Shepparton ○ Albury ○ Cooma ○
Horsham ○ Wangaratta ○
Bendigo ○ Merimbula ○ **206-207**
Ballarat ○ **MELBOURNE**
Geelong ○ Moe ○ **214**
Bairnsdale ○
**VICTORIA**

**211**

Burnie ○ Devonport ○
○ Launceston
**TASMANIA** **240-241**

HOBART ○

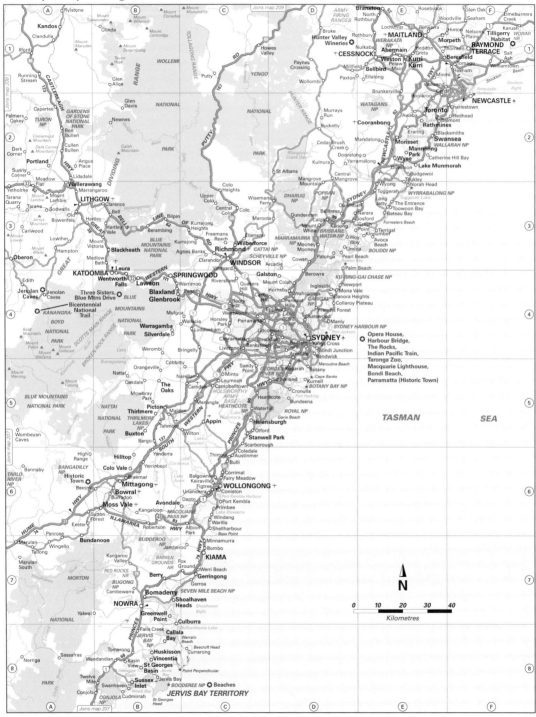

Opera House,
Harbour Bridge,
The Rocks,
Indian Pacific Train,
Taronga Zoo,
Macquarie Lighthouse,
Bondi Beach,
Parramatta (Historic Town)

**TASMAN       SEA**

N

0    10    20    30    40
Kilometres

★ BOODEREE NP ⊙ Beaches
**JERVIS BAY TERRITORY**

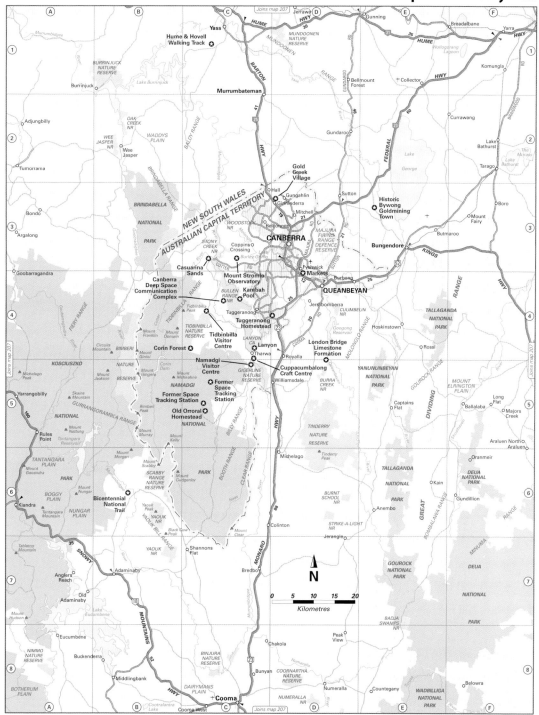

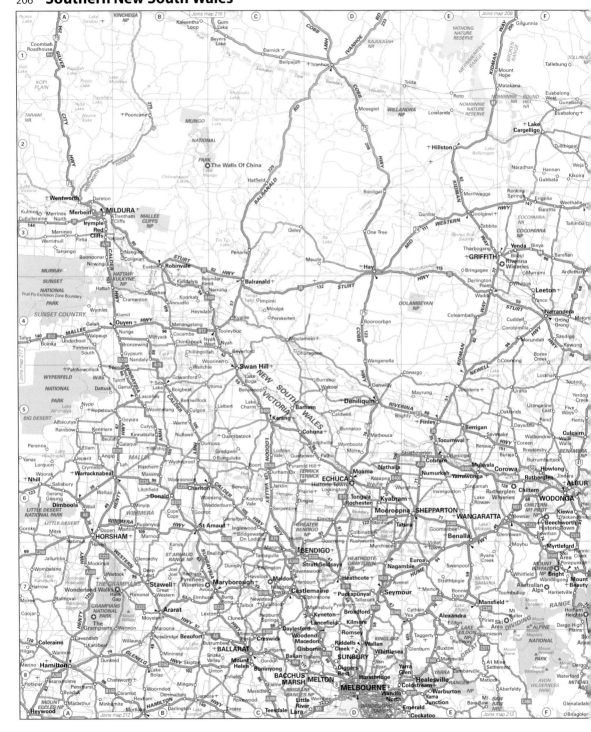

Joins map 208

Joins map 209

Joins map 214

For more detail on
Sydney & Region
see page 204

For more detail on the
Australian Capital Territory
see page 205

TASMAN          SEA

N

0    25    50    75    100
Kilometres

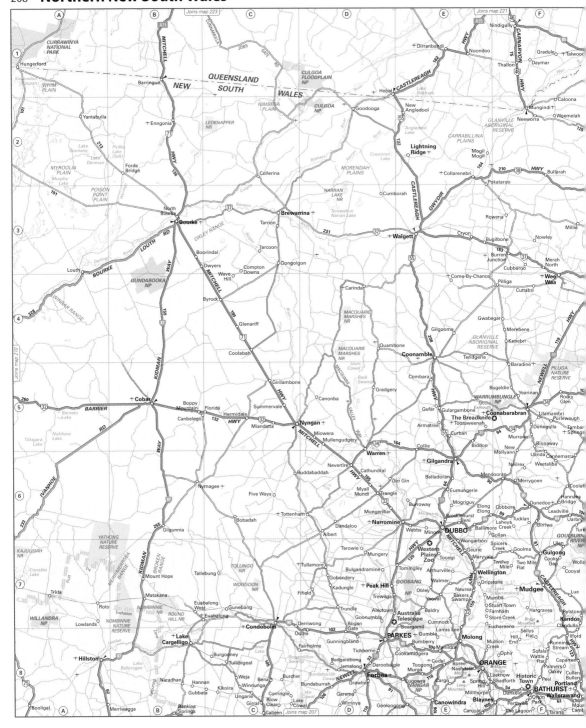

Joins map 221

Joins map 207

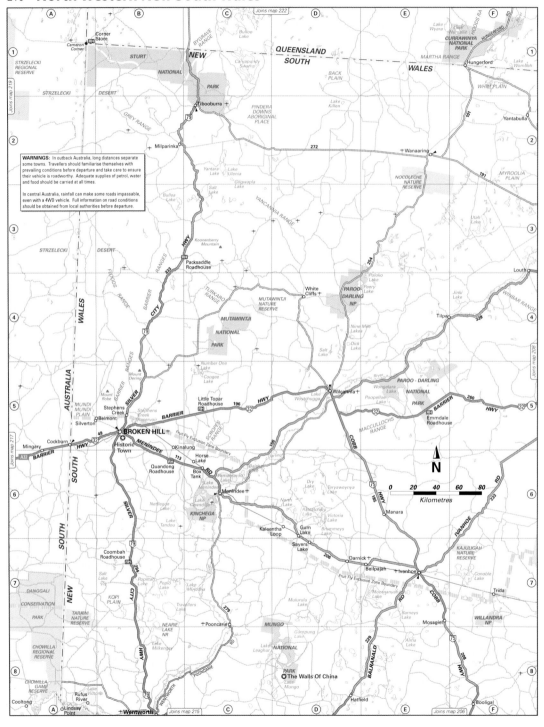

Joins map 222
Joins map 219
Joins map 208
Joins map 277
Joins map 215
Joins map 206

**WARNINGS:** In outback Australia, long distances separate some towns. Travellers should familiarise themselves with prevailing conditions before departure and take care to ensure their vehicle is roadworthy. Adequate supplies of petrol, water and food should be carried at all times.

In central Australia, rainfall can make some roads impassable, even with a 4WD vehicle. Full information on road conditions should be obtained from local authorities before departure.

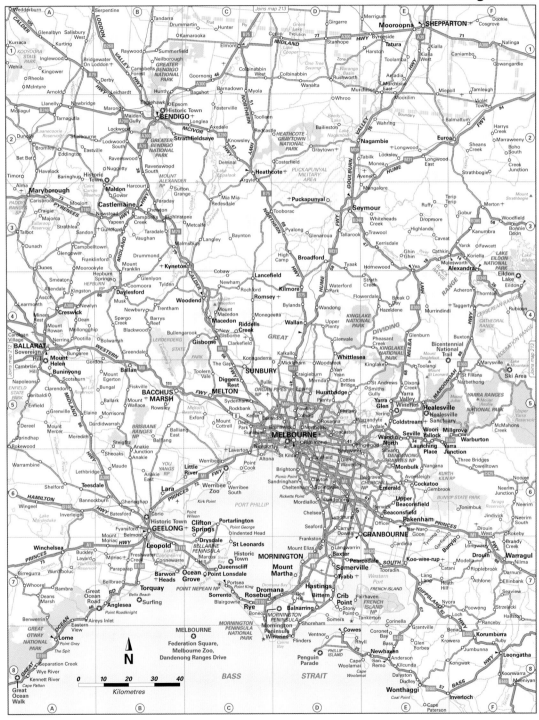

Joins map 215

NGARKAT
CONSERVATION
PARK

BIG
DESERT
WILDERNESS
PARK

WYPERFELD

NATIONAL

PARK

Lake
Albacutya

SOUTH AUSTRALIA
VICTORIA

MOUNT
RESCUE
CP

Keith

Brimbago
Lowan
Vale
Wirrega
Cannawigara

Kongal
Buckingham

Mundulla
Wolseley

DESERT
CAMP CR

Padthaway

Keppoch

Wallabrook
Minimay

Frances
Neuarpurr

Booroopki

FAIRVIEW
CP

Kybybolite
Hynam

Naracoorte
Naracoorte
Caves

NARACOORTE
CAVES NP

BOOL
LAGOON
GR

Struan

Joanna

Langkoop

BIG
HEATH
CP

Glenroy
Wrattonbully

Poolaijelo
Powers
Creek

Coonawarra

Comaum

Penola

Krongart

Nangwarry

Mount Burr
Kalangadoo

Tarpeena

Glencoe
Mil Lel

Tantanoola

MOUNT
GAMBIER
Blue Lake

Kongorong

Blackfellow
Caves
Mount
Schank

Nene
Valley

Allendale
East

Port
MacDonnell

Ewens
Ponds

PICCANINNIE PONDS CP

Nelson

LOWER
GLENELG
NATIONAL
PARK

Great South
West Walk

MOUNT RICHMOND NP

Heywood

Mount
Richmond

Heathmere

Tarragal

Cape
Bridgewater

Trewalla

Portland
Danger Point

Historic
Town

Cape Nelson
Lighthouse

BASS STRAIT

N

0  10  20  30  40  50
Kilometres

SOUTHERN        OCEAN

Joins map 206

For more detail on
Melbourne & Region
see page 211

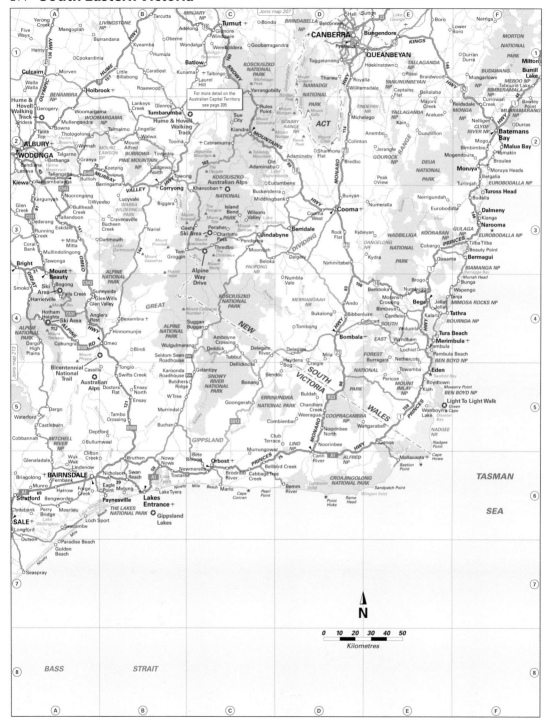

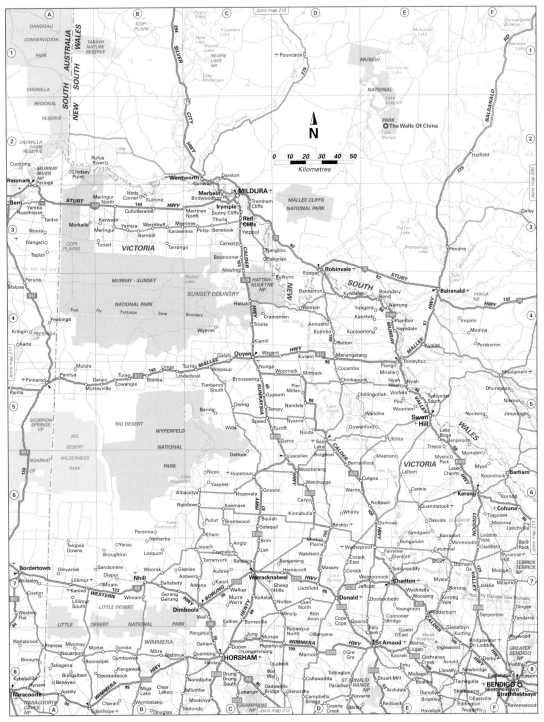

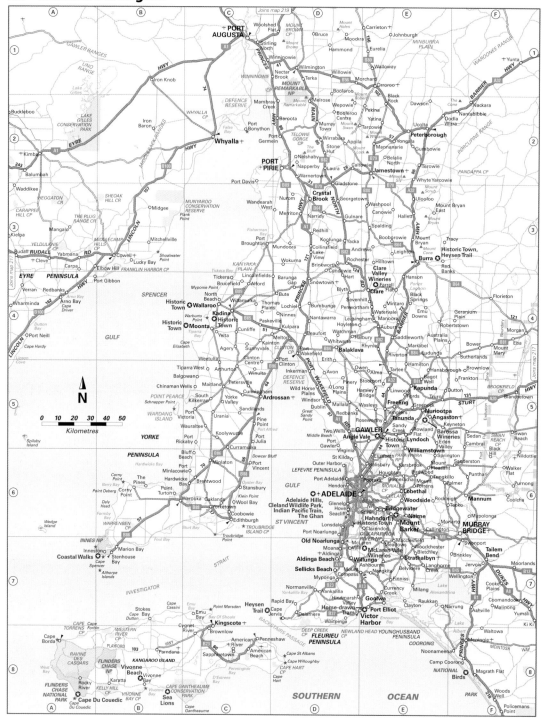

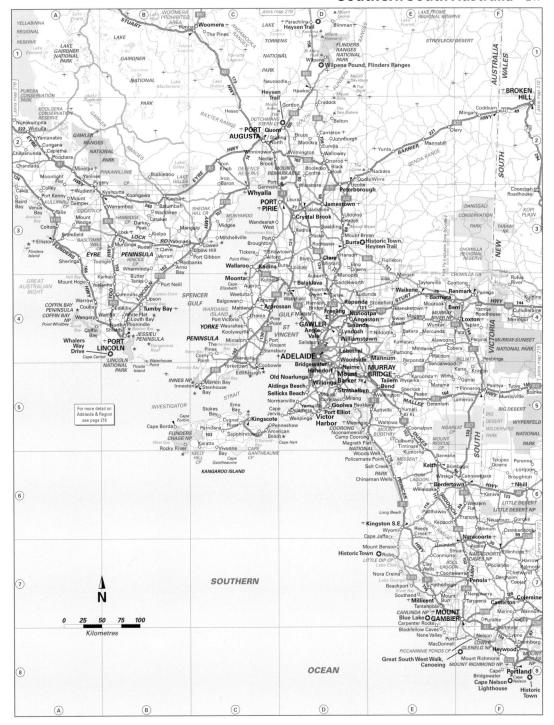

Southern South Australia

Joins map 238

Joins map 231

Joins map 229

WARNINGS: In outback Australia, long distances separate some towns. Travellers should familiarise themselves with prevailing conditions before departure and take care to ensure their vehicle is roadworthy. Adequate supplies of petrol, water and food should be carried at all times.

In central Australia, rainfall can make some roads impassable, even with a 4WD vehicle. Full information on road conditions should be obtained from local authorities before departure.

If visitors intend diverting off public roads within Aboriginal Land areas, a permit is required from the relevant Aboriginal authority.

**NORTHERN    SOUTH    AUSTRALIA    TERRITORY**

PETERMANN ABORIGINAL LAND TRUST

KATITI ABORIGINAL LAND TRUST

Surveyor Generals Corner

NGAANYATJARRA

TOMKINSON RANGES

MANN RANGES

THE MUSGRAVE RANGES

CENTRAL

ANANGU PITJANTJATJARA YANKUNYTJATJARA LANDS

BIRKSGATE RANGE

RESERVE

GREAT WESTERN VICTORIA DESERT

SOUTH AUSTRALIA / WESTERN AUSTRALIA

UNNAMED CONSERVATION PARK

WOOMERA PROHIBITED

TALLARINGA CONSERVATION PARK

AREA

GREAT VICTORIA DESERT NATURE RESERVE

MARALINGA

T.JARUTJA LANDS

WOOMERA PROHIBITED AREA

MARALINGA DEFENCE LAND (PROHIBITED AREA)

GOLDEA RANGE

NULLARBOR PLAIN

NULLARBOR REGIONAL RESERVE

YELLABINNA REGIONAL RESERVE

Nullarbor Plain Drive

NULLARBOR NATIONAL PARK

YALATA ABORIGINAL RESERVE

YUMBARRA CONSERVATION PARK

EUCLA NP

GREAT AUSTRALIAN BIGHT MARINE NP

HEAD OF GREAT AUSTRALIAN BIGHT

WAHGUNYAH CONSERVATION RESERVE

PUREBA CONSERVATION PARK

ROE PLAINS

GREAT AUSTRALIAN BIGHT

NUYTS ARCHIPELAGO CP

ISLES OF ST FRANCIS CONSERVATION PARK

NUYTSLAND NATURE RESERVE

FLINDERS

**SOUTHERN    OCEAN**

N

0   25   50   75   100
Kilometres

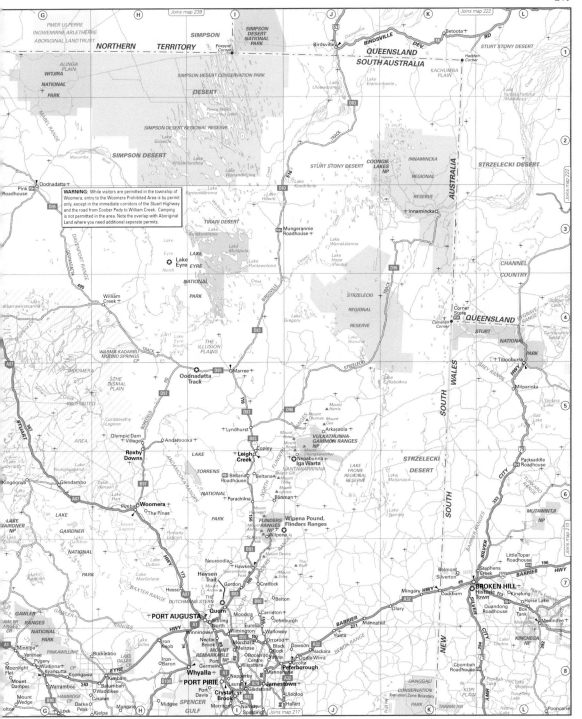

Joins map 239
Joins map 222
Joins map 222
Joins map 210
Joins map 217

**WARNING:** While visitors are permitted in the township of Woomera, entry to the Woomera Prohibited Area is by permit only, except in the immediate corridors of the Stuart Highway and the road from Coober Pedy to William Creek. Camping is not permitted in the area. Note the overlap with Aboriginal Land where you need additional separate permits.

NORTHERN TERRITORY

QUEENSLAND

SOUTH AUSTRALIA

NEW SOUTH WALES

SIMPSON DESERT

SIMPSON DESERT NATIONAL PARK

SIMPSON DESERT CONSERVATION PARK

SIMPSON DESERT REGIONAL RESERVE

STRZELECKI DESERT

STURT STONY DESERT

Birdsville

Innamincka

PORT AUGUSTA

PORT PIRIE

Whyalla

Quorn

BROKEN HILL

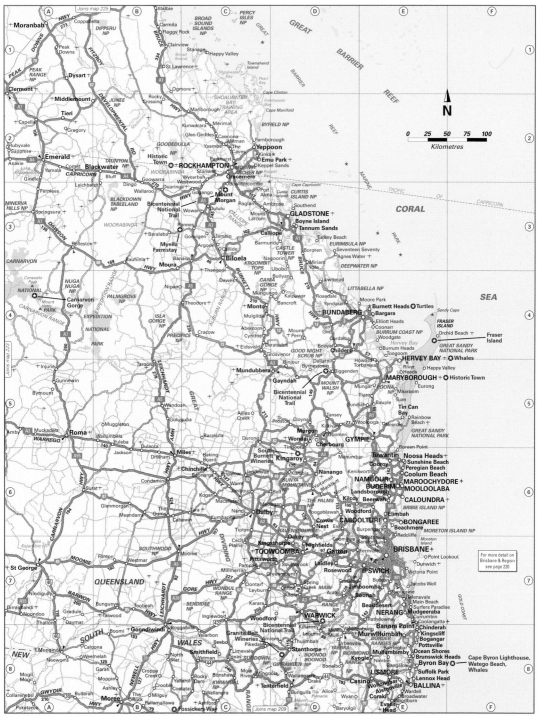

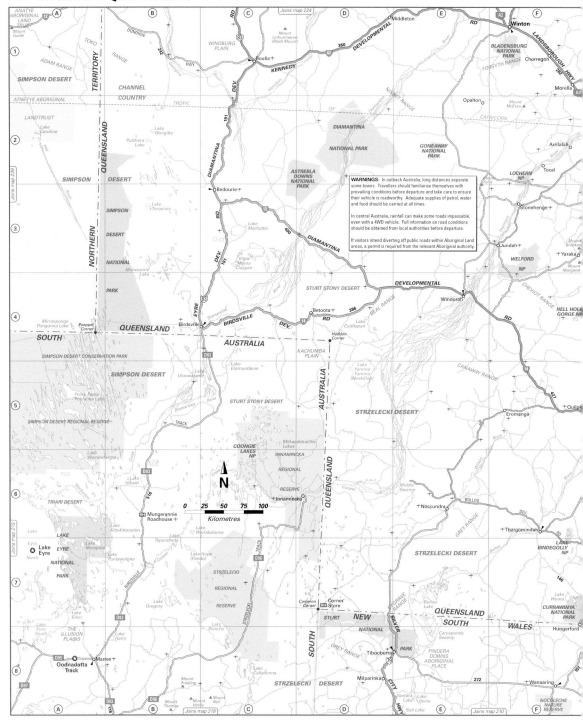

WARNINGS: In outback Australia, long distances separate some towns. Travellers should familiarise themselves with prevailing conditions before departure and take care to ensure their vehicle is roadworthy. Adequate supplies of petrol, water and food should be carried at all times.

In central Australia, rainfall can make some roads impassable, even with a 4WD vehicle. Full information on road conditions should be obtained from local authorities before departure.

If visitors intend diverting off public roads within Aboriginal Land areas, a permit is required from the relevant Aboriginal authority.

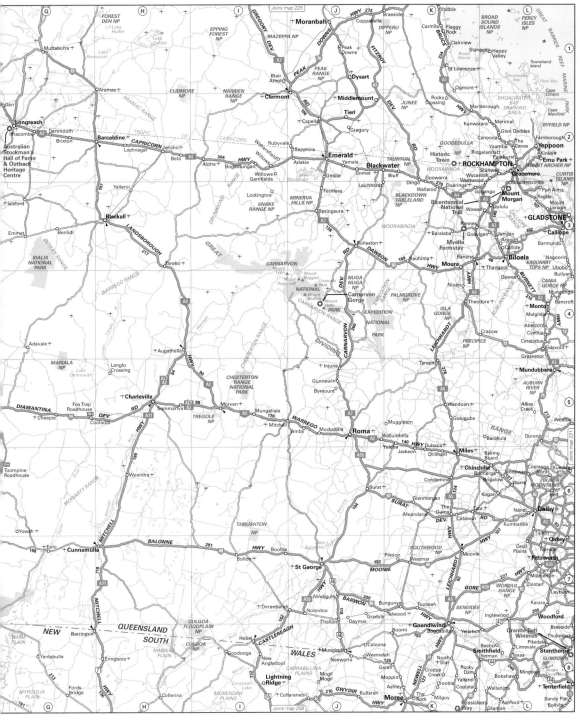

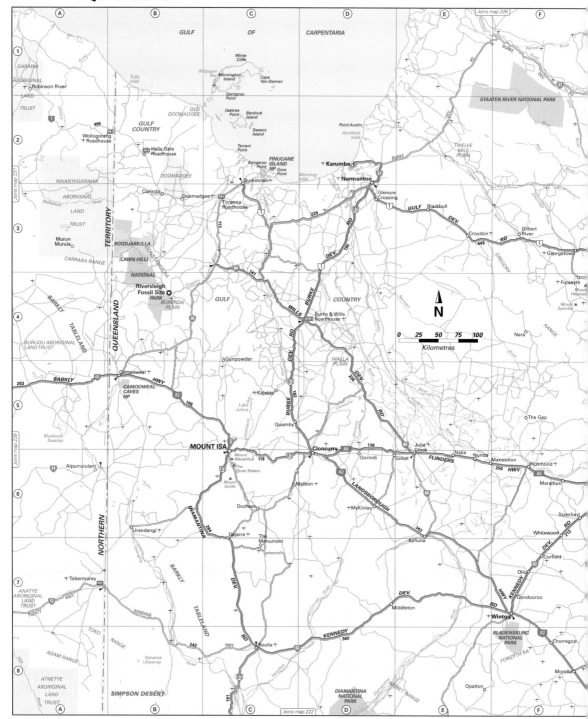

Joins map 226

CAPE YORK PENINSULA

WEST QUINKAN

QUINKAN

Walker Bay

Archer Point

BLACK MOUNTAIN NP

Rossville

Helenvale

PALMER GOLDFIELD

Palmer Mount Lukin

Lakeland

Wujal Wujal

Ayton

CEDAR BAY (MANGKAL-MANGKALBA) NP

Palmer River Roadhouse

Woods Peak

DAINTREE NATIONAL PARK

Daintree (World Heritage)

Cape Tribulation

Walsh

Mount Elephant

Cow Bay

DAINTREE NATIONAL PARK

Mount Carbine

Maryfarms

Mossman

Mialla

Wonga

Cape Kimberley

Low Isles Lighthouse

Mungana

Chillagoe

HANN TABLELAND

Mount Molloy

Koah

Port Douglas

Craiglie

Oak Beach

Four Mile Beach

Mount Mulligan

Dimbulah

Tabacum

Biboohra

Kuranda

Captain Cook Highway Drive

Kuranda Scenic Railway, Australian Butterfly Sanctuary

CHILLAGOE MUNGANA CAVES NP

Almaden

Mareeba

Watkamin

Edmonton

Palm Cove

CAIRNS

Ootann

Petford

Atherton

Kairi

Gordonvale

Aloomba

CRATER LAKES NP

GREAT

Lynd

Herberton

Tolga

Fishery Falls

BARRIER

Irvinebank

Malanda

Millaa

WOOROONOORAN NP

Bramston Beach

BULLERINGA NATIONAL PARK

MOUNT HYPIPAMEE NP

MILLSTREAM FALLS NP

Bullock Creek

Mount Garnet

Ravenshoe

Millaa Millaa

Babinda

MARINE

Innot Hot Springs

Mount Pope

TULLY GORGE NP

Flying Fish Point

Innisfail

Mourilyan

GREAT

Bicentennial National Trail

Mount Surprise

FORTY MILE SCRUB NP

Bilyana

Silkwood

South Johnstone

El Arish

Kurrimine Beach

Bingil Bay

Mission Beach

PARK

Great Barrier Reef

BARRIER

CORAL

Einasleigh

UNDARA VOLCANIC NP

Mount Tableland

BRETTS PLAIN

KINRARA NP

Whitewater Rafting

Tully

Euramo

Bellenden

Wongaling Beach

South Mission Beach

Tully Heads

EDMUND KENNEDY NP

Kennedy

Cardwell

Mount Misery

EMU PLAINS

GIRRINGUN

NATIONAL

Abergowrie

Kidston

Oasis Roadhouse

Greenvale

Michael Creek

Lannercost

Trebonne

Toobanna

HINCHINBROOK ISLAND NP

Hinchinbrook Island

Lucinda

Halifax

Forrest Beach

ORPHEUS ISLAND NP

Great Palm Island

GREAT

SEA

Mount Lookout

GREGORY

Bambaroo

Ingham

PALUMA RANGE NP

Mutarnee

Balgal Beach

Halifax Bay

BARRIER

REEF

Vineyard Mountain

BLACKBRAES

Blue Water Springs Roadhouse

Rollingstone

Jallonda

Bluewater

Pallarenda

MAGNETIC ISLAND NP

Nelly Bay

BLACKBRAES NP

DIVIDING

DEV

Thuringowa

TOWNSVILLE

Historic Town

Bobs Mountain

Clarke

GREAT BASALT WALL NP

TOWNSVILLE FIELD TRAINING AREA

Alligator Creek

Cungulla

BOWLING GREEN BAY NP

Mount Dick

Lake Cardoon

Mount Courtney

Mingela

Woodstock

BOWLING GREEN BAY

Giru

Brandon

Alva

Ayr

Home Hill

CAPE UPSTART NP

Mount James

Selheim

Reid River

Clare

Inkerman

Mount Pleasant

PORCUPINE GORGE NP

Balfes Creek

Macrossan

Gumlu

Guthalungra

Charters Towers

Ravenswood

Millaroo

Merinda

Bowen

GLOUCESTER ISLAND NP

WHITE MOUNTAINS NATIONAL PARK

Homestead

Dalbeg

MOUNT ABERDEEN NP

DRYANDER NP

Whitsunday Island

Whitsunday Islands, Whitehaven Beach

Hughenden

Pentland

Binbee

Cannonvale

Airlie Beach

WHITSUNDAY ISLANDS NP

FLINDERS

Prairie

Torrens Creek

GREAT

Lake Dalrymple

Proserpine

CONWAY NP

Conway Beach

LINDEMAN ISLANDS NP

Collinsville

Scottville

RANGE

Repulse Bay

Midge Point

SMITH ISLANDS NP

Great Barrier Reef

Bloomsbury

Mount Hector

NEWRY ISLANDS NP

BRAMPTON ISLANDS NP

Elaroo

Yalboroo

Seaforth

SOUTH CUMBERLAND ISLANDS NP

MIDORRINYA NATIONAL PARK

EUNGELLA NP

Calen

CAPE HILLSBOROUGH NP

Eungella

Mount Ossa

Bucasia

Eimeo

Lake Buchanan

BELYANDO

Belyando Crossing Roadhouse

Mount Coolon

Finch Hatton

Glenden

MACKAY

Walkerston

Bakers Creek

Tangorin

BLACKWOOD NP

NAIRANA NATIONAL PARK

HOMEVALE NP

Eton

Hector

NORTHUMBERLAND ISLANDS NP

WILANDSPEY CONSERVATION PARK

Nebo

Alligator Creek

Sarina Beach

Grasstree

Braeside

Sarina

Armstrong Beach

Cape Palmerston

FOREST DEN NP

Lake Galilee

MAZEPPA NP

Coppabella

DIPPERU NP

Koumala

CAPE PALMERSTON NP

Iblilbie

Mount Scott

WEST HILL NP

NORTHUMBERLAND ISLANDS NP

PERCY ISLES NP

Muttaburra

Moranbah

Carmila

BROAD SOUND ISLANDS NP

EPPING FOREST NP

DOWNS

Peak Downs

Flaggy Rock

Clairview

Stanage

Happy Valley

BLACKWOOD NP

PEAK

Blair Athol

PEAK RANGE NP

Dysart

FITZROY

JUNEE NP

St Lawrence

Townshend Island

CUDMORE NATIONAL PARK

NARRIEN RANGE NP

Browns

Ogmore

Cape Clinton

Aramac

CUDMORE RESOURCES RESERVE

Clermont

Middlemount

Rocky Crossing

Marlborough

SHOALWATER BAY TRAINING AREA

Cape Manifold

Longreach

Capella

Tieri

BRUCE

Kunwarara

BYFIELD NP

Joins map 223

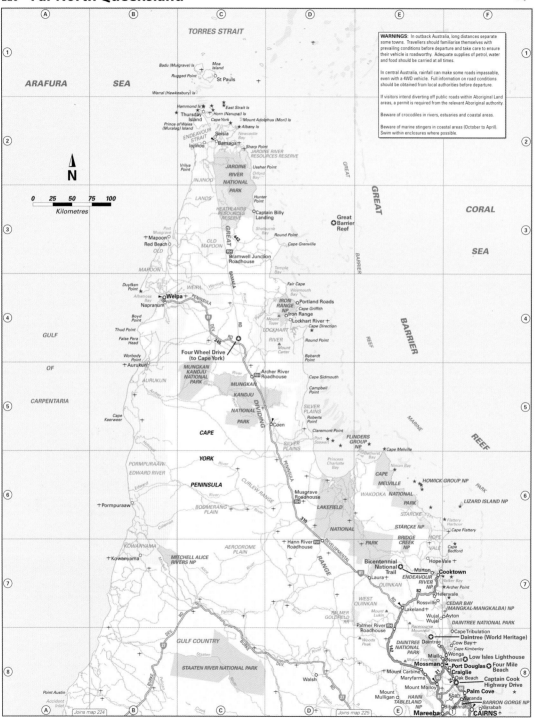

TORRES STRAIT

ARAFURA        SEA

WARNINGS: In outback Australia, long distances separate some towns. Travellers should familiarise themselves with prevailing conditions before departure and take care to ensure their vehicle is roadworthy. Adequate supplies of petrol, water and food should be carried at all times.

In central Australia, rainfall can make some roads impassable, even with a 4WD vehicle. Full information on road conditions should be obtained from local authorities before departure.

If visitors intend diverting off public roads within Aboriginal Land areas, a permit is required from the relevant Aboriginal authority.

Beware of crocodiles in rivers, estuaries and coastal areas.

Beware of marine stingers in coastal areas (October to April). Swim within enclosures where possible.

Badu (Mulgrave) Is
Moa Island
Rugged Point
St Pauls
Warral (Hawkesbury) Is

Hammond Is
East Strait Is
Horn (Narupai) Is
Thursday Island
Cape York
Mount Adolphus (Mori) Is
Prince of Wales (Muralag) Island
Albany Is
ENDEAVOUR STRAIT
Seisia
Newcastle Bay
Injinoo
Bamaga
Sharp Point
JARDINE RIVER RESOURCES RESERVE

Vrilya Point
Usher Point
INJINOO
Orford Bay
JARDINE
RIVER
NATIONAL
PARK
Hunter Point

LANDS

HEATHLANDS RESOURCES RESERVE
Captain Billy Landing
Great Barrier Reef

CORAL

Port Musgrave
Shelburne Bay
Round Point

Mapoon
Red Beach
OLD MAPOON
Cape Grenville

GREAT

SEA

OLD
MAPOON
Bramwell Junction Roadhouse
Temple Bay

Duyfken Point
Fair Cape
Weymouth Bay

Albatross Bay
Weipa
WEIPA
Wenlock
IRON RANGE NP
Portland Roads
Napranum
Cape Griffith
Iron Range
Boyd Point
Lockhart River
Cape Direction
Thud Point
LOCKHART
Round Point
RIVER
Mount Carter

GULF
False Pera Head
Four Wheel Drive (to Cape York)
Bobardt Point

Worbody Point
MUNGKAN KANDJU NATIONAL PARK
Archer River Roadhouse
Cape Sidmouth

Aurukun
AURUKUN
MUNGKAN
Campbell Point

OF
KANDJU
SILVER PLAINS
Roberts Point

Cape Keerweer
NATIONAL
Coen
Claremont Point

CARPENTARIA
PARK
CAPE
FLINDERS GROUP NP
Cape Melville

YORK
SILVER PLAINS
Princess Charlotte Bay
Bathurst Bay
Ninian Bay

PORMPURAAW
EDWARD RIVER
PENINSULA
CAPE MELVILLE
HOWICK GROUP NP

Pormpuraaw
CURLEW RANGE
Musgrave Roadhouse
WAKOOKA
NATIONAL
LIZARD ISLAND NP

BOOMERANG PLAIN
LAKEFIELD
STARCKE
Flattery Harbour

KOWANYAMA
AERODROME PLAIN
Hann River Roadhouse
NATIONAL
STARCKE NP
Cape Flattery

Kowanyama
MITCHELL ALICE RIVERS NP
PARK
BRIDGE CREEK NP
HOPE VALE
Cape Bedford

RANGE
Bicentennial National Trail
Hope Vale
Marton
Cooktown

QUINKAN
Laura
ENDEAVOUR RIVER NP
Walker Bay

WEST QUINKAN
Rossville
Archer Point
Helenvale

PALMER GOLDFIELD RR
Mount Lukin
Lakeland
CEDAR BAY (MANGKAL-MANGKALBA) NP

GULF COUNTRY
Palmer River Roadhouse
Wujal Wujal
Ayton
DAINTREE NATIONAL PARK

Woods Peak
Racecourse Mountain
Cape Tribulation
Daintree (World Heritage)

DAINTREE NATIONAL PARK
Daintree
Cow Bay
Cape Kimberley

Staaten
Miallo
Low Isles Lighthouse

STAATEN RIVER NATIONAL PARK
Mount Elephant
Mossman
Port Douglas
Four Mile Beach

Mount Carbine
Craiglie
Captain Cook Highway Drive

Walsh
Maryfarms
Oak Beach

Mount Molloy
Mount Mulligan
HANN TABLELAND NP
Koah
Palm Cove

Mareeba
Kuranda
BARRON GORGE NP
Biboohra
Yarrabah
CAIRNS

Point Austin
Accident Inlet

Joins map 224
Joins map 225

GREAT BARRIER REEF

GREAT BARRIER REEF

MARINE

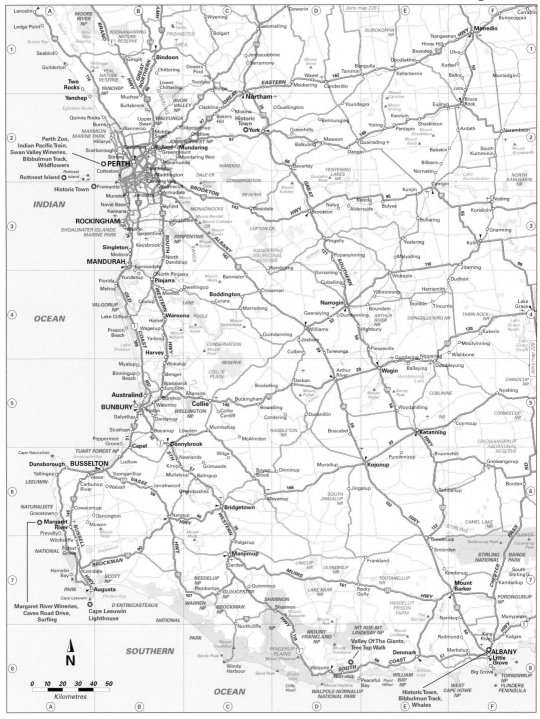

Joins map 228

Joins map 228

Lancelin
Ledge Point
MOORE RIVER NATURE RESERVE
Nine Mile Swamp
The Twins
PROHIBITED AREA
Wyening
Bolgart
Dowerin
Geomalling
DUROKOPPIN NR
Nangeenan
Hines Hill
HWY
Burracoppin
Carrabin
**Merredin**

Seabird
Breton Bay
Wilbinga Peak
BOONANARRING NATURE RESERVE
BRAND
GREAT NORTHERN
Gingin
Chittering
Dewars Pool
Jennacubbine
Yarramony
Mount Anne
Bungulla
Doodlakine
Baandee
Ulva
Korbel
Muntadgin

Guilderton
YEAL NATURE RESERVE
YANCHEP NP
**Bindoon**
Lower Chittering
Toodyay
Rines
Tammin
Meckering
Cunderdin
Waeel
162
Kellerberrin
Belka
Jura
Bruce Rock
Narembeen

Two Rocks
Yanchep
Eglinton Rocks
Muchea
Bullsbrook
AVON VALLEY NP
Clackline
Mokine
Bakers Hill
Quellington
**Northam**
Youndegin
Mount Caroline
Kwolyin
Eujinyn
Mount Stirling
Ardath
South Kummunin
Babakin

Quinns Rocks
Burns
Wanneroo
MARMION MARINE PARK
Hillarys
WALYUNGA NP
Upper Swan
Gidgegannup
Middle Swan
Chidlow
Historic Town
**York**
Greenhills
Belmunging
Mawson
Quairading
Dangin
Shackleton
Pantapin
Yoting
Mount Shackleton
Bilbarin
Nornakin
Lake Kurrenkutten
NORTH KARLGARIN NR

Perth Zoo, Indian Pacific Train, Swan Valley Wineries, Bibbulmun Track, Wildflowers
Scarborough
Stirling
Cottesloe
**PERTH**
Guildford
Midland
Greenmount
Mundaring
Kalamunda
**Mundaring**
Mundaring Weir
Beverley
Balkuling
66
Quaialbin Peak
YENYENING LAKES NR
Kunjin
Corrigin
Notting

Rottnest Island
Historic Town
Fremantle
Munster
Naval Base
Kwinana
**ROCKINGHAM**
Canning
Maddington
Canning Vale
Kalmscott
Armadale
Byford
DALE CR
WANDOO
CONSERVATION
RESERVE
Mount Dale
Mount Kokeby
Westdale
143
Brookton
Nalya
Aldersyde
Bulyee
Kweda
95
Bullaring
Kondinin
Gnarming

INDIAN
MARMION MARINE PARK
Rottnest Island
SHOALWATER ISLANDS MARINE PARK
Waikiki
Serpentine
Keysbrook
MONADNOCKS
Mount Randall
Mount Cuthbert CR
Mount Cooke
SERPENTINE NP
Mount Solus
LUPTON CR
Pingelly
Yealering
Kulin
55

Singleton
Madora
**MANDURAH**
Furnissdale
North Dandalup
North Pinjarra
Bannister
WANDERING ABORIGINAL RESERVE
Wandering
Popanyinning
Yornaning
Cuballing
Mslyalling
Jitarning
Dudinin
Lake Grace
69

Florida
Melros
Yunderup
**Pinjarra**
Dwellingup
Meelon
Curara
Marradong
Crossman
SOUTHERN
Williams
Yilliminning
Wickepin
Harrismith
Lake Grace North
Kukerin
Lake Grace South

OCEAN
YALGORUP NP
OLD COAST RD
WESTERN
Coolup
**Boddington**
**Waroona**
Hamel
Wagerup
Yarloop
Mount William
CONSERVATION
Mount Saddleback
Mount Rose
RESERVE
Geeralying
**Narrogin**
Boundain
**Dumberning**
Highbury
Toolibin
Tincurrin
ARTHUR RIVER NR
DONGOLOCKING NR
TARIN ROCK NR
120
Moulyinning
Wishbone

Lake Clifton
Preston Beach
**Harvey**
Lake Preston
Josbury
Culbin
Tarwonga
Plesseville
Gundaring
Nippering
Lake Grace

Myalup
Binningup Beach
Wokalup
Benger
Brunswick Junction
COLLIE PLAIN
Boolading
Darkan
Arthur River
29
**Wagin**
Ballaying
Dumbleyung
Mount Hugel
Dumbleyung Lake
CHINOCUP NR
Nyabing

**Australind**
**BUNBURY**
Picton
Waterloo
Burekup
Allanson
**Collie**
146
Collie Cardiff
Bowelling
Buckingham
107
Mount Fisher
Mount Arthur
Bunny Peak
120
COBLININE
Woodanilling
CORNECUP NR

Dalyellup
Dardanup
Lowden
Mumballup
Duranillin
Boscabel
**Katanning**
GNOWANGERUP ABORIGINAL RESERVE

Stratham
Peppermint Grove
WELLINGTON NP
McAlinden
HADDLETON NR
Cordering
59
Coyrecup
Broomehill

**Capel**
**Donnybrook**
COAST RD
Boyanup
Newlands
Wilga
Gnowangerup
RD

TUART FOREST NP
Geographe Bay
Ludlow
Kirup
Grimwade
Boyup Brook
Dinninup
Muradup
**Kojonup**
Punchmirup
Gnowangerup
Borden

Cape Naturaliste
**Dunsborough**
**BUSSELTON**
Yallingup
Vasse
Yoongarillup
Mullalyup
Balingup
166
Jingalup
Tambellup
STIRLING
CAMEL LAKE NR

LEEUWIN-NATURALISTE
Carbunup River
Walsall
VASSE
Jarrahwood
Greenbushes
Mayanup
SOUTH JINGALUP NR
102
122

Gracetown
Cowaramup
Osmington
**Bridgetown**
Nannup
WESTERN
Palgarup
Frankland
Cranbrook
Tenterden
STIRLING RANGE NATIONAL PARK
PORONGURUP NP

**Margaret River**
Prevelly
Witchcliffe
Mowen
Mount Yates
HWY
Mount Mark
**Manjimup**
Jardee
UNICUP NR
QUINDINUP NR
TOOTANELLUP NR
Kendenup
**Mount Barker**
South Stirling
Kambalup

Forest Grove
Blackwood
BROCKMAN
SCOTT NP
BEEDELUP NP
Pemberton
Quinninup
GLOUCESTER NP
LAKE MUIR NH
161
Rocky Gully
PARDELUP PRISON FARM
The Springs
Narrikup

Hamelin Bay
Karridale
Augusta
D'ENTRECASTEAUX
Cape Leeuwin Lighthouse
SHANNON
Shannon
MUIRS
HWY
Mount Roe
Manypeaks
King River
Kalgan

Margaret River Wineries, Caves Road Drive, Surfing
Cape Leeuwin
WARREN
107
BROCKMAN
NP
NATIONAL
Northcliffe
NP
118
MT ROE-MT LINDESAY NP
Mount Lindesay
Redmond
Marbelup
**ALBANY**
Little Grove
Big Grove

NATURALISTE
SOUTHERN
PARK
Mount Chudalup
Windy Harbour
Sandy Peak
Mount Pingerup
PINGERUP PLAINS
Broke Inlet
MOUNT FRANKLAND NP
Valley Of The Giants, Tree Top Walk
Denmark
William
Wilson Inlet
TORNDIRRUP NP
FLINDERS PENINSULA
WEST CAPE HOWE NP

OCEAN
Cliffy Head
Mount Hopkins
WALPOLE-NORNALUP NATIONAL PARK
Walpole
Nornalup
Peaceful Bay
Point Hillier
66
SOUTH COAST
WILLIAM BAY NP
Historic Town, Bibbulmun Track, Whales

N

0 10 20 30 40 50
Kilometres

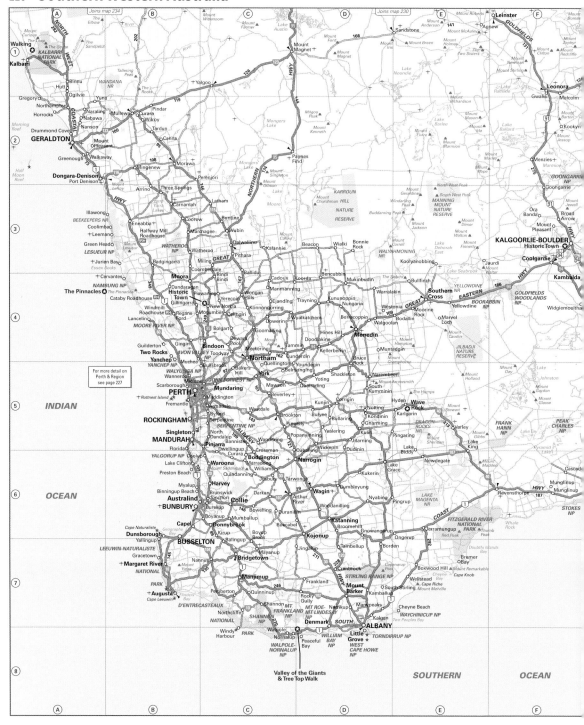

G H I J K L

Mount Clarke
Mount Vardell
COSMO NEWBERRY (WEST)
Mount Black
Mount Fleming
COSMO NEWBERRY (EAST)
YEO LAKE NATURE RESERVE
Neale Junction
NEALE JUNCTION NATURE RESERVE
Ilkurlka Roadhouse RH
Wanna Lakes
Serpentine

**WARNINGS:** In outback Australia, long distances separate some towns. Travellers should familiarise themselves with prevailing conditions before departure and take care to ensure their vehicle is roadworthy. Adequate supplies of petrol, water and food should be carried at all times.

In central Australia, rainfall can make some roads impassable, even with a 4WD vehicle. Full information on road conditions should be obtained from local authorities before departure.

If visitors intend diverting off public roads within Aboriginal Land areas, a permit is required from the relevant Aboriginal authority.

Windarra
Laverton
Mount Weld
Mount Sefton
COSMO NEWBERRY (SOUTH)
Mount Douglas
Mount Hickox
Mount Carlon
Mount Luck
Lake Rason
DOCTOR HICKS RANGE
SOUTH AUSTRALIA
WESTERN AUSTRALIA
UNNAMED
Lakes
MARALINGA TJARUTJA LANDS
CONSERVATION
PARK

Mount Keith
Mount Florence
Mount Colinda
Mount Howe
Lake Raeside
STELLARA
PLUMRIDGE LAKES NATURE RESERVE
Jubilee Lake
Lake Minigwal
GREAT VICTORIA DESERT NATURE RESERVE
MARALINGA TJARUTJA LANDS

Mount Balona
QUEEN VICTORIA SPRING NATURE RESERVE
GREAT
YAKADUNYA
VICTORIA
DESERT

Mount McLeay
Mount Eric
Lake Roe
CUNDEELEE MISSION
Cundeelee
SPINIFEX RA
Deakin
Hughes
NULLARBOR REGIONAL RESERVE

Lake Yindarlgooda
Quartz Peak
Mount Magnetic
Karonie
COONANA
Zanthus
Naretha
Rawlinna
Haig
Nurina
Loongana
Forrest
Reid

Stoneville
Mount Martin
Mount Belches
Lake Rivers
Kitchener
NULLARBOR PLAIN
Nullarbor NP
Nullarbor Plain Drive

**Kambalda**
Lake Lefroy
Mundrabilla Roadhouse RH
Eucla
Border Village
GREAT AUSTRALIAN BIGHT MARINE NATIONAL PARK
A1 HWY

Lake Cowan
EYRE
Mount Pleasant
Madura Roadhouse RH
340
ROE PLAINS
GREAT

**Norseman**
Mount Norcott
Mount Malcolm
FRASER RA
373
Balladonia Roadhouse RH
Caiguna Roadhouse RH
Cocklebiddy Roadhouse RH
Red Rocks Point
AUSTRALIAN

Mount Deans
Nullarbor Plain Drive
HWY
HWY
Scorpion Bight
BIGHT

Kurnarl
DUNDAS NATURE RESERVE
Lake Dundas
Mount Andrew
Point Dover
NUYTSLAND NATURE RESERVE
Toolinna Cove

Salmon Gums
Mount Coobaninya
Point Culver

Grass Patch
NUYTSLAND NATURE RESERVE
Mount Buramitya

Scaddan
Mount Ridley
Mount Heywood
BEAUMONT GROUP NR
Mount Dean

Gibson
KAU NR
Mount Ney
Mount Dean

Jayup
CAPE ARID NATIONAL PARK
Tower Peak
The Yatats Burden
Mobot
Mount Baring
The Pups
Israelite Bay
Point Dempster
Mount Malcolm
Point Malcolm
Daw Island

oomalbidgup
Condingup
Mount Pasley

**Beaches**
Butty Head
**Esperance**
Mount Le Grand
Hammer Head
Yokinup Bay
Sandy Bight
Cape Arid
Mount Arid
Middle Island
CAPE LE GRAND NP

Salisbury Island

**N**

0  25  50  75  100
Kilometres

**SOUTHERN**     **OCEAN**

1 2 3 4 5 6 7 8

G H I J K L

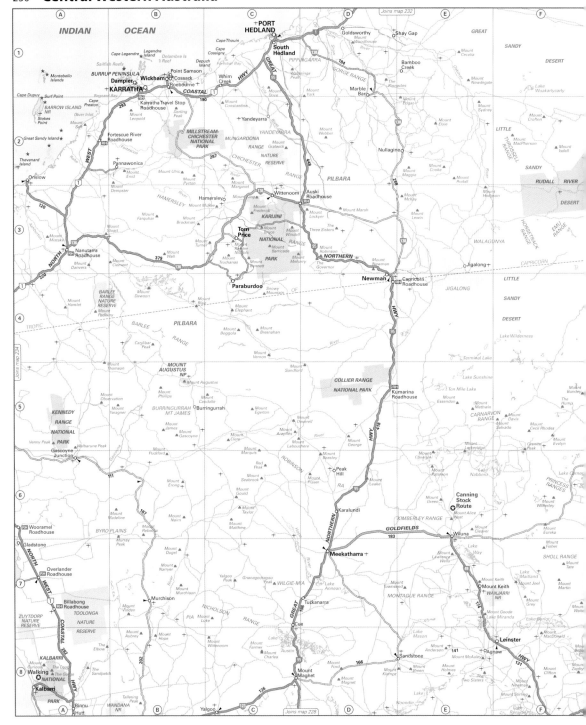

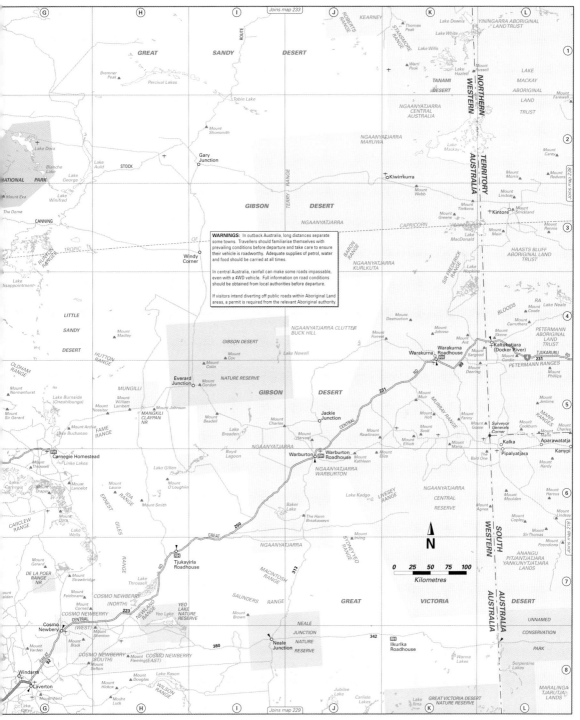

Joins map 238

Joins map 218

GREAT SANDY DESERT

KEARNEY

ROBERTS RANGE

SPANSMORE RANGE

Thomas Peak

Lake Dennis

YININGARRA ABORIGINAL LAND TRUST

Bremner Peak

Lake White

Percival Lakes

Lake Wills

TANAMI DESERT

Warri Peak

Lake Hazlett

Mount Russell

Mount Farewell

LAKE MACKAY

Mount Shoesmith

Tobin Lake

NGAANYATJARRA CENTRAL AUSTRALIA

ABORIGINAL

LAND

TRUST

Mount Carey

NGAANYATJARRA MARUWA

Lake Mackay

Mount Morris

Mount Redvers

Gary Junction

Kiwirrkurra

Mount Lindsay

Lake Dora

Blanche Lake

Lake George

Lake Auld

STOCK

Mount Webb

Mount Strickland

Kintore

NATIONAL PARK

Lake Winifred

GIBSON DESERT

TERRY RANGE

Mount Tietkens

Mount Renvia

Mount Eva

NGAANYATJARRA

CAPRICORN

Mount Greene

Mount Main

The Dome

CANNING

CAPRICORN TROPIC

OF

BARON RANGE

Lake MacDonald

HAASTS BLUFF ABORIGINAL LAND TRUST

RUDOLL RANGES

WARNINGS: In outback Australia, long distances separate some towns. Travellers should familiarise themselves with prevailing conditions before departure and take care to ensure their vehicle is roadworthy. Adequate supplies of petrol, water and food should be carried at all times.

In central Australia, rainfall can make some roads impassable, even with a 4WD vehicle. Full information on road conditions should be obtained from local authorities before departure.

If visitors intend diverting off public roads within Aboriginal Land areas, a permit is required from the relevant Aboriginal authority.

Windy Corner

NGAANYATJARRA KURLKUTA

SIR FREDERICK RANGE

Lake Hopkins

Lake Disappointment

LITTLE

SANDY

DESERT

Mount Madley

GIBSON DESERT

Mount Cox

Lake Newell

Mount Destruction

Mount Forrest

Mount Johnno

Mount Ant

Mount Skene

Warakurna

Warakurna Roadhouse

Kaltukatjara (Docker River)

BLOODS RA

Lake Neale

Mount Cowle

Mount Carruthers

PETERMANN ABORIGINAL LAND TRUST

TJUKARURU

OLDHAM RANGE

HUTTON RANGE

MUNGILLI

Mount Colin

NATURE RESERVE

Everard Junction

Mount Gordon

GIBSON

DESERT

Mount Sargood

Mount Deering

Mount Curdie

PETERMANN RANGES

Mount Phillips

Mount Normanhurst

Lake Burnside (Oneahibunga)

Mount William Lambert

Mount Noastier

Mount Johnson

MANGKILI CLAYPAN NR

Mount Beadell

Mount Charles

Jackie Junction

CENTRAL

Mount Muir

Mount Holt

Mount Fanny

Surveyor Generals Corner

Mount Jenkins

MANN RANGES

Mount Charles

Mount Sir Gerard

Mount Archie

Lake Buchanan

FAME RANGE

Lake Breaden

Mount Hervett

Mount Rawlinson

Mount Scott

Mount Gosse

Mount Cockburn

Mount Mann

Aparawatatja

Carnegie Homestead

Linke Lakes

NGAANYATJARRA

Boyd Lagoon

Warburton

Warburton Roadhouse

Mount Eliza

Mount Kathleen

Mount Elliott

Mount Matia

The Bald One

Kalka

Pipalyatjara

Kanypi

Mount Throssell

Mount Draper

Mount Lancelot

IDA RANGE

Mount Smith

Mount O'Loughlin

NGAANYATJARRA WARBURTON

Lake Gillen

Lake Kadgo

LIVESEY RANGE

NGAANYATJARRA

CENTRAL

RESERVE

Mount Agnes

Mount Moulden

Mount Harcus

Mount Lindsay

Lake Carnegie

Mount Dora

ERNEST GILES

Mount Laurie

Baker Lake

The Hann Breakaways

Mount Copley

Mount Sir Thomas

CARCLEW RANGE

Lake Wells

Mount Irving

SYDNEY YEO RANGE

Mount Hardy

Tjukayirla Roadhouse

GREAT

RANGE

Lake Throssell

NGAANYATJARRA

MACINTOSH RANGE

ANANGU PITJANTJATJARA YANKUNYTJATJARA LANDS

Mount Gerard

DE LA POER RANGE NR

Mount Strawbridge

SOUTH WESTERN AUSTRALIA

Mount Feldtmann

Mount Cornell

COSMO NEWBERRY (NORTH)

NEWLAND RANGE

YEO LAKE NATURE RESERVE

SAUNDERS RANGE

GREAT

VICTORIA

DESERT

Cosmo Newberry

COSMO NEWBERRY CENTRAL (WEST)

Mount Shenton

Mount Brown

NEALE JUNCTION

UNNAMED

CONSERVATION

Mount Varden

Mount Black

COSMO NEWBERRY (SOUTH)

Mount Sefton

Mount Fleming (EAST)

Neale Junction

NEALE JUNCTION NATURE RESERVE

Ilkurlka Roadhouse

Wanna Lakes

PARK

Windarra

Laverton

Mount Hickox

Mount Douglas

WILSON RANGE

Lake Rason

Jubilee Lake

Carlisle Lakes

Lake Ilma

GREAT VICTORIA DESERT NATURE RESERVE

Serpentine Lakes

MARALINGA TJARUTJA LANDS

Mount Weld

Mount Luck

NORTHERN TERRITORY WESTERN AUSTRALIA

N

0  25  50  75  100
Kilometres

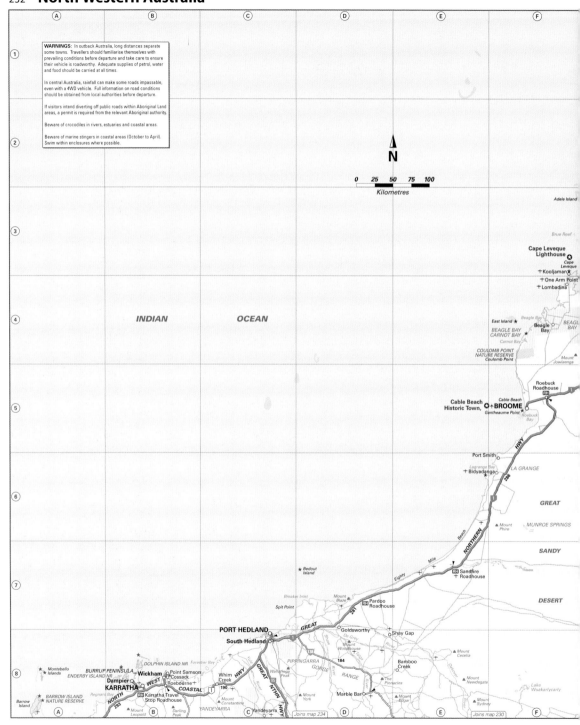

WARNINGS: In outback Australia, long distances separate some towns. Travellers should familiarise themselves with prevailing conditions before departure and take care to ensure their vehicle is roadworthy. Adequate supplies of petrol, water and food should be carried at all times.

In central Australia, rainfall can make some roads impassable, even with a 4WD vehicle. Full information on road conditions should be obtained from local authorities before departure.

If visitors intend diverting off public roads within Aboriginal Land areas, a permit is required from the relevant Aboriginal authority.

Beware of crocodiles in rivers, estuaries and coastal areas.

Beware of marine stingers in coastal areas (October to April). Swim within enclosures where possible.

N

0   25   50   75   100
Kilometres

Adele Island

Brue Reef

Cape Leveque
Lighthouse
Cape
Leveque
+ Kooljaman
+ One Arm Point
+ Lombadina

INDIAN    OCEAN

East Island
Beagle Bay
BEAGLE BAY
CARNOT BAY
Beagle
Bay
BEAGLE
BAY
Carnot Bay

COULOMB POINT
NATURE RESERVE
Coulomb Point

Mount
Jowlaenga

Roebuck
Roadhouse
RH

Cable Beach
Historic Town,
Cable Beach
BROOME
Gantheaume Point
Roebuck
Bay

HWY

Port Smith
Lagrange Bay
+ Bidyadanga
LA GRANGE
286

GREAT

NORTHERN

Mount
Phire
MUNROE SPRINGS

SANDY

Bedout
Island
Mile
RH Sandfire
+ Roadhouse

Eighty

DESERT

Breaker Inlet
Mount
Blaze
Spit Point
281
RH Pardoo
Roadhouse

PORT HEDLAND
GREAT
Goldsworthy
Shay Gap

South Hedland
De Grey
Mount
Wodehouse

PIPPINGARRA
184
Bamboo
Creek

Montebello
Islands
DOLPHIN ISLAND NR
Forrester Bay
GORGE
RANGE
RIVER
The
Pinnacles
Mount
Cecelia

BURRUP PENINSULA
ENDERBY ISLAND NR
Wickham
Point Samson
Cossack
Roebourne
GREAT
Wallareenya
Peak
Whim
Creek
HWY
Mount
Newdegate

Dampier
KARRATHA
WEST
COASTAL
190
N'THN
Mount
Elgar
Lake
Wuakarlycarly

BARROW ISLAND
NATURE RESERVE
RH Karratha Travel
Stop Roadhouse
Regnard Bay
NORTH
293
Mount
Constantine
Mount
York
Marble Bar
Mount
Sydney

Barrow
Island
HWY
Mount
Leopold
Darling
Peak
YANDEYARRA
Yandeyarra
Joins map 234
Joins map 230

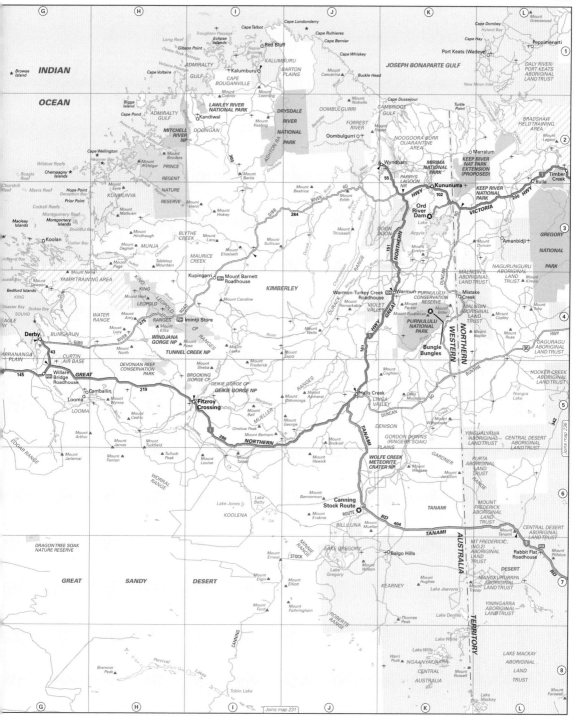

INDIAN

OCEAN

*Browse Island*
★

Cape Talbot
Cape Londonderry
Troughton Passage
Long Reef
Eclipse Islands
Napier Broome Bay
Red Bluff
Gibson Point
Oyster Rock Passage
Voltaire Passage
Cape Voltaire
Mount Leeming
Mount Codnor

ADMIRALTY GULF
CAPE BOUGANVILLE
◦ Kalumburu
Kalumburu
KALUMBURU

Cape Rulhieres
Cape Bernier
Cape Whiskey
Buckle Head
Cape Dussejour
BARTON PLAINS
Mount Casuarina

Cape Hay
Port Keats (Wadeye)

Cape Dombey
Hyland Bay
Peppimenarti
Mount Greenwood

DALY RIVER/ PORT KEATS ABORIGINAL LAND TRUST

New Moon Inlet

JOSEPH BONAPARTE GULF

Bigge Island
Cape Pond
ADMIRALTY GULF
Prince Frederick Harbour

LAWLEY RIVER NATIONAL PARK
★ Kandiwal

MITCHELL RIVER NP
DOONGAN

DRYSDALE RIVER NATIONAL PARK

OOMBULGURRI
Mount Keating

Mount Nicholls

FORREST RIVER

Oombulgurri ✛

CAMBRIDGE GULF
Turtle Point

BRADSHAW FIELD TRAINING AREA

Mount Lagana
Timber Creek

NOOGOORA BURR QUARANTINE AREA

Marralum

KEEP RIVER NAT PARK EXTENSION (PROPOSED)

Hanover Bay
Cape Wellington
Cape Pond
Wildcat Reefs
Beagle Reef
Champagny Islands ★
Hope Point
Deception Bay
Prior Point
Mount Trafalgar ✛
Mount Waghorn ▲

KUNMUNYA
Mount Hann

GIBB RIVER

NATURE RESERVE

PRINCE REGENT

Mount Beatrice ▲
Mount Edith

Wyndham ◦
55
PARRYS LAGOON NR

Kununurra ◦
102

MIRIMA NATIONAL PARK

KEEP RIVER NATIONAL PARK

Bulla ◦
200 HWY

Churchill Reef
Mavis Reef
Cockell Reefs
Macleay Islands
Montgomery Reef
Montgomery Islands
Doubtful Bay

Koolan ◦
Collier Bay
Charnley River

Mount Matheson ▲
Mount Daglish ▲
Mount Page ▲
Mount Hindhaugh ▲
Mount Elizabeth ▲

BLYTHE CREEK

MUNJA
MAURICE CREEK

Tabletop Mountain

Mount Hickey ▲

303

Mount Bertie ✛

Mount Sullivan ▲

GIBB RIVER

Mount Throssell ▲

284

RD

Ord River Dam ☼

Lake Argyle

DOON DOON

151 NORTHERN

Amanbidji ◦

Mount Duncan ▲

GREGORY

NATIONAL

PARK

NAGURUNGURU ABORIGINAL LAND TRUST ▲ Kimon

Mount Nellie ▲
scade Bay
Bedford Islands ◦
KING
Disaster Bay
Stokes Bay
EAGLE SOUND
rickland Bay

YAMPI TRAINING AREA
Mount Dawson ▲

Kupingarri ◦ RH
Mount Barnett Roadhouse

KING

LEOPOLD

Mount Hart ▲
Mount Amy ▲
375

Mount Lucy ▲

KIMBERLEY

Mount Caroline ▲

DURACK RANGE

Mount Lacy ▲

Warmun-Turkey Creek Roadhouse ◦

RANGE

Warmun ◦
PURNULULU CONSERVATION RESERVE

Mistake Creek ◦

MALNGIN ABORIGINAL LAND TRUST

MALNGIN ABORIGINAL LAND TRUST

Mount Toby ▲

Mount Rose ▲

Mount Evelyn ▲

Mount Remarkable ▲

VIOLET VALLEY

PURNULULU NATIONAL PARK

Mount Elder ▲

Mount Parker ▲

Mount Napier ▲

Mount Copley ▲

NORTHERN

HWY

Bungle Bungles

WESTERN

DAGURAGU ABORIGINAL LAND TRUST

HWY

95

Derby ◦
BUNGARUN
GIBB
43

WATER RANGE

LEOPOLD RANGES

RH Imintji Store

WINDJANA GORGE NP

TUNNEL CREEK NP

Mount North ▲

DEVONIAN REEF CONSERVATION PARK

BROOKING GORGE CP

GEIKIE GORGE CP

GEIKIE GORGE NP

Mount Sheba ▲

Mount Frederick ▲

Mount Lukie ▲

GREAT

HWY

161

Ord

Halls Creek ✛

Deka Mountain ▲

LINGA VALLEY

DUNCAN

BUNTINE RD

Mount Coghlan ▲

HOOKER CREEK ABORIGINAL LAND TRUST

Nongra Lake

342

RRANANGA PLAIN
CURTIN AIR BASE

Willare Bridge Roadhouse RH

145
GREAT

219

Looma ◦
Camballin ◦
LOOMA
LOOMA

Mount Wynne ▲
Mount Cedric ▲

Fitzroy Crossing ◦

Onslow Peak ▲
Mount Bertram ▲

MUELLER

288

NORTHERN

Margaret River

Mount Cummings ▲

RANGES

Mount Amherst ▲

Mount George ▲
Mount Dockrell ▲

TANAMI

DENISON

GORDON DOWNS (RINGERS SOAK)
PLAINS

Mount Wingdoom ▲

GARDNER

Mount Weeken ▲

YININGALYALYA ABORIGINAL LAND TRUST

PURTA ABORIGINAL LAND TRUST

CENTRAL DESERT ABORIGINAL LAND TRUST

Mount Arthur ▲
EDGAR RANGE

Mount Jarlemai ▲

Mount James ▲
Mount Fenton ▲

Mount Tuckfield ▲

Tulloch Peak ▲

Mount Louise ▲
Mount Talbot ▲

Mount Hawick ▲

WORRAL RANGE

WOLFE CREEK METEORITE CRATER NP

Mount Junction ▲

DUNCAN

Stud Creek

RANGE

MOUNT FREDERICK ABORIGINAL LAND TRUST

Mount Tanami ▲

CENTRAL DESERT ABORIGINAL LAND TRUST

Mount Bannerman ▲

Canning Stock Route ☼

Mount Erskine ▲

KOOLENA

Lake Jones
Lake Betty

ROUTE

BILLILUNA ◦

RD

Mount Mueller ▲

404

TANAMI

AUSTRALIA

MT FREDERICK (NO.2) ABORIGINAL LAND TRUST

Rabbit Flat Roadhouse ◦ RH

Mount Pilotus ▲

DRAGON TREE SOAK NATURE RESERVE

GREAT

SANDY

DESERT

CANNING

Mount Ernest ▲

STOCK

Mount Elgin ▲

Mount Elliott ▲

LAKE GREGORY

Lake Gregory

Balgo Hills ◦
Mount Wilson ▲

KEARNEY

Mount Hughes ▲

Mount Tracey ▲

DESERT

MANSKURURRPA ABORIGINAL LAND TRUST

YININGARRA ABORIGINAL LAND TRUST

Mount Farewell ▲

Mount Ford ▲
Mount Fothringham ▲

ROBERTS RANGE

Mount Jeavons ▲

Thomas Peak ▲

Lake Dennis

TERRITORY

Bremner Peak ▲
Percival Lakes

Tobin Lake

Lake White

Warri Peak ▲

NGAANYATJARRA

CENTRAL

AUSTRALIA

Lake Wills

Lake Mackay

Mount Russell ▲

LAKE MACKAY ABORIGINAL LAND TRUST

Mount Rose ▲

Joins map 236

Joins map 231

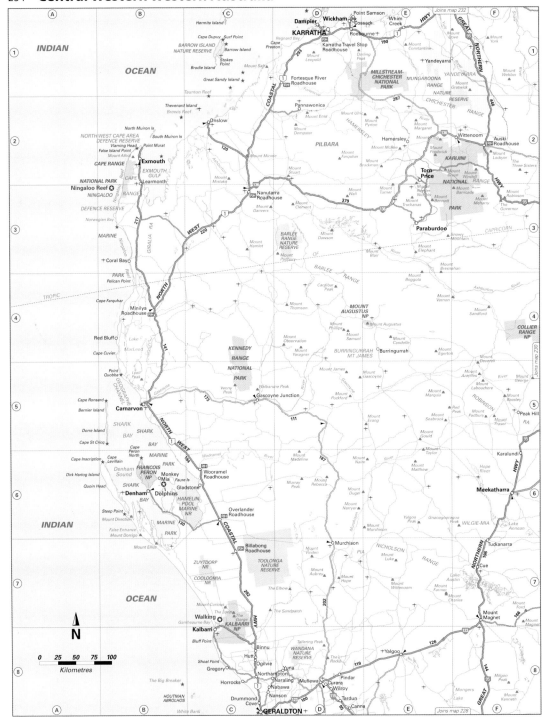

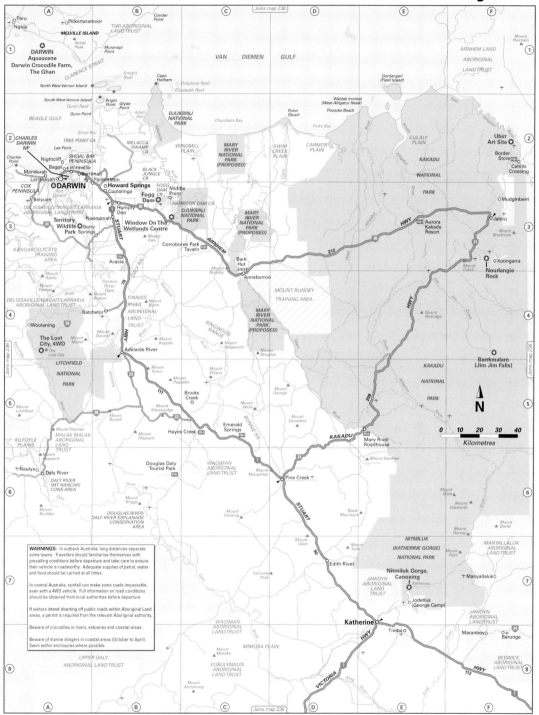

WARNINGS: In outback Australia, long distances separate some towns. Travellers should familiarise themselves with prevailing conditions before departure and take care to ensure their vehicle is roadworthy. Adequate supplies of petrol, water and food should be carried at all times.

In central Australia, rainfall can make some roads impassable, even with a 4WD vehicle. Full information on road conditions should be obtained from local authorities before departure.

If visitors intend diverting off public roads within Aboriginal Land areas, a permit is required from the relevant Aboriginal authority.

Beware of crocodiles in rivers, estuaries and coastal areas.

Beware of marine stingers in coastal areas (October to April). Swim within enclosures where possible.

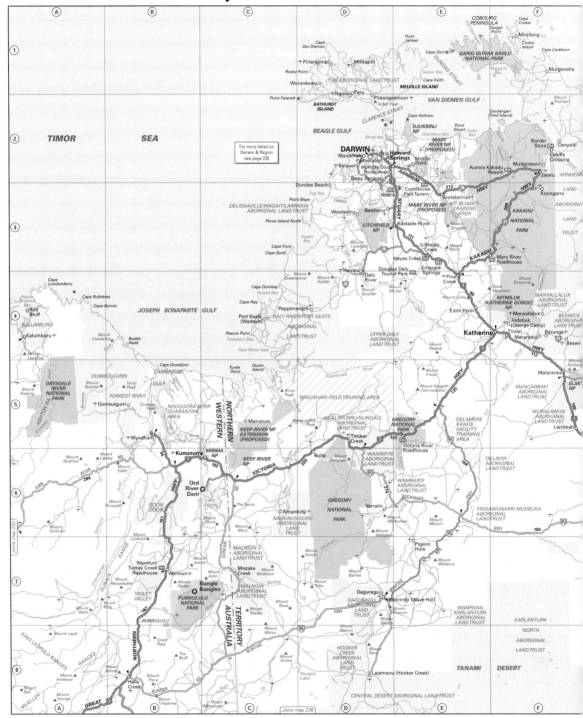

For more detail on
Darwin & Region
see page 235

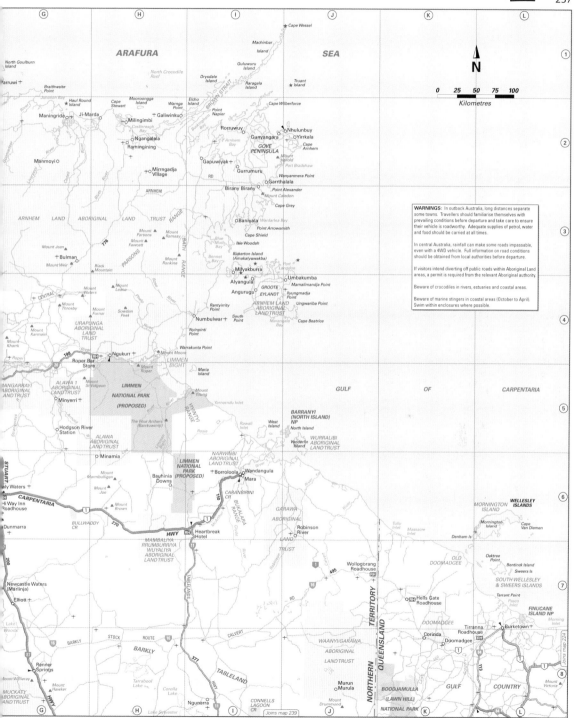

ARAFURA        SEA

N

0   25   50   75   100
Kilometres

GULF        OF        CARPENTARIA

**WARNINGS:** In outback Australia, long distances separate
some towns. Travellers should familiarise themselves with
prevailing conditions before departure and take care to ensure
their vehicle is roadworthy. Adequate supplies of petrol, water
and food should be carried at all times.

In central Australia, rainfall can make some roads impassable,
even with a 4WD vehicle. Full information on road conditions
should be obtained from local authorities before departure.

If visitors intend diverting off public roads within Aboriginal Land
areas, a permit is required from the relevant Aboriginal authority.

Beware of crocodiles in rivers, estuaries and coastal areas.

Beware of marine stingers in coastal areas (October to April).
Swim within enclosures where possible.

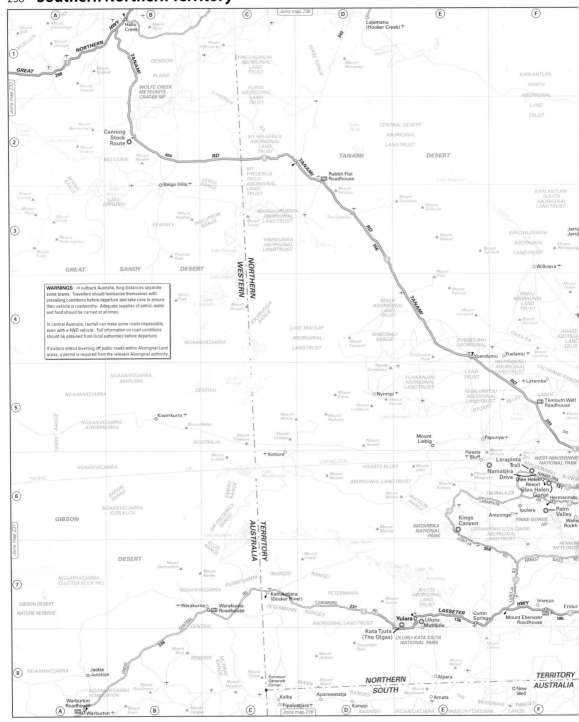

Joins map 236
Joins map 233
Joins map 231
Joins map 218

**WARNINGS:** In outback Australia, long distances separate some towns. Travellers should familiarise themselves with prevailing conditions before departure and take care to ensure their vehicle is roadworthy. Adequate supplies of petrol, water and food should be carried at all times.

In central Australia, rainfall can make some roads impassable, even with a 4WD vehicle. Full information on road conditions should be obtained from local authorities before departure.

If visitors intend diverting off public roads within Aboriginal Land areas, a permit is required from the relevant Aboriginal authority.

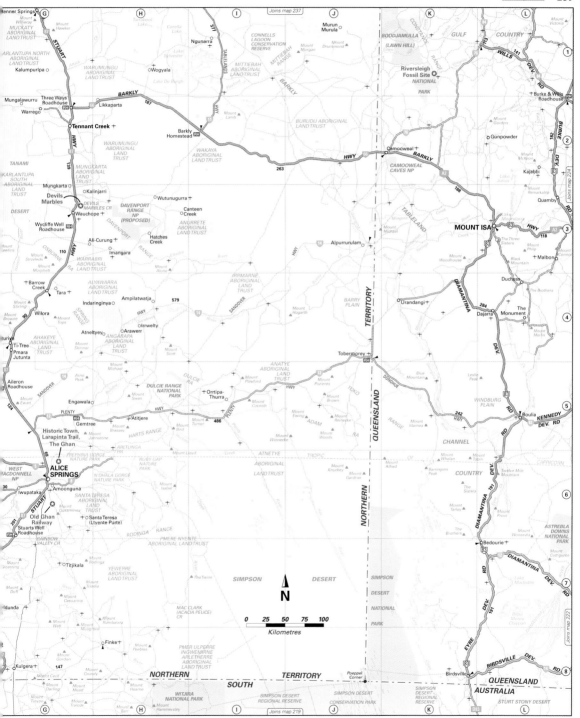

Renner Springs • **G**
Mount Wilmya ▲
Mount Hawker ▲
Tarrabool Lake
Corella Lake
**H**
**I**
Joins map 237
Murun Murula •
**J**
BOODJAMULLA (LAWN HILL) • GULF COUNTRY **K** • Mount Victoria **L**
**1**
Ngunarra •
CONNELLS LAGOON CONSERVATION RESERVE
Mount Morgan ▲
Mount Drummond ▲
Riversleigh Fossil Site • NATIONAL PARK
**WILLS** DEV
**141**
Burke & Wills Roadhouse •

MUCKATY ABORIGINAL LAND TRUST

ARLANTUPA NORTH ABORIGINAL LAND TRUST
Kalumpurlpa ○
WARUMUNGU ABORIGINAL LAND TRUST
Wogyala ○
Lake De Burgh
Lake Sylvester
MITTIEBAH ABORIGINAL LAND TRUST
BARKLY RANGE
Riversleigh Fossil Site
Mount Gordon ▲
Gunpowder •
BURKE DEV RD
**182**
**2**

Mungalawurru •
**STUART** **BARKLY**
Three Ways Roadhouse •
Likkaparta •
**187**
Mount Lamb ▲
BURUDU ABORIGINAL LAND TRUST
Camooweal • **BARKLY**
CAMOOWEAL CAVES NP **A2**
Mount McKison ▲
Kajabbi •
Mount Remarkable ▲
Lake Julius
Quamby •
Joins map 224
**3**

Warrego •
Tennant Creek +
Barkly Homestead •
**HWY**
**263**
WAKAYA ABORIGINAL LAND TRUST
**188**
TABLELAND
MOUNT ISA
The Three Sisters
**83** **HWY** A2 **118**

**TANAMI**
KARLANTUPA SOUTH ABORIGINAL LAND TRUST
**139**
WARUMUNGU ABORIGINAL LAND TRUST
MUNGKARTA ABORIGINAL LAND TRUST
Mungkarta ○ Kalinjarri ○
Wutunugurra +
**14**
Alpurrurulam ○
Mount Woodhouse ▲
Black Mountain ▲ Malbon •
Mount Isa •

Devils Marbles •
DEVILS MARBLES CR
Wauchope •
DAVENPORT RANGE NP (PROPOSED)
Canteen Creek •
ANURRETE ABORIGINAL LAND TRUST
Duchess •
The Brothers ▲

**DESERT**
Wycliffe Well Roadhouse •
Ali-Curung +
Hatches Creek •
**DIAMANTINA**
Urandangi +
Dajarra • **284** The Monument •
Mount Merlin ▲

Mount Strelecki ▲
**110**
Imangara +
WARRABRI ABORIGINAL LAND TRUST
Mount Alone ▲
**HWY**
IRRMARNE ABORIGINAL LAND TRUST
BARRY PLAIN
Mount Hogarth ▲

Barrow Creek +
Tara •
ALYAWARRA ABORIGINAL LAND TRUST
Ampilatwatja •
**579**
SANDOVER
**TERRITORY**
**DEV**

Mount Stirling ▲
Wilora •
SPRING RANGE
Mount Tops ▲
**HWY**
Atneltyey • Irrwelty • Arawerr +
ANGARAPA ABORIGINAL LAND TRUST
**11**
Mount Scott ▲
ANATYE ABORIGINAL LAND TRUST
Tobermorey •
Blue Mountain ▲
Leslie Peak ▲
WINDBURG PLAIN
Boulia • **KENNEDY**
**5**

Ti-Tree •
Pmara Jutunta •
AHAKEYE ABORIGINAL LAND TRUST
Arno Peak ▲
DULCIE RANGE NATIONAL PARK
Mount Playford ▲
Mount Pozieres ▲
**TEKO**
**DONOHUE**
**83** **DEV** **RD**

Aileron Roadhouse •
SANDOVER
Engawala •
Mount Swan ▲
Orrtipa-Thurra •
**PLENTY**
Mount Cornish ▲
Mount Brown ▲
Mount Reiniebar ▲
**242**
Mount Idamea ▲
**HWY**

**124**
**PLENTY**
Gemtree • Atitjere •
HARTS RANGE
**486**
Mount Bird ▲
Mount Turner ▲
**ADAM**
Mount Ewing ▲
Mount Woods ▲
CHANNEL

Historic Town, Larapinta Trail, The Ghan
TREPHINA GORGE NATURE PARK
ARLTUNGA
ARLTINGA THR
Mount Lloyd ▲
Mount Winnecke ▲
ATNETYE ABORIGINAL LAND TRUST
**TROPIC**
CAPRICORN
Mount Whelan ▲
Mount Tobin ▲
Twelve Mile Mountain ▲

WEST MACDONNELL NP
**30**
**ALICE SPRINGS**
Iwupataka •
Amoonguna •
N'DHALA GORGE NATURE PARK
RUBY GAP NATURE PARK
Mount Isabel ▲
Mount Knuckey ▲
Mount Alfred ▲
**COUNTRY**
The Sisters ▲

**STUART**
**201**
Old Ghan Railway
Stuarts Well Roadhouse •
SANTA TERESA ABORIGINAL LAND TRUST
Mount Quitnamme ▲
Santa Teresa (Ltyente Purte) +
RODINGA RANGE
PMERE NYENTE ABORIGINAL LAND TRUST
Mount Tarley ▲
Mount Prout ▲
Bedourie • **83**
**DIAMANTINA**
ASTREBLA DOWNS NATIONAL PARK
**6**

RAINBOW VALLEY CR
Titjikala •
Mount Rodinga ▲
YEWERRE ABORIGINAL LAND TRUST
The Brothers ▲
Mount Cuttapirie ▲
**DEV**
**191**
**7**

Idunda +
Mount Dutt ▲
Mount Caesurma ▲
Mount Triodia ▲
The Twins ▲
**SIMPSON** **DESERT**
**SIMPSON**
**DESERT**
Lake Machattie
Lake Mitchell

Mount Watt ▲
Mount Musgrave ▲
MAC CLARK (ACACIA PEUCE) CR
**N**
**NATIONAL**
**191**
**DEV**

Finke +
Mount Peebles ▲
PMER ULPERRE INGWEMIRNE ARLETHERRE ABORIGINAL LAND TRUST
**PARK**
Birdsville • **83**
**8**

Kulgera •
**147**
Mount Gravely ▲
**NORTHERN**
**SOUTH**
**TERRITORY**
Poeppel Corner •
Birdsville •
**QUEENSLAND**
**AUSTRALIA**
**BIRDSVILLE**
**DEV RD**

**WITJIRA NATIONAL PARK**
SIMPSON DESERT REGIONAL RESERVE
SIMPSON DESERT CONSERVATION PARK
SIMPSON DESERT REGIONAL RESERVE
STURT STONY DESERT

**G** **H** **I**
Joins map 219
**J** **K** **L**

0 25 50 75 100
Kilometres

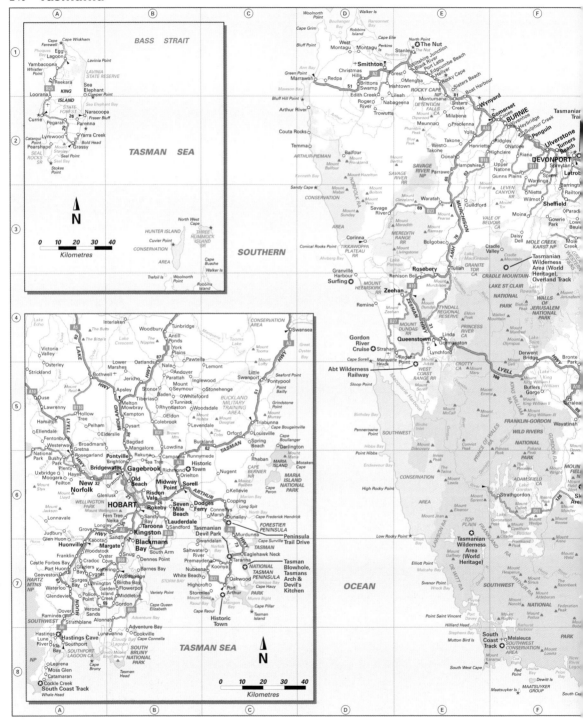

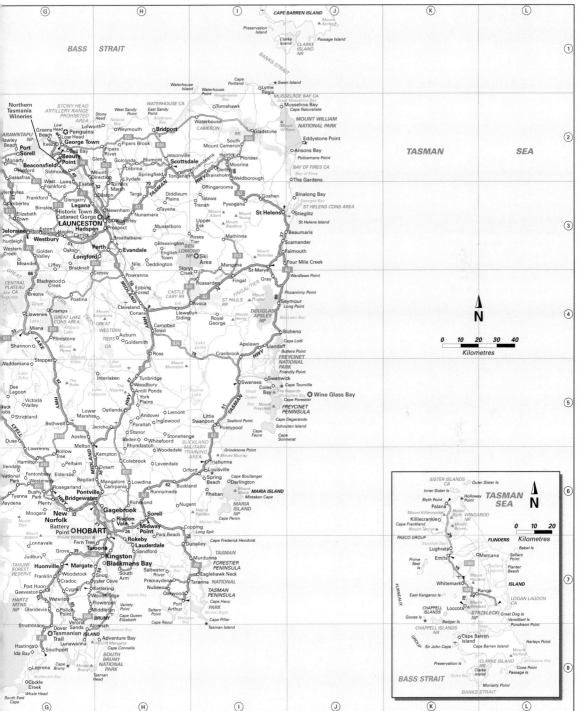

# Index

Abercrombie River National Park NSW 207 I3
Aberdeen NSW 207 K1, 209 H7
Abermain NSW 204 E1, 207 K2, 209 H8
Acacia NT 235 B3, 236 D3
Adelaide SA 216 E6, 217 D4, **152**
Adelaide Hills SA **161, 163**
Agnes Island National Park Qld 225 I3
Aileron Roadhouse NT 239 G5
Aireys Inlet Vic. 211 A7, 212 F7, **85**
Airlie Beach Qld 225 K6
Albany WA 227 F8, 228 D7
Albury NSW 206 F6, 213 J2, 214 A2
Aldinga Beach SA 216 D7, 217 D5
Alexander Morrison National Park WA 228 B3
Alexandra Vic. 206 E7, 211 F3, 213 H4
Alfred National Park Vic. 207 I8, 214 D6
Alice Springs NT 239 G6, **100, 115**
Alpine National Park Vic. 206 F7, 207 G7, 213 J4, 214 B3
Alstonville NSW 209 K2, 221 E8
Alton National Park Qld 221 B7, 223 J7
Angaston SA 216 E5, 217 D4
Angle Vale SA 216 E5, 217 D4
Anglesea Vic. 211 B7, 212 F7, **85**
Anna Bay NSW 207 L2, 209 I8
Apollo Bay Vic. 212 E7, **86**
Appin NSW 204 C5, 207 K4
Arakwal National Park NSW 209 K2, 221 E8
Ararat Vic. 206 B7, 212 D4
Archer River Roadhouse Qld 226 C5
Ardrossan SA 216 C5, 217 C4
Arkaroola SA 219 J5, **173**
Arltunga Historic Reserve NT 239 H6
Armidale NSW 209 I4
Arnhem Land NT 235 F1, 236 F2, 237 G3, **111, 113**
Arrawarra NSW 209 J4
Astrebla Downs National Park Qld 222 D2, 239 L6
Atherton Qld 225 H2, **59**
Auburn River National Park Qld 221 C5, 223 L5
Augusta WA 227 A7, 228 B7
Aurora Kakadu Resort NT 235 E3, 236 F2
Auski Roadhouse WA 230 D3, 234 F2
Australia Zoo Qld 220 D3, **42, 63**
Australian Alps Walking Track ACT, NSW & Vic. **10**
Australian Fossil Mammal Sites SA **10, 177**
Australind WA 227 B5, 228 C6
Avon Valley National Park WA 227 B2, 228 C4
Avondale NSW 204 C6, 207 J4
Ayers Rock *see* Uluru
Ayr Qld 225 J5
Babinda Qld 225 I2
Bacchus Marsh Vic. 206 D8, 211 B5, 212 F5
Badgingarra National Park WA 228 B3
Bago Bluff National Park NSW 209 J6

Bairnsdale Vic. 207 G8, 213 K6, 214 A6
Balaklava SA 216 D4, 217 D4
Bald Rock National Park NSW 209 I2, 221 D8, 223 L8
Balladonia Roadhouse WA 229 H5
Ballan Vic. 206 C8, 211 B5, 212 F5
Ballarat Vic. 206 C8, 211 A4, 212 F5, **96**
Ballina NSW 209 K2, 221 E8
Balnarring Vic. 211 D7, 213 G7
Balranald NSW 206 C4, 215 E4
Bangadilly National Park NSW 204 A6, 207 J4
Banora Point NSW 209 K1, 220 E7, 221 E8
Barakee National Park NSW 209 I6
Barcaldine Qld 223 H2
Bargara Qld 221 E4
Barham NSW 206 C5, 212 F1, 215 F6
Barkly Homestead NT 239 I2
Barmera SA 217 E4
Barnard Island Group National Park Qld 225 I3
Barool National Park NSW 209 I3
Barossa Valley SA **150, 161**
Barossa Valley wineries SA 216 E5, **162**
Barraba NSW 209 G4
Barranyi (North Island) National Park NT 237 J5
Barrington Tops National Park NSW 207 L1, 209 H7
Barron Gorge National Park Qld 225 H2, 226 F8
Barwon Heads Vic. 211 B7, 212 F6
Basin beaches WA **10, 132**
Bass Strait islands Tas. **178**
Batemans Bay NSW 207 J6, 214 F2
Bathurst NSW 207 I2, 208 F8
Batlow NSW 207 H5, 213 L1, 214 C1
Baw Baw National Park Vic. 206 E8, 213 I6, **94**
Baxter Vic. 211 D7, 213 G6
Beachmere Qld 220 D4, 221 E6
Beachport SA 217 E7, **175**
Beaconsfield Tas. 241 G2
Beaconsfield Vic. 211 E6, 213 H6
Beaudesert Qld 209 K1, 220 D6, 221 E7
Beaufort Vic. 206 B8, 212 E4
Beauty Point Tas. 241 G2
Beechworth Vic. 206 F6, 213 J3
Beedelup National Park WA 227 C7, 228 C7
Beerwah Qld 220 D3, 221 E6, **63**
Bega NSW 207 I7, 214 E4
Belair National Park SA 216 E6, 217 D5, **158**
Bellarine Peninsula Vic. **70**
Belford National Park NSW 204 E1, 207 K2, 209 H7
Bellbird NSW 204 E1, 207 K2, 209 H8
Bellingen NSW 209 J4, **30**
Bellinger River National Park NSW 209 J4
Bells Beach Vic. **10, 84**
Bells Line of Road NSW **28**

Beltana Roadhouse SA 219 I6
Belyando Crossing Roadhouse Qld 225 I7
Ben Boyd National Park NSW 207 I8, 214 E4
Ben Halls Gap National Park NSW 209 H6
Ben Lomond National Park Tas. 241 H3, **10**
Benalla Vic. 206 E6, 213 I3
Benambra National Park NSW 206 F5, 213 K1, 214 A1
Bendidee National Park Qld 209 H1, 221 C7, 223 K7
Bendigo Vic. 206 C7, 211 B2, 212 F3, 215 F8, **99**
Beresfield NSW 204 E1, 207 L2, 209 H8
Bermagui NSW 207 I7, 214 F3
Berri SA 215 A3, 217 F4
Berridale NSW 207 H7, 214 D3
Berrigan NSW 206 E5, 213 I1
Berry NSW 204 B7, 207 J4
Biamanga National Park NSW 207 I7, 214 F3
Bibbulmun Track WA **10, 137**
Bicheno Tas. **195**
Big Banana NSW **12**
Big Pineapple Qld **64**
Billabong Roadhouse WA 230 A7, 234 C7
Biloela Qld 221 C3, 223 L3
Bimberamala National Park NSW 207 J5, 214 F1
Bindarri National Park NSW 209 J4, **31**
Bindoon WA 227 B1, 228 C4
Bingara NSW 209 H3
Biriwal Bulga National Park NSW 209 I6
Bittern Vic. 211 D7, 213 G7
Black Mountain National Park Qld 225 H1, 226 E7
Blackall Qld 223 H3
Blackbraes National Park Qld 225 G5
Blackdown Tableland National Park Qld 221 B3, 223 K3
Blackheath NSW 204 B3, 207 J3, **27**
Blackmans Bay Tas. 240 B7, 241 H7
Blackwater Qld 221 B2, 223 J2
Blackwood National Park Qld 225 I7
Bladensburg National Park Qld 222 F1, 224 F8
Blaxland NSW 204 B4, 207 J3
Blayney NSW 207 I3, 208 F8
Bli Bli Qld 220 D2
Blue Lake National Park Qld 220 E5, 221 E7
Blue Mountains National Park NSW 204 B4, 207 J3, 209 G8, **10, 24, 25**
Blue Water Springs Roadhouse Qld 225 H4
Boambee NSW 209 J4
Boddington WA 227 C4, 228 C6
Bogangar NSW 209 K1, 220 E8, 221 E8
Bomaderry NSW 204 B7, 207 J5
Bombala NSW 207 I7, 214 D4
Bondi NSW **21**
Bongaree Qld 220 E4, 221 E6
Bongil Bongil National Park NSW 209 J4
Bonny Hills NSW 209 J6

Booderee National Park JBT 204 B8, 207 J5, **10**
Boodjamulla (Lawn Hill) National Park Qld 224 B3, 237 K8, 239 K1
Bool Lagoon Game Reserve SA 212 A3, 217 F7
Boonah Qld 209 J1, 220 C6, 221 D7
Boonoo Boonoo National Park NSW 209 J2, 221 D8
Boorabbin National Park WA 228 E4
Boorowa NSW 207 H4
Booti Booti National Park NSW 209 I7
Border Ranges National Park NSW 209 J1, 220 C8, 221 E8
Border Store NT 235 F2, 236 F2
Bordertown SA 212 A2, 215 A7, 217 F6
Botany Bay National Park NSW 204 D5, 207 K3
Bouddi National Park NSW 204 E3, 207 K3
Bourke NSW 208 B3
Bournda National Park NSW 207 I7, 214 E4
Bowen Qld 225 J5
Bowling Green Bay National Park Qld 225 I5
Bowral NSW 204 B6, 207 J4
Boyne Island Qld 221 D3
Brampton Islands National Park Qld 225 K6
Bramwell Junction Roadhouse Qld 226 C3
Branxton NSW 204 E1, 207 K2, 209 H7
Brewarrina NSW 208 C3
Bribie Island National Park Qld 220 E3, 221 E6
Bridge Creek National Park Qld 226 E7
Bridgetown WA 227 C6, 228 C7
Bridgewater SA 216 E6, 217 D5
Bridgewater Tas. 240 B6, 241 H6
Bridport Tas. 241 H2
Bright Vic. 206 F7, 213 J3, 214 A3
Brindabella National Park NSW 205 B3, 207 H5, 214 D1
Brisbane Qld 220 D5, 221 E7, **44**
Brisbane Ranges National Park Vic. 206 C8, 211 B5, 212 F5
Brisbane Water National Park NSW 204 D3, 207 K3, 209 H8
Broad Sound Islands National Park Qld 221 C1, 223 L1, 225 K8
Broadbeach Qld 220 E7, **54**
Broadford Vic. 206 D7, 211 D3, 213 G4
Broadwater National Park NSW 209 K2, 221 E8
Brockman National Park WA 227 C7, 228 C7
Broken Hill NSW 210 B5, 217 F2, 219 K7
Brook Islands National Park Qld 225 I3
Broome WA 232 F5, **120, 143**
Brunswick Heads NSW 209 K2, 220 E8, 221 E8
Bruny Island Tas. 241 H7, **191**
Bucasia Qld 225 K6
Budawang National Park NSW 207 J5, 214 F1
Budderoo National Park NSW 204 B7, 207 J4
Buderim Qld 220 E2, 221 E6
Bugong National Park NSW 204 B7, 207 J4
Bulahdelah NSW 207 L1, 209 I7
Bulleringa National Park Qld 225 G3
Bunbury WA 227 B5, 228 B6, **133**
Bundaberg Qld 221 E4, **68**
Bundanoon NSW 204 A6, 207 J4
Bundjalung National Park NSW 209 K3, 221 E8
Bungawalbin National Park NSW 209 K2, 221 E8
Bungendore NSW 205 E3, 207 I5, 214 E1
Buninyong Vic. 206 C8, 211 A5, 212 F5

Bunya Mountains National Park Qld 220 A3, 221 D6, 223 L6
Bunyip Vic. 211 F7, 213 H6
Burke & Wills Roadhouse Qld 224 D4, 239 L2
Burleigh Head National Park Qld 209 K1, 220 E7, 221 E7, **54**
Burleigh Heads Qld 209 K1, 220 E7, 221 E7, **54**
Burnett Heads Qld 221 E4
Burnie Tas. 240 F2
Burra SA 216 E3, 217 D3
Burrill Lake NSW 207 J5, 214 F1
Burrowa–Pine Mountain National Park Vic. 207 G6, 213 L2, 214 B2
Burrum Coast National Park Qld 221 E4
Busselton WA 227 B6, 228 B6, **134**
Butterleaf National Park NSW 209 I3
Buxton NSW 204 B5, 207 J4
Byfield National Park Qld 221 C2, 223 L2, 225 L8
Byron Bay NSW 209 K2, 221 E8, **12, 33**
Cable Beach, Broome WA **10, 143**
Caboolture Qld 220 D4, 221 E6
Cactus Beach SA **10**
Cadney Homestead SA 218 F3
Caiguna Roadhouse WA 229 I4
Cairns Qld 225 H2, 226 F8, **58, 59**
Callala Bay NSW 204 B8, 207 J5
Calliope Qld 221 D3, 223 L3
Caloundra Qld 220 E3, 221 E6, **64**
Camooweal Caves National Park Qld 224 B5, 239 K2
Camperdown Vic. 212 D6
Canberra ACT 205 D3, 207 I5, 214 D1, **12**
Cania Gorge National Park Qld 221 C4, 223 L4
Cannonvale Qld 225 K6
Canowindra NSW 207 H3, 208 E8
Canunda National Park SA 217 E7, **175**
Cape Arid National Park WA 229 H5, **149**
Cape Gantheaume Conservation Park SA 216 C8, **169**
Cape Hillsborough National Park Qld 225 K6
Cape Le Grand National Park WA 229 G6, **149**
Cape Melville National Park Qld 226 E6
Cape Leveque Qld 232 F3, **145**
Cape Palmerston National Park Qld 225 K7
Cape Range National Park WA 234 B2, **138, 142**
Cape Upstart National Park Qld 225 J5
Cape York Qld **42**
Capel WA 227 B6, 228 B6
Capoompeta National Park NSW 209 I3, 221 D8, 223 L8
Capricorn Coast National Park Qld 221 C2, 223 L2
Capricorn Roadhouse WA 230 E4
Capricornia Cays National Park Qld 221 D2
Cardwell Qld 225 I3
Carnarvon National Park Qld 221 A4, 223 J4
Carnarvon WA 234 B5, **141**
Carnegie Homestead WA 231 G6
Carrai National Park NSW 209 I5
Cascade National Park NSW 209 J4
Casino NSW 209 K2, 221 E8
Casterton Vic. 212 B5, 217 F7
Castle Tower National Park Qld 221 D3, 223 L3
Castlemaine Vic. 206 C7, 211 B3, 212 F4, **98**
Cataby Roadhouse WA 228 B4
Cathedral Rock National Park NSW 209 I4

Cattai National Park NSW 204 C3, 207 K3
Cedar Bay National Park Qld 225 H1, 226 F7
Ceduna SA 218 F7
Central Coast NSW **12**
Cessnock NSW 204 E1, 207 K2, 209 H8
Chaelundi National Park NSW 209 J4
Charles Darwin National Park NT 235 A2, 236 D2, **104**
Charleville Qld 223 H5
Charlton Vic. 206 B6, 212 E2, 215 E7
Charters Towers Qld 225 I5
Cherbourg Qld 220 B1, 221 D5
Chesterton Range National Park Qld 223 I5
Childers Qld 221 D4
Chillagoe–Mungana Caves National Park Qld 225 G2, 226 E8
Chiltern Vic. 206 F6, 213 J2
Chiltern–Mount Pilot National Park Vic. 206 F6, 213 J2
Chinchilla Qld 221 C6, 223 L6
Chinderah NSW 209 K1, 220 E7, 221 E8
Chowilla Game Reserve SA 210 A8, 215 A2, 217 F4
Chowilla Regional Reserve SA 210 A8, 215 A1, 217 F3
Churchill National Park Vic. 206 D8, 211 D6, 213 H6
Churchill Vic. 213 I7 Clare SA 216 E4, 217 D3
Claremont Isles National Park Qld 226 D5
Cleland Conservation Park SA 216 E6, **163**
Clermont Qld 221 A1, 223 J1, 225 J8
Cliff Island National Park Qld 226 D6
Clifton Springs Vic. 211 C6, 213 G6
Cloncurry Qld 224 D6
Clump Mountain National Park Qld 225 I3
Clyde River National Park NSW 207 J6, 214 F2
Coalstoun Lakes National Park Qld 221 D5
Cobar NSW 208 B5
Cobden Vic. 212 D6
Cobram Vic. 206 E6, 213 H2
Cockatoo Vic. 206 E8, 211 E6, 213 H6
Cocklebiddy Roadhouse WA 229 J4
Cocoparra National Park NSW 206 F3
Coffin Bay National Park SA 217 A4
Coffs Harbour NSW 209 J4, **31**
Cohuna Vic. 206 C5, 212 F1, 215 F6
Colac Vic. 212 E6
Coldstream Vic. 206 D8, 211 E5, 213 H5
Coleraine Vic. 206 A8, 212 B5, 217 F7
Collie WA 227 C5, 228 C6
Collier Range National Park WA 230 D5, 234 F4
Collinsville Qld 225 J6
Colo Vale NSW 204 B6, 207 J4
Condobolin NSW 207 G2, 208 C7
Conimbla National Park NSW 207 H3
Conjola National Park NSW 204 B8, 207 J5
Conondale National Park Qld 220 C2, 221 E6
Conway National Park Qld 225 K6
Coober Pedy SA 218 F4, **150, 170**
Cooktown Qld 226 E7
Coolah Tops National Park NSW 209 G6
Coolamon NSW 207 G4
Coolgardie WA 228 F3
Coolangatta Qld 209 K1, 220 E7, 221 E7, **54**
Coolum Beach Qld 220 E2, 221 E6
Cooma NSW 205 C8, 207 I6, 214 D3

Coombah Roadhouse NSW 206 A1, 210 B7, 217 F3, 219 L8
Coomera Qld 220 E6, **57**
Coonabarabran NSW 208 F5
Coonamble NSW 208 E4
Coonawarra SA 217 F7, 212 A4, **176**
Coongie Lakes National Park SA 219 K2, 222 C5
Coopracambra National Park Vic. 207 I8, 214 D5
Coorabakh National Park NSW 209 I6
Cooranbong NSW 204 E2, 207 K2, 209 H8
Coorong National Park SA 216 E8, 217 D5
Cooroy Qld 220 D2, 221 E6
Cootamundra NSW 207 H4
Coraki NSW 209 K2, 221 E8
Coral Bay WA 234 B3, **141**
Corner Store Qld 210 A1, 219 K4, 222 D7
Corowa NSW 206 F6, 213 J2
Corroboree Park Tavern NT 235 C3, 236 E3
Corryong Vic. 207 G6, 213 L2, 214 B2
Cottan–Bimbang National Park NSW 209 I6
Cowes Vic. 211 D8, 213 H7
Cowra NSW 207 H3
Cradle Mountain–Lake St Clair National Park Tas. 240 F4, **178, 198**
Craiglie Qld 225 H2, 226 F8
Cranbourne Vic. 211 D6, 213 H6
Crater Lakes National Park Qld 225 H2
Crescent Head NSW 209 J5
Creswick Vic. 206 C8, 211 A4, 212 F4
Crib Point Vic. 211 D7, 213 G7
Croajingolong National Park Vic. 207 H8, 214 D6
Crookwell NSW 207 I4
Crowdy Bay National Park NSW 209 J6
Crows Nest National Park Qld 220 B4, 221 D6
Crows Nest Qld 220 B4, 221 D6
Crystal Brook SA 216 D3, 217 D3, 219 I8
Cudmore National Park Qld 223 H1, 225 H8
Culburra NSW 204 B7, 207 J5
Culcairn NSW 206 F5, 213 K1, 214 A1
Culgoa Floodplain National Park Qld 208 D1, 223 I8
Culgoa National Park NSW 208 D2, 223 I8
Cunnamulla Qld 223 H7
Cunnawarra National Park NSW 209 I5
Currawinya National Park Qld 208 A1, 210 F1, 222 F7, 223 G7
Curtis Island National Park Qld 221 D3, 223 L3
D'Aguilar Range National Park Qld 220 C4, 221 D7
D'Entrecasteaux National Park WA 227 B7, 228 C7
Daintree National Park Qld 225 H1, 226 E8, **42, 62**
Danggali Conservation Park SA 210 A7, 215 A1, 217 F3, 219 K8
Dalby Qld 221 C6, 223 L6
Dalmeny NSW 207 J6, 214 F3
Dalrymple National Park Qld 225 H5
Dampier WA 230 B1, 232 B8, 234 D1
Dandenong Ranges National Park Vic. 206 D8, 211 E6, 213 H6, **89**
Darling Downs Qld **42**
Darling Range WA **120**
Darwin NT 235 A2, 236 D2, **100, 102**
Davenport Range National Park (Proposed) NT 239 H3
Davies Creek National Park Qld 225 H2, 226 F8

Daylesford Vic. 206 C7, 211 B4, 212 F4, **97**
Deep Creek Conservation Park SA 216 D7
Deepwater National Park Qld 221 D3
Deloraine Tas. 241 G3
Denham WA 234 B6
Denham Group National Park Qld 226 D2
Deniliquin NSW 206 D5, 213 H1
Denman NSW 207 K1, 209 G7
Denmark WA 227 E8, 228 D7
Derby WA 233 G4, **145**
Deua National Park NSW 205 F7, 207 I6, 214 E2
Devils Marbles Conservation Reserve NT 239 G3
Devonian Reef National Parks WA **145, 146**
Devonport Tas. 240 F2, **199**
Dharug National Park NSW 204 D3, 207 K3, 209 H8
Diamantina National Park Qld 222 D2, 224 D8
Diggers Rest Vic. 206 D8, 211 C5, 213 G5
Dimboola Vic. 206 A6, 212 C2, 215 C7
Dipperu National Park Qld 221 B1, 223 J1, 225 J7
Djukbinj National Park NT 235 B2, 236 E2
Dodges Ferry Tas. 240 B6
Donald Vic. 206 B6, 212 D2, 215 D7
Dongara-Denison WA 228 A2
Donnybrook WA 227 B5, 228 C6
Dooragan National Park NSW 209 J6
Dorrigo NSW 209 J4
Dorrigo National Park NSW 209 J4, **30**
Douglas Daly Tourist Park NT 235 B6, 236 E4
Douglas–Apsley National Park Tas. 241 I4, **194**
Dromana Vic. 211 D7, 213 G6
Drouin Vic. 211 F7, 213 H6
Drovers Cave National Park WA 228 B3
Dryander National Park Qld 225 K6
Drysdale River National Park WA 233 J2, 236 A4
Drysdale Vic. 211 C7, 213 G6
Dubbo NSW 207 H1, 208 E6
Dularcha National Park Qld 220 D3, 221 E6
Dulcie Range National Park NT 239 H5
Dungog NSW 207 L1, 209 H7
Dunsborough WA 227 A6, 228 B6, **134**
Dysart Qld 221 A1, 223 J1, 225 J8
Echuca Vic. 206 D6, 213 G2
Eden NSW 207 I8, 214 E5
Edmonton Qld 225 H2
Edmund Kennedy National Park Qld 225 H3
Eimeo Qld 225 K6
Elimbah Qld 220 D3, 221 E6
Ella Bay National Park Qld 225 I3
Elliminyt Vic. 212 E6
Elsey National Park NT 236 F5
Emerald Beach NSW 209 J4
Emerald Qld 221 A2, 223 J2
Emerald Springs NT 235 C5, 236 E3
Emerald Vic. 206 E8, 211 E6, 213 H6
Emmdale Roadhouse NSW 210 E5
Emu Park Qld 221 C2, 223 L2
Endeavour River National Park Qld 226 E7
Epping Forest National Park Qld 223 I1, 225 I8
Erringibba National Park Qld 221 B6, 223 K6
Errinundra National Park Vic. 207 H8, 214 C5
Esperance WA 229 G6, **148**
Eubenangee Swamp National Park Qld 225 I3

Eucla National Park WA 218 B7, 229 L4
Eudlo Creek National Park Qld 220 D2, 221 E6
Eungella National Park Qld 225 J6
Eurimbula National Park Qld 221 D3
Euroa Vic. 206 E7, 211 F2, 213 H3
Eurobodalla National Park NSW 207 J6, 214 F2
Eva Island National Park Qld 225 I3
Evandale Tas. 241 H3
Evans Head NSW 209 K3, 221 E8
Exmouth WA 234 B2, **142**
Expedition National Park Qld 221 B4, 223 J4
Fairlies Knob National Park Qld 221 D5
Falls Creek Vic. **10**
Family Islands National Park Qld 225 I3
Fannie Bay NT **108**
Ferntree Creek National Park Qld 220 D2, 221 E6
Finke Gorge National Park NT 238 F6, **118**
Finley NSW 206 E5, 213 H1
Finucane Island National Park Qld 224 C2, 237 L7
Fitzgerald River National Park WA 228 E6
Fitzroy Crossing WA 233 I5, **145**
Fitzroy Island National Park Qld 225 I2, 226 F8
Fleurieu Peninsula SA **150**
Flinders Chase National Park SA 216 A8, 217 B5, **168**
Flinders Group National Park Qld 226 E5
Flinders Island Tas. 241 L7
Flinders Ranges National Park SA 217 D1, 219 I6, **10, 150, 170, 172**
Forbes Islands National Park Qld 226 D4
Forbes NSW 207 H2, 208 D8
Forest Hill NSW 207 G5
Forest Den National Park Qld 223 H1, 225 H7
Forster–Tuncurry NSW 209 I7
Fort Lytton National Park Qld 220 D5, 221 E7
Fortesque River Roadhouse WA 230 A2, 234 D1
Fortis Creek National Park NSW 209 J3
Fortitude Valley Qld **50**
Forty Mile Scrub National Park Qld 225 H3
Foster Vic. 213 I7
Four Mile Beach, Port Douglas Qld **10, 61**
Fox Trap Roadhouse Qld 223 G5
Francois Peron National Park WA 234 B6, **140**
Frank Hann National Park WA 228 F5
Frankland Group National Park Qld 225 I2
Franklin–Gordon Wild Rivers National Park Tas. 240 F5, **178**
Fraser Island Qld 221 E4, **10, 42, 66**
Freeling SA 216 E5, 217 D4
Fremantle WA **120, 128**
French Island National Park Vic. 211 E7, 213 H7, **93**
Freshwater National Park Qld 220 D4, 221 E6
Freycinet National Park Tas. 241 I4, **194**
Gagebrook Tas. 240 B6, 241 H6
Galston NSW 204 D4, 207 K3
Gardens Of Stone National Park NSW 204 A2, 207 J2, 208 F8, 209 G8
Garig Gunak Barlu National Park NT 236 E1, **114**
Garigal National Park NSW 204 D4, 207 K3
Gatton Qld 220 B5, 221 D7
Gawler Ranges National Park SA 217 A2, 219 G7
Gawler SA 216 E5, 217 D4
Gayndah Qld 221 D5

Geelong Vic. 211 B6, 212 F6
Geikie Gorge National Park WA 233 I5, **146**
Gemtree NT 239 G5
George Town Tas. 241 G2
Georges River National Park NSW 204 C5, 207 K3
Geraldton WA 228 A2, 234 C8, **138**
Gerringong NSW 204 C7, 207 K4
Ghin-Doo-Ee National Park NSW 207 L1, 209 I7
Gibraltar Range National Park NSW 209 J3
Gilgandra NSW 208 E6
Gippsland Vic. 213 J6, **92, 94**
Girraween National Park Qld 209 I2, 220 A8,
    221 D8, 223 L8
Girringun National Park Qld 225 H4
Gisborne Vic. 206 D8, 211 C4, 213 G5
Gladstone Qld 221 D3, 223 L3
Glass House Mountains National Park Qld 220 D3,
    221 E6, **63**
Glen Innes NSW 209 I3
Glenbrook NSW 204 B4, 207 J3
Glenden Qld 225 J7
Glenelg SA **158**
Gloucester NSW 207 L1, 209 I7
Gloucester Island National Park Qld 225 K5
Gloucester National Park WA 227 C7, 228 C7, **137**
Gold Coast Qld **54**
Goldfields Vic. **96**
Goldfields Woodlands National Park WA 228 F4, **120**
Goneaway National Park Qld 222 E2
Goobang National Park NSW 207 H1, 208 E7
Good Night Scrub National Park Qld 221 D4
Goodedulla National Park Qld 221 B2, 223 K2
Goold Island National Park Qld 225 I3
Goolwa SA 216 E7, 217 D5
Goondiwindi Qld 209 G1, 221 B7, 223 K7
Goonengerry National Park NSW 209 K2, 220 E8, 221 E8
Goongarrie National Park WA 228 F2
Gooseberry Hill National Park WA 227 B2, 228 C5
Gordonvale Qld 225 H2
Goulburn NSW 207 I4
Goulburn River National Park NSW 207 J1, 208 F7,
    209 G7
Gourock National Park NSW 205 E7, 207 I6, 214 E2
Gracemere Qld 221 C2, 223 L2
Grafton NSW 209 J3
Grampians National Park Vic. 206 A7, 212 C4,
    215 C8, **84, 88**
Grasstree Qld 225 K7
Great Australian Bight Marine National Park SA
    218 C7, 229 L4
Great Barrier Reef Marine Park Qld 221 D2, 223 L1,
    225 K5, 226 E4, **10, 42, 58, 61**
Great Ocean Road Vic. **70, 84**
Great Otway National Park Vic. 211 A8, 212 E7, **86**
Great Sandy National Park Qld 220 E1, 221 E5, **66**
Great Southern WA **120**
Greater Bendigo National Park Vic. 206 D6, 211 B1,
    212 F3, 213 G3, 215 F8
Green Island National Park Qld 225 I2, 226 F8
Greenmount National Park WA 227 B2, 228 C5
Greenwell Point NSW 204 B7, 207 J5

Gregory National Park NT 233 L3, 236 D6
Grenfell NSW 207 H3
Grey Peaks National Park Qld 225 H2, 226 F8
Griffith NSW 206 F3
Gulaga National Park NSW 207 I7, 214 F3
Gulf of Carpentaria NT **100**
Gulgong NSW 207 I1, 208 F7
Gundabooka National Park NSW 208 B4
Gundagai NSW 207 H5
Gunnedah NSW 209 G5
Guy Fawkes River National Park NSW 209 I4
Guyra NSW 209 I4
Gympie Qld 220 D1, 221 E5
Hadspen Tas. 241 H3
Hahndorf SA 216 E6, 217 D5, **164**
Halfway Mill Roadhouse WA 228 B3
Halifax Bay Wetlands National Park Qld 225 I4
Halls Creek WA 233 J5, **146**
Hamilton Vic. 206 A8, 212 C5
Hanging Rock Vic. **98**
Hann River Roadhouse Qld 226 D7
Hann Tableland National Park Qld 225 H2, 226 E8
Hanson Bay Wildlife Sanctuary SA **168**
Harden NSW 207 H4
Harrington NSW 209 J6
Hartz Mountains National Park Tas. 240 A7, 241 G7
Harvey WA 227 B4, 228 C6
Hassell National Park WA 228 D7
Hasties Swamp National Park Qld 225 H2
Hastings Vic. 211 D7, 213 G6
Hastings Tas. 240 A8, **192**
Hat Head National Park NSW 209 J5
Hattah-Kulkyne National Park Vic. 206 B3, 215 C4
Hawkesbury NSW **12**
Hawks Nest NSW 207 L2, 209 I8
Hay NSW 206 D3
Haycock Island National Park Qld 225 I4
Hayes Creek NT 235 C5, 236 E3
Heads, Gold Coast Qld **54**
Healesville Vic. 206 E8, 211 E5, 213 H5, **91**
Heard Island WA **10**
Heartbreak Hotel NT 237 I6
Heartlands WA **120**
Heathcote National Park NSW 204 C5, 207 K4
Heathcote Vic. 206 D7, 211 C2, 213 G4
Heathcote–Graytown National Park Vic. 206 D7,
    211 D2, 213 G3
Helensburgh NSW 204 C5, 207 K4
Hell Hole Gorge National Park Qld 222 F4, 223 G4
Hells Gate Roadhouse Qld 224 B2, 237 K7
Hepburn Springs Vic. 206 C7, 211 B4, 212 F4, **97**
Hermannsburg *see* Ntaria
Hervey Bay Qld 221 E5, **67**
Heyfield Vic. 213 J6
Heysen Trail SA **172**
Heywood Vic. 206 A8, 212 B6, 217 F8
Hi Way Inn Roadhouse NT 237 G6
High Country Vic. **70**
Highfields Qld 220 A4, 221 D7
Hillston NSW 206 E2, 208 A8
Hilltop NSW 204 B6, 207 J4
Hinchinbrook Island National Park Qld 225 I3

Hobart Tas. 240 B6, 241 H6, **180**
Holbourne Island National Park Qld 225 J5
Holbrook NSW 207 G5, 213 K1, 214 A1
Home Hill Qld 225 J5
Homevale National Park Qld 225 J7
Hope Islands National Park Qld 225 H1, 226 F7
Horsham Vic. 206 A6, 212 C3, 215 C8
Howard Springs NT 235 B3, 236 D2
Howick Group National Park Qld 226 E6
Howlong NSW 206 F6, 213 J2
Hughenden Qld 225 G6
Hull River National Park Qld 225 I3
Hunter Valley wineries NSW 204 D1, 209 H8, **12, 40**
Huonville Tas. 240 A7, 241 G7, **191**
Hurstbridge Vic. 206 D8, 211 D5, 213 H5
Huskisson NSW 204 B8, 207 J5
Idalia National Park Qld 223 G4
Iga Warta SA 219 J6, **173**
Ilkurlka Roadhouse WA 218 A3, 229 K1, 231 K8
Iluka NSW 209 K3
Imintji Store WA 233 H4
Indwarra National Park NSW 209 H4
Ingham Qld 225 I4
Innamincka Regional Reserve SA 219 K2, 222 C6
Innes National Park SA 216 B7, 217 C5
Innisfail Qld 225 I3
Inverell NSW 209 H3
Inverloch Vic. 211 E8, 213 H7
Ipswich Qld 220 C5, 221 E7
Iron Range National Park Qld 226 D4
Irymple Vic. 206 A3, 215 C3
Isla Gorge National Park Qld 221 B4, 223 K4
Jamestown SA 216 E2, 217 D3, 219 I8
Japoon National Park Qld 225 H3
Jardine River National Park Qld 226 C2
Jenolan Caves NSW 204 A4, 207 J3, **28**
Jerrawangala National Park NSW 204 B8, 207 J5, 214 F1
Jervis Bay National Park NSW 204 B8, 207 J5
Jimbomba Qld 209 K1, 220 D6, 221 E7
Jindabyne NSW 207 H7, 214 C3, **35**
John Forrest National Park WA 227 B2, 228 C5
Joseph Banks (Round Hill Head) National Park Qld
    221 D3
Junction Hill NSW 209 J3
Junee NSW 207 G4
Junee National Park Qld 221 B2, 223 K2, 225 K8
Junuy Juluum National Park NSW 209 J4
Kadina SA 216 C4, 217 C3
Kakadu National Park NT 235 E3, 236 F3, **10, 100, 111**
Kalamunda National Park WA 227 B2, 228 C5
Kalbarri WA 228 A1, 230 A8, 234 C8, **139**
Kalbarri National Park WA 228 A1, 230 A8, 234 C7, **139**
Kalgoorlie–Boulder WA 228 F3
Kambalda WA 228 F4, 229 G4
Kanangra–Boyd National Park NSW 204 A4, 207 J3
Kandos NSW 204 A1, 207 J2, 208 F7
Kangaroo Island SA 216 B8, **150, 165**
Kapunda SA 216 E5, 217 D4
Karijini National Park WA 230 C3, 234 E2
Karoonda Roadhouse Vic. 207 H8, 213 L5, 214 C5
Karratha Travel Stop Roadhouse WA 230 B2, 232 B8,
    234 D1

Karratha WA 230 B1, 232 B8, 234 D1
Karumba Qld 224 D2
Katanning WA 227 E5, 228 D6
Katherine NT 235 E7, 236 F4, **100**
Katoomba NSW 204 B4, 207 J3, **25**
Keep River National Park Extension (Proposed) NT
　233 K2, 236 C5
Keep River National Park NT 233 K3, 236 C6
Keith SA 212 A1, 217 E6
Kelly Hill Caves Conservation Park SA 216 B8,
　217 C6, **169**
Kempsey NSW 209 J5
Kennedy Range National Park WA 230 A5, 234 C4
Keppel Bay Islands National Park Qld 221 C2,
　223 L2, 225 L8
Kerang Vic. 206 C5, 212 F1, 215 F6
Kiama NSW 204 C7, 207 K4
Kiewa Vic. 206 F6, 213 J2, 214 A2
Kilcoy Qld 220 C3, 221 D6
Kilmore Vic. 206 D7, 211 D4, 213 G4
Kimberley WA 233 I4, **120, 143**
Kinchega National Park NSW 206 B1, 210 C6, 219 L8
King Island Tas. 240 A1
Kingaroy Qld 220 A2, 221 D6
Kinglake National Park Vic. 206 D8, 211 D4, 213 H5
Kings Plains National Park NSW 209 H3
Kingscliff NSW 209 K1, 220 E8, 221 E8
Kingscote SA 216 C8, 217 C5, **166**
Kingsthorpe Qld 220 A4, 221 D7
Kingston S.E. SA 217 E6
Kingston Tas. 240 B6, 241 H7
Kinrara National Park Qld 225 H3
Kojonup WA 227 E6, 228 D6
Kondalilla National Park Qld 220 D2, 221 E6
Koo-Wee-Rup Vic. 211 E7, 213 H6
Kooraban National Park NSW 207 I6, 214 E3
Kootingal NSW 209 H5
Koreelah National Park NSW 209 J1, 220 B7,
　221 D8
Korora NSW 209 J4
Korumburra Vic. 211 F8, 213 H7
Kosciuszko National Park NSW 205 A5, 207 H6,
　213 L2, 214 C2, **12, 38**
Kroombit Tops National Park Qld 221 C3, 223 L3
Ku-Ring-Gai Chase National Park NSW 204 D4,
　207 K3, **12**
Kumarina Roadhouse WA 230 D5
Kumbatine National Park NSW 209 J5
Kununurra WA 233 K3, 236 C6, **147**
Kurri Kurri NSW 204 E1, 207 L2, 209 H8
Kurrimine Beach National Park Qld 225 I3
Kwiambal National Park NSW 209 H2, 221 C8, 223 L8
Kyabram Vic. 206 D6, 213 H2
Kyneton Vic. 206 D7, 211 C3, 213 G4
Kyogle NSW 209 K2, 220 D8, 221 E8
Laidley Qld 220 B5, 221 D7
Lake Bindegolly National Park Qld 222 F6
Lake Cargelligo NSW 206 F2, 208 B8
Lake Cathie NSW 209 J6
Lake Eildon National Park Vic. 206 E7, 211 F3, 213 I4
Lake Eyre National Park SA 219 I3, 222 A6
Lake Gairdner National Park SA 217 B1, 218 F6, 219 G6

Lake Mountain Vic. **11**
Lake Munmorah NSW 204 E2, 207 L2, 209 H8
Lake Torrens National Park SA 217 C1, 219 I6, 222 A8
Lake Tyers Forest Park Vic. 207 G8, 213 L6, 214 B6
Lakefield National Park Qld 226 D6
Lakes Entrance Vic. 213 L6, 214 B6
Lamington National Park Qld 209 K1, 220 D7,
　221 E7, **10, 55**
Lancefield Vic. 206 D7, 211 C4, 213 G4
Landsborough Qld 220 D3, 221 E6
Lane Cove National Park NSW 204 D4, 207 K3
Lara Vic. 206 C8, 211 B6, 212 F6
Larapinta Trail NT **10, 117**
Latrobe Tas. 240 F2
Lauderdale Tas. 240 B6, 241 H7
Launceston Tas. 241 H3, **195**
Launching Place Vic. 211 E5, 213 H5
Laurieton NSW 209 J6
Lawley River National Park WA 233 I2
Lawson NSW 204 B4, 207 J3
Leeton NSW 206 F4
Leeuwin–Naturaliste National Park WA 227 A6,
　228 B7, **136**
Legana Tas. 241 G3
Leigh Creek SA 219 I6
Leinster WA 228 F1, 230 F8
Lemon Tree Passage NSW 207 L2, 209 I8
Lennox Head NSW 209 K2, 221 E8, **32**
Leongatha Vic. 211 F8, 213 I7
Leonora WA 228 F1
Leopold Vic. 211 B7, 212 F6
Lesmurdie Falls National Park WA 227 B2, 228 C5
Lesueur National Park WA 228 B3
Leura NSW 204 B4, 207 J3, **25**
Lightning Ridge NSW 208 E2, 223 I8
Limestone Coast SA **174**
Limmen National Park (Proposed) NT 237 H5
Lincoln National Park SA 217 B4
Lind National Park Vic. 207 H8, 214 D5
Lindeman Islands National Park Qld 225 K6
Lismore NSW 209 K2, 221 E8
Litchfield National Park NT 235 A5, 236 D3, **110**
Lithgow NSW 204 A3, 207 J3, 209 G8
Littabella National Park Qld 221 D4
Little Desert National Park Vic. 206 A6, 212 B2,
　215 B7, 217 F6
Little Dip Conservation Park SA 217 E7
Little Grove WA 227 F8, 228 D8
Little River Vic. 206 D8, 211 C6, 213 G6
Little Topar Roadhouse NSW 210 C5, 219 L7
Livingstone National Park NSW 207 G5, 213 K1, 214 A1
Lizard Island National Park Qld 226 F6
Lobethal SA 216 E6, 217 D4
Lochern National Park Qld 222 F2
Longford Tas. 241 H3
Longreach Qld 223 G2, 225 G8
Lorne Vic. 211 A8, 212 F7, **85**
Lower Glenelg National Park Vic. 212 B5, 217 F8
Loxton SA 217 F4 Lyndoch SA 216 E5, 217 D4
Macedon Vic. 206 D8, 211 C4, 213 G5
Mackay Qld 225 K7
Macksville NSW 209 J5

Maclean NSW 209 K3
Macquarie Pass National Park NSW 204 B6, 207 J4
Madura Roadhouse WA 218 A7, 229 J4
Maffra Vic. 213 J6
Magnetic Island National Park Qld 225 I4
Main Range National Park Qld 209 J1, 220 B6, 221 D7
Maitland NSW 204 E1, 207 L2, 209 H8
Maldon Vic. 206 C7, 211 B3, 212 F4, **98**
Mallanganee National Park NSW 209 J2, 221 D8
Mallee Cliffs National Park NSW 206 B3, 215 D3
Mallee Country Vic. **70**
Malua Bay NSW 207 J6, 214 F2
Mandurah WA 227 B3, 228 B5
Manilla NSW 209 H4
Manjimup WA 227 C7, 228 C7
Mannering Park NSW 204 E2, 207 L2, 209 H8
Mannum SA 216 F6, 217 E4
Mansfield Vic. 206 E7, 213 I4
Mapleton Falls National Park Qld 220 D2, 221 E6
Mareeba Qld 225 H2, 226 F8
Margaret River WA 227 A6, 228 B7, **120, 135**
Margate Tas. 240 B7, 241 H7
Maria Creek National Park Qld 225 I3
Maria Island National Park Tas. 240 C6, 241 I6, **193**
Maria National Park NSW 209 J5
Mariala National Park Qld 223 G4
Maroochydore Qld 220 E2, 221 E6
Marramarra National Park NSW 204 D3, 207 K3, 209 G8
Marrawah Tas. **199**
Mary River National Park (Proposed) NT 235 C2, 236 E2
Mary River Roadhouse NT 235 E5, 236 F3
Maryborough Qld 221 E5
Maryborough Vic. 206 C7, 211 A3, 212 F4
Maryland National Park NSW 209 I1, 220 A8, 221 D8
Mazeppa National Park Qld 223 I1, 225 I7
McDonald Island WA **10**
Mebbin National Park NSW 209 K1, 220 D8, 221 E8
Meekatharra WA 230 D7, 234 F6
Megalong Valley NSW **27**
Melbourne Vic. 206 D8, 211 D5, 213 G5, **72**
Melton Vic. 206 D8, 211 C5, 213 G5
Merbein Vic. 206 A3, 215 C3
Meribula NSW 207 I7, 214 E4
Meroo National Park NSW 207 J5, 214 F1
Merredin WA 227 F1, 228 D4
Michaelmas And Upolu Cays National Park Qld
　225 I2, 226 F8
Middlemount Qld 221 A2, 223 J2, 225 J8
Midway Point Tas. 240 B6, 241 H6
Mid-west WA **138**
Mildura Vic. 206 A3, 215 C3, **70**
Miles Qld 221 B6, 223 K6
Millgrove Vic. 211 F5, 213 H5
Millicent SA 217 E7
Millstream Falls National Park Qld 225 H3
Millstream–Chichester National Park WA 230 B2, 234 E1
Milton NSW 207 J5, 214 F1
Mimosa Rocks National Park NSW 207 I7, 214 E4
Minerva Hills National Park Qld 221 A3, 223 J3
Minilya Roadhouse WA 234 B4
Minjary National Park NSW 207 H5, 213 L1, 214 C1
Mirboo North Vic. 213 I7

Mirima (Hidden Valley) National Park WA 233 K3, 236 C6, **147**
Mission Beach Qld 225 I3, **58**
Mitchell Alice Rivers National Park Qld 226 B7
Mitchell River National Park Vic. 206 F8, 207 G8, 213 K5, 214 A5
Mitchell River National Park WA 233 H2
Mittagong NSW 204 B6, 207 J4
Moama NSW 206 D6, 213 G2
Moe Vic. 213 I6
Mole Creek Karst National Park Tas. 240 F3
Molle Islands National Park Qld 225 K6
Molong NSW 207 I2, 208 E8
Monbulk Vic. 211 E6, 213 H6
Monga National Park NSW 205 F5, 207 I6, 214 F2
Monkey Mia WA 234 B6, **120, 140**
Monto Qld 221 C4, 223 L4
Mooball National Park NSW 209 K1, 220 E8, 221 E8
Moogerah Peaks National Park Qld 209 J1, 220 C6, 221 D7
Mooloolaba Qld 220 E2, 221 E6
Mooloolah River National Park Qld 220 E3, 221 E6
Moonta SA 216 C4, 217 C4
Moora WA 228 B4
Moore River National Park WA 227 A1, 228 B4
Mooroopna Vic. 206 E6, 211 E1, 213 H3
Moorrinya National Park Qld 225 G6
Moranbah Qld 221 A1, 223 J1, 225 J7
Moree NSW 209 G2, 221 B8, 223 K8
Moresby Range National Park Qld 225 I3
Moreton Island (Gnoorganbin) Qld 220 E5, 221 E7
Moreton Island National Park Qld 220 E4, 221 E6
Morialta Conservation Park SA 216 E6
Morisset NSW 204 E2, 207 K2, 209 H8
Mornington Peninsula National Park Vic. 211 C7, 213 G7, **70**
Mornington Vic. 211 D7, 213 G6
Morpeth NSW 204 E1, 207 L2, 209 H8
Morton National Park NSW 204 A7, 207 J5, 214 F1
Moruya NSW 207 J6, 214 F2
Morwell Vic. 213 I6
Morwell National Park Vic. 213 I7
Moss Vale NSW 204 B6, 207 J4
Mossman Qld 225 H2, 226 E8
Mount Aberdeen National Park Qld 225 J5
Mount Archer National Park Qld 221 C2, 223 L2
Mount Augustus National Park WA 230 B5, 234 E4
Mount Barker SA 216 E6, 217 D5
Mount Barker WA 227 F7, 228 D7
Mount Barnett Roadhouse WA 233 I4
Mount Barney National Park Qld 209 J1, 220 C7, 221 D7
Mount Bauple National Park Qld 221 E5
Mount Baw Baw National Park Vic. **11, 94**
Mount Beauty Vic. 206 F7, 213 K3, 214 A3
Mount Buffalo National Park Vic. 206 F7, 213 J3
Mount Buller Vic. 213 J4, 206 F7, **10**
Mount Chinghee National Park Qld 209 J1, 220 D7, 221 E8
Mount Clunie National Park Qld 209 J1, 220 B7, 221 D7
Mount Colosseum National Park Qld 221 D3
Mount Cook National Park Qld 225 H1, 226 E7
Mount Coolum National Park Qld 220 E2, 221 E6

Mount Ebenezer Roadhouse NT 238 F7
Mount Eccles National Park Vic. 206 A8, 212 C6, 217 F8
Mount Etna Caves National Park Qld 221 C2, 223 L2
Mount Field National Park Tas. 240 A5, 241 G6, **189, 190**
Mount Frankland National Park WA 227 D8, 228 C7
Mount Gambier SA 212 A5, 217 F7, **175**
Mount Helen Vic. 206 C8, 211 A5, 212 F5
Mount Hotham Vic. **10**
Mount Hypipamee National Park Qld 225 H2
Mount Imlay National Park NSW 207 I8, 214 E5
Mount Isa Qld 224 C6, 239 L3
Mount Jerusalem National Park NSW 209 K2, 220 D8, 221 E8
Mount Jim Crow National Park Qld 221 C2, 223 L2
Mount Kaputar National Park NSW 209 G4
Mount Lofty Summit SA **163**
Mount Martha Vic. 211 D7, 213 G6
Mount Martin National Park Qld 225 K6
Mount Mawson Tas. **10, 190**
Mount Morgan Qld 221 C3, 223 L3
Mount Nothofagus National Park Qld 209 J1, 220 C7, 221 D7
Mount O'Connell National Park Qld 221 C2, 223 L2, 225 L8
Mount Ossa National Park Qld 225 K6
Mount Pikapene National Park NSW 209 J2, 221 D8
Mount Pinbarren National Park Qld 220 D1, 221 E6
Mount Remarkable National Park SA 216 D1, 217 D2, 219 I8
Mount Richmond National Park Vic. 212 B6, 217 F8
Mount Roe–Mount Lindesay National Park WA 227 E8, 228 D7
Mount Royal National Park NSW 207 K1, 209 H7
Mount Stirling NSW **11**
Mount Tamborine Qld **56**
Mount Walsh National Park Qld 221 D5
Mount Warning National Park NSW 209 K1, 220 D8, 221 E8
Mount Webb National Park Qld 226 E6
Mount William National Park Tas. 241 J2
Moura Qld 221 B3, 223 K3
Mowbray National Park Qld 225 H2, 226 F8
Mudgee NSW 207 J1, 208 F7
Mudgeeraba Qld 209 K1, 220 E7, 221 E7
Mudjimba Qld 220 E2
Mullumbimby NSW 209 K2, 220 E8, 221 E8
Mulwala NSW 206 E6, 213 I2
Mummel Gulf National Park NSW 209 I5
Mundaring WA 227 B2, 228 C5
Mundrabilla Roadhouse WA 218 A7, 229 K4
Mundubbera Qld 221 D5, 223 L5
Mungerannie Roadhouse SA 219 I3, 222 B6
Mungkan Kandju National Park Qld 226 C5
Mungo National Park NSW 206 B2, 210 D8, 215 E1, 219 L8, **12**
Murgon Qld 220 B1, 221 D5
Murramarang National Park NSW 207 J6, 214 F2
Murray–Sunset National Park Vic. 206 A3, 210 A8, 215 B4, 217 F4
Murray Bridge SA 216 F6, 217 D5
Murray River Vic. **70**
Murray River National Park SA 210 A8, 215 A2, 217 F4

Murrumbateman NSW 205 C2, 207 I5
Murrumburrah NSW 207 H4
Murwillumbah NSW 209 K1, 220 E8, 221 E8
Musgrave Roadhouse Qld 226 D6
Muswellbrook NSW 207 K1, 209 H7
Mutawintji National Park NSW 210 C4, 219 L6
Myall Lakes National Park NSW 204 F1, 207 L1, 209 I7
Myrtleford Vic. 206 F7, 213 J3
Nagambie Vic. 206 D7, 211 D2, 213 H3
Nairana National Park Qld 225 I7
Nairne SA 216 E6, 217 D5
Namadgi National Park ACT 205 B5, 207 H5, 214 D1
Nambour Qld 220 D2, 221 E6, **64**
Nambucca Heads NSW 209 J5
Nambung National Park WA 228 B4
Nanango Qld 220 B2, 221 D6
Nangar National Park NSW 207 H2, 208 E8
Nanutarra Roadhouse WA 230 A3, 234 C3
Naracoorte SA 212 A3, 215 A8, 217 F7
Naracoorte Caves National Park SA 212 A3, 215 A8, 217 F7, **150, 177**
Narawntapu National Park Tas. 241 G2
Narooma NSW 207 J6, 214 F3
Narrabri NSW 209 G4
Narrandera NSW 206 F4
Narrien Range National Park Qld 223 I1, 225 I8
Narrogin WA 227 D4, 228 C6
Narromine NSW 207 H1, 208 E6
Nathalia Vic. 206 D6, 213 H2
Nattai National Park NSW 204 B5, 207 J4
Neerabup National Park WA 227 B2, 228 B5
Nelly Bay Qld 225 I4
Nelson Bay NSW 207 L2, 209 I8
Nerang Qld 209 K1, 220 E7, 221 E7
New England Qld **12**
New England National Park NSW 209 J4
New Norfolk Tas. 240 A6, 241 G6, **190**
Newborough Vic. 213 I6
Newcastle NSW 204 F2, 207 L2, 209 H8, **40**
Newhaven Vic. 211 E8, 213 H7
Newland Head Conservation Park SA 216 D7
Newman WA 230 D4
Newry Islands National Park Qld 225 K6
Nhill Vic. 206 A6, 212 B2, 215 B7, 217 F6
Nicoll Scrub National Park Qld 209 K1, 220 E7, 221 E8
Nightcap National Park NSW 209 K2, 220 D8, 221 E8, **34**
Nimbin NSW 209 K2, 221 E8, **34**
Ningaloo Marine Park WA 234 B3, **120, 141**
Nitmiluk (Katherine Gorge) National Park NT 235 E7, 236 F4
Ngarkat Conservation Park SA 212 A1, 215 A6, 217 E5
Noosa Heads Qld 220 E2, 221 E6, **65**
Noosa National Park Qld 220 E2, 221 E6, **10, 65**
Noosa Resources Reserve Qld 220 E2, 221 E6
Normanton Qld 224 D2
Norseman WA 229 G4, **149**
North Coast NSW **29**
North Coast, Kangaroo Island SA 216 C7, 217 C5, **167**
North Haven NSW 209 J6
North Hobart Tas. **186**
Northam WA 227 C1, 228 C4

Northumberland Islands National Park Qld 221 C1, 223 K1, 225 L7
Nowendoc National Park NSW 209 H6
Nowra NSW 204 B7, 207 J5
Ntaria NT 238 F6, **118**
Nuga Nuga National Park Qld 221 A4, 223 J4
Nullarbor National Park SA 218 B6, 229 L3, **150**
Nullarbor Plain WA **149**
Nullarbor Roadhouse SA 218 C6
Numurkah Vic. 206 E6, 213 H2
Nundroo Roadhouse SA 218 E7
Nuriootpa SA 216 E5, 217 D4
Nymboi–Binderay National Park NSW 209 J4
Nymboida National Park NSW 209 J3
Nyngan NSW 208 C5
Oakey Qld 220 A4, 221 D7, 223 L7
Oasis Roadhouse Qld 225 G4
Oberon NSW 204 A3, 207 J3
Ocean Grove Vic. 211 C7, 213 G6
Ocean Shores NSW 209 K2, 220 E8, 221 E8
Old Bar NSW 209 I7
Old Beach Tas. 240 B6
Old Noarlunga SA 216 D7, 217 D5
Onkaparinga River National Park SA 216 D6, 217 D5
Oolambeyan National Park NSW 206 E4
Orange NSW 207 I2, 208 E8
Orbost Vic. 207 H8, 213 L6, 214 C6
Organ Pipes National Park Vic. 206 D8, 211 C5, 213 G5
Orpheus Island National Park Qld 225 I4
Outback Coast WA **138**
Ouyen Vic. 206 B4, 215 C4
Overland Track Tas. **10, 198**
Overlander Roadhouse WA 230 A7, 234 C6
Oxenford Qld 220 E6, **57**
Oxley Wild Rivers National Park NSW 209 I5
Packsaddle Roadhouse NSW 210 C3, 219 L6
Pakenham Vic. 211 E6, 213 H6
Palm Cove Qld 225 H2, 226 F8
Palmer River Roadhouse Qld 225 H1, 226 E7
Palmerston Rocks National Park Qld 225 H3
Palmgrove National Park Qld 221 B4, 223 K4
Paluma Range National Park Qld 225 I4
Para Wirra Recreation Park SA 216 E6
Paraburdoo WA 230 C4, 234 E3
Pardoo Roadhouse WA 232 D7
Parkes NSW 207 H2, 208 D8
Paroo–Darling National Park NSW 210 E5
Paynesville Vic. 213 K6, 214 B6
Peak Charles National Park WA 228 F5
Peak Hill NSW 207 H1, 208 D7
Peak Range National Park Qld 221 A1, 223 J1, 225 J8
Pearcedale Vic. 211 D7, 213 H6
Pemberton WA 227 C7, 228 C7, **136**
Penguin Tas. 240 F2, **199**
Penneshaw SA 216 B8, 217 C5, **165**
Penola SA 212 A4, 217 F7
Percy Isles National Park Qld 221 C1, 223 L1, 225 L7
Peregian Beach Qld 220 E2, 221 E6
Perisher Blue NSW 207 H7, 214 C3, **10, 36**
Perth Tas. 241 H3
Perth WA 227 B2, 228 B5, **122**
Peterborough SA 216 E2, 217 D2, 219 I8

Phillip Island Vic. 211 D8, 213 G7, **70, 92**
Piccaninnie Ponds Conservation Park SA 212 A6, 217 F8
Picton NSW 204 B5, 207 J4
Pilbara WA **120**
Pinjarra WA 227 B4, 228 C5
Pink Roadhouse SA 219 G3
Pioneer Peaks National Park Qld 225 K6
Pipeclay National Park Qld 221 E5
Piper Islands National Park Qld 226 D3
Pittsworth Qld 221 D7, 223 L7
Point Lonsdale Vic. 211 C7, 213 G6
Point Nepean National Park Vic. 211 C7, 213 G6
Pontville Tas. 240 B6, 241 H6
Poona National Park Qld 221 E5
Popran National Park NSW 204 D3, 207 K3, 209 H8
Porcupine Gorge National Park Qld 225 G5
Porongurup National Park WA 227 F7, 228 D7
Port Arthur Historic Site Tas. 240 C7, 241 G7, **178, 189**
Port Augusta SA 216 C1, 217 C2, 219 I7, **171**
Port Campbell National Park Vic. 212 D7, **86**
Port Douglas Qld 225 H2, 226 F8, **61**
Port Elliot SA 216 E7, 217 D5
Port Fairy Vic. 212 C6, **87**
Port Hedland WA 230 C1, 232 C8
Port Lincoln SA 217 B4, **150**
Port Macquarie NSW 209 J6, **29**
Port Pirie SA 216 D2, 217 D3, 219 I8
Port Sorell Tas. 241 G2
Port Stephens NSW **39**
Portarlington Vic. 211 C6, 213 G6
Portland NSW 204 A2, 207 J2, 208 F8
Portland Vic. 212 B6, 217 F8
Possession Island National Park Qld 226 C2
Pottsville NSW 209 K1, 220 E8, 221 E8
Precipice National Park Qld 221 B4, 223 K4
Proserpine Qld 225 K6
Puckapunyal Vic. 206 D7, 211 D3, 213 G4
Purnululu National Park WA 233 K4, 236 B7, **10, 147**
Quandong Roadhouse NSW 210 B6, 219 L7
Queanbeyan NSW 205 D4, 207 I5, 214 E1
Queenscliff Vic. 211 C7, 213 G6
Queenstown Tas. 240 E4
Quirindi NSW 209 G6
Quoin Island National Park Qld 226 D4
Quorn SA 217 D2, 219 I7
Rabbit Flat Roadhouse NT 233 L7, 238 D2
Rainbow Valley Conservation Reserve NT 239 G7
Raine Island National Park Qld 226 E3
Ramornie National Park NSW 209 J3
Rathmines NSW 204 E2, 207 L2, 209 H8
Ravensbourne National Park Qld 220 B4, 221 D7
Raymond Terrace NSW 204 F1, 207 L2, 209 H8
Red Cliffs Vic. 206 A3, 215 C3
Reliance Creek National Park Qld 225 K6
Renmark SA 215 A2, 217 F4
Repulse Islands National Park Qld 225 K6
Restoration Island National Park Qld 226 D4
Richmond NSW 204 C3, 207 K3
Richmond Tas. 240 B6, 241 H6, **188**
Richmond Range National Park NSW 209 J2, 220 C8, 221 D8
Riddells Creek Vic. 206 D8, 211 C4, 213 G5

Risdon Vale Tas. 240 B6, 241 H6
Robe SA 217 E7, **174**
Robinvale Vic. 206 B3, 215 D4
Rochester Vic. 206 D6, 213 G2
Rockhampton Qld 221 C2, 223 L2, **69**
Rockingham WA 227 B3, 228 B5
Rocky Cape National Park Tas. 240 E1
Rocky Islets National Park Qld 226 F6
Roebuck Roadhouse WA 232 F5
Rokeby Tas. 240 B6, 241 H7
Roma Qld 221 A5, 223 J5
Romsey Vic. 206 D8, 211 C4, 213 G4
Roper Bar Store NT 237 H4
Rosebery Tas. 240 E4
Rosebud Vic. 211 C7, 213 G7
Rosedale Vic. 213 J6
Rosewood Qld 220 C5, 221 D7
Rottnest Island WA 227 A2, 228 B5, **120, 131**
Round Top Island National Park Qld 225 K7
Roxby Downs SA 219 H5
Royal National Park NSW 204 D5, 207 K4
Ruby Gap Nature Park NT 239 N6
Rudall River National Park WA 230 F2, 231 G2
Rundle Range National Park Qld 221 C3, 223 L3
Russell River National Park Qld 225 I2
Rutherglen Vic. 206 F6, 213 J2
Rye Vic. 211 C7, 213 G7
St Arnaud Vic. 206 B6, 212 E3, 215 E8
St Arnaud Range National Park Vic. 206 B7, 212 E3, 215 E8
St George Qld 221 A7, 223 J7
St Georges Basin NSW 204 B8, 207 J5
St Helena Island National Park Qld 220 E5, 221 E7
St Helens Tas. 241 I3, **195**
St Kilda Vic. **81**
St Leonards Vic. 211 C7, 213 G6
Sale Vic. 213 J6
Sandbanks National Park Qld 226 D5
Sandfire Roadhouse WA 232 E7
Sandy Beach NSW 209 J4
Sarabah National Park Qld 209 K1, 220 D7, 221 E7
Sarina Qld 225 K7
Saunders Islands National Park Qld 226 d3
Savage River National Park Tas. 240 E2
Sawtell NSW 209 J4
Scheyville National Park NSW 204 C3, 207 K3
Scone NSW 207 K1, 209 H6
Scott National Park WA 227 B7, 228 B7
Scottsdale Tas. 241 H2
Seal Bay Conservation Park SA **169**
Seldom Seen Roadhouse Vic. 207 G8, 213 L4, 214 C4
Sellicks Beach SA 216 D7, 217 D5
Serpentine National Park WA 227 B3, 228 C5
Seven Mile Beach National Park NSW 204 C7, 207 J5
Seven Mile Beach Tas. 240 B6
Seville Vic. 211 E5, 213 H5
Seymour Vic. 206 D7, 211 D3, 213 H4
Shannon National Park WA 227 D7, 228 C7
Shark Bay Marine Park WA 234 B5, **10, 177**
Sheffield Tas. 240 F3
Shepparton Vic. 206 E6, 211 E1, 213 H2
Shoal Bay NSW 209 I8

Shoalhaven Heads NSW 204 B7, 207 J5
Silverdale NSW 204 B4, 207 J3
Simpson Desert Conservation Park SA 219 I1, 222 A5, 239 J8
Simpson Desert National Park Qld 219 I1, 222 B2, 239 K7
Simpson Desert Regional Reserve SA 210 A1, 219 H2, 222 A5, 239 I8
Single National Park NSW 209 H3
Singleton NSW 207 K1, 209 H7
Singleton WA 227 B3, 228 B5
Sir Charles Hardy Group National Park Qld 226 D3
Sir James Mitchell National Park WA 227 C7, 228 C7
Six Foot Track NSW 26
Smith Islands National Park Qld 225 K6
Smithfield Qld 209 H2, 221 C8, 223 L8
Smithton Tas. 240 D1
Snake Range National Park Qld 223 I3
Snow towns NSW 36
Snowy Mountains NSW 35
Snowy River National Park Vic. 207 H8, 213 L5, 214 C5
Somerset Tas. 240 F2
Somerville Vic. 211 D7, 213 G6
Sorell Tas. 240 B6, 241 H6, 188
Sorrento Vic. 211 C7, 213 G6
South Burnett Qld 42
South Bruny National Park Tas. 240 B8, 241 G8, 191
South Coast Track Tas. 10
South Cumberland Islands National Park Qld 225 K6
South East Forest National Park NSW 207 I7, 214 E4
South Hedland WA 230 C1, 232 C8
South Stradbroke Island Qld 57
South West Rocks NSW 209 J5
Southwest National Park Tas. 192
South-west WA 133
South-west Wilderness Tas. 178
Southern Cross WA 228 E4
Southern Moreton Bay Islands National Park Qld 209 K1, 220 E6, 221 E7
Southport Qld 220 E7, 56
Southwest National Park Tas. 240 F7, 241 G8
Southwood National Park Qld 221 B7, 223 K7
Sovereign Hill Vic. 70, 96
Spa Country Vic. 96, 97
Springbrook National Park Qld 209 K1, 220 E7, 221 E7
Springwood NSW 204 B4, 207 J3
Staaten River National Park Qld 224 F1, 226 C8
Stanthorpe Qld 209 I2, 220 A8, 221 D8, 223 L8
Stanwell Park NSW 204 C5, 207 K4
Starcke National Park Qld 226 E6
Stawell Vic. 206 B7, 212 D4
Stirling Range National Park WA 227 F7, 228 D7
Stokes National Park WA 228 F6
Strahan Tas. 178
Stratford Vic. 213 J6, 214 A6
Strathalbyn SA 216 E7, 217 D5
Strathfieldsaye Vic. 206 D7, 211 B2, 212 F3, 215 F8
Streaky Bay SA 218 F8
Strzelecki National Park Tas. 241 K7
Stuarts Well Roadhouse NT 239 G6
Sturt National Park NSW 210 B1, 219 L4, 222 D7
Suffolk Park NSW 209 K2, 221 E8
Sunbury Vic. 206 D8, 211 C5, 213 G5

Sundown National Park Qld 209 I2, 221 C8, 223 L8
Sunshine Beach Qld 220 E2, 221 E6
Sunshine Coast Qld 63
Surfers Paradise Qld 209 K1, 220 E7, 221 E7, 42, 55
Sussex Inlet NSW 204 B8, 207 J5
Swain Reefs National Park Qld 221 D1
Swan Hill Vic. 206 C5, 215 E5
Swan Valley WA 120
Swansea NSW 204 E2, 207 L2, 209 H8
Sydney Harbour National Park NSW 204 D4, 207 K3, 14
Sydney NSW 204 D4, 207 K3, 14
Tahune Forest Reserve Tas. 241 G7
Tailem Bend SA 216 F7, 217 E5
Tallaganda National Park NSW 205 E4, 207 I6, 214 E1
Tamar Valley Tas. 197
Tamborine National Park Qld 209 K1, 220 D6, 221 E7, 57
Tamworth NSW 209 H5
Tannum Sands Qld 221 D3
Tanunda SA 216 E5, 217 D4, 161
Tapin Tops National Park NSW 209 I6
Taree NSW 209 I6
Tarlo River National Park NSW 204 A6, 207 J4
Tarong National Park Qld 220 A2, 221 D6
Taroona Tas. 240 B6, 241 H7
Tarra–Bulga National Park Vic. 213 I7, 95
Tasman National Park Tas. 240 C7, 241 I7, 189
Tasmanian Devil Conservation Park Tas. 240 C7, 178, 189
Tasmanian wilderness Tas. 240 E6, F3, 10
Tasmanian wineries Tas. 178, 197
Tathra NSW 207 I7, 214 E4
Tathra National Park WA 228 B3
Tatura Vic. 206 D6, 211 E1, 213 H3
Taunton National Park Qld 221 B2, 223 K2
Teesdale Vic. 206 C8, 211 A6, 212 F6
Temora NSW 207 G4
Tennant Creek NT 239 G2, 100
Tenterfield NSW 209 I2, 221 D8, 223 L8
Terang Vic. 212 D6
Terrick Terrick National Park Vic. 206 C6, 212 F2, 215 F7
Tewantin Qld 220 E2, 221 E6
The Dutchmans Stern Conservation Park SA 217 C2, 219 I7
The Grampians Vic. 70, 88
The Oaks NSW 204 B5, 207 J3
The Lakes National Park Vic. 213 K6, 214 B6
The Palms National Park Qld 220 A3, 221 D6
Thirlmere NSW 204 B5, 207 J4
Thirlmere Lakes National Park NSW 204 B5, 207 J4
Thredbo NSW 207 H7, 213 L3, 214 C3, 10, 36
Three Islands Group National Park Qld 226 F6
Three Sisters NSW 12
Three Ways Roadhouse NT 239 G2
Thrushton National Park Qld 223 I6
Tieri Qld 221 A2, 223 J2, 225 J8
Tilmouth Well Roadhouse NT 238 F5
Timbarra National Park NSW 209 J2, 221 D8
Tin Can Bay Qld 221 E5
Tirranna Roadhouse Qld 224 C3, 237 L8
Tiwi Islands NT 100
Tjukayirla Roadhouse WA 231 H7
Tobermorey NT 224 A7, 239 J4

Tocumwal NSW 206 E5, 213 H1
Tom Price WA 230 C3, 234 E2
Tomaree National Park NSW 207 L2, 209 I8
Tongala Vic. 206 D6, 213 G2
Tooloom National Park NSW 209 J1, 220 B8, 221 D8
Toompine Roadhouse Qld 223 G6
Toonumbar National Park NSW 209 J1, 220 C8, 221 D8
Toowoomba Qld 220 A5, 221 D7
Topaz Road National Park Qld 225 H2
Torndirrup National Park WA 227 F8, 228 D8
Toronto NSW 204 E2, 207 L2, 209 H8
Torquay Vic. 211 B7, 212 F6, 84
Towarri National Park NSW 207 K1, 209 G6
Townsville Qld 225 I4, 42
Trafalgar Vic. 213 I6
Traralgon Vic. 213 I6
Tregole National Park Qld 223 I5
Trephina Gorge Nature Park NT 239 G6
Tropics Qld 58
Triunia National Park Qld 220 D2, 221 E6
Tuart Forest National Park WA 227 B6, 228 B6
Tully Qld 225 H3
Tully Gorge National Park Qld 225 H3
Tumbarumba NSW 207 G6, 213 L2, 214 B2
Tumby Bay SA 217 B4
Tumut NSW 207 H5, 213 L1, 214 C1
Tunnel Creek National Park WA 233 H4, 146
Tura Beach NSW 207 I7, 214 E4
Turners Beach Tas. 240 F2
Turon National Park NSW 204 A2, 207 J2, 208 F8
Tuross Head NSW 207 J6, 214 F3
Turtle Group National Park Qld 226 E6
Twelve Apostles Vic. 212 D7, 86
Two Islands National Park Qld 226 F6
Two Rocks WA 227 A1, 228 B4
Tyabb Vic. 211 D7, 213 G6
Ulidarra National Park NSW 209 J4
Ulladulla NSW 207 J5
Uluru (Ayers Rock) NT 238 E7, 100, 119
Uluru-Kata Tjuta National Park NT 238 E7, 10, 119
Ulverstone Tas. 240 F2
Undara Volcanic National Park Qld 225 G3
Upper Beaconsfield Vic. 211 E6, 213 H6
Uralla NSW 209 H4
Urunga NSW 209 J4
Venman Bushland National Park Qld 220 E5, 221 E7
Victor Harbor SA 216 E7, 217 D5
Victoria River Roadhouse NT 236 E5
Vincentia NSW 204 B8, 207 J5
Vulkathunha–Gammon Ranges National Park SA 219 J5, 222 B8, 173
Wadbilliga National Park NSW 205 E8, 207 I6, 214 E3
Wagga Wagga NSW 207 G5
Wagin WA 227 E5, 228 D6
Waikerie SA 217 E4
Walcha NSW 209 I5
Walgett NSW 208 E3
Walhalla Vic. 213 I6, 94
Walkerston Qld 225 K7
Wallan Vic. 206 D8, 211 D4, 213 G5
Wallarah National Park NSW 204 E2, 207 L2, 209 H8
Wallaroo SA 216 C4, 217 C3

Wallerawang NSW 204 A3, 207 J2, 208 F8
Wallingat National Park NSW 209 I7
Walls Of Jerusalem National Park Tas. 240 F4
Walpole–Nornalup National Park WA 227 D8, 228 C8, **137**
Walyunga National Park WA 227 B2, 228 C5
Wandin North Vic. 206 E8, 211 E5, 213 H5
Wangaratta Vic. 206 F6, 213 I3
Warakurna Roadhouse WA 231 K4, 238 C7
Warburton Vic. 206 E8, 211 F5, 213 H5
Warburton Roadhouse WA 231 J6, 238 A8
Warialda NSW 209 H3
Warmun–Turkey Creek Roadhouse WA 233 K4, 236 B7
Waroona WA 227 B4, 228 C6
Warra National Park NSW 209 I4
Warrabah National Park NSW 209 H4
Warracknabeal Vic. 206 B6, 212 D2, 215 C7
Warragamba NSW 204 B4, 207 J3
Warragul Vic. 211 F7, 213 I6
Warren NSW 208 D5
Warren National Park WA 227 C7, 228 C7, **137**
Warrnambool Vic. 212 D6, **87**
Warrumbungle National Park NSW 208 F5
Warwick Qld 209 I1, 220 A7, 221 D7
Washpool National Park NSW 209 J3, 221 D8
Watagans National Park NSW 204 E2, 207 K2, 209 H8
Watarrka National Park NT 238 E6, **118**
Watego Beach NSW 209 L2, 221 F8, **10, 33**
Watheroo National Park WA 228 B3
Waychinicup National Park WA 227 F8, 228 E7
Weddin Mountains National Park NSW 207 H3
Wee Waa NSW 208 F4
Weipa Qld 226 B4
Welford National Park Qld 222 F3
Wellington NSW 207 I1, 208 E7
Wellington National Park WA 227 C5, 228 C6
Wellington Park TAS 240 A6, 241 G6
Wentworth NSW 206 A3, 210 B8, 215 C2
Wentworth Falls NSW 204 B4, 207 J3, **24**
Werakata National Park NSW 204 E1, 207 K2, 209 H8
Werrikimbe National Park NSW 209 I5
Werris Creek NSW 209 G5
West Cape Howe National Park WA 227 F8, 228 D8
West Hill National Park Qld 221 B1, 223 K1, 225 K7

West MacDonnell National Park NT 238 F6, 239 G6, **117**
West Wyalong NSW 207 G3
Westbury Tas. 241 G3
Weston NSW 204 E1, 207 K2
White Mountains National Park Qld 225 G6
Whitehaven Qld **10**
Whitsunday Islands National Park Qld 225 K6, **42**
Whittlesea Vic. 206 D8, 211 D4, 213 G5
Whyalla SA 216 C2, 217 C3, 219 I8
Wickham WA 230 B1, 232 B8, 234 D1
Wilberforce NSW 204 C3, 207 K3
Wild Cattle Island National Park Qld 221 D3
Willandra National Park NSW 206 D2, 208 A7, 210 F7
Willare Bridge Roadhouse WA 233 G5
Willi Willi National Park NSW 209 I5
William Bay National Park WA 227 E8, 228 D8
Williamstown SA 216 E5, 217 D4
Willunga SA 216 D7, 217 D5
Wilsons Promontory National Park Vic. 213 I8, **10, 95**
Winchelsea Vic. 211 A7, 212 F6
Windjana Gorge National Park WA 233 H4, **146**
Windmill Roadhouse WA 228 B4
Windsor NSW 204 C3, 207 K3
Wineglass Bay Tas. **10, 178, 194**
Wingham NSW 209 I6
Winton Qld 222 F1, 224 F7
Witjira National Park SA 219 G1, 239 H8
Wodonga Vic. 206 F6, 213 J2, 214 A2
Woko National Park NSW 209 I6
Wolfe Creek Meteorite Crater National Park WA 233 J6, 238 B2
Wollemi National Park NSW 204 B1, 207 J2, 209 G7
Wollogorang Roadhouse NT 224 B2, 237 J7
Wollongbar NSW 209 K2, 221 E8
Wollongong NSW 204 C6, 207 K4
Wollumbin National Park NSW 209 K1, 220 D8, 221 E8
Wondai Qld 220 A1, 221 D5
Wondul Range National Park Qld 209 H1, 221 C7, 223 L7
Wonthaggi Vic. 211 E8, 213 H7
Woodbridge Tas. 240 B7, 241 G7, **191**
Woodend Vic. 206 D8, 211 C4, 213 G4
Woodford Qld 209 I1, 220 D3, 221 E6, 223 L7
Woodside SA 216 E6, 217 D4
Woolgoolga NSW 209 J4

Woomargama National Park NSW 207 G6, 213 K2, 214 B2
Woomera SA 217 C1, 219 H6
Wooramel Roadhouse WA 230 A6, 234 C6
Woori Yallock Vic. 211 E5, 213 H5
Wooroonooran National Park Qld 225 H2, **58**
Wycliffe Well Roadhouse NT 239 G3
Wyee NSW 204 E2, 207 K2, 209 H8
Wynyard Tas. 240 E2
Wyperfeld National Park Vic. 206 A5, 212 B1, 215 B5, 217 F5
Wyrrabalong National Park NSW 204 E3, 207 L3, 209 H8
Yabbra National Park NSW 209 J2, 220 B8, 221 D8
Yalata Roadhouse SA 218 D6
Yalgorup National Park WA 227 B4, 228 B6
Yallourn North Vic. 213 I6
Yamba NSW 209 K3
Yamba Roadhouse SA 215 A3, 217 F4
Yanchep WA 227 A2, 228 B4
Yanchep National Park WA 227 B1, 228 B4, **130**
Yanununbeyan National Park NSW 205 E5, 207 I5, 214 E1
Yarra Glen Vic. 206 D8, 211 E5, 213 H5
Yarra Junction Vic. 206 E8, 211 E5, 213 H5
Yarra Ranges National Park Vic. 206 E8, 211 F5, 213 H5, **91**
Yarra Valley wineries Vic. 211 E5, **70, 90**
Yarrahappini National Park NSW 209 J5
Yarram Vic. 213 J7
Yarrangobilly Caves NSW 214 C1, **38**
Yarrawonga Vic. 206 E6, 213 I2
Yass NSW 205 C1, 207 H4
Yenda NSW 206 F3
Yengo National Park NSW 204 C1, 207 K2, 209 G8
Yeppoon Qld 221 C2, 223 L2
York WA 227 C2, 228 C5
Yorke Peninsula SA 216 B5, 217 C4, **150**
Young NSW 207 H4
Yulara NT 238 E7
Yungaburra National Park Qld 225 H2
Yuraygir National Park NSW 209 K3
Zeehan Tas. 240 E4

# ACKNOWLEDGEMENTS

**Publications manager**
Astrid Browne

**Project managers**
Melissa Krafchek (editorial)
Bruce McGurty (cartography)

**Editors**
Melissa Krafchek, Dale Campisi, Clare Coney

**Proofreader**
Clare Coney

**Cartographers**
Bruce McGurty, Emily Maffei

**Cartography assistance**
Adrian Goodman, Samantha Gough, Kaye Hannam

**Design**
saso content & design pty ltd

**Writers**
*Before you go* Samantha Gough and Kaye Hannam *New South Wales*
Frances Bruce *Queensland, Northern Territory and South Australia*
Anthony Roberts *Victoria* Rachel Pitts *Western Australia* Heather Pearson
*Tasmania* Sue Medlock

**Index**
Lucy Rushbrooke

**Photo selection**
Melissa Krafchek

**Prepress**
Publishing Prepress Pty Ltd

## Photography credits

Cover Australian flip-flops on the beach (Tim Starkey/iStock International)
Back cover Beach signs (Adam Booth/iStock International)
Title page Beach signs (Adam Booth/iStock International)
Contents pages Surfing at Currumbin (Tourism Queensland); Uluru (John Baker/Explore Australia Publishing)
Other pages 3 MK; 4 KS/EAP; 5 NR/EAP; 6 Courtesy Spirit of Tasmania; 7 Bill Bachman/Stock Photos; 8 Courtesy Reserve Bank of Australia; 11 Courtesy of Tourism Queensland; 13 (a) Adam Taylor, Aubergine Productions. Courtesy Tourism New South Wales (b) NR. Courtesy Tourism New South Wales (c) Courtesy Tourism New South Wales; 14 Jann Tuxford. Courtesy Tourism New South Wales; 16 Courtesy Tourism New South Wales; 18 (a) GL/EAP (b) Tony Yeates. Courtesy Tourism New South Wales; 21 Courtesy Tourism New South Wales; 22 Hamilton Lund. Courtesy Tourism New South Wales; 23 Courtesy Tourism New South Wales; 25 Peter Lik. Courtesy Tourism New South Wales; 26 (a) Adam Taylor, Aubergine Productions. Courtesy Tourism New South Wales (b) Courtesy Scenic World Blue Mountains; 27, 28 & 29 Courtesy Tourism New South Wales; 30 Hamilton Lund. Courtesy Tourism New South Wales; 32 Robbi Newman. Courtesy Tourism New South Wales; 33 (a) Adam Taylor, Aubergine Productions. Courtesy Tourism New South Wales (b) Mike Newling. Courtesy Tourism New South Wales; 34 EAP; 36 (a) Susan Wright. Courtesy Tourism New South Wales (b) Courtesy Tourism New South Wales; 37 Courtesy Thredbo Media; 38 Jann Tuxford. Courtesy Tourism New South Wales; 39 & 40 Courtesy Tourism New South Wales; 41 NR. Courtesy Tourism New South Wales; 43 (a), (b) & (c), 45, 46, 51, 52, 55 & 56 Courtesy of Tourism Queensland; 57 Courtesy Zorb Gold Coast; 59, 60 & 61 Courtesy of Tourism Queensland; 62 Jean Paul Ferrero-Labat/AUS; 63, 65 (a) & (b), 66, 67, 68 & 69 Courtesy of Tourism Queensland; 71 (a) & (b) KS/EAP (c) David Simmonds. Courtesy Fed Square; 72 (a) John Golings. Courtesy Fed Square (b) David Simmonds. Courtesy Fed Square; 74 (a) DB (b) Tim Webster. Courtesy Tourism Victoria; 75 David Hannah. Courtesy Tourism Victoria; 76

DB; 80 Mojo Advertising Partners. Courtesy Tourism Victoria; 85 (a) Gavin Hansford. Courtesy Tourism Victoria (b) Courtesy Tourism Victoria; 86 KS/EAP; 88 Craig Lewis; 89 DB; 90 (a) John Krutop/EAP (b) & (c) MK; 92 GL/EAP; 95 (a) JB/EAP (b) NR/EAP; 96 KS/EAP; 97 Courtesy Tourism Victoria; 99 JB/EAP; 101 (a) JB/EAP (b) NR/EAP (c) Barry Skipsey. Courtesy Tourism NT; 102 Peter Eve. Courtesy Tourism NT; 104 DS. Courtesy Tourism NT; 105 & 107 Bruce Molloy. Courtesy Tourism NT; 108 David Haigh. Courtesy Tourism NT; 109 Barry Skipsey. Courtesy Tourism NT; 110 (a) DS. Courtesy Tourism NT (b) David Silva. Courtesy Tourism NT; 112 (a) NR/EAP (b) & 113 GL/EAP; 114 David Silva. Courtesy Tourism NT; 116 John Henshall. Courtesy Tourism NT; 118 (a) & (b) NR/EAP; 119 JB/EAP; 121 (a) Len Stewart/Lochman Transparencies (b) & (c) NR/EAP; 122 Len Stewart/Lochman Transparencies; 124 Courtesy AQWA – The Aquarium of Western Australia; 125 KS/EAP; 127 (a) & (a) NR/EAP; 131 EAP; 132 DS/EAP; 134 JB/EAP; 136 (a) NR/EAP (b) Heidi Marfurt/EAP; 138 & 139 DS/EAP; 140 GMH/EAP; 141 NR/EAP; 143 & 144 GMH/EAP; 145, 146 & 147 NR/EAP; 148 JB/EAP; 151 (a) Courtesy South Australian Tourism Commission (b) EAP (c) NR/EAP; 152, 154 & 157 Courtesy South Australian Tourism Commission; 159 & 160 EAP; 162, 163, 164 & 166 Courtesy South Australian Tourism Commission; 168 NR/EAP; 169 Courtesy South Australian Tourism Commission; 171 (a) Boris Hlavica (b) NR/EAP; 172 Courtesy South Australian Tourism Commission; 173 KS/EAP; 174 & 175 NR/EAP; 176 & 177 Courtesy South Australian Tourism Commission; 179 (a) Courtesy Tourism Tasmania (b) & (c) JB/EAP; 180 RE/EAP; 182 NR/EAP; 184 Courtesy Tourism Tasmania; 185 RE/EAP; 188 MK; 189 Courtesy Tourism Tasmania; 190 NR/EAP; 192 Courtesy Tourism Tasmania; 194 (a) RE/EAP (b) & 195 NR/EAP; 196 & 197 MK; 199 JB/EAP.

**Abbreviations** AUS Auscape International; DB David Browne; DS Don Skirrow; EAP Explore Australia Publishing; GL Gary Lewis; GMH Graeme & Margaret Herald; JB John Baker; MK Melissa Krafchek; NR Nick Rains; KS Ken Stepnell; RE Rick Eaves

Explore Australia Publishing Pty Ltd
85 High Street
Prahran, Victoria 3181, Australia

10 9 8 7 6 5 4 3 2 1